THE
Native Tongue
And The Word

THE

NATIVE TONGUE
AND THE WORD

Developments in English Prose Style
1380–1580

JANEL M. MUELLER

THE UNIVERSITY OF CHICAGO PRESS
Chicago & London

JANEL M. MUELLER is professor of English
at the University of Chicago.

The University of Chicago Press, Chicago 60637
The University of Chicago Press, Ltd., London
© 1984 by The University of Chicago
All rights reserved. Published 1984
Printed in the United States of America
93 92 91 90 89 88 87 86 85 84   5 4 3 2 1

Publication of this work was made possible in part by
a grant from the Publications Program of the National
Endowment for the Humanities, an independent
federal agency.

LIBRARY OF CONGRESS CATALOGING IN PUBLICATION DATA

Mueller, Janel M., 1938–
    The native tongue and the word.

    Includes index.
    1. English language—Middle English, 1100–1500—
Style.   2. English language—Early modern, 1500–1700—
Style.   3. English prose literature—Middle English,
1100–1500—History and criticism.   4. English prose
literature—Early modern, 1500–1700—History and
criticism.   5. Bible. English—Language, style.
6. Bible—Influence.   I. Title.
PE877.M83   1984   420′.9′024   83-15817
ISBN 0-226-54562-8

To my father and mother—
Scripturalists too, though rarely in prose

CONTENTS

Contents

Acknowledgments

In the decade since this study began to take shape in my mind, my manifold indebtedness has mounted. I gratefully acknowledge receipt of a John Simon Guggenheim Memorial Fellowship for 1972/73, which launched my work under the fostering eye of the foundation's director, Gordon Ray. Thanks mainly to Dean Karl J. Weintraub and to former president John T. Wilson, the University of Chicago, my home institution, has seen fit to invest generously in my enterprise by granting me research leave and supplementary assistance during 1972–74 and 1977/78; for this help my appreciation remains great. I acknowledge also the courteous hospitality and research opportunities afforded me by the British Library, London, and the Folger Shakespeare Library, Washington, D.C., during my two periods of leave from Chicago.

Nearer to home, I have been the beneficiary of Jim McCawley's and Jerry Sadock's kind toleration of a colleague from elsewhere in the Humanities Division in their graduate linguistics courses at intervals from 1974 to 1977; to borrow a phrase of Jim's, with respect to myself I found their teaching at least "a minor service to mankind," although neither is to be held responsible for any of my errors or failures of comprehension. In the graduate English program, part of my own precincts, I have been fortunate in receptive yet independent-minded students on whom I have tried out ideas and from whom I have learned: my special acknowledgment is due to Alan Golding, Marshall Harvey, Anne Higham, Margaret Lynch, Cristanne Miller, Judith Page, James Shapiro, and Ellen Stauder. In a special category all her own, Julie Carlson has my thanks for conscientiously preparing the typescript of an earlier draft from my handwritten copy; somehow such circumstances engendered friendship. Among colleagues at Chicago and elsewhere who have lent their ears and wits, as well as timely and much-valued encouragement, I have to thank especially Anne Burnett, the late Arthur Friedman, Gwin Kolb, Barbara Lewalski, Norman Maclean, Jerry McGann, Jason Rosenblatt, Ned Rosenheim, John Paul Russo, Richard Strier, and Stuart Tave. For their investment of confidence, my deep thanks go also to Jehanne

Williamson, to John Mark Mulder, Martha Mulder, and, supremely, to my parents, John and Nella Mulder, who are offered the dedication of this study as a token of my love and gratitude. Finally, in the innermost familial circle, the support and forbearance I have had from Ian, my husband, and from our daughters, Maria and Monica, cannot even be reckoned for acknowledgment, but they and I know what I owe to them. I have found my "blessed case of conjunctivitis" protracted, certainly, but not noticeably disabling—thanks to the forenamed and to the wider circle of friends (although unnamed here, they will recognize themselves) who have contributed to my thinking and well-being over the long run.

1. Introductory

"MODERNITY" IN PROSE AND PROSE STUDY

As twentieth-century readers, we agree widely in principle on what we expect from a piece of prose. We ask, on the one hand, that it be a serviceable instrument of its writer's thought and, on the other, that it show a vital connection with spoken English, to the extent of sustaining an idiomatic if not always colloquial or conversational mode of discourse. While we vary in our particular judgments regarding "good" prose—a specification that corresponds to our distinction between "poetry" and mere "verse," according to Ian Gordon[1]—we nevertheless typically share a sense of disappointment when we cannot "hear a writer's voice" in what we read, and a reflex of exasperation when sentences (and paragraphs) of prose do not yield up their meaning to us at a single reading. Generally we are willing to linger and take greater pains over what a poem has to "say" to us, without dreaming that such differential treatment reflects anything other than a generic distinction between poetry and prose. In our century, moreover, writers on English prose style and composition have dignified our pair of expectations with the claim that they constitute a peculiarly "modern" awareness of what prose should be and what good prose is. Yet, as long as we stay within contemporary range, there is not likely to be much difficulty in defining modern prose as the proper vehicle of our cognition in language, just as mathematics and logic are its vehicles in formalization, or, as Bonamy Dobrée notes, in identifying the voices which speak in modern prose with those of our own age.[2]

---

[1] Ian A. Gordon, *The Movement of English Prose* (London: Longmans, Green & Co., 1966), pp. 7–8.

[2] Bonamy Dobrée, *Modern Prose Style*, 2d ed. (Oxford: Clarendon Press, 1964), p. 5. For an absorbing account of how the distinction between poetry and prose became fixed on the basis of later nineteenth-century assertions of imaginative and aesthetic autonomy in the use of language, see K. G. Hamilton, *The Two Harmonies: Poetry and Prose in the Seventeenth Century* (Oxford: Clarendon Press, 1963), pp. 2–9, 39–44, 98–112, 130–38, 143–50, 195–202.

Difficulties can arise, however, when our expectations about prose are projected backward in an effort to locate some specific point at which "modern" English began to be written in a fashion that continues to be recognizable as our own. Proceeding more or less intuitively, a number of influential critics and scholars from the first half of the twentieth century—J. Middleton Murry, Sir Herbert Read, H. C. Wyld, James Sutherland, F. P. Wilson, and others—purported to find such a turning point in the Restoration era, roughly, at the end of the seventeenth and the beginning of the eighteenth century.[3] While with these men the impetus to periodize English prose in terms of its modernity remained subservient to other interests, it erupted concurrently as the central issue in a protracted controversy between Richard Foster Jones and Morris W. Croll as chief opponents. Since the Croll-Jones controversy is a well-known literary-historical crux that has also received Robert Adolph's book-length retrospective assessment,[4] there is no need here for any detailed recounting. What I wish to bring out in a summary way are the values I consider to have been established by the controversy and the thoroughly relative nature of the term "modernity" in an other than contemporary application.

Jones's position, articulated and elaborated through a series of articles published in the 1930s,[5] grounds itself in a positivistic slant on the history of ideas; it affirms a causal link between the enterprises of the Royal Society and a "new prose" of a secular and, ultimately, also of a religious kind. Beginning with work on antitraditionalism in intellectual pursuits at the end of the seventeenth century—the so-called battle of the ancients and the moderns[6]—Jones went on to argue that the repercussions of

[3]See, variously, J. Middleton Murry, *The Problem of Style* (London: Humphrey Milford, 1922), pp. 5, 55–68; Sir Herbert Read, *English Prose Style* (London: G. Bell & Sons, 1928), pp. xii–xiv; Henry Cecil Wyld, *A History of Modern Colloquial English*, 3d ed. (Oxford: Basil Blackwell, 1936), pp. 148–49; James R. Sutherland, *On English Prose* (Toronto: University of Toronto Press, 1957), pp. 9–19, 58–78; F. P. Wilson, *Seventeenth-Century Prose* (Cambridge: Cambridge University Press, 1960), pp. 5–10.

[4]Robert Adolph, *The Rise of Modern Prose Style* (Cambridge, Mass., and London: MIT Press, 1968). On balance, Adolph sides with Jones over Croll in stressing a "utilitarian ethic" and a late seventeenth-century date as the key aspects of modernity in English prose; see especially pp. 242–43, 301–3.

[5]Richard Foster Jones, "Science and English Prose Style in the Third Quarter of the Seventeenth Century," *PMLA* 45 (1930): 977–1009; "The Attack on Pulpit Eloquence in the Restoration: An Episode in the Development of the Neo-Classical Standard for Prose," *Journal of English and Germanic Philology* 30 (1931): 188–217; "Science and Language in England of the Mid-Seventeenth Century," *JEGP* 31 (1932): 315–31. These essays are republished with minor revisions in *The Seventeenth Century: Essays by Richard Foster Jones and Others Writing in His Honor* (Palo Alto: Stanford University Press, 1951).

[6]Richard Foster Jones, "The Background of *The Battle of the Books*," Washington University Studies no. 7, Humanistic Series no. 2 (St. Louis, 1920), pp. 97–162; *Ancients and Moderns: A Study of the Background of "The Battle of the Books*," Washington University Studies no. 5, Language and Literature no. 6 (St. Louis, 1936).

Baconianism in Restoration England, not only the prescriptions for conducting philosophical and scientific discourse but also the rationalism and antienthusiasm manifested in the period's preaching reforms, comprised the crucial determinants of modern English prose. His account therefore identified modernity with the period 1660–1700, the same reference point as that of the critics and scholars named earlier. Croll, however, saw modern English prose as originating with Bacon himself, not with his followers, in the period 1580–1630. Croll's guiding conception of modernity exhibits an older, Burckhardtian cast in its insistence that Renaissance style is the outgrowth of individualistic self-discovery and self-expression all the while that it incorporates, too, the Renaissance's own conception of the Renaissance as the bringing of classical antiquity to rebirth.[7] Thus, for him, the significantly modern dynamic was the alleged reenactment in the sixteenth century of an opposition dating to classical times between a florid, "Asiatic" school of prose composition and a restrained, "Attic" one. In Croll's representation, "anti-Ciceronianism" or "Atticism" was a rhetorical program for stylistic revolt that came into its own in England with Bacon, Robert Burton, Sir Thomas Browne, and other writers who somehow combined imitation of such models as Seneca and Tacitus with transmutation of the restless, inquisitive, and even skeptical trains of their own thought into prose in the native tongue.

For all of the erstwhile heat generated by its original participants and by George Williamson's efforts to carry Crollian interpretation deep into the Jonesian territory of the later seventeenth century,[8] this controversy has left us not at the site of a victory or of an impasse but with something which Earl Miner remarks as more curious still: a de facto accommodation of the rival orthodoxies, so that the usual approach to teaching or discussing seventeenth-century English prose at present is to splice together Croll on the earlier half of the period with Jones on the later

[7]See *Style, Rhetoric, and Rhythm: Essays by Morris W. Croll,* ed. J. Max Patrick et al. (Princeton: Princeton University Press, 1966), a volume that supplements with useful annotations its reprintings of the following pieces: "Juste Lipse et le mouvement anticicéronien," *Revue du seizième siècle* 2 (1914): 200–242; " 'Attic Prose' in the Seventeenth Century," *Studies in Philology* 18 (1921): 79–128; "Attic Prose: Lipsius, Montaigne, Bacon," *Schelling Anniversary Papers by His Former Students* (New York: Century Co., 1923), pp. 117–50; "Muret and the History of 'Attic Prose,' " *PMLA* 39 (1924): 254–309; and "The Baroque Style in Prose," *Studies in English Philology: A Miscellany in Honor of Frederick Klaeber,* ed. Kemp Malone and Martin B. Ruud (Minneapolis: University of Minnesota Press, 1929), pp. 427–56. For some usefully skeptical reflections on the Renaissance's view of the Renaissance, see C. S. Lewis, *English Literature in the Sixteenth Century, Excluding Drama* (Oxford: Clarendon Press, 1954), pp. 1–65.

[8]See the review, by Croll and R. S. Crane, of Jones's "Science and English Prose Style" in *Philological Quarterly* 10 (1931): 85; and George Williamson, *The Senecan Amble: A Study in Prose Form from Bacon to Collier* (London: Faber & Faber, 1951); Phoenix Books reprint (Chicago: University of Chicago Press, 1966).

half.[9] Miner asks how such an eventuality came about, and what, in the light of it, we can regard ourselves as having learned about how to set our historical and critical referents for the study of English prose. These are excellent questions.

My answer to the first would be that, upon reflection, Croll's and Jones's work discloses a considerable amount of shared perspective in which accommodation can find a place: both invested intellectual history with primary importance as a determinant of literary history, and both absorbed themselves in the historian's concern with tracing forces and setting time spans for crucial developments. As for the second question, what we can regard ourselves to have learned from the Croll-Jones controversy reaches, I think, well beyond their staked-out range of opposition. The extraordinary fruitfulness of their work in engendering solid and sensitive interpretations by other students of earlier prose style[10] shows the rightness of their assumption that such study must reckon, on the analytical plane, with the interconnections of a writer's thinking and the forms and constructions in which that thinking receives expression, and, on the historical plane, with larger relations between the ideas of an age and the language of an age. Proportionally, we have Jones more to thank for basing prose study in the issues of a specifically English cultural context, and Croll more to thank for instruction in how to scrutinize and construe sentence forms as vehicles of authorial design. Together they have demonstrated the essentials of what modern prose study includes.

But what of the issue of "modernity" itself, which figures so constantly in our intuitions as contemporary readers of prose? Surely the Croll-Jones controversy also shows us how variable and malleable a referent this is in interpreting the past; we will find this or that "modern" in accordance with how we conceive of modernity. Since this is true, should we not dispense with the concept altogether as a referent in the historical study of prose? My decision in this study has been to retain "modernity" as a referent because it carries associations of what is continuing or

[9]Earl Miner, "Patterns of Stoicism in Thought and Prose Styles, 1530–1700," *PMLA* 85 (1970): 1023–34, esp. 1023–24.

[10]Since Williamson, Croll's influence has been notable in work by Don Cameron Allen, "Style and Certitude," *ELH* 15 (1948): 167–75; Floyd Gray, *Le style de Montaigne* (Paris: Librairie Nizet, 1958); Jonas A. Barish, *Ben Jonson and the Language of Prose Comedy* (Cambridge, Mass.: Harvard University Press, 1960); Joan Webber, *Contrary Music: The Prose Style of John Donne* (Madison: University of Wisconsin Press, 1963); Wesley Trimpi, *Ben Jonson's Poems: A Study of the Plain Style* (Stanford: Stanford University Press, 1962), chaps. 1–4; and Lisa Jardine, *Francis Bacon: Discovery and the Art of Discourse* (London and New York: Cambridge University Press, 1974). Jones's principal continuators have been F. P. Wilson (*Seventeenth-Century Prose*), Robert Adolph (*Rise of Modern Prose Style*), and Andrews Wanning ("Some Changes in the Prose Style of the Seventeenth Century" [Ph.D. diss., Cambridge University, 1936], regrettably, never published).

common to us in past ages that I am prepared to welcome. I think it is no bad thing to ask, with the needed allowances, about the degree to which prose of earlier eras "speaks" to us or functions as the instrument of its writer's (and readers') thought. The needed allowances, of course, are explicit and viable definitions. I am aware—I hope sufficiently—that in using terms like "modern" and "modernity" I will have to indicate what I mean by them. While I shall attempt to do this where required throughout this study, my particular concern in this section of chapter 1 will be to spell out the various senses and ramifications of "modernity" on which the subsequent parts of my discussion depend.

Prior to any considerations of "modernity" as such, although they later came to have a bearing, has been the working assumption on my part that English prose of a given era could be approached as a self-contained body of materials, a subject in its own right. This assumption may seem innocuous enough—even, perhaps, self-evident—until it is recalled that Croll thought the advent of modernity in English prose depended on the vernacular replay of Latin stylistic developments. He is by no means the only scholar of earlier English literature to have thought along such lines; I hope to give a better sense presently of why this should have been the case. As a first preliminary to reflect our intuitive "modern" expectation that prose be the instrument of thought, I have chosen the sentence unit—in which the clause figures vitally as identical with the simplest type of sentence—for the focus of my analysis. This choice is easily accounted for on all fronts, beginning with Croll's precedent and the regular practice of stylisticians who take their cue from the consensus found among linguists of every persuasion. Simeon Potter may declare for them on the fundamental place of the sentence in English: "Because English is, in the main, an analytic language . . . , the sentence is the most important unit. The sentence is more important even than the word."[11] But for the connection between sentence form and thought that is so indispensable to mentalistic approaches like mine, the more significant evidence has been adduced by psycholinguists like Thomas Bever who have explored "the psychological reality of clause structure." Bever's most germane finding for my purposes is that the construction of English sentences is governed by what he calls a "canonical-sentoid strategy." A "sentoid" is a single, intact clause or simplex sentence that is isolable within a larger sentential unit; he defines it as "a subtree of the base structure whose highest node is S [for "Sentence"] and which contains no embedded sentences."[12] A "canonical" sentoid is canonical by virtue of the word order of modern English. It has the

[11]Simeon Potter, *Our Language* (Harmondsworth: Penguin Books, 1950), p. 90.

[12]Thomas G. Bever, "The Interaction of Perception and Linguistic Structures: A Preliminary Investigation of Neo-Functionalism," *Current Trends in Linguistics*, ed. Thomas A. Sebeok et al. (The Hague: Mouton & Co., 1972), 12:1159–1233; especially 1169, 1176–77.

form of a noun phrase followed by a verb followed by a noun phrase followed by optional modifiers—*NP + V + NP* (*+Modifier*)—a form which, Bever shows, both elicits and imposes interpretation of the internal relations of the elements as subject, verb, and object, respectively. Since there appear to be only a limited number of quite simple variants on canonical sentoid form, the predictive implication of the strategy is that sentence forms resistant to its application ought to be hard to understand. This has been shown experimentally to be the case.[13] What the work on the "canonical sentoid" offers the study of prose style is a view of the thoroughgoing cognitive consistency and transparency of the clausal unit in English and an invitation to consider how syntax serves—and perhaps also projects—the functional capacities and limits of our minds.[14]

Given the suggestiveness of the findings regarding the "canonical sentoid" as a basic link forged between thought and language, an obvious next question involving "modernity" relates to the history of English—a dimension unfortunately lacking in Croll's and Jones's work: When did the stipulated order of elements in the clause (or simplex sentence) attain a set form? The answer would supply one basis for defining a "modern" English sentence in terms of word-order rules, while also preserving our insistence that it function, for us, as an instrument of thought. A substantial monographic literature has clarified the outlines of emergent modern—that is, *Subject Verb* (*Object*) (*Complement*)—order for clauses in English. While clauses in Old English prose conform to one of three types of word order, so-called common order, conjunctive order, and demonstrative order,[15] Middle English is characterized by a gradual evolution toward the all but uniform and single "modern" type. The order *Verb Object* was dominant by 1300 and firmly fixed for both independent and dependent clauses in prose texts by 1400; declarative (*Subject Verb*) order and interrogative (*Verb Subject*) order became generalized as distinct types during the same period. Furthermore, the conditions under which inversion still applies in clause structure—e.g., 'Through the darkness came a beam of light,' 'So am I'—

---

[13]For summaries of experimental work with the "canonical sentoid" and the so-called click-location tests used to probe subjects' perceptions of language in terms of constituent structure, see Jerry A. Fodor, Thomas G. Bever, and Merrill F. Garrett, *The Psychology of Language: An Introduction to Psycholinguistics and Generative Grammar* (New York: McGraw-Hill, 1974), pp. 252–53, 328–42, 352–53, and bibliographical references given there.

[14]For a suggestive discussion, see Thomas G. Bever and D. Terence Langendoen, "A Dynamic Model of the Evolution of Language," *Linguistic Inquiry* 2 (1971): 433–63, esp. 454–55, on perceptibility and learnability as the parameters for language change.

[15]See S. O. Andrew, *Syntax and Style in Old English* (Cambridge: Cambridge University Press, 1940). "Common order" is the specific ancestor of the "canonical sentoid."

were stabilized in all essentials in prose texts by 1600.[16] Regarding the major constituents within the clause (*Noun Phrase, Verb Phrase*), Barbara Strang observes that "the general principles governing the structure of *NP*s have been unchanged since late Middle English," while for *VP*s "the main outlines of present usage were established by the sixteenth century." She adds: "By *NP* I mean such structures as serve as subject, object, or complement in simple sentences; by *VP* such structures as serve as predicators."[17] John McLaughlin offers the following general summation on what we can see is the modernity of English word order, judged according to the canonical sentoid, by the turn into the fifteenth century: "For both transitive and intransitive sentences the order subject-verb clearly predominates in the late fourteenth century, as does the order subject-verb-object. Apparently, too, at this stage in the development of word-order patterns, such order is not, as it was to some extent in Old English, contingent upon whether a given sentence is or is not embedded in another."[18]

But if we agree to identify our modern insistence that prose be the instrument of thought with the stabilization of clausal word order into canonical sentoid form, what, if anything, else can we look to find in English prose of the later fourteenth and fifteenth centuries that will tally with our other criteria for "modernity"? The answer given in Margaret Schlauch's work may startle us at first. She emphasizes that the sentence structures in writing of this period bear an exceptionally close relation to those of actual speech, arguing that such prominent traits as

---

[16]See Charles C. Fries, "On the Development of the Structural Use of Word-Order in Modern English," *Language* 16 (1940): 199–208; and discussion by Fred West, "Some Notes on Word Order in Old and Middle English," *Modern Philology* 71 (1973): 48–53, and by T. P. Dolan, "On Claims for Syntactical Modernity in Early English Prose," *MP* 74 (1977): 305–10. On vital aspects of constituent structure in the clause, see Bohumil Trnka, *On the Syntax of the English Verb from Caxton to Dryden*, Travaux du Cercle Linguistique de Prague no. 3 (Prague: Jednota Československých Matematiků a Fysiků, 1930); Victor Engblom, *On the Origin and Early Development of the Auxiliary 'Do'*, Lund Studies in English no. 6 (Lund: Berlingska, 1938); Alvar Ellegård, *The Auxiliary Do: The Establishment and Regulation of Its Use in English* (Uppsala: Almqvist & Wiksells, 1953); Hans Marchand, "The Syntactic Change from Inflectional to Word-Order System and Some Effects of This Change on the Relation 'Verb to Object' in English," *Anglia* 70 (1951): 70–89; Walerian Świeczkowski, *Word Order Patterning in Middle English: A Quantitative Study Based on Piers Plowman and Middle English Sermons*, Janua Linguarum, ser. minor, no. 19 (The Hague: Mouton & Co., 1962); and Bengt Jacobsson, *Inversion in English, with Special Reference to the Early Modern English Period* (Uppsala: Almqvist & Wiksells, 1951).

[17]Barbara M. H. Strang, *A History of English* (London: Methuen & Co., 1970), pp. 96, 98.

[18]John C. McLaughlin, *Aspects of the History of English* (New York: Holt, Rinehart & Winston, 1970), pp. 242–43. Cf. Gösta Langenfelt, *Select Studies in Colloquial English of the Late Middle Ages* (Lund: Håkan Ohlsson, 1933), p. xxi: "Generally, one may say that the fifteenth century, as well as part of the fourteenth, in syntactical matters belongs as much to New English as does the sixteenth century."

their doublings back, their loosely continuative progression, and their elliptical turns can be given a unified analysis as close replications of what still are the fundamental syntactic features of conversational—or "free"—spoken English.[19] It seems, then, that if our readerly ears as moderns are attuned to idiomatic expression and the sound of a voice from a page of prose, here is a promising area in which to inquire further. Because the notion of "speech-based prose" requires appreciable discussion in order to be defined adequately for my purposes, I shall postpone consideration of the evidence supporting Schlauch's claim and its ramifications for prose study until the final section of chapter 2. Here I remark only that Schlauch finds nothing at all pejorative to literary interests and values in prose tied closely to the spoken language; she praises the prodigious versatility and liveliness, the constantly maintained premium on communicative transmission of meaning, and even the authorial self-consciousness which imposes "a kind of literary screening to eliminate incoherencies, dialect, and vulgarisms" within prose of the era reaching from Chaucer's time to Shakespeare's.[20] Her praise, while unusual, is not solitary. A philologically trained literary historian of the generation preceding Croll and Jones, John Earle, could affirm in his *English Prose* (1890) that its preservation as a spoken medium for more than a century and a half after the Norman Conquest had "the effect of stamping the English language with one of its most peculiar and most valuable characteristics": "that larger measure of popularity, that greater breadth of contact with the nation, than is found in any other of the great literary languages of the West." Earle adds: "It is in the English of the fifteenth century that this character manifests itself in conspicuous maturity."[21]

In pinpointing texts of the fifteenth century, Earle is referring to the striking phenomenon of the widespread resurgence of English as a written medium which Basil Cottle has subsequently surveyed in *The Triumph of English, 1350–1400*.[22] To students of literature, the most familiar manifestations of this phenomenon are the decisions of the two principal court poets of this half century—the elder, John Gower's, to shift from writing in French to writing in English; the younger, Geoffrey Chaucer's,

[19]Margaret Schlauch, "Chaucer's Colloquial English—Its Structural Traits," *PMLA* 67 (1952): 1103–16; "Early Tudor Colloquial English," *Philologia Pragensia* 1 (1958): 97–104; *The English Language in Modern Times (Since 1400)* (Warsaw: Państwowe Wydawnictwo Naukowe, 1959), pp. 56–61, 145–49.

[20]*The English Language in Modern Times*, pp. 30, 34–37, 111–21.

[21]John Earle, *English Prose: Its Elements, History, and Usage* (London: Smith, Elder & Co., 1890), p. 389, and cf. pp. 422–23.

[22]Basil Cottle, *The Triumph of English, 1350–1400* (London: Blandford Press, 1969), pp. 13–25, citing earlier scholarship. Albert C. Baugh provides an excellent discussion of the reestablishment of written English in *A History of the English Language*, 2d ed. (New York: Appleton-Century-Crofts, 1957), chap. 6.

to write in English alone. But other than literary developments in Richard II's reign extend the movement to reinstate the native tongue as the national medium: in 1362 the law courts were ordered to use English for their proceedings; in 1363 and 1365 Parliament was opened in English; and in 1399 Henry IV accepted the crown with a speech in English.[23] A southwestern deed of 1376 is the oldest private legal instrument surviving in English; the oldest English petition to the Crown is that of the mercers' gild of London in 1386; the oldest English wills in the London Court of Probate date from 1387; and in 1389 returns of the ordinances, usages, and holdings of the guilds were made in English, principally for London, Norwich, and King's Lynn. It is widely recognized from the nature of this evidence that the readoption of writing in English had what in broader historical terms must count as a "modern" impetus: at base, the upsurge of patriotic and nationalistic sentiment as results of political unification and centralization of rule in a capital. But these results are inseparably bound up with and accompanied by others, one of the most important being the growth in numbers, activity, and power of a manufacturing, commercial, and bureaucratic sector of the population. Manifestations of such growth in fourteenth- and fifteenth-century England appear variously in the organization of guilds, trading companies, municipal corporations, and a civil service. In turn these emergent classes, localized in cities, find or make places for themselves in a political and economic power base which was formerly controlled by a nobility and the ecclesiastical hierarchy.[24] Thus, "modern" trends embracing urbanization, secularization, and enlarging popular participation in the national economy and culture become motives or factors for the writing of various kinds of English prose texts in this period. Chapter 3 of this study takes selective measure of this larger picture, but on the whole I place much greater continuing weight on the shaping influence in English prose of the determination to have the Bible, no less, also freely available in the native tongue. This determination, which I call "Scripturalism" when it manifests itself as a stylistic impetus in prose writing, is equally and thoroughly a product of early modern English confidence in the capacities of the native tongue and its users to deal requisitely with the supreme instance of a text, the very Word

[23]Remarkably, the racial memory had preserved to Shakespeare's time the association of the Lancastrians with speaking English, on principle. See the wooing of French "Kate" and her crash efforts at bilingualism in *Henry V*.

[24]For further pertinent treatment of the "modern" aspects of the period with which this study is concerned, see Francis R. H. DuBoulay, *An Age of Ambition: English Society in the Late Middle Ages* (New York: Viking Press, 1970), pp. 27–30, 61–66, 116–19, 160–63, 178; George Holmes, *The Later Middle Ages, 1272–1485* (London: Nelson, 1962), pp. 131–81, and *Europe: Hierarchy and Revolt, 1320–1450* (London: Fontana-Collins, 1975), pp. 105–33, 154–67, 195–213, 230–38, 301–13; and Sylvia L. Thrupp, *The Merchant Class of Medieval London, 1300–1500* (Chicago: University of Chicago Press, 1948), pp. 191–319.

of God. Subsequent discussion, starting in chapter 2, will clarify and expand upon the paramount significance which I find in Scripturalism for developments in English prose style between 1380 and 1580.

Thus far I have adduced various considerations based on accepted senses of "modernity" to indicate why I propose to expand the scope of what we receive both intuitively and critically as modern English prose as far back as the later fourteenth century, and I expect that these considerations will be genuinely predisposing. We now come to a sticking point in some understandable reservations, which can be captured as a sequence of queries. What, after all, is the strength of the claims that the prose of this earlier era can lay to literary attention? Why did Croll trace the inception of English prose with a fully "modern" literary stature only to a date some two centuries later, and Jones to one three centuries later? Is there something inherently deficient in this earlier prose when regarded, specifically, as literature? The key issue here is what one means by "literary" and "literature," but the reservations are real ones, and they are not likely to be allayed by Schlauch's call for banishing the distinction between the literary and the subliterary in addressing this prose or by Gordon's contention that students of style cannot bypass the vernacular legacy of chronicle histories, wills, charters, guild records, familiar letters, and even recipes and written instructions of other kinds if they are to reckon fairly with the prodigious phenomenon of English prose.[25] To the unconvinced, those less restive with traditional notions of the literary canon than some contemporaries (including myself), such pronouncements may smack of special pleading. I hope that it will be acceptable to propose, as a manner of proceeding, that a text can be acknowledged to have a minimally literary character if its handling of language displays some combination of the qualities of clarity, exactness, directness, and naturalness of expression that figure in our judgments of prose as good by "modern" (contemporary) standards. I hope as well that a text can be granted to be "literary" in kind if it exhibits signs of a self-aware handling of the medium of language in the act of writing. If these working definitions are acceptable for the purpose of continued discussion, we can now take note of a body of evidence that substantiates yet another "modern" aspect of the period and the prose being considered, namely, the emergence of so-called standard English as the single, dominant dialect that the native tongue would assume in writing (and, to an appreciable extent, also in speech).

[25]Schlauch, *The English Language in Modern Times*, pp. 112, 117; Gordon, *The Movement of English Prose*, pp. 7–8, 36–41, 58–64. See, further, Norman Blake, *The English Language in Medieval Literature* (Totowa, N.J.: Rowman & Littlefield, 1977), pp. 11–12.

The following review pretends to do no more than trace broad outlines, for the investigation of emerging standard English—identified as the language of the capital, the London-Westminster complex—has proceeded laboriously through scrutiny of phonological and morphological features as reflected in spelling practices in relevant texts, and interpretation of the evidence has altered over time. The widely prevalent view in historical linguistic scholarship until quite recently stressed the primacy of spoken London English in effecting the replacement of what Wyld termed the "regional dialects" of the post-Conquest era with the more or less uniform "class dialect" of the capital. This stress reflected the generally acknowledged principle that language change manifests itself first in spoken usage, thereafter in written. In Wyld's words: "London speech, or one type of it, as it existed in the fourteenth century, is the ancestor of our present-day Received Standard," having been promoted by a cultural "recognition of the superiority of the one type over the others" that had taken place "as early as the fifteenth century, and perhaps earlier still."[26] While sustaining his stress on the spoken origins of standard English, Wyld also was concerned with representing the thoroughgoing speechlikeness—the affinities between speech and prose—manifested by the texts as a positive stylistic feature, one which led ultimately to the glories of Shakespearian dialogue, supremely colloquial and literary at once.[27]

As long as a century ago, however, Lorenz Morsbach took exception to the prevailing stress on the spoken origins of standard English—not, of course, to set aside the role of speech in constituting and disseminating a standard, but rather to contest the straightforward identification of the language found in late fourteenth- to mid-fifteenth-century English texts with the language of London speech during the same period. Focused on three categories of texts—City of London records, royal documents, and Parliamentary documents—written between 1380 and 1475, Morsbach's work yielded evidence of a crucial half-century of transition (1380–1430), during which the royal and Parliamentary documents that at first displayed a preponderance of southern dialectal features assimilated themselves more and more nearly to the east Midland features of the City records. It was Morsbach's view that this process of standardization to a London norm on the written front outran related developments on the spoken front. He accordingly proposed a date of 1430 for the essential completion of developments toward a written standard, and 1460 or

[26]Wyld, *History of Modern Colloquial English*, 3d ed., pp. 4–5. Also see Francis P. Magoun, Jr., "Colloquial Old and Middle English," *Harvard Studies and Notes in Philology and Literature* 19 (1937): 167–73; and Langenfelt, *Select Studies in Colloquial English of the Late Middle Ages*, p. 3.

[27]Wyld, *History of Modern Colloquial English*, pp. 70, 76, 97–99, 101–3.

shortly thereafter for the felt establishment of a spoken standard (Caxton's testimony playing a decisive part in the latter case).[28]

Building upon Morsbach's findings that the origins of modern standard English were "literary," that is, standardizations self-consciously produced in writing, H. M. Flasdieck showed that this new official medium constituted by the language of City legal documents strongly influenced the language of deeds, wills, and other such writings drawn up in other parts of the country in the middle decades of the fifteenth century. In a still further enlargement of the "literary" picture to be drawn from spelling and compositional practices, Asta Kihlbom reached the following conclusion from a study of the great fifteenth-century letter collections, the Cely, Paston, Stonor, and other remains of communications to and from private individuals in various parts of England: "It is evident that the London language was felt as a Standard to be followed as closely as possible, for the dialectal deviations that do occur, are more or less occasional and generally appear by the side of the 'Standard' forms. . . . Often the influence of regional dialect is apparent only in the marked preference of one spelling, when the Standard vacillates between two."[29] The most recent study in this line, John H. Fisher's "Chancery and the Emergence of Standard Written English in the Fifteenth Century," gives us a circumstantial picture of the self-conscious handling of the written language in Chancery English (the texts produced by a well-trained cadre of official Westminster scribes who serviced both the Crown and Parliament). Tracing the influence toward nationwide uniformity that Chancery English exerted on the preparation of vernacular legal documents between 1420 and 1460, after attaining "a mature form" by 1430, Fisher graphically evokes a sense of the force for linguistic standardization that issued from the authorized production of documents in mainly formulaic language by professionals under regulated procedures for transcription.[30] Summing up on the readjustments in interpretation that have now accorded temporal priority to self-con-

[28]Lorenz Morsbach, *Ueber den Ursprung der neuenglischen Schriftsprache* (Heilbronn: Henniger, 1888), pp. 7–9, 165–70.

[29]Asta Kihlbom, *A Contribution to the Study of Fifteenth-Century English*, I, Uppsala Universitets Årsskrift: Filosofi Språkvetenskap och Historiska Vetenskaper, Band 2 (1926): 193–94. The earlier reference in this paragraph is to H. M. Flasdieck, *Forschungen zur Frühzeit der neuenglischen Schriftsprache*, Tom. 1–2, Studien zur englischen Philologie, Heft 65–66 (Halle, 1922). I have not seen two other contributions in this line: R. E. Zachrisson, *Pronunciation of English Vowels, 1400–1700*, Göteborgs Kungliga Vetenskaps- och Vitterhets-Sämhalleshandlingar, Heft 14–15 (1913); and Julius Lekebusch, *Die Londoner Urkundensprache von 1430–1500: Ein Beitrag zur Entstehung der neuenglischen Schriftsprache*, I, II, Studien zur englischen Philologie, Heft 14–15 (Halle, 1906).

[30]John H. Fisher, "Chancery and the Emergence of Standard Written English in the Fifteenth Century," *Speculum* 52 (1977): 870–99.

scious writing practices in the emergence of standard English, Strang has this to say:

The rise of this special form of English was a very complicated matter, and, which is rarely true, the more we find out about it, the more complicated it looks. The unique position of London in even earlier centuries had long ago set its speech apart from ordinary dialects, giving it a social stratification. . . . What was new in [the period 1370–1570] was a threefold development: first, the evolution of a City of London written standard, which need not imply a spoken one; second, the evolution of a sequence of competing types, of which one (the direct ancestor of P[resent] E[nglish] Standard) dominated from about 1430; third, the rise and spread of a spoken standard (subject to many subsequent variations, but in principle the ancestor of R[eceived] P[ronunciation]) not later than the sixteenth century.[31]

My purpose in the foregoing brief review of scholarship on the origins of standard English has in part been to call attention to another momentous modern development with a bearing on the present study, but even more to emphasize the existence of a good deal of circumstantial evidence—in textual specifics that can be construed phonologically and morphologically—of the deliberate regulating and standardizing of language in the process of writing which, as I have claimed, can be equated with at least a minimal level of literary or stylistic self-consciousness.[32] My emphasis has been the more pointed in view of a regrettable fact which we have now to confront squarely, both in itself and for its undoubted influence on the thinking of Croll and Jones (among many others). The fact is that the subtlety and control which philologists were willing to attribute to earlier writers' spellings and word-groupings as registers of distinctive features in phonology and morphology by and large stopped there. The tradition to which we still owe much illumination of other aspects of earlier English prose scanted the study of sentence form overall, and, where it did not, it took at best a condescending view. A survey of this work and its implications will conclude this section of my introductory reflections on "modernity" in prose and prose study.

The pioneering study of sentence form according to the methods and procedures of late nineteenth-century historical philology was Leon Kellner's *Historical Outlines of English Syntax* (1892). Notwithstanding a careful use of descriptive terminology, Kellner presents a view of the development of English sentence form that is conspicuous for a kind of evolutionary grand design resting on the supposition that syntax in the

---

[31]Strang, *A History of English*, p. 161, and see further, pp. 162–65.

[32]For illuminating discussion, see Henry Bradley, *On the Relations between Spoken and Written Language, with Special Reference to English* (Oxford: Clarendon Press, 1919); and David Abercrombie, "Conversation and Spoken Prose," *English Language Teaching* 18 (1963): 10–16.

classical languages is normative for all others. He envisaged English to have arisen, like other languages, out of a primitive phase in which there was not yet even full clausal structure, only juxtaposed linguistic primaries (in Tarzan-like sequences), for example, 'Man see,' 'Pot empty,' 'Enemy near.' This stage, called "bald parataxis," was alleged to have close surviving analogues in folk sayings like "The more, the merrier," "Like father, like son," "Here today, gone tomorrow," "Easy come, easy go," "Out of sight, out of mind," and the like.[33] After the emergence of clausal units, the next step in Kellner's hypothesized reconstruction of syntactic structure was the joining together of clauses: the step at which his bias toward the classical languages as models for linguistic usage and cultivation is most clearly perceptible. He not only represents co-ordination—with or without a conjunctive particle—as historically prior to subordination of one clause to another; he also holds up hypotaxis as inherently superior to parataxis according to an ideal typology which discloses its conceptual provenance in phrasing at key pionts. Kellner sums up as follows on "Old English (A.D. 500–1200)": "The structure of sentences is in its infancy; co-ordination is frequent, conjunctions are not always made use of in connecting sentences and clauses." And here is the opening of his summary on "Modern English (A.D. 1500–Present)":

> The most characteristic feature of Modern English syntax is *perfection in the structure of sentences*. Both Old and Middle English are wanting in unity and proportion; in Modern English both are attained, favoured, in all probability, by the models of Greek and Latin prose-works. . . . The well-constructed period is of comparatively recent date.[34]

Kellner held comparable evolutionary views about human consciousness (indeed, self-consciousness) in the use of language, and he invoked these as an ultimate explanation for the historical dynamic which he attributed to sentence form. Suggestive in themselves, his mentalistic predilections were unfortunately used to buttress such facile generalizations as the one advanced in the introduction to *Historical Outlines*, where English prose written subsequent to the sixteenth century is alleged to show a *"proportion and unity in the structure of the sentence"* which prior English prose lacks altogether. These are, says Kellner, "the philological facts. But how are we to account for them in a psychological way?" This was his answer:

[33]Leon Kellner, *Historical Outlines of English Syntax* (London and New York: Macmillan & Co., 1892), secs. 97–99. Charles Bally also retails this evolutionary myth about sentence formation in *Linguistique générale et linguistique française* (Paris: E. Leroux, 1932), p. 79. For a sensible attack on the myth, with discussion of the linguistic applicability of logical concepts of coordinate and dependent relationships, see M. Sandmann, "Subordination and Coordination," *Archivum Linguisticum* 2 (1950): 24–38.

[34]Kellner, *Historical Outlines*, secs. 432, 484. His italics.

The syntax of older periods is natural, *naïf,* that is, it follows much more closely the drift of the ideas, of mental images; the diction, therefore, looks as if it were extemporised, as if written on the spur of the moment, while modern syntax, fettered by logic, is artificial, and therefore far from being a true mirror of what is going on in the mind.[35]

While the very sentence form of the foregoing explanation belies its putative truth by pursuing "modern" logic with the *"naïf"* devices of parataxis (including coordinate, appositive, and nonrestrictive relative constructions), the attitudinal effect of Kellner's *Historical Outlines* was powerful and extremely prejudicial, in particular, to English prose which relied extensively on the resources of conjunctive syntax. A later essay, written in German, which sought to adduce other explanations than crudity and ineptitude for redundancy and "shifted" constructions in Old and Middle English sentences, had nothing like the circulation of its predecessor.[36] On this side of the Atlantic, the *Syntax* volume of George O. Curme's *A Grammar of the English Language* adopted the evolutionary grand design of Kellner's view of English sentence form without cavil or modification.[37] The view also deeply influenced Samuel K. Workman's *Fifteenth-Century Translation as an Influence on English Prose*, a study which has properly won respect for its analytical rigor although it is based on the questionable premise that the way to the writing of English prose of literary quality in the fifteenth century lay through exercise in translating from Latin or French into the native tongue. While the results of his qualitative comparisons of translations and original writing from early, middle, and late points in the century are equivocal,[38] interesting evidence of Kellnerian influence emerges in Workman's treatment of the vernacular prose chronicle as a continuous genre of original composition. He duly distinguishes a first stage (1400–1470), "almost invariably char-

---

[35]Ibid., sec. 9. Kellner's italics. Also see Wilhelm Havers, *Handbuch der erklärenden Syntax* (Heidelberg: C. Winter, 1931), secs. 45–48, where coordinating conjunction is classified as a primitive syntactic resource because it conveys only "successive thinking" (*das sukzessive Denken*).

[36]Leon Kellner, "Abwechselung und Tautologie: Zwei Eigenthumlichkeiten des Alt- und Mittelenglischen Stiles," *Englische Studien* 20 (1895): 1–24. Here he offers the appeal of variety and the desire to make meaning maximally explicit as explanations for the syntactic anomalies he identifies.

[37]George O. Curme, *Syntax* (Boston: D. C. Heath & Co., 1931), pp. 28–30, 89, 176.

[38]Samuel K. Workman, *Fifteenth-Century Translation as an Influence on English Prose* (Princeton: Princeton University Press, 1940), pp. 11–13, 20–23, 28–32, 145–50. Based on Workman's own assessments, John Wyclif and Nicholas Love, from the beginning of the period, are equally good at original writing and translating; John Capgrave and Sir John Fortescue, from the latter part of the century, are also equally good at both. Caxton, again at the end of the century, is uneven on both counts. Only Edward of York, working early in the century (ca. 1405), affords direct confirmation of the controlling hypothesis by emerging as a significantly better translator than original writer. Workman distinguishes compositional phases for the vernacular prose chronicle on pp. 42–46.

acterized by an elementary simplicity of structure," in which paratactic sentence form prevails; an overlapping second stage (1460–75), in which hypotactic constructions begin to make inroads; and a third stage (1475–1504), in which hypotaxis moves into the ascendancy over paratactic form. Apart from questions we might now raise about the categorization of various constructions, the interest attaching to these compositional phases for the fifteenth-century vernacular prose chronicle lies, first, in the constant implication that hypotaxis is the means to improved (and superior) style and, second, in the puzzling relation between this evolutionary paradigm and the larger argument. Since the vernacular output of these mostly anonymous chronicle writers is not known to have been connected with any translating activity, if it improves on its own, by Workman's own accounting, in the course of the century in question, then is it really necessary to learn to write English prose by way of translation? The puzzle attests the force of the prevailing pejorative outlook on the heavily conjunctive syntax of what I have been attempting to define as early "modern" English prose.

To be sure, dissent was registered notably by S. O. Andrew and Erich Auerbach in their respective treatments of coordinate sentence structure.[39] But the crucial point is that the scholarly majority had its reasons for the outlook it had adopted—good reasons, too, of a sort. There was nothing in the methods or findings of the syntactic analysis at their disposal to make them suppose that there could be any real interest in the workings of conjunction—anything of cognitive or stylistic value. George Williamson's generalizations from the hypotaxis-parataxis dichotomy to principles for interpreting sentence form are both representative and revealing; as the passage runs its course in ascribing potential functions, it is clear why "the coordinate sentence" was disparaged in comparison with "the complex sentence":

The coordinate sentence, which is most fully exploited in balance, equates thought, emphasizes alike, and disperses unity and coherence. Structurally the relation between members of a coordinate sentence devoid of balance is the same as that between sentences. Members when united in paratactic structure and unified in thought do not advance logically; they repeat or vary the main idea, or present different aspects of it. When thrown into parallel form they acquire a formal unity. The complex sentence, which is most fully exploited in the cumulative period, subordinates thought to thought, distributes emphasis, and promotes or focuses unity or coherence. It provides its thought with an articulate logic, and in periodic form is well-knit both grammatically and rhetorically; for when so compacted it is shaped so as to accumulate force and sonority. Hypotaxis is

---

[39]Andrew, *Syntax and Style in Old English*, pp. 87–100; Erich Auerbach, *Mimesis: The Representation of Reality in Western Literature*, trans. Willard R. Trask (Princeton: Princeton University Press, 1953), chap. 1.

the structural principle of climax in a sentence or period; it permits the energy and meaning of a sentence to be centered in a comprehensive rounding.[40]

If it were indeed true that, by contracting likeness or identity relations among its members, the "coordinate sentence" both dispersed "unity and coherence" and failed to "advance logically," it is hard to see how the added felicities of "balance" or "parallel form" could save it from its users' willed extinction. Williamson can plainly be seen to be handicapped here by a critical outlook on conjunction which is so rudimentary that it discloses no more "relation between members of a coordinate sentence devoid of balance" than discrete sentences would show. Despite the limitations of his mode of analysis, he properly claimed of the syntactic configurations which he called "figures" that "For the accurate definition of a prose style it is necessary to determine not only what figures are used but how they are used," and, of his own work, that it was a history of the "most incisive pattern" in "prose style in the seventeenth century." In accepting Williamson's lead with regard to the stylistic significance of syntax, if I am to further my claim that English prose from the era I have designated meets our "modern" expectations of literary interest and accomplishment, I will have to show some reason to think that such interest and accomplishment might attach to the conjunctive sentence forms which surely are the "most incisive pattern" in this prose. I make a beginning with some needed theoretical and critical referents in the following section.

A STYLISTICS OF THE SENTENCE: THE SYNTAX AND SEMANTICS OF CONJUNCTION

Conjunction, centrally constituted by coordination with *and*, *but*, and *or*, is a fundamental resource in natural language, as familiar a staple of writing as of speech. Traditional grammar captures one of its essentials in defining conjunction as a linkage of elements on an equal syntactic basis, whether or not any semantic dependency can be seen to operate as well. However, an approach by way of a perspective opened mainly by transformational-generative analysis allows us to recognize in conjunction one of a restricted but very powerful group of operations that make for inexhaustible potential in the production of new sentences—the very core of linguistic creativity. What this group of only three operations, conjunction, relativization, and complementation, does is to provide for incorporating sentences within sentences within sentences in an ongoing fashion that has no grammatically determined limits, only the pragmatic ones imposed on all human activities by the limits of

[40]Williamson, *The Senecan Amble*, p. 38. The following references are to p. 31 and p. 7.

energy, attention, and purpose. Because they are potentially so creative, it is not surprising to find them as objects of linguistic play. The play is on conjunction in "And the hip bone is connected to the thigh bone, and the thigh bone is connected to the knee bone, and the knee bone is connected to the leg bone . . ."; the play is on relativization in "This is the dog that worried the cat that chased the rat that plagued the miller that ground the corn . . ."; and the play is on complementation in "We know that they know that you know that I know . . . that I love you." The power of these three sentence-combining operations is such that we cannot call a halt at any juncture on the grounds that the end product is an impossibility in English. Each successive result of these operations is always a possible sentence of English—perhaps more of a sentence than one wants or can see need for, but still, incontestably, a sentence.[41] On analogy with certain functions in mathematics, indefinitely repeatable linguistic operations are called recursive. Recursion in conjunctive sentence forms will be a major focus of concern in the present study.

It is not difficult to see the stylistic interest and, even, complexity that attaches to recursion. In the continuing option to proliferate or not to proliferate sentence form by means, say, of conjunction, the creative potential of language converges with the creativity but also the self-conscious restraint of the human user of language who has an expressive or communicative end in mind. What kind of sentence units are produced by the exercise of recursion can be of vital significance in prose style. Complexity enters, also, with the *and*s of conversational English and with the *and*s of the prose I will be discussing because it is not always certain where a sentence unit ends. For example, at the opening of the Gospel of Matthew where there are forty-five consecutive conjunctions of simplex sentences ("Abraham begat Isaac, and Isaac begat Jacob, and Jacob begat Judas and his brethren, and . . ."), we may wonder whether we are dealing with a compound sentence or a discourse. Probably no principled cutoff between sentence form and discourse structure can be formulated. I have proceeded by taking my cues from punctuation (or its lack) in the prose under discussion—admittedly still a developing means for signaling to a reader how the energies unleashed in recursion are also being directed. But there can be no satisfactory

[41]Sanford A. Schane proposed a formal characterization of recursion and other functions in *A Schema for Sentence Coordination*, Information System Language Studies no. 10 (Bedford, Mass.: Mitre Corp., April 1966), pp. 1–60, which serves as the basis of the treatment of sentential conjunction in Robert P. Stockwell, Paul Schachter, and Barbara Hall Partee, *The Major Syntactic Structures of English* (New York: Holt, Rinehart, & Winston, 1973), pp. 23–24, 296, 320–67. For pertinent discussion of recursion and grammar-writing, see Paul Ziff, "The Number of English Sentences," *Foundations of Language* 11 (1974): 519–32; and P. Stanley Peters and R. W. Ritchie, "On the Generative Power of Transformational Grammars," *Information Sciences* 6 (1973): 49–83.

alternative to taking the frequently prodigious amplitude of these sentence forms on their own terms in the study of style.

Although conjunction, relativization, and complementation are all and equally sentence-creating recursive operations of natural language, conjunction is unique in kind, precisely because of its linkage of elements on an equal syntactic basis. Relativization and complementation proceed by adjoining, or embedding, newly produced sentences at nodes of a containing sentence which can properly—that is, grammatically—receive them. Recursion of these two operations is like stuffing an envelope. However, since sentences being conjoined with *and*, say, are not being subordinated to each other syntactically, a totally new, higher-order sentence requires to be brought into being in order to sustain equality while creating linkage. The resulting whole is indeed more than the sum of its parts—a singular superstructure which differentiates the "sentence" it is from the "clause" units that can only be its members, or members subordinated to one another in relativization and complementation. The compound sentence is, thus, the defining instance of sentencehood.[42] Lest this point about the unique structure-creating effects of conjunction be thought a mere theoretical nicety, we may directly consider several tests for identifying coordinate structure in the composition of actual sentences. What these tests reveal is a distinctive resistance in compound sentences to having their own internal structure altered or to being absorbed in the internal structure of other sentences.[43]

The first test shows that the main and subordinate clauses of a complex sentence can interchange freely, while the clauses of a compound sentence cannot. Thus, 'She went to the chapel although he was not there' and 'Although he was not there, she went to the chapel' are acceptable sentences. 'She went to the chapel, but he was not there' is acceptable also; *'But he was not there, she went to the chapel' is unacceptable (as the asterisk denotes). A second test shows that it is possible to question an element in the main clause of a complex sentence but not to question

[42]The point is Roger Fowler's, in "Sentence and Clause in English," *Linguistics* 14 (1965): 5–13. He observes that the phenomenon of a compound sentence is the sole basis on which we can distinguish a "sentence" from a "clause." For a clause shares with a sentence the feature of an S node immediately dominating $(NP + VP)$; and, likewise, clauses as well as sentences are sites for the embedding operations of relativization and complementation. Only the structural description of a compound sentence as an entity whose S node immediately dominates $(S + S + \ldots)$ gives us the characterization of a sentence which is also, emphatically, not a clause.

[43]I owe the formulation of the four coordinate structure tests to my colleague James D. McCawley. A fifth test involving the clear anaphoric referencing of pronouns in complex sentences but not in compound ones may be found in Lila R. Gleitman, "Coordinating Conjunctions in English," *Language* 41 (1965): 260–93; reprinted in *Modern Studies in English: Readings in Transformational Grammar*, ed. David A. Reibel and Sanford A. Schane (Englewood Cliffs: Prentice-Hall, 1969), pp. 80–112, and see esp. p. 94 n.

an element in a coordinated clause. Thus, to the sentence 'The servants gathered in the hall when the earl entered' it is possible to put the question 'Where did the servants gather when the earl entered?' But to the sentence 'The servants gathered in the hall and the earl entered' it is not possible to put the question *'Where did the servants gather and the earl entered?' The third test shows it is possible to relativize a complex sentence but not a compound one. Thus, 'The English proceeded to Agincourt because the French held Harfleur' can be relativized as 'The English who proceeded to Agincourt because the French held Harfleur were the archers.' But 'The English proceeded to Agincourt and the French held Harfleur' cannot be relativized as *'The English who proceeded to Agincourt and the French held Harfleur were the archers.' A fourth test yields parallel results with *for . . . to* complementation. Thus, 'Hastings did not appear at court until Richard summoned him' can undergo complementizing as 'For Hastings not to appear at court until Richard summoned him was a provocative gesture.' But 'Hastings did not appear at court and Richard summoned him' cannot be complementized as *'For Hastings not to appear at court and Richard summoned him was a provocative gesture.' Obviously, the fixity of structure and imperviousness to transformation shown by coordinate sentences are important defining characteristics.[44] Their syntactic independence and self-containedness, I think, may have figured importantly in their stylistic designation as vehicles for sententious form in the prose we shall consider in chapters 5 and 6.

The foregoing tests have revealed some basic constraints on sentential conjunctions already in existence. What about bringing sentential conjunctions into existence? Can any two (or more) sentences be conjoined freely? Chomsky's pioneering account of the subject in *Syntactic Structures* recognized that there had to be some motivating condition for sentential conjunction, and he attempted to define it purely syntactically, in terms of constituents of the same type playing analogous roles in the deep structures of their respective sentences. Thus, in his example, from 'The scene of the movie was in Chicago' and 'The scene of the play was in Chicago' we can proceed to form the conjunction 'The scene of the movie and of the play was in Chicago.'[45] This straightforward example clarifies what, in general, is required to conjoin sentences: first, some

[44]John Robert Ross has articulated these qualities in his proposed Coordinate Structure Constraint: "In a coordinate structure, no conjunct may be moved, nor may any element contained in a conjunct be moved out of that conjunct." See his "Constraints on Variables in Syntax" (Ph.D. diss., Massachusetts Institute of Technology, 1967; mimeographed text distributed by Indiana University Linguistics Club), sec. 4.84.
[45]Noam Chomsky, *Syntactic Structures* (The Hague: Mouton & Co., 1957), pp. 35–36 (sec. 5.2).

measure of relevant sameness (in this case, both conjuncts have the following same constituents: *the scene, was, in Chicago*), and, second, some measure of relevant difference which, nevertheless, takes the form of likeness (in this case, *of the movie* and *of the play* are the different, but like constituents). This requisite motivation is called an identity condition—a useful term, so long as it is recalled that the relevant sameness must include relevant difference. If the identity condition were totally met, sentential conjunction would be vitiated by tautology: *'The scene of the movie was in Chicago and the scene of the movie was in Chicago.' The unacceptability of the foregoing conjunction also points to another aspect of the overall operation recognized in Chomsky's early account: in conjoining, the separate occurrences of identical constituents reduce—or collapse—into a single occurrence (hence, in the sentential conjunction of his example, *the scene, was, in Chicago* occur only once). This elimination of surface sameness is known as conjunction reduction; there is a powerful predisposition toward it, although it is not, strictly speaking, obligatory.

As future discussion—beginning with the material now under review—will show, the heightening of sensitivity to the nature and limits of linguistic sameness and difference which attends on the use of conjunctive syntax is of extreme importance both in the creation of new sentence forms by this means and in any stylistic interpretation of them. Subsequent to *Syntactic Structures*, one major line of inquiry addressed in more detail the formation and properties of coordinate phrases as outcomes of sentential conjunction (and conjunction reduction). Lila Gleitman offered an important generalization regarding the difference in identity conditions for conjunction reduction involving *NP*s and *VP*s.[46] Reducing identical *NP*s do so under strong identity: identity, that is, of (*a*) linguistic form, (*b*) sense, and (*c*) reference. Thus, it is impossible to interpret 'A woman entered and began weeping' as referring to two women, one who entered and another who began to weep. In 'Cromwell trusted to Providence but acted energetically,' to understand the *Cromwell* of 'Cromwell trusted to Providence' as Thomas and the *Cromwell* of 'Cromwell acted energetically' as Oliver is equally impossible. The semantic content of the identity condition on conjoining *NP*s may be stated in Gleitman's rule: nonrepetition indicates identity; repetition indicates nonidentity. The rule requires reading Donne's line in "The Indifferent" ("I can love her and her and her . . .") as referring to different women, which is how we do naturally read it. This is a tidy situation, but the one regarding reducible *VP* conjuncts is messier. The condition on the

[46]Gleitman, "Coordinating Conjunctions in English," in *Modern Studies in English*, ed. Reibel and Schane, pp. 88–93.

latter is weak identity: identity of (*a*) linguistic form, (*b*) sense, and (*c*) *parallel* reference only.[47]

The semantic consequences of this difference between strong and weak identity conditions are momentous, and easy to illustrate. Conjunctively reduced *VP*s are widely unspecific in English with respect to the possibilities of "unit" or "individual" interpretation. For instance, the sentence 'Mary and Elizabeth left London' does not convey definite information as to whether the two left together, as a "unit" (one action) or separately, as "individuals" (two actions). This unspecificity may affect an object *NP* within a conjunctively reduced *VP*; in 'Mary and Elizabeth want a cat' it is unclear whether one or two animals are at issue. Further reflection showed that "individual" interpretation of a conjunctively reduced *VP* seems quite certainly to trace to a source in sentential conjunction: the sense of separate actions derives from the separate predicates of the conjoining sentences. But "unit" interpretation has struck certain theorists as having much more in common with plural expressions and number expressions, which are formed as phrases, and, in any case, as having no straightforwardly demonstrable source in sentential conjunction.[48] Thus, to take Curme's long-standing example, the source of 'The king and queen are an amiable pair' is apparently "not an abridgement of two or more sentences"—not, that is, derived from a conjunction of *'The king is an amiable pair' and *'The queen is an amiable pair,' to which reduction of identical material has applied.[49] The unsatisfactoriness of a proposed source in sentential conjunction for the 'king and queen' phrase comes to the fore, likewise, in the unit interpretation of 'Mary and Elizabeth left London.' How can its source be a conjunction of 'Mary left London' and 'Elizabeth left London' when the whole gist of unit interpretation is, in Anna Wierzbicka's

---

[47]"Strong identity" is a term from formal logic, which builds upon Gottlob Frege's definitions of "sense" (*Sinn*) and "reference" (*Bedeutung*). The sense of a sentence is a proposition (*Gedanke*); the reference of a sentence is a truth-value. Under strong identity, both sense and reference coincide; in the analogous syntactic relation, linguistic form as well as sense and reference do. See "Ueber Sinn und Bedeutung," *Zeitschrift für Philosophie und philosophische Kritik* 100 (1892): 25–50; also T. Schiebe, "Zum Problem der grammatisch relevanten Identität," in *Generative Grammar in Europe*, ed. Ferenc Kiefer and Nicholas Ruwet (Dordrecht: D. Reidel, 1973), pp. 482–527. On weak identity and its ramifications, see, further, Östen Dahl, "On So-Called 'Sloppy Identity,' " *Synthèse* 26 (1973): 81–112.

[48]For discussion, see Carlota A. Smith, "Ambiguous Sentences with *And*," in *Modern Studies in English*, ed. Reibel and Schane, pp. 75–79; Anna Wierzbicka's (influential but unpublished) paper, "Against Conjunction Reduction" (MIT, 1967), as discussed in Stockwell, Schachter, and Partee, *Major Syntactic Structures of English*, pp. 305–6; and James D. McCawley, "The Role of Semantics in a Grammar," in Emmon Bach and Robert T. Harms, ed., *Universals in Linguistic Theory* (New York: Holt, Rinehart, & Winston, 1968), pp. 167–68, revised in "A Program for Logic," in *Semantics of Natural Language*, ed. Donald Davidson and Gilbert Harman (Dordrecht: D. Reidel, 1972), pp. 538–39.

[49]Curme, *Syntax*, p. 161.

words, to affirm a "general proposition" and not to make discrete predications? A much closer source for the unit meaning of 'Mary and Elizabeth' would seem to be 'The two women left London' or 'The pair left London.'

While theoretical debate has confirmed the indispensability and enormous power of sentential conjunction as a source of coordinate structures, the existence of "unit" (sometimes also called "phrasal") meaning has continued to challenge adequate formulation—the more so as its ramifications have been recognized in other constituent structures than *NPs*. For example, unit meaning is present, and sources in sentential conjunction apparently lacking, in the following (italicized) adjective and adverb phrases: 'His trousers were *black-and-white checked*'; 'They returned *time and again*'; 'They wandered *to and fro*'. Any temptation we might feel to treat such locutions as isolated and infrequent anomalies, moreover, is checked by confronting the wealth of unit meaning that opens before us in certain categories and uses of verbs. By far the most important of these are reciprocal and reflexive verbs. What sentential conjunction can possibly be the source of 'Henry and Anne embraced' or of 'Bushy, Bagot, and Green killed each other'?[50] Equally, though less obviously, it is surely possible to say 'She laughed and cried' with the necessary sense that the laughing and crying were one complex, simultaneous action—a unit of meaning.[51] The existence of significant ambiguity in coordinate structure between individual and unit interpretations can prove stylistically crucial, as we shall be seeing at various points in this study. In general, I have found such ambiguity figuring vitally in theological contexts—which is not surprising when one considers that the central Christian paradoxes have received formulation as conjunctions with unit meaning: the Trinity (three Persons and one God), the incarnation (God and man), the virgin birth (mother and maid), transubstantiation and Lutheran consubstantiation (Body and bread). But in secular contexts also, an author's awareness of joint or separate connotations of coordinate phrasing can be conveyed to us in what becomes as much a literary as a linguistic transaction.

[50]For discussion, see Ray C. Dougherty, "A Grammar of Coordinate Conjoined Structures," Parts I and II, *Language* 46 (1970): 850–98 and 47 (1971): 298–339; Robert Fiengo and Howard Lasnik, "The Logical Structure of Reciprocal Sentences in English," *Foundations of Language* 9 (1973): 447–68, and Dougherty's reply in "The Syntax and Semantics of *Each Other* Constructions," *FL* 12 (1974): 1–47; also George Lakoff and P. Stanley Peters, "Phrasal Conjunction and Symmetric Predicates," in *Modern Studies in English*, ed. Reibel and Schane, pp. 121–22; Robert P. Stockwell, *Foundations of Syntactic Theory* (Englewood Cliffs: Prentice-Hall, 1977), pp. 14, 53.

[51]For discussion of this and other aspects of 'unit' meaning, see R. A. Hudson, "On Clauses Containing Conjoined and Plural Noun Phrases in English," *Lingua* 24 (1969–70): 205–53.

Another major line of inquiry subsequent to *Syntactic Structures* focused on clausal rather than phrasal units under the operation of sentential conjunction. By all odds the most important contribution in this line for students of prose style is Robin Lakoff's "Ifs, Ands, and Buts about Conjunction."[52] She begins by refining a purely syntactic definition of the identity condition motivating sentential conjunction. We cannot, she shows, conjoin any two internally well-formed sentences of English by virtue solely of their identity as sentences. There are relatively more acceptable and relatively less acceptable sentential conjunctions, as the following graded series (adapted from her examples) illustrates:

> The king acquired Hampton Court and he also held title to Whitehall.
> The king acquired Hampton Court and the queen took title to Greenwich.
> ? The king acquired Hampton Court and Latimer preached jeremiads.
> ?? The king acquired Hampton Court and vagabonds plague England.
> * The bishop is childless and he has three daughters.
> ** London is on the Thames and London is on the Thames.

The decreasing acceptability of the foregoing sentences has a semantic explanation. We have already observed that the identity required of conjoining sentences must include a measure of difference-in-sameness in order to block tautology. Now, to proceed from the head of the list, it is clear that the first sentence is thoroughly acceptable as a compound of different predications about a same subject (*the king* = *he*) and that the second sentence is also thoroughly acceptable as a compound of different predications about perceptibly like subjects (*the king* and *the queen*). The third sentence is questionable, despite the correspondent subject + transitive verb + direct object structure of its conjuncts, because it is hard for us to carry interpretation beyond "Two men kept busy in their own ways—so what?" Acceptability will depend on knowing that Hampton Court is a lavish palace and that the prophet Jeremiah denounced sins of worldliness. The fourth sentence is still more unacceptable than its predecessor because it complicates the search for relevant semantic identity with linguistic anomaly: a predication referring to an action and a specific time (the verb *acquired*) is paired with one referring to a state holding for an indefinite time (the generic verb *plague*). Yet this conjunction may become acceptable if we know or can intuit a connection, say, between royal extravagance and the circumstances under which vagabondage emerges as a national problem. The last two examples, however, seem more or less firmly unacceptable. At the opposite extreme from tautology, contradiction works powerfully to disqualify sentential conjunction by denying a motivation in sameness; all

---

[52]Robin Lakoff, "Ifs, Ands, and Buts about Conjunction," in *Studies in Linguistic Semantics*, ed. Charles J. Fillmore and D. Terence Langendoen (New York: Holt, Rinehart & Winston, 1971), pp. 114–49.

is (or appears to be) difference. The only shift for saving the sentence with a single asterisk is somehow to find, in irony or innuendo, the needed measure of likeness—the possibility of reading, say, with the following intonation: 'The bishop is "childless"—and he has three daughters!' Extrapolating from the observable gradation in acceptability which I have just illustrated, Lakoff concludes that "paired constituents must be reducible to partial or complete identity . . . for a conjunction to be appropriate"; they must, that is, have a *common topic*." This name, she continues, points to the localization of motivating identity in the "pair of constituents in the two conjuncts that are *what the sentence is particularly about*. This, I think, is the normal way in which conjoined sentences are interpreted."[53]

Much more than the advance it registers on earlier, purely syntactic definitions of the identity condition motivating sentential conjunction, Robin Lakoff's formulation in terms of a "common topic" signals sharp divergence from a then prevalent literary and stylistic outlook on the "coordinate sentence" as an entity that, to requote Williamson, "emphasizes alike, and disperses unity and coherence." Lakoff's common topic both specifies what the emphasis on "alike" consists in and recognizes its effect as the promoting of "unity and coherence." The enabling implications for the analysis of sentence form are immediate, as her own essay proceeds to show. After identifying in the notion of a common topic the semantic core of the condition governing the conjoining of sentences, Lakoff examines the types of sentential conjunction and the specific properties of conjunctive particles from her continuing semantic perspective. The point of departure for her typology is the standardly drawn distinction between "symmetric" conjunction (conjuncts in interchangeable positions) and "asymmetric" conjunction (conjuncts in fixed, invariant positions). Symmetric conjunction is observably the more demanding and binding relation, for there are many sentences that cannot be put together in an indifferent order. Those that can, therefore, tend to display clear set membership or other overarching connections—for example, 'Patricia does needlework, and Larry watches television, and Ruth rebinds books, and Elizabeth reads spy thrillers, and Steve breeds gerbils.' The common topic is unmistakable: leisure-time activities. By contrast, asymmetric conjunction, especially with *and*, is easily entered upon—so easily, in fact, that a loosely continuative series of coordinated sentences is the most common pattern for spontaneous speech.

Significantly, however, Lakoff notes a further principle operative in asymmetric sentential conjunction with *and:* a superimposed binary division that offsets the looseness of connection by giving the larger sen-

[53]Ibid., p. 122, and cf. pp. 118, 148. Her emphases.

tence unit a discernible turn or break. Its force is semantic: one of the conjoining sentences will serve as a crux or pivot. In her example, the crux is in the initial conjunct, 'the police came in': 'Well, the story is as follows: the police came in, and everyone swallowed their cigarettes, and Bill choked on his, and they had to take him to the hospital, and his mother just about went frantic when she heard, and I had to placate her by lending her my copy of *Portnoy's Complaint*.'[54] How much my own analysis of symmetric and, especially, asymmetric sentential conjunction owes to Lakoff's will be evident throughout the ensuing sections of this study, particularly chapter 3. My increased attentiveness to the crux or pivot superstructure which is part of my debt to her work tends to indicate, however, that a late or final conjunct is a far likelier site for a semantic turning point, since it will give the asymmetric sentential conjunction a climax form (*pace* Williamson and others under Kellnerian influence, who ascribe climax distinctively to hypotaxis). I illustrate, once again, from the Gospel of Matthew (7:25, 27), with italicizing to indicate the climactic conjunct:

And the rain descended, and the floods came, and the winds blew, and beat upon that house, *and it fell not:* for it was founded upon a rock.

And the rain descended, and the floods came, and the winds blew, and beat upon that house, *and it fell,* and great was the fall of it.

It is advisable to interrupt exposition of Lakoff's essay and turn attention briefly to Francis Christensen's *Notes toward a New Rhetoric*, a manifesto for the teaching of writing that advanced slightly earlier and much stronger claims than Lakoff's for the stylistic potentiality of asymmetric sentential conjunction, though without the incisiveness of her analysis. According to Christensen, "The foundation for a generative or productive rhetoric of the sentence is that composition is essentially a process of addition." In explaining what he means, he comes close to anticipating Bever's "canonical sentoid" strategy in his focus on the "main clause" and he emphatically anticipates my claim for the modernity of the prose which is the subject of this study in characterizing "the typical sentence of modern English" as "what we may call the *cumulative* sentence":

The main clause, which may or may not have a sentence modifier before it, advances the discussion; but the additions move backward, as in this clause, to modify the statement of the main clause or more often to explicate or exemplify it, so that the sentence has a flowing and ebbing movement, advancing to a new position and then pausing to consolidate it. . . . Thus the . . . form of the sentence . . . serves the needs of both the writer and the reader, the writer by

---

[54]Ibid., p. 127.

compelling him to examine his thought, the reader by letting him into the writer's thought.[55]

I find Christensen's account of the "cumulative sentence" somewhat too rigid in allowing only for "backward" addition from a main clause located at the head of a larger sentence unit, but its sturdy insistence that an additive, asymmetrically progressing sentence is the optimal (and "modern") vehicle—in English—for pursuing and developing a train of thought is well taken, indeed.

Returning, now, to Lakoff's essay, we note her signal perception that the distinction between symmetric and asymmetric types of sentential conjunction (1) holds for *or* and *but* as well as *and*, while also (2) intersecting in definite ways with the recursive potential of these conjunctions. *Or* in natural language is quite unlike its counterpart in formal logic: it places propositions in relation to each other as exclusive alternatives. So basic is this semantic function of *or* conjunction that the positing of alternatives is its "common topic." Symmetric *or* seems to be freely recursive: 'We'll take a drive or we'll walk in town or we'll go to a movie or. . . .' Asymmetric *or*, the less common type, seems nonrecursive in allowing only two conjuncts. Its semantic force is a causal or contingent implication extending from the first alternative to the second. Interestingly enough, this asymmetry diminishes the possibility of actual choice between the specified alternatives. Thus, we find asymmetric *or* used in ultimatums or other "no-choice" situations: 'You'll be back by one or you'll be grounded'; 'It's do or die'; 'Your money or your life'; 'Give me liberty or give me death.'[56]

Lakoff's analysis of sentential conjunction with *but* incorporates various prior insights in transformational-generative analysis,[57] among them Gleitman's to the effect that *but* is always nonrecursive. Apparent recursions involving *but* are actually separate conjunctions at discrete levels of underlying structure, as can easily be seen in 'The prince was tall but sickly' (lower node), 'but his page was healthy' (higher node). In discussing the common topic in *but* conjunction, she also builds on an observation first made by Zellig Harris in purely syntactic terms: sentences conjoined with *but* standardly exhibit a minimum of two elements of difference-in-sameness, while sentences conjoined with *and* and *or* exhibit a minimum of one. The usual manifestation of this minimal twofold difference is in different lexical material at corresponding points of constituent structure; thus, 'The army marched on Rochester but it

[55]Francis Christensen, *Notes toward a New Rhetoric* (New York: Harper & Row, 1967), pp. 4, 6–7. His emphasis.

[56]Lakoff, "Ifs, Ands, and Buts," p. 144.

[57]Ibid., pp. 133–36, building on Gleitman, "Coordinating Conjunctions in English," p. 82; and Zellig Harris, "Transformational Theory," *Language* 41 (1965): 363–401.

did *not* march on *Canterbury*'; 'The friar ate meat, but the *monk* did *not.*'
Moreover, the overt presence of a negative particle endows these *but*
conjunctions with a kind of normative status, for, as Lakoff's semantically oriented analysis makes clear, the common topic in *but* conjunctions
is a "combination of similarity and difference"—more precisely, the registering of difference over against similarity. She distinguishes two senses
of *but:* one, more impersonal in tenor, termed "semantic opposition";
and another, more subjective and personal, termed "denial of expectation."[58] Semantic opposition *but* is the ordinary type: 'Wolsey is wealthy
but Bilney is penniless.' Denial of expectation *but* may be illustrated by
'They scheduled the landing for dawn, but it was stormy'; 'Anne prayed
long for a son, but she bore the princess Elizabeth.' In rounding out her
typology of symmetric and asymmetric conjunction, Lakoff is inclined
(understandably enough) to rank denial of expectation *but*, with its built-
in dual time reference, among the asymmetric conjunctions, and semantic opposition *but* among the symmetric ones. Such a division of
semantic labor appears feasible while offering the additional theoretical
advantage of bringing *but* into alignment on syntactic and semantic criteria as, by and large, an antitype—a negative counterpart—of *and.*

For stylistic reasons, it is worth prolonging reflection on the factor of
semantic opposition that identifies *but*, for antithesis is sometimes made
so blurry a concept that mere structural (or other) responsion passes for
its defining feature. Specifically, just as the semantics of *and* proscribe
the total identity of tautology, so too the semantics of *but* rule out the
total opposition of antonymy unless the subjects of the conjuncts themselves differ. Thus, unless irony or other special interpretation comes to
the rescue, we cannot accept *'Wolsey is wealthy but he is penniless,'
while the acceptability of 'Wolsey is wealthy but Bilney is penniless' is
a matter of course. This essential semantic opposition, controlled with
regard to how little and how much is predicated, probably explains why
the occurrence of *but* is restricted to two conjuncts: to focus the required
balance of difference and sameness. Osgood and Richards have shown
in interesting experimental work that the presence of negative connotation is the sole known psycholinguistic determinant for the choice of
but over *and* in sentential contexts that could admit either connective.[59]
But, in a literary-critical quarter, the strongest recognition I know of the
tight oscillation of *but* in balancing semantic polarities comes from Kenneth Burke, who comments as follows on antithesis in *A Rhetoric of
Motives:*

[58]Lakoff, "Ifs, Ands, and Buts," p. 132.
[59]Charles E. Osgood and Meredith M. Richards, "From Yang and Yin to *and* or *but*,"
Language 49 (1973): 380–412.

Once you grasp the trend of the form, it invites participation regardless of subject matter. Formally, you will find yourself swinging along . . . even though you may not agree with the proposition that is being presented in this form. Or it may even be an opponent's proposition which you resent—yet for the duration of the statement itself you might "help him out" to the extent of yielding to the formal development, surrendering to its symmetry as such. . . . But in cases where a decision is still to be reached, a yielding to the form prepares for assent to the matter identified with it. Thus, you are drawn to the form, not in your capacity as a partisan, but because of some "universal" appeal in it. . . . You feel how it is destined to develop—and on the level of purely formal assent you would collaborate to round out its symmetry by spontaneously willing its completion and perfection as an utterance.[60]

While antithesis—*but* conjunction—is the only nonrecursive form in the core group also including *and* and *or*, there is a considerably larger group of connectives that impose an insistent binary design on or within coordinate sentence form: these are the so-called correlative conjunctions (sometimes also called emphatic conjunctions). The staples of this group include *both . . . and, not (only) . . . but (also), either . . . or, neither . . . nor, as . . . so.* It is noteworthy that clauses connected by correlatives show the same resistance to the manipulations of the coordinate structure tests as do those joined by *and, but,* or *or.* What is more, they exhibit a cognitive and rhetorical dynamic analogous to that identified by Burke in antithesis. Virginia Tufte aptly observes that "the correlative creates an order all its own, one of *logical* progression or inevitability in which the idea introduced [by the first member of the pair] is known to be incomplete and remains in a kind of suspension until finally . . . the missing material is supplied as introduced by the conjunction." Not only is such an insight into the specific workings of correlative conjunction accurate in itself and useful in correcting the Kellnerian imputations of "logic" and "suspension" only to hypotaxis, but it will also prove important to my developing formal argument in chapters 4 through 6 that the prose of the long period with which I am concerned undergoes a comprehensive shift from what I call "open sentences" to "directed syntax." Tufte, in summing up on correlative conjunction for her purposes, gives an introduction in brief to mine: "This quality of the correlative to direct the reader to the intended logical and syntactic conclusion allows its use, even without the ordering effects of a strong parallelism, as a 'ready-made' source of control over the arrangement of some rather lengthy and complex structures."[61]

[60]Kenneth Burke, *A Rhetoric of Motives* (New York: Prentice-Hall, 1950), pp. 58–59.
[61]Virginia Tufte, *Grammar as Style* (New York: Holt, Rinehart, & Winston, 1971), pp. 107, 109. See, further, on the range and effects of diverse placement of conjunctive particles in phrase structure, Simon C. Dik, *Coordination: Its Implications for the Theory of General Linguistics* (Amsterdam: North-Holland Publishing Co., 1968), p. 53; and Georgia M. Green,

Besides the precision and intensiveness that transformational-generative analysis has contributed to our understanding of sentential conjunction, an almost equal benefit has been the expansion of our awareness of its resources. Application of the concept of deep structure has disclosed the hitherto unsuspected origins in sentential conjunction of a number of ostensibly dissimilar constructions, the most important of which are nonrestrictive relatives, so-called sentential relatives, parentheticals, and appositives. It is vital to our estimate of the specifically literary potential of coordinate structure that these constructions should be recognized as family members, for, as I shall indicate in the following selective discussion, they make apertures in sentence form through which the author can put in an appearance—that is, interject a voice, often with something pointed to say.

In the formation of nonrestrictive relative constructions, an underlying symmetric conjunction of two sentences with *and* is transformed by the adjoining of one of the sentences within the other, in accordance with the following procedure.[62] Given a pair of sentential conjuncts, each of which contains a coreferential—that is, identical—*NP*, one of the sentential conjuncts can be moved to a position immediately following the coreferential noun in the other conjunct and adjoined there (with minor attendant alteration of its internal structure). Notably, however, the syntactic independence—or coordinate status—of the affected sentences is not compromised in either case. Thus from an underlying symmetric conjunction like the following, 'The Englishman was a skilled archer and the Englishman won the flitch of bacon,' either of a pair of nonrestrictive relatives can be derived: 'The Englishman, who won the flitch of bacon, was a skilled archer,' 'The Englishman, who was a skilled archer, won the flitch of bacon.' For this pair, the respective intermediate step in derivation would be sentential conjunctions of the form 'The Englishman, and the Englishman won the flitch of bacon, was a skilled archer,' 'The Englishman, and the Englishman was a skilled archer, won the flitch of bacon.' To generate a nonrestrictive relative conjunction is to exercise an option with respect to stylistic focus. At the same time that two independent pieces of information are being vouched for—or, more

---

"The Lexical Expression of Emphatic Conjunction: Theoretical Implications," *Foundations of Language* 10 (1973): 197–248.

[62]This analysis was first proposed by John R. Ross, *Constraints on Variables in Syntax,* secs. 4.2.3, 6.2.4.1; the argument for the coordinate origins of relative clauses generally was first made by Sandra A. Thompson, "The Deep Structure of Relative Clauses," *Studies in Linguistic Semantics,* ed. Fillmore and Langendoen, pp. 79–94. Stockwell concurs with Thompson in *Foundations of Syntactic Theory,* pp. 162–63. The coordinate origins of nonrestrictive relative constructions are not in dispute.

precisely, "two predications" are being made "on the same argument"[63]—one of these (the adjoined clause) is nevertheless relegated to what, on the surface, is a secondary status while the other (the "matrix" clause) retains its primary status. Still, the matrix clause does not absorb the adjoined clause as in the sentence-within-sentence embeddings found in nominalization and relativization. The nonrestrictive relative preserves and continues to (we might say) assert its syntactic independence through a characteristic intonation contour, reflected more or less acutely in the punctuating of written English over time. The contour is a segmenting one; its force can be seen in these clearly nonidentical sentences: 'Lovers who exalt their mistresses are idealistic,' 'Lovers, who exalt their mistresses, are idealistic.'

At this point, transformational-generative analysis empowers a further fundamental observation: we see that the essential syntactic and semantic difference between nonrestrictive relative and restrictive relative clauses corresponds to that between coordinate NPs with individual and unit meanings. Specifically, restrictive relative constructions, like coordinate NPs with unit meaning, are set-creating: 'lovers who exalt their mistresses' are constituted together as a unit within the class of lovers generally. Nonrestrictive relative constructions, by contrast, exhibit individual meaning. The characteristic comma intonation (or punctuation) operates to maintain the discreteness of the sentential components: thus we have 'Lovers, who are idealistic. . . .' (It is interesting, moreover, that analogous comma intonation or punctuation can be employed to signal individual meaning for coordinated NPs: note the lack of ambiguity with regard to unit or individual meaning in 'Henry danced, and Anne,' 'Henry, and Anne, danced.') Compounding the indications given by such correspondences of a source in sentential conjunction for nonrestrictive relatives, their attendant stylistic focus strongly suggests the same source. For nonrestrictive relatives function as commentary elements injected into the matrix sentence whose truth or validity is vouched for independently of the matrix. Thus we have as a typical instance: 'Polonius, who trusted his own shrewdness, persuaded the king that Hamlet was lovesick.' The assertion of self-trust has nothing to do, one way or the other, with the persuading. The commentary function may, moreover, occasion ambiguity if there is more than one possible commentator: for example, 'Ophelia related how Hamlet, who was in a fit of madness, paid her a visit'; 'Hamlet declared that the murder of Claudius, which was long overdue, was justified revenge.' Whose views of

[63]Thompson, "The Deep Structure of Relative Clauses," p. 87. See, further, Roderick A. Jacobs and Peter S. Rosenbaum, *Transformations, Style, and Meaning* (Walthan, Mass.: Xerox Publishing Co., 1971), pp. 101–2.

madness and murder are these? Only the context informs us that Ophelia says no such thing about Hamlet but that Hamlet does berate himself about delay. These semantic and stylistic dimensions are of special interest in the confirmation they lend to the view that the effect of extraneousness—created by nonrestrictive relatives as they project content into a matrix sentence from a source outside—derives from the syntactic independence conferred by origins in sentential conjunction. For, as we have been noting, the workings of nonrestrictive relatives make explicit the presence of a "speaker" in the sentence, and they do so twice over: once in the commentary function itself, and once in the content of the commentary as an addition to the "common topic" by someone with a store of knowledge.

We are now in a position to examine other conjunctively originating structures which, moreover, point at their family resemblance to nonrestrictive relatives through the same features of adjunction and segmenting intonation or punctuation. "Sentential" relatives are cousins at two syntactic removes from nonrestrictive relatives: (1) a sentential relative clause takes a whole sentence, or at least a *VP* and not just an *NP*, as its referent; and (2) its source is an underlying conjunction of an asymmetric rather than a symmetric type.[64] Sentential relatives are exceedingly common in speech and writing alike, for example, 'The lecture took only an hour, which pleased me' (the referent for *which* is the full clause, 'The lecture took only an hour'); 'She climbed right over the fence, which she had no business doing' (the referent for *which* is the *VP*, 'climb over the fence'). It will be obvious from the examples that the semantic and stylistic functions of sentential relatives are more transparent than those of nonrestrictive relatives; we always know that the producer of the sentence is the commentator.

Unlike sentential relatives, which trail their clausal or *VP* referent, and more like nonrestrictive relatives, appositive and parenthetical constructions tend to be positioned within matrix clauses; this is so because they, too, like nonrestrictive relatives, are adjoined to *NP*s under a motivating identity condition.[65] Bespeaking their source, they may optionally undergo a kind of conjunction reduction from clauses into phrases. With their optionally reducible elements parenthesized, one example of an appositive and two examples of parenthetical constructions follow: 'Henry VII,

[64]John R. Ross, "Adjectives as Noun Phrases," in Reibel and Schane, ed., *Modern Studies in English*, p. 357; also Thompson, "The Deep Structure of Relative Clauses," pp. 84–94.

[65]On appositives, see Otto Jespersen, *Analytic Syntax* (New York: Holt, Rinehart, 1969; rpt. of 1937 ed.), pp. 17, 21, 123; Ross, *Constraints on Variables in Syntax*, secs. 4.2.1, 4.2.3, 6.2.4.1; Charles F. Hockett, "Attribution and Apposition," *American Speech* 30 (1955): 99–102; and Orin D. Seright, "On Defining the Appositive," *College Composition and Communication* 17 (May 1966): 107–9.

(who was) the king of all England, knelt in the tiny chapel'; 'He called for the destruction of Antichrist, that is (to say), the papacy, from the pulpit at Paul's Cross'; 'Arriving at Dover, which she had longed to do, put the countess in good spirits.' In their reduced form, especially, appositives may seem indistinguishable from coordinate NPs. Yet there is a fundamental semantic difference: coordinated elements are understood as referring to different things, appositives to the same thing.[66] This marked separation of function reflects still further on the wealth of nuance regarding semantic and syntactic likeness-and-difference that comprises the resources of sentential conjunction. Because the difference between identity and nonidentity is always vital in language, it is important to note that certain syntactic cues signal the respective relations of apposition or coordination—for instance, serial apposition never takes an *and* connective while serial coordination nearly always does. Thus, if *and* is omitted from a serial coordination, it may become correspondingly ambiguous. Compare in this connection 'They hailed Sir Francis Bacon, Lord Chief Justice, Baron Verulam, Viscount St. Albans' (apposition: one object of the action); 'They hailed the knight, the lord, the baron, the viscount' (serial coordination: four objects of the action). But the more routinely difficult distinction to draw is that between coordinate *or*—always disjunctive, as noted previously—and appositive *or*, which multiplies alternative names for the same referent. Only comma intonation or comma punctuation, again the surface sentential reflex of syntactic independence deriving from conjunctive origins, can be looked to for cues to the presence of appositive *or:* 'He sailed for Constantinople, or Istanbul'; 'Steenie, or the duke of Buckingham, was the king's favorite.'

The parting reflection to be made on the extended family members among those constructions having a source in sentential conjunction is stylistic, and it turns on a possible effect of their syntactic peculiarity as a group: their adjunction within a matrix or containing clause. The feature of adjunction carries with it a remarkable latitude, for it can produce suspensive or successive effects that completely confound the simplistic distinction drawn between hypotaxis and parataxis in traditional philology. If adjunction occurs at the head or at some internal node of clause structure, and if the material being adjoined is of any bulk, the effect will be to suspend the progression of main elements in the clause and to complicate perception of the clause as an integral unit, no matter whether the source of the adjunct is conjunction or one of the two embedding operations, relativization or complementation. Conversely, if adjunction is performed only at the tail end of clause units, the effect

[66]George L. Dillon, *Language Processing and the Reading of Literature: Toward a Model of Comprehension* (Bloomington: Indiana University Press, 1978), pp. 90–91.

will be trailing, additive, and inherently more perspicuous.[67] Thus the resources of conjunctive syntax—especially as augmented by analysis tracing nonrestrictive relatives, appositives, and parentheticals to origins in subsurface coordination—emerge in a much more dazzlingly various light than that shed upon them by earlier means. Yet, as we shall have occasion to see, there may be correspondingly deeper shadows—obfuscations and obscurities—produced if these staple resources are exploited in ways that frustrate the "canonical sentoid" strategy for English sentences by encumbering its $NP + V + NP$ progression with adjuncts: thereby, in Christensen's picturesque phrase, "loading the patterns" on which we rely for understanding what we hear and read.[68]

To draw this introduction to a close, and to prepare the way for future discussion of a major aspect of Scripturalism in English prose style in the period with which I am concerned, I wish to make a summary review of the features of sentential conjunction that characterize so-called Semitic or Hebraic sense parallelism, the parallelism characteristic of lyric, oracular, and sententious passages, even whole books, of the Bible. Although sense parallelism is now, properly, regarded as a poetic device, this knowledge of its character had long been lost to sight, in Jewish tradition as well as more generally, until Bishop Robert Lowth's momentous rediscovery in the eighteenth century. The fact of this rediscovery bears rehearsing in the present context for several reasons: the first, to clarify that Biblical parallelism was construed and appreciated, prior to Lowth, as a species of heightened prose. In those eras, when Biblical parallelism was imitated, it was imitated in prose.[69]

How poetic form could have been transmitted (and translated, and retranslated) for centuries in such a fashion that the form was preserved, ready for recognition and yet unrecognized, becomes less a puzzle when one takes account of its fundamentally syntactic and semantic, rather than lexical and phonological, composition. Lowth lucidly set out the

---

[67]The distinction to which I am alluding has been formulated in an important way for linguistic study as one between "left-branching" (suspensive) and "right-branching" (successive) constructions by Victor H. Yngve in "A Model and an Hypothesis for Language Structure," *Proceedings of the American Philosophical Association* 104 (1960): 444–66. For useful discussions, see Judith Greene, *Psycholinguistics: Chomsky and Psychology* (Harmondsworth: Penguin Books, 1972), pp. 148–54, 169–83; and Fodor, Bever, and Garrett, *The Psychology of Language*, pp. 406–19.

[68]Christensen, *Notes toward a New Rhetoric*, p. 5. His injunction is: "Don't load the patterns."

[69]For accounts of relevant developments in England, see Israel Baroway, "The Bible as Poetry in the English Renaissance: An Introduction," *JEGP* 32 (1933): 447–80; "The Hebrew Hexameter: A Study in Renaissance Sources and Interpretation," *ELH* 2 (1935): 66–91; " 'The Lyre of David': A Further Study in Renaissance Interpretation of Biblical Form," *ELH* 8 (1941): 119–42; William Whallon, "Hebraic Symmetry in Sir Thomas Browne," *ELH* 28 (1961): 335–42; Harold Fisch, *Jerusalem and Albion: The Hebraic Factor in Seventeenth-Century Literature* (London: Routledge & Kegan Paul, 1964).

principles of composition in sense parallelisms in the Preliminary Dissertation appended to his translation of Isaiah (1778): "The correspondence of one Verse, or Line, with another, I call Parallelism. When a proposition is delivered, and a second is subjoined to it, or drawn under it, equivalent, or contrasted with it, in Sense; or similar to it in the form of Grammatical Construction; these I call Parallel Lines; and the words or phrases answering one to another in the corresponding Lines Parallel Terms."[70] He proceeded to distinguish and describe three main kinds of "Parallel Lines." Synonymic lines "correspond one to another by expressing the same sense in different, but equivalent terms; when a Proposition is delivered, and it is immediately repeated, in the whole or in part: the expression being varied, but the sense entirely, or nearly the same." Antithetic lines "correspond with one another by an Opposition . . . sometimes in expressions, sometimes in sense only. Accordingly the degrees of Antithesis are various; from an exact contraposition of word to word through the whole sentence, down to a general disparity, with something of a contrariety, in the two Propositions." What becomes remarkable about Lowth's definitions in the context of the preceding linguistic excursus is that Hebraic sense parallelism makes creative capital of the very sameness-and-difference relations that inform the workings of sentential conjunction. Thus, as Lowth indeed recognized, synonymic and antithetic sense parallelisms comprise the paradigmatic types of composition in this mode; they subsist together in syntactic and semantic complementarity.

Over against this paradigmatic complementarity, Lowth defined a third type of Biblical parallelism which he termed "Synthetic or Constructive": in it the joint syntactic and semantic specifications are relaxed so that "the Parallelism consists only in the similar form of Construction." In other words, synthetic parallelism is what we ourselves mean by "parallelism" as a stylistic term. The lines in a synthetic parallelism are bound together by the "mere correspondence between different Propositions, in respect of the shape and turn of the whole sentence, and of the constructive parts: such as noun answering to noun, verb to verb, member to member, negative to negative, interrogative to interrogative." In fact, subsequent scholarship has disclosed even more possibility for variety in synthetic parallelism than Lowth recognized: it may retain a form parallel to a preceding line while being shorter (containing fewer constituents); or it may depart from parallel form at some point in its sequence. To bring out more explicitly these possibilities for variation

---

[70]Robert Lowth, Preliminary Dissertation to Isaiah, pp. xix, xx, cited in George Buchanan Gray, *The Forms of Hebrew Poetry* (London, New York, Toronto: Hodder & Stoughton, 1915), pp. 48–49.

from the norms of the synonymic and antithetic types, synthetic parallelism is today more commonly known as the "incomplete" type.[71]

The still definitive study of the subject in English, George Buchanan Gray's *The Forms of Hebrew Poetry*, provides a number of literal translations of Biblical sense parallelisms in which hyphens are inserted to mark the units of constituent structure that become the correspondent parts of the Hebrew composition. The following illustration of the three types derives from Gray:

(a) *Synonymic parallelism:*
I-will-divide-them   in-Jacob,
And-I-will-scatter-them   in-Israel.   (Genesis 49:7)
For-the-heavens   like-smoke   shall-vanish-away,
And-the-earth   like-a-garment   shall-wax-old.   (Isaiah 52:6)

(b) *Antithetic parallelism:*
The-glory-of   young-men   is-their-strength;
But-the-beauty-of   old-men   is-their-gray-hair.   (Proverbs 20:29)
A-soft   answer   turneth-away   wrath,
But-a-grievous   word   stirreth-up   anger.   (Proverbs 15:1)

(c) *Incomplete (or synthetic) parallelism:*
I-will-restore   thy-judges   as-at-the-first,
And-thy-counsellors   as-at-the-beginning.   (Isaiah 1:26)
As-for-man   his-days   are-as-grass;
as-a-flower-of   the-field   so-he-flourisheth.   (Psalm 103:15)
Her-hand   to-the-tent-peg   she-stretched-forth,
And-her-right-hand   to-the-workman's-mallet.   (Judges 5:26)
For-Yahweh   knows   the-way-of   the-righteous;
But-the-way-of   the-wicked   will-perish.   (Psalm 1:6)[72]

A very considerable portion, well over a third, of the Old Testament is composed in sense parallelisms, with paired lines forming the staple verse unit out of which larger thematic responsions are built. In the overall binary patterning, single lines and groups of threes and fours are rare. The pervasive effect is rhythmic, either that of "balancing rhythm," in which a complete parallelism in a second line matches a first, or that of "echoing rhythm," in which an incomplete parallelism answers only partly to the form and sense of its predecessor. The resulting intensity of this shaped, reduplicated mode of expression con-

---

[71]Gray discusses incomplete parallelism extensively (ibid., pp. 59–74). Other useful discussions in English include Theodore H. Robinson, *The Poetry of the Old Testament* (London: Duckworth, 1947); and Norman K. Gottwald's entry, "Poetry, Hebrew," in *The Interpreter's Dictionary of the Bible*, ed. George A. Buttrick (New York: Abingdon Press, 1962).

[72]Gray, *The Forms of Hebrew Poetry*, pp. 60–62, 75–78.

duces to song, to prophecy, to aphorism, and other kinds of consciously charged or weighty utterance. Accordingly, parallelistic composition characterizes the whole of Proverbs, Lamentations, and Canticles, extensive portions of the Psalms and Job, and parts of Ecclesiastes as well as Isaiah and the nonbiographical part of Jeremiah among the major prophets, while among the minor prophets too, from Hosea through Malachi, such composition is quite continuously maintained. In addition, interpolated parallelisms are found sporadically in the Old Testament historical books, in victory songs, cultic hymns, words of counsel, blessings, denunciations, and curses. (A snatch of a victory song is illustrated in the parallelism from Judges 5:26 cited above.) Finally, while parallelistic composition is comparatively much rarer in the New Testament, it nevertheless makes notable appearances in the Magnificat (Luke 1:46–55), in the Beatitudes (Matthew 5:1–11), in stretches of the Pauline Epistles (particularly in Ephesians, Philippians, Colossians, and 1 and 2 Timothy), and in extended passages of 1 John and the visionary evocations of Revelation.[73]

Some excellent recent discussion by Roman Jakobson and Ruth apRoberts has focused literary attention on the singular amenability of Hebraic sense parallelism to replication from language to language—a characteristic that qualifies it as a poetic universal.[74] Jakobson's articles cite evidence from Chinese and Vedic traditions, which, of course, are independent of the Hebrew, to show that synonymic and antithetic parallelisms undergird the most ancient verse productions of discrete cultures. The analysis offered by apRoberts addresses itself more to the psychological impact of this mode of composition—what she finely calls "the ideational rhyme of parallel members" that at once engages and heightens consciousness:

The essential pattern prevails, the parallelisms that are the radical formal element of Hebrew verse. By these patterns the poem refers back to itself, sets up expectations within itself, and resolves itself. . . . For the reader or hearer actively correlates the two members, the pair of "rhyming" ideas, by discovering the logic of similarity or contrast. . . . Those who are familiar with traditional musical form will recognize a strong similarity here: repetitions with variations, paired phrases, refrains, da capos, resolutions, and tonality. But the remarkable thing is that although the form is "musical," the patterns are not of sound but of

---

[73]Ibid., pp. 132–57. The listing of parallelistic composition in the Old Testament is taken from pp. 37–40; information on its occurrence in the New Testament derives from Amos N. Wilder, *Early Christian Rhetoric: The Language of the Gospel* (Cambridge, Mass.: Harvard University Press, 1971), pp. 104–15.

[74]Roman Jakobson, "Grammatical Parallelism and Its Russian Facet," *Language* 42 (1966): 399–429; and "Poetry of Grammar and Grammar of Poetry," *Lingua* 21 (1968): 597–609; Ruth apRoberts, "Old Testament Poetry: The Translatable Structure," *PMLA* 92 (1977): 987–1004.

meaning. The sense unit coincides with the form unit, constitutes, in fact, the form unit. It is what Ernest Renan called a *rime des pensées,* a rhyme of thoughts, or a music of ideas. . . . The Old Testament poem is intelligible—as indeed many poems are; but, by virtue of the way in which its members explain each other, it reaches a consummate degree of intelligibility; it is an art form that has been used, or understood, perhaps more than any other in history.[75]

To supplement apRoberts's focus on the cognitive and perceptual effects of sense parallelism as heard or read, observations from rabbinical scholarship, as reported by Gray, offer insights into the motives of writers employing the mode. Ibn Ezra (1093–1163) first commented that the repetition of a thought in synonymous words was a stylistic elegance befitting prophetic utterance, while D. Kimhi (ca. 1160–1235) identified the power of the style of Isaiah with the "reduplication of meaning by means of synonymous terms" practiced by the book's author.[76] Louis Newman, a twentieth-century Hebrew scholar, has sought to extend insight into the authorial perspective still further by grounding parallelistic composition in two of the "deepest psychological principles": (1) the specific sensation of strong feelings as successive "waves of emotion" and (2) the common human inability to "leave with one statement what is felt as a profound insight." He postulates a pair of corresponding rules that harness these psychological principles in parallelistic composition: (1) a "demand for orderliness" confronts the waves of emotion, imposing stichic form and binary responsion on their expression, while (2) a countervailing "demand for repetition" is accommodated, but at the price of stylization that rules out indulgence in verbatim reiteration.[77]

It will by now have become evident, from historical and formal vantage points in the linguistic domain, why seeking to trace the impact of Scripture upon vernacular English prose has a commanding stylistic interest for me: writers whose native mode of composition abounds in conjunctive sentence forms encounter in the immediacy of their own tongue what to them is divine utterance, and it abounds in the same mode. What are the effects of such an encounter on the writing of prose? Yet, stated only linguistically, such a question remains insensitive to the intense additional interest that accrues specifically from the context of the English national experience during the two centuries from 1380— above all, the singularly deflected and delayed process of securing the

---

[75]ApRoberts, "Old Testament Poetry," pp. 988, 990, 998, 999, 1000.

[76]Gray, *Forms of Hebrew Poetry,* pp. 17–18.

[77]Louis I. Newman, *Studies in Biblical Parallelism,* I: *Parallelism in Amos,* University of California Publications in Semitic Philology no. 1.2 (Berkeley: University of California Press, 1918), pp. 57–59.

Bible in English before any absorption into popular consciousness can be assessed for its literary effects. Of necessity, then, the principal critical referent for my study—Scripturalism—is as much an ideological term as a formal one. I shall undertake to make its calculated duality both cogent and fruitful in the pages which follow.

2. Prose in the Later Fourteenth and Fifteenth Centuries: Scripturalism and the Oral Basis of Composition

WYCLIF'S ENGLISH SERMONS

If, as I propose, the term Scripturalism is used to denote a writer's absorption with the text of the Bible and with rendering its meaning in English—an absorption so intense as to mark the writer's own style with the impress of Biblical modes of expression—then, admittedly, Wyclif's Scripturalism was nothing absolutely new in English prose. John Alford has shown, for example, that Richard Rolle's prose, both Latin and English, is pervaded by networks of Biblical associations and allusions.[1] The first of my concerns in this chapter can be viewed as expanding on Alford's salutary claim that Scripturalism—what he calls "Biblical *imitatio*"—should command a good deal more attention as a shaping influence in late medieval English literature. Such a claim for the influence of Scripturalism points in an essentially new direction for criticism and scholarship, since Chambers, Croll, and Williamson all categorically declared (without, however, adducing arguments) against the Bible as an influence upon the style of English prose during the formative developments of the two centuries that are the focus of my study.[2]

---

[1]John A. Alford, "Biblical *Imitatio* in the Writings of Richard Rolle," *ELH* 40 (1973): 1–23.

[2]Raymond Wilson Chambers, "The Continuity of English Prose from Alfred to More and His School," in *Harpsfield's Life of More*, ed. Elsie V. Hitchcock, Early English Text Society o.s. 186 (London: Humphrey Milford, 1932); Morris W. Croll, "The Sources of the Euphuistic Rhetoric," in John Lyly, *"Euphues: The Anatomy of Wit" and "Euphues and His England,"* ed. Morris W. Croll and Harry Clemons (New York: Dutton, 1916), p. xxvi; George Williamson, *The Senecan Amble: A Study of Prose Form from Bacon to Collier* (Chicago: University of Chicago Press, 1966), p. 87. Certain nineteenth-century scholars had, however, asserted the impact of Scripturalism on English prose composition in diverse eras; see, e.g., C. Hardwick, "Notes on the Study of the Bible among Our Forefathers," Parts I and II, *Journal of Classical and Sacred Philology* 1 (1854): 83–91, 299–309; and Albert S. Cook, ed., *The Bible and English Prose Style: Selections and Comments* (Boston: D. C. Heath & Co., 1892), p. xxiv.

Even though Wyclif's Scripturalism was no absolutely new phenomenon, its most pronounced characteristics set it apart within its own time and, as a group, constitute a distinctive stylistic impulsion. By contrast with the vernacular Scripturalism of Rolle or that of a nearer contemporary, Walter Hilton, which aims at spiritual enrichment for a circumscribed number of "religious"—persons living devout lives prescribed by a more or less formal vow—the Scripturalism of Wyclif's vernacular writings envisages a broad audience ("the puple") who are to be instructed in doctrine and morals through renderings of Holy Writ that will be both respectfully literal and intelligible as English speech. An innovation in its day, Wyclif's conception of the Word of God as idiomatic, even familiar address to be brought over into the native tongue of English Christians has been seen in its due importance since Margaret Deanesly's work.[3] She showed that, prior to Wyclif, the only operative notion of Biblical translation in England was that of a scrupulous construe of the Vulgate text, adhering as closely as possible to its Latin vocabulary and word order. This is the notion embodied in Rolle's English Psalter, where it serves devotional ends,[4] and in the so-called Earlier Version of the Wycliffite English Bible, where the objectives are quite different.

Deanesly observed that the received notion of painstakingly literal and therefore unidiomatic Englishing of Scripture could accommodate Wyclif's first, legalistic objectives: to redress the abuses and evils in the Church and society of the later fourteenth century by compelling a return to the authority of the Bible from that of canon law. On this basis she accounted for the mode of translation that produced the Earlier Version. However, the so-called Later Version of the Wycliffite Scriptures, which came into circulation some years after Wyclif's death, bespeaks, in Deanesly's view, a significantly evolved conception of what God's Word was and was for. By this time it had become to Wyclif the voice of divine authority in all things—personal belief and morality as much as social and ecclesiastical governance—and it spoke with immediacy to every Christian soul. Even so, current scholarly consensus regards neither the Earlier nor the Later Version as Wyclif's own work. Another large body of material, the two hundred and ninety-four English sermons that Thomas Arnold's edition ascribed to Wyclif on the strengths of Thomas Netter's near-contemporary attribution (ca. 1430) and their thematic af-

---

[3]Besides her major work, *The Lollard Bible and Other Medieval Biblical Versions* (Cambridge: Cambridge University Press, 1920), Deanesly develops the particular interpretation to which I refer in *The Significance of the Lollard Bible* (London: Athlone Press, 1951), pp. 8–9.

[4]See H. R. Bramley's old-spelling edition, *The Psalter or Psalms of David, and Certain Canticles, with a Translation and Exposition in English by Richard Rolle of Hampole* (Oxford: Clarendon Press, 1884).

finities with Wyclif's known Latin works, is now under dispute regarding its authorship.[5] Since, however, it is agreed that if the sermons are not Wyclif's, they are the compositions of a single hand and a mind steeped in every aspect of Wyclif's thought, the absence of a clear alternative determination justifies retaining his name. It is on these considerations, and this body of evidence, that I base the following discussion of Wyclif's vernacular Scripturalism, both as a translator and as a writer of original prose.

The norm of immediate, personal, oral communication that Wyclif associates with Scripture derives from the Gospel characterization of Christ as the living Word. Christ in Scripture is radically self-disclosing. He is all truth or "soth," and cannot lie; he is also the Word of life in the sense of being the sole means of salvation. Thus he must be attended to with the utmost care, which for Wyclif means hearing Christ speak in Scripture:

And for this parable is ful good for many men to knowe, therfor biddith Crist aftir that, *he that hath eeris to heeren, here he* thes wordis, with ere and herte.

Therfor Jesus seide to the Jewis, . . . Whi knowen ȝe not my speche? Certis, for ȝe may not here my word. . . . And therfore Crist axith the Jewis, . . . *Ʒif Y seie thus treuthe, whi trowe ȝe not to me? He that is on Goddis half, heerith Goddis wordis;* and sith it is al oon, to be on Goddis half, and to heere his wordis, he that is not on Goddis half, herith not hise wordis.

As men shulden trowe in Crist that he is bothe God and man, so men shulden trowe bi his wordis that thei ben sothe, and wordis of liif. . . . For as no word of Goddis lawe hath ony strengthe, but as Crist spekith it, so no word of mannis lawe shulde be loved but if Crist speke it. For Crist is treuthe, and noo word shulde be loved but for it is trewe. Take we noon heede to beestis skynnes, ne to ynke, or other ornamentis, but to treuthe that Crist spake, in which stondith oure bileve. For as we trowen that Crist was man, so we trowen that he spake

[5]In his edition of *Select English Works of John Wyclif*, 3 vols. (Oxford: Clarendon Press, 1871), Thomas Arnold discusses the authenticity of Wyclif's English sermons at two junctures: I, xii–xv, and II, v–vi. Netter of Walden excerpted and excoriated a pair of passages from these sermons in his *Doctrinale* (ca. 1430); to one he added the following attribution: "quod in vulgari dicat in sermone evangelii natalis festi Joannis Baptistae Witcleff." Edmund D. Jones considered the English sermons a reliable guide to establishing Wyclif's English canon ("Authenticity of Some English Works Ascribed to Wyclif," *Anglia* 30 [1907]: 261–68), but E. W. Talbert first argued from a wide spread of alleged topical references that their author cannot be Wyclif ("The Date of the Composition of the English Wycliffite Collection of Sermons," *Speculum* 12 [1937]: 464–74). Most recently, Peggy Ann Knapp has undertaken to defend the position which I adopt as a matter of convenience, namely, that Wyclif's authorship of the English sermons has not been disproven; see her "John Wyclif as Bible Translator: The Texts for the English Sermons," *Speculum* 46 (1971): 713–20; and *The Style of John Wyclif's English Sermons* (The Hague: Mouton, 1977), pp. 5–8.

thus; and his wordis my3ten not be amended, sith he is God that seith this treuthe.[6]

Wyclif's Christocentric and communicative sense of Scripture entails several important consequences. One is the strikingly sustained focus in the great cycle of English sermons on what Christ did say during his life and ministry on earth. Of the total of 294 sermons, no fewer than 239 are on lengthy texts from the Gospels: the lesser part on narrative sections, the greater part on Christ's own teaching and preaching, especially the parables and precepts, but also the prophecies. In sustaining this focus on the actual words of Christ, Wyclif reverts often to his forthright and singular insistence that Scripture is "opin" to human understanding.[7] This insistence encompasses great faith in God, in language—specifically, the vernacular, English—and in human capacities, for to Wyclif Scripture redounds with the expressibility of divine meaning, the communicability of divine intention. The grounds alleged in support of all this faith are the Gospels' accounts of Christ's preaching ministry combined with the self-revelatory character of the living Word. Wyclif translates and comments on the opening of the Sermon on the Mount as follows:

Jesus seying the puple wente into an hil, and whanne he was sett his disciplis camen to *him. And he openede his mouth and tau3te hem and seide, Blessid be pore men in spirit,* *for hern is the rewme of hevene.* Ech word of this gospel is of greet wisdoom. For it is ful notable that Jesus saw this peple able to be lerned, and hadde mercy on hem, and 3af hem so plenteously thes 3iftis of goostli mercy. . . . For what man of bileve trowith that Crist openede thus his mouth, (and he is wisdom of the Fadir and the same God with him, and as he openede his mouth to speke, so he openede hertis of men to heere and undirstonde thes wordis, and teche hem men that camen aftir), that he ne wolde bisyen him to knowe hem, bothe for worshipe and for profit? [*SEW*, I, 406–7]

Briefer incidental remarks reinforce Wyclif's insistence on the communicative and intelligible nature of the Gospels in particular. "We shal bileve that al the gospel, be it nevir so literal, techith what thing shal bifalle, and how that men shal lyve." "It is knowun bi Goddis lawe that heering of Goddis word is shapen of God for this ende, to teche it and do it in dede" (*SEW*, I, 338; II, 299). Notably, Wyclif identifies the communicative and intelligible nature of the Gospels with Christ's method

---

[6]*Select English Works of Wyclif*, ed. Arnold, II, 28, 54–55, 1–2. In these and all subsequent citations of the English sermons (which are denoted *SEW* and incorporated in my text) I have substituted *th* where Arnold prints the thorn. Note that Arnold italicizes all verbatim Biblical quotation in Wyclif's sermons—a practice which my citations necessarily respect.

[7]For a literarily suggestive discussion of Jesus' use of the parable form, see Amos N. Wilder, *Early Christian Rhetoric: The Language of the Gospel* (Cambridge, Mass.: Harvard University Press, 1971), pp. 71–88.

of teaching in parables. He remarks of the parable of the woman who mixed leaven with three measures of barley meal, "This thing is knowe to wyves, and includith myche witt, for of comoun thing and knowun shulden the comouns beste take ther witt"; and of the parable of the grain of mustard seed, "Men undirstonden comunly this parable " (*SEW*, II, 195, 194). In another context he expatiates more broadly on the parabolic mode of Scripture:

For God spake ofte in parablis; as David propheciede of him, and seith, in Cristis persone, *Y shal opene my mouth in parablis and shal speke in proposiciouns that weren beyng and hidd at the bigynnynge of the world*. Parablis on good manere tellen many faire treuthis; and thus, for many causis, Crist spake ofte in parablis. . . . For every part of Holi Writt tellith Goddis word, the olde law in figure, and the gospel expressly. [*SEW*, I, 284–85; cf. I, 105]

The consequences of Wyclif's Christocentric understanding of scripture, however, extend well beyond the settled preference for Gospel texts in the great program of the English sermons. Since Christ declared openly to the people the saving truth about himself which they needed above all else to know, two inescapable imperatives confront the Church in present times. First, there must be a tirelessly active preaching ministry, after Christ's own example, and secondly, the Scripture must be made available to all in English, not merely preached in English. Only thus can the life-giving power of the Word attain its true and requisite impact. In the following passage Wyclif holds up the example of Christ's preaching from vernacular Scriptures and then judges accordingly the preaching of his own day:

And as Crist turnede the book, he fond the place where it was writun, The Spirit of the Lord is upon me, wherfore he anoyntide me; to preche to pore men he sente me, and so the Holi Ghost bad me, *preche to prisoneris forʒyvenes, and to blynde men siʒt, to leeve broken men in remissioun, to preche the ʒeer that the Lord acceptith, and the daie of forʒyvyng*. This preching is al disusid, and turnid to pride and coveitise. For how ever men mai plese the peple, and with moneie wynne hem worship, that thei prechen, puttith abak the profit of the peplis soule. This book was ordeyned of God to be red in this place, for alle thingis that felden to Crist weren ordeyned for to come thus. . . . And thus Crist mut nedis preche to meke men that wolden take it, for this is the beste dede that man doith here to his bretheren. . . . Certis traveile of the prechour or name of havyng of good witt shulde not be the ende of preching, but profit to the soule of the peple; and however this ende come beste, is moost plesing to God. And curiouse preching of Latyn is ful fer fro this ende; for many men prechen hemsilf, and leeve to preche Jesus Crist, and so sermouns done lesse good than thei diden in meke tyme. [*SEW*, II, 18–19]

Indictments of the present age as a nonpreaching one because Scripture is not preached abound in the English sermons, where they typically give point to strident anticlerical outbursts directed at worldly and dissolute prelates or at Wyclif's special targets, the new, self-styled "preaching orders" of friars. In one passage, however, a markedly personal expression of the crisis mentality engendered by the resolve to bring God's Word to the people in their native tongue infuses Wyclif's attack on the ecclesiastical hierarchy and their opposition. These powers must be of Antichrist's party; England's hopes for good governance and eventual licensing of vernacular Scripture lie with a lay party of knights (then including John of Gaunt, later Sir John Oldcastle) who savor the Bible in English:

And this lore is nedeful now in this world, for Anticrist; for he hath turned his clerkes to coveitise and worldli love, and so blindid the peple and derkid the lawe of Crist, that hise servantis ben thikke, and fewe ben on Cristis side. And algatis thei dispisen that men shulden knowe Cristis liif, for bi his liif and his loore shulde help rise on his side, and prestis shulden shame of her lyves, and speciali these hiȝe prestis, for thei reversen Crist bothe in word and dede. And herfore oo greet Bishop of Engelond, as men seien, is yvel apaied that Goddis lawe is writtun in Englis, to lewide men; and he pursueth a preest, for that he writith to men this Englishe, and somonith him and traveilith him, that it is hard to him to roowte. O men that ben on Cristis half, helpe ȝe now aȝens Anticrist, for the perilous tyme is comen that Crist and Poul telden bifore. But oo confort is of knyȝttis, that thei savoren myche the gospel and han wille to rede in Englishe the gospel of Cristis liif. For aftirward, if God wole, this lordship shal be taken from preestis, and so the staaff that makith hem hardi aȝens Crist and his lawe. . . . Crist helpe his Chirche from these fendis, for thei fiȝten perilously. [SEW, I, 208–9]

Despite the emphasis in these sermons on the direct, immediate impact of Christ's speaking in Scripture, Wyclif does not by any means associate the divine Word, or true human preaching of it, with spontaneous oral discourse. Rather, his thinking is summed up in his ubiquitous epithet for Scripture—"Goddis lawe." While constantly alleging that Scripture and sermon alike must be in the vernacular for the people, he just as constantly scorns the currently popular mode of the exemplum, or story sermon, as tale-telling and not truth (e.g., SEW, II, 216–17, 274). Instead, the nature of preaching must derive from the nature of Scripture, which itself derives from the nature of Christ who, as God and man, mediates between the two. What can man know of God through God's Word? Wyclif has much to say by way of answer; and the answer, while bearing the marks of his age and training, exhibits still more the rigorously intellectual and moral cast of his own mind. How God determines to style himself to man determines Wyclif's perceptions of the style of Scripture.

To some extent, the analytical character Wyclif finds in Scripture—what God's Word is by virtue of being God's Word—traces to established traditions in Biblical interpretation and to the scholasticism of Oxford.

Since Christ characterizes himself as the Word of truth and the sole means of salvation, Wyclif holds the paramount meaning of Scripture to be spiritual: what a Christian soul must be and do in order to gain eternal life. There are only two allusions in the English sermons to the fourfold senses, but one of these praises the "allegorik," the other the "allegorik" and "anagogik" strains cultivated by Paul (*SEW*, I, 30; II, 277–78). Another remark, utilizing the traditional kernel and shell figure, calls "the moral sense of these wordis . . . more swete than sense of the storye" (*SEW*, I, 114). However, Wyclif implements such received conceptions in an original fashion: he insists on respecting the literal sense and acknowledging a relation of identity rather than opposition between the literal and the spiritual sense of most of Christ's words.[8] The latter point, notable for the literarily sensitive view of textual integrity which it reflects, arises in connection with the Gospel parables and prophecies around which the vast cycle of the English sermons principally revolves. Wyclif's handling of the texts of these parables and prophecies shows a systematic tendency to translate them as larger units of discourse before proceeding, as a separate and subsequent step, to interpretation. In this respect he loosens the hold of the word-by-word or phrase-by-phrase glossing technique which was the standard means of extracting the sense of Scripture in his time.

Beyond its primacy of spiritual significance inseparably bound up with the literal sense, the text of Scripture furnished a plenum of knowledge: all and only the things a Christian soul needed to understand. Thus the English sermons virtually preclude both abstruseness and ineffability in warning against curiosity about matters that remain untouched or unspecific in the Bible. Wyclif sees good reasons why God withholds from men knowledge of the day of their death, of the day of doom, and of whether they are among the elect (*SEW*, I, 236). He also declares the state of eternity inexpressible (*SEW*, I, 127), but this is one of the very few exceptions to his emphasis on the articulateness of God's Word, which he prodigiously emulates in his own preaching. Thus he stresses the sum of meaning in Scripture and man's duty toward it: "Holi writt conteyneth al treuthe, sum treuthe expresli, and that shulden men thus trowe; and sum treuthe pryvyli, and that shulden men trowe in comune"; "And thus we may see worthinesse of Goddis word. Wordis of God ben many by diversite of resoun, but al thei rennen to gidere in o myddil poynte, and so thei ben alle Goddis word, that is him silfe" (*SEW*, I, 330, 156; cf. I, 302). In the Gospels, moreover, Wyclif discerns and praises a quality that most writers of his time seem not to have remarked: a

---

[8]See *SEW*, II, 343. Barbara Kiefer Lewalski has shown that a comprehensive conception of Scriptural meaning which resists dividing the literal from the spiritual sense is a defining characteristic of Reformation exegesis; see her *Protestant Poetics and the Seventeenth-Century Religious Lyric* (Princeton: Princeton University Press, 1979), pp. 72–86.

systematic economy and succinctness of expression, which allows us to distinguish among the four Evangelists' accounts of the essentials of Christ's life and ministry according to what they include or omit. By the same token, Wyclif infers that any apparent reiterations must in fact denote different things, for otherwise "it hadde be superflue to thus have told this" (*SEW*, II, 117; I, 63)—and there is nothing "superflue" in Scripture.

Above all else, for Wyclif the essence of Scripture, like that of Christ himself, is purely rational. The following odd translation stems from the Vulgate wording, but the added comment is characteristic and revealing:

Therfore seiden the Jewis to Crist, Who art thou? And Jesus seide to hem, I am a principle that speke to 30u. A principle is an out cause, as Crist was cause of alle thingis, and as he seide, he tolde hem his godhede in a manere. [*SEW*, II, 59]

Scholastic conceptions imbue the insistence on divine rationality in being and language that reechoes in these sermons. It is by analogy, proportionality, and consistency that the body of divine truth coheres and "Goddis lawe" endures. Ramifications of this line of thinking appear variously; the most notorious (and negative) is Wyclif's rejection of the dogma of transubstantiation as a physical and logical impossibility, the positing of "accidents withouten suget" (e.g., *SEW*, II, 82, 91, 274, 358). But the positive significance he discovers in divine rationality is equally telling and ultimately more effectual in shaping his ideas and style.

Fundamentally Wyclif does not—and, it would seem, cannot—allow for paradox in Scripture or Christian doctrine. While the gift of grace is acknowledged in numerous contexts, salvation is chiefly represented as a reward that one earns. It is only logical that this be so, Wyclif thinks: "For ech man that shal be dampned is dampned for his owne gilt, and ech man that shal be saved is saved bi his owne merit" (*SEW*, II, 117). Again, "In this we thenke ever on hevenli blisse, and traveile therfore, ni3t and dai, in hope for to gete this blisse. . . . Lord, sith a tiliyng man hopith ofte to have his fruyt, how moche more shulden we have hope to come to blisse of hevene" (*SEW*, I, 63). Thus Wyclif labors to dispel any imputation of illogic to "Goddis lawe." Christ's commandment to love one's enemies is praised as a clever means of combatting evil because it shames and converts the offender: "For love of God is ful of resoun, and holdith no thing a3ens resoun; for 3if it held a3en resoun, thanne it were a3ens God. And thus clene love puttith out al synne" (*SEW*, II, 253; cf. I, 55). In larger terms, a voluntaristic view of God is outright heresy to Wyclif, for "blessid men shulen clerely see the opyn resoun of Goddis wille, and thanne thei shulen scorne thes foolis that wenen that God may chaunge his wille" (*SEW*, II, 235).

In particular, as suggested in the analogy between a tiller's expectation of harvest and the cultivation of virtue, divine truth renders itself intelligible in orderly modes of expression and correlation. Thus Wyclif expatiates:

And men shulden not muse on this, that ther ben diverse meritis. For as ther ben in ech man diverse degrees of bileve, so ther ben in Cristis apostlis diverse degrees of meritis. And for to quiete hem in this Crist seith to his apostles, *That in the hous of his Fadir ben many dwellingis:* as who seith, Have 3e sum degree of feith and hope and charite, and last 3e, creessyng therinne to 3our lyves eende, and 3our place is ordeyned in hevene after that 3e ben worth. . . . For Crist wole teche his disciplis bi litil and litil alle thes. [*SEW*, I, 358]

The supreme graduated lesson of Scripture is, of course, knowledge of God through the incarnate Christ of the Gospels: "For it fallith bi grace of God that knowing of Cristis manheede bringith in the knowing of the Godhede" (II, 102). Nevertheless, Wyclif discerns degrees and correspondences in every aspect of the truth of Scripture:

Cristene men shulde lerne Goddis lawe, and holden hem paied therof; and in this mesure, and in this nombre, and in this wei3te, shulden thei lyven here, and abiden lore in hevene that men shulden have over this. For this lore that Crist tau3te ys ynou3 for this liif. . . . For God coude ordeyne noo kyn thing, but in mesure, noumbre and wei3te. [*SEW*, I, 310]

It is not too much to assert what the foregoing passage intimates: the proportionality of divine reason finally assumes an overtly arithmetical character in Wyclif's representations. The English sermons are rife with passages in which the process of understanding, the unfolding interpretation, takes the form of enumeration. There are four comings of Christ, which correspond to the four cruxes of human history; Christ's six sufferings in his Passion are reflected in the six kinds of trials that virtuous souls undergo in this world; Christ meetly manifested himself in the flesh exactly ten times between his resurrection and ascension; and so on (*SEW*, I, 65, 106, 132). The enumerations are the most conspicuous signs of the intellectual and verbal confidence that pervades these sermons: the Word says all, and that plenum of meaning can be comprehended and articulated in the vernacular for the people.

We are now in a position to examine the stylistic implications of Wyclif's Scripturalism—to ask in what ways and to what extent it affects, first, his responsiveness to Biblical language as revealed in his translations and, then, the sentence forms of his own prose. As we turn to the style of Wyclif's translations, his preference for Gospel texts is the great fact to be kept in view. It entails that the English renderings are, by and large, passages of narration (Christ's life and ministry, the parables) or passages of sequential discourse of other kinds (Christ's preaching, prophecies). Accordingly, the syntax and semantics of these passages are preponderantly those of asymmetric conjunction. As we shall see,

Wyclif's Englishings go remarkably far in preserving the speech continuum, the additive and consecutive character of such blocs of sentences,
either by foregoing the intrusive gloss technique or by expanding upon
the recursive potential of the conjunctive syntax through insertions of
appositive or parenthetical constructions within larger sequences of connectives. The effect of Wyclif's Gospel translations is emphatically to
"opin" the sense by reproducing the discursive quality and the specific
forms of utterance used by the living Word in speaking to man.

In this regard it is significant that the parable translations, on the
whole, exhibit the greatest textual integrity, the least incidence of interruption. Here is Wyclif's version of Christ's parable of the good Samaritan:

*But this lawier wolde justifie himsilf, and therfore he axide, who was his neiȝbore. And
Crist tolde him a parable,* that was sutil in witt, *for Crist lokynge on him seide him
this parable,* how *a man wente doun fro Jerusalem into Jerico and felde in thefes handis,
that dispuyliden him and fastiden many sores on him and wenten and leften him halfe
quyke. And it fell that a preest passide the same way; and he siȝ him lye thus hirt, and
wente awey and helpide him not. And a deken, whan he was niȝ the place, and siȝ him
sich, passide a wey. But a Samaritan making his weie bi that place came bi side him, and
siȝ his state, and hadde mercy on him. And he cam nyȝe, and bond his woundis, and
helde in hem bothe oile and wyn, and put him upon his hors, and brouȝt him in to stable
of a toun, and there he did cure of him. And anothir dai he toke two pens, and ȝaf hem
to the hosteler, and bade him have cure of him, and seide thus, What ever thou ȝyvest
over, whan Y come aȝen Y shal pay thee.* And whan Christ hadde seide this parable,
he axide of this man of lawe, *which of these three men semed him to be neiȝbore
unto this syke man that thus fell into theves handis. And he seide,* that *the thridde man,
that dide mercy on him. And Jesus seide* to this legistre, *Go thou and do riȝt so.* [SEW,
I, 32]

By comparison with his handling of the parables, Wyclif is consistently
more intrusive in rendering stretches of Gospel narrative. The following
treatment of the risen Christ's appearance to Mary Magdalene is
characteristic:

This gospel tellith how Crist apperide to Marie Mawdeleyn. For Crist wolde that
womman kynde hadde this privylege tofore man, that he shewide him aftir his
deth rather to womman than to man. For wymmen ben freel as water, and taken
sooner printe of bileve. Joon tellith how this *Marie at the sepulcre stood withouten,
wepyng.* And licly she wente bifore withinne, and wantide Cristis bodi, but her
brennynge in love nedide hir to abide more. *And while this Marie wepte thus, she
bowide and lokide into the tombe;* for hoot love makith many lokingis to that thing
that it loveth. *And she saw two aungels sittinge in white, one at the heed, another at
the feet, wher the bodi of Jesus was put. The aungels seyn to her, Womman, whi wepist
thou?* She seith to hem, For *thei han taken awey my Lord, and Y noot where thei han
doon him. Whanne she hadde seid thes wordis, she turned abac fro the sepulcre, and
she saw Jesus stondinge, and she wiste not that it was Jesus. Jesus seide to Magdaleyn,
Womman, whi wepist thou? whom sekist thou?* She, *gessinge that he was a gardyner,*

seide to him, Sire, ʒif thou hast taken him awey, telle me where thou hast put him, and Y shal take him thennes, and thus he shal not be chargious to this gardyn. *Jesus seith to hir, Maria.* And so she knewe bi vois and name that this persone was Jesus, *and she was turned, and seide to him, Rabony,* that is to seie, Mastir. And it semeth that she wolde have kist Christis feet as bifore. *Jesus seith to hir, Nyle thou touche me, for ʒit Y have not steied to my fadir.* Marie lovede here fleishli Crist, and he was not steyed in her herte as a bodi glorified, as he shal be after assencioun. And bifore this ascencioun shal he not be fleishly tretid, for bi his ascensioun his body shal be goostly knowun, and not bi sich fleishly kissyng as Marie wolde have kissid Crist. [*SEW,* II, 139–40]

The self-consciousness of Wyclif's Scripturalism as a translator emerges most markedly in his differential treatment of Christ's discourse as compared with other portions of Scripture. We find a paramount respect for the orality of the living Word: that which Christ speaks is transmitted intact, with careful preservation of its speech features, including redundancies (e.g., *But a Samaritan . . . cam bi side him. . . . And he cam nyʒe . . . ; and bade him . . . and seide thus . . .*). Sentence form, too, is clearly governed by the dynamic that Robin Lakoff has noted in recursive asymmetric conjunction: one clause will stipulate a crux or decisive occurrence to which the other clauses in the series are accessory. Wyclif's strong stylistic preference is to make a crux a climax, the last clause in its semantically related series. We note in this connection *and wenten and leften him halfe quyke, and there he did cure of him* in the good Samaritan parable; and in the narrative of Christ and Mary Magdalen, *and she wiste not that it was Jesus.*

Nevertheless, where the written account of a human (if divinely inspired) author comprises the text at hand, Wyclif's Scripturalism tends to leave itself more scope for interpolated commentary to drive home the rationality and the spiritually charged significance of all of Christ's doings, including his conversational exchanges with various persons, which are treated as a species of action in the English sermons.[9] In addition, Wyclif takes pains to specify motives, causes, and other attendant factors so that Christ will emerge in a verbal fullness of perfection. To be sure, the then standard exegetical option, which Wyclif often exercises, of proposing an inclusive figurative interpretation after translating a parable in its entirety did gravitate against piecemeal interpolations of the kind found in other contexts. Yet it remains a fact that

[9]See, e.g., Wyclif's explanations of why Christ spoke sharply to his mother at the wedding feast at Cana (*SEW*, I, 86–87), why he answered the Pharisees' question with a question (*SEW*, I, 56–58), why he waited in silence after hearing the woman taken in adultery accused (*SEW*, II, 86–87). Analogous passages in a rationalist strain include *SEW*, I, 279, and II, 12. I do not suggest that Wyclif proceeds in an original fashion, for indeed what he says at several junctures derives from patristic commentaries. The essential point is Wyclif's unshakeable certainty that every aspect of Scripture is accessible to reason.

Wyclif accords the spoken discourse of Christ far more unitary and uninterrupted treatment than he does other portions of Scripture. In particular, this fundamental difference between the treatment of Christ's words and all others evinces its principled nature in Wyclif's translations from the apostle Paul.

Of the fifty-five English sermons that are not on Gospel texts, forty are on the reading appointed for the day from the Pauline Epistles. Wyclif expresses high regard for the apostolic New Testament writings, at one point even going so far as to characterize them as Gospel too: "And . . . not oonly thes foure gospels, but epistlis of Poul and of othere apostlis ben cleped evangelies . . . , and thes ben men out of bileve, that denyen that thes ben gospelis" (*SEW*, II, 339). Paul, however, claims the highest regard of all:

And al3if the Holi Goost spekith ech word of holi writt, netheles Crist spake in Poul more plenteousely and sutilli. And this moveth sum men to telle in Englishe Poulis pistelis, for sum men may betere wite herbi what God meneth bi Poul. . . . And so Cristene men shulden wite that Poulis wordis passen otheres writingis in two thingis: thei ben sutil and plenteous to preche the puple. . . . For ech treuthe that Poul spekith is knyttid with ech point of bileve, and so after speche of oon may come speche of anothir, after that it profitith to the heerers. [*SEW*, II, 221, 224]

Such praise notwithstanding, Wyclif regularly breaks up sections of text Englished from the Pauline Epistles and subjects them not only to glossing but also to wholesale syntactic recasting, in which clauses are separated off as discrete propositions from the cumulative wholes of their containing sentences. Such handling, illustrated by the enumerative style of the next quotation, confirms that the integrity accorded Christ's own words in the English sermons must derive from the Christocentric character of Wyclif's Scripturalism. What follows is part of the dismemberment process undergone by the serial clauses of 1 Corinthians 13, a chapter whose allegedly consummate rationality he represents as a list of "sixtene condiciouns by which men may knowe . . . charite":

The thrittenthe condicioun of this love is that *it trowith all thingis;* ffor thing and treuthe is al oon, and so al treuthis ben trowid of it. . . . The fourtenthe condicioun of this love is that, *it hopith alle thingis;* for it hopith that ordeyned treuthe helpith to alle good men, and this charite hopith to have parte of this helpe. . . . The fiftenthe condicioun of this love is that, *it susteyneth al thingis;* for it helpith to holde al treuthe, and abidith the ende therof. . . . The sixtenthe condicioun and the laste that folwith this charite, is that *it fallith never awey,* neither in this world ne in the tother. For Goddis love may not faile, sith God mai not ceese to ordeyne thes men to come to blis, the which he wol ever have blis. And this love that is in God mut have sich charite in man. Loke thou thes condiciouns, whether thou have hem al in thee; and 3if thou hast not, be aboute for to have hem al hool, and than thou hast withouten doute this love that mut bringe to blis. [*SEW*, II, 268]

Over against such strenuous reshaping of an eloquent Pauline formulation, it is the more striking and extraordinary that Wycliff's Scripturalism should compel him as a translator to reproduce the looseness and repetitiousness of the asymmetrically conjoined sentences in Christ's parables and preaching. On the evidence of the English sermons Wyclif was far from insensitive to the stylistic potentialities of conjunctive syntax. However, the means by which he attains a distinctive lucidity among prose writers of his age lead away from looseness, repetitiousness, and asymmetric sentence form toward symmetry, parallel coordinate structures, and articulated responsions of phrasing and sense. Given such stylistic predilections together with his convictions regarding the economy and logicality of Biblical language, it is no wonder we find Wyclif baffled by a Hebraic sense parallelism, struggling to account for the locution by imposing distinctions and sequencing on its conjuncts—as in this example:

Certis *God seith* to these men, *In covenable tyme Y have herd thee, and in day of helthe Y have helpid thee.* First, men bidden to God ther prier, that he helpe hem in tyme of nede; and ȝif this be resounable, God helpith hem in covenable tyme; and whanne tyme cometh that God ȝyveth helthe, he helpith men as he hath bihiȝt. And thes wordis of Ysaye ben general and in good ordre. [*SEW*, II, 270; cf. II, 241–44; I, 72–73]

Yet for every such incapacity to deal in kind with Biblical language, there are many times that number of passages in which Wyclif acutely renders the syntax of the original and proceeds to implementation of his own in the same vein. The results embrace a wide spectrum of the resources of conjunctive syntax, applied in the service of reason and in the course of reasoning about the Word.

One recurrent rhythm in the thought and style of the English sermons is that of antithesis arising from *not . . . but . . .* constructions in Scripture which convey moral or metaphysical oppositions. Here is a quite typical instance in which Wyclif's own style adapts itself to the syntax of the texts he cites:

And thus seith Crist, that kyngis and gentilefolk have lordship. . . . But ȝe shal not thus lyve, in noon of thes thre pointis. For worldli lordshipis shal not be among ȝou; ne power to prisoune shal be in oon upon othir; ne ȝour goode dedis shal not stonde in ȝyvynge of worldli goodis; *but he that is more amonge ȝou be maad as ȝonger, and he that goith bifore, be he as a servere.* That is to sei, the mekere of ȝou is the more, and oon shal go bifore anothir, not for worldli worship, but to serve more mekeli to othir of his fellowship. [*SEW*, I, 386; cf. I, 393; II, 111]

Similarly, alternative *or* undergoes elaboration from Wyclif in contexts and for purposes like those of *but:*

And Crist seide to hem, Wher it be leveful to do wel in the Sabot, or men shulden do yvel in the Sabot? wher it is leveful to make a mannis liif saaf, or lese mannis liif in the Sabot? *But thes foolis holden ther pees.* . . . Mathew tellith that Crist seith first that, *Whoever is not with him, he is aʒens him.* For generalte of this Lord, sith he is both God and man, he axith service of ech man, for ech man must serve Crist, other doinge or suffring. . . . And this sentence shulden lordis lerne, and all maner of ydel men, to wite wher thei ben with Crist, or thei ben aʒens him. [*SEW,* II, 22]

Above all, it is the synthesizing and combinatory power of sentential conjunction that compels Wyclif stylistically as he applies his conviction regarding the "oonhede" of Scripture. Thus correlatives, to some extent, but especially emphatic forms of *and* play a pervasive role in his own style. One reliable mark of Wyclif's signature in conjunctive syntax is his polysyndeton—reiteration of connectives—and his retention of phrasal structure for conjuncts. From the abundance of possible examples, here is a sampling (with polysyndetic elements italicized): "And Jesus profitide in wisdom, *in* age, and *in* grace *bothe* to God and *to* man"; "And thus this lond is undisposid bi three enemyes of a man, *the which be,* the fend, *and* the world, and *the* fleish wanton of a man" (*SEW,* I, 84, 104). The local effect of such polysyndeton is to give explicit indication of the sentential derivation of such conjoined phrases while at the same time welding them together through the articulation of identical elements. When, as frequently, these smaller polysyndetic units are incorporated within overarching correlative or emphatic conjoining constructions (*bothe . . . and, aswel as, riʒt as . . . riʒt so*), the net result is powerfully integrative, as part answers to part. Even semantic opposition in the contained material docs not inhibit this result, as the two following passages illustrate:

But, as men that ben in feveris desire not that were best for hem, so men here in sinne coveiten not the best thing for hem. For the world seide that the apostlis weren fooles and forsaken of God, and so it wolde seie todaie of men that lyveden lyke to hem. . . . For as a mouth of a syke man distempered fro good mete moveth him for to coveite thingis contrarie to his helthe, so it is of a mannis soule that savoureth not Goddis lawe. And as wanting of appetit is a signe dedly to man, so wanting of Goddis witt is signe of his secounde deeth. [*SEW,* I, 150]

And thus *ech good tree* that God hath ordeyned to the hous of heven *bereth here good fruyte* and *ech yvel tree berith venym,* for riʒt as Goddis children may not do but good thing, so children of the fend may not do but harmful thing. For riʒt as fendis semen to do good, and it turneth at the ende to ther harm, so Goddis children semen to do yvel, but God turneth it to ther good. [I, 21]

Besides polysyndeton, correlation, and emphatic conjunction, the other specially identifying mark of Wyclif's handling of conjunctive syntax is his frequent recourse to parallel construction, oftenest in full clauses or even in sentence wholes. Parallelism of form is, of course, an amenable stylistic option for enforcing likeness of sense through likeness of shape. If Wyclif fails to make much of Hebraic sense parallelisms alone, he does nevertheless respond acutely to promptings toward formal parallelism that emanate from his Scriptural texts.[10] Again, instances are plentiful; one occurs in the parallelistic cast of the clauses at the end of the quotation just preceding. The two examples below document the productivity of the device as Wyclif's style elaborates syntactic or semantic aspects of identity in his Biblical materials by way of serial parallelism:

And Crist helide al languyshing and al sykenesse in the peple. . . . And thei offriden to Crist al tho that hadden hem yvel bi diverse siiknesse, as lunatikes and paralitykis, and Crist heelide hem. And myche folk sueden Crist. Sum men sueden Crist for lore of Goddis lawe and weye to hevene; sum men sueden Crist for helthe, for Crist heelide many bodies; sum men sueden Crist for mete, for Crist fedde men ofte by myracle; sum men sueden Crist for woundris that thei sawen Crist do, for Crist dide more wonderful werkes than men don in somer games; and sum men sueden Crist to accuse him in word and in dede. And thus, for summe of these or manye, summe folk sueden Crist. [*SEW*, II, 23]

And herfore seith Crist, *If the world hate you, ȝe shulden wele wite that it hatide me bifore. . . .* If thou grutche aȝens poverte, and coveite worldeli worshipe, wite thou that Crist biforne was porer than thou, sith he hadde not bi his manhede place to rest his heed ynne. If thou grutchist that thi sugetis wolen not ȝyve thee goodis, thenke how Cristis sugettis wolden neither ȝyve him mete ne herberwe; and ȝit herfore he curside hem not, but dide hem moche good. And if thou grutche that the world doith thee ony injurie, and thou profitist to the world aȝen in love and in mekenesse, thenke how Crist bifore thee profitide thus more to the worlde, and ȝit Crist suffride more wronge of his sugettis than thou maist. And thus if thou woldist thenke on Crist, how he suffride for love of man, it were the beste ensample that thou shuldist have to suffre, and to cese thi grutching. [*SEW*, I, 172–73]

It is noteworthy that the serial parallelisms in the first passage exfoliate from a plural expression, *And myche folk sueden Crist,* displaying in the process Wyclif's typical enumerative mode for "opening" the rationality of the Word. In addition, the parallelisms bespeak the fundamental affinities between the semantics of plurals and the semantics of conjunction. The second passage is at first sight somewhat less than transparent in its stylistic wellsprings, for why should a Scriptural *if . . . (then)* construction trigger Wyclif's series of parallel and semantically symmetric

---

[10]Knapp (*Style of Wyclif's English Sermons*, pp. 62–64) remarks upon the incidence of parallelism, balance, and antithesis, but associates these features with a penchant for "orderliness" apparently independent of Scripturalism.

sentences? The association between conditionals and coordination is neither inadvertent nor fortuitous, however, to Wyclif's mind. An extraordinarily interesting reflection on Scriptural language in another sermon explains how Christ's conditional locutions are equivalent to sentential conjunctions:

And for to make hem siker of this, Crist seith this word, *ȝe trowen in God, and trowe ȝe in me.* As who seith, ȝe moten nedis trowe in God, or ellis ȝou faileth charite; and ȝe mai not trowe in God, but ȝif ȝe trowen in me, for Y am the same God, that is God the Fadir. . . . ȝif God tell us a thing, who of us wolde drede therof, sith we ben certyn of bileve that God mai not disseyve us. [*SEW,* I, 357]

The equivalence of a conditional and a coordinate expression which Wyclif affirms here is a notion drawn from the formal logic in which he was trained; he applies it to the speech of the Word. The claim is that the conditional '*if* x, *then* y' is an alternative way of expressing the conjunction '*not both not-*y *and* x.' Under Wyclif's logical analysis, Christ is saying 'You cannot both not believe in me and believe in God' (or, in the equivalent conditional, 'If you believe in God, then you believe in me'). As Wyclif explains, the equivalent truth value of the coordinate and the conditional expressions is assured by Christ's identity with God. Since Christ is God, he divinely authenticates all his utterance with binding exactitude and rational force. It is this conviction that forges the connection between Wyclif's respectfully idiomatic and "opin" renderings of Christ's speech in the Gospels, with its additive, asymmetric sentence conjunctions, and the more incised, polysyndetic, and parallelistic design of the sentences of his own prose.

HILTON'S *SCALE OF PERFECTION*

The foregoing discussion of Wyclif's Scripturalism invests the motive of Biblical translation with primary interest and importance as a shaping factor in the development of English prose style. For such theoretical emphasis on Biblical translation as a stylistic determinant, there is precedent to cite in the critical approach offered by Elizabeth Salter as a corrective to Chambers's sweeping and simplistic affirmation of "continuity" in English prose from King Alfred to Thomas More. The gist of Salter's approach, as set out in her monograph on Nicholas Love,[11] is that two distinct strains appear in vernacular religious prose as early as

---

[11]Elizabeth Salter, *Nicholas Love's "Myrrour of the Blessed Lyf of Jesu Christ,"* Analecta Cartusiana no. 10 (Salzburg: Institut für englische Sprache, 1974); also see her "Continuity in Middle English Devotional Prose," *JEGP* 55 (1956): 417–22. The best account I know of the ornate prose tradition is Margery M. Morgan's "*A Talkyng of the Love of God* and the

Aelfric, who reflects his awareness of them by writing in both by turns. The distinction between the two strains turns on the degree and manner in which sound similarities—especially at the beginnings and endings of words—are cultivated in the prose. Sound similarities are the chief sources of the rhetorical ornamentation that exercises a double appeal on vernacular writers: in part through postclassical Latin rhetorical treatises, in part through native propensities toward alliterative composition. Lavish use of sound similarities to produce insistent, even incantatory patternings marks for Salter a vernacular "high style" which is traceable in Aelfric's *Lives of the Saints*, Wulfstan's *Sermo Lupi*, the saints' lives of the "Katherine Group" and the "Wooing" texts associated with it, as well as in Rolle's English *Epistles* and *Meditations on the Passion*, the near-contemporary *A Talkyng of the Love of God*, and in the work of two fifteenth-century translators: Richard Misyn, who Englished Rolle's *Incendium amoris*, and William Atkynson, who prepared an aureate version of the *Imitatio Christi* for the countess of Richmond, mother of Henry VII.[12]

The high style characterized by Salter receives consistent generic application. It is used on materials and in contexts that aim at affective transport, at achieving the heights of contemplation in mysticism or ecstasy—which is to say, its appeal is all but exclusively to readers with a formal religious vocation. Over against this high style, Salter discerns a "simpler, more moderate" style in which sound similarities are less densely evident and, where they do appear, are made to serve semantic functions—for example, the marking of phrases and clauses that contain key ideas or thematic relationships.[13] This moderate style is found in Alfred's translations, the Old English Biblical renderings, and a substantial portion of Aelfric's English works among prose of the pre-Conquest era; it persists thereafter in the *Ancrene Wisse*, in the *Book of Vices*

Continuity of Stylistic Tradition in Middle English Prose Meditations," *Review of English Studies*, n.s. 3 (1952): 97–116. Morgan has particularly good comments on the vexed debate over the provenance of the syntactic patternings (figures) which are so conspicuous in this tradition of prose. On the one hand, she concedes that an ultimate stimulus toward antithesis, parallelism, isocolon, and other commonly used figures probably derives from the Latin of the Vulgate and from patristic Latin writings which extensively quote and elaborate upon Vulgate texts. On the other hand, Morgan stresses that these types of syntactic patterning were fully domesticated and cultivated as a native English aspect of style in devotional and meditative prose well before the fourteenth century. Hence there is unimpeachable critical reason to regard this ornate prose as a vernacular tradition rather than a Latinate import by this point in its history.

[12]Salter, *Love's "Myrrour,"* pp. 193–98, 203–14. She also calls attention to the prior challenge posed to Chambers's continuity thesis by Dorothy Bethurum, "The Connection of the Katherine Group with Old English Prose," *JEGP* 34 (1935): 553.

[13]See, further, the application and extension of Salter's two traditions made in Norman F. Blake's introduction to his edition of *Middle English Religious Prose* (Evanston: Northwestern University Press, 1972), pp. 1–3.

and Virtues, in Walter Hilton's *Scale of Perfection*, and in Nicholas Love's *Myrrour of the Blessed Lyf of Jesu Christ*. Again, definitive generic associations attach to the objectives of the moderate style. It appeals to a broad audience, lay as well as clerical, by means of direct, unaffected, idiomatic English, and it eschews mystical transport to pursue doctrinal and devotional ends. It is within the framework of this "simpler, more moderate" style that Salter proposes to locate the English sermons and the Scripturalism of Wyclif and his collaborators.[14]

There is substantial validity and value in Salter's two stylistic traditions, particularly in her composite definitions of materials, aims, audiences, and figuredness of form. Hers is a critical approach of considerably greater utility than Norman Blake's proposal that fifteenth-century prose be divided into two classes according to the types of reader courted, respectively, by the printers William Caxton and Wynkyn de Worde: on Caxton's side, mainly secular works, especially, prose romances derived from French models and appealing to a courtly or otherwise modish readership; on de Worde's side, mainly religious works produced in accordance with Latin models for the members of conventual foundations who may have been his official patrons.[15] While Blake's classification along religious and courtly lines seems more germane to the late sixteenth century than the fifteenth, Salter's differentiation between a high, decorated prose style and a simpler, more moderate one provides for extension of both traditions to secular applications and analogues by the start of the sixteenth century. For the high style, the extension is the cult of aureation; for the moderate style, it is the emergence of an advisory, even admonitory prose which has various political, social, and moral ends in view—a prose which I shall be linking with its religious counterpart and terming "the prose of counsel" in discussing the later sixteenth century in chapters 5 and 6 of this study.

While I welcome Salter's contributions in distinguishing concurrent traditions of "high" and "moderate" vernacular prose styles on formal and generic grounds and in emphasizing the "moderate" strain as the crucial one for the development of English prose in the fifteenth century (the era of the great influence of Hilton's *Scale* and Love's *Myrrour*), it will not do, in my view, to group Wyclif and the Lollards together with Hilton, Love, and other orthodox writers of vernacular prose as cohorts in a great enterprise centered in Biblical translation—or, at least, transmission—that began with Alfred and Aelfric. Anglo-Saxon efforts on behalf of the Gospels in English find no analogues in the ideology and politics obtaining in England at the close of the fourteenth century. At that time, vernacular Biblical versions were incurring such hostility be-

---

[14]Salter, *Love's "Myrrour,"* pp. 196–97, 215–29, 248–50.
[15]Norman F. Blake, "Middle English Prose and Its Audience," *Anglia* 90 (1972): 437–55.

cause of the countercultural program of Lollardy that, in 1408, Archbishop Arundel's *Constitutions* effectually prohibited all translating, reading, or possessing of the Scripture in English. Accordingly, the single greatest factor in the fifteenth-century popularity of Love's *Myrrour* and its survival in numerous manuscripts was Arundel's commissioning of the work, a free translation of pseudo-Bonaventure's Latin original, to circulate among would-be readers of the life of Christ, as a substitute for the Gospels in English.[16] In my view, when the climate of received opinion undergoes such drastic sensitizing to the issue of vernacular Scripture, one can no longer postulate an English prose tradition in which attitudes and practices with respect to the Bible continue unaltered.

In the next three sections I shall be arguing for a discernible difference in the handling of Biblical materials by prose writers after Wyclif—a difference that emerges most suggestively in Hilton's *Scale* and Love's *Myrrour*, two works which Salter links closely in purpose and style. Since Hilton died in 1396, and the *Myrrour* appeared in 1410, there is circumstantial plausibility in inferring from the suppression of the Lollards to the changed handling of Scripture in English. Although glancing disapproval of Lollardy has been noted in Hilton,[17] the authorial consciousness of the work appears, in its straightforward, unperturbed incorporation of Scriptural translation or paraphrase as its purposes demand, to predate the hue and cry (and worse) that very shortly ensued upon Wyclif's supporters. Although he neither translates en bloc nor respects the ipsissima verba as Wyclif does, there is a real sense in which Hilton can be called a transmitter of Scripturalism. In Love, however, the attitude toward Scripture and its concomitant treatment become very different. The *Myrrour*, as a deliberate surrogate, consistently filters its Vulgate materials through paraphrase, or summary, or affective dilation, or combinations of these. Love, then, is not a Biblical translator or transmitter even in the sense that Hilton is one; and evidence from their prose styles will bear out the difference. Thus the perspective which I shall implement here parts company with Salter's precisely in insisting on divorcing the motive of Biblical translation from consideration of the development of a "simpler, more moderate" vernacular prose style for the period intervening between Wyclif and Tyndale—roughly, the du-

---

[16]Further evidence of the popularity of Love's *Myrrour* emerges from surviving fifteenth-century wills, in which copies frequently figure among bequests. See Margaret Deanesly, "Vernacular Books in England in the Fourteenth and Fifteenth Centuries," *MLR* 15 (1920): 354–55.

[17]See Evelyn Underhill's introduction to her modernized version of *The Scale of Perfection* (London: John M. Watkins, 1923), pp. xiii–xviii; and Doms. M. Noetinger and E. Bouvet, eds. and trans., *Scala perfectionis* (Tours: A. Mame et fils, 1923), II, 39 n. There is also a brief discussion of possible anti-Lollard passages in Joseph E. Milosh, *The Scale of Perfection and the English Mystical Tradition* (Madison: University of Wisconsin Press, 1966), pp. 117–22.

ration of the fifteenth century. In the sixteenth century, however, we shall find the motive of Biblical translation rejoining the composite of characteristics that define the "simpler, more moderate" style, so that once again this hardy native tradition comes to operate at full strength.

The severance of Scripturalism from the motives informing prose style in the fifteenth century had momentous consequences for vernacular religious writing. Since direct reliance on Scripture as a source and model for authoritative utterance was ruled out as a stylistic option, English writers who remained committed to the materials, aims, and audience of the moderate prose tradition found themselves thrown back upon their native linguistic resources. What we therefore observe, in their continued avoidance of rhetorical excess, is a growing body of original composition in fifteenth-century religious prose that bases itself in the locutions and sentence forms of actual speech, thereby attesting the orality of its conception. Not the least value of utilizing Salter's tradition of a simple, moderate style as a framework for considering this prose is to dispense with the condescending imputations of crudity, naivete, adventitiousness, and the like that have attached to many critics' and scholars' treatments of later fourteenth- and fifteenth-century writing in English. Instead we can examine this style as a matter of principled and pragmatic authorial decisions. An additional advantage in viewing the religious prose of this era positively in the light of speech norms is that it can be related, by way of the same norms, to the secular prose contemporaneous with it. Some consideration of the comprehensive oral basis of composition for both religious and secular prose in the later fourteenth and fifteenth century will follow the next three sections on the receding influence of Scripturalism and will serve to conclude this chapter.

It is disconcerting to begin reading *The Scale of Perfection* with an eye to its location in Salter's two traditions, for its opening announcement to a "ghostly syster" that its purpose is to bring her to "ghostly closing" in contemplation with "the blessed trinite" would appear to exclude the work on two counts from all possibility of being written in the simpler, more moderate style which we in fact find Hilton using.[18] Since Hilton's choice does appear exceptional in view of his address to an individual

---

[18]Walter Hilton, *Scala perfectionis*, I.i; II.xlvi. In the absence of a critical old-spelling edition, I have cited from a microfilm copy (University Microfilms no. 1402) of the earliest complete surviving print, Wynkyn de Worde's 1525 edition, which bears the title *Scala perfectionis* (STC 14044). The original is in the British Library, London (B.M. 1.A.47940[1]). Because signature notation is characteristically sporadic and inaccurate, I have chosen to cite by book and chapter numbers since these are supplied throughout. In my citations (subsequently denoted *SP* and incorporated in my text) I expand all contractions (except ampersands), and I modernize consonantal *i* and *u* and long *s*. Otherwise I reproduce de Worde's spelling and accidentals.

anchorite, not a wider readership, on aspiring to the mystical knowledge of God in his essence, we are naturally inclined to look for an explanation of the style of the *Scale*. Joseph Milosh has usefully emphasized the integral connection between the notion of contemplation and the emphasis on moderation, degree, and proportionality that informs Hilton's thought.[19] As Hilton represents spiritual progress, it comes always as a gift of God's grace in gradual, sometimes almost imperceptible movements from relatively lower to relatively higher states of responsiveness and moral capability; at best this life affords only momentary and evanescent access to mystical experience. Hilton's sustained attention in the *Scale* to what is technically the second part of contemplation—"a lytell tastynge of the swetnes of the love of god" attained "comynly of symple & unlettred men/ whiche gyve them holy to devocion" (*SP*, I.v, vi)—in preference to the first part, intellectual and rational knowledge, or the third, the mystical heights, seems to have been the aspect of its spirituality which attracted a broad English audience from early on. Yet conceding this much to thought content must not preclude acknowledgment of the accessibility, measuredness, and expressiveness of Hilton's style, whose principal features can be traced and accounted for by relation to the two prominent Biblical sources used in the *Scale*—the affective and introspective portions of Paul's Epistles, and the lyrical and gnomic books of the Old Testament, especially the Psalter.

The ladder image of the title signals the sense of degree which for Hilton controls progress in the spiritual life as well as his authorial proceeding:

/For refourmynge in fayth is the lowest state of al chosen soules/ for byneth that myght they not well be/ But refourmynge in felyng is the hyest state in this lyfe that the soule may come to/ But as fro the lowest to the hyest maye not a soule sodenly styrte, no more than a man that wol clymbe upon a ladder hye, and setteth his fote upon the lowest stele, may at the nexte flee up to the hyest/ But hym behoveth go by processe one after another untyl he maye come to the overest/ Ryght so it is ghostly. [*SP*, II.xvii]

Loo I have tolde thee a lytyl as me thynketh fyrst of contemplatyf lyf what it is/ and sythen of the wayes whiche by grace leden therto/ not for I have it in felyng & in werchynge as I have it in sayenge/ . . . And therfore yf ony worde be therin that styreth thee or comforteth thee more to the love of god/ thanke god, for it is his gyfte, & not of thi worde/ And yf it comforte thee not or elles thou takest it not redely/ studye not to longe theraboute but laye it besyde thee tyl a nother tyme/ and yeve thee to thy prayer or to other ocupacyon/ Take it as it wol come and not al at ones/ . . . And therfore/ yf thou think that I have herbefore spoken to hye to thee/ for thou myghtest not take it nor fulfill it/ as

---

[19]Milosh, *The Scale of Perfection*, pp. 24–110.

I have sayde or shall saye/ I wyl now fall downe to thee as lowe as thou wylt/ for my profyt as wel as for thyne. [*SP*, I.xciii]

Hilton recurrently counsels degree, measure, and moderation as the soul's conformable response to divine grace through expressive use of correlative and binary conjunctions and degree constructions with parallelism. Examples in the foregoing passages include: "as fro the lowest to the hyest maye not a soule sodenly styrte, no more than a man that wol clymbe upon a ladder . . ./ Ryght so it is ghostly . . ."; "I have it in felyng & in werchynge as I have it in sayenge"; "And yf it comforte thee not or elles thou takest it not . . ."; "yf . . . I have herbefore spoken to hye to thee/ . . . I wyl now fall downe to thee as lowe as thou wylt/ for my profyt as wel as for thyne"; "for thou myghtest not take it nor fulfill it." Nevertheless here, as in numerous other passages in the *Scale*, outcroppings of antitheses work to counteract and qualify the scalar dynamic—for example, "For refourmynge in fayth is the lowest state . . ./ But refourmynge in felyng is the hyest state . . ."; "Loo I have tolde thee a lytyl . . . of contemplatyf lyf what it is/ . . . not for I have it"; "thanke god, for it is his gyfte, & not of thi worde"; "studye not to longe theraboute but laye it besyde thee"; "Take it as it wol come and not al at ones."

These characteristic interminglings of correlative and degree constructions with antitheses bespeak the strong semantic associations in Hilton's prose between this kind of binary conjunction and the oscillating or contrarious turns of human psychology and earthly existence. The provenance of these associations as well as the syntactic means of expressing them appears in the main to be Pauline. Hilton often composes by quoting, translating, and commenting on excerpts from the Epistles, and, in the process, his sentence forms begin more and more to replicate the Apostle's, as illustrated in the following passage:

> It is good that a man have pees with al thynge save with the feende & with this ymage of synne/ . . . /And therfore saye I that every man behovyth stryffe ayenst this ymage of synne/ . . . / In the person
> [Gal. 5] of which men sayth saynt poul/ *Caro concupiscit adversus spiritum & spiritus adversus carnem*, That is, A soule refourmed to the lyknes of god fyghtyth ayenst the flesshly styrynges of this ymage of synne/ & also this ymage of synne stryveth ayenst the wyll of the spyryte. This maner of fyghtyng of this dowble ymage saynt poule knewe
> [Rom. 7:23] whan he sayd thus/ *Inveni legem in membris meis repugnantem legi mentis meae & captivum me ducentem in legem peccati/* That is/ I have founde two lawes in myself/ One lawe in my soule within/ and a nother in my flesshly lymmes without fyghtyng with it . . . / In thyse two lawes a soule refourmed ledeth hys lyfe as saynt poul sayth/
> [Rom. 7:25] *Mente enim servio legi dei, carne enim legi peccati/* In my soule that is

in my wyl and in my reason I serve to the lawe of god/ but in my flessh that is in my flesshly appetyte I serve to the lawe of synne/ Nevertheles that a soule refourmed shal not dispeyre though he serve to the lawe of synne by felynge of the vycyous sensualyte ayenste the wyl of the spyryte by cause of corrupcyon of the bodely kynde, saynt poul excusyth it sayeng thus of his owne persone/ *Non enim quod volo bonum hoc ago sed malum quod odi hoc facio. Si autem malum quod odi hoc facio, non ego operor illud sed quod habitat in me peccatum.* I do not that good that I wolde do, That is I woulde fele no flesshly styryng/ & that do I not/ But I doo that evyl that I hate, That is, The synful styrynges of my flesshe I hate/ and yet I fele hem/ Nevertheles syth it is so that I hate the wycked styrynges of my flesshe/ & yet I fele hem and ofte delyte in hem ayenst my wyl, they shal not be reherced ayenst me for dampnacyon as yf I hadde done hem/ And why? For the corrupcyon of this ymage of synne doth hem & not I. Loo saynt poul in his persone comforteth al soules. [*SP*, II.xi]

[Rom. 7: 19,20]

Hilton reflects more extensively on passages from the Pauline Epistles than he does on any other portion of Scripture, with the result that the psychology and style of these reflections exhibit marked assimilation to the thought and expression of the original. Hilton is especially drawn to introspective and self-scrutinizing passages, and he adopts as his own their sharp flesh-spirit dichotomy, their emphasis on the constants in human nature which make it possible to generalize from the self to all humankind, and their equally sharp dichotomy between sin and grace.[20] Because antithesis is the vehicle for expressing and eliciting such perceptions in the Apostle's style, it plays a correspondingly prominent role in Hilton's too. From beginning to end in the *Scale*, the mighty metaphysical opposition between the devil and God for possession of each Christian's soul, along with the experiential implications of this opposition in each Christian's personal battle against sin, finds its projection in antithetical sentence forms, oftenest side by side with quotations and translations from Paul. (See, for further verification of the scope of the antithetical Pauline play of style, *SP*, I.iv, I.ix, and the conclusion of *SP*, II.xlv.)

The influence of Paul's thought and mode of expression reaches beyond antithesis to another conspicuous feature of Hilton's sentence form, namely, the many-membered *NP* catalogues which give specificity to exhortations against sin as well as encouragements to virtue. In the Pauline Epistles the substance of these great catalogues evinces serious

[20]For a discussion of Hilton's teachings on grace in the context of the disputes of his age, see Milosh, *Scale of Perfection*, pp. 78–89. Also see Helen L. Gardner's "Walter Hilton and the Mystical Tradition in England," *Essays and Studies by Members of the English Association* 22 (1937): 103–27.

performing of the pastoral office. Their structure demonstrates the recursive power of sentential conjunction and conjunction reduction, as this is harnessed to the Apostle's largeness of moral concern. Since Paul attracts Hilton more as a model for spiritual effort and dedication to the cure of souls than as a theologian, he responds to the catalogues as a preeminently functional stylistic device for conveying moral urgency on both fronts of the ceaseless spiritual combat. Here is an example:

With devocyon shalt thou se thy wretchednes thy synnes/ and thy wickednes as pryde/ covetyse/ glotony/ slouth/ lechery/ & wycked sterynge of envy/ Ire/ hatred/ melancoly/ angrynese/ ye bytter & unskylfull hevynesse. . . . Also in meditacyon thou shalt se vertues whiche be nedefull to thee for to have/ as mekenes/ myldnesse/ pacyence/ ryghtwysnes/ ghostly strength/ temperance/ clennes/ peas & sobernes/ fayth/ hope/ & charite. [*SP*, I.xv]

Hilton's Pauline catalogues cluster with unusual frequency in the protracted serial treatment of the deadly sins which occupies forty of the ninety-three chapters of the first book of the *Scale* (I.lii–xci). This section has long been remarked as an unusual obtrusion of practical morality into a treatise on the contemplative life. Equally, however, this section affords vital evidence of the connections between the *Scale* and the aims and audience that typify what I, following Salter, have been calling the "simpler, more moderate" tradition in religious prose style, and what Milosh calls "the religious-handbook tradition."[21] Thematic and stylistic indications together bear out the weight of Pauline influence in the shape and content of this section of the *Scale*, where Hilton's scalar progression assimilates itself to urgent, particularized moral counsel in the manner of the Apostle.

Thus far I have argued that, beyond Hilton's seemingly innate predilection for conceiving and representing the contemplative life in terms of measure and proportionality, the thought and style of the *Scale* exhibit the deep impress of Paul in treating the psychology and applied morality of sin and grace. A scarcely less determinative factor in Hilton's writing is, however, Old Testament parallelistic composition, which orders and intensifies the affectivity of the *Scale* as the Pauline influence does its morality. Hilton is superbly responsive to the lyrical and visionary expressiveness of Biblical parallelism in numerous contexts, from which the following passages comprise a representative sampling:

The hande of our lord is full nere/ & helpeth ryght soone. For he kepeth hym full sykerly/ & the man woteth not how/ as the prophete
[Psal. 91]   Davyd sayeth in the persone of our lorde/ *Cum ipso sum in tribulatione:*

[21]Milosh, *Scale of Perfection*, pp. 150–64.

eripiam eum et glorificabo eum: I am with hym in his tribulacyon/ & in his temptacyon I shall delyver hym/ & I shall make hym gloryous in my blysse. [*SP*, I.xxxvii]

[Eze. 28]   Thus behyght our lorde by his prophete saying thus/ *In quacumque hora conversus peccator et ingenuerit vita vivet et non morietur/* That is In what tyme that it be that the synful man is tourned to god from synne and he have sorow therfore/ he shal lyve and he shall not deye endelesly/ [*SP*, II.x]

Have ye no wonder though the felynge of grace be withdrawe som-tyme fro a lover of Jhesu. For holy wrytte sayth the same of the
[Cant. 3]   spouse that she fareth thus/ *Quesivi et non inveni illum. Vocavi et non respondit mihi.* I serched & I founde hym not/ I called & he answered not. But at the last whan he wol he comyth ayen ful of grace & of sothfastnes . . .: and then cryeth the soule to Jhesu in ghostly voys
[Cant. 1]   with a glad herte thus/ *Oleum effusum nomen tuum/* Oyle yshedde is thy name Jesu/ Thy name is Jesu. That is hele . . . to me/ . . . For oonly thy gracyous presence helyth me fro sorowe & fro synne. [*SP*, II.xli]

So integrally bound up with Old Testament song and prophecy and with its allegorical exegesis are Hilton's own strains of devotion and mysticism that to read the *Scale* with understanding is to recognize that he composes by enlarging on Biblical texts according to traditional principles of spiritual interpretation. Two of the most celebrated excursuses in the work—the passages on the name of Jesus and on the twinned paradoxes of "good derknesse" and "ryche noughte"—develop as exfoliations from centers in Scriptural formulations. Milosh is surely correct to insist on the disparity between Rolle's sensory transports and Hilton's intimations of the plenitude of divine meaning which emerges from comparison of the two writers' respective meditations on the Holy Name.[22] The Hebraic character of Hilton's apperceptions harks back to their source in Joel 2:32: *Omnis enim quicumque invocaverit nomen domini, salvus erit,* rendered as "Every man what that he be that calleth the name of god, that is to saye/ askith salvacyon by Jhesu & his passion: he shall be saaf." The sense of Hilton's language is to enforce the futility of any periphrastic or discursive means of conveying what it is to experience the presence of God. When God is present, all the soul can do in affirming the fact is to name him, vocatively and hence evocatively for others. The reiterated synonymy that becomes the locus of the meaning of such experience prompts Hilton to a magnificent use of the resources of conjunctive syntax, illustrated in the serial appositives and parallel constructions of the following quotation:

[22]Ibid., pp. 55–68.

I shall tell thee oon worde for all/ the whych thou shalt seke/ desyre and fynde: for in that one worde is al that thou hast lost/ This worde is Jhesu/ I meane not this worde Jhesu paynted upon the walle/ or wrytten by letters on the boke/ or fourmyd by lyppes in sounde of the mowthe/ or feyned in thy herte by traveyle of thy mynde/ For in thys maner wyse maye a man oute of charyte fynde hym. But I meane Jhesu cryst that blessyd persone god and man/ sonne of vyrgyn mary/ whom this name betokenith that is al goodnes, endles wisdom/ love/ and swetnes/ thy joye, thy worshyp, and thyn everlastyng blysse/ thy god: thy lorde, and thy salvacyon. [*SP,* I.xlvi; cf. I.xliv]

In the strikingly formulated paradoxes of "good derknesse" and "ryche noughte"—locutions for the phase of contemplation in which all earthly attachments have been rooted out of the soul and it awaits the advent of divine illumination—it is the affirmative character, the connotations of goodness and richness attaching to the soul's darkness and emptiness, that set Hilton's treatment of the *via negativa* apart from those of other mystical writers.[23] Significantly, Hilton himself furnishes the contextual key to the source of what are usually alleged to be original elements in his thought and expression. Displaying his characteristic Scripturalism, he purports in formulating these paradoxes only to be drawing upon the Psalms and the prophets, and subjecting them to the unusual allegorical interpretation. After several preparatory excursuses (*SP,* II.xxiv–xxvi), Hilton proceeds to offer his conclusive elaboration in the form of concatenation and commentary that merge a text from Psalm 73 with several from a Messianic portion of Isaiah. The resultant interplay of Scriptural thought and style comprises a beautifully transparent demonstration of its shaping influence in Hilton's own writing:

This is thenne a goode derknesse and a ryche noughte that bringeth a soule to soo moche ghostly ease and so stylle softenesse/ I trowe davyd meaned of the nyghte or of this noughte whan he sayd

[Psal. 73] thus/ *Ad nichilum redactus sum et nescivi/* That is: I was broughte to noughte and I wyste not/ That is: The grace of our lorde Jhesu sente in to myn herte hath slayne in me/ and broughte to noughte all the love of the worlde and I wyste not how/ For thrugh noo worchynge of myself ne by myn owne wytte I have it not/ but of the grace of

[Isa. 50] oure lorde Jhesu/ And therfore . . . byddeth the prophete/ *Qui ambulavit in tenebris et non est lumen ei, speret in domino et invitatur super deum suum/* Who soo gooth in derkenes and hath noo lyghte/ That is: who soo woll hyde hym fro the love of the worlde/ and may not redily fele lyght of ghostly love/ dispeyre not/ torne not ayen to the worlde but hope in oure lorde and leen upon hym/ That is: truste in god/ & cleve to hym by desyre/ and abyde awhyle and he shall have lyght/ . . . Thus semith it that the prophete behight sayeng

[Isa. 58] thus/ *Orietur in tenebris lux tua, et tenebrae tuae erunt sicut meridies: et*

---

[23]See ibid., pp. 98–102.

> *requiem dabit tibi dominus deus tuus, et implebit animam tuam splendor-
> ibus/* Lyghte shall sprynge to thee in derkenesse/ That is: Thou that
> forsakest sothfastly the lyghte of all worldly love and hydest thy
> thoughte in this derknes/ lyghte of blessyd love & ghostly knowyng
> of god shall sprynge to thee/ *And thy derknes shall be as myddaye/* That
> is thy derkenes of traveylynge desyre & thy blynde truste in god
> that thou hast fyrste shall torne in to clere knowynge & in to sykernes
> of love/ *And thy lorde god shall yeve rest to thee/* . . . That is: Whan
> thou arte broughte in to this ghostly reste thenne shalt thou more
> easely tende to god and noughte elles doo but love hym/ and thenne
> he shall wyth bemes of ghostly light fulfyll all the myghtes of thy
> soule. Have thou noo wonder though I calle the forsakinge of worldly
> love derkenes/ for the prophete calleth it soo saynge thus to a soule/
> [Isa. 47] *Intra in tenebras tuas filia Chaldaeorum/* Goo in to thy derkenesse thou
> doughter of chaldee/ That is: thou soul that arte as a doughter of
> Chaldee for love of the worlde/ forsake it and goo in to thy derkenes.
> [*SP,* II.xxvii]

I have dwelt at some length on the formative impact of Scripture on
Hilton's thought and prose style in the *Scale of Perfection* because the
phenomenon is tremendously suggestive with respect to the history of
ideas and style—and yet, for all that, it emerges as an isolated phenomenon in the context of English prose in the later fourteenth and fifteenth
centuries. In fact, the category-crossing which the *Scale* displays—in
pursuing the objectives of the high style, systematic contemplation leading to mystical union with God, by means of the moderate style—arises
from the scope of Biblical expression to which Hilton assimilated his
own. Thus it seems natural as well as noteworthy that Hilton (if assigned
dates can be trusted) was the first English religious writer to recommend
the reading of Scripture to the laity.[24] The acuteness and breadth of the
response to Biblical modes of thought and style in Hilton's *Scale* are
remarkable; joined as they are with their author's unimpeachable orthodoxy, they move us to ponder what might have been.

What came to be the future course of Scripturalism in England emerged
from underground after a century and a quarter with the inception of
the Reformation, and it is not until that period, in Tyndale and his
successors, that a response to Pauline composition and Old Testament
parallelism comparable to Hilton's can be found among writers of vernacular prose. Even so, the Reformers, while steeped in Paul and the
prophets, fail to reach Hilton's depth of sensitivity to the lyrical dimensions of parallelistic composition revealed in the Song of Songs and

---

[24]Hilton makes his recommendation in *A Treatise on Mixed Life,* thought to have been
composed about 1370 for "a worldlye lorde"; for comment, see Carl Horstman, ed.,
Yorkshire Writers: Richard Rolle of Hampole and His Followers (London: S. Sonnenschein &
Co., 1895–96), I, 264.

preeminently in the Psalter. To my best knowledge, one must await the sermons of Donne before this strain of Hebraic influence again becomes a discernible factor in the writing of English prose.[25] Thus, while Hilton's immersion in the sacred text has behind it a long line of distinguished native precedents, he figures in his own time as the last of a line in which Catholic orthodoxy combines overtly and unproblematically with Scripturalism, in the sense in which I define and apply this term in the study of style.

THE CLOUD OF UNKNOWING

Before proceeding to examine, in Love's *Myrrour*, the perceptibly altered mode of dealing with Scripture in vernacular prose that ensued on the rise of Lollardy, it is instructive to augment what we have observed about Hilton with some consideration of the thought and style of the author of *The Cloud of Unknowing* in order to work from a fuller picture of trends at the turn from the fourteenth to the fifteenth century. The seventeen known manuscripts of the *Cloud* attest to considerable circulation in the fifteenth century, though less than that attained by Hilton's *Scale* (of which forty manuscripts of Book I and at least twenty-four of Book II are known) or by Love's *Myrrour* (extant in its entirety in forty-seven known manuscripts, and in excerpts in six others).[26]

The unidentified and seemingly unidentifiable author of *The Cloud of Unknowing* exhibits external likeness to Hilton in date, in the contemplative objectives that inform his work, and in his conscious adoption of an affective rather than an intellectual route to his objectives.[27] Such

[25]On Donne's explicit appreciation and emulation of the literary qualities of Psalmic language, see Dennis Quinn, "Donne's Christian Eloquence," *ELH* 27 (1960): 276–97, and "John Donne's Principles of Biblical Exegesis," *JEGP* 61 (1962): 326–29; Janel M. Mueller, ed., *Donne's Prebend Sermons* (Cambridge, Mass.: Harvard University Press, 1971), pp. 6–7, 39–40; and Barbara K. Lewalski, *Protestant Poetics and the Seventeenth-Century Religious Lyric*, pp. 72, 84–85, 99–100.

[26]Phyllis Hodgson, Introduction, *"The Cloud of Unknowing" and "The Book of Privy Counselling,"* Early English Text Society o.s. 218 (London: Humphrey Milford, 1944), pp. ix–xix; Milosh, *The Scale of Perfection*, p. 3; and Salter, *Love's "Myrrour,"* pp. 1–9.

[27]There has been some recurrent scholarly predisposition to attribute *The Cloud of Unknowing* to Hilton; for discussion, see Helen L. Gardner's review of Hodgson's edition of the *Cloud* (*Medium Aevum* 16 [1947]: 41–42), and Hodgson's own lack of receptivity to the idea (Introduction, *Deonise Hid Divinite and Other Treatises on Contemplative Prayer Related to "The Cloud of Unknowing,"* Early English Text Society o.s. 231 [London: Geoffrey Cumberlege, 1955], pp. xxxiv–xxxv). The case for single authorship has most recently been renewed in Wolfgang Riehle's "The Problem of Walter Hilton's Possible Authorship of *The Cloud of Unknowing* and Its Related Tracts," *Neuphilologische Mitteilungen* 78 (1977): 31–45; the case for separate authorship is reaffirmed in Louis C. Gatto's "The Walter Hilton—*Cloud of Unknowing* Authorship Reconsidered," *Studies in Medieval Culture* 5 (1975): 181–89. My discussion indicates my strong commitment to the view of separate authorship.

likeness, however, is confined to externals, for the underlying view of language which determines the style of the *Cloud* is very unlike Hilton's. This author sustains a wary if not dismissive attitude toward the use of linguistic formulations to promote the soul's union with God.

The *Cloud* author's denigration of language manifestly affects even his handling of Scripture, which he cites infrequently in free paraphrase. Phyllis Hodgson's notes record only a dozen instances of quotation or allusion combined[28]—an astonishing contrast with the *Scale* and the *Myrrour*. These uses of Scripture are also brief and isolated; a typical instance looks like this: "& herfore seith Seinte Poule of himself & many other thus: 'Thof al oure bodies ben presently here in erthe, nevertheles ʒit oure levyng is in heven.' He ment theire love & theire desire, the whiche is goostly theire liif."[29] In addition to these few, scattered references, the *Cloud* author develops two extended and minutely allegorized process descriptions that have their points of departure in Biblical narratives: one in the story of Mary and Martha, the other in the story of Moses, Aaron, and Beseleel. Not only does the allegory progressively obscure the Scriptural character of these stories, but the untextual claim is also made that such allegorizing has divine authorization. Hodgson's commentary on these process descriptions of the contemplative life and its mystical goal properly explains, however, that the *Cloud* author is synthesizing and elaborating materials that derive from several patristic and Victorine sources.[30] Indeed, there is no Biblical warrant to be found for the thought or style or any other feature of these conspicuously drawn-out passages except the names of the personages being allegorized.

More compelling evidence of the *Cloud* author's relatively low esteem for Scripture among possible means conducing to the mystical life takes the form of direct testimony. Scripture has no special status; it is placed on a plane with all other uses of language, like "other mens techyng," which is acknowledged to have an elementary spiritual value in aiding "byginners" to become "profiters" in contemplation. Scripture has value in convicting souls of their sinfulness and prompting them to avail themselves of prayer and the sacrament of confession. Thus, language, including God's Word, is simply a point of departure:

[28]The following is an exhaustive list of the Biblical quotations and allusions identified by Hodgson in her edition of *The Cloud of Unknowing* (I adopt her page and line referencing here and throughout): 38.16, 41.8, 44.13, 45.1, 47.3, 55.15, 56.8, 75.5, 75.14, 111.12–13, 112.15, 120.12. In addition, Hodgson signals a possible distant allusion at 99.1.

[29]*Cloud of Unknowing*, ed. Hodgson, 112.15–18; cf. 44.22–45.1. In my citations (subsequently denoted *CU* and incorporated in my text) I depart from Hodgson's text only in substituting *th* for thorn.

[30]Introduction, *Cloud of Unknowing*, pp. lxxi–lxxv. The two allegories are developed in chapters 17–21 and 71–73, respectively. In this connection, the author's pronouncement at 53.6–54.9 about the nature of divine meaning is also significant.

Withouten redyng or heryng of Godes worde, . . . or a teching of another than itself, . . . it is impossible to mans understondyng that a soule that is bleendid in custom of synne schuld see the foule spot in his concyence. . . . & thus maist thou see that no thinkyng may goodly be getyn in byginners & profiters withoutyn redyng or heryng comyng before, ne preyng withouten thinkyng. [*CU*, 72.4–22]

By definition, however, one leaves a point of departure behind. This author goes on to exempt advanced contemplatives like the addressee of the *Cloud* from the reading and hearing of Scripture and other teaching. Finally what he holds out is not so much an exemption as a prohibition from using such means to pursue exalted mystical ends:

But it is not so with hem that contynuely worchen in the werk of this book. For theire meditacions ben as thei were sodein conseites & blynde felynges of their owne wrechidnes, or of the goodnes of God, withoutyn any menes of redyng or heryng comyng before, & withoutyn any specyal beholdyng of any thing under God. [*CU*, 72.24–73.5]

Not just in the foregoing passage—distinctive only in its specificity regarding "Goddes worde, outher wretyn or spokyn"—but from end to end of the work, the author of *The Cloud of Unknowing* belabors his conviction that contemplation is optimally cultivated by repudiating every natural or human means of intellection, including all recourse to language. This is the cardinal principle of the works of pseudo-Dionysius the Areopagite, the acknowledged primary influence on the author of the *Cloud*.[31] Hence is is precisely the nature or conception of the Bible as God's proffering of a humanly accessible means for relating to him that makes Scripturalism an impossibility for this English author.

The logical outcome of the view of language, including Scripture, which is expressed in *The Cloud of Unknowing* would be no book at all. While stopping short of such rigor, the author applies himself to developing a surcharged rhetoric of negativity. In his notable extended attack on the misconceptions that such words as "in," "up," "above," "under," and even "heaven" precipitate in evocations or elicitations of mystical experience, the *Cloud* author is understandably concerned to deny to language any referential or predicative functions. For if these functions are viewed as world-positing in the twentieth century, in this earlier author's sterner view they operate as materialistic distractions or even delusions.[32] Ultimately, he presses toward the denial of all cognitive validity in linguistic formulations. This crucial extreme of thought is

---

[31]See, further, Hodgson's Introduction, *Cloud of Unknowing*, pp. lviii–lxix.

[32]See the diverse attacks on the use, in mystical contexts, of locatives like "in" and "up" (95.6–100.4, 105.3–106.15) or "upwards" and "heaven" (111.18–112.21) as well as the related admonitions to construe "above" and "under" spiritually (120.6–121.4). These passages are usually interpreted as criticisms of Rolle and his school.

reached, significantly, in a disquisition on the key term "nought," which the *Cloud* author shares with Hilton. Here is this author, in an equally characteristic display of psychology and style, admonishing his reader to seek the way to the nowhere where God is solely to be found:

But this wil I bid thee. Loke on no wyse that thou be withinne thiself & schortly withoutyn thiself wil I not that thou be, ne ʒit aboven, ne behynde, ne on o side, ne on other.

"Wher than," seist thou, "schal I be? Noʒwhere by thi tale!" Now trewly thou seist wel; for there wolde I have thee. For whi noʒwhere bodely is everywhere goostly. . . . & thof al thi bodely wittes kon fynde ther nothing to fed hem on, for hem think it nouʒt that thou dost, ʒe! do on than this nouʒt, . . . & lete nouʒt, therfore, bot travayle besily in that nouʒt with a wakyng desire to wilne to have God, that no man may knowe. For I telle thee trewly that I had lever be so nowhere bodely, wrastlyng with that blynde nouʒt, than to be so grete a lorde that I miʒt when I wolde be everywhere bodely, merily pleiing with al this ouʒt as a lorde with his owne.

Lat be this everiwhere & this ouʒt, in comparison of this noʒwhere & this nouʒt. Reche thee never ʒif thi wittys kon no skyle of this nouʒt; for whi I love it moche the betir. . . . What is he that clepith it nouʒt? Sekirly it is oure utter man, & not oure inner. Oure inner man clepith it Al; for of it he is wel lernid to kon skyle of alle thinges, bodely or goostly, withouten any specyal beholdyng to any o thing by itself. [*CU*, 121.5–122.17]

To go "nowhere" with thought and language, to reduce them to "nought," would seemingly eliminate all grounds for syntax, for putting words into sentence form. In fact, this is the position which the *Cloud* author takes with respect to the mystical use of utterance as he assembles his instructions on contemplation and its affiliated mode of prayer. He is fortunate that English was rich in monosyllabic words by the late fourteenth century, for the monosyllable figures centrally in his striking injunctions on how to confound one's human thought by reducing language to a bare minimum:

Thefore, what tyme that thou purposest thee to this werk, & felest bi grace that thou arte clepid of God, lift than up thin herte unto God with . . . a naked entent directe unto God, withouten any other cause then himself.

& ʒif thee list have this entent lappid & foulden in o worde, for thou schuldest have betir holde therapon, take thee bot a litil worde of o silable; for so it is betir then of two, for ever the schorter it is, the betir it acordeth with the werk of the spirite. & soche a worde is this worde GOD or this worde LOVE. Cheese thee whether thou wilt, or another as thee list: whiche that thee liketh best of o silable. & fasten this worde to thin herte, so that it never go thens for thing that bifalleth.

This worde schal be thi scheeld & thi spere, whether thou ridest on pees or on werre. . . . With this worde thou schalt smite doun al maner thouʒt under the cloude of forʒeting; insomochel that ʒif any thouʒt prees apon thee to ask thee what thou woldest have, answere him with no mo wordes bot with this o worde. [*CU*, 28.3–29.3]

Subsequently the *Cloud* author demonstrates how to utilize the minimum of a monosyllable in exciting and intensifying one's spiritual faculties during the practice of contemplation, whether negatively through awareness of sin or positively through disciplined concentration on the being of God. In either case, the value of the monosyllable is to force the mind to be abstract, to leave off what this author calls "any specyal beholdyng unto any kynde" of particular sin or particular divine attribute. To admit consideration of any such particularity will cause the contemplative to lose sight of the unitary goal at which he aims. Thus, says this author, proceed similarly with the monosyllables "SYNNE" and "GOD":

Do thou . . . fille thi spirit with the goostly bemenyng of this worde SYNNE. . . . What recche contemplatives what synne that it be, or how mochel a synne that it be? For alle synne hem thinkyth—I mene for the tyme of this werk—iliche greet in hemself, when the leest synne departeth hem fro God. . . . & fele synne a lumpe, thou wost never what, bot non other thing than thiself. & crye than goostly ever upon one: "Synne synne synne, oute oute oute!" This goostly crie is betyr lernid of God by the proef then of any man by worde. For it is best whan it is in pure spirit, withoutyn specyal thou3t or any pronounsyng of worde. . . .

On the same maner schalt thou do with this lityl worde GOD. Fille thi spirit with the goostly bemenyng of it. . . . What recche contemplatives? For alle vertewes thei fynden & felyn in God; for in hym is alle thing, bothe by cause & by beyng. For hem think, & thei had God, thei had alle good; & therfore thei coveyte nothing with specyal beholdyng, bot only good God. [*CU*, 78.9–79.10]

Significantly, the author of the *Cloud* spurns all Hiltonian degree and proportionality in delineating the soul's access to metaphysical absolutes; the contemplative is to associate any sin with all sin, and any virtue with the source of all virtue, God. With the removal of discursive thought, of attention to particulars "whether thei be good, betir, or alther best, bodily or goostly," goes the reduction of language to a monosyllabic minimum—preferably unvoiced except in sore emotional need. At most this author finally allots language the role of an affective escape valve, an emergency exit for welling feelings. The closest approach to syntax for such a contemplative is ejaculation: "Synne synne synne, oute oute oute!" (There is a prima facie resemblance to be remarked between this kind of ejaculation and the "bald parataxis" stage of language hypothesized by Kellner: 'Enemy near,' etc. No true resemblance, however, can be sustained. For Kellner such forms of utterance are both natural and primitive; for the *Cloud* author they are acquired late and only through stringent self-conditioning.) But these ejaculatory cries have further force, according to this author; God will receive them as appeals for help which cannot be denied. In enforcing his claim that language can be permitted to operate for a contemplative on the rudimentary semiotic level of an alarm bell, the *Cloud* author is driven, despite his principles, to a homely analogy with the response we would make on hearing a neighbor whom we despised "crye in the hei3t of his spirit this lityl worde FIIR or this worde OUTE." "For pure pite," "stirid & reisid with the doelfulnes of this crie," we would rise—"3e! thof it be aboute midwintirs ni3t— & helpe hym to sleck his fiir, or for to stylle hym & rest hym in hys disese." "A, Lorde!" continues this author,

sithen a man may be maad so mercyful, to have so moche mercy & so moche pitie of his enmye, not a3enstonding his enmite, what pite & what mercy schal God have than of a goostly crye in soule, maad & wrou3t in the hei3t & the depnes, the lengthe & the breed of his spirit, the whiche hath al by kynde, that man hath by grace, & moche more? [*CU*, 76.4–18]

In the style of the author of *The Cloud of Unknowing*, the steady, virtually obsessive repudiation of all cognitive and nearly all communicative functions of language issues in a particular mode of incantatory, rhythmical utterance. This mode is replete with sound similiarities stemming from verbatim repetitions and unreduced identical conjuncts as well as word-play; it is highly oral-aural.[33] Illustrations of this mode from foregoing quotations include the spellbinding of "Lat be this everiwhere & this ou3t, in comparison of this no3where & this nou3t"; or "This worde schal be thi scheeld & thi spere, whether thou ridest on pees or on werre"; or "For hem think, & thei had God, thei had alle good; & therfore . . . nothing . . . bot only good God." To the appreciable extent that the *Cloud* author undertakes, through the linguistic options he exercises, to heighten identity relations in his prose—the sameness of sounds, of lexical items, of phrasal and clausal structures—to the same extent his style merges with the native high tradition that had been functioning for several centuries as a vehicle of mystical transport (cf. the "Wooing" group of lyrical prayers and *A Talkyng of the Love of God*).

Yet it must also be observed that the aim of the repetitions and the insistent rhythms of this author is not to race the heartbeat and the pulses, but instead to induce a sort of suspended animation, a lulling and stilling of the faculties into a state of quiescence that will negate individual consciousness and prepare the soul for union with God. In accordance with this aim, there is not only the oral strain of patterned elaboration to be found in the prose of the *Cloud*, but also, side by side and interfused with it, another very different oral strain, to which Ran-

[33]Oral-aural is a useful as well as playful McLuhanism. See Marshall McLuhan, *The Gutenberg Galaxy* (Toronto: University of Toronto Press, 1962), p. 21.

dolph Quirk has given the name "phatic."[34] Phatic expressions are the filler elements of colloquial speech: oaths, expletives, greetings, farewells, expressions of thanks, approval, commiseration, and so on. Quirk defines phatic expressions as phonetically, lexically, or syntactically fixed units which—and this point is significant with regard to *The Cloud of Unknowing*—are almost altogether devoid of semantic content. (In Quirk's example, to take 'How do you do?' as a request for information about one's state of health is to misunderstand the phatic nature of the expression.) However, if they are mainly meaningless, we may ask: Why are there so many phatic devices in spoken language? Quirk sees their principal function as setting up and maintaining conditions of sociable interchange. Thus as a speaker literally extends himself or herself in a flow of emitted sounds, a hearer reciprocally signals adoption of the role of listener: 'Um-hmm,' 'Oh, no!' 'Really?!' Without the phatic dimension of language, ordinary human communication would soon dissipate in alienation and silence.

The paradoxical linguistic goals of the author of *The Cloud of Unknowing* are to merge the states of communion and silence. In pursuit of silence, he ruthlessly pares utterance to monosyllables. Still he will not have silence at the cost of communion—whether with God, the paramount objective, or with his addressee, the young contemplative whom he is prompting and guiding. Thus, phatic expressions are a necessity to this author, and he knows it. They recommend themselves uniquely yet doubly to his use, for they join psychological supportiveness with minimal articulation of meaning. Accordingly, two traits of style predominate in the *Cloud:* one, sentence structures saturated with linguistic identity of various kinds; the other, a fellowly frequency of phatic expressions. In particular, this author encloses the body of his treatise within an urgent prologue-envoi frame in which phatic expressions and large amounts of identity in clausal and phrasal structures combine more densely than anywhere else in the *Cloud.* These phatic expressions compounded with parallelisms work to ward off inappropriate or unqualified readers and to ratify the personal trust between the author and his specific addressee. The present discussion of the un-Scriptural and, for the most part, antilinguistic bias of this author and his style may fittingly conclude and reinforce its findings with excerpts from the phatic envelope of *The Cloud of Unknowing.* The two that follow, taken from the beginning and ending respectively, specify and solemnly enjoin the right use of this singular work:

[34]Randolph Quirk, *The Uses of English,* 2d ed. (New York: St. Martin's Press, 1968), pp. 62–65. Quirk credits the anthropologist Bronislaw Malinowski with identifying "phatic communion" as a social function of language.

I charge thee & I beseche thee, . . . that neither thou rede it, ne write it, ne speke it, ne ȝit suffre it be red, wretyn, or spokyn, of any or to any, bot ȝif . . . thou charge hem, as I do thee, for to take hem tyme to rede it, speke it, write it, or here it, al over. For paraventure . . . ȝif a man saw o mater & not another, paraventure he miȝt liȝtly be led into errour. & therfore, in eschewing of this errour bothe in thiself & in alle other, I preye thee par charite do as I sey thee. [*CU*, 1.8–2.18]

Lo! goostly freende, in this werk, . . . thou maist worche ȝif thou wilt . . . fer betir & more worthely then I do, . . . that is to say, contynuely worching therin for thee and for me. Do then so, I prey thee, for the love of God Almiȝty. & sithen we ben bothe clepid of God to worche in this werk, I beseche thee for Goddes love fulfille in thi partye that lackith of myne. [*CU*, 129.4–11]

LOVE'S *MYRROUR OF THE BLESSED LYF OF JESU CHRIST*

Elizabeth Salter's admirable monograph on Nicholas Love's *Myrrour of the Blessed Lyf of Jesu Christ* sets a precedent for study of a number of literary aspects of this widely circulated work, among them its style. Salter documents a fundamental homogeneity in the style of the *Myrrour*, both in its translated and its original passages, which in purely formal, compositional terms emerges as a major achievement in early fifteenth-century vernacular prose writing. Even more important for my purposes than her findings with regard to the stylistic cohesiveness of the *Myrrour*, however, is the critical perspective she develops on modes of religious prose writing in English at this period, especially, the continuing native tradition of simple, moderate prose style in which Love is seen to figure centrally.

According to Salter, this simple, moderate prose style developed— "for reasons which are in origin socioreligious but ultimately literary"— as the medium for disseminating to a broad English-speaking audience the truths and teachings required for salvation. Hence its practitioners in the fourteenth and fifteenth centuries are, in the main, "translators of Biblical and devotional Latin material, of whom Love is one."[35] One particularly significant finding to emerge from Salter's examination of these translators' efforts is their explicit self-consciousness about using the vernacular and harnessing its resources of expression to effective discharge of their chiefly didactic aims. This testimony that these writers both knew what they wanted to do and what the nature of their linguistic medium was poses a challenge to S. K. Workman's hitherto widely accepted theory that the intensive translating activity of the fifteenth century engendered an English stylistic awareness that had not

[35]Salter, *Love's "Myrrour,"* pp. 263, 251.

previously existed.[36] The evidence Salter adduces from the native tradition of simple, moderate prose writing suggests, rather, that the stylistic awareness engendered the translating and informed its character. The following are excerpts from her account of the stylistic awareness manifested by English translators working in this tradition:

The nature of their theory was always influenced by the fact that they composed for the unlearned; but the way in which they transcended the limitations thus imposed upon them, and developed a mature sense of literary criticism, reveals the power of native resources. Theirs is not the only good prose . . . , but the best composition of the time answers to their requirements. In the Prefaces and Prologues to their works they made familiar discussion of translation and style in general, thereby laying the foundation of literary prose criticism; in their extension of the field of vernacular prose—scope and method—they provided new material for original writing. Thus they enriched and disciplined the English language.

Even in earliest times we can see that, in spite of their utilitarian motives, the translators had some feeling for the natural prose idiom of the language, as distinct from that of their Latin originals. Moreover, their easy acceptance of the criteria of simplicity and directness, however prompted, proved to be an excellent basis for the development of one major kind of English prose style. . . . The medieval English translators knew how to preserve a subtle relation with their original text, reconciling independence with submission.

In the matter of prose style also there is agreement of theory and practice, . . . linked by a dominant interest in communication, the conveying of important material from one language to another. Significant control over style is exercised by this constant awareness of the need for easy comprehension, which may also be reinforced, even delicately modified, by a proper desire to betray neither the essential characteristics of the Latin original, nor the essential characteristics of the English language.[37]

In relating Love's *Myrrour* to the native tradition of moderate style in English religious prose, Salter does not merely claim that the work exemplifies what is best and most characteristic in the tradition but, additionally, that Love must be credited with certain strategic adjustments which enhanced its stylistic vitality and effectiveness in addressing an

---

[36]Samuel K. Workman's *Fifteenth-Century Translation as an Influence on English Prose* (Princeton: Princeton University Press, 1940) develops the view that, during the period in question, English prose style underwent substantial upgrading primarily because of widespread activity in translating from Latin and French into English. Workman argues for a causal connection between appreciation of the relatively more advanced stylistic cultivation of sentence form in Latin and French, gained through the close syntactic work of translation, and the ability to replicate or emulate such formal accomplishments in English. Salter's position, on the contrary, is that stylistic awareness and competence in English translation was well established—for the moderate no less than the high tradition in religious prose—well before the fifteenth century.

[37]Salter, Love's *"Myrrour,"* pp. 228, 257, 263.

English readership at the beginning of the fifteenth century. In documenting the homogeneous stylistic composition of the translated and original portions of the *Myrrour* and variously considering "grammatical structure, vocabulary, ornament, and rhythmical design,"[38] Salter brings into sharp relief the specific features of ease and expansiveness that mark Nicholas Love's signature in prose. The openwork of his sentence forms consistently enlarges on abrupt or concise locutions in the Latin. Since ablative absolutes and participials are typically rendered as finite verb phrases if not as full clauses, the staple of Love's style becomes the loosely additive sentence resulting from abundant recourse to various conjoining operations.[39] Symmetric conjunction and conjunction reduction together account for numerous word pairs, while asymmetric conjunction, in general less stringently reduced, creates trailing series of larger (phrasal and clausal) units. Reiteration further compounds the volubility of the style.

In the functional fluency that characterizes Love's composition, it is natural that loose, asymmetrically assembled sentences become the principal conveyances for the materials of the *Myrrour,* a work that elaborates narratively and reflectively on events from the life of Christ. Love, however, is by no means content merely to replicate in English the substance and the emphases of his Latin, pseudo-Bonaventuran source. He is much more attracted by affective implications in the Gospel story than by the apocryphal and allegorical minutiae that engage the Latin writer's attention. Accordingly, Love abridges the *Meditationes vitae Christi* radically in his vernacular account of Christ's ministry. The space gained through such abridgment is in turn consigned to verbal elaboration on the Nativity, Baptism, Transfiguration, Ascension, and, supremely, the stages of the Passion which functions to intensify the dramatic and emotional immediacy of this sequence of events. For such purposes Salter finds Love typically deploying a pair of rhythm- and pattern-inducing devices which, we may note, derive from underlying clausal conjunction: parallel constructions and catalogues of lexical primaries (especially nouns, verbs, participles, and adjectives). Her stylistic observations empower, finally, the following pronouncement on Love's place and importance in the history of English prose: "While he cannot be ranked as a highly original writer, he has command of a fuller, more accomplished range of prose

---

[38]See chaps. 7 and 8, "Love's Prose Style" and "Love's Methods of Translation," in Salter, *Love's "Myrrour,"* pp. 264–321.

[39]See Elizabeth Zeeman [Salter], "Nicholas Love—A Fifteenth-Century Translator," *RES* n.s. 6 (1955): 120–21, for a discussion of the characteristic proceeding by which Love combines several sentences in his Latin source into one "long sentence composed of a series of loosely linked clauses."

expression than was the possession of many other more famous literary figures."[40]

What my own discussion of Love will address is the operative relation to be discerned between his expansive, diffuse mode of expression and his undertaking to fashion an orthodox substitute for the (now proscribed) vernacular Gospels, to offer the laity at large. In this connection, there is a pertinent passage in the Preface which Love himself composed for the *Myrrour.* Alluding first and matter of factly to the existence of other aids than "holy writt" for "men and women" who devoutly seek the way to salvation, he proceeds to affirm with mounting emphasis that the "sovereynly" appropriate text for him to English is "the forsaide book of cristes lyf," the *Meditationes vitae Christi,* because it best serves the devotional and affective ends he considers primary in addressing an unscholarly native readership of both sexes. Love maneuvers adroitly in justifying his alternative account of Christ's life, not least in alleging warrant for his enterprise out of Scripture itself. This is the force of his application of Hebrews 5:12–14, the famous passage on the distinction between the meat which may be given to strong men and the milk appropriate for babes:

Wherefore now bothe men and women and every age and every dignyte of this worlde is stired to hope of everelastyng lyf. And for this hope and to this intente/ with holy writt also ben writen dyverse bokes and tretees of devouȝt men: not onliche to clerkes in latin but also in english to lewed men and wommen and hem that ben of symple understondynge. . . . The whiche scripture and writynge/ for the fructuose mater therof sterynge specially to the love of Jesu/ semeth amonge othere sovereynly edifienge to symple creatures: the whiche as children haven nede to be fedde with mylke of lyȝte doctrine/ and not with sadde mete of grete clergie and hiȝe contemplacioun. Wherefore/ at the instaunce and the prayer of somme devoute soules/ to edificacioun of suche men or wommen/ is this drawynge out of the forsaide book of cristes lyf wryten in english.[41]

Love holds true to his announced intent of "sterynge specially to the love of Jesu" the readership of the *Myrrour.* As already mentioned, his curtailed treatment of Christ's ministry makes for an English work quite differently apportioned; Love reduces to a total of 63 the 161 chapters of his Latin original. But the firm hand he is taking with overall design comes through most clearly at junctures where Love articulates for the reader what he is doing and why. For instance, he signals his omission,

[40]Salter, *Love's "Myrrour,"* pp. 269–71, 261–62.

[41]Nicholas Love, *The Mirrour of the Blessed Lyf of Jesu Christ: A Translation of the Latin Work Entitled Meditationes Vitae Christi Attributed to Cardinal Bonaventura,* ed. Lawrence F. Powell (Oxford: Clarendon Press, 1908), p. 8. In my citations of Love (subsequently cited as *Mirrour* and incorporated in my text) I have departed from Powell's edition only in modernizing consonantal *i* and *u* and long *s*.

except for a capsule summary, of the Sermon on the Mount and the Lord's Prayer, presumably because the *Myrrour* is not a repository of doctrine in its compiler's eyes:

When oure lorde Jesu had chosen and gadered his disciples/ as it is seide/ willynge to teche hem and enforme hem the perfeccioun of the newe lawe/ he ladde hem up in an hille/ that is cleped Thabor/ aboute two myle fro Nazareth after the comoun opinioun: and there he made to hem a longe sermoun and full of fruyte: It conteneth all the perfeccioun of cristen lyvynge: for in that sermoun he tau3te hem firste whiche men ben blessed of god and worthy to have his blisse. Also he tau3te hem the trewe manere of prayere/ of fastynge/ and of almesdede/ and othere vertues longynge to the perfite lyf of man: as the texte of that gospelle opounly telleth/ and dyvers doctoures and clerkes expownen it sufficiently: the whiche processe we passen over here/ for as moche as it is writen bothe in latyn and in englische in many other places: and also it were ful longe processe to touche alle the poyntes thereof. [*Mirrour*, p. 109]

Similarly and equally characteristically, Love offers a carefully worded rationale for not including in the *Myrrour* a full narration of Jesus's teachings, healings, and various visitations in the Gospels. In his disparagement of these materials as "long . . . and peraventure tedyouse/ bothe to the rederes and the hereres hereof/ . . . that semeth litel edificacioun inne as to the manere of symple folk/ that this book is specially writen too," there may well be an unexpressed inhibition, for these are precisely the materials that bulk largest in Wyclif's English sermons. In their place, Love tells us, he will provide a sustained treatment of the Passion, "as the mater that is moste nedefulle and moste edifienge" (*Mirrour*, p. 100).

Whatever inhibitions may have operated to make the *Myrrour* an impeccably orthodox production, Love also has a constructive motive for the doctrinal and narrative excisions he performs, namely, to make room for repeated evocations of Christ as the supreme object of the soul's wonder and love. The affective priorities served by Love's mode of composition can be seen in his handling of the following episode in Christ's ministry, to which the relative stylistic elaboration provides a significant index. While the climactic event, the healing, is summarily related at the very end in indirect discourse, the greater part of the passage is given over to concatenated physical details and side remarks which are as vital to a pious response as they are incidental to the narrative:

There was in the citee of Jerusalem/ in the manere of a ponde/ a standynge water closed about with fyve dores: in the whiche water the schepe were waschen that were offred in to sacrifice: in the whiche water also/ after the opinioun of some clerkes/ lay the tre of the holy crosse: where it byfel as by wey of myracle that ones in the 3ere that water was gretly stered and meved of the aungel of god. And than what seke man my3te firste entre in to the water he was heled of his infirmyte: wherfore many seke men dwelleden contynuelly by that water/ abydynge the mevynge therof by the aungel: among the whiche there was one liggyng in his bedde of the palesye xxxviii 3ere. The whiche man oure lord Jesu heled on the sabbot day/ and badde hym bere awey his bedde and goo/ as the processe of the gospelle telleth more plenerly. [*Mirrour*, p. 152]

For all of its brevity and simplicity, the foregoing passage admirably illustrates a fundamental point about the larger workings and effects of the prose style of the *Myrrour:* that the wealth of affective particulars with which Love supplements his narrative of the life of Christ finally supplants any potential for Scripturalism as I have defined it. In this connection, the most conspicuous feature of Love's style is the recursive filling out of sentence units with various parenthetical and appositive constructions that use *and* and *or* almost indifferently. As noted in the second section of chapter 1, this group of constructions derives under transformational-generative analysis from a deep source in clausal conjunction through an intermediate adjoining operation that also produces nonrestrictive relative clauses. All such constructions provide quite literal linguistic outlets within sentence form for a speaker's or writer's locally associated bits of information, observations, or feelings. Nothing could be more instrumental than such outlets to Love's program as a stylist. Again and again in the *Myrrour* he is to be observed in the act of inserting edifying additions at relevant junctures in the Gospel story or other discourses, and doing so to such an extent that the interpolations swamp the Biblical modes and rhythms of expression. The effacement of the impress of Scripturalism in the *Myrrour* sets it apart from the prose of such diverse and yet near contemporaries as Wyclif and Hilton. Here, to illustrate, is Love at work interpolating commentary in the Christmas story as narrated in the well-known second chapter of Luke:

What tyme that nyne monthes fro the concepcioun of blissed Jesu drowen to ende Cesar Auguste/ the Emperour of Rome/ sente oute a maundement/ or an heste/ that all the world sugette to hym schulde be descryved: so that he my3te knowe the noumbre of regiouns/ of citees/ and of the hevedes longynge to hem/ that weren subdyte to the Emperour of Rome: and herfore he ordyned and bad that alle men where so evere they dwelleden schulde goo to the citee of hir firste birthe and propre lynage. Wherfore Joseph/ that was of the lynage of david/ whos citee was bethleem/ toke with hym his spouse/ blissed marie/ that was that tyme greet with childe/ and wente fro Na3areth unto the citee Bethleem/ there to be noumbred among othere as sugett to the Emperour. And so ledyng with hem an oxe and an asse/ they wenten al that longe wey to gidre/ as pore folk/ havynge no more worldely good bot tho tweyne bestes. And what tyme they comen to Bethleem/ for the grete multitude that was there in the same tyme for the selve cause/ they my3te gete none herborwe in none house but in a comoun place/ bytwixe tweyne houses/ that was . . . icleped a dyversorie/ they were neded to reste ynne and abide all that tyme. In the whiche place Joseph/ that was a carpunter/ made hem a closere and a cracche for her bestes. . . . Whan tyme of that blissed byrthe was come/ that is to say the sonday at mydny3t/ goddis sone of hevene/ as he was conceyved in his moder wombe by the holy goost with outen seede of man/ so goynge out of that wombe with outen travaille or sorwe/ sodeynely was uppon hey at his moder feete. And anon sche/ devoutly enclynande/ with sovereyne joye toke hym in hir armes and swetely clippyng and kessynge leyde hym in hir barme/ and with a fulle pap/ as sche was tau3t of the holy goost/ wisshe hym al aboute with hir swete mylk; and so wrapped hym in the keverchiefes of hir heved and leide hym in the cracche. [*Mirrour,* pp. 45–46]

In such a style, the presiding regard for the reader's spiritual welfare is everywhere manifest. Since Love will not leave his reader uninstructed or unaffected at any juncture, the appositives and parentheticals swarm in to explain Caesar's decree and why it was issued, the specifics in which Joseph could (and could not) provide for Mary, and even the instantaneous, painless fashion in which the virgin birth was brought to delivery. But to stir devotion Love systematically employs another category of nonrestrictive relative constructions: the reduced participial forms in parallel ("devoutly enclynande," "and swetely clippyng and kessynge") whose rocking rhythmical responsions are always a cue to affective design in the *Myrrour*.

Thus, in the Friday (or *Die Veneris*) section devoted to the Passion, "the moste nedefulle and most edifienge" subject in the entire work, Love draws upon the medieval tradition of devotion to Christ's manhood for thematic and stylistic intensification of his appeal to his readership, whom he aims to confront with their Lord in his extremities of weakness and suffering.[42] Admitting to a sense of strain in seeking to evoke the "most fructuous" scenes from the end of Christ's life, he says his "chapitres schullen be writen as god wole 3eve grace" (*Mirrour,* p. 100). As he labors to articulate to his readers their unique opportunity to relate intimately to their Savior in his voluntary submission to the worst infirmities which humankind can experience, the rising tide of theological and emotional signification comes to the fore in waves of parallel attributive constructions:

Wherfore thou schalt ymagyne and ynwardely thinke of hym in his passioun as of a faire 3onge man of the age of xxxiii 3ere/ that were the faireste/ the wiseste/ and the most ri3twysse in his levinge: and moost goodly and innocent that evere was or my3t be in this world: so falsely accused/ so enviously pursewed/ so wrongfully demede/ and so despitously slayne/ as the process of this passioun afterward telleth/ and all for thy love. [*Mirrour,* pp. 216–17]

[42]On Love's place in this devotional tradition, see Salter, *Love's "Myrrour,"* pp. 119–78.

The pattern of the elements in parallel—the superlative predicate adjectives ("the faireste," "the wiseste," etc.) and the participial degree constructions ("so falsely accused," "so enviously pursewed," etc.)—becomes the more effective, or affective, because the reduced conjuncts also serve as bearers of semantic intensification. But, even without reinforcement of the latter kind, syntactic recursion alone can produce a powerful rhythmic arousal when, as in Love's evocation of the scourging of Jesus, each parallel clause arrives in linear succession like another blow of the lash:

And wolde thou knowe in what conflicte and bataile he was/ byholde and see. First/ oon dispitiously leieth hond upon hym and taketh hym: another is redy and hard byndeth hym: another/ crienge/ putteth uppon hym blaspheme: another spitteth in his face: another sotelly asketh of hym meny questiouns in desceyte forto accuse hym: another is besy to brynge false witnesse aȝenst hym: another draweth hym forth bifore the Justice: another stifly accuseth hym: another buffeteth hym: another hydeth his eiȝen: another skorneth hym: another after despoilleth him: another byndeth hym harde to the piler; another with scharpe skorges sore beteth hym: another unbyndeth hym: another casteth on hym that olde silken mantel: another setteth a scharpe crowne of thornes uppon his heved: another putteth into his hande a reede; another takith it woodly fro hym/ and smyteth his sore heved ful of thornes: another in skorne kneleth byfore hym: and so forth/ now one and now another/ and dyverse and menye with all hir wittes and myȝte besien hem to turment hym in the worste manere. [*Mirrour*, p. 235]

Always performed with the best of intentions, Love's authorial intrusions upon the text of Scripture can easily modulate from additions to recastings of its language, as the foregoing quotation shows. Yet, whether the motive is to supplement or intensify, the pleonastic, expatiating tendencies remain prominent in the *Myrrour*. An illuminating case in point is the following passage of original composition in which Love shows how paraphrase and elaboration can increase one's emotive response to the message brought by the angel of the Annunciation:

The whiche greting after the commone understondynge may be thus seide in Englische tonge: Heyle marye/ ful of grace/ oure lorde is with the. Blissed be thou sovereynly in wymmen/ and the fruyte of thy wombe/ Jesu/ evere blessid be. And ȝif the liste in this gretynge specifye the fyve joyes with the fyve vertues byfore seid/ Thou mayst seie thus in schort wordes: Heile marie/ mayden mekest/ gret of the aungel gabriel in Jesu gracious conceyvynge: Ful of grace/ as moder chast withouten sorowe or peyne thi sone Jesu berynge. Oure lord is with thee by trewe feith and byleve at Jesus joyful uprisynge. Blessid be thou sovereinly in wommen/ by sadde hope seynge thy sone Jesu to hevene myȝtily upstyenge. And blessed be the fruyte of thi wombe/ Jesu/ in evere lastynge blisse: thorw perfit charite the quene of hevene gloriously crownynge. Gete us thise vertues as for our spede to thy sone Jesu and thy plesynge. Be thou oure help in al oure nede and socoure at oure last ending. Amen. Thus thinketh me may be had contemplacioun more conveniently after the ordre of the fyve joyes of our lady seynt marye in the forseide gretynge *Ave maria* &c. than was bifore writen to the Ankeresse as scheweth here. Chese he that liste/ to rede or write this processe as hym semeth best/ or in other better manere 3if he can/ so that be it one be it othere/ that the ende and the entent be to the worschippe and the plesynge of our lord Jesu and his blessed moder marye. [*Mirrour*, pp. 36–37]

In this passage Love discloses a good deal of information and awareness regarding the methods and the motives of his style. We are permitted to watch how he employs his ascriptive, reiterative direct address to set in motion a lovingly devout access of the spirit to the Virgin and, simultaneously, the process of composition. Love invites others to such composition—to surpass him in it, if possible—but he does so with a revealing warning that style divorced from proper spirituality is profitless. One must sustain a worshipful and gracious intent toward the persons of Christ and Mary, as if one were actually in their presence. Accordingly, in Love's writing no less than in his thinking about prose the situation of direct address, immediate and personal speaking contact, plays an altogether central role. Here is one explanation for the wealth of appositives, parentheticals, and related constructions in the *Myrrour*: they aid in evoking a sense of situation by signalling the presence of a speaker within sentence form. These syntactic means contribute powerfully to making Love's prose style such a functional instrument of his pious designs upon a wide English audience.

But, beyond the central role played by direct address in Love's affective mode of composition, it remains to be noted how extensively features of oral language interpenetrate the more deliberate rhetorical designs constituted by the catalogues and serial parallelisms. Undoubtedly the most recurrent oral feature of Love's prose is pleonasm—his speakerlike tendency to repeat himself, often without the slightest trace of so-called elegant variation. Here are some typical examples of pleonasm in passages from the *Myrrour* that have already been cited: "a longe sermoun and full of fruyte: It conteneth all the perfeccioun of crysten lyvynge . . . and othere vertues longynge to the perfite lyfe of man"; "the whiche processe we passen over here/ for as moche as it is writen . . . in many other places: and also it were ful longe processe to touche alle the poyntes thereof"; "Cesar Auguste/ the Emperour of Rome/ sente oute a maundement/ or an heste/ that all the world sugette to hym schulde be descryved/ so that he my3te knowe the noumbre . . . of the hevedes longynge to hem that weren subdyte to the Emperour of Rome"; "in his birthe and first comynge in to this worlde." Surely the most egregious single instance of pleonasm among passages already cited is Love's recommended paraphrase of the Ave Maria so as to incorporate in it "in schort wordes" the five joys as well as the five virtues of Mary; the resulting paraphrase, as we have had occasion to note, is anything but "schort." Still another recurrent oral feature of Love's prose is his tendency to conjoin clauses of different types in making fluid transitions from declaratives to questions or imperatives or exclamations—for example, "And wolde thou knowe in what conflicte and bataile he was/ byholde and see"; "as the process of this passioun afterward telleth/ and all for thy love."

Indeed, it is arguable that the oral basis of Love's prose style, its affinity with spoken language, is ultimately a more crucial aspect than is the rhythmic heightening found at strategic junctures in the *Myrrour.* For his greatest imperative in composing this work, as he well knew, was to project an authoritative presence, to create a voice that would be listened to, in the sense of believed and obeyed, so that Holy Church would remain the fold of all Christian souls in England. This sense of purpose regarding his authorial self-assertion is so strong that it acts as a framework in which the various features of Love's style find their place and function: the direct address, the intrusive appositives and parentheticals, the insistent sound similarities, the pleonasm, the conjunctions of differing clause types. Above all, this sense of purpose infuses Love's stance as an intermediary between the Bible and the people. It is thus we see him at work in his prose—preselecting, predigesting, instructing, and exhorting—to the end that his readership will receive aright what they are given of the Word and of the Sacrament as well.

In the latter connection, it is indicative both of the author and his time that the longest stretches of original composition in the *Myrrour* are attempts to confute the Wycliffite attack on transubstantiation. One of these is a basically independent piece, "A schort tretys of the hiȝeste and moste worthy sacrament of Cristes blessed body and the merveyles there of," which furnishes what again is not at all a "schort" last word to the *Myrrour* proper. This "tretys" of Love's is strongly oral in its features of style and mode of address which culminate in an ejaculatory prayer to the consecrated Host.[43] Orality is, however, no less marked in Love's other major addition to his source materials—an excursus of several pages on the subject of sacramental reception which he inserted in the *Die Jovis* or Thursday section immediately following the narration of the Last Supper. I shall close with some fairly lengthy excerpts from this excursus because of the uniquely illuminating insights which it affords into Love's projection of an authoritative voice through the dynamics of his style:

Take now good hede here thou cristen man/ but specially thou preost/ how devoutly/ how dyligently and trewely thy lorde Jesu criste firste made this

[43]Love, "A schort tretys," in *Mirrour*, ed. Powell, pp. 323–24. The "tretys" is on pp. 304–24.

preciouse sacrament: and after with his blissed handes mynystred it and communed that blissed and his byloved meigne. And on the tother side take hede with what devoute wondre firste they seie hym make that wonderfulle and excellent sacrament: and after with what drede and reverence they toke it and resceyved it of hym. Sothely at this tyme they lefte al their kyndely resoun of man/ and onely restede in trewe byleve to alle that he seide and didde/ bylevynge with oute eny dowte that he was god and my3t not erre. And so moste thou doo that wolt fele and have the vertue and the gostly swetnesse of this blissed sacrament.

These termes I touche here so specially by cause of the lewed lollardes that medlen hem a3enst the feith falsely. And more over this feith of this excellent sacrament/ tau3t by holy doctoures and worthy clerkes/ is conhermed by many maneres of myracles/ as we reden in many bookes and heren all day preched and tau3t. But here lawheth the lollarde and skorneth holy chirche in allegeaunce of suche myracles/ holdynge hem bot magge tales and feyned illusiouns: and by cause that he tasteth nou3t the swettenesse of this precious sacrament/ ne feleth the gracious worchynge thereof in hym self/ therfore he leveth no3t that eny othir dothe. But here in confusioun of alle false lollardes/ and in comforte of alle trewe loveres and worschipperes of this holy sacrament/ and principally to the lovynge and honour of the hi3e auctor and makere there of/ oure lorde Jesu/ I schal seie more over somwhat in specialle that I knowe sothely of the gracious worchynge in sensible felynge of this blissed sacrament: the whiche marveylous worchynge and felynge above comoun kynde of man scheweth and proveth sovereynely the blessid bodyly presence of Jesu in that sacrament.

A lorde Jesu/ in what delectable paradyse is he for that tyme that thus feleth that blessed bodily presence of the in that preciouse sacrament: thoru3 the whiche he feleth him sensibily/ with unspekeable joye/ as he were joyned body to body? Sothely I trowe that there may no man telle it or speke it: and I am siker that there may no man fully and sothefastly knowe it/ but onely he that in experience feleth it: for with outen doute this is specially that hidde manna/ that is to say aungelles mete/ that no man knoweth bot he that feleth it. [*Mirrour*, pp. 204, 207, 209]

In the foregoing excerpts the pattern-creating elements of parallelism and catalogue are held in abeyance, despite the crescendo of feeling, so that the speech features are brought into highest prominence in the texture of the prose. In thus clarifying and maintaining under pressure the comparatively greater importance of colloquialism as over against rhetorical design, Love reveals that his priorities in composing the *Myrrour* lay, above all, in harnessing the power and appeal of oral expression in a written text. He needed to attain the force of a voice that would be able to command both the assent and the affections of a broad popular readership.

To pursue these ends, this sacramental excursus develops out of a narrative sequence from Scripture which Love repeatedly interrupts and interlards in his typical fashion. As the excursus proceeds, it converts more and more to a spoken mode—first in the reiterated exhortations and imperatives, finally in the vocal outpouring of feeling that accompanies the attempt to articulate the "unspekeable joye" of sacramental union with Christ. However, the affective climax here does not reduce, as in "A schort tretys," to a lyric apostrophe. Rather it inheres in the singular attestation of personal mystical experience to which Love, in his urgency to repel Lollardy, has recourse.[44] With only a trace of indirection (the intermittent shift to "he" from "I"), Love here exerts to the fullest the authoritativeness of his voice and his powers of expression as he affirms in ringing tones a sense of transport which, at the same time, he professes to find inexpressible. The passage indeed reaches its heights in language as Love jointly ascribes the grace of mystical communion to Jesus in prayerful direct address and yet maintains unbroken discourse with his English audience. This is a style, then, which in its furthest reaches hazards the spanning of heaven and earth in the interest of asserting a comprehensive and conclusive vernacular authority. Nonetheless Love's enterprise in the *Myrrour* is not merely significant for the resulting character of its literary achievement. It is equally important in foreshadowing the nature of the role that later self-styled champions of Catholic authority, most notably, Pecock and More, would take upon themselves and subject to different interpretations in the writing of English prose.

THE ORAL BASIS OF PROSE COMPOSITION

In tracing the chequered fortunes of Scripturalism within the prose styles of the four most widely circulated English religious writers from the turn of the fourteenth to the fifteenth century, I have repeatedly had reason to refer to oral features as an additional factor in vernacular prose composition. Why should this be so? What relation is there between Scripturalism and orality in the prose of this period? The relation which we have seen variously affirmed or avoided by Wyclif, Hilton, the author of *The Cloud of Unknowing*, and Love leads toward the finding that Scripturalism depends on the factor of orality for whatever implementation it receives. In other words, to the extent that Biblical modes and forms of expression leave their impress on a writer's style, they are empowered to do so by the writer's own declared understanding of Scripture as a living—that is, personally addressed and spoken—Word from God to man. Such primacy of emphasis upon speech in the self-conscious cul-

[44]Salter ("Nicholas Love—A Fifteenth-Century Translator," p. 116) takes the view that the intimately circumstantial particulars in this passage bespeak "Love's own knowledge of spiritual ecstasy" while at the same time conceding that such first-person disclosures are "rare" with this author.

tivation of an open, communicative style in the vernacular suggests that orality should be examined in its own right as a factor in prose composition. For not only does the contingent relation of Scripturalism to orality raise the possibility of the latter's being the more fundamental of the two factors in shaping vernacular writing at this period, but also orality, by its very nature, offers itself as a potentially more comprehensive referent in studying style, one equally applicable to secular and religious prose. Thus, what we may term "the oral basis of composition" will absorb our attention for the remainder of this chapter, and it will remain an object of interest in much of the next as well.

In my view, a viable perspective on the oral basis or oral features of vernacular prose style in this period requires as much comprehensiveness in one's chronology as in one's subject matter. Here and in chapter 3 I shall be using an essentially synchronic framework for discussing works and authors from an era spanning more than a century—the close of the fourteenth to the beginning of the sixteenth century. My justification for this synchronic framework hinges on the very different circumstances under which works were disseminated in manuscript and during the first tentative decades of printing (the incunabula era), as compared with the level of circulation achieved after printing had firmly established itself in Europe and England by the 1530s. The phenomenon of multiple translation usefully illustrates the local, uncoordinated character of literary enterprises in the later fourteenth and fifteenth centuries. Among works that became popular in English versions, we know of seven or eight separate translations of Friar Laurent's *Somme des vices et des virtus* as well as of Birgitta's *Revelations* and *Life*, four separate translations of the *Secreta secretorum* and the *Life of Alexander*, and three each of the *Imitatio Christi* and Mandeville's *Travels*—all cases in which the translators were oblivious of reduplicating one another's efforts.[45] However, after printing gained a surer foothold, retranslation was undertaken wholly with an eye to the market, the motive being either to improve or to update the English of durable items. Multiple translation of the former kind simply disappeared. Such a drastic alteration in the circumstances that determined the currency of a work provides sanction for a nonlinear, nondevelopmental approach to English prose in the later fourteenth and fifteenth centuries.[46] Equally, it requires acknowledgment of the vast alteration brought about by the success of the printing press

[45]William Matthews, ed., *Later Medieval English Prose* (New York: Goldentree Books, 1963), pp. 5–6. On the disputed relationship of the English translations of Mandeville, see B. D. H. Miller's review of M. C. Seymour's edition of *The Bodley Version of Mandeville's Travels* in *Medium Aevum* 35 (1966): 71–78.

[46]Further justification for such an approach to this era may be found in Workman's conclusion (*Fifteenth-Century Translation*, pp. 53–58) that original prose composition in English undergoes marked stylistic development only about 1480 and thereafter.

with movable type—acknowledgment which I shall render by adopting a chronological framework in my discussion of sixteenth-century English prose in chapters 4, 5, and 6.[47]

It is convenient to pursue an understanding of the oral basis or oral features of prose composition by reviewing the principal received conclusions in areas of scholarship that bear on this subject at this period. Such a review necessarily raises three interrelated questions: (1) What are the literary, that is, textual, characteristics underlying the judgment that a given prose specimen is a close reflection of actual speech in its period? (2) What sorts of specific evidence support the labeling of certain textual characteristics as "speech-based" or "speech-derived"? (3) What implications, finally, for stylistic study can be drawn from a relatively technical notion of an oral basis for prose composition that owes its origin and most of its applications to the philological tradition and to the subsequent rise of historical linguistics?

The premise that English prose existed in a close and vital relation to spoken English from the later fourteenth to the earlier sixteenth century, if not for an even longer period, has been a hardy perennial in literary study. Histories of English prose by authors trained in the philological methods of the later nineteenth and earlier twentieth centuries regularly affirm the speechlikeness of this prose as fact. John Earle's *English Prose* remarks on the great frequency of what he calls "word-coalitions" or "the reverse"—the common practice of running together or separating morphemes in writing—which seem to him to give a text a voice.[48] "Shalbe," "welynoughe," "theschequer" are word-coalitions; "bi cause," "with owt," "owre selff" are the reverse. In due course Earle's sense of the affinities between spoken English and textual characteristics would receive massive documentary confirmation in H. C. Wyld's *A History of Modern Colloquial English* (1st ed., 1920).

Wyld grounds his study in painstaking analyses of writers' spelling practices in the later fourteenth century and following. Figuring prominently in these analyses are the works of Gower, Chaucer, Wyclif, Pecock, and Fortescue, the letters of John Shillingford (1447–50), and of the Pastons, and Celys, William Gregory's *Chronicle* (completed ca. 1470), and the original prologues and epilogues Caxton added to works he translated and printed.[49] Among these diverse writers, Wyld finds only

---

[47]See, further, Elizabeth L. Eisenstein, *The Printing Press as an Agent of Change: Communications and Cultural Transformations in Early Modern Europe* (Cambridge and New York: Cambridge University Press, 1979); Lucien P. V. Febvre and Henri-Jean Martin, *The Coming of the Book: The Impact of Printing, 1450–1800*, tr. David Gerard (London: NLB, 1976).

[48]John Earle, *English Prose: Its Elements, History, and Usage* (London: Smith, Elder & Co., 1890), p. 409.

[49]Henry Cecil Wyld, *A History of Modern Colloquial English*, 3d ed. (Oxford: Basil Blackwell, 1936), pp. 46–98.

Caxton deviating in any marked degree from highly phonetic procedures for spelling and dividing words and word groups; Caxton's texts distinguish themselves in adhering quite punctiliously to the conventions of Westminster scribal practice. The explanation he proposes for such hyperconformism invokes Caxton's reiterated expressions of uncertainty regarding his command of English—for example, the admission in the Prologue to *Eneydos* (1492) that he stands "abasshed" at the variety of English usage confronting him, and the more celebrated deference paid to "my ryght redowted lady mylady Margarete," duchess of Burgundy and "suster unto the kynge of Englond and of france, my soverayn lorde" (Edward IV). According to Caxton's Prologue to *The Recuyell of the Historyes of Troye* (1475), "Her sayd grace . . . anone she fonde a defaute in myn englissh whiche she comanded me to amende."[50] Overall, however, Wyld's analyses of spelling lead him to discount the anomaly of Caxton and to infer the existence of considerable numbers of literate persons of both sexes who took their own flexible, pragmatic views on the formulas observed by professional secretaries and copyists. Thus he summarizes regarding the vernacular remains from the later fourteenth and fifteenth centuries: "Many more people can and do write. In their great variety of spelling documents freed from the shackles of professional scribes, we almost seem to overhear real people actually speaking in what they record of pronunciation."[51]

Besides spelling, Wyld's *History of Modern Colloquial English* investigates features of vocabulary and phrasing that seem to originate in spoken language. His work yields a wealth of stock expressions—especially proverbs, oaths, and popular clichés—that came over from speech to writing, together with listings of a whole congeries of expletives, questions, rejoinders, and other socially meaningful but otherwise meaningless linguistic commonplaces which played an indispensable phatic role in conversation. It was Wyld's contribution to identify the types of expressions that bespoke the closeness of prose to speech and to substantiate that closeness by collecting instances of the most common expressions. What is more, Wyld tended to see a connection between the social and ceremonial functions of spoken English and the literary impulse to record experience in the chronicles, letters, and diaries of the fifteenth century. He cites the colloquial vitality exuded by the report made of an official business visit to London in 1447 by John Shillingford, mayor of Exeter, all the while that Shillingford is trying to maintain formality by calling himself "the mayer." A portion of Shillingford's

---

[50]*Prologues and Epilogues of William Caxton*, ed. W. J. B. Crouch, Early English Text Society o.s. 176 (London: Humphrey Milford, 1928), pp. 4–5, 109. For discussion of Caxton's linguistic self-consciousness, see Norman F. Blake, *Caxton and His World* (New York: London House & Maxwell, 1969), pp. 171–93.

[51]Wyld, *History of Modern Colloquial English*, 3d ed., p. 362.

report (with stock oral phrases and phatic expressions italicized) reads as follows:

The Saterdey next ther after the mayer came to Westminster *sone apon ix. atte belle*, and ther mette w⁺ *my lorde* Chaunceller, atte brode dore *a litell fro* the steire fote comyng fro the Sterre chamber, y yn the courte and by the dore, knellyng and salutyng hym *yn the moste godely wyse* that y cowde, and recommended yn to *his gode and gracious lordship* my feloship and all the comminalte . . . of the Cite of Exceter. He sayde to the mayer ii. tymes *Well come*, and the iii.de tyme *Right well come Mayer*, and helde the mayer *a grete while faste by the honde*, and so went forth to his barge and w⁺ hym *grete presse*, lordis and other, and yn especiall the tresorer of the kynges housholde, with wham he was at *right grete pryvy* communicacion. And therfore y, mayer, drowe me apart, and mette w⁺ hym at his goyng in to his barge, and ther *toke my leve* of hym, seyyng these wordis, *My lord, y wolle awayte apon youre gode lordship and youre better leyser* at another tyme.[52]

Two more recent studies have extended Wyld's emphasis on the large number of conventional speech locutions to be found in fifteenth-century English prose. R. K. Stone instances such "common, everyday expressions" as these from the *Book of Margery Kempe*: "at the last," "ryth wel," "as kynde wolde," "on a tyme," "wyth good wil," and these from Julian of Norwich's *Showings of Divine Love*: "as to myne understondyng," "so far forth," "and after this," "withoute ende."[53] P. J. C. Field records the following among "familiar stock phrases" from Malory's *Morte Darthur*: "berdles boye," "fyghtynge as a wood lyon," "blood up to the fittlockys," "grete tray and tene," "went to have gone the same way," "both towarde and frowarde," "for fayre speache nother for foule," "say hym a good worde."[54] Both Stone and Field stress that locutions of this type comprise so large a dimension of the style of their respective authors that an exhaustive listing would be impractical.

Beyond local features of spelling, vocabulary, and idiom, one can infer the closeness of prose to speech from the fluid modulations in fourteenth- and fifteenth-century prose texts between the grammatical third person, on the one hand, and either the first or the second person, on the other. (I have noted in passing Love's as well as Shillingford's mod-

---

[52]*Letters and Papers of John Shillingford*, ed. S. A. Moore (London: Camden Society, 1871), pp. 5–6, cited in Wyld, p. 81.

[53]Robert Karl Stone, *Middle English Prose Style: Margery Kempe and Julian of Norwich* (The Hague and Paris: Mouton & Co., 1970), p. 55.

[54]P. J. C. Field, *Romance and Chronicle: A Study of Malory's Prose Style* (London: Barrie & Jenkins, 1971), p. 59. See, further, Mark Lambert, *Malory: Style and Vision in "Le Morte Darthur"* (New Haven: Yale University Press, 1975), pp. 30–33, 44. Lambert usefully remarks that Malory's constant recourse to adjectival constructions like "fayre," "noble," "the goodliest," and so on is not unlike present-day colloquial uses of "wonderful," "fine," "the greatest."

ulations in this vein.) Gösta Langenfelt, in his *Select Studies in Colloquial English of the Late Middle Ages*,[55] was apparently the first scholar to record and link this discourse feature with the distinctly colloquial effect it creates in a text. We can observe something of the ease with which texts shift grammatical person in moving from indirect to direct representation of speech by considering part of a homely allegory, composed about 1425, on the subject of hallowing Sunday. Other residual oral features will be obvious in the writing; I have italicized the pertinent shifts in the representation of speech in the passage. The scene is the great hall of the house of the Seven Deadly Sins, where they gather to drink and jest at day's end. Pride, Covetousness, Sloth, and Lechery have already assembled and greeted the company:

Then cometh in glotonee the stuard of that howsolde, & *he* cherith *tham* alle, & bidith tham sitte stille & be mery and glad, so that *noon of 3ow* go hoom bot it be so *he* be sad, or a staf in his hoonde for allynge. Than slowthe herith this maundement, that is the marchel of that halle, & then he overloketh tham alle. And then he chargeth Ydulnes to cheren tham alle, & to sitte stille, and that the cuppe, be not empte no tyme. Than at the laste ende comith in wrath & he bringeth with him envye, & rekunneth ther acuntes, for that he is treasureer of that howsoolde, *he* chargeth that *noon of hem* parte from other in charite, & loke he saith wen that ever *3e* come togedur that *noon* speke good of other, ne of *3owre* neibures. And than saide *thai* alle, Amen.[56]

A no less lively but far more controlled modulation of this sort from indirect to direct representation of speech in writing occurs in a letter Margaret Paston wrote in 1448 to her husband when he was away on business. The news is the kind that would prompt a long-distance phone call today; a petty incident erupted into a brawl in which Margaret and her mother became involved. To begin with, Margaret reports, their neighbor Wymondham was standing at his gate with two of his serving men, when the parish priest, James Gloys, returned from town, hat on head, and approached Wymondham's gate in his usual fashion. At that moment Gloys, the priest, decided to stand on his clerical rank with a show of superiority toward Wymondham, which Margaret dramatizes in direct discourse:

And whanne Gloys was a-yenst Wymondham he seid thus, "Covere thy heed!" And Gloys seid ageyn, "So, I shall for thee." And whanne Gloys was forther passed by the space of iii or iiii stryde, Wymondham drew owt his dagger and seid, "Shalt thow so, knave?" And therwith Gloys turned hym and drew owt

---

[55]Gösta Langenfelt, *Select Studies in Colloquial English of the Late Middle Ages* (Lund: Håkan Ohlsson, 1933), pp. 93–96.

[56]*A Middle English Treatise on the Ten Commandments*, ed. J. F. Royster (Chapel Hill: University of North Carolina Press, 1911), p. 22, cited in Workman, *Fifteenth-Century Translation*, p. 42, as a typical specimen of original prose of the period.

his dagger and defendet hym, fleyng in-to my moderis place. And Wymondham and his man Hawys kest stonys and dreve Gloys into my moderis place. And Hawys folwyed into my moderis place and kest a ston as meche as a forthyng-loaf into the halle after Gloys.

But the drama of the brawl is only the smaller part of Margaret's message to her husband; the larger part is the role which she and her mother played in defending the priest and restoring order. Interestingly, as she signals the women's intervention her voice asserts control too by shifting into indirect discourse for the report of the final exchanges:

And with the noise of this a-saut and affray my modir and I come owt of the chirche from the sakering; and I bad Gloys go in to my moderis place ageyn, and so he dede. And thanne Wymondham called my moder and me strong hores. . . . And he had meche large langage, as ye shall knowe her-after by mowthe.[57]

The closeness to dialogue found at all levels of prose writing in the period is further attested in Reginald Pecock's vernacular tracts against the Lollards. The austerely intellectual argument in both *The Donet* and *The Folewer to the Donet* develops as a familiar discussion between a son and his father (a form that anticipates the English controversial works of Thomas More and other writers); accordingly, the phatic interchanges display the following character: "Ffadir how schal y wite that this is trewe?" "Sone thou seist sooth."[58] By contrast, Pecock's *Repressor of Overmuch Blaming of the Clergy* strikes a distinctly more formal note while still using a mode of oral interchange, the elaborate courtesy which permits adversaries to debate with one another: "Seie to me, good Sire, and answere herto . . ."; "But for to turne here fro aȝen unto oure Bible men, y preie ȝe, seie ȝe to me. . . ." Even so, the authorial persona is not too dignified to exclaim against the ilk of Oldcastle: "Fy fy fy therefore upon presumpcioun and obstynacie in the lay party."[59] Thus Pecock's formal mode as well as his familiar one bespeaks the accessibility of colloquialism in vernacular prose writing.

Probably no literary historian has labored more tirelessly than H. S. Bennett to establish respect for fifteenth-century writers "who owed

---

[57]*Paston Letters and Papers of the Fifteenth Century*, ed. Norman Davis (Oxford: Clarendon Press, 1971), I, 224. For other examples of a strongly indicated speech context, see *The Cely Papers*, ed. Henry E. Malden, Camden Society, 3d ser., no. 1 (London: Longmans, Green, & Co., 1900), pp. 57–59; and the 1481 letter by Richard Cely included among the illustrative materials in Wyld, *History of Modern Colloquial English*, pp. 79–80.

[58]Reginald Pecock, *The Folewer to the Donet*, ed. Elsie V. Hitchcock, Early English Text Society o.s. 164 (London: Humphrey Milford, 1924), pp. 78, 84.

[59]Reginald Pecock, *The Repressor of Overmuch Blaming of the Clergy*, ed. Churchill Babington, Rolls Series no. 19 (London: Longman, Green, Longman, & Roberts, 1860), I, 28, 86, 221. Also see Bruno Zickner's remarks on speech locutions in his *Syntax und Stil in Reginald Pecocks "Repressor"* (Berlin: Mayer & Müller, 1900), p. 118.

little or nothing to French or Latin" but gave proof of the self-sufficiency of their native tongue by exercising it freely. Bennett insisted on the stylistic merits of the prose which these writers produced by "constantly attempting to put down their thoughts in a clear and unornamented fashion, . . . almost as simply as if they were talking."[60] Unquestionably valid perceptions underlie such stress on the literary interest and importance of much fifteenth-century prose, but it is nevertheless true that Bennett's claims have had little impact on literary-historical thinking. One reason for this, I think, lies in his failure to move beyond generalized and impressionistic representations of the stylistic significance of speech-likeness in fifteenth-century English prose; in this regard, Bennett's ideas join with Chambers's continuity hypothesis. Another reason, however, may trace to the dichotomy between a "fine" style practiced by authors versed in both French and Latin and a plain, popular style utilized by writers who knew only English which Bennett's pronouncements about prose always imply. The implication of such a dichotomy is unfortunate, for it fosters a misconception. The presence or absence of colloquial features in vernacular prose writing of the fifteenth century does not correlate at all neatly or necessarily with a line dividing "writers who owe little or nothing to French or Latin" from those who do; the example of Pecock, just referred to, is a telling case in point. Thus Bennett's position has proved rather more suggestive than compelling to date.

After the first great gains of philological investigation which mostly identified the affinities between prose and speech with the reflection of phonological and morphological features in spelling, students of earlier English gradually expanded their interest in the speechlikeness of prose to considerations of syntax. Here the central fact to reckon with was the ubiquity of sentential conjunction, with all its attendant multiplicity and variety of applications. As such reckoning was undertaken, however, the evolutionary myth of the superiority of hypotaxis to parataxis and of subordination to coordination which we have already remarked in the work of Kellner and Curme gave a strong coloration to the interpretive approaches taken by literary historians to English sentence form. George P. Krapp, one of the most influential of these literary historians, offered a typical run of negative if not dismissive judgments. While he credits the *Melibee* and the *Parson's Tale* with being "idiomatically expressed in a simple, straightforward, and unmannered style," in the main Chaucer's prose registers with him as "crude and inferior," an "imperfect adaptation of the thought to the English idiom." Wyclif's prose is similarly decried for being "crude and experimental" in its intellectualism, while Pecock's ranks lowest of all in quality and interest;

[60]Henry Stanley Bennett, *Chaucer and the Fifteenth Century* (Oxford: Clarendon Press, 1947), p. 180.

in Krapp's words, it is "heavy and repetitious without being dignified," "often labored and tediously verbose."[61] Easily the most favorable notice goes to the "prose of simple narration" found in Mandeville's *Travels* and in John Trevisa in the later fourteenth century, as well as in *The Brut* and other chronicles in the fifteenth; these writers are commended for "utter, guileless simplicity," "childlike and effortless expression." But the patronizing undertones here suddenly reveal their source in the evolutionary myth as Krapp expatiates on the disparity between such style and the "more mature manner of modern English": "The sentences are short and direct, never complex. Few connectives are used, and those of the most obvious kind. . . . The whole tone of the expression is naive, the language of a grown-up child."[62] Similarly, the force of this evolutionary myth in the thinking of earlier twentieth-century literary historians is felt in George Saintsbury's slightly later echo of Krapp on Mandeville; Saintsbury observes of the *Travels* that they are "arranged for the most part in very short sentences introduced (exactly like those of a child telling stories) by *And.*"[63]

It is to the concomitant efforts of language historians rather than literary historians that one must look for any signs of the diminishing force of this evolutionary myth, for language historians have shown markedly greater readiness to take the features of earlier English prose for what they are as objects of analysis and understanding. (This is true even though it must be admitted that the methodology of these language historians trained attention on those features of fourteenth- and fifteenth-century English which differed from those of later English, and as a result scanted recognition of the far greater number of features which would—and do—register as natural and normal by present standards.) The principal sources for the extension of philological concerns to English sentence structure include Kellner's own "Abwechselung und Tautologie" essay and the discussion of Caxton's style that prefaces Kellner's edition of *Blanchardyn and Eglantine*, Urban Ohlander's *Coordinate Expressions in Middle English*, and Margaret Schlauch's "Chaucer's Colloquial English—Its Structural Traits."[64]

[61]George P. Krapp, *The Rise of English Literary Prose* (New York: Oxford University Press, 1915), pp. 5, 8, 50, 73.

[62]Ibid., pp. 19–20.

[63]George Saintsbury, *A History of English Prose Rhythm*, 2d ed. (London: Macmillan & Co., 1922), p. 64.

[64]Leon Kellner, "Abwechselung und Tautologie: Zwei Eigenthumlichkeiten des Alt- und Mittelenglischen Stiles," *Englische Studien* 20 (1895): 1–24; Introduction, *Caxton's Blanchardyn and Eglantine*, ed. Kellner, Early English Text Society e.s. 58 (London: N. Trübner & Co., 1890); Urban Ohlander, *Studies on Coordinate Expressions in Middle English* (Lund: C. W. K. Gleerup, 1936); Margaret Schlauch, "Chaucer's Colloquial English—Its Structural Traits," *PMLA* 67 (1952): 1103–16. Also relevant are Schlauch's "Early Tudor Colloquial English," *Philologica Pragensia* 1 (1958): 97–104; and her *English Language in Modern Times (Since 1400)* (Warsaw: Pánstwowe Wydawnictwo Naukowe, 1959), pp. 35–37, 56–61, 112–21, 145–49.

Although Kellner's and Schlauch's analyses do not focus exclusively, as Ohlander's study does, on conjunctive syntax, nevertheless the representation of significant features is strikingly akin in all three. So is the connection between the significant features identified and the workings of sentential conjunction (and conjunction reduction). With unimportant differences in terminology, Kellner, Ohlander, and Schlauch agree in isolating a triad of defining features for the handling of sentence form in fourteenth- and fifteenth-century English prose. These features include (1) ellipsis; (2) pleonasm (Kellner's "Tautologie," Schlauch's "repetition"); and (3) anacoluthon (Kellner's "Abwechselung," Schlauch's "special syntax"). It is additionally germane to my concerns in this study that the bulk of the examples adduced by these three language historians involve some operation or result associated with the use of *and* as a structure-building resource.

It would be pleonastic to illustrate pleonasm as identified by Kellner, Ohlander, and Schlauch in any way but briefly, since the commonness of its occurrence is impossible to miss. I mention merely, from passages recently cited, the allegory author's reiterated "& cherith them alle" and Margaret Paston's "And therwith Gloys turned hym . . . , fleying in-to my moderis place. And Wymondham and his man Hawys kest stonys and dreve Gloys into my moderis place. And Hawys folwyed into my moderis place." While pleonasm is used in these analyses to denote all kinds of reiteration, especially reiterated function words (pronouns, negative and conjunctive particles, double genitives and double comparatives),[65] it is obvious all the same that its single largest source lies in the option of unreduced coordination which, when exercised, leaves varying amounts of identical phrase structure as a residue in surface sentence form.

Ellipsis is used as a covering term for elements which are absent from the sentence forms of earlier English prose but which a twentieth-century reader either requires or expects. Inspection of examples reveals, again, that sentential conjunction is centrally involved—in particular, with ambiguities arising from coordinated verb phrases. The following are Ohlander's illustrations taken from John Mirk's *Festial*, a popular mid-fifteenth-century cycle of story-sermons for feast days; I have added questions in brackets to focus the ambiguities:

But when Thomas herd the knyghtes yarmed yn the cloystyr, and wold have comen yn, and myght not. . . . [Who wanted to come in but might not, Thomas or the knights?]

They saw Jhesu Cryst bodyly with blody wondys stondyng before the seke mannys bed, and sayde to hym thus. . . . [Who is the subject of *sayde*—Jesus, the sick man, or the onlookers? and who is the *hym?*]

[65]Kellner, "Abwechselung und Tautologie," pp. 8–10.

They seen arows of fuyr comyng from the erthe, and slogh men, an huge nowmbyr. [Are persons or arrows doing the slaying?][66]

Mirk is fully representative with respect to ellipses of this sort. Further instances could readily be multiplied from other writers of the period.

Anacoluthon, in its more general meaning, denotes any kind of internal syntactic inconsistency that causes a sentence to end otherwise than it began. Applied, however, to the heavily conjunctive sentence structures of fourteenth- and fifteenth-century prose, the term becomes essentially synonymous with what teachers of English composition call "faulty parallelism." Ohlander devotes more than sixty pages—the entire second part of his monograph—to this phenomenon. Here are a few characteristic specimens from his collection (I retain Ohlander's references in quoting):

From Chaucer's *Parson's Tale:* "Now been ther generale signes of gentilesse; as eschewinge of vyce . . . ; and usinge vertu, curtesye, and clennesse, and to be liberal, that is to seyn, large by mesure" (Cant. I, clause 300). "Wepinge and nat for to stinte to doon sinne, may nat avaylle" (Cant. I, clause 90).

From *The Brut:* "The Erl Godwyn . . . hade muchel herd of the godenesse of Edward, and that he was ful of mercy and of pitee" (129:13). "He remembred his soul, and also that he was mortal, and must dye" (495:17).

From Wyclif's *English Works:* "Litel thenk these woode men and wommen on cristis povert and cold and povert of his modir and what lif he lyvede in this world" (206:5 from bottom). "Thes anticristis clerkis cursen men al day for money, for techyng of goddis lawe and for werkis of mercy and riȝtwisnesse, and for that thei wolen nat assente to errouris aȝenst holy writt" (95:3 from bottom).

From Mirk's *Festial:* "He told hom the case, and how Cryst dyd to hym" (96:22). "I rede that ther was summetyme a mawmet in a cite, that wold tell of all stolen thyngys, and who hyt had" (111:35).[67]

On the interpretive front, Kellner and Schlauch, at least, take genial stances in seeing pleonasm as one manifestation of the rhetorical intensity that courses in a considerable body of earlier English prose. An analogous stance emerges in their characterization of ellipsis and anacoluthon as informalities countenanced by writers and readers out of a love of variety. Yet, for all of their laudable attempts to understand this

---

[66]Ohlander, *Coordinate Expressions*, p. 159, citing *Mirk's Festial: A Collection of Homilies*, Part I, ed. Theodor Erbe, Early English Text Society e.s. 96 (London: Kegan Paul, Trench, Trübner & Co., 1905), pp. 42, 92, 259.

[67]Ohlander, *Coordinate Expressions*, pp. 121–22, 129, 131, 156, 166. I have substituted the term "faulty parallelism" for Ohlander's "asymmetric coordination" because "asymmetric" has another, technical meaning in my study. An interesting sidelight on faulty parallelism—its apparent disappearance from present-day American English prose written for publication—is provided by Mary P. Hiatt, *Artful Balance: The Parallel Structures of Style* (New York: Teachers College Press, 1975), pp. 108–9, 121.

vernacular prose on its own terms, the net effect of the analyses by language historians working to extend the scope of philological methods to sentence structure remains at best a kindly condescension. At less than best, the strictures of linguistic as well as literary historians can become quite severe, especially when a connection is postulated between allegedly unfunctional language constructions and inept or insensitive language users. Ohlander is prone at times to invoke such a connection, partly because his outlook on his subject is colored by the evolutionary grand design. Remarking, for example, that "Coordination by means of *and* . . . exhibits a striking frequency in Middle English," he proceeds to assert that this is "what might be expected on a priori grounds . . . in a comparatively underdeveloped and rough-hewn language"—namely, the lack of more semantically differentiated connectives and the appearance of "constructions that may often be ascribed to a certain primitivism of expression." In Ohlander's view, "The primary function of Middle English *and* . . . is merely to add a new thought to a preceding one. . . . The use of the *and*-construction under discussion springs no doubt very often from a certain inability on the part of the speaker (writer) to find the exact expression on the spur of the moment."[68] A later series of remarks interprets the incidence of faulty parallelism as a sign of the closeness of this English prose to "colloquial speech," a closeness which, in Ohlander's words, permitted an earlier writer to be "not so scrupulous as a reasonably careful modern writer" and even to succumb periodically to "mental confusion" in handling sentence form.[69]

So far as I am aware, the harshest interpretive implications to be drawn from the traits of crudity and inattention that have been imputed to vernacular writers of this period are Workman's, in *Fifteenth-Century Translation as an Influence on English Prose* (1940) and James Sutherland's, in *On English Prose* (1957). Sutherland faults what he considers an almost universal inability to synchronize "the shorter rhythm of the individual sentences and the longer rhythm of the general argument," at one juncture disparaging an unnamed but allegedly typical "our author" as follows:

We rarely feel that we are being taken straight to the point. . . . If the individual sentences have no tension, if they lie spread out before us like a collapsed tent, the writer's general argument will fail to emerge, and if his argument is not constantly present in his mind as he writes, the separate sentences will wander into every sort of digression and parenthesis and amplification.[70]

[68]Ohlander, *Coordinate Expressions,* pp. 8–9.

[69]Ibid., pp. 115–16. A closely analogous line of thinking informs Robert Ray Aurner's diachronic analysis, *Caxton and the English Sentence,* University of Wisconsin Studies in Language and Literature no. 18 (Madison, 1923), pp. 22–59.

[70]James Sutherland, *On English Prose* (Toronto: University of Toronto Press, 1957), pp. 5–6.

Workman at first glance seems to proceed very differently from Sutherland, for *Fifteenth-Century Translation* consists of wide-ranging and intensive textual analyses geared, for the most part, to the triad of defining features: pleonasm, ellipsis, and anacoluthon. While Workman's acute attention to particulars commands respect, his monograph is marred by local interpretations that turn on an a priori supposition that writers either could not or did not keep their minds on seeing sentences through to completion. Thus he remarks of an anonymous sermon of 1400: "The writer of this appears to have had a pattern present in his mind, a pattern of short equal blocks of thought. But lacking a consciousness of the grammatical cast of the blocks, he simply added any thought he wanted in the most convenient construction at hand." Similarly, a sentence in Lydgate's *Serpent of Division* draws this fire: "Here it is hard to trace even any pattern of thought. Before he has gone very far Lydgate himself seems to have forgotten what he started out to say. Certainly he paid no attention to how he started to say it." However, it is an early generalization that best summarizes Workman's recurrent outlook on interpretation of the prose with which he deals: "Many fourteenth and fifteenth century writers would seem from their prose to have been unaware of any thought-relationship which cannot be expressed by *and*."[71] This generalization captures the broader sense of disappointment rather than promise which has affected the majority of scholars and critics who have worked on the vernacular prose of the two centuries spanned by my study.[72]

It is, of course, a truism of intellectual advance that the means for finding a subject lively and significant must accompany any finding of liveliness or significance. Personally I think that such means lie ready to hand and that we have only to apply them analytically to discover their positive interpretive implications. Although they themselves have rarely broached language history, the contributions made in recent decades by transformational-generative linguistics and psycholinguistics to our understanding of natural language can be used to open a substantially altered perspective on the characteristics of English prose in the period in question—an alteration for the better, as I hope to show.

In particular, I find in the concept of deep structure a consistent and unifying backdrop against which to view the features of pleonasm, ellipsis, and anacoluthon. Rather than requiring us to conceive these as fortuitously arising cases of too much or too little language at a given juncture because a writer was forgetful or out of control, deep structure

[71]Workman, *Fifteenth-Century Translation,* pp. 37–38, 3, and cf. pp. 29, 34–35.
[72]Field's *Romance and Chronicle* is especially revelatory in this regard; on p. 10 he claims that Malory was "the reverse" of "a conscious artist," and on pp. 35, 36, that because of its "basic parataxis," there is "no hint of the future in Malory's prose"; "the style is a very limited one, . . . and it is doomed to extinction by the proliferation of the printed word."

can help us account for ellipsis as something other than an inherently deficient sentence, and pleonasm as something other than its equally problematic opposite. For the deep structure of every sentence, theoretically, is its full or exhaustive linguistic representation, on which transformations operate in a stipulated, systematic, and orderly fashion to produce the surface sentences of actual speech and writing. It seems obvious to me that if one regards occurrences of ellipsis, pleonasm, and anacoluthon as possible evidence of some transformational or detail rule that has changed in English through time, there are two likely results. First, if the aspect of system or "rule-governedness" emerges—and it has, enough to permit Ohlander's elaborate classifications of types of coordinate expressions—then one is less inclined to think, in received terms, of lapses, inadvertences, and crudities. Second, it becomes harder to impose one's own present-day conceptions and standards of sentence formation as criteria (let alone desiderata) for judging earlier prose if the features of earlier linguistic usage are treated as being just as interpretable as later features in terms of the creativity, versatility, completeness, economy, and system that we now know to be the attributes of all natural languages. To illustrate, if 'a bonny lass and a merry' and 'a bonny and merry lass' are seen as minor variants of one another and as equally finished outputs of conjunction reduction, can the later phase structure—representable as (ab + bc)—be judged formally or in any other way superior to the earlier (abc + ab) pattern? I think not; the perspective afforded by a transformational-generative analysis levels out any presumed qualitative differences. Likewise, when we bring this perspective to bear on a number of the cases of "faulty parallelism" categorized by Ohlander, we find discriminations which he classes as obligatory but which we do not find the grammar of English obliging a native speaker to make. Accordingly, we reverse judgments of ungrammaticality leveled against such acceptable sentences as "He remembred his soul, and also that he was mortal, and must dye" and "He told hom the case, and how Cryst dyd to hym."

To move from particulars to a broader point: it seems to me that the appreciation of system is especially vital for the study of style. The language historians whose work we have been surveying knew—to take one instance—that Middle English afforded the option of deleting a subject pronoun in second and following coordinate clauses which had the same subject as the first clause, or, more generally, the option of deleting a subject pronoun from any coordinate clause where it could be understood from a reference in a preceding clause.[73] This option, as

[73]W. F. J. Roberts, "Ellipsis of the Subject-Pronoun in Middle English," *University of London Mediaeval Studies* 1 (1937–39): 100–115.

Workman acknowleged,[74] produced quantities of the subjectless verb phrases whch Ohlander and he persistently treated as major sites of ellipsis and recurrent sources of ambiguity. Such a split between grammatical analysis and interpretation was possible because, at the time of Ohlander's and Workman's studies, there was not enough impetus from philological theory about linguistic creativity and syntactic structure to prompt looking for system in what was perceived as aberration. The point is all the clearer where considerations of power, comprehensiveness, and variety accompany those of system. Thus C. S. Baldwin can comment in his study of syntax in Malory's *Morte Darthur* that "at times . . . the *and* is practically expletive,"[75] that is, an "empty" or "filler" element; and Ohlander and Workman can talk about "merely" the "linkage" and "only" the "thought-relationships" of *and* because they had no account of its syntax and semantics that could engage their respect on a stylistic—that is, a jointly communicative and expressive—plane. A present-day student of prose style is in a position to be better provided with an understanding and appreciation of the fundamental creativity of natural language before sallying forth to exercise the prerogatives of literary judgment.

This discussion has temporarily run ahead of itself in taking up its third guiding question before addressing the second, the question to which we now turn: What sorts of specific evidence support the labeling of certain textual characteristics as "speech-based" or "speech-derived"? The only available evidence from spoken English that can be brought to bear on this question is of necessity contemporary, but the recourse is warranted by the stability of human cognitive and physiological development during the time span involved. Further warrant appears in the striking measure of agreement between contemporary experimental findings and the pronouncements of literary and language historians (though some important qualifications must also be added). Findings from both quarters indicate that spoken English is preponderantly conjunctive in its syntax, and that its sentence forms do prominently exhibit the triad of features discussed above. Here, to illustrate, is a passage of transcribed speech from a study by V. V. Valian:

Uh, my earliest, earliest memory—
Uh, my birthday is November 15 and my earliest memory of my only birthday. It's the only really mem—good memory I have, like the birthday that I remember the best (laugh). Can I start again? Uh, uh, O.K. My birthday is November 15, and uh, I remember my fourth, my fourth birthday the most. I didn't know it was my fourth birthday until about three weeks ago because I happened to ask

[74]Workman, *Fifteenth-Century Translation*, p. 36.
[75]Charles Sears Baldwin, *The Inflections and Syntax of the Morte D'Arthur of Sir Thomas Malory* (Baltimore: Johns Hopkins University Press, 1894), sec. 359.2.

my mother what happened to this, uh, red chicken that I used to play with when I was a kid and she told me uh, you know, the one that you got on your fourth birthday and, uh, I didn't realize it was my fourth birthday until then, but I always have memories of it because that chicken was, uh, like I used to sleep with it all the time and I remember the time that I first learned how to dance with that chicken, at my fourth birthday party, because then the Lindy was the big dance and, uh, I wanted to learn how to do it and all my relatives were doing it.[76]

Spontaneous speech is typically nonfluent, replete with hesitations, "paralinguistic" sounds (*uh*s, throat-clearing),[77] and left-off or revised constructions. These traits reflect, in part, the usual conditions of speaking and, in part, the psychology of speakers and hearers. There is a socially imposed requirement that spoken language be produced rapidly and that the speaker signal fairly clearly the scope of an utterance—that is, at what points a stretch of speech is continuing and at what point it is likely to stop. The hearer needs these signals as cues to understanding as well as leads for determining when his own turn to speak has come. Nonfluency results from the speaker's changing decisions about what to say and how to say it, under the pressure of the constraints governing utterance in a social context. Offsetting this nonfluency (which is ordinarily taken for granted by speaker and hearer alike) are two facts: first, that the act of speaking is much richer in resources of tone, gesture, facial expression, and reference to shared knowledge for the purposes of communication than is the act of writing; and second, that the hearer can usually ask the speaker to clarify or repeat, either immediately, by interrupting, or within a short interval thereafter.

In another study of spoken English, David Crystal and Derek Davy transcribe two conversations: one conducted face to face, the other over the telephone. The analysis they offer of the sentence forms used in their transcripts of conversational English is so suggestive for the concerns of the present study that it necessitates quoting at some length:

Informal conversation is characterised by a large number of loosely coordinated clauses, the coordination being structurally ambiguous: it is an open question whether one takes these as sequences of sentences or as single compound sentences. The situation is complicated by phonetic and phonological ambiguity

---

[76]V. V. Valian, "Talking, Listening, and Linguistic Structure" (Ph.D. diss., Northeastern University, 1971), quoted in Jerry A. Fodor, Thomas G. Bever, and Merrill F. Garrett, *The Psychology of Language: An Introduction to Psycholinguistics and Generative Grammar* (New York: McGraw-Hill, 1974), p. 419.

[77]See David Crystal and Randolph Quirk, *Systems of Prosodic and Paralinguistic Features in English* (The Hague: Mouton, 1964).

other than that caused by the intonation: the generally rapid speed of speech and the absence of interclausal pause, in particular, e.g., I / ÀM CÓLD / and I'll / be all 'right. . . .

The choice of solution has implications for the stylistic analysis. Thus if we take all such sequences as separate sentences, then we can make a statement such as "Sentence length is relatively short, and in structure displays predominantly the simple type." On the other hand, if we take such sequences as units, then our analysis must point to a significantly high proportion of longer, more complex, and more varied sentence types. We have adopted the former solution here, on the grounds that it produces a simpler description. . . .

Having said this we may now qualify the point made above by noting that if sentences do reach any substantial length, it is because of this phenomenon of loose coordination. It might be better, indeed, to refer to such a feature without using the term "sentence" at all, talking instead of "clause complexes." Such a procedure would certainly clarify a very important point about the way in which conversation progresses, more in a series of loosely coordinated sentence-like structures than in a series of sharply defined sentences.

Other than these loosely coordinated types, sentences tend to be short. Minor [i.e., freestanding but grammatically "unfulfilled"] sentences are extremely frequent. . . . One should also note the high proportion of parenthetic compound types of sentences . . . , particularly through the introduction of *you know* . . . though other interpolations could have been just as appropriately used (e.g., *I mean, you see*). . . .

The use of minor sentences, along with the loose coordination discussed above, is almost certainly the basis of the impression of "disjointedness" which many people feel is characteristic. . . . [But] to refer to conversation as if it were "disjointed," or to talk about [hesitation and on-line revision] features as if they were "errors," without further qualification, . . . is in fact to judge conversation against some other (usually written) standard, such as is manifested by the regular omission of these features in written forms of conversation, novels or dramatic dialogue. Considered in its own situation (that is, with gestures, facial expressions, and so on all included), conversation does not seem "disjointed" at all.

The disjointedness referred to, moreover, is increased by the fact that many sentences and clauses are incomplete. This is sometimes due to a "syntactic anacoluthon" on the part of a speaker, a restarting of a sentence to conform more to what he wanted to say . . . ; but it is also fairly common for A to complete B's sentence, or vice versa. . . . In this way the characteristic "give and take" of a successful conversation is maintained . . . : the pace of the dialogue is kept up by the "agreement" question tags and the phatic interpolations.[78]

With regard to the naivete or immaturity that earlier literary historians and philologists imputed to conjunctive, speech-based syntax (likening

[78]David Crystal and Derek Davy, *Investigating English Style* (London: Longman Group, 1969), pp. 105, 110–12.

it to "a child telling stories"), experimental evidence shows no distinction in kind between children and adults: both typically string sentences together with *and*s when they speak. However, there are some pertinent specifics to note about children's language acquisition and sentence perception. The utility of the so-called canonical sentoid—the $N + V + N$ clausal sequence that Bever has shown to be central to adult "cognitive strategies" for language processing—is equally vital to children's understanding of sentences.[79] Moreover, the order in which various sentence types appear in the speech of two- to six-year-olds correlates with the closeness of any given sentence type to that of an active, affirmative, transitive $N + V(+ N)$ "kernel" sentence. The same order and correlation persist in the acquisition patterns for NP complement constructions shown by children ranging in age from five to twelve years. In progressing to reading, children at the fourth- as well as the second-grade level showed "generally better" comprehension "where the written material coincided syntactically with frequent patterns of oral language."[80]

Another group of findings indicates two broader trends in the handling of sentence form as children grow older. First, in speaking (and then in writing), they become able to conjoin more and more clauses in their sentences; and, second, their writing styles gradually become differentiated from their speaking styles through diversification of clausal relationships.[81] A virtually exclusive reliance on *and* as a sentence connective characterizes the spoken English of young children. Preschoolers typically conjoin only two clauses, while lower elementary-school children use sentence conjunction four to five times as often in their speaking

[79]On the canonical sentoid, see Thomas O. Bever, "The Interaction of Perception and Linguistic Structures: A Preliminary Investigation of Neo-Functionalism," *Current Trends in Linguistics*, ed. Thomas A. Sebeok et al. (The Hague: Mouton & Co., 1972), 12:1169, 1176–77. Related research includes P. A. DeVilliers and J. G. DeVilliers, "Early Judgments of Semantic and Syntactic Acceptability by Children," *Journal of Psycholinguistic Research* 1 (1972): 299–310; Hermine Sinclair-de Zwart and J. P. Bronkhard, "SVO a Linguistic Universal?" *Journal of Experimental Child Development* 14 (1972): 329–48, as cited in Fodor, Bever, and Garrett, *Psychology of Language*, pp. 499–502.

[80]Reference is, respectively, to Carol Chomsky, *The Acquisition of Syntax in Children from Five to Ten* (Cambridge, Mass.: MIT Press, 1969); R. F. Cromer, " 'Children Are Nice to Understand': Surface Structure Clues for the Recovery of Deep Structure," *British Journal of Psychology* 61 (1970): 397–408; and F. S. Kessel, *The Role of Syntax in Children's Comprehension from Ages Six to Twelve*, Monographs of the Society for Research in Child Development, vol. 35, no. 139 (1970)—cited in Fodor, Bever, and Garrett, *Psychology of Language*, pp. 495–99. Also see S. M. Tatham, "Reading Comprehension of Materials Written with Select Oral Language Patterns: A Study at Grades 2 and 4," *Reading Research Quarterly* 5 (1970): 402–26.

[81]Roy C. O'Donnell, William J. Griffin, and R. C. Norris, *Syntax of Kindergarten and Elementary School Children: A Transformational Analysis* (Champaign, Ill.: National Council of Teachers of English, 1967), cited in Kellogg W. Hunt, "How Little Sentences Grow into Big Ones," *Readings in Applied Transformational Grammar*, ed. Mark Lester (New York: Holt, Rinehart, & Winston, 1970), pp. 178–79.

as twelfth graders do in the same number of words. By the fifth grade, children tend to use sentence-conjoining *and*s two to three times as often in their speech as they do in their writing (although the difference may reflect composition pedagogy—"Never begin a sentence with *And*"— rather than a developmental phenomenon). Finally, there seems to be some correlation between intelligence and the rate and extent to which preschool and lower elementary-school children utilize sentence conjunction. While sentence conjunction remains the staple of both oral and written expression throughout this phase of development, increasing age (and intelligence) correlates with increasing use of sentence connectives other than *and*.[82]

What implications, if any, for the study of prose style can be drawn from experimental studies of the syntactic features of spoken English and of the characteristics of children's language? I would emphasize two, above all. On the one hand, we now have sufficient data on which to base a characterization of written English, as, say, close to or derived from spoken English. But, on the other hand, we must remain aware of the considerable stylization imposed on spoken English even to produce "speech-based prose." Valian's speech transcript—as well as those of Crystal and Davy, which I have not quoted—manifestly cannot constitute more than a partial approximation, an imperfect analogue, for even the most informal or colloquial written English of any era. Writing, by comparison with transcribed speech, remains consistently more connected and fluent. In this regard, the study of fifth-grade children to which I have just referred is illuminating, for it indicates that the stylization which distinguishes writing from speech is a process well underway by age ten or so (however it is set in motion). It seems to me legitimate to analogize between the written English of fifth-graders and earlier English prose, in this fashion: that where closely comparable deployment of syntactic resources to differentiate writing from speech can be documented, the earlier writers should be credited with a comparable stylistic self-consciousness.

If the first of my suggested implications—that there is literarily significant sense to be made of the notion of an "oral basis of prose"— were pursued for an even earlier period of English than that covered by this study, it might be possible to ascribe more substance to Chambers's continuity hypothesis than is usual at present. Norman Davis and Ian Gordon have separately taken the position that the "continuity of English prose" from King Alfred to Sir Thomas More reduces to a truism about spoken English only—namely, that it never became a dead tongue

[82]Kellogg W. Hunt, "Recent Measures in Syntactic Development," in *Readings in Applied Transformational Grammar*, ed. Lester, pp. 185–89. Also see John Limber, "The Genesis of Complex Sentences," *Cognitive Development and the Acquisition of Language*, ed. Timothy E. Moore (New York and London: Academic Press, 1973), pp. 168–85.

but preserved its existence through a precarious period, mostly the late eleventh and the twelfth centuries, in the speech of the lower classes. In this period (to judge from surviving evidence), English virtually ceased to be used as a written medium. On Davis's and Gordon's view, therefore, English prose can only be said to be continuous in the rudimentary, dependent sense that the language itself was.[83] A literarily viable notion of an "oral basis" for prose could, however, permit us to move from truism to genuinely useful truth. For, if such a notion has a relatively stable and comparable meaning with regard to native speakers of English from one period to another, as the experimental findings just surveyed give reason to suppose, then Chambers can be confirmed in his intuition that considerations of stylistic and not merely linguistic continuity are the rightful business of prose study.

The second of my suggested implications—the one about the inevitable stylization that attends on writing and therefore complicates the speech-prose relationship—requires further pursuit, some of which is already underway. We have become much more circumspect about disparaging speech-based prose as naive or colloquial, both because we know more about the mastery and sensitivity which native speakers of all ages demonstrate in their so-called ordinary language and because we have become more attentive to the functional adjustments involved in adapting oral features and oral devices to presentation on the page. Thus, Elizabeth Salter has protested against Workman's overall charge of "looseness of texture" in Love's sentence forms. "It would be a mistake," retorts Salter, "to assume that length and informal plan must imply confusion. . . . Nothing is gained, therefore, by objecting to such usages on purely formal grounds; each sentence or sentence group must be judged by its effectiveness in the immediate context."[84] In fact, however, Workman himself anticipated the possibility of making more positive assessments than the ones he was to offer of the features of sentence form that predominate in later fourteenth- and fifteenth-century vernacular writing. At one point he reflects as follows:

Much medieval prose has for modern readers the effect of *naïveté*. The cast of its thoughts is so unvaried or so random, or the thoughts themselves seem so unselected, that we incline to call it primitive, forgetting that twentieth-century psychology has released a somewhat similar prose which we call stream-of-consciousness. The difficulty of pre-Tudor prose writers can scarcely have been

[83]Norman Davis, "Styles in English Prose of the Late Middle and Early Modern Period," Actes du 12ᵉ Congrès de Langue et Littérature, *Les Congrès et Colloques de l'Université de Liège* 21 (1961): 165–81, especially pp. 179–80; and Ian A. Gordon, *The Movement of English Prose* (London: Longmans, Green, & Co., 1966), pp. 8–9. Also see Astley C. Partridge, *Tudor to Augustan English: A Study in Syntax and Style from Caxton to Johnson* (London: André Deutsch, 1969), pp. 21, 32, 68.

[84]Elizabeth Zeeman [Salter], "Nicholas Love—A Fifteenth-Century Translator," p. 121.

their unawareness of the nature of the thought-relationship within any given sequence or period. In fact, it is possible that there was no "difficulty" or "inadequacy" at all: the modern judgement may be based only on a change of usage.[85]

Nevertheless, as we have been seeing, the received tradition in philology and literary history at the time Workman was writing was one that effectually precluded adopting a positive critical perspective. Indeed, the weight of the received tradition is felt even in the foregoing passage when Workman alludes to "a change of usage" to account for the differences he sensed between fifteenth-century standards for prose style and his own. As Francis Christensen has shown, both the magnitude and the permanence of a change in usage were exaggerated by later nineteenth- and earlier twentieth-century critics and scholars. The staple of good present-day English prose style is the loosely additive progression made possible by the resources of sentential conjunction.[86]

To my knowledge, besides Nicholas Love, Sir Thomas Malory is the only prose writer to have profited thus far from sympathetic study of the capabilities of a style that shares fundamental features with oral expression. Mark Lambert's *Malory: Style and Vision in "Le Morte Darthur"* opens with a suggestive discussion of the wide-ranging authority that a narrative voice can project through fluid and frequent shifts from indirect to direct representation of speech, for by these means an authorial voice can literally "speak for" any and every character—but never a character for an author. Throughout, Lambert's book on Malory challenges the prevailing conventional view of an artlessly and unselfconsciously produced *Morte Darthur*. Lambert asks, for example, why it seems "natural to assume . . . that Malorian parataxis is a colloquial feature" purely and simply, while it is acknowledged that "in fifteenth-century French prose parataxis may suggest dignity and solemnity rather than artlessness"? He pursues the point:

I believe it suggests these things in Malory also. . . . I would speak of the sobriety and dignity rather than the colloquial simplicity of Malory's style, but my point here is not that Malory is not colloquial but that it is more difficult than it seems to demonstrate that he is, and more difficult still to show that he is an unselfconscious stylist.[87]

As I have been suggesting, a possible and even promising way out of the difficulty which Lambert acknowledges in ascribing artistry—and,

[85]Workman, *Fifteenth-Century Translation*, pp. 33–34.

[86]Francis Christensen, *Notes toward a New Rhetoric* (New York: Harper & Row, 1967), pp. 16–17.

[87]Lambert, *Malory: Style and Vision in "Le Morte Darthur,"* pp. 2–8, 40–41, n. 36. The discussion also reckons with Caxton's *Paris and Vienne* (1485) and the fifteenth-century English *Life of St. Catherine of Siena*.

hence, stylistic interest—to fourteenth- and fifteenth-century English prose is to posit a functionalism akin to that of speech for the features that claim attention in this writing, and then to see where analysis of such features will take us. It is the possibility or potentiality of such an approach that I will be exploring in chapter 3. But, before testing the critical adequacy of a posited functionalism for speech-based prose, it is well to pause and review at least the major pieces of testimony in which English writers in the fourteenth and fifteenth centuries registered their sense of the functionalism attaching to the medium of prose.

In all likelihood, only Chaucer's sidelights on prose will spring to mind. Harry Bailly, the host of the *Canterbury Tales*, is cast as a spokesman for some of the apparent commonplaces about the subject in the later fourteenth century. Exasperated by what he terms the "rym dogerel" of Chaucer the pilgrim's *Tale of Sir Thopas*, the host peremptorily calls for the opposite of verse, the other medium: "Tell in prose somwhat, at the leeste, / In which ther be some murthe or some doctrine." Chaucer "gladly" obliges with his *Tale of Melibee*, an obvious submission in the second category, "doctrine," although not at all so clearly the promised "litel thing in prose / That oghte liken you, as I suppose." One reason why the *Melibee* becomes a big rather than a little thing in prose may be gathered from Chaucer's Preface to his *Treatise on the Astrolabe* in which he addresses a larger readership than "litel Lowys," the son for whom he originally wrote. In this Preface Chaucer self-consciously admits and attempts to excuse the "superfluite of wordes" in his exposition, appealing for agreement to the principle that "it is better to wryten unto a child twyes a good sentence than he forgete it ones."[88] Here pleonasm is expressly assigned a function geared to the instructional purpose of the vernacular prose work and to the capacities of an unlearned—that is, un-Latined—reader. Before inferring, however, that condescension is also implicit in Chaucer's explanation of the need for "superfluite," we should recall that all reading at this period was ordinarily done aloud, even reading by oneself.[89] Thus an oral mode of composition was an entirely natural functional model for English prose, since the purposes assigned to the medium required intelligibility and accessibility. "Murthe" and "doctrine" depend equally on getting the point.

Very nearly contemporaneous with these Chaucerian passages is the revealing question-and-answer exchange which John Trevisa represents

[88]F. N. Robinson, ed., *The Complete Works of Geoffrey Chaucer*, 2d ed. (Boston: Houghton Mifflin, 1957), pp. 167, 546.

[89]On various aspects of reading in the period, see Margaret Deanesly, "Vernacular Books in England in the Fourteenth and Fifteenth Centuries," *MLR* 15 (1920): 349–58; J. W. Adamson, "The Extent of Literacy in England in the Fifteenth and Sixteenth Centuries," *The Library* 10 (1929): 163–93; H. S. Bennett, "Caxton and His Public," *RES* 14 (1943): 113–19; Marshall McLuhan, *The Gutenberg Galaxy*, pp. 82–90.

as having occurred between his patron Lord Berkeley and himself. Berkeley had commissioned Trevisa to translate Ranulf Higden's *Polychronicon* from Latin into English, whereupon this clerk asked his lord: "Whether is you liefer have a translation of these chronicles in rhyme or in prose?" The lord responded: "In prose, for comunely prose is more clear than rhyme, more easy and more plain to know and understand."[90] The same conception of prose had been recorded roughly half a century earlier, in 1338, by Robert Mannyng, who noted of the French legends of King Arthur that "In prose al of hym ys writen / The bettere til understande and wyten." To Mannyng's mind, however, there was a crucial difference between French prose and English prose in their capacities for clear, comprehensible expression. Because he was committed to writing in English at this era, he chose to write in verse.[91]

Subsequent writers do not sustain Mannyng's reservations about the adequacy of English prose. Nor is Chaucer's and Trevisa's confidence about its functionalism and purposes only an isolated phenomenon. The latter half of the fourteenth century witnessed a quite encompassing linguistic and literary self-confidence in which English prose composition had a central place.[92] One symptomatic document is the popular and widely disseminated *John* (or *Dan*) *Gaytryge's Sermon* (1357), which provides an abridgment of the fundamentals of the faith "opynly yn Ynglysche" so that priests throughout the archdiocese of York can preach and teach them as "our haly fadir the beshope, of his gudnes, has ordaynede and bedyn that thay be schewede opynly yn Ynglysche amanges the folke."[93] With time, the emphasis on the potential of English prose to reach and affect a wide audience grows to a chorus that unites both orthodoxy and Lollardy. On the orthodox side we may consider the original English prologue written to serve as a personalized introduction to a *Life of St. Catherine of Siena* that had been translated from Latin. As the anonymous translator describes to the spiritual "doughter" for whom he Englished the *Life* the benefits of having "in englysshe tongue the legende and the blessed lyf of an holy mayde and virgyn," his vocabulary takes on a ringing intensity. What she "heres" or "redes"

---

[90]John Trevisa, "Dialogue between a Lord and a Clerk," in Alfred W. Pollard, ed., *Fifteenth-Century Prose and Verse* (Westminster: A. Constable & Co., 1903), p. 207.

[91]*The Story of England by Robert Mannyng of Brunne*, ed. Frederick J. Furnivall, Rolls Series no. 87 (London: Longman & Co., 1887), lines 10973–78.

[92]See, further, Basil Cottle, *The Triumph of English, 1350–1400* (London: Blandford Press, 1969).

[93]The phrase "openly yn Ynglysche" is repeated as indicated in *John Gaytryge's Sermon*, a freely augmented English rendering of Archbishop Thoresby's Latin catechism made by a monk of St. Mary's Abbey, York. The sermon survives in four separate versions (including an adaptation and further enlargement by a Wycliffite writer) and in eight other manuscripts. The excerpt quoted here is from Robert Thornton's version, as printed in Norman F. Blake, ed., *Middle English Religious Prose*, pp. 74–75.

in her native tongue, he tells her twice over, she will instantly "see" as if physically before her: the "fructuous example of vertuous livinge to edyfycacion of thy sowle and to comforte and encrese of thy gostly labour in all werkes of pyte." This example will not fail of its effect, in part because it is in English, in part because, as he again tells her twice over, he has exactly fitted his prose to her own needs and capacities.[94]

Analogous views and analogous intensity are to be found in the Wycliffite tracts. In the letter, "Five Questions on the Love of God," the writer balances his sense of the inherent difficulty of the questions that have been put to him with his sturdy faith in the communicative power of the vernacular, which he represents as a common possession: "But ʒit charite dryveth men to tell hem sumwhat in Englische, so that men may best wite by this Englisch what is Goddis wille. . . . And thus it helpith heere to Cristen men, to studie the gospel in that tunge in whiche thei knowen best Cristis sentense." However, it is the Wycliffite treatise on the Pater Noster that rises to the heights of forthrightness and force at this period in arguing for teaching the people by the medium of "wryten" English:

And syththe the treuthe of God stondeth nouʒt in one langage more than another, bot whoevere lyveth best, techeth best, pleseth most God, of what langage evere he be, therfore this prayere, declared en Englyssche, may edifye the lewed peple, as it doth clerkes in Latyn. And syththe it is the gospel of Crist, and Crist bad it be preched to the peple, for the peple scholde lerne it and kunne it and worche therafter, why may we nouʒt wryte in Englyssche the gospel and othere thynges declaryng the gospel, to edificacion of Cristen mennus soules, as the precheour telleth it trewelyche en Englyssche to the peple? For by the same resoun yf it scholde nouʒt be wryte, it scholde nouʒt be preched.

And here is a reule to Cristen men, of what langage evere they be, that it is an heye sacrifice to God to kunne here Pater Noster, the gospel, and other poyntes of holy wryt ytolde to hem or wryten in Latyn, or in Englyssche, or in Frensche, or in Duchyssche, other in eny other langage, after that the peple hath understondyng. And thus clerkes scholde joye that the peple knewe Godes lawe, and travayle hemself busylyche, by alle the goede menes that they myʒte, to make the peple know the treuthe. . . . And yf any clerke wolde contrarye this, who schal be dampned bot such a quyke fende?[95]

A related development arising from the closeness of English speech and English prose composition in this period seems in some ways even more remarkable than the widespread insistence on writing English. This is the extremity of effort to which ostensibly illiterate persons would

[94]*The Lyf of Saint Katherin of Senis* (printed by Wynkyn de Worde, 1493), ed. Carl Horstman, *Archiv für das Studium der neueren Sprachen* 76 (1886): 33–34, cited in Workman, *Fifteenth-Century Translation*, pp. 24–25.
[95]Wyclif, *Select English Works*, ed. Arnold, III, 183, 184; I, 98–100.

go in order to become English prose authors when they were convinced they had something to convey by means of a text. Julian of Norwich may or may not have been illiterate when she began to compose her *Showings of Divine Love;* in either case, the work contains extensive evidence of self-consciously conducted revisions that may have occupied as much as fifty years and, perhaps, the labors of an amanuensis as well as her own.[96] Invaluable direct insights into the process of oral composition and supervised dictation-taking that produced the *Book of Margery Kempe* are afforded in its opening pages, which undertake to convince the reader that the text in hand preserves the illiterate Margery's very words. We learn that she brought to a second scribe a gathering of pages which another scribe had taken down at her dictation. The second scribe's inability to read her text back to her made Margery suspicious of the quality of the transcript. It in fact proved so bad that it could not even be deciphered by a "good man" who had known her first scribe before his death. Hence a new beginning was made by a new method on the *Book of Margery Kempe:* she and the second scribe worked by turns in long sessions, she remembering and associating for a while aloud, he writing and then reading back to her what he had written. On rehearsing the difficulties of authorship which she had surmounted, Margery concedes her frequent departures from narrative sequence: "Thys boke is not wretyn in ordyr, every thyng aftyr other as it were done, byt lych as the mater came to the creature in mynd whan it schuld be wretyn." Yet she will concede nothing with regard to her accuracy in having to redo her entire *Book:* "And therfore sche dede no thing wryten but that sche knewe it ryth wel for very trewth."[97]

So much, then, by way of direct testimony from later fourteenth- and fifteenth-century writers on the conceptions and objectives which they associated with English prose will establish a predisposition, at least, toward analysis geared to the semantic functionalism shared by spoken and written language—a mode which I have been advocating for the study and interpretation of style. The testimony reviewed here suggests not merely that vernacular writers were cognizant of the functional resources of their native language but also that they deliberately undertook

[96]Edmund Colledge and James Walsh argue strongly that Julian possessed considerable learning, despite her characterization of herself as "a woman that could no letter"; see their two-text edition, *A Book of Showings to the Anchoress Julian of Norwich* (Toronto: Pontifical Institute of Medieval Studies, 1978), pp. 41–52, 198. On her authorial labors and self-consciousness, see B. A. Windeatt, "Julian of Norwich and Her Audience," *RES* n.s. 28 (1977): 1–17. For relevant discussion and a helpful bibliography, see Christina von Nolcken, "Julian of Norwich," in *Middle English Prose: A Guide to Major Authors and Genres,* ed. A. Edwards (New Brunswick: Rutgers University Press, forthcoming).

[97]*The Book of Margery Kempe,* ed. Sanford B. Meech, ann. Hope Emily Allen, Early English Text Society o.s. 212 (London: Humphrey Milford, 1940), 4.14–5.18.

to cultivate these resources in their prose. In the next chapter I shall attempt to substantiate and particularize the functional relation between speech and style by examining the diverse uses made of conjunctive syntax in a number of representative writers, both religious and secular, from this formative period of English prose.

3. Prose in the Later Fourteenth and Fifteenth Centuries: The Reaches of Recursion

"Open Sentences"

For a discussion of semantics and style in the conjunctive syntax of later fourteenth- and fifteenth-century English prose, there is an all but obligatory point of departure. It is found in the observations on English in general, and conjunctive syntax in particular, which Nicholas Purvey, Wyclif's literarily gifted collaborator, developed in the General Prologue to the Later Version of the Wycliffite Bible (ca. 1395).[1] The value of these observations lies in their articulated consciousness of the indigenous resources of English sentence form. Since Purvey acknowledges no stylistic considerations other than his concern with meaning in its expressive and communicative aspects, "sentence," as he uses the term, denotes semantics (sententia) quite as much as it does syntax. His overall statement of purpose equates his efforts in translating with opening the "sentence" of Scripture in English:

At the begynning I purposide with Goddis helpe to make the sentence as trewe and open in English as it is in Latyn, either more trewe and more open than it is in Latyn. And I preie for charite and for comoun profyt of Cristene soulis that if ony wiys man fynde ony defaute of the truthe of translacioun, let him sette in the trewe sentence and opin of Holy Writ.

Purvey also explains what his objective of "open sentence" is and what the resources of English are for attaining it:

First it is to knowe, that the best translating is out of Latyn into English, to translate aftir the sentence, and not oneli aftir the wordis, so that the sentence

---

[1]Purvey's authorship of the General Prologue has been established by Margaret Deanesly, *The Lollard Bible and Other Medieval Biblical Versions* (Cambridge: Cambridge University Press, 1920), pp. 260–67, 376. Its date can be determined from an allusion to a scandal "made known at the last Parliament," presumably that of January–February 1395, at which the Lollard Conclusions were presented. See Herbert B. Workman, *John Wyclif: A Study of the English Medieval Church* (London: Oxford University Press, 1926), and Herbert E. Winn, ed., *Wyclif: Select English Writings* (London: Oxford University Press, 1929), p. 8.

be as opin either openere in English as in Latyn, and go not fer fro the lettre; and if the lettre mai not be suid in the translating, let the sentence evere be hool and open, for the wordis owen to serve to the entent and sentence, and ellis the wordis ben superflu either false.

In translating into English, manie resolucions moun make the sentence open, as an ablative case absolute may be resolvid into these thre wordis, with co-venable verbe, *the while, for, if*—as gramariens seyn. As thus: *While the maistir redith, I stonde,* either *If the maistir redith,* either *For the maistir* etc. And sumtyme it wolde accorde wel with the sentence to be resolvid into *whanne* either into *aftirward.* Thus:– *Whanne the maistir red, I stood,* either *Aftir the mastir red, I stood.* And sumtyme it may wel be resolvid into a verbe of the same tens, and into this word *et,* that is, *and* in English. And thus: *Arescentibus hominibus prae timore:* that is, *And men shulen wexe drie for drede.*

Also a participle of a present tens, either preterit, of active vois, either passif, mai be resolvid into a verbe of the same tens and a conjunccioun copulatif. As thus:– *dicens,* that is, *seiynge,* mai be resolvid thus, *and seith,* either *that seith.* And this wole in manie placis make the sentence open where to Englisshe it aftir the word wolde be derk and douteful.[2]

One of the most remarkable strains in this remarkable series of ob-servations is Purvey's attitude toward working in English at this date. There is not the slightest insinuation that English might be inferior to Latin, or inadequate in itself, as a medium for God's Word. Instead, Purvey proceeds on the assumption that his native English is at least as good a language as Latin, if not, possibly, better in certain respects. His minimal standard for his work is to make "the sentence as trewe and open in English as it is in Latyn," but sometimes the English sentence can be made "more trewe and more open than it is in Latyn." This working assumption that natural language will prove adequate to the expressive and communicative demands placed on it by its users is a facet of early modern consciousness first clearly attested in England as an outgrowth of Wycliffite—or Lollard—advocacy of vernacular Scrip-tures. While it might at first seem implausible that the source of confi-dence in the vernacular should trace to fervently religious and literalistic conceptions of the Bible as the Word of God rather than to incipient humanistic beliefs in man's self-defining capacities in language, the facts are, nevertheless, as I state them. Expressions of humanism in England long reflected uneasiness, if not overt feelings of inferiority, about the "rudeness," "barbarousness," and "poverty" of the vernacular.[3] It is the

[2]Nicholas Purvey, "The General Prologue to the Second Version of the Bible," in J. Forshall and E. Madden, eds., *The Holy Bible . . . Made . . . by John Wycliffe and His Followers* (London: Oxford University Press, 1850); also printed in *Wyclif: Select English Writings,* ed. Winn, p. 27. Italics are reproduced from Forshall and Madden.

[3]See chap. 1, "The Uneloquent Language," and chaps. 3 and 4, "The Inadequate Lan-guage," in Richard Foster Jones, *The Triumph of the English Language: A Survey of Opinions concerning the Vernacular from the Introduction of Printing to the Restoration* (Stanford: Stanford University Press, 1953), pp. 3–31, 68–141.

advocates of an English Bible for the English people who initially and most insistently affirm the worth of English as a linguistic medium. They were prompted by the belief that a God who had made saving knowledge of Christ necessary had also made human souls and human languages capable of receiving and transmitting this necessary knowledge; such a belief, in turn, could only acquire the force it did from popularizing motives within Christendom.[4] As we have noted at the beginning of chapter 2, the intent of producing a readable, accessible text rather than a scholarly construe differentiates Purvey's Later Version from Hereford's Earlier Version, and it also bespeaks the increasing emphasis placed on reaching the people as the Wycliffite movement gained strength. Yet, in view of the vigorous official efforts at suppression that this movement soon encountered, it is significant that its claims for the adequacy of English did not suffer the fate of the rest of its doctrinal program. So far from being branded as heretical delusion, respect for the vernacular and for its native readers grows beyond its Lollard origins into something like a universal and self-evident truth in the course of the fifteenth century.

Thus the arch-opponent of Lollards at mid-century, Reginald Pecock, is found declaring without apology or discomfiture that he writes in "the comoun peplis langage" in order to clear it of the feigned and diabolical misrepresentations that heretics have disseminated among "cristen lay men." He displays his linguistic attitude and his commanding authorial manner at the beginning of *The Donet*, where he says that English is as fit as Latin "forto knowe what myn undirstonding and meenyng is, and schal be, in wordis of my writingis," if his readers will only closely "attende to the circumstauncis in the processis whiche y make there bifore and aftir." In *The Folewer to the Donet* Pecock advances the more extravagant and more equivocal claim that English can not only convey a writer's full meaning to a reader's understanding, but can also overmaster a reader's understanding.[5] Such a claim is material to his project of demonstrating to his own satisfaction and that of his native readership, in English, that they should be tractable to a Church whose authorities know more than they do. But no less confidence in the capabilities of the native tongue and its users reechoes in secular prose of the period, whether we look to such casual evidence as Margaret Paston's recurrent sentence opening, "I shal schortly declare to you," in her letters to her husband or follow Malory's self-possessed conduct of his interlaced narrative: "Now leve we thes knyghtes presoners, and speke we of sir

---

[4]For a forthright declaration of these beliefs, see chap. 15 of the English version of Wyclif's *De officio pastorali* in *Wyclif: Select English Writings*, ed. Winn, pp. 19–20.

[5]See Reginald Pecock, *The Donet*, ed. Elsie Vaughan Hitchcock, Early English Text Society o.s. 156 (London: Humphrey Milford, 1921), pp. 3, 5; *The Folewer to the Donet*, ed. Hitchcock, Early English Text Society o.s. 164 (London: Humphrey Milford, 1924), pp. 7–8.

Launcelot de Lake that lyeth undir the appil-tre slepynge."[6] An especially interesting sidelight is provided in the mixed tones of John Capgrave's address to his readers in the universal history section of his *Chronicle of England*, a vernacular compilation dating to ca. 1460–64. In apologizing for the skimpiness of his entries for "thoo ʒeres fro Adam to the Flood of Noe," Capgrave goes to some lengths to explain that what failed him was not his English, but rather his sources of information. He pleads for assistance from "othir studious men that have more red than I, or can fynde that I fond not," to help him "make more expression" in the later, larger version of his work which he is already preparing: "The velim lith bare, . . . redy to recyve that thei wille set in."[7]

Yet, while a chorus of voices soon joins Purvey in expressing confidence in the medium of English, at the same time his observations on the specific workings of English syntax are so incisive as to make Purvey unique. Basic to his procedures for translating Scripture is an emphatic distinction between "close" or closed, compacted phrasing and "open," "hool," "resolvid" expression. Purvey ascribes to English a special capacity for openness—that is, accessibility, communicability—in its sentence forms, explaining quite precisely its resources and the operations to be performed in order to make a closed sentence an open one. He instances two closed constructions from Latin: the ablative absolute (consisting of a subject *NP* and a participle in the ablative case) and a subjectless participle—*dicens* is his example. A transformational-generative analysis would account for both constructions as altered and reduced clauses whose fuller underlying structure can be retrieved by tracing back and reassembling their *NP + VP* constituents. Purvey, of course, does not invoke deletions and deformations in explaining what he means by "closed" sentences, but his recommended means for "opening" their sense all aim at reconstituting the affected clausal units on the surface level of discourse. In a striking anticipation of Bever's canonical sentoid—the basic Subject *NP + V +* Object *NP* unit in English sentence processing—Purvey conceives of bound and elliptical phrasing as needing loosening and expansion; that is the force of his nomenclature of "resolve" and "resolucion": "Manie resolucions moun make the sentence open."

He is, moreover, notably explicit that clause structure is the mainstay of open sentence form. He points out that a minimum of "thre wordis"— conjunction plus subject noun plus verb—are required for an English equivalent of a Latin ablative absolute. However, it is also possible to

---

[6]*Paston Letters and Papers of the Fifteenth Century,* ed. Norman Davis (Oxford: Clarendon Press, 1971), I, 218, 229, 242; Sir Thomas Malory, *Morte Darthur,* in *The Works of Sir Thomas Malory,* 2d ed., ed. Eugene Vinaver (Oxford: Clarendon Press, 1967), I, 256.

[7]John Capgrave, *The Chronicle of England,* ed. Francis Charles Hingeston, Rolls Series no. 1 (London: Longman, Brown & Green, 1858), p. 2.

accommodate a subjectless Latin participle to clausal recasting in English by either of two means, using only two words. The choice is between a coordinate *VP* (*and seith*) and a nonrestrictive relative clause (*that seith*): "As thus:– *dicens,* that is, *seiynge,* mai be resolvid thus, *and seith,* either *that seith.*" Again, Purvey's recognition of the potential substitutability of coordinate and nonrestrictive relative constructions is a remarkable display of intuition regarding the syntax and semantics of conjunction. After explaining and illustrating the vital connection he sees between open meaning and the wholeness exhibited by unreduced and untransformed clauses, Purvey adduces a further reason for composing in clausal units if one holds, as he does, that "wordis owen to serve to the entent and sentence"—namely, that a clause has a more articulated semantic structure than a phrase does, due to the presence of an extra word, a conjunction. The sum of his observations on the semantics of conjunction is widely applicable to the prose of the later fourteenth and fifteenth centuries, which makes wholesale reliance on the "conjunccioun copulatif," *and.* Not only does Purvey stress the Englishness of rendering a participial or an ablative absolute by a clause (or verb phrase) with *and,* he also indicates that *and* in certain contexts in English may be interchanged with *for, if, when, the while,* and *after.* The inescapable implication left by Purvey is a sense of the semantic richness and utility of *and* constructions which "let the sentence evere be hool and open."

It would be difficult to say whether Purvey's syntactic insights are more remarkable for their foreshadowings of formulations in twentieth-century linguistics and psycholinguistics or for the critical guidance they can provide to the style of fourteenth- and fifteenth-century English prose. Fortunately, choice in this matter is as unnecessary as it is difficult, and we can begin directly to consider representative specimens of prose in the light of both his emphases on the Englishness of conjunctive syntax and on openness of sentence as a deliberate stylistic norm. In this prose, where for the most part clausal units are left intact and unaltered except for their relatively minimal reduction into verb phrases, the regular semantic consequence of the syntactic conjunctions is that of asymmetry—in the sense in which asymmetry has been defined in the second section of chapter 1. It is not hard to see why asymmetry would predominate in this prose, for sentences that retain full clauses and verb phrases in their surface form carry a heavy predicative load. Predication, in turn, tends to presuppose and depend upon sequencing, on arrangement in a set order—whether that of events, or of steps in an argument, or of a process of another kind. Asymmetry, then, is a natural and understandable hallmark of the conjunctive syntax which figures so largely in the "open" sentence forms of the earliest modern English prose.

Less predictable, however, except on the basis of its frequency in oral language, is the conspicuous exercise of recursion to sustain the asymmetric sentential conjunctions found throughout this prose. Although Crystal and Davy warn that the reiterated *and*s of speech may be performing an articulating and segmenting function rather than a sustaining and connective one, the medium of prose is less equivocal than speech in indicating how writers conceive of their *and*s: whether the objective is discrete, simple sentences or cumulative, compound ones. In this regard, it is illuminating to return to the self-conscious Capgrave and his *Chronicle of England*, which embodies a marked stylistic contrast between its earlier and later sections. The earlier sections record milestones of universal history in a high concentration of short, simplex sentences. Here is a typical entry:

Anno 4044.—This 3ere deied Samson with deceyt of a woman; whech was the Juge of Israel xx. 3ere. His strength passed all men. He rent a leon. He brak the bondis that he was bound with. The gates of a town, and the postis, he bare hem away. And at the last, by stering of the Holy Goost, he pullid down too postis; where a hous felle, and oppressed him and mech othir puple.

Capgrave expects that his readers will react negatively to the choppy style of these early sections, and he tries to excuse himself from time to time, at one point acknowledging their deficiency as prose by representing them as "rather Abbreviacion of Cronicles than a book," as "schort remembraunces of elde stories, that whanne I loke upon hem and have a schort touch of the writing I can sone dilate the circumstances." The later sections of Capgrave's *Chronicle* include no such authorial self-excusings, but they are also written in a style that makes considerably more use of clausal coordination and continuative constructions, as can be seen from part of the description of the battle of Agincourt (1415):

So in the xxiii. day of Octobir the hostis met not a myle asunder, and the Kyng coumforted gretely his men, that thei schuld trost in God, for her cause was rithful. The Frensch part stod on the hille, and we in the vale. Betwix hem was a lond new heried, where was evel fotyng. Schort for to say, the feld fel onto the Kyng, and the Frensch party lost it, for al her noumbyr and her pride.[8]

As Capgrave's pronouncement and practice together attest, "dilation of the circumstances" by recursive application of sentential conjunction is, in combination with semantic asymmetry, the most conspicuous stylistic impulse to be discerned in English prose in the later fourteenth

[8]Ibid., pp. 36, 312. Capgrave's demurrer about his "Abbreviacion" is cited by Alice D. Greenwood, "English Prose in the Fifteenth Century—I: Pecock, Fortescue, the Paston Letters," *Cambridge History of English Literature* (Cambridge: Cambridge University Press, 1908; 1948 reprint), II, 287.

and fifteenth centuries. The recursion, a fundamental and repeatable process that generates new sentences from serial conjoinings of other sentences, at once exhibits and exploits the linguistic creativity associated with the vernacular by writers of this period. The asymmetry, a unidirectional, cumulative dynamic for sentence form, proves in the handling of these writers a varied and versatile modality for saying what they want to say. The twin thrust of this stylistic impulsion is perceptible especially in the body of secular documents—ordinances, wills, instructions, and specifications of other kinds—which evince the resumption of English as a written medium for ordinary, utilitarian purposes. We may take as our first example the compact by which the members of the barbers' guild of Norwich constituted themselves a religious brotherhood in 1389:

And a bretherhode ther is ordened of barbres, in the cite of Norwyche, in the worschep of God and ys moder and Seynt Johan the Babtis, that alle bretherin and sisterin of the same gylde, als longe as xii. persones of hem lyven, they schulen offeryn a candel and ii. torches of wax. And this light they hoten and a-vowen to kepyn and myntenyn, and thes other ordenances that ben under wreten, up-on here power and diligence, in worschepe of Crist and ys modyr and Seyn John Babtis; and the ii. torches schul bien of xi. *lib.* weyght; and alle the bretherin and sisterin schullen offeryn this candel and the ii. torches everi ᴣer a misomere day, and they heeren here messe at the heye auter in Cristis Cherche. And everi brother and sistir offeryn an *ob.* wyth here candel and here ii. torches, in honour of God and Oure Lady and Seynt Johan the Babtis. And the ii. torches, everi day in the ᴣer, schullen ben light and brennynge at the heye messe at selve auter, from the levacioun of Cristis body sacrid, in til that the priest have usid. Thes bien the names of the men that ben maystris and kepers of the gyld:

Philippus Barbur	And thes men han in
Jacobus Barbir	kepyng, for the same
Thomas Barbyr at Prechors	light, ii. *s.* in here box.[9]

In this document a motivated progression is clearly in evidence. First the membership of the compacting parties is stipulated, along with the purpose for the compact ("the worschep of God and ys moder and Seynt Johan the Babtis") and the terms of its performance ("they schulen offeryn a candel and ii. torches of wax"). After this preamblelike first sentence, the bringing into being of the compact as an agreement binding the whole membership is asserted and elaborated in a separate sentence beginning "And this light they hoten and a-vowen to kepyn and myntenyn." (We note parenthetically the solemnizing effect and possible legal overtones of the reduplicated verbs.) To conclude the Norwich barbers'

---

[9]*English Gilds,* ed. Toulmin Smith, Early English Text Society o.s. 40 (London: N. Trübner & Co., 1870), p. 27; also cited in Basil Cottle, *The Triumph of English, 1350–1400* (London: Blandford Press, 1969), p. 25.

compact, two additional sentences specify further vital particulars—respectively, the obligations of an individual member and the requisite daily duration of the candle-and-torch burning at divine service. The compositional principle informing this document is the very one observed by Robin Lakoff to govern asymmetrical conjunction generally: one conjunct supplies a crux or core of predication (here, the members' agreement contracted in the second sentence); and preceding and following conjuncts serve as accessories of one kind or another to the sense of the crux or core predication.

The same compositional principle informs the texts of the earliest English wills in Furnivall's collection. Richard Yonge, a London brewer, disposed thus of his personal belongings in 1413:

After my dedtis an rement of my testament be fulfyllyt, y wyl that my moder have xx^s. Al-so y wyl that Jon, my prentys, have a reles of to 3er of hys hol termys, of thys condicyon, that he be gode an trewe to my wyf. Al-so·y be-quethe to the for-sede Jon, 1 graner, an a flot, an a planer. Al-so y be-quethe to William, my sone, a new bras pot, an a panne, an a bedde, an a potel pot of peuwter. The residue of my gode, y be-quethe to Amys my wyf, an my son, to kepe hem bothe wyl. Al-so y make Richard Roos, Glover, and Jon man, Corwaner, myn executours, & ayder of hem to have for ther trayvall, a gode bow.[10]

This excerpt from Yonge's will follows a series of stipulations about his outstanding business debts and nonfamilial obligations. He begins a new series of bequests with a respectable lump sum for his mother, who is deferentially placed at the head of the list. While there is no way to ascertain if she is a member of Yonge's immediate household, the three persons next mentioned clearly are. The passage unfolds as a projection of the dying brewer's thoughts on how best to ensure their domestic well-being when he is not there to regulate matters himself. Yonge recognizes in the loyalty of his apprentice, Jon, to his wife's interests a precondition of the settledness he wants. Hence Yonge shrewdly angles for Jon's loyalty by releasing him from two years of his indentures, "of thys condicyon, that he be gode an trewe to my wyf." William, the son, is next willed some estimable household necessaries—all but one are metal. Yet William is evidently still a dependent, for Yonge, having circumscribed his concerns and bequests by degrees, now comes to the heart of the matter. All the residue of his "gode" will go to the maintenance of his wife, Amys, and of William, "to kepe hem both wyl." Mother and son are the conjoint central concern in Yonge's mind and phrasing. Having provided for them, he rounds off his efforts to ensure the orderly disposition of his estate by naming a pair of executors and prescribing their remuneration. Again, accessory considerations lead

---

[10]*The Fifty Earliest English Wills in the Court of Probate, London: 1387–1454*, ed. Frederick J. Furnivall, Early English Text Society o.s. 78 (London: N. Trübner & Co., 1882), p. 22.

toward and away from a manifest core of meaning. In serving to frame and offset that core of meaning, the series of asymmetrically conjoined sentences acquires a formal and functional unity alike.

The dynamic inherent in asymmetrical conjunction works itself out quite differently, however, in the instructions which the countess of Warwick drew up in 1439 to supplement an earlier "lyst" of specifications for her funeral monument in Tewkesbury Abbey:

And my Image ys to be made all naked, and no thyng on my hede but myn here cast bakwardys, and of the gretnes and of the fascyon lyke the mesure that Thomas Porchalyn hath yn a lyst, and at my hede Mary Mawdelen leyng my handes a-crosse, And seynt John the Evangelyst on the ryght syde of my hede; and on the left syde, Seynt Anton, and at my fete a Skochen of myn Armes departyd with my lordys, and ii Greffons to bere hit uppe; And all a-bowt my tumbe, to be made pore men and wemen In theire pore Array, with their bedys In theire handes.[11]

The countess immediately addresses what for her is the main consideration: how the effigy of herself in death is to look. It is to be fashioned in the latest Burgundian style, macabre and melodramatic in its representation of her "all naked," with uncoiffed hair "cast bakwardys." She next specifies how the three saints who will comprise a statuary group with her on top of the tomb are to be stationed; here, significantly, Mary Magdalen figures in first place as the only one portrayed as actually ministering to the countess. The grouping instructions lead into a further congeries of specifications regarding symbolism that bears on the countess's sense of herself: the directions for the coat of arms uniting her descent and her marriage, and how this badge of identity is to be presented (by the paired griffins) and positioned (at the foot of her tomb). Hereafter the countess's level of imagined vision drops, and so does the degree of her interest, as indicated in the brevity and unspecificity of her decorative program for the sides of the tomb: "pore men and wemen In theire pore Array." Her social inferiors, who presumably also were the recipients of her charity, count for little in the countess's overriding involvement with her own representation on her tomb. Thus the expressive and communicative use of conjunctive syntax in these early English wills reflects the "intendments" of individual minds in the face of death.

The new secular prose of the fifteenth century is in general, however, at least as preoccupied with the conduct of life as with that of death. This age is notable throughout for its production of how-to-do-it manuals and books of practical information in the vernacular. These treat basic subjects like hunting, husbandry, medicine, the rearing of children, and

[11]Ibid., pp. 116–17.

various household arts including cooking, carving, and serving.[12] The functional virtues of such prose can be considerable, as Ian Gordon has noted; here, for example, is a fifteenth-century recipe for apple fritters, which perspicuously groups into separate sentences the respective steps of mixing the batter, coating and frying the apple slices, dishing out the fritters, and bringing them to the table (the last presumably involving not the cook but a serving person):

Take yolkes of egges, drawe hem thorgh a streynour, caste therto faire floure, berme and ale, and stere it togidre til hit be thik. Take pared appelles, cut hem thyn like obleies, & lay hem in the batur, then put hem into a ffrying pan and fry hem in faire grece or buttur till thei ben browne yelowe. Then put hem in disshes, and strawe sugur on hem ynough. And serve hem forthe.[13]

In gauging the interworkings of the temper of the age with the development of vernacular prose style, the large measure of attention accorded to properly ordered and ceremonial behavior or utterance in Malory's *Morte Darthur* lays claim to critical notice. These fictional evocations, no less than the matter-of-fact stipulations which we have been surveying, develop through recursive asymmetrical conjunctions of what for the most part are unreduced or minimally reduced clausal units. The following stately description occurs in Book I of the *Morte:*

And than they made an othe, and the first that began the othe was the deuke of Canbenet, that he wolde brynge with hym fyve thousand men of armys, the which were redy on horsebakke. Than swore kynge Brandegoris of Strangore that he wolde brynge with hym fyve thousand men of armys on horse backe. Than swore kynge Clarivaus of Northumberlonde that he wolde brynge three thousand men of armys with hym. Than swore the Kynge with the Hondred Knyghtes that was a passyng good man and a yonge, that he wolde brynge four thousand good men of armys on horse backe. Than there swore kynge Lott, a passynge good knyght and fadir unto sir Gawayne, that he wolde brynge fyve thousand good men of armys on horsebak. Also there swore kynge Uryens that was sir Ulwaynes fadir, of the lond of Goore, and he wolde brynge six thousand men of armys on horsebak. Also there swore kynge Idres of Cornwaile that he wolde brynge fyve thousand men of armys on horsebak. Also there swore

[12]For discussion, see H. S. Bennett, "Fifteenth-Century Secular Prose," *RES* 21 (1945): 257–63, and his *English Books and Readers, 1475–1557* (Cambridge: Cambridge University Press, 1952).

[13]*Two Fifteenth-Century Cookery Books,* ed. T. Austen, Early English Text Society o.s. 91 (London: N. Trübner & Co., 1888), p. 73; also cited in Ian A. Gordon, *The Movement of English Prose* (London: Longmans, Green & Co., 1966), pp. 59–60. For other examples of this handbook prose, see Wynkyn de Worde's *The Boke of Kervynge,* in *The Babees Book, Etc.,* ed. Frederick J. Furnivall, Early English Text Society o.s. 32 (London: N. Trübner & Co., 1862), pp. 265–86, and *A Generall Rule to teche every man that is willynge for to lerne, to serve a lorde or mayster in every thyng to his plesure,* in *A Fifteenth-Century Courtesy Book,* ed. R. W. Chambers, Early English Text Society o.s. 148 (London: Kegan Paul, Trench, Trübner, 1914).

kynge Angwysshauns of Irelonde to brynge fyve thousand men on horsebak. Also there swore kynge Nentres to brynge fyve thousand men on horsebak. Also there swore kynge Carados to brynge fyve thousand men of armys on horsebak. So hir hole hoste was of clene men of armys: on horsebacke was fully fyffty thousand, and on foote ten thousand of good mennes bodyes.[14]

The cumulative employment of asymmetric sentential conjunction in this passage which so strongly evokes the marshaling and massing of an army may be adjudged a deliberate stylistic effect on the basis of the last conjunct, the crux of the series: "So hir hole hoste was of clene men of armys." Malory's signature, however, is read most surely in the quantity and character of the pleonasm in the passage. His is a prose style rife in identical conjuncts that remain unreduced in surface structure although they meet the relevant conditions for conjunction reduction. In this passage, for example, the stylistic option which would recommend itself to anyone committed to the information-conveying function of prose would be a systematic reduction of sentence structure along these lines: 'King Uryens of Goore swore to bring with him six thousand men of arms on horseback, and the Duke of Canbenet, King Brandegoris of Strangore, King Lot, King Idres of Cornwall, King Cradilmaus, King Angwysshauns of Ireland, King Nentres, and King Carados each swore to bring with him five thousand, and the King with the Hundred Knights swore to bring with him four thousand, and King Clarivaus of Northumberland swore to bring with him three thousand.' Certainly, if the criterion for judging this prose were a matter of keeping count, Malory's arithmetic would be clearer if his syntax were more succinct. However, another criterion seems to be operating here and in many other Malorian contexts where pleonasm involving identical and not merely synonymous material regularly conduces to rhythmical effects that evoke the formulaic character of life lived according to the chivalric code. Of course, the aural resonance of such pleonasm is essential to the effects created, and a shared mode of oral-based composition may account for the arresting likeness between the present passage (and other similar ones) in Malory and the epic Catalogue of Ships in the second book of the *Iliad*.

While augmentation of recursion and asymmetry by means of pleonasm is more concentrated in descriptive passages of the *Morte* than in narration or dialogue, there is, nonetheless, an exceptionally notable use made of these means in an ostensible speech context. The passage is doubly notable, first in displaying the unreduced identical conjuncts which mark original Malorian composition, and second, in appropriating

[14]*Works of Malory*, 2d ed., ed. Vinaver, I, 12; cf. I, 361. Mark Lambert (*Malory: Style and Vision in "Le Mort Darthur"* [New Haven: Yale University Press, 1975], pp. 34–35) remarks on an analogous passage in *The Brut*.

to secular use a means of rhetorical heightening that had hitherto been confined to the ornate tradition in religious prose. The passage is Sir Ector's justly famous lament over the dead Launcelot, his brother:

"A, Launcelot," he sayd, "thou were hede of al Crysten knyghtes! And now I dare say," sayd syr Ector, "thou sir Launcelot, there thou lyest, that thou were never matched of erthely knyghtes hande. And thou were the curteyst knyght that ever bare shelde. And thou were the truest frende to thy lovar that ever bestrade hors, and thou were the trewest lover of a synful man that ever loved woman, and thou were the kyndest man that ever strake wyth swerde. And thou were the godelyest persone that ever cam emonge prees of knyghtes, and thou was the mekest man and the jentyllest that ever ete in halle emonge ladyes, and thou were the sternest knyght to thy mortal foo that ever put spere in the reeste." Then there was wepyng and dolour out of mesure.[15]

The taut emotional pitch of Sir Ector's lament makes it possible to read the passage as an instance of semantic symmetry rather than asymmetry—that is, one in which the conjuncts have an order that could be varied, in which the thoughts apparently issue as they occur, by happenstance, to a griefstricken mind. A symmetrical reading would naturally emphasize the extent of the pleonasm: the reiterated superlatives and, in addition, the considerable semantic overlapping between the third sentence ("And thou were the curteyst knyght that ever bare shelde") and the final clause ("and thou were the sternest knyght to thy mortal foo that ever put spere in the reeste"). Given the large amount of syntactic identity, there is indeed some basis for concluding that the passage is purely emotive and lyric—a threnody—and that the sentential conjunction is not, so to speak, going anywhere semantically.

On closer examination, however, the passage can be found to yield a richer but still unforced reading in asymmetric terms that register its structural particularities. From this perspective, the semantic core or crux of the asymmetrical conjunction is the one idea that has behind it the force of all the syntactic identity in the passage—simply, the superlativeness of Launcelot. And this idea launches the passage. Immediately thereafter this core idea is signalled as such, and intensified, by two synonymous though nonidentical expressions, each accompanied with an expletive ("A," "now I dare say"): "A, Launcelot! thou were hede of al Crysten knyghtes! And now I dare say, thou sir Launcelot, . . . thou were never matched of erthely knyghtes hande"). In turn Malory reinforces the effect of the expletives, oral elements, in two successive reminders that this personal outpouring takes the form of speech: "he sayd," "sayd syr Ector." In the remainder of the passage, the accessory considerations that sustain the core idea develop serially within a kind of pleonastic, though by no means identical, framing structure com-

[15]*Works of Malory*, 2d ed., ed. Vinaver, III, 1258–59.

prised of the two conjuncts, "And thou were the curteyst knyght," "and thou were the sternest knyght." An asymmetrical reading of this sequence of conjunctions will necessarily focus on the semantic opposition presented by the adjectives "curteyst" and "sternest." Is this passage after all so emotional a transport that its speaker, Sir Ector, cannot be bound by rudimentary self-consistency? Or does Malory give us means for integrating the two apparently contradictory attributes being ascribed to Launcelot in the framing conjuncts? I think the latter. The intervening conjuncts work to mediate between superlative courtesy and superlative sternness by predicating a number of other aspects of knightly conduct which divide into two broad categories: individual (one-to-one) relationships and social (group) relationships. The net implication of this series is that, whatever each relationship called for in the way of perfect conduct, Launcelot met the demand superlatively. Thus Sir Ector's lament over Launcelot evokes the contradiction as well as the glory of the chivalric code at the same time that its grammar reiterates as a fact of personal loss (in the serial *thou weres*) the passing of the knight who was the best exemplar of this code. In the final sentence of the quotation, moreover, the semantic crux of the lament—Launcelot's superlativeness—is brought to a still further head in the simple account of the general reaction to his death. The excessive grief, by virtue of its excess, becomes a tribute in kind to the greatness of the man: "Then there was wepyng and dolour out of mesure."

Malory's great stylistic achievements in the "open sentences" of conjunctive syntax belong to a larger literary program in the fifteenth century: the ongoing enterprise of Englishing French prose romances for a growing readership, and one particularly central to William Caxton's successful establishment of a printing press at Westminster in 1476. Because the majority of the romances are translations and not original compositions, they fall outside the confines of this study. Yet to restrict attention to original prose writing in the vernacular is by no means to rule narrative out of consideration. Well beyond the precincts of romance, narration offered an appealing mode for earlier modern English prose writers both because storytelling is a perennially effective way of reaching a popular audience and because it offers plentiful opportunities for exploiting the creative resources of recursive—and, specifically, asymmetric—sentential conjunction. Much religious prose composition in the later fourteenth and fifteenth century assimilates itself to the narrative mode and in doing so places stress on the truths of the stories told. Wyclif's English sermons are entirely symptomatic of the temper of the age in conceiving of Scripture for "the puple" in terms of Christ's parables and the acts of his ministry—that is, in narrative form. A pair of orthodox sermon collections of the fifteenth century, the anonymous *Jacob's Well* and John Mirk's *Festial*, bear out the extent to which the art of popular preaching devolved into the art of telling stories. In the *Festial*, a sermon cycle probably composed before 1415, doctrinal exposition and devotionalism are distinctly subservient to the flow of animated exempla—in Mirk's own nomenclature, *narraciones*—that bespeak their origins in the all-time favorite among such compilations, the *Legenda aurea*. To judge from the easy, anecdotal style of the *Festial*, Christian truth may reduce on occasion to folktale. This story on the "out of the mouths of babes" theme is characteristic:

> I rede of a gret mayster of divinyte that studyet bysily, forto have broʒt into won boke why God wold be won God in thre persons. Then, on a day, as he walket by the se-syde deeply studiyng in thys mater, he was warre of a fayre chyld syttyng on the see-sond: and had made a lytyll pyt in the sonde, and wyth his hond wyth a lytyll schell he toke of the see-watyr and powret in to that pyt. Then thought thys mayster he was a fole for to do so, and spake to hym, and sayde: "Sonne, wherabouts art thow?" Then sayde he: "Syr, I am about for to helde all the watyr yn the see ynto this pyt." Then sayde the mayster: "Lef of, sonne, for thou schalt never do that." "Syr," quod he aʒeyne, "I schall als sone do thys, as thow schalt do that, that thow art abowte." And when he had sayde so, he vanesched away. Then the mayster bethoght hym how hyt was not Godys wyll that he was abowte, and laft of his studiyng, and thonket God that so fayre warnet hym.[16]

The oral basis of Mirk's composition shows in his loosely continuative use of *and*s (and *then*s), in his subject pronoun ellipsis ("and ˄ had made a lytyll pyt"), in his ambiguously reiterated *hym*s and *he*s, and in his pleonasm ("and spake to hym, and sayde"). But the narrative is stylistically accomplished in a number of respects: its economy, its deft shift from narration to dialogue; and, above all, its placement of a correlative in the midst of the predominant asymmetry of the syntax, to constitute the semantic pivot of the incident. The master thinks himself wise and the child foolish; he admonishes the child initially across a presumed great divide. But the child's rejoinder, cast as a correlative ("Syr, . . . I schall *als sone* do thys, *as* thow schalt do that, that thow art abowte"), brings home to the master the likeness between his and the child's undertakings, which in turn precipitates the perception of futility. Pleonasm functions beautifully to underscore the force of the master's perception: he who had told the child to "lef of" himself "laft of his studiyng." Moreover, the "open sentence" employed throughout renders the narrative both natural and preternatural in the manner of folktale at its best: there is familiar, colloquial interchange with a child who plays as children

---

[16]*Mirk's Festial: A Collection of Homilies*, Part I, ed. Theodor Erbe, Early English Text Society e.s. 96 (London: Kegan Paul, Trench, Trübner & Co., 1905), pp. 167–68. A revision made about 1483 with the intention of updating this appealing collection for a later popular audience is discussed by Lillian L. Steckman, "A Late Fifteenth-Century Revision of Mirk's Festial," *Studies in Philology* 34 (1936): 36–48.

do, but who can also deliver a telling—and tellingly expressed—insight and, having done so, can forthwith "vanesch away."

Despite the extensive assimilation of vernacular religious prose in this period to a narrative mode of composition, secular prose affords still more striking evidence of its appeal for a variety of purposes in a variety of contexts—some of them somewhat surprising. One such context is the legal realm, in particular, the formulation of petitions for official action or redress. Probably the best-known English document of this type, because of its early date of 1386, is the "Petition of the Folk of Mercerie," a request presented to the lords of the King's Council by the mercers' guild of London. The request is that Sir Nicholas Bembre, mayor of London, be arraigned and made to stand trial for acts of intimidation and terrorism against citizens of the city, by which he sought to extend his term in office:

For in the same yere the forsaid Nichol, with-outen nede, ayein the pees made dyverse enarmynges bi day & eke bi nyght & destruyed the kynges trewe leyges, some with open slaughtre, some bi false emprisonement3, & somme fledde the Citee for feere as it is openlich knowen. And so ferthermore for to susteyne thise wronges & many othere, the next yere after, the same Nicholus, ayeins the forsaide fredam & trewe comunes, did cry openliche that no man sholde come to chese her Mair but such as were somned; & tho that were somned were of his ordynaunce & after his avys. And in the nyght next after folowynge, he did carye grete quantitee of Armure to the Guyldehalle, with which as wel straungers of the contree as othere of with-ynne were armed on the morwe, ayeins his owne proclamacion, that was such that no man shulde be armed. And certein busshment3 were laide, that, when free men of the Citee come to chese her Mair, breken up armed, cryinge with loude voice sle! sle! folwyng hem; wherthourgh the peple for feere fledde to houses & othere hidynges, as in londe of warre, adradde to be ded in comune.[17]

The "Petition of the Folk of Mercerie" is an adroit composition. Within a framework of recursive, asymmetrical sentential conjunction it exercises a number of options for constructions of other types (chiefly the participles which Purvey noted as equivalents for clauses) and for varied placement of phrasal components. A favored device in the latter regard is that of fronted adverbials or complements: "For *in the same yere* the forsaid Nichol . . ."; "And so ferthermore *for to susteyne thise wronges* . . . , *the next yere after*, the same Nicholus . . ."; "And *in the nyght next after folowynge*, he did carye. . . ." The variety afforded by this device registers conspicuously in overall sentence form, for the preposed elements repeatedly counterbalance the trailing, additive development produced by asymmetric conjunction. Other felicitous consequences of the

[17]*A Book of London English, 1384–1425*, ed. R. W. Chambers and Marjorie Daunt (Oxford: Clarendon Press, 1931), p. 34.

fronting practiced by this writer include the tendency to create a clean, direct line of progression within the clausal unit from subject *NP* to *V* and, further, to ensure comprehensibility by only preposing phrases which could not be mistaken for subject *NP*s: "in the same yere," "in the nyght," "for to susteyne." Nevertheless, this writer's practice of also inserting adverbials between main elements within clausal units is a potential source of stylistic complication—for example, "the forsaid Nichol, *with-outen nede, ayein the pees* made dyverse enarmynges"; "the same Nicholus, *ayeins the forsaide fredam & trewe comunes*, did crye openliche"; "the peple *for feere* fledde." Yet, since the interposed adverbials are kept brief, the sentence form can be said to remain "open." Finally, beyond the handling of syntax, a noteworthy aspect of the vitality of style and expression in the "Petition of the Folk of Mercerie" emerges in its easy movement from quasi-legal formulations to the immediacy of reported speech ("sle! sle!") and colloquialisms ("bi day & eke bi nyght," "with-outen nede"). As the Malory and Mirk excerpts also demonstrate, range of this kind from comparative formality to colloquialism is highly characteristic of the narrative mode in later fourteenth- and fifteenth-century prose.

Probably the single most momentous manifestation of the appeal of the narrative mode in this era, compounded with new confidence in English as a written medium, is the resumption of vernacular chronicle history in the form of continuations—original compositions covering more recent events—which were added to the most popular of the chronicles, *The Brut*. The following passage from one of these continuations narrates the last events in the life of William de la Pole, the powerful and much despised duke of Suffolk, who was implicated, among other things, in the death of Humphrey, duke of Gloucester, and in the loss of Normandy:

And for to Apease the comons, the Duke of Southfolk was exiled out of Englond v yere; & so, during the Parlement, he went in to Northfolk, & ther toke shipping for to go out of the Reame of Englond unto Fraunce. And this yere, as he sayled on the See, A shipp of Werre called Nicholas of the Tour mett with this shippe, & founde him ther-in; whome thei toke out, & brought hym into there shipp tofore the Maister & Capitayns; & ther he was examined, & at last Juged to the deth. And so thei put him in A Cabone, & his chapeleyn for to shryve him; And that done, thei brought him in to Dover Rood, & ther sett him in-to the boot, & there smote of his hede, & brought the body Alonde, upon the sondes, & sett the hede ther-by. And this was done the fyft day of Maye. Loo! whatt Availed him now, al his deliverance of Normandy &c. And here yhe may leer how he was rewarded for the deth of the Duke of Gloucestre. This began sorow upon sorew, & deth for deth.[18]

[18]Continuator G (after 1461), *The Brut, or the Chronicle of England*, ed. Frederick W. D. Brie, Early English Text Society o.s. 131, 136 (London: Kegan Paul, Trench, Trübner, 1906,

In this passage the semantic groupings comprised by the successive sentence units attest the writer's stylistic control in shaping expression of his understanding of the course of events. First there are two compounded summarizing sentences: one narrates the exile pronounced on the duke of Suffolk and his attempt to reach asylum in France, the other his interception and (extrajudicial) condemnation to death. The modulation from active, transitive conjuncts ("& founde him . . . whome thei toke out, & brought hym") to passive ones ("& ther he was examined, & at last Juged to the deth") in the second sentence effectively conveys Suffolk's helplessness in his captors' hands. Yet this effect might well elicit sympathy for the duke—a response clearly counter to this writer's design of impressing the reader with the overthrow of a dangerous and powerful force for evil in the kingdom.

Accordingly, the third sentence works in an unobtrusive but masterful fashion to reduce the crucial series of actions to a flat process description: Suffolk was confined to a cabin; his chaplain was sent in to hear his confession; at the entrance to the port of Dover he was transferred to a boat; his beheading took place in the boat; and, finally, the duke's severed head and body were rowed ashore and displayed as those of a capital offender against the Crown (in an extension of the practice of mounting severed heads on pikes above the gateway to London's Tower Bridge). Taken in isolation, virtually every one of the conjuncts in this larger asymmetric sequence prompts some disturbing question. Why, for example, was the duke beheaded in the small boat, privately, and not more publicly on the ship or on land? Did he have sympathizers in either place who would have rallied to his support? Obviously these are the tactics of a kangaroo court, but the skill of the writer's presentation is such as to override the questionable character of each step by treating it as part of an ordered (and implicitly orderly) proceeding. Implications of order and even of the mechanical handling of the duke as a thing, a mere physical object, serve the writer's larger ends by evoking a sense of justice done in a regular, businesslike manner which he needs to predispose the reader to the climactic section of this passage: the lesson in the history, the rendering of explicit ethical judgment against Suffolk. Here the syntax shifts once again, to shorter sentences—which, however, include diverse types: an exclamation and a sentence in direct address. This shift bespeaks its manifest stylistic function; it sets out with equal starkness the ended life and power of the duke and the simple moral which the writer has to enforce.

1908), p. 516. A perceptive and appreciative discussion of prose style in this genre, as represented by the *Peterborough Chronicle,* may be found in Cecily Clark, "Early Middle English Prose: Three Essays in Stylistics," *Essays in Criticism* 18 (1968): 376–82.

For all of the narrative scope and nuance attained by means of recursive, asymmetric sentential conjunction in fifteenth-century continuations to vernacular chronicle history, it is autobiographical recounting, where the author is close to personal experience and to the circumstances of actual speech, that encompasses the greatest psychological depth to be found in the English prose of this period. Illustration may be made by a sequence near the beginning of the *Book of Margery Kempe*, which relates the events of her marriage, her first pregnancy and delivery, her attendant despair, her interchange with her confessor, and her subsequent torments and delirium:

When this creatur was xx. ʒer of age or sumdele mor, sche was maryed to a worschepful burgeys and was wyth chylde wyth-in schort tyme, as kynde wolde. And aftyr that sche had conceyved, sche was labowred wyth gret accessys tyl the chyld was born, & than, what for labowr sche had in chyldyng & for sekenesse goyng beforn, sche dyspered of hyr lyfe, wenyng sche mygth not levyn. And than sche sent for hyr gostly fadyr, for sche had a thyng in conscyens wheech sche had nevyr schewyd be-forn that tyme in alle hyr lyfe. For sche was evyr lettyd by hyr enmy the Devel evyr-mor seyng to hyr whyl sche was in good heele hir nedyd no confessyon but don penawns by hir-self a-loone, & all schuld be forʒovyn, for God is mercyful i-now. . . . And whan sche was any tym seke or dysesyd, the Devyl seyd in her minde that sche schuld be dampnyd, for sche was not schrevyn. . . . And whan sche cam to the poynt for to seyn that thing which sche had so long conselyd, hir confessour was a lytyl to hastye & gan scharply to undyrnemyn hir er that sche had fully seyd hir entent, & so sche wold no more seyn for nowt he mygth do. And a-noon, for dreed sche had of dampnacyon on the to syde & hys scharp reprevyng on that other syde, this creature went owt of hir minde & was wondyrlye vexid & labowryd wyth spyritys half ʒer, viii wekys, & odde days. And in this tyme sche sey, as hir thowt, develys opyn her mowthys al inflaumyd wyth brennyng lowys of fyr as thei schuld a swalwyd her in, sum-tyme rampyng at hyr, sum-tyme thretyng her, sum-tym pullyng at hyr & halyng hir bothe nygth & day duryng the forseyd tyme. And also the develys cryed up-on hir wyth greet thretyngys, & bodyn hir sche schuld forsake hir Crystendam, hir feyth, and denyin hir God, Hys Modyr, & alle the seyntys in Hevyn, hyr goode werkys & alle good vertues, hir fadyr, hyr modyr, & alle hire frendys. And so sche dede. Sche slawndred hir husbond, and hir frendys, and her owyn self; sche spak many a reprevows worde and many a schrewyd worde; sche knew no vertu ne goodnesse; sche desyrd all wykkydnesse; lych as the spyrytys temptyd hir to sey & do, so sche seyd & dede. Sche wold a fordone hir-self many a tym at her steryngys & a ben damnyd wyth hem in helle, & in-to wytnesse therof sche bot hir owen hand so vyolently that it was seen al hir lyfe aftyr. And also sche roof hir skyn on hir body a-ʒen hir hert wyth hir nayles spetowsly, for sche had noon other instrumentys, & wers sche wold a don saf sche was bowndyn & kept wyth strength both day & nygth that sche mygth not have hir wylle.[19]

[19]*The Book of Margery Kempe,* ed. Stanford B. Meech, ann. Hope Emily Allen, Early English Text Society o.s. 212 (London: Humphrey Milford, 1940), pp. 6–11.

The language of this passage, like that of the Mirk *narracione,* is strongly marked by oral characteristics: phonetic spellings ("schuld a swalwyd" for "schuld have swalwyd"), colloquialisms ("as kynde wolde," "a lytyl to hastye"), pleonasm ("sche dyspered of hyr lyf, wenyng sche mygth not levyn," "hyr good werkys & alle good vertues"), and, above all, the suffusion of continuative sentence forms beginning with *And.* Yet these sentence forms are in no way fortuitous productions; rather, the style constantly and variously attests its author's self-consciousness of expression. For example, the autoreferential locutions used in the *Book of Margery Kempe* are "thys creatur" and "sche," not *I;* by these grammatical means Margery takes up and sustains an outside perspective on herself. This perspective is that of other persons and how they react, judge, and behave regarding her. It remains constant even in the subjective disclosures and probings where, as here, it produces a simultaneous, double view—interior and exterior—of Margery and her experiences.

The quoted passage subdivides into three clearly articulated but unequal sections in which differing content coalesces suggestively with different use of the resources of conjunctive syntax. A long opening section is dominated by runs of asymmetric and largely unreduced clauses which crowd the page with predication. The function of this section is to supply an expository background, to build up information both from the recent and the more distant past that will help to authenticate the experience of crisis: "sche was labowred wyth gret accessys," "sche dyspered of hyr lyfe," "And than sche sent for hyr gostly fadyr," "For sche was evyr lettyd by hyr enmy the Devel." As the asymmetric conjuncts accumulate, the information about the recent past (Margery's fear of death and summons to her "gostly fadyr") and the more distant past (her acquiescence in the devil's suggestion that she could do without confession) together lead the reader to anticipate a crux in this section, perhaps in the form of some great sin divulged to her confessor. Indeed, the implicit lead of the conjunctive syntax ultimately becomes explicit ("And whan sche cam to the poynt for to seyn that thing which sche had so long conselyd"), whereupon it is "scharply" checked: "& so sche wold no more seyn for nowt he mygth do."

With the checking and deflecting of this anticipated crux, the second section of the narrative shifts away from social and external referents (Margery's marriage, her physical symptoms, her dealings with her confessor) and into Margery's internal, diabolical promptings and torments. This redirection of energy and attention toward subjective experience and introspective awareness eventually precipitates a crux that climaxes the whole passage; hence the shift is marked by an onset of syntactic patterning. First correlatives appear: "for dreed sche had of dampnacyon *on the to syde &* hys scharp reprevyng *on that other syde,*" "*sum-tyme* rampyng at hyr, *sum-tyme* thretyng hyr, *sum-tym* pullyng at hyr & halyng hir *bothe* nygth & day." The correlatives are followed by a great catalogue of *NP*s produced by sentential recursion and conjunction reduction, which literally gathers the devils' temptations to an overwhelming head: "& bodyn hir sche schuld forsake hir Crystendam, hir feyth, and denyin hir God, Hys Modyr, & alle the seyntys in Hevyn, hyr goode werkys & alle good vertues, hir fadyr, hir modyr, & alle hir frendys." In seeking to recover the semantic impetus underlying the syntax of this catalogue, we need to find the shared feature that makes these *NP*s a set. The conceptual bond linking God, the saints, Margery's virtues and good works, her parents and friends would appear to be expressible as "x matters or should matter greatly to Margery." Outward identity (good works) and human relations figure importantly beside heavenly beings in this catalogue. Margery is "boden" to "denyin" all this—essentially to repudiate all her values.

To experience such a temptation with enough presence of mind to be able to articulate it as exactly as Margery does must entail a state of mind close to assent. Assent, in fact, comes next: the crux of the whole narrative. It is expressed in a brief *do so* construction: "And so sche dede." The syntax here is highly instrumental to the meaning, for *do so* is an unfailing indicator of *VP* identity: in the act of denial, what the devils bid and what Margery does are all one. Now a massive run of sentential conjunctions follows to enforce, by elaboration, the terrible consequences of Margery's going over to the devils' party; a larger-scale catalogue of symmetrically conjoined clauses focuses its growing burden of predication of Margery as agent of sin, expanding on "so sche dede": "sche slawndred . . . ," "sche spak . . . many a schrewyd worde," "sche knew no vertu ne goodnesse; sche desyrd all wykkydnesse; lych as the spyrytys temptyd hir to sey & do, so sche seyd & dede." Again the syntactic signals of crisis, intensified patternings, appear, as the catalogue is compounded toward its end with correlatives (*"no* vertu *ne* goodness," *"lych as* the spyrytys tempted hir to sey & do, *so* sche seyd & dede"). The correlatives, particularly, betoken the collapse of what otherwise would have been moral opposition if Margery had resisted denying the set of coordinates that determined her values and, with them, her moral being. But, on her own account, she did not resist.

In the crucial progression from the first to the second section of the narrative which we have been examining, the sentence forms are not merely "open" in their clarity and explicitness but also in their function as vehicles for authorial self-disclosure. In the first section, the bulk of the clauses have the similar surface structure of attributives or passives: "was xx. ʒer of age," "was maryed," "was wyth chyld," "was labowred wyth gret accessys," "was ever lettyd." The experiences recounted by Margery, uniquely female ones for the most part, happen to her in the sense of being acts done to and not by her. A serious illness brings to the fore both her sense of being helpless ("sche dyspered of hyr lyfe") and her ingrained impulse to take charge of her own religious state, which, if a sin, can also be viewed more benignly as a species of self-determination. Surely it is no accident that Margery's delirium sets in after her confessor interrupts and reproves her sharply in the midst of her attempt to declare herself; the great evocation of her consent to diabolical promptings follows. This consent, like the early stages of Margery's recuperation that succeed it, is represented as a deep ambivalence. On the one hand, she is acting and asserting herself strongly (it may not be immaterial that "hir husbond" is the first to be "slawndred," although the devils had not expressly "bodyn" this); but, on the other hand, these same actions make her the devils' thrall and require the humans about her to bind her physically. Eventually "thys creatur" is to attain an extraordinary measure of self-direction and self-assertion by divine authorization in familiar colloquy, as the *Book of Margery Kempe* will go on to tell. What the introductory narrative sequence serves to reveal is the complementary nature of the obstacles and the character traits that make this attainment both difficult and imperative for its author-subject.

The third and final section of the passage which we have been examining reverts to asymmetric sentential conjunction for the purpose of detailing the series of violent actions which Margery in this state directs against herself. Although a considerable amount of additional quotation would be needed to trace her full recovery of self-possession, the restoration of her sanity and her identity in her human community, the style can be observed to be preparing for these developments here through the use of syntactic constructions that incorporate an external as well as internal perspective on her experience. Margery bites her hand "in-to wytnesse" that she willed her damnation, and the bite was so severe "that it *was seen* al hir lyfe aftyr." The resumption of passive locutions in this asymmetric sequence heralds the return of some sense of social surroundings even though the option of agent deletion is repeatedly exercised: thus it was unspecified persons who saw Margery's scar "al hir lyfe aftyr." Likewise, and nearer at hand, unspecified human agents persist in caring for Margery: "sche *was bowndyn & kept* wyth strength . . . that sche mygth not have hir wylle." Margery here begins to represent the process of being reclaimed for life among fellow human beings, but this first stage, as the passive conjuncts show, is a precarious one. Nonetheless, there is a glimmer of prospective cooperation from the patient: if "hir wylle" runs counter to that of her ministrants in the biting and binding, her sharing of their attitudes is implied in other locutions, such as "sche wold a *fordone* hir-self many a tym," "& *wers* she wold a don" (in which we register the effective ambiguity between future conditional *wold* and volitional *wold*). Thus a psychologically rich, even sensational account of an interval lived as one of the damned confirms all the while that it employs the communicative versatility of a style whose principal syntactic resource is recursive, asymmetric sentential conjunction.

The Range of Resources and Pecock's Program for English Prose

Although the foregoing discussion has been highly selective, I think it will also be found representative of English prose of the later fourteenth and fifteenth century in the dominant linear dynamic which results from heavy reliance on the type of "open sentence" form that we have been examining. We are now in a position to reflect somewhat more broadly on contributory as well as potentially offsetting features of the stylistic dynamic produced by asymmetric sentential conjunction and the option of recursion. Although *and* is by all odds the most common coordinator to figure in recursive series, it is not uncommon to find series with *not* (or *ne*), *or* (or *other, either*), or *for*, with *but* being excepted by its semantic constraint noted in chapter 1. Thus Julian of Norwich expresses her intense reprehension of sin by means of recursive negation: "But I saw *nott* synne, for I beleve it hath *no* maner of substaunce, *ne no* part of beyng, *ne* it myght *not* be knowen but by the payne that is caused therof"; and the "Pistle of Discrecioun of Stirings" attributed to the *Cloud of Unknowing* author uses recursive *or* to delimit alternatives: "It is ful perilous to strein the kynde to any soche werk of devocioun, as is silence *or* spekyng, comoun dietyng *or* singuleer fastyng, dwelling in companye *or* in onliness" (italics mine).[20] Recursive *for*, not surprisingly, occurs in contexts where the linear movement of the syntax is directed into argument. The three writers who make conspicuous use of recursive *for* (or *therefore*)—Wyclif, Reginald Pecock, and Sir John Fortescue—span the period under discussion and thus attest its vitality as a stylistic option. Fortescue's *The Governance of England* (ca. 1470) illustrates this live connection in arguing that English subjects must provide their king with greater properties and revenues if he is ever to make the rule of law effective in the realm:

Ffor his reaume is bounde by right to systeyne hym in every thyng necessarie to his estate. *Ffor*, as Seynt Thomas saith, *Rex datur propter regnum, et non regnum propter regem. Wherfore* all that he doth owith to be referred to his kyngdome.

---

[20]*A Book of Showings to the Anchoress Julian of Norwich*, ed. Edmund Colledge and James Walsh (Toronto: Pontifical Institute of Medieval Studies, 1978), pp. 406.26–28; "A Pistle of Discrecioun of Stirings," *Deonise Hid Divinite and Other Treatises on Contemplative Prayer Related to "The Cloud of Unknowing,"* ed. Phyllis Hodgson, Early English Text Society o.s. 231 (London: Geoffrey Cumberlege, 1955), p. 62.

Ffor though his estate be the highest estate temporall in the erthe, yet it is an office, in wich he mynestrith to his reaume defence and justice. And *therfore* he mey say off hym selff and off his reaume, as the pope saith off hym selff and off the churche, in that he writithe, *servus servorum Dei*. By wich reason, ryght as every servant owith to have his sustenance off hym that he serveth, so aught the pope to be susteyned by the chirch, and the kyng by his reaume. *Ffor nemo debet propriis expensis militare.*[21]

On observing the strong causal or conditional force of recursive *for* in this (and other) prose passages of the period, we might well question whether there is any real affinity between it and the far more neutral-seeming *and* of asymmetric conjunction. (Twentieth-century handbooks of English grammar dispute whether to class *for* as a coordinating conjunction.) Under close examination, however, the fixed succession of clauses linked by asymmetric *and* in the prose of the period we are discussing frequently carries quite definite implications of contingency, the fundamental kinds being relations of temporal, causal, or conceptual priority between an earlier conjunct and a later one.[22] Despite the semantic unspecificity of *and*, its role in asymmetric conjunction as an ordering connective gave rise to a usage which became commonplace in earlier modern English but which strikes the present-day reader as curious: the substitutability, under certain conditions, of clause-initial *and* or *if*. Employment of *and* to express conditionality has been widely commented on by philologists and historians of English.[23] Apparently the usage began in early spoken Middle English and reached highest frequency at the beginning of the seventeenth century, all the while preserving its colloquial associations; the plays of Shakespeare and Jonson abound in examples. But *and* (or *an*, as it is often spelled) is already much in evidence as a substitute for *if* in the speech-based texts of the later fourteenth and fifteenth centuries. Here, with a mere sampling, are the *Cloud* author: "For hem think, & thei had God, thei had alle good"; *The Book of Margery Kempe*: "A, Lord Jhesu, I trowe, *and* thu were

---

[21]Sir John Fortescue, *The Governance of England: Otherwise Called, The Difference between an Absolute and a Limited Monarchy*, ed. Charles Plummer, rev. ed. (Oxford: Clarendon Press, 1885), pp. 126–27. Emphasis on connectives mine.

[22]See Part I of Urban Ohlander's *Studies on Coordinate Expressions in Middle English* (Lund: C. W. K. Gleerup, 1936), pp. 7–106, where the comprehensive semantic contingency in what I call asymmetric *and* is treated under five heads: (1) "the adversative relation," (2) "the cause and effect relation," (3) "the final relation," (4) "the temporal relation," and (5) "*and* introducing the equivalent of a relative clause."

[23]See Tauno F. Mustanoja, *A Middle English Syntax*, Mémoires de la Société Néophilologique de Helsinki no. 23 (Helsinki: 1960), pp. 469–70; Edwin A. Abbott, *A Shakespearian Grammar* (London and New York: Macmillan & Co., 1869), sec. 101; Wilhelm Franz, *Die Sprache Shakespeares in Vers und Prosa: Shakespeare-Grammatik*, 4th ed. (Halle: Max Niemeyer, 1939), p. 441; Otto Jespersen, *A Modern English Grammar on Historical Principles* (London: Allen & Unwin, 1931), III.2, 46.

here to prechyn in thin owyn persone, the pepyl shulde han gret joy to heryn the"; and Malory's *Morte Darthur:* "Moche harme he wille doo *and* he lyve," "*And* there ryse warre, there wille be many kynges hold with syr Launcelot" (italics mine).[24]

The substitution of *an(d)* for *if* has two identifying features: (1) the finite verb of the clause headed by *an(d)* is in the subjunctive mood— e.g., "*&* thei *had* God," "*and* thu *were* here," "*and* he *lyve*"; (2) there is no conjunctive particle heading the clause to which the *an(d)* clause stands in a conditional relation. The clause lacking a conjunctive particle must, moreover, be adjoined directly at either end of the *an(d)* clause. However, such optional interchangeability in turn violates the Coordinate Structure Constraint formulated by Ross (see chap. 1, n. 44), and, together with the subjunctive verb of the *an(d)* clause, presents traits that defy analysis by straddling the boundary between hypotaxis and parataxis. Some light may be thrown on the substitutability of *an(d)* for *if*, however, by the intermingling of certain correlative and comparative constructions with sentential conjunction throughout the two centuries encompassed by this study. Workman has aptly remarked on the great incidence of "loose connective devices" like *if . . . then, where . . . there, wherefore . . . therefore, although . . . yet, as much as* in original English prose of the fifteenth century.[25] What these devices share with *an(d)* is (1) the fundamental binary, that is, two-term, nonrecursive, relation which they set up between clauses, and (2) their optional interchangeability. Not to be lost sight of, either, is the fact that emphatic conjunction with *as well as* is itself both binary and interchangeable, that is, symmetric. Indeed, *as well as* appears to constitute another boundary phenomenon, this time straddling coordination and correlation-comparison, although the nature and extent of the affinities between these types of linkage still await adequate characterization.[26] What I am suggesting as a possibility is that conditional *an(d)* came into being as a hybrid com-

---

[24]*The Cloud of Unknowing" and "The Book of Privy Counselling,"* ed. Phyllis Hodgson, Early English Text Society o.s. 218 (London: Humphrey Milford, 1944), 79.8; cf. 77.14, 83.7, 104.19–20; *The Book of Margery Kempe,* ed. Sanford B. Meech, ann. Hope Emily Allen, Early English Text Society o.s. 212 (London: Humphrey Milford, 1940), p. 49; Charles Sears Baldwin, *The Inflections and Syntax of the Morte D'Arthur* (Baltimore: Johns Hopkins University Press, 1894), secs. 210, 260(a), 261, 399. Baldwin also offers the following interesting observation on Malory's usage: "*Yf* is comparatively infrequent except in the combination *and if.*"

[25]Samuel K. Workman, *Fifteenth-Century Translation as an Influence on English Prose* (Princeton: Princeton University Press, 1940), p. 50; cf. Baldwin's observation that *in as moch as, in so moche (that),* and *ferthermore* are increasingly frequent syntactic connectives in fifteenth-century English prose (*Inflections and Syntax of the Morte D'Arthur,* secs. 367, 373).

[26]The nature of the eventual analysis is likely to be more logical (or semantic) than formal (or syntactic) only. See Robert P. Stockwell, *Foundations of Syntactic Theory* (Englewood Cliffs: Prentice-Hall, 1977), pp. 150–53.

bining basic aspects of asymmetric conjunction (contingency associated with adjunction) and symmetric conjunction (interchangeability, tendency toward binary form); and, further, that this apparent hybridizing of types within the syntax and semantics of conjunction was facilitated by the free intermingling of coordinate structures with correlatives and comparatives in discourse.

But what of these freely intermingled correlatives and comparatives, and, more generally, the binary "loose connective devices" remarked by Workman as a staple of fifteenth-century prose? Do they play a shaping role in overall sentence structure? The question is all the more interesting because the two-member, symmetric relations set up by these connective devices carry real potential for countervailing the aggregative tendencies of recursive, asymmetric conjunction with effects of balance and responsion. Workman answers this question in the negative by sweeping imputations of proliferated chaos in shorter stretches of sentence form: "Loose connective devices . . . were the chief ones employed by original writers. . . . In between the two semi-correlative words would be thrown any number of sentence members in any type of construction."[27] While it is demonstrably mistaken to speak of "any type of construction" thrown in between pairs of higher-clause symmetric connectives, Workman is correct that the dynamic of sentence form in this period is not notably characterized by balance and that a factor working quite as much against balance as clausal recursion is the recursion of local elements of syntactic structure. By far the greatest source of this recursion of local elements is the option of conjunction reduction, with its range of operations and effects. We shall note two of the most characteristic of these effects in the prose of this period, leaving a third, socalled word pairs or doublings, for separate treatment in the next and final section.

Conjunction reduction is in a manifestly transitional phase in early modern English. While the formation of many coordinate phrase structures utilizes the same collapsing rule that holds for present-day English, there are certain others that are produced through the exercise of an option that the language no longer offers. This is an option not to regroup, according to constituent type, the elements remaining after conjunction reduction, but instead to leave this residue in its underlying sentential order.[28] The difference made by the option available to fourteenth- and fifteenth-century writers, but not to us, is easy to illustrate. Purvey can write of "trewe sentence and opin," Malory of Launcelot as

27Workman, *Fifteenth-Century Translation*, p. 50.

28For formalizing this option in earlier English, a number of leads can be found in Andreas Koutsoudas's objections to empowering conjunction reduction with the obligatory function of regrouping constituents. See his "Gapping, Conjunction Reduction, and Coordinate Deletion," *Foundations of Language* 7 (1971): 367–72.

"the mekest man and the jentyllest," but we are constrained to *true and open sentence, the meekest and gentlest man.* The *Brut* continuator can write, "Thei put him in a Cabone, & his chapelyn," but we must write: *They put him and his chaplain in a cabin.* Mirk can write: "he toke of the seewatyr and powret in to that pyt," while we must regroup the conjoined verbs with a single object, thus: *He took and poured some of the seawater into that pit.* Only a trace of the option remains in our handling of certain coordinated auxiliaries; we can say, for example, *They wanted to come and did; I must go and will.*[29] Commenting on what we might call the unconsolidated type of coordinate phrase in earlier English writing, Henry Sweet appositely notes "a tendency to avoid suspensiveness" by putting only one of two or more conjoined elements in a specified position within a clause and appending the other(s) at the end of the clause.[30] For us, it is the stylistic effect that matters; clearly this option gives more momentum to the additive, trailing movement that predominates in the sentence forms of later fourteenth- and fifteenth-century vernacular prose. The obligatory collapsing rule of present-day English systematically ensures that coordinate phrase structure will show a balance which was formerly left to chance.

Another conspicuous aspect of coordinate phrase structure in the prose of this period is the extremely frequent incorporation of appositives, parentheticals, and nonrestrictive relative constructions. The comma intonation, which, as noted in the second section of chapter 1, distinguishes these structures as a group, also constitutes a significant link between them and spoken language. Stylistically considered, there is a real possibility that appositives, parentheticals, and nonrestrictive relatives will function as interrupting or suspending factors in overall sentence form, since such constructions are adjoined in rightmost position within their receiving constituent, having not infrequently undergone little or no reduction from full clauses. The absolutely crucial variable with regard to this group of constructions and their role in a writer's prose is the degree of structural complexity introduced by any given one. Greatly reduced adjuncts can easily be assimilated in phrase structure; but long, elaborate ones are liable to subvert both the achievement of "open sentence" and the reader's syntactic bearings.

[29]For discussion, see Frederikus T. Visser, *An Historical Syntax of the English Language,* III.1 (Leiden: E. J. Brill, 1969), sec. 1756, as well as his earlier account, "Two or More Auxiliaries with a Common Verbal Complement," *English Studies* 31 (1950): 11–27.

[30]Henry Sweet, *A New English Grammar, Logical and Historical* (Oxford: Clarendon Press, 1892), sec. 1863. Further comment may be found in Leon Kellner, *Historical Outlines of English Syntax* (London and New York: Macmillan & Co., 1892), secs. 473–74; H. C. Wyld, "Aspects of Style and Idiom in Fifteenth-Century English," *ESEA* 26 (1940): 41; and Fernand Mossé, *A Handbook of Middle English,* tr. J. A. Walker (Baltimore: Johns Hopkins University Press, 1952), p. 123.

In general, prose with the greatest affinities to speech makes the most successful use of these adjuncts by keeping them assimilably compact. Thus Margaret Paston's appositives, "John Norwode *his man*" and "Thomas Hawys *his other man*," set the scene at Wymondham's gate deftly for her husband; thus too the author of the allegory on the Seven Deadly Sins uses appositives to work information into the flow of his narration: "Than cometh in glotonee *the stuard of that howsolde*." The fifteenth-century continuations of *The Brut* particularly abound in felicitous uses of appositives—for instance:

In the ix yere of his regn, upon saynt Nicholas Day in December, was borne Henry, *the Kynges first begoten son* at Windesore, whose god-fadres at fount-stone was Henry *Bisshop of Wynchestre*, & John, *Duke of Bedford*; & the Duches of Holand was god-moder; And Henry Chicheley, *Erchebisshop of Canterbury*, was god-fader at confirmyng.[31]

The frequent parentheticals in the prose of this period show a variety ranging from near-formulaic expletives to full-scale excursuses. The following examples from previously discussed passages illustrate this range: "some fledde the Citee for feere *as it is openlich knowen*" ("Petition of the Folk of Mercerie"); "And in this tyme sche sey, *as hir thowt*, develys opyn her mowthys" (*Book of Margery Kempe*); "For what man of bileve trowith that Crist openede thus his mouth, (*and he is wisdom of the Fadir and the same God with him, and as he openede his mouth to speke, so he openede hertis of men to heere and undirstonde thes wordis, and teche hem men that camen aftir*), that he ne wolde bisyen him to knowe hem, bothe for worship and for profit?" (Wyclif's English sermons). Yet probably the single most common parenthetical in this prose is the "that is to say" locution or its equivalents, which play the semantic role of appositives to clauses and phrases and thus serve the earnestly communicative purposes of these vernacular writers. Love, as befits his self-styled authoritativeness, is an especially fecund source: "Whan tyme of that blissed byrthe was come/ *that is to say* the sonday at mydny3t/"; "with outen doute this is specially that hidde manna/ *that is to say* aungelles mete/ that no man knoweth bot he that feleth it." So, too, in a secular vein is Caxton, who almost compulsively glosses by interrupting the sentence forms of his prologues: "Thuse and thexercyse of a knyghte/ *that is to wete* that he knoweth his hors/ & his hors hym/ *that is to saye/* he beynge redy at a point to have al thyng that longeth to a knyght."[32]

The use of nonrestrictive relative constructions in this prose tends, on the whole, to enforce the trailing movement of sentence form rather than to suspend and complicate clausal units. This is so because most

---

[31]Continuator F (1419–61), *The Brut*, ed. Brie, p. 492; my italics.
[32]*Prologues and Epilogues of William Caxton*, ed. W. J. B. Crouch, Early English Text Society o.s. 176 (London: Humphrey Milford, 1928), p. 77. Italics mine.

writers avail themselves of the so-called continuative relative: the option of adjoining a nonrestrictive relative to the end of the clause and not the end of the phrase containing the identical conjunct.[33] A pair of previously quoted passages yield perspicuous illustrations: Capgrave's "This 3ere deied Samson with deceyt of a woman; *whech was the Juge of Israel xx. 3ere*" and *The Brut* continuator's "A shipp of Werre called Nicholas of the Tour mett with this shippe, & founde him ther-in; *whome thei toke out*, & brought hym into there shipp." Over against such easily absorbed accretions of coordinate structure we may again set Caxton, whose habit it is to multiply continuative relative constructions so recursively that they may swamp overall sentence form, as in this example from the Prologue to *The Recuyell of the Historyes of Troye*:

Than I havynge no grete charge of ocupacion folowynge the sayd counceyll/ toke a frenche booke and redde therin many strange and mervayllous historyes/ *where in I had grete pleasyr and delyte/ as well for the novelte of the same as for the fayr langage of frenshe/ whyche was in prose so well and compendiously sette and wreton/ which me thought I under stood the sentence and substance of every mater.*[34]

It may be the stylistic miscarriage of appositive, parenthetical, and nonrestrictive relative constructions in the prose of writers like Caxton and, as we shall see, Pecock that has given rise to the commonplace among historians of English that two of the three in this group, appositives and parentheticals, came into the language through imitation, primarily humanist imitation, of Latin models for learned and eloquent prose. On the contrary, as we have seen, this group of constructions is thoroughly indigenous in the vernacular composition of the period. The difference is only that the less learned writers in general employ compact specimens which remain unobtrusive in the "open sentence"—that is, the largely intact clausal structure—of their prose. We are now in a position to examine another kind of response to the creative potential of conjunctive syntax: the problematic but, to my mind, no less symptomatic phenomenon of Pecock's style, which testifies supremely to the linguistic high-spiritedness of this period when writers who used their native tongue were all too happy to be left, quite literally, to their own resources.

Although a fraction, only, of his total output survived the suppression and burning of his writings after his conviction for heresy in 1457, Reginald Pecock still ranks as the most prolific vernacular author of his century on the basis of six substantial works: *The Reule of Crysten Religioun* (1443), *The Donet* (ca. 1443–49), *The Poore Mennis Myrrour* (ca. 1443–49), *The Repressor of Overmuch Blaming of the Clergy* (ca. 1449), *The Folewer to*

---

[33]On "continuative relatives," see Mats Rydén, *Relative Constructions in Early Sixteenth-Century English with Special Reference to Sir Thomas Elyot* (Uppsala: Almqvist & Wiksells, 1966), p. xlviii.

[34]*Prologues and Epilogues of William Caxton*, ed. Crouch, p. 4; italics mine.

the Donet (1453–54), and *The Book of Faith* (1456).[35] Intensely serious by temperament, Pecock engrossed himself in contemporary problems, determined to help solve the gravest one then confronting the Church in England: the laity's widespread disillusionment and animosity toward what they saw as depravity and spiritual betrayal on the part of the clergy at every level, including the papacy itself (then in contention between a French and an Italian claimant). The imperative facing the ecclesiastical hierarchy as viewed by Pecock—successively bishop of St. Asaph and bishop of Chichester and, hence, one of its members—was to vindicate the due authority of the Church over its lay membership. Thus he deliberately began to write doctrinal instruction and admonition to English Christians at large, launching a project that not only entailed the choice of the native tongue and the medium of prose but also located his efforts squarely in Salter's simpler, more moderate tradition—at least with respect to subject matter, audience, and objectives.

Ironically, the utmost efforts of Pecock to engage with the crisis of the Church in his day resulted in greater and greater alienation from all possible quarters of reception and support, ecclesiastical no less than lay. What we can reconstruct of the conduct of his heresy trial confirms his isolation and his failure to secure any kind of political influence, while consideration of his literary and intellectual reputation, in his time or any other, leads to similar conclusions. Moreover, the isolation and the failure are quite readily understood.[36] All this notwithstanding, Pecock's stylistic project is instructive in the context of this study: conceptually, in the opposition it posed to Scripturalism, and linguistically, in what it reveals of an important distinction between the wider potential capacities of the native tongue and the narrower limits of actual human toleration for their exercise. In pursuing his project, Pecock had a threefold aim: to reach an authoritative determination of the essentials of Christian dogma, to formulate these essentials in the most authoritative thought system possible, and to articulate his formulations in the most authoritative English at his command. When we confront the results, the stepwise, interlocking, minutely subdivided and cross-referenced exposition and argument of the six surviving treatises (which also indicate the place of the destroyed and unwritten works in the whole), it

---

[35]See the useful biographical summary in Joseph F. Patrouch, Jr., *Reginald Pecock* (New York: Twayne Publishers, 1970), pp. 17–46. Also see Ernest F. Jacob, "Reynold Pecock, Bishop of Chichester," *Proceedings of the British Academy* 37 (1951): 121–54, an account on which Patrouch materially depends.

[36]Patrouch (*Reginald Pecock*, pp. 33–34, 84–88) argues convincingly that, on the one hand, Pecock alienated the ecclesiastical hierarchy and orthodox laity by conceding as a precondition of argument with the Lollards that the Church might err in determining matters of faith, but that, on the other hand, he no less affronted the Lollards by insisting that the Church was to be obeyed, right or wrong.

is hard to avoid the inference that Pecock, who never undervalued himself or his pretensions, was seeking to gain for the credit of the English Church in this highly nationalistic era the achievement of an updated, streamlined, and unassailable *Summa* of theology and morality that would command universal assent in England. For true universality in England, he would have to write in English.

We know from his own testimony that his efforts at recasting and defending the faith were prompted by virulent criticism from laymen whom Pecock names from time to time as Lollards. The demand they were sounding—for the first but far from the last time in England—was that the Church show express warrant in the text of Scripture for everything it taught and practiced. Pecock assessed the strength of these Scripturalizing impulsions among the English laity as requiring an all-out answer, in the form of a rebuttal. He did not merely find the Lollards' position insubordinate or extreme; he judged it outright error, on the basis of his own estimate of the authority of Scripture. In *The Book of Faith* he explains that he has devoted a considerable portion of his writings, the first part of the *Repressor* and "the book callid *Just apprising of Holy Scripture*" as well as the work in hand, to confuting the fundamental heresy of the time, Scripturalism itself:

> If twey thingis ben the principal causis of heresie in the lay peple which ben clepid lollardis, ȝhe and if thei ben causis, as it were, of alle her erringis generaly, sotheli forto remove and take awey fro hem tho twey causis muste nedis be the gretist remedie doyng aȝens her erringis, which may be do therto . . . in this present book. . . . But so it is that of these ii thingis the first is this, over myche leenyng to Scripture, and in such maner wise as it longith not to Holi Scripture forto receyve; and the ii^e is this, setting not bi forto folowe the determynaciouns and the holdingis of the chirche in mater of feith.[37]

As he explains here, Pecock finds Scripturalism heretical on two counts. One of these is utterly unsurprising, although it does evoke some remarkable speechlike echoes in these massive tomes: adherents of Scripturalism contest "the determynaciouns and the holdingis of the chirche." The *Repressor* collects examples of their "smert" and "wantoun" questions "whanne ever eny clerk affermeth to hem eny governaunce being contrarie to her witt or plesaunce": " 'Where groundist thou it in the Newe Testament?' or 'Where groundist thou it in Holi Scripture in such place which is not bi the New Testament revokid?' " In due course, as he labors his more conventional claim that only the learned clergy could be trusted to interpret so infinite and abstruse a source of divine wisdom as the Bible, Pecock tellingly imagines what might well come to pass in

---

[37]Reginald Pecock, *The Book of Faith*, ed. J. L. Morison (Glasgow: J. Maclehose & Sons, 1909), pp. 114–15.

"Ynglon" if "the lay parti wolen attende and truste to her owne wittis, and wolen lene to textis of the Bible oonli":

Y dare weel saie so many dyverse opinions schulden rise in lay mennys wittis bi occasioun of textis in Holy Scripture aboute mennys moral conversacioun, that al the worlde schulde be cumbrid therwith; and men schulden accorde togidre in keping her service to God, as doggis doon in a market, whanne ech of hem terith otheris coat. For whi oon man wolde understonde a text in this maner, and an other man wolde understonde it in an other dyvers maner, and the iiiᵉ man in the iiiᵉ maner; namelich for that weelniȝ in ech place where Holi Writ spekith of eny point of moral lawe of kinde, it is so spoken that it nedith forto have a redressing of it into accordaunce with lawe of kinde and with doom of reson; and than if no juge schulde be had forto deeme bitwixe hem so diversely holding, eende schulde ther nevere be of her striif, into tyme that thei schulde falle into fiȝting and into werre and bateil; and thanne schulde al thrift and grace passe awey, and noon of her holdingis schulde in eny point be therbi strengthid or confermid.[38]

While such decrying of currish wrangling over some Biblical bone of contention is only to be expected, given Pecock's authoritarian objectives with regard to the disaffected laity, it is important to register the far greater weight of the other count of heresy charged against Scripturalism: that of "over myche leenyng to Scripture, and in such maner wise as it longith not to Holi Scripture forto receyve." What does Pecock mean by asserting that it is possible to be too reliant on Scripture, and that there are ways in which it is not to be relied upon? The loss of his *Just Apprising of Holy Scripture* may have deprived us of the definitive answer to this question, but its gist is certainly given in other, surviving works. What spurs Pecock to the writing of prose is no deep conviction about the sacrosanct character of the Bible, but rather his total commitment to what he calls the "doom of reson": judgment on the basis of formal argument.[39] As he represents matters, the ultimate error of taking one's stand on the sufficiency of Scripture emerges from the insufficiency it displays as a source of authority. Acknowledging the three means by which divine revelation is dispensed to humankind—Scripture, miracle, and reason—Pecock proceeds to argue that God would not tolerate any overlap in these means; hence, the "doom of reson" apprehends what is rational and reasonable in God's will, and Scripture and miracle absorb the residue. The two latter means, however, are so residual in Pecock's thought that they pale before the full blush of reason. He advances to

[38]Reginald Pecock, *The Repressor of Overmuch Blaming of the Clergy*, ed. Churchill Babington, Rolls Series no. 19 (London: Longman, Green, Longman & Roberts, 1860), I, 5–7, 85–86.
[39]Essential discussions include Ernest F. Jacob, "The Judgment of Reason: Bishop Pecock's Contentions," *Times Literary Supplement*, 29 September 1945, p. 462; and E. H. Emerson, "Reginald Pecock: Christian Rationalist," *Speculum* 31 (1956): 236–42.

the following unequivocal assertion of the superiority of the "doom of reson" to Scripture as part of his "first principal conclusioun" in the *Repressor:*

Of whiche first principal conclusioun thus proved folewith ferther this core-larie, that whanne evere and where evere in Holi Scripture be writen eny point or eny governaunce of the seide lawe of kinde it is more verrili writen in the book of mannis soule than in the outward book of parchemyn or of velym; and if eny semyng discorde be bitwixe the wordis writen in the outward book of Holi Scripture and the doom of resoun writen in mánnis soule and herte, the wordis so writen withoutforth ouȝten be expowned and be interpretid and brouȝt forto accorde with the doom of resoún in thilk mater.[40]

This conclusion regarding the sovereignty of reason over the text of Scripture is no onetime twist of the argument, but the core of Pecock's thought and his program for prose. He far exceeds Love's objective of supplying the English readership of a half-century earlier with an adaptation of pseudo-Bonaventure in place of the vernacular Scriptures. If the relevant passage in Love's Preface (examined in chapter 2) can be taken as downgrading anything, it is surely not Scripture but at most the popular capacity to receive Scripture. Pecock, however, asserts that "God not so reulith him in his governauncis, that he ȝeveth a reule which is not sufficient forto reule, or that he puttith the worthier thing undir reule of the unworthier thing." Hence, in accordance with this divine principle, God sets as supreme over Scripture "thilk doom of resoun which is a formal complete argument clepid a syllogism. . . . And certis this doom of resoun . . . faillith nevere." The implications of the supremacy of reason for how a defender of the Church will proceed in speech and writing emerge in Pecock's unusual (not to say subversive) elaboration of the Pauline distinction between letter and spirit: in these times, "the outward writing of the Oold Testament and of the Newe" is to give precedence to the "inward Scripture of the lawe of kinde writen bi God him silf in mannis soule, whanne he made mannis soule to his ymage and liknes."[41] This "inward Scripture," we discover, is syllogistic. Unquestionably, Pecock's bold and forthright move to exalt syllogistic over Scripture would have precipitated a total reorientation of the tradition of moderate English prose style applied to popular religious instruction and counsel if his views and his program for vernacular writing had met with acceptance.

In *The Book of Faith*, Pecock's last work, which he propounded as an ultimate refutation of Lollardy but which instead brought on his heresy

---

[40]Pecock, *Repressor*, ed. Babington, I, 25–26.

[41]Ibid., 73, 51–52. Cf. I, 8, where Pecock presses his notorious but characteristic and sincere claim that there is no appeal—not even in heaven—against a properly conducted syllogistic argument.

trial, we find strong first-person testimony to the author's pride in his syllogistic prowess over his opponents:

I have spoke ofte tyme, and bi long leiser, with the wittiest and kunnyngist men of thilk seid soort, contrarie to the chirch, and which can be holde as dukis among hem, and which han loved me for that y wolde pacientli heere her evydencis, and her motyves, without exprobracioun. And verrili noon of hem couthe make eny motyve for her parti so stronge as y my silf couthe have made therto. And noon of hem couthe make eny motive which schulde meve a thrifti clerk nedis into concent, but a thrifti sad clerk in logik, philosophie, and divinite schulde soone schewe her motive to be over feble to a cleer and undoubtable proof.[42]

Yet Pecock claimed no abilities for himself in the framing of "a cleer and undoubtable proof" that he was not also willing to ascribe to the popular mind as early as the writing of the *Repressor*. There his outspoken optimism about the cognitive capacities of "the comon peple" for syllogistic is extremely significant, and his optimism regarding the use of English, "her modiris langage," no less so:

What propirtees and condiciouns ben requirid to an argument, that he be ful and formal and good, is tauȝt in logik bi ful faire and sure reulis. . . . Wolde God it were leerned of all the comon peple in her modiris langage, for thanne thei schulden therbi be putt fro myche ruydnes and boistosenes which thei han now in resonyng; . . . and thanne thei schulden kepe hem silf the better fro falling into errouris, and thei myȝten the sooner come out of errouris bi heering of argumentis maad to hem, if thei into eny errouris weren falle. . . . And miche good wolde come forth if a schort compendiose logik were devysid for al the comoun peple in her modiris langage. . . . Into whos making, if God wole graunte leve and leyser, y purpose sumtyme aftir myn othere bisynessis forto assaie.[43]

Although it appears that Pecock never wrote an *Introduction* (or, as he might well have entitled it, a *Donet*) *to Syllogistic Logic*, he exercised his readers continually in the art with every passage of argument that he wrote in English. What is more, he incorporated the progression from major premise to minor premise to conclusion—or the inverse—into the very structure of his sentences, so that the mainstay of Pecock's vernacular prose is not merely syllogistic argument but, in fact, an equally syllogistic style. As one might expect, the most amenable syntactic resource for Pecock's syllogistic style is asymmetric sentential conjunction, in which clausal order enchains the logical progression. Here is an unusually clear because uncharacteristically succinct illustration: "Lo, sone, this argument is a good sillogisme, *and* the first premysse nedis is to be grauntid, *and* the ii^e premysse is moche probable, *and* likli, for his notable

[42]Pecock, *The Book of Faith*, ed. Morison, p. 234.
[43]Pecock, *Repressor*, ed. Babington, I, 4.

greet evydence, *and* no man kan gretter evydence bringe into the contrarie." However, in such a style it is far more characteristic for the sentence unit to be expanded through recursive applications of conjunction to a quite considerable length, its compendiousness being the by-product of its development as a container for an entire three-step proof. Here, from the same source as the preceding shorter quotation, is a passage which undertakes to demonstrate the superiority of the syllogism to all other modes of acquiring knowledge and ascertaining truth. It demonstrates the inseparability of logical argument from additive, trailing form in Pecock's prose:

And thanne thus: sithen thilk cleerli knowun trouthe may not gendre the knowing of this derke or unknowun trouthe, in the mannes resoun or undirstonding, in lasse than thilke cleer treuthe be coupled and applied in the undirstonding of the man to the derke trouthe; and this now seid coupling and appliyng may not be maad without two proposiciouns goyng bifore, in teermes and wordis of the bothe treuthis, forto conclude and drive out of hem the iii^e proposicioun, which is the derke trouthe to be leernyd and not erst knowe; and the coupling togidre of suche proposiciouns in the now seid maner is an argument, which is clepid a sillogisme; therfore nedis this foloweth out of what is now bifore seid, that ech treuthe which a man leerneth and knoweth, aftir that bifore he thilk treuthe not knewe for hardnes and derknes therof, it folowith that the leernyng and knowing of ech treuthe and conclusioun of feith must nedis be hadde and gete bi argument, which is a sillogisme; or bi sum other reducible into a sillogisme, and may not be get and had, without such seid argument being in the undirstonding of the leerner, whilis he it leerneth.[44]

If the asymmetric, trailing progression occasioned by Pecock's allegiance to a syllogistic mode of argument were the sole determinant of his style, his sentence forms probably would remain coherent despite their length and intricacy. Many do remain coherent. There is, however, another identifiable impetus in Pecock's bid to achieve an ultimate authoritativeness in his prose: his unflagging resolve to cover everything that can be said, to leave unnoted no possible facet, detail, or even objection pertaining to the subject at hand. This impetus to have the last, exhaustive word connects with his decidedly tempered regard for the Church Fathers as well as the Bible; he became convinced that he could outdo all predecessors with his systematic formulation of Christian doctrine for the laity of England. Joseph Patrouch's study of Pecock rightly emphasizes that his intellectual achievement rests with whatever value is found to inhere in the tabulations and interlocking divisions and expositions of the "Seven Matters" of knowledge needful for a

---

[44]Pecock, *The Book of Faith*, ed. Morison, pp. 173, 125–26; italics mine. My discussion is indebted to Patrouch's suggestive brief comments on some formal connections between Pecock's study of dialectics and his prose style (*Reginald Pecock*, pp. 54–59).

Christian.[45] My concern is more specific: the influence of Pecock's compendious thought system on his prose style. If, as we have seen, the influence of syllogistic leads in the direction of additive clausal sequences, the influence of compendiousness makes for constant additions to the structure of individual clauses. These additions take the form of compounded lexical primaries (especially nouns, verbs, and adverbs) and of appositive, parenthetical, and nonrestrictive relative constructions. Pecock's resort to pleonasm for the purposes of vernacular prose composition may be interpreted simply as a link with his age, but in the lavish recursion of his coordinate phrase structures he stands unmatched by any other writer. His introduction of a core concept, the "Four Tables" of "meenal" (instrumental) virtues and "eendal" (intrinsic) virtues in *The Donet*, will begin to illustrate the complications produced by the recursions incorporated in his sentence forms:

And so, at this tyme, forto sette oute and expresse goddis moral lawis, as it is sufficient into cristen mennys necessarye leernyng, the first table of goddis lawe schal conteyne these viii poyntis of meenal vertu: that is to sei, forto governe us leernyngly, preisyngly, dispreisingly, preiyngly, thankingly, worschipingly, disworschipingly, and sacramentingly.

And that the ii[e], iii[e], and iiii[e] tablis conteyne eendal vertues thus: that the ii[e] table conteyne these vii poyntis: that is to seie, forto lyve and governe us anentis god at the next, goostly, obediently, ri3twisly, mekely, treuly, benyngneli, and largeli.

And that the iii[e] table conteyne these viii poyntis: that is to sei, forto lyve and governe us silf anentis us silf at the next, goostly, fleischely, worldly, clenly, honestly, paciently, dou3tili, and largely.

And that the iiii[e] table conteyne these viii poyntis: that is to seie, forto lyve and governe us anentis oure nei3boris at the next, Goostly, attendauntly, ri3tfully, mekely, accordingli, treuly, benyngnely, and largely.[46]

An extraordinarily sanguine attitude toward the reader emanates from Pecock's proliferating lists of terms and qualities: it is assumed that one will find and keep one's bearings in all of these intersecting sets (although, to be sure, the members of the sets are reviewed, as reminders, at frequent junctures). It is also assumed that the reader will await and then register information on the different senses to be assigned to "goostly" in tables two, three, and four, or to "largely" in tables two and four, or to "ri3twisly" in table two and "ri3tfully" in table four, or to the contradictory-seeming pairs, "preisyngly" and "dispreisingly," "worschipingly" and "disworschipingly," in table one. Unwavering in his trust in the "doom of reson," Pecock extends his confidence from himself as author, over the English in which he writes, to the whole of

[45]Patrouch, *Reginald Pecock*, pp. 123–24, 141–43.
[46]Pecock, *The Donet*, ed. Hitchcock, p. 24.

his readership. Thus, by the end of *The Donet*, Pecock affirms the matter to be beyond question: his systematic formulations have met the criteria for completeness ("no vertu of goddis lawe can be assigned which is not evidentli and openly conteyned undir oon of the seide xxxi vertues") and for finality ("this foorme of teching goddis commaundementis and lawis . . . nedith not to be chaungid or amendid"). In comparison with his authoritativeness, "othir mennys foormes, taking upon hem forto teche and trete goddis commaundementis and lawis, ben insufficient and inconvenient to thilk purpose," for they are a "heepe" of "pacchis" which do not constitute "an hool sufficient foorme of leernyng, re-membring and reporting upon godis commaundementis." A flurry of compounded adjective phrases sums up the disadvantages of others' heaps of terms before a redoubled flurry of compounded infinitive phrases and adverbial phrases drives home the benefits of the Pecockian system:

Also this heepe schal be as long in noumbre of poyntis as is the foorme of the iiii tablis in the first party of this book y tau3t, . . . or, certis, moche lengir. And therwith al it schal be oute of cours, of joynt, and oute of lithth, oute of ordre, and oute of dewe processe to gider clumprid, that it schal never serve to teche, to leerne and to remembre and to report so fair and so esili and so profitabli as schal therto serve the foorme of the iiii seid tablis aftir that thilk foorme be had a while in haunt and use of remembring.[47]

The Donet is entirely representative of Pecock's style and thought as it unfolds through the eliciting suggestions of a "sone" to a "fadir" figure—for example, "Wherfore a man my3t argue that neither crist, neither the apostle powle sawe so fer as thei schulde have seen in assignyng tablis of goddis moral lawe; or that 3e seen therynne over fer, or ferthir than they sawen." In return, the "fadir" is nothing loath to claim that his single, comprehensive scheme of thirty-one virtues in "Four Tables" has superseded such piecemeal listings as the seven works of mercy, the four cardinal virtues, the seven gifts of the Holy Ghost, and the Ten Commandments, to the end that we see "fruytfully, easily and redily every poynt of oure moral governaunce": "And therfore it is necessarye to resolve moral vertues into a widder noumbre, so that thilk nowmbre be not over large, but compendiose, and in a meene bitwixe to schort and to long, as is the noumbre of xxxi poyntis expressid and noumbrid in the seid iiii tablis."[48] Pecock apparently continued to believe that his doctrinal system and the swelling sentence units that serve as its vehicles were "compendiose" yet "not over large," but it becomes impossible for a reader to agree with him. Bever's concept of the "ca-nonical sentoid" (the intact clausal unit that figures crucially in linguistic perception) and Christensen's notion of "loaded patterns" (major con-

[47]Ibid., pp. 145–47.
[48]Ibid., pp. 25, 102–3, 110.

stituents of a clause that undergo enlargement and complication by embeddings of other constituents within them) can be used in combination to diagnose what goes wrong with the impetus toward ultimate authority in Pecock's style. While coordinate phrases located anywhere but in sentence- (or clause-) final position introduce some amount of suspensiveness into overall syntactic form, an incomparably greater potential for complication arises from the class of appositives, parentheticals, and nonrestrictive relatives. This is so in part because constructions belonging to this class markedly interrupt the progression of the clause in which they are adjoined (with their identifying comma intonation), and in part because this class of constructions is far more likely to be unreduced, closer to full clausal form, than are coordinate lexical primaries. Pecock's sentence forms, like his cast of mind, are imbued with forensic force. His particular impetus to be authoritative by specifying and including everything may be compared with the "fine print" of present-day legal and contractual English: the difficulty verging on unreadability and incomprehensibility can be accounted for in an essentially similar way.[49] Exhaustive stipulations prove exhausting when the stylistic options exercised load the patterns and obscure the form of the affected clausal units. Pecock's prose surges with recursions that all too frequently produce the linguistic equivalent of an overloaded circuit— with the attendant power outage as its inevitable result. Yet such moments when the reader's mind goes blank, frequently enough encountered in his pages, reflect no discredit either on Pecock's conceptual or his linguistic energies. They reflect only on his failure to harness these energies in a style that could at once transmit his meaning to the readership he sought so tirelessly and withstand the strain created by its very expression.

Doublings and Caxton's Program for English Prose

I have reserved for separate treatment in this discussion of the interworkings of semantics and syntax in later fourteenth- and fifteenth-century prose style the surface feature of sentence form conventionally known as "word pairs" or "doublings." Although I have been stressing the more comprehensive aspects of sentence form in focusing on asymmetric and recursive clausal conjunction, there is no question either that word pairs are an equally pervasive, if more local aspect of linguistic organization in the prose of this period or that critics and scholars have

[49]See the useful discussion by Crystal and Davy, "The Language of Legal Documents," which comprises chap. 8 of their *Investigating English Style* (London: Longman Group, 1969), esp. pp. 201–8.

attended more carefully to them than to any other syntactic feature for their role, variously characterized, in style. Even casual notice will verify how common doublings are in the prose we have been considering. While they are more common in some writers than in others, and most common in Pecock and Caxton, no writer lacks the device. Wyclif seems to use it most sparingly, yet a single sentence can on occasion furnish two examples: "Specially sithen alle Cristen men, *lerid and lewid*, that shulen be savyd, moten algatis sue Crist, and knowe *His lore and His lif.*"[50]

Certain rhetorical tendencies assert themselves over merely sporadic occurrences: for example, writers in the frequently employed narrative mode resort regularly to word pairs in building to a pivot or climax. It is at just such a point that Margaret Paston calls the quarrel between Wymondham and Gloys an "a-saut and affray" in writing her letter to her husband. Analogously, in the "Petition of the Folk of Mercerie," where the complaints about Sir Nicholas Bembre's strongarm tactics come to a head, we find "bi day & eke bi nyght," "the forsaide fredam & trewe comunes." In Malory, however, the word pairs are not deployed at climactic junctures only; they constitute a steady undercurrent in the narration: "gentyl and courtois knyght," "homage and fealte," "with play and game," "my prowesse and hardynesse," "ye may see Syr Palomydes beholdeth and hoveth," "repose yow and take your rest."[51] Caxton, in translating romances, increases the trend in Malorian doublings toward greater saturation and greater pleonasm: "a kynge of benewred and happy fame," "prest and redy," "privated and voyde," "bewayllynges and lamentaciouns," "of lignage or yssue of his bodye," "by his behavoure and contenaunce," "to gyve socoure and helpe," "come of noble extraction and hyghe parentage," "she wolde putte in oblyvyon and forgete hym," "right grete was the effucyon or shedyng of blode."[52]

Wyld has collected the following word pairs from legal and administrative writings of the fifteenth century: from the letters between Henry V and the mayor of London, "the ancien usage and custume of the same reaume," "your kyngly might and power," "that ye mowe . . . in eternel glorie perpetuelly duelle and abyde," "and so ben the sayd castell and Town yolden and delivered," "our soveraign lord, whom god save and kepe," "gret pees and tranquillite," "your plein luste and plesaunce," "to receyve and accepte"; from the Guildhall Letter Book, "it is shame and dole for to here," "resonable gayne and gettyng," "yf eny strif and debate falle"; from the Brewers' Book, "and ʒiff John Pekker breke or

[50]*Wyclif: Select English Writings,* ed. Winn, p. 20. Italics mine.

[51]Cited in Wyld, "Style and Idiom in Fifteenth-Century English," p. 40.

[52]Cited by Leon Kellner, Introduction, *Caxton's Blanchardyn and Eglantine,* Early English Text Society e.s. 58 (London: N. Trübner & Co., 1890), p. cxiii.

empeire eny werk of Tylynge," "meschief and disese," "they wysten and knewen," "wonte to selle or retaille"; from a memorial to Henry VI from John Paston: "ambyguytees and doubtes," "hertye devoyr and dewtee," "trust or confidence," "joie and felicitie"; and from the indenture of Richard Wittington's executors: "the makyng and edificacion of two new houses," "to make, edifie, and set up."[53]

Both climactic and what may be called incremental doublings occur profusely in religious prose, too; Stone gives twelve pages of listings (pairs mainly, but also triplets and foursomes) from Julian's *Showings of Divine Love* and the *Book of Margery Kempe*.[54] Moreover, the incidence of doublings linked by such sound similarities as alliteration or rhyme correlates generally in religious writing with intensified hortatory or affective appeal: hence, conjuncts like "might and ryght," "pomp and pryde," "wepyng and weyling," "bawme and blisse." While catalogues are proportionately rarer, there is some evidence to suggest that they shared stylistic associations of markedness and intensity with doublings as well as an underlying origin in sentential conjunction. In the following evocation of paradise from the *Book of Vices and Virtues*, the sustained catalogue is interrupted periodically by doublings that contribute a touch of rhetorical balance as they round off successive sentence endings:

There is the joyeful companye of God, of aungeles, and of halewen. There is plente of al goodnesse, fairenesse, richesse, worschipe, joye, vertues, love, wit, and *joye and likynge* everemore lastynge. There is non ypocrisie, ne gile, ne losengerie, ne non evel-acord, ne non envye, ne hunger, ne thrist, ne to moche hete, ne colde, ne non yvele, ne non akynge of heved, ne drede of enemyes, but everemore *festes grete and realle*, and *weddynges with songes and joye* withouten ende.[55]

Obviously it is not just the wide currency of doublings that attracts scholarly and critical attention to this stylistic device. There are at least two further reasons for their conspicuousness in English sentence form: (1) the paired (or multiplied) elements are lexical primaries—nouns, verbs, adjectives, adverbs—which accordingly produce concentrations of strong stresses in their containing phrases; and (2) the structure-building effect of conjunction is such, in any case, that it renders a coordination a more obtrusive feature of surface phrasal structure than

---

[53]Wyld, "Style and Idiom in Fifteenth-Century English," pp. 39–40. The suggestion recurs that word pairs may trace, in written form, to origins in the traditional language of law and administration, but I know of no systematic examination of pertinent evidence.

[54]Robert Karl Stone, *Middle English Prose Style: Margery Kempe and Julian of Norwich* (The Hague and Paris: Mouton & Co., 1970), pp. 121–33. Also see Colledge and Walsh's comments on Julian's use of rhetorical figures that employ conjunctive syntax (*A Book of Showings*, pp. 49–51).

[55]*Middle English Religious Prose*, ed. Norman F. Blake (Evanston: Northwestern University Press, 1972), p. 137. Italics mine.

any single item would be. Allowing for differences in languages that mark lexical primaries by means other than stress, it seems nevertheless that there is an inherently emphatic character to doublings that would recommend them for rhetorical purposes—not just in English, but indeed as a kind of universal resource of style. This hypothesis garners considerable support, if not full confirmation, from the extensive philological literature on doublings which documents them as a general feature of Indo-European languages (Sanskrit, Greek, Latin, Gothic, Old High German, Celtic) in their earliest periods, as well as in Hebrew and Chinese, among languages outside the Indo-European group.[56] However, in English and in Germanic languages generally, the syntax of doublings is highly constrained; the conjunctive particle must be positioned between the coordinated elements. In Latin, by contrast, the corresponding construction (*ave atque vale, sudore et sanguine*) is only one of several available, including conjunctionless juxtaposition and the *-que* suffixed to the second member of a pair (e.g., *usus et fructus = usus fructus = usus fructusque*).

The contrast between the accommodating nature of Latin and the exacting nature of English in the formation of word pairs has not hindered the development of a fairly standard line of philological interpretation which accounts for the English origins of the device in imitations of Latin. Alfred's translation of Boethius, the Old English translation of Bede's *Ecclesiastical History*, Aelfric's and Wulfstan's sermons, and the *Blickling Homilies*—all works of a markedly rhetorical character with recognized Latin sources or prototypes—have been used to ground an inference that these English writers followed the precedent of their sources or prototypes in their frequent employment of word pairs.[57] Questions of compositional precedent aside, there is a substantial amount of commentary in Latin rhetorical treatises on the device of *synonymia*, the usual term for word pairs.[58] In this connection, what Cicero has to say in

[56]For an extensive bibliography, see Inna Koskenniemi, *Repetitive Word Pairs in Old and Early Middle English Prose: Expressions of the Type 'Whole and Sound' and 'Answered and Said' and Other Parallel Constructions*, Annales Universitatis Turkuensis, Ser. B, Tom. 107 (Turku, 1968), pp. 98–108. On the differences between Germanic and Latin coordinate syntax, see Herman A. Hirt, *Indogermanische Grammatik* (Heidelberg: C. Winter, 1921–37), IV, 44–48.

[57]See J. W. Tupper, "Tropes and Figures in Anglo-Saxon Prose" (Ph.D. diss., Johns Hopkins University, 1897); J. M. Hart, "Rhetoric in the Translation of Bede," *An English Miscellany Presented to Dr. Furnivall* (Oxford: Clarendon Press, 1901), pp. 150–54; and P. Fijn van Draat, "The Authorship of the Old English Bede," *Anglia* 39 (1916): 322, where it is suggested that the "double expressions" appearing mostly at the ends of clauses in English are imitations of Latin *cursus* effects.

[58]The remainder of this paragraph draws upon two treatments of word pairs from the perspective of Latin rhetoric and style: Jules Marouzeau, *Traité de stylistique appliquée au latin*, 2d ed. (Paris: Société des Études Latines, 1946), pp. 278–80, and Heinrich Lausberg, *Handbuch der literarischen Rhetorik: Eine Grundlegung der Literaturwissenschaft* (Munich: M. Hueber, 1960), I, 330, 374, 386, 413.

chapter 20 of *De partitione orationis* is predictably concerned with the attaining of *copia:* "Illustris est oratio si verba . . . duplicata et idem significantia [ponuntur]." Figures of synonymy are also discussed in the *Ad Herennium* and by Quintilian (*Institutio oratoria*, IX.3.45). In addition to its usefulness as a means of amplification, *synonymia* was recognized as enhancing the effects of other figures like *expolitio* (the "polishing-up" of phrasing by reiterated variations and refinements), *correctio* (self-conscious pausing to emend wording), and *interpretatio* (parenthetical glossing or paraphrasing of a term); this group of devices was regarded as particularly apposite for rounding off a period. Hence, to return again from precept to practice, paired words and phrases emerge as one of the foremost aspects of style in the Latin of the Church Fathers, especially in Augustine, who retained a Ciceronian partiality for them and integrated them in the Christianized rhetorical program of his *De doctrina christiana*, a work of wide influence. Gregory the Great was hardly less influential in his use of doublings. All in all, this continuous transmission of rhetorical machinery and motive must be accorded a real measure of plausibility as a factor in the frequency of word pairs in the Old English translations of Bede and Boethius as well as the sermons of Aelfric and Wulfstan—not least because of the Augustinian stamp of thought in these works, which might easily be accompanied by an effect upon style.

The difficulty with tracing word pairs in English to Latin precedents, according to the most recent treatment of the subject, is not so much that it is incorrect as that it is seriously incomplete. Inna Koskenniemi's study of an entire range of Old and early Middle English prose texts has uncovered many demonstrably indigenous and extraliterary doublings (e.g., "whole and sound," "hale and hearty," "kith and kin," "hearth and home," "toil and moil," "friend or foe," "answered and said," "wax and wane") that have no likely connection with Latin rhetorical models. Moreover, this study documents the consistent naturalness and ease with which extremely heterogeneous writers utilize word pairs, whether as nonce or stock formulations.[59] It is Koskenniemi's overall contention that a more profitable line of inquiry than the pursuit of supposed sources lies in the analysis of function and form in English word pairs: first, as devices to meet broad cultural needs for impressive or well-turned or memorable or even binding locutions (hence the frequency of word pairs not only in religious and legal texts but also in proverbs, spells, and oaths); and, second, as constructs that exploit specifically English resources of phonology, vocabulary, and phraseology for a telling effect. Koskenniemi's emphases arise out of a specific concern with identifying the properties that enable a word pair to become established as an item of usage, but this specific concern does not exhaust

---

[59]See the Index of Word Pairs in Koskenniemi, *Repetitive Word Pairs*, pp. 120–62.

the force of the emphases. Indeed, the fact that word pairs are so widely distributed a feature of natural language suggests that a correspondingly broad perspective is in order.[60] Although a cultural approach goes beyond my own competence and the limits of the present study, certain aspects of the telling effect attributed to doublings can be elucidated through analysis of their stylistic and semantic function within the domain of English. The appreciable body of discussion already in existence merits a brief review for its suggestive observations and insights which have lacked critical notice of late.

Dietrich Behrens originally proposed a functional-semantic explanation for English word pairs which was widely disseminated after its adoption and extension by Otto Jespersen in successive editions of his *Growth and Structure of the English Language*.[61] The Behrens-Jespersen view fastened on an allegedly systematic common feature in the word pairs of the *Ancrene Wisse* and other late twelfth- and early thirteenth-century English texts, namely, that these pairings combined a French loanword or derivate with a native English word. Behrens hypothesized that the first Middle English instances (e.g., "cherite other luve") were interpretive in character, that they came into being as responses to the needs of an enforcedly bilingual society during a period of gradual adjustment. Jespersen claimed additionally that this type of locution acquired a different rationale which accounts for its persistence in Chaucer's time: "The reader is evidently supposed to be equally familiar with both [words of the pair], and the writer uses them to heighten or strengthen the effect of the style; for instance, 'He coude songes *make* and wel *endyte*.' "[62]

Despite the fair number of exceptions to be cited against this generalization about the character of French-English doublings in early Middle English, the Behrens-Jespersen view has remained broadly persuasive. One literary advantage which it offers is a latitude of explanation encompassing both expository and rhetorical motives without assuming

[60]These are among the points made in Koskenniemi's General Discussion, ibid., pp. 75–112. In another brief but suggestive section entitled Psychological Factors (pp. 108–12), Koskenniemi identifies four general features of word pairs in English: (1) emphasis and the prolonging of a listener's or reader's attention, (2) the motive of "clarity and precision", (3) "the enumerative tendency of human speech", and (4) an instinct toward rhythmical phrasing, seen in the positioning of an unstressed conjunctive particle between two stressed conjuncts. Koskenniemi also invokes "bipolar organization" (p. 111) as a basic perceptual and cognitive tendency that receives linguistic expression in word pairs. On this last point, see the interesting discussion by Charles E. Osgood and Meredith M. Richards, "From Yang and Yin to *and* or *but*," *Language* 49 (1973): 380–412.

[61]See Dietrich Behrens, "Beiträge zur Geschichte der französischen Sprache in England," *Französische Studien* 5 (1886): 8–9. The first edition of Jespersen's *Growth and Structure of the English Language* appeared in 1905.

[62]Otto Jespersen, *Growth and Structure of the English Language*, 9th ed. (Oxford: Basil Blackwell, 1948), p. 90. Jespersen's italics.

or insisting that these be separated from each other. Yet, in postulating a rhetorical motive for Chaucerian word pairs, Jespersen regrettably says nothing about how they might operate to "heighten or strengthen the effect of the style." We, for our part, have already noted phonological and syntactic properties that enhance the markedness of a word pair in an English sentence. There may also be cultural attitudes that contribute to the saliency of word pairs. As Barbara Strang observes in discussing vocabulary-building in English at different eras, associations of cultural prestige or superiority as well as a delight in linguistic variety and curiosity provide far more powerful motivations for borrowing and assimilation than do imputed gaps in the lexicon.[63] Strang's point about cultural predilections toward appropriating words from French, in particular, gains plausibility with distance in time from the Norman Conquest. There is express substantiation for it in Caxton's praise of Chaucer in the famous Prologue to his second edition of the *Canterbury Tales* (1484). Here Caxton acknowledges an eminent forerunner in what he perceived as an ongoing struggle to upgrade English to the level of French as a literary medium. How closely doublings, if not recursions, are connected with such upgrading in Caxton's mind emerges clearly as the Prologue proceeds:

Grete thankes laude and honour/ ought to be gyven unto the clerkes/ poetes/ and historiographs that have wreton many noble bokes of wysedom of the lyves/ passions/ & myracles of holy sayntes/ of hystories/ of noble and famous Actes/ and faictes/ And of the cronycles sith the begynnyng of the creacion of the world/ unto thys present tyme/ by whyche we ben dayly enformed/ and have knowleche of many thynges/ of whom we shold not have knowen/ yf they had not left to us theyr monumentis wreton/ Emong whom and inespecial to fore alle other we ought to gyve a synguler laude unto that noble & grete philosopher Gefferey chaucer the whiche for his ornate wrytyng in our tongue may wel have the name of a laureate poete/ For to fore that he by hys labour enbelysshyd/ ornated/ and made faire our englisshe/ in thys Royame was had rude speche & Incongrue/ as yet it appiereth by olde bookes/ whyche at thys day ought not to have place ne be compared emong ne to hys beauteuous volumes/ and aournate wrytynges/ of whom he made many bokes and treatyces of many a noble historye as wel in metre as in ryme and prose/ and them so craftyly made that he comprehended hys maters in short/ quyck and hye sentences/ eschewyng prolyxyte/ castyng away the chaf of superfluyte/ and shewyng the pyked grayn of sentence/ utteryd by crafty and sugred eloquence/ [64]

---

[63]Barbara M. H. Strang, *A History of English* (London: Methuen & Co., 1970), pp. 92–96, 120–31, 184–87, 250–57.

[64]*Prologues and Epilogues of William Caxton,* ed. Crouch, pp. 89–90. For comment on this passage (including specifics on its borrowings from Lydgate's *Siege of Thebes*), see Norman F. Blake, *Caxton and His World* (London: London House & Maxwell, 1969), pp. 166–67. Blake also comments on Caxton's use of word pairs (pp. 185–87), as does Kellner (Introduction, *Caxton's Blanchardyn and Eglantine,* pp. cxii–cxiii).

Considerably before Strang, J. B. Greenough and G. L. Kittredge proposed a different angle of functional-semantic explanation encompassing stylistic concerns which they saw persisting in doublings from the Old English period onwards. The two authors contended that doublings were a "literary habit" that set an exceedingly durable "fashion in language" from the ninth century to the eighteenth, and they defined this fashion as a valuing of explicitness, even overexplicitness, above the power of suggestion. The values of "the older fashion," according to Greenough and Kittredge, are "energy" above all, but also "dignity and copiousness of style," unless semantic motives become severed from stylistic ones and "tiresome verbiage" ensues. The two authors offer this reconstruction of the optimal situation they discerned when semantic and stylistic motives converge in "the use of synonymous nouns or verbs or adjectives where one would suffice to convey the meaning":

> The rationale of such phrases is evident enough. A single noun or verb seldom expresses the full scope of an idea. The pair of words covers the whole meaning intended by the writer, since the synonyms that he chooses have somewhat different senses. To be sure, some repetition is involved, since the second word repeats a large part of the meaning of the first, though adding some meaning of its own. Yet the author prefers to express his thought one-and-a-half times to the opposite method of expressing three-quarters of it and leaving the rest to be inferred.[65]

One may discount the imperious intentionalism in this passage ("the author prefers") and still emerge with a significant insight. Examination of two areas, at least, of later fourteenth- and fifteenth-century English prose—religious controversy and official and business correspondence and legal documents—bears out the operation of some kind of principle of maximal explicitness, by which loopholes in meaning or alternative interpretations are closed off, at the cost of some redundancy. Although writers of controversy implement the principle to varying degrees (Wyclif, for example, far less than Pecock), it is manifestly at work in the *will and bequeaths*, *defend and protects*, *without let or hindrances* of the *Early English Wills*, the Paston records, the guild proceedings, and royal (and other) proclamations and formal correspondence. These applications notwithstanding, the more problematic side of Greenough and Kittredge's proposal is that, despite the light shed on certain areas of earlier prose writing, the principle as formulated does not encompass a universal "fashion in language" with a thousand-year history.

In apparent dissatisfaction with the multiplication of competing theories about the interworkings of semantics and style in the creation of word pairs, J. F. Royster undertook to argue that a unifying motive

[65]J. B. Greenough and George Lyman Kittredge, *Words and Their Ways in English Speech* (New York: Macmillan Co., 1901), pp. 113, 115.

(insofar as one could be identified) derived from an ornamental conception of writing. Taking the twelfth through the sixteenth centuries as his sphere of discussion, Royster proposed to account for bilingual word pairs in terms of "the author's vanity of desiring to display a knowledge of two languages," concluding as follows: "The examples of French-English word pairs assembled in the Behrens-Jespersen collection are probable instances in early Middle English of a stylistic affectation which Shakespeare mocked in Holofernes (*Love's Labours Lost*, IV.ii.3 ff.)."[66] Whatever its explanatory appeal, Royster's imputation of "vanity" and "stylistic affectation," as sweeping in its way as Behrens and Jespersen's or Greenough and Kittredge's more positive hypotheses, incurs perhaps the greatest difficulties of all on the score of authorial intention. For it is an easier task by far to argue that a linguistic construction has some kind of expressive or communicative function than that it has none but show. However, by the contrary nature of the case he tried to make, Royster's entry into the ongoing debate exposed the futility of assuming that any blanket motivation, whether seriousness or vanity, would serve to account for the word pairs in an individual author's work, let alone in a comprehensive body of prose writing. Subsequent discussion has therefore concentrated on delimiting the field of investigation, on the one hand, and on exploring possibilities of compatible joint explanations, on the other. This work opens a number of interesting perspectives on semantic and psychological dimensions to be found in the phenomenon of doublings.

In an essay on Chaucer's prose, W. Héraucourt postulated as a principle of the social psychology of style that a writer reinforces and lingers over what matters to him; hence, the lexical content of word pair items can be investigated as an index to the set of values that find expression in a given text. Adopting the Greek term *hendiadys*—literally, "one-by-way-of-two"—as a functional specification of the semantics of doubling, Héraucourt purported to reconstruct the "universe of value" (*Wertwelt*) embodied in the *Parson's Tale*. On his account, Chaucer's word pairs fall into three main groupings under heads that are spelled out as goods of nature, goods of fortune, and goods of grace (lines 450 ff.). Particular word pairs—"myght and strengthe," "fayth and ful credence," "straunge or foreine goodnesse"—reify values by the standard mode of affirmation. But word pairs in the less standard mode of negation (e.g., "the feeblesse and infirmitee of wikkede folk") play a complementary role by enforcing the same values inversely. Héraucourt went on to argue that word pairs created by a translator can reveal values that indicate why a work is being brought over by him or her, into English, at a paticular era. While his own applications of the joint social and psychological significance of word pairs remain moral and thematic, he insists that the principle is capable of accommodating quite diverse impulsions to verbal reduplication—among them, intensity, emphasis, display, and conformity to current stylistic conventions and cultural norms. One of Héraucourt's more arresting generalizations concerns the locus of value to be inferred from clusterings of "strong forms" (his special term for doublings) in certain contexts in late medieval literature; he states it thus: "Suffering and its expression became pleasurable and directly experienceable through their aesthetic stylizing and pathetic presentation in strong forms in the Middle Ages."[67] Rather than the *Parson's Tale,* Julian of Norwich's visionary evocation of the bleeding head of the crucified Christ springs to mind in this regard, especially its tripled doublings: "Thys shewyng was quyck and lyvely, and hidows and dredfulle, and swete and lovely."[68]

Although Lambert has carefully considered the ways in which Malory's word pairs reflect the world of chivalric values immortalized in *Morte Darthur,*[69] the most detailed and exacting study that has been made, so far as I know, of a single author's use of this resource is Ernst Leisi's monograph on Caxton's *Aenydos.* At the outset Leisi makes an important point about the interpretive challenge which doublings present. He says, in effect, that they are as risky to construe as to use because their pleonastic quality defies the usual conditions governing conjunction in natural language:

Especially astonishing in this context is the function of the connective (most often, *and*). We are absolutely accustomed to expect something new and different from the preceding word to follow an *and,* just as in counting 'one and two and . . .' we also regard what comes after *and* as something independent of its predecessor and additional to it, of the sort that the sum of the two things is an enriching of the first with the second.[70]

However, he continues, the operation involved in many doublings seems tantamount to $(x + y = x)$. Then "one somehow has the feeling of being tricked by the language." (Or, as I think, one might put the situation from the opposite perspective and see language itself as the victim, its syntax drained of functionality and expressiveness, trivialized into empty

---

[67]W. Héraucourt, "Das Hendiadyoin als Mittel zur Hervorhebung des Werthaften bei Chaucer," *Englische Studien* 73 (1938–39): 190–201. The quotation is from p. 196: "der Schmerz und sein Ausdruck wurde in Mittelalter in ästhetischer Stilisierung und pathetischer Aufmachung in strenger Formen ausgekostet und geradezu genossen." My translation.

[68]Julian of Norwich, *A Book of Showings,* ed. Colledge and Walsh, 313.31–32.

[69]Lambert, *Malory: Style and Vision,* pp. 30–33.

[70]Ernst Leisi, *Die tautologischen Wortpaare in Caxton's "Eneydos": Zur synchronischen Bedeutungs- und Ursachenforschung* (Cambridge, Mass.: Murray Printing Co., 1947), p. 2. My translation.

form.) Whatever one's intuitive picture, the gist of Leisi's point about the problematics of doubling anticipates Gleitman's succinct formulation of the semantics of conjunction (as reviewed in the second section of chapter 1): reiteration implies nonidentity; nonreiteration implies identity. What tautological word pairs give us is both repetition and identity. Leisi finds the vast majority in Caxton's *Aenydos* to be of the tautologous type, which he defines as pairs exhibiting "no conceptual differentiation" or pairs in which the second item is less specific than the first and merely repeats part of what the first conveys (e.g., "Juno prayede them to *breke* and *destroye* all the navye").[71] Why, then, we are brought to ask, are tautological word pairs tolerated at all, let alone cultivated as a stylistic device?

Leisi's painstaking attempt to answer this question on virtually a case-by-case basis reaches the conclusion that, for Caxton, the motives of exposition or ornamentation are relevant to very few instances. Nor does moral outlook, *pace* Héraucourt, seem to be an identifiable determinant. Rather, according to Leisi, Caxton's purpose in using tautological word pairs is to call attention to the manifold sources of energy in lexical primaries: in the nouns, greatness or intensity; in the verbs, kinetic activity or force; in the adjectives, intensity once more. His final characterization of the stylistic motive for word pairs of this type touches on features of stress, syntactic balance, and semantic potency, but only insofar as these combine in word pairs to set forth the vigor and imposingness (*die Emphase*) inherent in language itself, especially when conceived as much in oral as in written terms:

Since we have seen that the demands of precision and beauty scarcely come into question as driving forces, and since we have established, finally, that tautology as a rule occurs with words that are stressed and with reference to something powerful, it seems probable enough that emphasis is the sole objective, and, consequently, the cause of the doubling.[72]

Whatever interpretation(s) one makes of doublings in earlier writers of English, Caxton's practice is of considerable historical importance, as Leisi recognized—both because Caxton's own and translated prose achieved, through print, an unparalleled circulation in his time and because Caxton compounded his practice with outspoken advocacy of the "aureate" school of writing. His admiration for Lydgate's and Skelton's productions in this vein is well known. Leisi's work makes it clear

[71]Ibid., pp. 58, 60.

[72]Ibid., pp. 133–34: "Nachdem wir gesehen, dass die Bedürfnisse der Deutlichkeit und Schönheit kaum als auslösende Kräfte in Frage kommen, nachdem wir schliesslich festgestellt, dass die Tautologie in der Regel bei akzentuierten Worten und bei Bezeichnung des Gewaltigen vorkommt, scheint es wahrscheinlich genug, dass Emphase der einzige Zweck und damit die Ursache der Verdoppelung ist." My translation.

that Caxton is to be credited with genuine stylistic intuitions regarding the creative potential of recursive conjunction in general and the "emphasis" on the power of language inherent in word pairs in particular. Nevertheless, Caxton's genuine intuitions about style and syntax combined with two misguided assumptions that went far toward vitiating the intuitions. One of these was that orality in written language should be cultivated in a direction counter to that of actual speech, that prose should resonate with curious polysyllables and flocks of suspended constructions; the other assumption was that the more removes from the spoken language there were, the better the prose was likely to be.[73] (The latter may, perhaps, be the recursion principle in an altered guise. Enlisted in the service of anticolloquialism, recursive syntax will merely compound oddities and eccentricities.)

With the attempted repudiation of speech-based prose that accompanies aureation in the later fifteenth century, the creative potential of language seems at times to be turning back on itself. Openness of sentence gives way before involution and distension of clausal structure: the twin result of lexical exoticism (a subject deserving of study in its own right)[74] and of syntactic recursion. Interesting evidence of its effects may be found in various rewritings or revisions of earlier fifteenth-century prose that were made at the end of the century. Consideration of efforts other than Caxton's in this line will be deferred to the opening section of chapter 4. Here we may conclude by examining a specimen of the revisions Caxton made of Malory, for the most part in book 5 of the *Morte*, while readying for print the edition entitled *King Arthur* (1485). Malory's version had read as follows:

And than come there an husbandeman oute of the contrey and talkyth unto the kyng wondourfull wordys and sayde, "Sir, here is a foule gyaunte of Gene that turmentyth thy peple; mo than fyve hundred and many mo of oure chyldren

---

[73]See Norman Blake's comments on the nature of Caxton's interest in English prose style: *Caxton and His World*, pp. 175, 181; *Caxton's Own Prose* (London: André Deutsch, 1973), pp. 32–36. Also pertinent is Morton Donner's "The Infrequency of Word Borrowings in Caxton's Original Writings," *English Language Notes* 4 (1967): 86–89.

[74]Scholars and critics of Renaissance literature, so far as I am aware, take the mid- and later sixteenth-century outcry against "inkhorn terms" at face value and assume that a recent rash of neologisms must have precipitated the reaction. There is lexical and morphological evidence, however, that the prolonged high point of consequential activity in English word-formation was the period 1100–1400 (see Strang, *A History of English*, pp. 189–96). It would seem that literary history should be brought more explicitly into line with linguistic history in this stylistically important matter. For thoughtful discussion (which, however, gives uncritical acceptance to the representations about the native tongue made by writers from Caxton to Jonson), see Anne Drury Hall, "Tudor Prose Style: English Humanists and the Problem of a Standard," *English Literary Renaissance* 7 (1976): 267–96. Also pertinent is Alvin Vos's "Humanist Standards of Diction in the Inkhorn Controversy," *SP* 73 (1976): 376–96.

hath bene his sustynaunce all this seven wynters. Yet is the sotte never cesid, but in the contrey of Constantyne he hath kylled all our knave chyldren, and this nyght he hath cleyghte the duches of Bretayne as she rode by a ryver with her ryche knyghtes, and ledde hir unto yondir mounte to ly by hir whyle hir lyff lastyth. Many folkys folowed hym, mo than fyve hundird barounes and bachelers and knyghtes full noble, but ever she shryked wondirly lowde, that the sorow of the lady cover shall we never."

Caxton recast the passage in this fashion:

Thenne came to hym an husbond man of the countrey and told hym how there was in the countre of Constantyn besyde Bretayne a grete gyaunt whiche hadde slayne, murthered, and devoured moche peple of the countreye, and had ben susteyned seven yere with the children of the comyns of that land in soo moche that alle the children ben alle slayne and destroyed. And now late he hath taken the duchesse of Bretayne as she rode with her meyne and hath ledde her to his lodging which is in a montayne for to ravysshe and lye by her to her lyves ende. And many people folowed her, moo than vC., but alle they myghte not rescowe her. But they lefte her shrykyng and cryenge lamentably, wherfore I suppose that he hath slayne her in fulfyllynge his fowle lust and lechery.[75]

The points of comparison speak largely for themselves; they need not be indicated at any great length. Significantly, both texts are pleonastic, although in different ways; as a result Caxton's stylistic flourishes do not appreciably expand Malory's text. Caxton does, however, betray his concern with removing prose from speech in endeavoring to turn Malory's husbandman's report into indirect discourse. (The endeavor is not wholly self-consistent; the "I suppose" inserted in the last sentence of Caxton's version breaks conclusively with the indirect mode, but there are already signs of its erosion in the shift from past to present perfect tenses between the first and second sentences of the quotation.) Caxton also appears to be aiming at some elegant variation in Malory's asymmetrically conjoined sentences, but little beyond the "how there was" and the "in soo moche that" substitutions in the first sentence ultimately leads in this direction. Caxton retains all of Malory's sentence units except for splitting the last sentence in half. Thus the doublings become the major focus of Caxton's alterations.

In Malory's original, by comparison, the syntax and semantics interrelate more functionally and perspicuously. The crux of the giant of Gene story, in this version, is the supreme threat which the giant poses to knightly valor and prowess and to a society dependent on these: children are slain and eaten, a duchess ravished, and yet (here Malory strategi-

---

[75]Both passages are cited in Blake, *Caxton and His World*, pp. 183–84. On the relation of the two versions, see Arthur O. Sandved, *Studies in the Language of Caxton's Malory and That of the Winchester Manuscript* (Oslo: Norwegian Universities Press, New York: Humanities Press, 1968).

cally introduces his one catalogue) "mo than five hundird barounes and bachelers and knyghtes full noble" are powerless to "cover [recover?] the sorow of the lady." The passage functions as a despairing report to a remote authority figure; what is "wondourfull" in its "wordys" is how bleak the situation looks for the massed local power of chivalry. Thus the passage ends with a *VP* inversion that appropriately places sentence-final stress on "never."

Caxton's syntactic reworking alters the semantics considerably through rhetorical emphases achieved by doublings. Interestingly, Malory's pleonastic coordination ("and talkyth unto the kyng wondourfull wordys and sayde") is excised. Caxton's "wondourfull wordys" are the doublings themselves. These cluster markedly in the articulation of one theme: not the threat to chivalric society as such (which in this version becomes "many people"), but the colossal wickedness of the giant of Gene. Formerly, the giant "hadde slayne, murthered, and devoured moche peple . . . in soo moche that alle the children ben alle slayne and destroyed"; just lately, he took a duchess "for to ravysshe and lye by her to her lyves ende." The semantic crux of this passage is the sensationalism which the emphatic language infuses into "supposed," not reported particulars: "But they lefte her shrykyng and cryenge lamentably, wherfore I suppose that he hath slayne her in fulfyllynge his fowle lust and lechery." This sentence-final doubling, "his fowle lust and lechery," encapsulates the difference between Caxton's passage and Malory's original, with its ending on "never." Is "his fowle lust and lechery" a climactic reinforcement, by antonymy, of Caxton's "universe of value," as Héraucourt would have it? Or is this doubling, and the others, an exhibition of Leisi's "emphasis," the inherent vigor and power of language? I do not think it is possible or necessary to exclude Héraucourt's perspective, but I would accord greater weight to Leisi's interpretation of Caxton's stylistic efforts as an attempt to maximize the vitality of language in what he conceived as an enduring—specifically, a written and an ornamented—form. An original addition by Caxton to the Prologue of the *Mirror of the World* (1481) bears out the force of his personal investment in ornamented, written English:

Consideryng that wordes ben perishyng vayne and forgeteful/ and writynges dwelle & abide permanent as I rede *Vox audit perit littera scripta manet*/ thise thinges have ben causes that the faites and dedes of auncyent menn ben sette by declaracion in fair and aourned volumes/ to thende that science and artes lerned and founden of thinges passed myght be had in perpetuel memorye and remembraunce.[76]

[76]Cited in Blake, *Caxton and His World*, p. 155.

By his own accounting, then, we gather that Caxton embraced aureation, which for him centered in the use of doublings, because he was embarked on a quest for linguistic permanence. In all likelihood his choice of the precarious new vocation of a printer bore some relation to such a quest. Although we in the twentieth century know that linguistic permanence is an impossibility, unless the language in question is "dead," nevertheless we may view Caxton's yearnings in that direction with a measure of sympathy for the fervent patriotism and literary aspirations which they encompassed. Even so, there are definite limits to the sympathy that can be felt either for Caxton's stylistic objectives or for his style. Two factors weigh especially heavily, I think, in this regard.

In the first place, Caxton made the gratuitous—and stylistically fatal—assumption that written language was to be severed from spoken language and cultivated in an altogether separate fashion in order to preserve it from the effects of language change that one can observe in speech during one's own lifetime. Such a governing assumption leads, however, to false notes and fantastic strains in prose composition, sentences all but unimaginable as English because they flout the practical norms of idiom and comprehensibility that arise in the course of language use. A second adverse factor in Caxton's stylistic program for prose is a kind of corollary or extension of the first, namely, that inherent linguistic "emphasis," the vitality and power of language, can be exercised and exploited simply for its own sake. But here, again, the peril of ignoring the essential functionality of language as a system soon becomes manifest. If, as often in Caxton's doublings, distinctions are multiplied without discernible differences, or specifications without substance are reiterated, then, indeed ($x + y = x$) to the point of becoming a negative equation. As we have noted, one can describe the result either as the feeling of being tricked by the language or as the feeling that the language is suffering from being tricked out. "Strong forms" used as ostensible ends in themselves do not long retain their linguistic vitality and power. No more in style than in speech can syntax operate to the exclusion of semantics, for the latter supplies not only the contents of sentence forms but also the implication of meaningfulness that disposes us to attend on the forms of use. Such is the conclusion that Caxton would have reached if he had been able to reflect with equanimity rather than anxiety on the achievements of a century and more of native, speech-based, and eminently functional prose.

4. Prose in the Earlier Half of the Sixteenth Century: Resurgent Scripturalism and the Stylings of Authority

At the turn from the fifteenth to the sixteenth century in England, vernacular prose yields little intimation either in its content or in its modes of expression that sweeping change would soon beset the life of the nation. Malory's *Morte Darthur*, a celebration of a vanished feudal society which held great appeal for a turn-of-the-century readership, provides the most familiar literary-historical illustration of the retrospective character of the age. But Malory was no isolated phenomenon, as the larger vogue of Englished prose romances among the early printers and their readers indicates.[1] Indeed, the sustained enterprise of translating from Latin as well as French into English, which Workman considers definitive of the fifteenth century, was to proceed unabated for the better part of three decades in the sixteenth century. Even the phenomena that are genuinely new in kind at this period fail to produce like effects in the writing of vernacular prose. The initial phase of English humanism that took shape in the illustrious circle of William Grocyn, Thomas Linacre, William Lily, John Colet, Erasmus, and Thomas More ended by infusing only a modicum of its enthusiasm for rediscovered Latin and Greek classics into the native tongue.[2] On balance, the total written output of the Englishmen (in contrast to that of Erasmus) was meager, and what they did write tended as a policy to be written in Latin, not in English. Similar conservatism attaches to the most momentous innovation of all, the printing press with movable type. The record of publications from

---

[1]The character of this vogue is illuminated by William A. Ringler, Jr.'s "A Chronological List of Long Fictional Prose Narratives in English to 1558" appended to his article, "*Beware the Cat* and the Beginnings of English Fiction," *Novel* 12 (1979): 124–26.

[2]The standard account remains Douglas Bush's *The Renaissance and English Humanism* (Toronto: University of Toronto Press, 1939). Elizabeth M. Nugent's *Thought and Culture of the English Renaissance: An Anthology of Tudor Prose, 1481–1558* (Cambridge: Cambridge University Press, 1956) admirably introduces English humanism in its beginnings through selections—including translations from Latin works—and commentary by several hands.

the first half century and more shows that Richard Pynson and Wynkyn de Worde, Caxton's successors, selected markedly more traditional works to print than Caxton himself had.[3]

The traditionalism of late fifteenth- and early sixteenth-century English printers had a double effect on the character of vernacular prose: in the first place, higher priority was accorded to religious than to secular works; in the second place, preference was shown for saints' lives and instructional and devotional treatises in long-established modes. Of the seventy-four books that Caxton saw into print between 1470 and 1490, only twenty-nine can be identified with certainty as religious works. But de Worde published thirty religious works out of a total of fifty-four in the single decade from 1490 to 1500, and this proportion remains constant in the output of his press until his death in 1535. More particularly, vernacular works on the saints—whether as subjects of hagiography or objects of devotion—immensely outnumbered all other religious publications. Mirk's *Festial*, the main English collection of pious legends and exempla, went through nineteen editions between 1483 and 1532, while its counterpart, Jacob de Voragine's *Legenda aurea*, went through seven editions between 1483 and 1527 in an enlargement containing seventy new saints' lives.[4] What is remarkable, though surely symptomatic, about the widespread popular appetite for traditional religious works at the end of the fifteenth and the beginning of the sixteenth century is the hold of the institutional Church as the ultimate and encompassing authority over human life which such works attest. The publishing record gives no evidence of the mounting anticlericalism and disillusionment with the papacy that are signaled throughout England and Europe by other sources of historical information. Various official registers—but no printed books—supply clear readings in the manifold consequences of more than a century of warring popes and contending French, Italian, and Spanish interests for control of the Holy See. In England specifically, as A. G. Dickens notes: "From about the year 1490 we hear with ever-increasing frequency of Lollard heretics and of official attempts to obliterate the sect."[5]

It is puzzling, but a fact to be reckoned with nonetheless, that English prose is so utterly silent and uninformative with regard both to religious

---

[3]See H. S. Bennett, *English Books and Readers, 1475–1557* (Cambridge: Cambridge University Press, 1952), pp. 182–93, and his handlist of de Worde's publications (pp. 239–76), and Norman F. Blake, "Wynkyn de Worde: The Early Years," *Gutenberg Jahrbuch* 46 (1971): 62–69.

[4]On the divergent audiences which Caxton's and de Worde's publishing records suggest, see Norman F. Blake, "Middle English Prose and Its Audience," *Anglia* 90 (1972): 437–55; on the character of late medieval religion, see Arthur G. Dickens, *The English Reformation* (New York: Schocken Books, 1964), pp. 1–21.

[5]Dickens, *The English Reformation*, pp. 25–26.

and to political ferment—in the latter case, the urgent need of the new royal house of Tudor to establish its authority over the entire realm on a solid financial and administrative footing. Perhaps the national sentiment bred through several decades of the Wars of the Roses and compounded by wars with France could only gravitate against engagement with the affairs of the Crown and subside into the worldweariness and *contemptus mundi* that J. W. Blench finds everywhere in late fifteenth- and early sixteenth-century vernacular sermons.[6] However one tries to rationalize or account for the situation, English prose at this era shows a steady orientation toward modes of composition that presuppose or reinforce the authority of the Church in all its traditional accoutrements: the hierarchical sway of the clergy, the elaborated sacramental and penitential systems by which spiritual jurisdiction was exercised over the laity, and the cults of the saints whose merits might be appropriated by various means to aid the soul in its moral accountability. Yet despite the traditionalism of belief, devotion, and practice displayed in vernacular religious prose, there are concomitant signs that one rather recent stylistic trend, at least, was conducing to the exercise and affirmation of ecclesiastical authority: this was the cultivation of grandiosity in expression. We have just been remarking how Caxton furthered the vogue of aureation in prose chiefly through the doublings that crowd and load his sentence forms. Manifestly, for him, the objective was to attain a maximally authoritative style deriving from the combined resources of learning and eloquence which he channeled into the proliferation of constituents for his sentences—mainly through the structure-creating operation of conjunction—until the desired mass and weight were obtained. We have also traced in the prose of Pecock as well as Caxton the effects of a systematic shift in the use of the resources of coordinate constructions which replaces the prevailing "open sentences"—intact clausal units—of vernacular composition with what Christensen calls "loaded patterns"—distensions and interruptions within a clause, which obscure its perception as a unit.[7] What we shall now proceed to consider are the developing implications in this era that "open sentences" and "loaded patterns" were understood as divergent stylistic options, and that pattern-loading, in particular, bespoke the dignity and gravity of ecclesiastical authority.

[6]J. W. Blench, *Preaching in England in the Late Fifteenth and Sixteenth Centuries: A Study of English Sermons, 1450–ca. 1600* (Oxford: Basil Blackwell, 1964), pp. 228–63.

[7]Francis Christensen, *Notes toward a New Rhetoric* (New York: Harper & Row, 1967), p. 5. J. McH. Sinclair's "arrest," "a sentence in which the onset of a predictable *alpha* [free clause] is delayed or in which its progress is interrupted" by adjunctions to its major constituents, is an essentially equivalent notion. See his "Taking a Poem to Pieces" in *Essays on Style and Language,* ed. Roger Fowler (London: Routledge & Kegan Paul, 1966), p. 72.

There is plenty of circumstantial evidence in Caxton and other turn-of-the-century prose writers for regarding open sentences and loaded patterns as alternative approaches to composition, for they do not mingle. Caxton is typical in laboring to excess the phrase structures of the sentences in his prologues and epilogues but then sustaining only his penchant for doublings in the more open sentences of his translated prose.[8] Evidently the degree of effort required to compose in the aureate manner is part of the explanation for Caxton's purple patchwork, but it is still only a part. Caxton reserves his utmost capabilities in pattern-loading for subjects and contexts that are of paramount importance, in his view, and hence in need of authoritative articulation: the supreme value of history, the superlative achievement of Chaucer, the lengths to which he has gone to acquire the best copy-text of a work, and so on. Although the division of stylistic labor between loaded patterns and open sentences remains crudely obvious in Caxton, other vernacular writers resort to aureation in the form of pattern-loading at junctures in their discourse when a potent source of imposingness and intensification requires to be tapped in the exercise of stylistic authority. But precisely because it was conceived as a resource for use in extremities, aureation tends to remain localized in short stretches of prose composition.[9]

What endows aureation with more than mere curiosity value for my purposes will perhaps become clearer from some notice of its origins. Standard literary-historical accounts agree in tracing its determined pursuit of grandiloquence to the exalted esteem in which the "colors of rhetoric" and "terms of art" were held in medieval Latinity.[10] More specific and suggestive still are the supposed origins of vernacular aureation in the *ars dictaminis:* the devices and procedures for composing official Latin letters and proclamations that had been evolved over centuries by scribes in the service of the papal Curia and the Holy Roman Empire. Such origins comport well with the types and modes of English prose in which aureation figures as an all but obligatory stylistic attribute: for example, in formal letters of address, especially dedicatory epistles and prefaces setting out the scope and intent of a work, and in high-level official decrees and regulations issued by bishops or the Crown.

---

[8]For discussion, see the introduction to *Caxton's Blanchardyn and Eglantine,* ed. Leon Kellner, Early English Text Society e.s. 58 (London: N. Trübner & Co., 1890), pp. cxii–cxiii, and Norman F. Blake, *Caxton's Own Prose* (London: André Deutsch, 1973), pp. 36–43.

[9]The rule-proving exception is the huge first half of Edward Hall's *Union of the Two Noble and Illustre Famelies of Lancastre and Yorke* (STC 12722) (London: Richard Grafton, 1548). Hall sustains aureate composition for hundreds of pages.

[10]See John M. Berdan, *Early Tudor Poetry, 1485–1547* (New York: Macmillan, 1920), pp. 139–45; J. W. H. Atkins, *English Literary Criticism: The Medieval Phase* (London: Methuen & Co., 1952), pp. 168–71; and John Conley, " 'Aureate,' A Stylistic Term," *Notes and Queries* 211 (1966): 369.

As a fashion of composition that embraced not just lexical choice but also sentence form,[11] aureation recommended itself as the means for emulating and extending into English the officialese employed by those Latin clerks who, by the standards of popes and emperors, were the most highly skilled practitioners in their day of the art of verbal majesty and authority.

As a first piece of evidence that aureate style had not merely a recognized set of mannerisms but also distinctly ecclesiastical connotations in the sixteenth century, we may consider the parody Thomas Wilson inserted in *The Arte of Rhetorique* (1553). Adept parody is an index of stylistic consciousness in any age, and Wilson's is no exception. Although he claims to be reproducing the actual text of "A letter devised by a Lincolneshire man, for a voyde benefice, to a gentleman that then waited upon the Lorde Chauncellour, for the time being," the breadth of his strokes eventually tips Wilson's hand. Absurd contrivance that it is, the letter is considerably more instructive than the treatments of aureation in latter-day literary histories because it parodies sentence forms as well as vocabulary, thus signaling the style as the joint product of lexical and syntactic elaboration. Here is the text Wilson offers:

Pondering, expending, and revoluting with my selfe, your ingent affabilitie, and ingenious capacity for mundaine affaires: I cannot but celebrate & extol your magnifical dexteritie above all other. For how could you have adepted such illustrate prerogative, and dominicall superioritie, if the fecunditie of your ingenie had not been so fertile and wonderfull pregnant. Now therefore being accersited to such splendente renoume, and dignitie splendidious: I doubt not but you will adjuvate such poore & adnichilate orphanes, as whilome ware condisciples with you, and of antique familiaritie in Lincolneshire. Among whom I being a Scholasticall panion, obtestate your sublimitie, to extoll mine infirmitie. There is a Sacerdotall dignitie in my native Countrey contiguate to me, where I now contemplate: which your worshipfull benignitie could sone impetrate for mee, if it would like you to extend your sedules, and collaude me in them to the right honourable lord Chaunceller, or rather Archgrammacian of England. You know my literature, you know the pastorall promotion, I obtestate your clemencie, to invigilate thus much for me, according to my confidence, and as you knowe my condigne merites for such a compendious living. But now I relinquish to fatigate your intelligence, with any more frivolous verbositie, and therfore he that rules the climates, be evermore your beautreur, your fortresse, and your bulwarke. *Amen.*

---

[11]The only discussion of aureation with a syntactic orientation that I know is Samuel K. Workman's "Versions by Skelton, Caxton, and Berners of a Prologue by Diodorus Siculus," *MLN* 56 (1941): 252–58. He concludes that "the most pervasive element in the aureate style—and the most vitiating—was periphrasis" (p. 256).

Dated at my Dome, or rather Mansion place in Lincolneshire, the penult of the moneth Sextile. *Anno Millimo, quillimo, trillimo.*

Per me Ioannes Octo.[12]

In the style of this mock letter, aureation gets underway with a grand syntactic flourish: the tripled conjoined participials which load the subject pronoun *I* and displace it from head position in the first sentence. Over the longer run, however, the syntax subsides typically into the serial, end-to-end progression of clauses found in asymmetric conjunction, while pattern-loading becomes the more localized function of the word pairs. These load sentential structure effectively by doubling adjectives along with nouns at a number of points, often in egregiously tautological fashion ("celebrate & extol," "fertile and wonderfull pregnant," "splendente renoume and dignitie splendidious," "poore & adnichilate"). The acuteness of Wilson's syntactic perceptions is further demonstrated in several parenthetical locutions that interrupt the sequence of main elements in the clauses in which they occur, only to supply pleonastic material; noteworthy in this connection are the two appositive *or* constructions ("the right honourable lord Chaunceller, or rather Archgrammacian of England," "my Dome, or rather Mansion place") and the conjunction "whilome ware condisciples with you, and of antique familiaritie." Although the parody is most masterful in its handling of periphrastic and suspended sentence form, the compulsion to find or coin Latinisms for dealing officially with ecclesiastical matters also figures as a defining feature of aureation that shades into disclosure of its author's religious views. Wilson, an avid Protestant publishing the *Arte* in the first year of Queen Mary's reign, represents this inept bid for spiritual preferment as a recent composition (if the dog Latin of the date means "1553") sent from the heavily Catholic north country to a courtier in Stephen Gardiner's retinue. At this date Gardiner, who had been deprived of the bishopric of Winchester under Edward but immediately reinstated and named Lord Chancellor under Mary, ranked without question as the most prominent spokesman for the old faith in England. The innuendoes connecting slavish Latinisms with Romish adherence in this letter "for a voyde benefice" are as relentless as they are devastating; aureation, as Wilson represents it, is the ridiculous jargon of papists.

Even if one grants the general accuracy of the foregoing analysis of Wilson's parody, it is still germane to inquire whether the associations

[12]Thomas Wilson, *The Arte of Rhetorique*, ed. G. H. Mair (Oxford: Clarendon Press, 1909), p. 163. Further documentation of a link between aureate style and ecclesiastical authority may be had in Sir Francis Bygod's *A Treatise concernynge Impropriations of Benefices* (STC 4240) (London: T. Godfray, 1535?).

between aureation and the exercise of ecclesiastical authority had been in force as much as fifty years earlier, when there was only one Church for Englishmen. I am confident that the following discussions of prose style in John Fisher and John Skelton will confirm that such associations were in force at least by the entry of Lutheran ideas into England (about 1517). In the absence of comparable evidence for the turn of the century, any position must necessarily be more speculative. Nonetheless, I am inclined to posit the associations for the earlier era as well since they help to provide an explanation for the otherwise unexplained fact that wholesale aureate recastings were made about 1500 of two works which had become exceptionally popular with vernacular readers in the course of the fifteenth century—Mirk's *Festial* and *The Imitation of Christ*. Regarding the appearance of these two works in aureate versions, the central place of homily and devotion in religious literature might seem to support the existence of the associations in question, were it not that homily and devotion also have durable ties with what we have been calling the simpler, more moderate tradition of prose composition. Actually, aureation is the last style we should expect to encounter at any date in these quarters. That we do encounter it nevertheless in versions of the *Festial* and *The Imitation of Christ* made about 1500 can always be dismissed as modish and ill-advised affectation. Alternatively, however, we might generalize from the analysis of word pairs at the end of chapter 3 and impute some analogous functions to the aureate style in which they figure so prominently. Under this approach it becomes possible to refer the impetus behind the aureate recastings of these two works to one or more factors of expressiveness, maximal articulation of essential values, intensity of emphasis—all means of asserting or establishing authority in stylistic terms. Perhaps, then, the tensions of the period following the Wars of the Roses and preceding the English Reformation find oblique reflection in the imposing phraseology with which vernacular prose writers continued to exercise the traditional ministry of the Church to the faithful: that is, in linguistic forms as strong as they knew how to use.

Mirk's *Festial* was revised by an unknown writer about 1483, with the result that loaded patterns (mostly in the form of doublings and catalogues) became an added feature of its predominantly asymmetric and trailing sentence forms at points of reinforcement for pious lessons. The details are often telling; for example, "mongkes come to him" becomes "There came unto this sike man a devoute and an holy preest"; and the clause "the sike is more comfortid" swells to "more comfortid, slakid, and allevyed of his payne." The writer also makes original interpolations, one of which adverts feelingly to the Wars of the Roses in a rash of loaded patterns:

Experiens sheweth that in the absence of a kyng, or ellis if a kyng be not in reputacion and favour of the peple as such a sovereyn oweth to be, oft tymes there growes and enkreses moche malice; and shortly to speke of, falshede, syn and untrewthe have than grete dominacion. For then the spoliacions, robereis, decytis, treasons, and many wronges done without correccions causeth oft tymes the peple to rebell and rise ageyn the pees, as it was like to have bene in the reeme within fewe yeres, had not Gode shewed to us of his gode grace.[13]

In the case of *The Imitation of Christ*, matter for comparison is provided by an anonymous earlier fifteenth-century translation which may be set against the one made by William Atkynson for Margaret Beaufort, countess of Richmond and Derby, the mother of Henry VII. Atkynson's heavily aureate version was printed by de Worde in 1504, thus giving appreciably greater circulation to a stylistic performance that encompassed such characteristic elaborations as this one on the *ubi sunt* theme which the period found so congenial:

Where be now all the royall poetes with theyr craftye conveyed poemes, and elegant oratours with theyr oracions garnisshed with eligancy: the philosophers with theyr pregnaunt reasons and sentences? Divers of these maner of clerkes we have knowen in oure days: but now their curiosite is passed and other men occupie their prebendes and promocions that they possessed: if they were here now agayne, I suppose they wolde never labour so busily for curiosite in knowlege ne temporall promocyons. . . . O howe many in maner of every state perisshith in this worlde by vayne glory that more desyre to plese pry018nces and prelates and other patrons for a temporall promocyon than truly and inwardly to serve God for the promocions eternall.

The earlier English translation—which, as the editor of the two versions notes, is far more faithful to à Kempis's original—gives this rendering of the same passage:

Telle me now, where are the lordes and maistres that thou knewist somtyme, whiles thei lyved and florished in scoles? Now othir men have her prebendes, and I wote not whethir thei ones thenke upon hem. In her lyves somewhat thei apperid; and now of hem spekith almost no man. O lorde, how sone passith the glory of this worlde. . . . How many ben there that perisshith in this worlde by veyn konnyng, that litel recchith of the service of God.[14]

Syntactically, Atkynson's aureation displays the loaded patterning that creates a now familiar contrast with the more open sentence of the earlier

[13]These quotations from the unpublished revision contained in two British Library manuscripts, Harl. 2247 and Roy. 18.B.XXV, are given in Lilian B. Steckman, "A Late Fifteenth-Century Revision of Mirk's *Festial*," *SP* 34 (1936): 38, 43.

[14]*The Earliest English Translation of . . . De Imitatione Christi . . . Also the Earliest Printed Translation*, ed. John K. Ingram, Early English Text Society e.s. 63 (London: Kegan Paul, Trench, Trübner, 1893), pp. xxiv, xxv. On the popularity of the *ubi sunt* theme, see Blench, *Preaching in England in the Late Fifteenth and Sixteenth Centuries*, pp. 228–35.

anonymous translation, although it is interesting to observe that word pairs are a principal feature of both styles. The sharpest difference between the simpler and the aureate version consists in the comparative closeness of the anonymous writer to actual speech. The direct address ("Telle me now," "that thou knewist somtyme") and the expletive ("O lorde") find no counterparts in Atkynson. The anonymous writer even invokes the act of speaking ("and now of hem spekith almost no man"), another detail that the aureate version significantly lacks. Instead Atkynson pontificates at the corresponding juncture, where he takes it upon himself to speak *for* the persons in question: "If they were here now agayne, I suppose they wolde never labour so busily for curiosite in knowlege ne temporall promocyons." Overall in employing the aureate manner Atkynson eschews any idiomatic or colloquial phrasing along with any suggestion of familiarity in the stance adopted toward his reader, presumably so as not to undercut the imposing, authoritative presentation which this mode of composition fosters. Therefore only the anonymous writer can admit, "I wote not whethir. . . ." Atkynson is constrained to pronounce for himself and his reader—or perhaps only for himself, if he is here appropriating the "plural of majesty": "Divers of these maner of clerkes we have knowen in oure days."

The turn from the fifteenth to the sixteenth century in England was not conspicuous for its output of original vernacular prose, whether religious or secular. A rule-proving exception, however, emerges in John Fisher, bishop of Rochester, whose prominence as an ecclesiastic ranked second only to that of Wolsey after his rise to power. Fisher's English sermons establish him not only as the most distinguished preacher in the realm and a uniquely prolific writer and publisher, but they also provide strong confirmation for the associations I have been proposing between aureation and authoritative utterance on the Church's behalf. His major production, initially delivered as a series of sermons, was the prolix *Treatyse concernynge the fruytful saynges of Davyd the kynge & prophete in the seven penytencyall psalmes*. Despite (or because of) its prolixity, Fisher's *Treatyse* became a popular favorite, going through seven editions between 1508 and 1555. A sense of its appeal can still be gathered from the assurance projected in the work that a tirelessly conscientious pastor has the state of one's soul under minute review and knows how to prescribe for it. Fisher achieves this effect by laboring verse by verse through the Vulgate text of each penitential Psalm. There is a kind of phatic continuum set up by the asymmetrically conjoined clauses and phrases and by the sentential relative constructions that are Fisher's staples of composition. When he expounds a text, his profuse word pairs—many of them synonymous or near-synonymous—seem to usurp all possibility of additional or alternative meaning; when he applies a text, his barrages of pleonastic correlatives enforce the consolatory likenesses between the Psalmist and every Christian soul. Here is a typical progression (in which, to facilitate the reader's course, pleonastic correlation is italicized):

Whiche of us now that were seke in ony parte of his body beynge in Jeopardye of deth, wolde not dylygently *serche for a medycyne wherwyth he myght be heled, and fyrst make inquysycyon of hym that had the same sekenesse before,* and wolde we not also put very trust & *hope to have remedy of our dysease by that medycyne wherby lyke maner sekenes & dyseases were cured before.* Sooth we now therfore have herde tell for a trouth *how gretely seke and dyseased* this prophete *Davyd was,* not with sekenes of his body, but of his soule, *and also with what medycyne he was cured and made hole. Let us* take hede and *use the same whan we be seke in lyke maner as he was by our synnes* shortely to be cured, *for he was a synner as we be, but* he dyde holsome penaunce and made this holy psalme wherby *he* gate forgyvenes and *was restored to his soules helth.*[15]

The foregoing is representative of Fisher's style in affective address. Although pleonastic and rhetorical in its deployment of doublings, this is not in itself an aureate manner; the *Treatise on the Penitential Psalms* reserves aureation, significantly, for use in Englishing Scripture. Not every text elicits such treatment, but the ones which advance Fisher's doctrinal and devotional purposes and which promise to advance them even further if elaborated are the ones which duly receive aureate paraphrases. For example:

Davyd sayth *Multa flagella peccatoris.* Many dyvers and grevous punysshementes be for the obstynate & harde herted synner that never wyll be penytent.

Therfore the prophete sayth *Quoniam lumbi mei impleti sunt illusionibus.* The partes of my flesshe wherin the nourysshynge of flesshely volupty be resydent & abydynge are replete & fulfylled with mockes & scornes.[16]

What may be observed repeatedly in Fisher's handling of Scripture is a process very similar in some ways to the authorial intrusiveness exhibited by Love a century earlier in his *Myrrour.* Both clerics, professing the best of pastoral intentions toward a broad English readership, manifestly feel compelled to function as intermediaries between that readership and Scripture in the native tongue. To judge from their proceedings, the Bible is unsuitable for straightforward transmission, and the problem they perceive, interestingly enough, seems less to be one of difficulty or profundity than of inexplicitness. Love's interpolations, as we have seen, operate to heighten the concreteness, immediacy, and affective

---

[15]*The English Works of John Fisher, Bishop of Rochester,* ed. John E. B. Mayor, Early English Text Society e.s. 27 (London: N. Trübner & Co., 1876), Part I, p. 7. For discussion of the transitional character of Fisher's conceptions and style, see Thomas M. C. Lawler, "Fruitful Business: Medieval and Renaissance Elements in the Devotional Method of St. John Fisher," *Medievalia et Humanistica,* n.s. 4 (1973): 145–59.

[16]*English Works of John Fisher,* ed. Mayor, pp. 41, 64.

impact of what passes with him as too bald a narrative mode in the Gospels. We can feel reasonably assured about such an inference, because Love's syntax runs so consistently to parenthetical and nonrestrictive insertions in his sentences. What he inserts presumably indicates what he found lacking in the original. By contrast there are no such uniform syntactic clues for tracing a relation beween the phrasing of Scripture and the morass of Fisher's doublings and expatiations. At different points the relation varies a good deal between close and free paraphrase of the Vulgate Latin; it is not a relation which an unlearned person could intuit, let alone verify. Hence Fisher's aureate handling of Scripture in English constitutes a major appropriation and exercise of verbal authority in the name of the Church. It is very much a late pre-Reformation Church, too, that is refracted in Fisher's *Treatyse:* bit by bit his "saynt" David works through the stages of penance—contrition, confession, satisfaction—in order to shorten "the pangs of purgatorye" whose existence is asserted to have Scriptural warrant.

Another revealing aspect of the style of Fisher's English sermons consists in the extension of aureation and loaded patterns from the enforcement of ecclesiastical authority, which I take to be its primary function in prose of this period, to contexts where the dominant connection appears to be with temporal authority. In 1509 one such context was provided by the funeral of Henry VII, which happened to coincide with the first month's anniversary of the death of the king's mother, Margaret Beaufort. Fisher was commissioned to preach the king's funeral sermon. The heavily embellished and loaded sentence cited below develops an interesting dual perspective according to which Henry's public image of worldliness as a monarch is offset by Fisher's own testimony to the otherworldliness displayed by the late king in the midst of "these worldly pleasures":

Thyrdely touching these worldly pleasures wherin men set grete parte of theyr comforte bothe in body & soule, he had than full lytell comforte or pleasure in them but rather dyscomforte & sorowe, al his goodly houses so rychely dekte & appareyled, his walles & galaryes of grete pleasure, his gardyns large & wyde with knottes curyously wrought, his orcheyardes set with vines & trees most dilicate, his mervaylous rychesse & treasour, his metes & drynkes were they never so dilycately prepared might not than helpe hym, but rather were paynfull to hym, so moche that longe before his deth his mete was to hym so lothsome (were it never so dilycately prepayred) that many a tyme he sayd, but onely to folowe counseyle he wold not for all this world receyve it, wherin he well perceyved the myseryes of this wretched worlde.[17]

The surging thrusts of the recursively multiplied *NP*s in this sentence seem, from their contents, to be just so many detriments on the king's

---

[17]Ibid., p. 278.

way to the kingdom of heaven, but as Fisher marshals and transmutes them from creaturely delights to spiritual goads, his verbal authority reaches imperturbable assurance: Henry, we are given to know, is with God.

A work of paramount importance in confirming Fisher as a stylist and an authoritative figure in Church and State is the public sermon which Wolsey commissioned and subsequently ordered printed under the explanatory title, *A Sermon . . . made agayn the pernicyous doctryn of Martin luuther . . . by the assignement of the moost reverend father in god the lord Thomas Cardinall of Yorke & Legate ex latere from our holy father the pope* (1521). In making the first public response in English to the gathering forces of the Reformation, Fisher relied on his expertise in the equally traditional modes of allegory and aureation. Since allegory—to say nothing of aureation—would soon be denied any role in establishing doctrine, Fisher's imperturbability is remarkable as he claims to refute the Lutheran doctrine of justification by faith on analogy with the ways trees cooperate with the sun in bringing forth their "leves & floures" after the seeming dead of winter:

This example yf ye perceyve it maye enduce us to conceyve how wonderfully the spyrytuall sonne almyghty god worketh by his spyrytuall and invysyple bemes of his lyght spred upon the soule of man or upon the chyrche, both whiche is called in scrypture a spyrytuall erthe. *Dominus dabit benignitatem et terra nostra dabit fructum suum,* that is to saye, our lorde shall gyve his gracyous influence and our erthe shal yelde fruytfull workes. The bemes of almyghty god spred upon our soules quyckeneth them & causeth this lyfe in us and the fruyte of good workes. Fyrst they cause the lyght of faythe but this is a veray sklender & weke lyght withouten the reboundynge of hope and the hete of charite. . . . Have a man never so moche lyght of faythe onlesse he have also this hete of charyte sterynge his soule and bryngyng forthe lyfely workes he is but a deed stock & as a tree withouten lyfe. For as I sayd, though the naturall sonne shyne never so bryght upon a tree, yf this tree have in it no grenenes nor puttynge forthe of buddes & lefes this tree is not alyve.

But now to what purpose serveth this instruccyon? To this, it subverteth one grete grounde of Martyn luther, which is this, that fayth alone withouten workes doth Justifye a synner, upon the whiche ground he byldeth many other erroneous artycles & specyally that the sacramentes of Christes holy Chirche dothe not Justyfye but onely faythe.[18]

If Fisher's employment of aureation in combination with loaded patterns can be taken as representative of the functions and associations of these features of prose style in the opening decades of the sixteenth century—a move sanctioned, in my opinion, by his unparalleled status and productivity as an original writer at this era in the vernacular—then

---

[18]Ibid., pp. 324, 326–27.

the very range of application which these features receive in his English sermons supplies presumptive confirmation that the enforcement of ecclesiastical authority is, indeed, primary at this time. By contrast, aureation and loaded patterns serve the ends of secular authority only in extremely restricted contexts in early sixteenth-century prose: the contexts of formal letters, prefaces, and proclamations. But, further, if the ecclesiastical associations are primary, it ought to be possible to find instances of aureation and loaded patterning in secular contexts that bespeak their connection with the primary set of associations and do so by revealing themselves as essentially dependent developments, offshoots. The possibility is all the greater if Héraucourt is right that word pairs, the largest component in aureation and loaded patternings, reflect the universe of values operative in a style and work (see the third section of chapter 3). Although I cannot claim to have inquired exhaustively, I have discovered a fair number of explicit connections with ecclesiastical or religious authority in the secular applications of aureation and loaded patterning made by writers of the early sixteenth century. Excerpts from a pair of prefaces will illustrate. The first is from Henry Watson's preface to his translation of Sebastian Brant's *Ship of Fools* (1509):

> To the honour of the ryght hye and ryght sacred trynyte/ fader/ sone/ and holy ghost in one essence/ and of the ryght gloryous moder of god/ and of all the sayntes of paradyse I have begon to make this translacyon for to exhorte the poore humaynes the whiche by imbesylytes & pusyllanimytes/ have ensued the fooles of this presente worlde/ & theyr werkes. And to the ende that they may eschewe al mondanytes and folyes/ I praye them that they have regarde unto this present booke/ and that they comprehende the substaunce/ to the ende that they maye wysely governe themselfe in the tyme to come/ and that thorugh theyr labour they may be of the nombre of the saved.[19]

The second illustration comes from the opening of Lord Berners's preface to his translation of Froissart's *Chronicles* (1523):

> What condygne graces and thankes ought men to gyve to the writers of historyes, who with their great labours have done so moche profyte to the humayne lyfe? They shewe, open, manifest and declare to the reder, by example of olde antyquite, what we shulde enquere, desyre, and folowe; and also what we shulde eschewe, avoyde, and utterly flye: for whan we beynge unexpert of chaunces se, beholde, and rede the auncyent actes, gestes, and dedes, howe and with what labours, daungers, and paryls they were gested and done, they right greatly admonesh, ensigne, and teche us howe we maye lede forthe our lyves. . . . Wherfore I say that historie may well be called a divyne provydence; for as the

---

[19] Henry Watson, "Prologue of the Translatour," *The Shyppe of Fooles* (STC 3547) (London: Wynkyn de Worde, 1509), sigs. Ai^v–Aii^r; modern-spelling text in Nugent, *Thought and Culture of the English Renaissance*, p. 43.

celestyall bodyes above complecte all and at every tyme the universall worlde, the creatures therin conteyned, and all their dedes, semblably so dothe history.[20]

To conclude this discussion of aureation and loaded patterns and to substantiate further the interpretation I have been proposing for these two features of style, I turn to consider John Skelton's curious *Replycacion agaynst Certayne Yong Scolers Abjured of Late* (1528). A twofold enterprise is discernible in the *Replycacion*, described by its author as a "lytell pamphilet . . . canonically prepensed, professed, and with good delyberacion made." Skelton first reviles Thomas Arthur and Thomas Bilney, two Cambridge scholars recently arraigned for heresy, who had abjured their preaching against pilgrimages and the veneration of images. Undeterred by their abjuration, Skelton addresses himself to rectifying Bilney's and Arthur's presumed inattention to the Thomistic distinctions of *latria, dulia,* and *hyperdulia,* which would have prevented them from identifying images with idols. Invoking his credentials as rector of Diss in Norfolk and as a "laureate poete," Skelton explicitly puts himself forward in this work as a spokesman for the Church against heresy. The latter and major part of the *Replycacion* is written in Skeltonic meter. Prior to the Skeltonics, however, the work displays remarkable stylistic instability: once launched in aureate prose, it makes a temporary transition to verse, and then resumes for a stretch in aureate prose before reverting again to verse. The transitional section develops as follows:

Howe yong scolers nowe a dayes enboldned with the flyblowen blast of the moche vayne glorious pipplyng wynde, whan they have delectably lycked a lytell of the lycorous electuary of lusty lernyng, in the moche studious scolehous of scrupulous Philology, countyng them selfe clerkes excellently enformed and transformed and transcendingly sped in moche high connyng, . . .

Than forthwith by and by
They tumble so in theology,
Drowned in dregges of divinite,
That they juge them selfe able to be
Doctours of the chayre in the Vyntre
At the Thre Cranes,
To magnifye their names:
But madly it frames,
For all that they preche and teche
Is farther than their wytte wyll reche.
Thus by demeryttes of their abusyon,
Finally they fall to carefull confusyon,
To beare a fagot, or to be enflamed:
Thus are they undone and utterly shamed.

---

[20]"The Preface of Johan Bourchier, Knyght, Lord Berners, Translatour," in *The Chronicle of Froissart,* ed. William E. Henley, Tudor Translations, 1st ser., no. 27 (London: David Nutt, 1901), I, 3.

Over this, for a more ample processe to be farther delated and contynued, and of every true christenman laudably to be employed, justifyed, and constantly mainteyned; as touchyng the tetrycall theologisacion of these demy divines, and Stoicall studiantes, . . . they were but febly enformed in maister Porphiris problemes, and have waded but weakly in his thre maner of clerkly workes, analeticall, topicall, and logicall: howbeit they were puffed so full of vaynglorious pompe and surcudant elacyon, that popholy and pevysshe presumpcion provoked them to publysshe and to preche to people imprudent perilously, howe it was idolatry to offre to ymages of our blessed lady, or to pray and go on pylgrimages, or to make oblacions to any ymages of sayntes in churches or els where.[21]

What I find significant in the foregoing passage is the fact that so intensely self-conscious a stylist as Skelton should undertake to reprove heresy in English with prose sentence forms conspicuous for their loaded patterns and aureation. His choice of means tells in favor of the argument I have been making about the associations obtaining between these features of style in that era and the production of authoritative ecclesiastical utterance. Rainer Pineas has remarked upon another salient consideration: the unmistakable implication conveyed by Skelton in his dedicatory preface that his old nemesis, Cardinal Wolsey, had requested the *Replycacion* of him.[22] Thus we are led to believe that Skelton had been expressly charged with authority to declare authoritatively for the Church. Notwithstanding his charge and his credentials, however, Skelton has trouble settling into the appropriate mode of composition and, once he does, he deploys it improperly. He vituperates, turning the aureation and loaded patterns of the style back on themselves in derisive jingles and mocking echoes, forfeiting all possibility of gravity and grandiloquence. On the evidence of the opening of *A Replycacion*, Skelton was incapable of practicing the ecclesiastically authoritative style in English prose of that era without subverting it. That the prose is replaced by Skeltonic verse would seem once again to bespeak the author's literary self-consciousness: he elects not to continue working in a medium which he was simultaneously working against. For in so doing, obviously, he was working against himself.

Pineas, who has researched extensively in the religious polemic that ushered Reformation ideas into England, is inclined to find still more significance in Skelton's *Replycacion* for the history of sixteenth-century vernacular prose. He hypothesizes that Wolsey's dissatisfaction with Skelton prompted the now famous Latin letter of 1528 to Thomas More: a tribute to More's superlative learning and abilities compounded with

---

[21]*A Replycacion* in *The Poetical Works of John Skelton*, ed. Alexander Dyce (London: Thomas Rodd, 1843), I, 207–9.

[22]Rainer Pineas, *Thomas More and Tudor Polemics* (Bloomington: Indiana University Press, 1968), pp. 38–39.

a charge to assume the defense of the Church and faith of Rome against the Reformers in the native tongue. In the absence of known evidence either for or against Pineas's hypothesis it is impossible to pronounce more certainly on Wolsey's motivation, but the fact of his charge to More remains one of the most momentous developments in this period for a study of the associations between the exercise of ecclesiastical authority and the resources of vernacular style. More's first response to Wolsey's charge was the work now commonly called the *Dialogue concerning Heresies* (1529). Its original title, however, specifies the "dyvers maters treatyd": "The veneracyon & worshyp of ymagys & relyques/ prayng to sayntis/ & goynge on pylgrymage/ wyth many othere thyngys touchyng the pestylent secte of Luther & Tyndale/ by the tone bygone in Saxony, and by the tother laboryd to be brought in to Englond."[23] In the light of Pineas's hypothesis, this listing reads as putative confirmation that More began where Skelton left off as a polemicist, with the issues raised by the Arthur and Bilney cases. In fact, however, the text belies the title, for the continuing preoccupation of More's *Dialogue concerning Heresies* is William Tyndale's English New Testament and his attendant vernacular writings. Wolsey's charge to More, therefore, is surely to be seen as a momentous development, but one made defensively in reaction to a greater development still. The appearance of Tyndale as translator and author on the English scene marks the onset of what, despite Wycliffite beginnings, registered in that era as a radically new view of religious authority and a radically altered set of conceptions and approaches regarding the exercise of religious authority in prose. In keeping with the magnitude of their respective importance as vernacular writers, the next two sections of chapter 4 are given over to consideration of Tyndale first, then of More, as exponents of rival influences that proved determinative for the future course of stylistic developments in early modern English prose.

TYNDALE'S SCRIPTURALISM

Both the guiding concerns of this study and the eventual course of English history make it inevitable that Tyndale and his work be accorded a pivotal position, for it was with him that vernacular Scripturalism achieved its ultimately enduring reappearance within English life and letters. During the brief decade of Tyndale's literary activity, however, there was no reason whatever to suppose that the main thing he was doing was readying a text of which nine-tenths would come down in successive authorized editions as, quite simply, the Bible in English.

[23]Cited from the title page of the first (1529) edition of More's *A Dyaloge* (STC 18084).

Although two years, only, would intervene between his burning as a heretic in Flanders, where he had gone in the hope of finding a safe place to work, and Henry VIII's granting of a license for an official English Bible (which incorporated all the translating that had been finished), no authorization of any kind attached to Tyndale's enterprise while he lived. On the contrary, his chief contemporary opponents—Cuthbert Tunstal, then the bishop of London, and Thomas More—found Tyndale doubly opprobrious as a heretic and a traitor, for they imputed his Scripturalism to a foreign source of contagion: Luther. Since Tyndale did come under the influence of Lutheran theology after removing to the Continent in 1524, decisive questions about the provenance of the convictions on which he acted continue to draw debate. We are in no doubt about the Englishness of Tyndale's literary sensibility.[24] But the Englishness of his dedication to translating the Bible into the native tongue is still in the process of being confirmed by a mounting body of evidence and interpretation.

Until fairly recently, historians have tended to shy away from the question of continuity between Lollardy and the onset of the English Reformation. A. G. Dickens, a leading figure in the move to address the question, has declared as follows on "the distribution and nature of heresy in early Tudor England": "That its inspiration was overwhelmingly Wycliffe, at least until about 1530, would not for a moment be disputed by anyone who read the original texts and who had even an elementary acquaintance with earlier Lollard processes."[25] By far the most crucial factor conducing toward continuity, as Deanesly's work has shown, was the configuration of circumstances that made England a case unparalleled by any other Western European country with respect to a vernacular Bible. The challenge to ecclesiastical authority mounted by Wyclif and his associates, and perpetuated in an underground Lollard movement through the fifteenth century, came to a head in an acutely polarized situation focusing on Scripture as the central issue. Anxious, resistant churchmen faced a pertinacious lay desire both to have the forbidden knowledge of God's Word in English and to know why such

---

[24]The following trio of pronouncements is indicative. "Tyndale is the man to whom, above all other, the literary merit of the English Bible is due, because he impressed upon his translation his own character of simplicity, strength, and truth"—R. W. Chambers, "Tyndale and Our Bible: The English Prose Tradition," *TLS* 3 October 1936, pp. 773–74, rptd. *Man's Unconquerable Mind* (London: Jonathan Cape, 1939), pp. 200–201; "Tyndale did more than anyone else to firm up a simple, all-purpose prose style"—Simeon Potter, *Our Language* (Harmondsworth: Penguin Books, 1950), p. 53; "Clerics, as scholars, would normally have written treatises in Latin. . . . Without Christianity and Biblical translators like Tyndale, English would have been a different instrument from what it became"—A. C. Partridge, *Tudor to Augustan English* (London: André Deutsch, 1969), p. 15.

[25]Dickens, *The English Reformation*, p. 27; cf. Margaret Aston, "John Wycliffe's Reformation Reputation," *Past and Present* 30 (1965): 23–51.

a thing remained forbidden in England when, by the turn into the six-teenth century, vernacular Bibles were being circulated and printed in increasing numbers on the Continent.[26] The "original texts" in which Dickens grounds his certainty of a sustained protest movement uniting the Scripturalism of the later fourteenth century with the Scripturalism of the earlier sixteenth do, indeed, afford striking correspondences, as we find in comparing relevant passages in Wyclif's English sermons or the treatise on the Pater Noster with Tyndale's epistle "To the Reader" prefacing *The Obedience of a Christian Man* (1528). Differences of articu-lation aside, the convictions, the protestations, the recriminations stay fixed over a dozen or more decades.

To Tyndale, quite as much as to Wyclif, opposition to vernacular Scrip-ture was the work of Antichrist and his adherents. Thus Tyndale actually argues for the authenticity of Scripture as "the true worde of God: which worde is ever hated of the worlde, neyther was ever without persecu-tion" because the authorities have forbidden Scripture in English "on payne of life and goods, or . . . made breaking of the kinges peace, or treason unto his highnesse to read the worde of thy soules health." Tyndale's "To the Reader" also adduces the same reasons as the treatise on the Pater Noster why "the scripture ought to be in the mother tounge":

First God gave the children of Israell a law by the hande of Moses, in their mother tounge, and all the prophetes wrote in theyr mother tounge, and all the Psalmes were in the mother tounge. . . . Christ commaundeth to search the scriptures. John 5. Though that miracles bare recorde unto hys doctrine, yet desired he no fayth to be geven eyther unto hys doctrine, or unto hys miracles, without recorde of the scripture. When Paule preached. Act. 17. the other searched the scriptures dayly, whether they were as he alleaged them. Why shal I not likewise see, whether it be the scripture that thou alleagest: yea, why shall I not see, . . . whether thou be about to teache me, or to disceave me.

The Sermons which thou readest in the Actes of the Apostles, and all that the Apostles preached, were no doubt preached in the mother tounge. Why then might they not be written in the mother tounge? As if one of us preach a good sermon, why may it not be written? Saint Hierome also translated the Bible into his mother tounge: Why may not we also?

If the Scripture were in the mother tounge, they will say, then would the lay people understande it, every man after his owne wayes. Wherfore serveth the Curate, but to teach hem the right way? Wherfore were the holy dayes made, but that the people shoulde come and learne? Are yee not abhominable schole-maisters, in that ye take so great wages if ye will not teach? If ye would teach, how could ye do it so well, and with so great profite, as when the lay people have the scripture before them in theyr mother tounge?

[26]Margaret Deanesly, *The Lollard Bible and Other Medieval Biblical Versions* (Cambridge: Cambridge University Press, 1920), pp. 351–53; cf. John A. F. Thomson, *The Later Lollards, 1414–1520* (London: Oxford University Press, 1965).

Furthermore, Tyndale reflects the full breadth of the Wycliffite Scripturalist program in the sturdy confidence he shares with Purvey regarding the superiority of English over Latin as a linguistic medium for the transmission of God's Word to the people:

They will say it cannot be translated into our tounge it is so rude. It is not so rude as they are false lyers. For the Greeke tounge agreeth more wyth the Englishe, then wyth the Latin. And the properties of the Hebrue tounge agreeth a thousand tymes more wyth the Englishe, then wyth the Latyn. The maner of speaking is both one, so that in a thousand places thou needest not but to translate it into the English, worde for worde, when thou must seeke a compasse in the Latin, and yet shalt have much worke to translate it welfavouredly, so that it have the same grace & sweetnesse, sence & pure understanding with it in the Latin, & as it hath in the Hebrue. A thousand partes better maye it be translated into the English, then into the Latin.[27]

Notwithstanding the demonstrable ties that bind Tyndale to the indigenous thought heritage of Lollardy, the Englishness of his Scripturalism is also to be traced in more contemporary contacts and experiences. Notably, he was in the right place at the right time to encounter the vanguard of the English Reformation movement in the universities. Having proceeded B.A. and M.A. at Oxford by 1515, he moved to Cambridge (perhaps attracted by the prospect of studying Greek) and stayed for approximately three years. He had certainly left by 1521.[28] While there is no evidence that Tyndale was in Cambridge while Erasmus taught Greek there from 1511 to 1514, it is beyond question that Tyndale's stay coincided with the height of Erasmus's influence in Cambridge in the three years following the publication of his Greek-Latin New Testament at Basel in 1516. Against such a backdrop, it becomes the more significant that Tyndale repeatedly cites the precedent of Erasmus to support his own arguments for the Bible in English. For example, the epistle "To the Reader" just quoted ends by alleging "A thousand reasons moe might be made (as thou mayst see in Paraclesis Erasmi, & in his preface to the paraphrasis of Matthew)."[29] Although the English translation of the *Paraclesis*, which appeared in 1529, is regarded as the work of William

---

[27]"To the Reader," *The Obedience of a Christen Man*, in *The Whole Workes of William Tyndall, John Frith, and Docter Barnes* (STC 24436) (London: John Daye, 1573), fols. 101, 102, 104. For these passages in modern spelling, see *Doctrinal Treatises, and Introductions to Different Portions of the Holy Scriptures, by William Tyndale*, ed. Henry Walter, Parker Society vol. 43 (Cambridge: Cambridge University Press, 1848), pp. 131, 144–47, 160–61.

[28]For discussion of biographical probabilities in this obscure period, see C. H. Williams, *William Tyndale* (London: Thomas Nelson & Sons, 1969), pp. 3–8.

[29]Tyndale, *Whole Workes*, fol. 104; modern-spelling text in Parker Society vol. 43, pp. 161–62. On Erasmus's opinions regarding vernacular Scripture, see Craig R. Thompson, "Scripture for the Ploughboy and Some Others," *Studies in the Continental Background of Renaissance English Literature: Essays Presented to John L. Lievsay*, ed. Dale B. J. Randall and George Walton Williams (Durham, N.C.: Duke University Press, 1977), pp. 3–28.

Roye, Tyndale's assistant on the first edition of the English New Testament, nevertheless the famous envisaging of a Bible-conversant laity of ploughboys, weavers, and wayfarers contained in this work had a profound impact on Tyndale's mind. His Erasmianism, indeed, demonstrated its strength as a literary impetus in this formative period, for Tyndale Englished the *Enchiridion militis Christiani* in 1521–22 to clarify his convictions for Sir John and Lady Walsh in whose household he was employed after leaving Cambridge.[30]

The verve and resolve brought by Erasmus to the enterprise of recovering the literature of antiquity and, above all, the original text of Scripture through arduous study of the ancient tongues became mainly though not only an inspiration to Englishmen, for it was their country that felt his full personal influence as a scholar. No other quarter than that of Erasmus, the charismatic advocate of philological scholarship, can be looked to for the spark that ignited Tyndale's zeal to master Greek and Hebrew in preparation for translating the Bible into English. Thus there is interesting testimony to the sustaining force of his Erasmianism to be found in a play on nomenclature which Tyndale made near the midpoint of his brief career as a translator and writer. Noting that his opponents try to discredit his work by branding it "new learning"—that is, heresy—Tyndale proposes to embrace the term as a badge of honor. His response to his opponents is Erasmian in two ways: first, in his frank owning to the charge of innovation, and, second, in his insistence that its connotations are necessarily positive. His efforts must be understood, Tyndale says, in relation to late successes in restoring God's Word from the accretions and distortions of centuries, so that it can truly be learned anew. As Allan G. Chester has shown, these affinities between Tyndale's thought and Erasmus's have been aptly (if unwittingly) reinforced by the appropriation of the term "new learning" in the nineteenth century to serve as a synonym for the "revival of learning," which was the rallying cry of Renaissance humanism.[31]

Yet, while the stamp set by Erasmus's influence on Tyndale's scholarly and programmatic outlook was deep and genuine, the gap between the two men could not have been wider in two vital matters: the use of the vernacular and the style for rendering Scripture into another tongue. Erasmus, as is well known, wrote and by preference spoke only Latin of a studiedly elegant kind. As a philologist he produced a text of the

[30]Foxe's life of Tyndale in *Acts and Monuments* is the source for this information. On the *Enchiridion* as the distillation of Erasmus's unique blend of humanism and reform which more greatly influenced the early English Reformers than any other of his works, see James K. McConica, *English Humanists and Reformation Politics* (Oxford: Clarendon Press, 1965), pp. 17–22.

[31]See, further, Allan G. Chester's important essay, "The 'New Learning': A Semantic Note," *Studies in the Renaissance* 2 (1955): 139–47.

Greek New Testament and a Latin parallel version that were major critical advances of the day, but as a stylist he was anything but a Scripturalist in the sense in which I have defined the term. Erasmus's procedure as a stylist exhibits an exactly inverse motive in his voluminous Latin *Paraphrase upon the New Testament* (1535); he reworks the language of the Gospels and Epistles to accord with the elegant variation and circumlocution which his immensely influential textbook, *De duplici copia verborum ac rerum* (1513), had promoted as the basis of all good literary composition. Since Erasmus's *Paraphrase* was Englished in 1548–49 by a team of translators including such able men as Nicholas Udall, Thomas Caius, and Miles Coverdale, it is fortunately possible to document the great stylistic contrast between this faithful and near-contemporary version of Erasmus and a corresponding selection from Tyndale's work both as translator and as expositor of Scripture. For this threefold comparison, I have chosen a short passage from the Sermon on the Mount (Matthew 6:32–33), which reads as follows in Tyndale's translation: "For youre hevenly father knoweth that ye have neade of all these thynges. But rather seke ye fyrst the kyngdome of heven and the rightwisnes therof/ and all these thynges shalbe ministred unto you."[32] Here, next, is the English of Erasmus's *Paraphrase* on this verse and a half:

Emong men, who is so wicked a father, that wil not provide for his children thynges necessary for the sustentation of their life? Ye have a father so riche, so bounteful, so circumspect, that he is sufficient for al, to enriche all, and leve nothing unprovided for, be it never so litill or vile. And feare ye that he wil not provide for his children these thynges, without the whiche they can not lyve? Lay this carefulnes upon him, he knoweth wel that ye have nede of al these thinges: and he is not so harde that he wil withdrawe thynges necessary from such as be occupied in his busines. . . . For your matters are greater than that the carefulnes of light, trifelyng, & corruptible thinges should withdrawe you from them. Let your chefe care be aboute that good thyng, in comparison of the whiche, these worldly thynges be of no value nor reputacion. The kyngdom of god must be set up, that is to say, the doctrine of the gospell, by the which we attayne unto the heavenly inheritaunce. Wherof I have chosen you to be the preachers and setters furth, & have showed you what excellent vertues be nedeful to the doyng of this thyng: whyche, because they be the chyefe and hyghest, cum not unto you from youre father withoute your diligence and carefulnes: but ye must fyrst & chyefely seke for them. The other smaller thinges whyche pertayne unto the necessitie of this lyfe, the good and gracious father wyll cast unto you as an augmentation, & that of his owne accorde, wythoute any carefulnes on youre behalfe: that for both causes ye shoulde render thankes unto hys bountefulnes, bothe because he hath geven you those high & chefe

[32]William Tyndale, *An Exposition uppon the v. vi. vii. Chapters of Mathew,* in *Whole Workes,* fol. 235; modern-spelling text in *Expositions and Notes on Sundry Portions of Holy Scriptures, Together with "The Practice of Prelates," by William Tyndale,* ed. Henry Walter, Parker Society vol. 44 (Cambridge: Cambridge University Press, 1849), p. 108.

thinges, you endevoryng unto the same: and also because he hath cast unto you these thynges, without any carefulnes on your behalfe.[33]

And here, finally, is Tyndale's *Exposition upon the 5. 6. 7. Chapters of Matthew* (1532) on the same verse and a half:

The kyngdome of God, is the Gospel and doctrine of Christ: and the righteousnesse therof, is to beleve in Christes bloud for the remission of sinnes. Out of which righteousness springeth love to God, & thy neighbour for his sake, which is also righteousnesse as I have sayd afore, so farre as it is perfect, and that which lacketh is supplied by faith in Gods word, for he hath promised to accept that, til more come. Then foloweth the outward righteousnesse of workes, by the which, and diligent recording of Gods word together, we grow and waxe perfect and keepe our selves from goyng backe and losyng the spirite agayne. And these have our spiritualtie with their corrupt doctrine myngled together: that is to say, the righteousnes of the kyngdome of God, which is fayth in Christs bloud: & the outward righteousnes of the members, that we ascribe to the one that pertaineth to the other. Seke the kingdome of heaven therfore and the righteousnesse of the same, and be sure thou shalt ever have sufficient, and these thynges shalbe ministered unto the: that is to say, shall come of their owne accord by the promise of God, yea, Christ promiseth thee an hundredfolde even in this life, of all that thou leavest for his sake.[34]

The stylistic contrast between Erasmus's *Paraphrase* and Tyndale's *Exposition* turns on divergent conceptions of what God's Word conveys and what its implications are for human uses of language. To Erasmus the text spells encouragement; it does not so much speak as elicit a response in terms of a sanguine psychology of spiritual effort: God is so bountiful, and man so well endowed with the capacity both to live as God wills and to avail himself of God's goodness, that the injunction against worldliness in the text becomes transmuted into a series of almost unctuous promptings: "Ye have a father so riche, so bounteful, so circumspect. . . . Lay this carefulnes upon him. . . . For your matters are greater than that the carefulnes of light, trifelyng, & corruptible thinges should withdrawe you from them. Let your chefe care be about that good thyng, in comparison of the whiche, these worldly thynges be of no value nor reputacion. . . . The other smaller thinges whyche pertayne unto the necessitie of this lyfe, the good and gracious father wyll cast unto you as an augmentation." The expansiveness of this style, with its pleonastic doublings and periphrastic constructions, bespeaks a correspondingly expansive and composed view of man's relationship to God. If man only applies himself, this relationship will be one of genial co-

---

[33]Nicholas Udall et al., trans., *The First Tome or Volume of the Paraphrase of Erasmus upon the Newe Testamente* (STC 2854) (London: E. Whitchurche, 1548), fols. xxxᵛ–xxxiʳ.

[34]Tyndale, *An Exposition*, in *Whole Workes*, fol. 235; modern-spelling text in Parker Society, vol. 44, pp. 108–9.

operation: man doing his part, and God doing his, as evoked in the balanced constructions with conjunction pairs ("for both causes," "both because," "and also because") that shape the rhetorical climax in the last sentence of the quotation. Tyndale, however, reads the text as a "promise," and, hence, as an epitome of the message and the language of Gospel. He brings to bear an appreciably different psychology of spiritual effort: one which offers fierce resistance to a religion of works (castigated as the "corrupt doctrine" of "our spiritualtie") while relying utterly on the efficacy of "Christes bloud," which is twice characterized as the only "righteousness." The inherent tension of the Christian life, in Tyndale's view, is reflected in his additive clausal sequences which resist closure as sentence units, until a conjunct specifying God's agency makes good his Word as promise (e.g., "for he hath promised to accept that, til more come" in the second sentence, and "yea, Christ promiseth thee an hundredfolde even in this life, of all that thou leavest for his sake" in the last). Tyndale's is also a more homely and colloquial sense of the Word as speech; he rephrases the key text thus:

Seke the kingdome of heaven therfore and the righteousnesse of the same, and be sure thou shalt ever have sufficient, and these thynges shalbe ministered unto the.

Erasmus's grandiloquence, however, recasts the text as a communal program for action of which he himself seems to become the propounder (for his "we" could not come from Jesus' mouth):

Let your chefe care be aboute that good thyng, in comparison of the whiche, these worldly thynges be of no value nor reputacion. The kyngdom of god must be set up, that is to say, the doctrine of the gospell, by the which we attayne unto the heavenly inheritaunce.

What I have been attempting to delineate with regard to Erasmus and Tyndale is at once a substantive and a circumscribed connection—one most operative on the plane of scholarly dedication and confidence in establishing the text of Scripture, least so in aspects of temperament, religious outlook, and stylistic expression. Accordingly, if Tyndale is not simply to be regarded as sui generis among his contemporaries in these latter aspects, affinities beyond those with Erasmus must be sought. It appears likely that some of these affinities—and, very possibly, a live influence—were provided in the intense personality of Thomas Bilney, an agemate of Tyndale's and a student at Cambridge during the period to which Tyndale's stay is dated. John Foxe preserves in his *Acts and Monuments* Bilney's own account of his powerful conversion experience and his telling apprehension of the message of Scripture, both of which overtook him when he settled down to savor the eloquence he expected to find in his new copy of Erasmus's New Testament:

And at the first readyng, as I remember I chaunced upon this sentence of S. Paul (O most swete and comfortable sentence to my soule) in his first Epistle to Timothy and first chapter: *It is a true saying and worthy of all men to be embraced, that Christe Jesus came into the world to save sinners, of whom I am the chiefe & principall.* This one sentence, through Gods instruction, and inward workyng, whiche I dyd not then perceve, did so exhilarate my hart, beyng before wounded with the gilte of my sinnes and beyng almost in dispayre, that immediately, I felt a mervelous comforte and quietnes, in so much, *that my brused bones leapt for joye.* Psal. 50. After this, the Scripture began to bee more pleasaunt to me then the hony or the hony combe: wherin I learned that all my travailes, all my fastyng and watchyng, all the redemption of Masses and pardons, beyng done without trust in Christ, whiche onely saveth his people from their sinnes: these, I say, I learned to bee nothyng elles but even (as S. Augustin sayth) a hasty and swift runnyng out of the right way.[35]

Although we have from Tyndale no such witness to the impact of this man as we have from Hugh Latimer, the most eminent preacher among the earliest English Reformers, who attributed his entire reorientation toward an affective Scripturalism to Bilney,[36] nevertheless Bilney's conversion, and the role of the Word in it, can be regarded as a contemporary English analogue to developments that Tyndale must have undergone himself in order for his work to have taken on the character and direction that it did.

To begin with, the date is important: Bilney's experience with Scripture predated the advent of Lutheran ideas in England by two or more years and thus qualifies for viewing as a native English phenomenon. From this angle, certain correspondences with Wyclif's Scripturalism and with emphases in later Lollardy become apparent—the focus on Christ and, hence, on the Gospels and Pauline Epistles as the core of the Word; the revulsion against penitential and expiatory practices that are allowed to substitute for "trust in Christ." These correspondences extend equally to the psychology and theology of Tyndale, where they are confirmed as the basic constants in an English Scripturalism which traces, however obliquely, from the later fourteenth to the earlier sixteenth century. Even so, the proportionally greater weight placed by Bilney on the Gospel content of the Pauline text from 1 Timothy is a critical shift away from Wyclif's Scripturalism, a new emphasis in this later age, and one wholeheartedly espoused by Tyndale. This paramount esteem for Paul, in turn, emerges as the most important eventual link between Luther's Scripturalism and Tyndale's. Bilney's account, then, which furnishes

[35]John Foxe, *The . . . Ecclesiasticall History, contayning the Actes & Monumentes of . . . the Church of England* (STC 11224) (London: John Daye, 1576), fol. 978ᵃ. For a modern-spelling text, see *The Acts and Monuments of John Foxe,* ed. Stephen Reed Cattley (London: R. B. Seeley & W. Burnside, 1837), IV, 635.

[36]See Allan G. Chester, *Hugh Latimer: Apostle to the English* (Philadelphia: University of Pennsylvania Press, 1954), pp. 11–13.

such an apt analogue for Tyndale's own dual rapport with Lollardy and Lutheranism, will remain a useful standing referent as we turn to consider more particularly how Tyndale implemented his Scripturalism stylistically as a translator and as a prose writer.

On the whole, it has been the literary ramifications of what we might call the Lollard strain in Tyndale's work that have chiefly drawn critical notice. He has often earned praise as a Biblical translator for his earnest fidelity to the conceptual and syntactical forms of expression found in the original Greek and Hebrew of the New Testament and Pentateuch, respectively—the two major portions of Scripture that stood in finished English versions at the time of his death.[37] As the excerpts already quoted from his prefatory epistle to the *Obedience of a Christian Man* attest outright, Tyndale was cognizant of the fundamental likenesses between the sentence forms of the Gospels and the Old Testament historical books, on the one side, and the native resources of English expression, on the other. His best work as a translator has been found to lie in his management of asymmetric sentential conjunction and in the speechlikeness of his renditions of direct address and dialogue. A characteristic illustration of both is provided by the close of the parable of the prodigal son (Luke 15:25–32) in Tyndale's rendering:

The elder brother was in the felde/ and when he cam and drewe nye to the housse, he herde minstrelcy and daunsynge/ and called one of his servauntes/ and axed what thoose thinges meante. And he sayde unto him: thy brother is come/ and thy father hath kylled the fatted caulfe/ because he hath receaved him safe and sounde. And he was angry/ and wolde not goo in. Then came his father out/ and entreated him. He answered and sayde to his father: Loo these many yeares have I done the service/ nether brake at eny tyme thy commaundement/ and yet gavest thou me never soo moche as a kyd to make mery with my lovers: but assone as this thy sonne was come/ which hath devoured thy goodes with harlottes/ thou hast for his pleasure kylled the fatted caulfe. And he sayd unto him: Sonne/ thou wast ever with me/ and all that I have/ is thyne: it was mete that we shuld make mery and be glad: for this thy brother was deed/ and is a lyve agayne: and was loste/ and is found.[38]

At first it seems remarkable as well as gratifying that Tyndale, who had as strong convictions about the supreme authoritativeness of Scripture as any predecessor or contemporary, displays not the slightest inclination to render the Word of God in the doublings, loaded patterns, and

[37]The classic discussion remains Gavin T. Bone's "Tindale and the English Language," in S. L. Greenslade's *The Work of William Tindale* (London and Glasgow: Blackie & Son, 1938), pp. 50–68. A corrective is proposed by Dahlia M. Karpman, "William Tyndale's Response to the Hebraic Tradition," *Studies in the Renaissance* 14 (1967): 110–30.

[38]The version cited here and subsequently is that of Tyndale's revised New Testament (1534), reprinted in *The English Hexapla: Six Important English Translations of the New Testament Scriptures, 1380–1611* (London: Samuel Bagster & Sons, 1841).

circumlocutions of the ecclesiastically authoritative style in vogue in his day. But, on further acquaintance, it emerges that Tyndale's Gospel translations could sustain the same literalistic respect for the words of the living Word as could Wyclif's English sermons, and for much the same reasons: an anticlerical and antiestablishment virulence which cast the Bible and the institutional Church in terms so mutually exclusive that no accommodation, let alone appropriation of language from one by the other, was even imaginable. It is much more likely to be vitriol than tact that we have to thank for the colloquial vigor, the speech-based prose, of Tyndale's version of the English Bible.

All the same, tact arising from reverence for the Word cannot be excluded entirely. If Tyndale's radicalism as a Reformer operated to free his sentence forms from the period fetters of aureate and grandiloquent expression, his readiness to polemic posed a potentially graver danger to the exactness of his renderings. For Tyndale was anything but a detached and dispassionate philologist in his view of the Bible and his work upon it, as his violently partisan glosses and marginalia show.[39] But, happily for the history of the English Bible, the sacredness of the text effectually inhibited interpolation and other kinds of interference on his part as a translator. In this regard, he and Purvey stand together. Yet it is also somewhat misleading to raise, even in passing, the possibility of Tyndale working at odds with the text of Scripture, for his entire output as translator and author shows that he conceived the Bible in terms of the immediacy of spoken language, the "promises" or the "message" of God to humankind, and that he conceived of his own vernacular writings as discourse in a like telling fashion. (The orality so central to Tyndale's conceptions may well be a Lollard inheritance; the very name derives from *lallen*, a verb of Dutch origin for the murmuring tones in which these sectaries passed from mouth to mouth the portions of the Word which they had learned by heart.)

The strength of Tyndale's stylistic predilection for colloquial discourse in keeping with his Scripturalism has perhaps not received its critical deserts. Having acquired the reputation, from his controversy with More, of a castigator of such devices as the dialogue framework and the invented character of an eager but ignorant young questioner who engages with the authorial persona—both of these functional mainstays of the *Dialogue concerning Heresies*—the "literal" Tyndale has been too easily contrasted with the "literary" More. In fact, at later junctures in *An Answer unto Sir Thomas More's Dialogue* (1530), the very work that takes More to task for his use of invented speech as a weapon of controversy, Tyndale crafts dialoguelike exchanges himself. Apprehensive about the

[39]See Stanley R. Maveety, "Doctrine in Tyndale's New Testament: Translation as a Tendentious Art," *Studies in English Literature* 6 (1966): 151–58.

size to which his *Answer* is growing, he distills far longer and wordier allegations from More's *Dialogue* into short charges which he then "speaks to," albeit on the page. Tyndale's quarrel is not with colloquialism, but with the feigning which he regards the issues and the times as being too serious for.[40] Here, to corroborate the point, are two of the dialogue-like exchanges from the later parts of his *Answer:*

More. The constitution of the Byshops is not that the Scripture shall not be in English, but that no man may translate it by his owne authoritie or read it, untill they had approved it. *Tyndall.* If no translation shalbe had untill they geve licence or till they approve it, shal it ever be had? And so it is all one in effect: to say there shalbe none at all in English, and to say, till we admitte it.

More. What good deede will he do, that beleveth Martin, how that we have no frewill to do any good with the helpe of grace? *Tyndall.* O Poete, without shame. *More.* What harme shall he care to forbeare, that beleveth Luther, how god alone, without our will worketh all the mischiefe that they do? *Tyndall.* O naturall sonne of the father of all lies.[41]

The irony, however, which we noted in Wyclif's Scripturalism arises again in Tyndale's Scripturalism—at least as far as the Gospels go as a potential model for vernacular prose composition. Tyndale's own writing accords only in its general colloquial or speech-based character with the utterances of the living Word; we find only intermittently at best the sudden first-person affirmations (e.g., "I am the way," "No man cometh unto the Father but by me") or the homely narrations and aphorisms that are the staples of Jesus' teaching and preaching.[42] While we cannot rule out the possibility that a certain intuited decorum—the sense of the inimitability of the Word made flesh—may have been in force with Tyndale (and Wyclif), nevertheless in Tyndale's case there is pervasive and compelling evidence that the Scriptural model for his own writing derived, for whatever reason, from elsewhere—that elsewhere being the Epistles of Paul. Thus to trace the most incisive imprint of Tyndale's Scripturalism involves crossing from the Lollard to the Lutheran side of his thinking and feeling. For Tyndale, as for Luther, the great route to an apprehension of the core meaning and the paramount authority of the Biblical message lay in the nexus of teachings on human faith and human works, on the law of God and the grace of God, for which the

[40]For discussion of the literary side of Tyndale, see Pineas, *Thomas More and Tudor Polemics,* pp. 77–79, and Peter Auksi, " 'So Rude and Simple Style': William Tyndale's Polemical Prose," *Journal of Medieval and Renaissance Studies* 8 (1978): 235–56.

[41]William Tyndale, *An Aunswere unto Syr Thomas Mores Dialogue,* in *Whole Workes,* fols. 318, 327. Henry Walker has a modern-spelling edition under the same title, as Parker Society vol. 45 (Cambridge: Cambridge University Press, 1850), pp. 166, 188.

[42]See, further, Amos N. Wilder, *Early Christian Rhetoric: The Language of the Gospel* (Cambridge, Mass.: Harvard University Press, 1971), pp. 40–54, 71–77.

locus classicus is the opening sequence of chapters in the Epistle to the Romans. Its very heartland is this urgent set of claims, as Englished by Tyndale:

I am not ashamed of the Gospell of Christ/ because it is the power of God unto salvacion to all that beleve/ namely to the Jewe/ and also to the gentyle. For by it the righteweses which commeth of god/ is opened/ from fayth to fayth. As it is written: The just shall live by faith.

There is none righteous/ no not one: there is none that understondeth/ there is none that seketh after God/ they are all gone out of the waye/ they are all made unprofytable/ . . . For by the lawe commeth the knowledge of synne.

The righteweses no dout which is good before God/ commeth by the fayth of Jesus Christ/ unto all and upon all that beleve. There is no difference: for all have synned/ and lacke the prayse that is of valoure before God: but are justified frely by his grace/ through the redemcion that is in Christ Jesu/ whom God hath made a seate of mercy thorow faith in his bloud/ . . . that he myght be counted juste/ and a justifiar of him which beleveth on Jesus. Where is then thy rejoys-inge? It is excluded. By what lawe? by the lawe of workes? Naye: but by the lawe of fayth. For we suppose that a man is justified by fayth without the dedes of the lawe. . . . Do we then destroye the lawe thorow fayth? God forbid. But we rather mayntayne the lawe.[43]

Tyndale concurred wholly with Luther in identifying the Pauline proc-lamation of justification by faith as the epitome of what the Gospel means and how its language works: to put reason in abeyance with the paradox of wholly undeserved and unearned salvation through Christ's "bloud," and to overwhelm the heart which alone can feel the force of such a promise by believing it, that is, taking it personally to heart. Such faith in Christ's promise, in turn, maintains the Law in the sense that the believing heart responds in joy, love, and thankfulness to what God would have it do or suffer.[44] What makes an understanding of the central and emphatic place of Pauline theology in Tyndale's outlook a requisite step in the study of his prose style is, above all, his utter conviction that the Apostle had gotten the message of the Gospel right and the Church of his day had gotten it all wrong. Joining with Wyclif as much as with Luther in utilizing the account of primitive Christianity in the New Testament as a standard by which to judge the conduct of the current ecclesiastical establishment, Tyndale, like them, reached a scathingly negative verdict. The clergy were hypocritical in professing spiritual living and guidance while in fact giving themselves over to worldliness, and in exhorting the laity to do penance, give alms, offer to saints, endow

[43]Romans 1:16–17, 3:10–12, 22–25, 27, 31, reprinted in *The English Hexapla*.

[44]For a superb handling of the relevant theology, see chaps. 1 and 5 of John S. Coolidge's *The Pauline Renaissance in England* (Oxford: Clarendon Press, 1970), a study often useful for Tyndale although he is too early to figure explicitly as one of its subjects.

chantries, and go on pilgrimage, as if it were possible to be saved by one's own efforts rather than by God's grace. Beyond these ills, however, Tyndale saw a worse evil yet that ensued upon the lapse of a Pauline understanding of Scripture: the presumption of the clergy in claiming to dispense God's grace and salvation. He is the first English writer in whom the Protestant emphasis on the individual soul's accountability before God is fully articulated, and articulated as a concomitant of the true apprehension of the Word which is the goal of his own efforts in Englishing and expounding Scripture. Thus Tyndale again and again admonishes his readers to the reading of Scripture, often, as here, by Scripture:

God is nothyng but hys law, and his promises, that is to say, that which he biddeth thee to doe, and that which he biddeth thee beleve and hope. God is but his worde, as Christ sayth, John 8. I am that I say unto you, that is to say, that which I preach am I. My words are spirite and life. . . . Therfore saith the 118. Psalme, Happy are they which search the testimonies of the Lord, that is to say, that which God testifieth, and witnesseth unto us.[45]

Even though the explicit references in the foregoing quotation are to the Gospel of John and the Psalms, the vocabulary of "law" and "promises" which shapes the admonition also reveals that Paul's conception of Scripture undergirds Tyndale's own. The perception emerges all the more forcefully from two notable passages, one in *The Obedience*, and one in *An Answer*, where he attempts to articulate and verify his identification of Gospel "promise" with the doctrine of justification by faith, as found in Paul. In the earlier of the two, the passage in *The Obedience*, Tyndale proceeds by way of what he claims is an intuitively clear and important distinction between believing that "the kyng is rich, & that he is rich unto me":

When I beleve that the kyng is rich I am not moved: but when I beleve that he is rich unto me, & that he will never faile me at my nede, then love I, and of love am ready to worke unto the uttermost of my power. . . . Paule in the 8. chapter to the Romaynes, after that he hath declared the infinite love of God to us ward, in that he spared not hys owne sonne, but gave hym for us, cryeth out saying: who shall separate us from the love of God? shall persecution, shall a sworde? &c. No, sayth he, I am sure that no creature shall separate us from the love of God, that is in Christ Jesus our Lord: as who should say, we see so great love in God to us warde in Christes death, that though all misfortune should fall on us, we can not but love agayne. Now how know we that God loveth us? verely by fayth. . . . But let us see the text. Paule sayth thus. In Christ Jesu, neither circumcision is any thyng worth, nor incircumcision: but fayth which worketh thorow love, or which thorow love is strong or mighty in

[45]"To the Reader," *The Obedience*, in *Whole Workes*, fol. 102; Parker Society (hereafter cited PS) vol. 43, p. 145.

working. . . . For Paules fayth is to beleve Gods promises. Fayth (sayth he) Rom. 10, commeth by hearing, and hearing commeth by the worde of God. Neither doth any that consenteth in the hart to continue in sinne, beleve that Christ dyed for him. For to beleve that Christ dyed for us, is to see our horrible damnation, and how we were appointed unto eternall paines, and to feele, and to be sure that we are delivered therefrom thorough Christ: in that we have power to hate our sinnes, and to love Gods commaundements. All such repent and have their hartes loosed out of the captivitie and bondage of sinne, and are therefore justified thorough fayth in Christ.[46]

Manifestly, the Pauline and Tyndalian "faith" which is characterized in this passage is preeminently a response of "the hart" whose knowledge and surety come through feeling love, first God's, then its own. The premium placed on the affectivity of Biblical meaning when taken aright, that is personally ("the kyng is rich unto me"), receives still further and more explicit elaboration in *An Answer*, where Tyndale undertakes to represent the difference between what the clergy of his day make of Scripture and what he desires to have made of Scripture in terms of a distinction between a "historical" and a "feeling" faith.[47] As he explains it, "historicall fayth," what we would call credence, "hangeth of the truth and honestie of the teller, or of the common fame and consent of many." Thus, he says, he might believe "that the turke had wonne a citie," taking one man's word, until "an other that seemeth more honest or that hath better perswasions" causes him to think that the first man "lyed" and so to lose his faith. On this plane, Tyndale adds acerbically, it makes no difference whether one believes "that the scripture is Gods" or "that Roben Hode had bene the scripture of God," because such "fayth is but an opinion, and therfore abideth ever fruitless and falleth away, if a more glorious reason be made . . . , or if the preacher live contrary." To this "historicall fayth" Tyndale opposes "a feelyng fayth," that is, conviction, gained solely through personal experience which he images with a return to his example of the captured city: "And a feeling fayth is, as if a man were there present when it was wonne, and there were wounded and had there lost all that he had, and were taken prisoner there also. That man should so beleve that all the worlde could not turne him from hys faith." At this point Tyndale turns to apply his distinction to Scripture, and to the individual's answering for its felt

[46]Ibid., fols. 266, 267, 268; PS vol. 43, pp. 222–24.
[47]William A. Clebsch, *England's Earliest Protestants, 1520–1535* (New Haven: Yale University Press, 1964), pp. 293–94, notes that More accused Tyndale of cribbing the distinction between historical and feeling faith from Philipp Melanchthon. However, I have found something of an indigenous English prehistory in Pecock's distinction between 'believing to' (= believing in as authoritative) and 'believing to be' (= believing that something or someone merely exists). See Reginald Pecock, *The Book of Faith*, ed. J. L. Morison (Glasgow: J. Maclehose & Sons, 1909), pp. 283–84; and, for discussion, Joseph F. Patrouch, Jr., *Reginald Pecock* (New York: Twayne Publishers, 1970), pp. 32–33, 36–38.

meaning in terms of "a feelyng faith" characterized by increasingly explicit Pauline references:

But of a feeling fayth it is written, John 6. They shall be all taught of God. That is, God shall write it in their harts with his holy spirite. And Paule also testifieth, Rom. 8. The spirite beareth record unto our spirite that we be the sonnes of God. And thys fayth is none opinion, but a sure feling, and therefore ever fruitfull. . . . For Christes preaching was with power and spirite that maketh a man feele and know and work too, and not as the Scribes and Pharisies preached.

And therfore when thou art asked, why thou belevest that thou shalt be saved thorough Christ and of such like principles of our fayth, aunswere thou wottest and felest that it is true. And when he asketh how thou knowest that it is true? aunswere because it is written in thyne hart. And if he aske who wrote it? aunswere the spirite of God. . . . And if he aske whether thou belevest it not because it is written in bookes or because the Priestes so preach, aunswere no, not now, but onely because it is written in thyne hart and because the spirite of God so preacheth and so testifieth unto thy soule.

It hath pleased God of his exceding love wherewith he loved us in Christ (as Paul sayth) before the worlde was made, and when we were dead in sinne and his enemies, in that we did consent to sinne and to live evill, to write with his spirite ii. conclusions in our harts, by which we understand all thyng: that is to wete, the fayth of Christ, and the love of our neighbours. For whosoever feleth the just damnation of sinne, and the forgevenes and mercy that is in Christes bloud for all that repent & forsake it, and come and beleve in that mercy, the same onely knoweth how God is to be honoured and worshipped, and can judge betwene true serving of God in the spirite, and false Image serving of God with workes. . . . And on the other side, he that loveth his neighbour as himselfe, understandeth all lawes, and can judge betwene good and evil, right & wrong, godly and ungodly, in all conversation, deedes, lawes, bargaines, covenauntes, ordinaunces and decrees of men.[48]

On the strength of his own testimony, then, Tyndale's Scripturalism is predicated upon an urgently affective sense, contracted from Paul, of the workings of the Word upon the human heart. The theological paradigm duly becomes a compositional paradigm, as the Scripturalism of Tyndale's own style manifests itself in the assimilation of native resources of expression to the sentence forms and rhetorical devices that characterize the Pauline Epistles where apostolic authority takes the guise of an irresistible call for a feeling response.[49] Probably the most con-

---

[48]*An Aunswere*, in *Whole Workes*, fols. 266–68; PS vol. 45, pp. 50–52, 55–56.

[49]Some remarks by Astley C. Partridge in *English Biblical Translation* (London: André Deutsch, 1973) anticipate in a general fashion the argument which I pursue regarding the Pauline character of Tyndale's style. Partridge notes that "no Isocrates is needed" to account for the "nervous balance and rhetorical impact" of many passages in Tyndale if one registers that "this style was fundamental to many Pauline passages in Tyndale's New Testament" (pp. 39, 47).

spicuous feature of Pauline style is the binary linkage of sentences (or verb phrases) in an antithetical, correlative, or comparative relation. The at once oscillating and balancing movement created by runs of such constructions infuses the discourse with a highly characteristic nervous intensity, as excerpts from Tyndale's translation of Romans readily demonstrate:

There is no difference: for all have synned, and lacke the prayse that is of valoure before God: but are justified frely by his grace/

For we knowe that the lawe is spirituall: but I am carnall/ I delite in the lawe of God/ concerning the inner man. But I see another lawe in my membres rebellinge agaynst the lawe of my mynde/

It is not written for him only/ that it was reckened to him for rightewesnes: but also for us/ to whom it shalbe counted for rightewesnes/

For yf when we were enemyes/ we were reconciled to God by the deeth of his sonne: moche more/ seing we are reconciled/ we shall be preservid by his lyfe.[50]

Tyndale's own prose is also strongly marked by binary conjunctions and correlatives in dense clusters and extended sequences. The following excerpt from his *Parable of the Wicked Mammon* (1527) interestingly assimilates Christ's teaching to this Pauline dynamic:

If we be sonnes, so are we also heires. Roma. 8. and Ga. 4. How can or ought we then to worke, for to purchase that inheritaunce withall, wherof we are heyres already by fayth? . . . Christ sayth, Mat. 10. freely have ye receyved, freely geve agayne. For looke, as Christ with all his workes did not deserve heaven, for that was hys already, but did us service therewith, and neither looked, nor sought his owne profite, but our profite, and the honour of God the father only: even so we with all our workes may not seke our own profite, neither in this worlde, nor in heaven, but must and ought freely to worke, to honoure God withall, and without all maner respecte, seek our neighboures profite, and do hym service.

At certain relatively infrequent junctures, as in this later passage from the *Parable of the Wicked Mammon*, the urgent instrumentality of such binary composition can take on a schematic cast:

Marke now how much I love the commaundement, so much I love God, how much I love God, so much beleve I that he is mercifull, kynde, and good, yea, and a father unto me, for Christes sake; how much I beleve that God is mercifull unto me, and that he will for Christes sake fulfill all hys promises unto me: so much I see my sinnes, so much do my sins greve me, so much do I repent, and

---

[50]Romans 3:22, 7:14, 22–23, 4:23–25, 5:10, reprinted in *The English Hexapla*.

sorrow that I sinne, so much displeaseth me that poyson that moveth me to sinne, and so greatly desire I to be healed.[51]

Much more characteristically, however, the antithetical or correlative responsions of Tyndale's sentence forms retain the looser cast of the Apostle's own, as shown in the following continuation of a passage quoted just previously from *An Answer.* Especially noteworthy is the close approximation of the patterning of its last sentence to those found in 1 Corinthians 13 (e.g., in Tyndale's rendering, "And though I bestowed all my gooddes to fede the poore/ . . . and yet had no love/ it profiteth me nothing"):

And thys fayth is none opinion, but a sure feling, and therefore ever fruitfull. Neyther hangeth it of the honestie of the preacher, but of the power of God and of the spirite, and therefore if all the preachers of the world would goe about to perswade the contrary, it would not prevayle. . . . For Christes preaching was with power and spirite . . . and not as the Scribes and Pharisies preached. . . . For if I have none other feeling in my fayth than because a man so sayth, then is my fayth faithles and fruitles.

Nearly as conspicuous as the binary connectives of Pauline prose are the outcroppings of *erotema,* or short question-and-answer pairs, by which an objection is dispelled, an alternative raised, or a likely first impression countered with a second, better formulation. Amos Wilder remarks on the provenance of this syntactic figure as follows: "In Paul's letters we are taught to recognize the familiar Hellenistic *diatribe* style, according to which the writer simulates objectors and inquirers and answers them."[52] Despite their formalization as a stylistic device, which affords a further source of binary organization, these brief question-and-answer exchanges impart a strong flavor of orality as well as an accelerated pace to the writing. They contribute to the affective strain in Pauline prose, especially when the answer to the question is—or is coupled with—an expletive. Again, Tyndale's renderings of excerpts from Romans (3:27, 29, 31) are illustrative:

Where is then thy rejoysinge? It is excluded. By what lawe? by the lawe of workes? Naye: but by the lawe of fayth.

Is he the God of the Jewes only? Is he not also the God of the Gentyles? Yes: even of the Gentyles also.

Do we then destroye the lawe thorow fayth? God forbid. But we rather mayntayne the lawe.

---

[51]William Tyndale, *Parable of the Wicked Mammon,* in *Whole Workes,* fols. 90–91; PS vol. 43, pp. 112–14.
[52]Wilder, *Early Christian Rhetoric,* p. 46.

Pauline *erotema* is likewise a staple of Tyndale's style, where the question-and-answer pairs function similarly to heighten the speechlikeness, the tempo, and the feeling of the prose. The following examples come, respectively, from the prefatory epistle to *The Obedience*, from the body of *An Answer*, and from a previously quoted section of *An Answer*:

What is the cause that we may not have the olde Testament, with the new also, which is the light of the olde, and wherin is openly declared before the eyes, that there was darckly prophesied? I can imagine no cause verely, except it be that we should not see the woorke of Antechrist, & jugglyng of hipocrites. . . . Came Christ to make the world more blinde? By this meanes, Christ is the darknes of the world, and not the light, as he saith himselfe, John 8. [*Whole Workes*, fol. 101; PS vol. 43, p. 131]

And when they aske whether we receaved the scripture of them? I aunswere, that they which come after receave the scripture of them that go before. And when they aske whether we beleve not that it is Gods worde by the reason that they tell us so? I aunswere, that there are two manner faythes, an historicall fayth, and a feelyng fayth. [*Whole Workes*, fol. 266; PS vol. 45, p. 50]

And therfore when thou art asked, why thou belevest that thou shalt be saved thorough Christ . . . , aunswere thou wottest and felest that it is true. And when he asketh how thou knowest that it is true? aunswere because it is written in thyne hart. And if he aske who wrote it? aunswere the spirite of God.

In assessing the imprint of Scripturalism upon Tyndale's own prose style, we find that his accommodation of his mode of composition to that of the Pauline Epistles is so systematically predisposed toward binary forms that the option of recursive elaboration by means of asymmetric sentential conjunction with *and* plays at best a sporadic role. This binary predisposition of sentence forms attests all the more to the force of the particular paradigm he found in the Apostle, for we have noted his care to preserve the asymmetric conjunctive syntax of Gospel (and Old Testament) narrative while Englishing those Biblical books. There is, nonetheless, one aspect in which Tyndale does avail himself of the recursive potential of conjunctive syntax, and it again corroborates the power of Pauline precedent; this is the amassing of large NP catalogues to buttress the making of some larger essential point. The catalogues in the Epistles have consistently to do with fundamental moral concerns: the vices of contemporary urban society, the fruits of the Spirit, the trials and tribulations of the faithful, the attributes of godly living, and so on. Here, in Tyndale's translations, is a pair of semantically contrasting but equally typical examples—the first a chastisement of the Corinthians (1 Corinthians 6:9–11), the second an encouragement to the Colossians (Colossians 3:12–13):

Be not deceaved. For nether fornicators/ nether worshyppers of ymages/ nether whormongers/ nether weaklinges/ nether abusars of them selves with mankynde/ nether theves/ nether the coveteous/ nether dronkardes/ nether cursed speakers/ nether pyllers/ shall inheret the kyngdome of God. And soche ware ye, verely.

Now therfore as electe of god/ holy and beloved/ put on tender mercie/ kyndnes/ humblenes of mynde/ mekenes/ long sufferynge/ forbearynge one another/ and forgevynge one another. And if eny man have a quarrell to an other/ even as Christ forgave you/ even so do ye.

Tyndale's own recurrent utilizations of *NP* catalogues reflect exactly the same semantic and rhetorical principles of composition as those that govern his Pauline prototypes. An example of a negative catalogue, punctuated with native alliteration, surges forth in an admonition to the laity to exercise independent judgment on the clergy and its accoutrements of priestly authority in *An Answer unto Sir Thomas More:*

Judge whether it be possible that any good should come out of their domme ceremonies & Sacramentes unto thy soule. Judge their penaunce, pilgrimages, pardons, purgatorie, praying to postes, domme blessynges, domme absolutions, their domme pateryng and howlyng, their domme straunge holy gestures with all their domme disguisinges, their satisfactions and justifyinges. And because thou findest them false in so many thynges, trust them in nothyng but judge them in all thinges.[53]

Affirmative catalogues are appreciably rarer in Tyndale's prose, but they do have some currency as, for example, this evocation of the acts and offices of Christ as Saviour in *A Pathway into the Holy Scripture* (1530?):

His bloud, his death, his pacience, in suffering rebukes and wronges, his prayers and fastynges, his mekenes and fulfillyng of the uttermost point of the law, peased the wrath of God. . . . He is our redemer, deliverer, reconciler, mediator, intercessor, advocate, attorney, soliciter, our hope, comfort, shield, protection, defender, strength, health, satisfaction and salvation. His bloud, his death, all that he ever dyd, is ours. And Christ him self, with all that he is or can do, is ours.[54]

Seen against the backdrop of recent stylistic developments in English prose, the advent of Tyndale's translation of Scripture together with his original writings in a studied Pauline mode registered a sharp challenge to various received features of vernacular prose composition. It is not difficult, for instance, to recognize in the strategic placement of the *NP* catalogues an effectual alternative to word pairs as means for maximal articulation of meaning, or delineating a universe of values, or projecting the energy intrinsic in "strong forms" of language. To the extent that

[53]Preface to the Reader, *An Aunswere*, in *Whole Workes*, fols. 248–49; PS vol. 45, pp. 8–10.

[54]*A Pathway into the Holy Scripture*, in *Whole Workes*, fol. 382; PS vol. 43, pp. 18–19. Considerable portions of the *Pathway* translate Luther's preface to his German Bible (1522).

NP catalogues can substitute with equal or greater semantic and rhetorical effectiveness for word pairs, to that extent they call for a corresponding adjustment in the all but exclusive standing associations of the latter with authoritative utterance. But the matter of word pairs and catalogues is minor compared with the implications stemming from the insistent binary responses in sentence form which Tyndale, emulating Paul, infused on a wide scale into the writing of English prose. Eventually, in chapter 6, we shall have occasion to note the far-reaching literary impact and repercussions of the resurgence of English Scripturalism in the peculiar and forceful Pauline strain that originates with Tyndale as, within half a century, the staple of prose composition becomes no longer asymmetric and recursive clausal conjunction but, rather, sentence forms of a binary, symmetric, and even schematic, cast. These developments, however, lie in the future. Here the more pressing stylistic question is that of the possible rhetorical or semantic function of these insistent binary constructions. Are there any contextual clues to their great appeal for Paul and for Tyndale?

There are. In the Apostle's conception of the meaning of Scripture, the affectivity of the saving Word arises from the complementary working of the two great halves of the message, the Law that condemns and the Gospel that saves, within the believer's heart. The binary responses of Pauline sentence forms recurrently mirror this specific apprehension of Biblical meaning, and with sustained insistence in the fifth and sixth chapters of Romans. Indicative formulations (5:19–21, 6:8–11, 14) read as follows in Tyndale's translation:

Lykewise then as by the synne of one/ condemnacion came on all men: even so by the justifyinge of one commeth the rightewesness that bringeth lyfe/ upon all men. For as by one mannes disobedience many becam synners: so by the obedience of one shall many be made righteous. Neverthelater where aboundance of synne was/ there was more plenteousnes of grace: that as synne had raigned unto deeth/ even so might grace rayne thorow rightewesnes unto eternall lyfe/ by the helpe of Jesu Christ.

For as touchynge that he dyed/ he dyed concernynge synne/ once: and as touching that he liveth/ he liveth unto God. Lykewise ymagen ye also/ that ye are deed concernynge synne: but are alive unto God thorow Jesus Christ oure Lorde. . . . For ye are not under the lawe/ but under grace.

Tyndale himself absorbed the thrust of the great Pauline oppositions which at the same time were complementarities, registering them as the core of the Scriptural message and at the same time projecting them as the dynamic of his own prose style. *A Pathway into the Holy Scripture*, his short tract on how to read God's Word rightly, abounds so in these binary responses that it becomes the purest—that is, most extreme—exemplification of the Tyndalian stylistic program and its tendency toward what might be called "directed syntax" in the service of divine meaning. Here is an illustration from its pronouncement on the complementarity of Law and Gospel:

> The old Testament is a booke, wherein is written the law of God, & the dedes of them which fulfill them, & of them also which fulfill them not. The new Testament is a booke, wherein are conteined the promises of God and the dedes of them which beleve them or beleve them not. . . . In the old Testament are many promises, which are nothyng els but the *Evangelion* or Gospel, to save those that beleved them from the vengeaunce of the law. And in the new Testament is oft made mention of the law, to condemne them, which beleve not the promises. Moreover the law and Gospell may never be separate: for the Gospel and promises serve but for troubled consciences, which are brought to desperation and feele the paynes of hell and death under the law: and are in captivitie and bondage under the law. In all my dedes I must have the law before me to condemne myne unperfectnes: . . . I must also have the promises before myne eyes, that I dispayre not.[55]

It is therefore transparent from these passages that the binary responsions in the styles of Paul and Tyndale are semantic vehicles, and it seems clear that they are rhetorical instruments as well. Indeed this would almost have to be the case, given the sweeping character of Paul's theological convictions and their adamant espousal by Tyndale. According to these convictions, each soul must be brought individually and personally to confront its condemnation for sin and the promise offered to it of salvation in Christ. Yet, at the same time, the highly paradigmatic representation made of this personal confrontation with the core message of Scripture by both writers presupposes that these separate individual experiences will show a uniform character—at least, insofar as they prove to be redemptive ones. But here a no less vexing than fundamental question arises. How can it possibly be assumed that individual responses to the Law and Gospel will have such a uniform character? Theologically, we find, this assumption is empowered for Paul and Tyndale by certain views about the universality of God's purposes, the workings of grace, and the accessibility of the meaning of the Word. Yet stylistically, too, both writers aim to ensure that the unifying assumption about individuals and their response to Scripture will hold as far as possible. It is here that the directed syntax, the heavily predetermined sentence forms enter as key resources of prose expression for literally bearing out this fundamental assumption about the affective working of Scripture upon the soul. Thus the exercise of linguistic authority in the impulsion toward schematic sentence form in Paul and Tyndale arises from the resolve to provide for individual responses to Scripture and nonetheless warrant that all of them will be like in kind.

[55]Ibid., fols. 377, 379; PS vol. 43, pp. 8, 11.

Some such inference, I think, is inescapable, given the systematic patterning of form and vital content in both writers' prose.

A discussion of Tyndale's style, however, would be incomplete if it failed to reckon with his claim that a soul justified by faith begins to think and express itself altogether differently than it did before. Perhaps, then, some allowance for a distinctively Protestant spirituality is requisite in any attempt to account for the determinants of his mode of composition. In a central passage of his *Parable of the Wicked Mammon*, Tyndale develops the claim that justification by faith profoundly alters one's sense and representation of experience. His point of departure is the condition of time-bound natural man, who registers and reflects on events as they occur. Serial perception and sequential reasoning are thus the order of nature, according to Tyndale; and as such they are also the source of continual error or misinformation in how we conceive and speak of things. He gives three homely examples. When "we first see the Moone darke, and then serche the cause," we determine that "the puttyng of the earth, betwene the sunne and the Moone is the naturall cause of the darknes, and that the earth stoppeth the light. Then," says Tyndale, "dispute we backeward saying: The Moone is darkned, therfore is the earth directly betwene the sunne and the Moone." Similarly, we observe regarding a man we know that "he hath a sonne, therfore is he a father, and yet the sonne is not cause of the father, but contrarywise." Again, in observing the round of the seasons, "This is the maner of speaking, as we say. Sommer is nie, for the trees blossome. Nowe is the blossomyng of the trees not the cause that sommer draweth nie, but the drawyng nie of sommer is the cause of the blossoms, and the blossomes put us in remembraunce that sommer is at hand."

What Tyndale's three examples show about human minds and human language may be paraphrased as follows. We have a natural bent, first of all, toward asymmetric clausal conjunction as the basic mode of representing our experience. But then we go on to transform these asymmetric conjunctions into causal or conditional constructions, reasoning that what to us is a later event must somehow, by virtue of this temporal order, be dependent on an earlier one. (This is the *post hoc ergo propter hoc* fallacy which Tyndale is faulting, though not by name.) As a result of the causal and conditional significance which we impute to asymmetric conjunction, we falsify the very experiences we think we are representing truly. In short, we get things backwards. Tyndale sums up: "We for the most part because of our grossenes, in all our knowledge procede from that whiche is last and hindmost, unto that which is first, begynnyng at the latter end, disputyng and makyng our argumentes backeward."[56]

[56]*Parable of the Wicked Mammon*, in *Whole Workes*, fols. 67, 77; PS vol. 43, pp. 58–59, 83.

It is, however, the natural "backeward" application of human thought and expression in the sphere of religious experience that leads to the gravest and most irreparable kind of error, according to Tyndale. In particular, one can be led to conclude as the institutional Church teaches: that since God is all goodness and enjoins man to the same, man may be saved by good works. But this is precisely the imputing of conditionality and causality to asymmetric conjunction that Tyndale is so fiercely determined to repudiate and combat with his own binary correspondences. Hence, in the following characteristic and revealing passage, the dynamic of the style is directed at superseding asymmetrical *and* conjunction with a set of binary, mainly antithetical constructions that have been drawn, unsurprisingly, from the text of Scripture:

> Thou mayest not thinke that our deedes blesse us first, and that we prevent God and his grace in Christ, as though we in our naturall giftes, and beyng as we were borne in Adam, looked on the lawe of God, and of our owne strength fulfilled it, and so became rightewes, and then with that rightewesnes obtayned the favour of God. . . . For contrarie to that, readest thou John 15. Ye have not chosen me (sayth Christ) but I have chosen you, that ye goe and bring forth fruite, and that your fruite remayne. And in the same chapter. I am a vine, and ye are the braunches, and without me can ye do nothing. With us therefore so goeth it.

> Moreover, if the reward should depend, and hang of the workes, no man shoulde be saved: for as much as our best deedes, compared to the lawe, are damnable sinne. By the deedes of the lawe is no fleshe justified, as it is written in the thirde chapter to the Romanes. The lawe justifieth not, but uttereth the sinne onely.[57]

The fatal error made by natural, time-bound human thought and syntax in representing salvation as the outcome of good works is that, on Tyndale's reading of Scripture, the envisaged process is an actual impossibility. For the truth is that man, left to his own workings, can never be anything other than a sinful creature, while God continues as the sole source and agent of good. This binary cleavage, this radical antithesis, goes to the very root of Tyndale's Scripturalism. Hence, while the much desired means of bridging this antithesis can partially be expressed as a correlation between God as promiser of salvation and man as believer of that promise, due care must be exercised with such a formulation. In it the roles of God and man are mutual, for both are parties to the same promise. At the same time, and paradoxically, however, the roles of God and man cannot be understood as reciprocal, since man receives all and God receives nothing. To this extent, reciprocal constructions are less than adequate vehicles of the Gospel message; thus it is probably not accidental that they remain an infrequent and subor-

[57]Ibid., fols. 90–91; PS vol. 43, pp. 112–14.

dinate feature of Tyndale's prose style. Instead, his staple resources are the class of binary conjunctions, correlatives, and comparatives which to his linguistic intuitions more truly articulate the vital convergence between human faith and the totality of what God does for his faithful in the gift of salvation.

More versus Tyndale

Thus far we have been occupied with the intrinsic interest of the prose style that Tyndale developed as a translator of Scripture and as an original vernacular writer in the course of spearheading the resurgence of Scripturalism in England. Now we must reckon additionally with the fact that Tyndale's efforts both as a translator and as an original vernacular writer incurred a massive counterattack, almost from the day that their influence began in England. This counterattack, in turn, gave the challenge to authority posed by Tyndale's Scripturalism an even greater importance than it would otherwise have attained. The importance stems from the identity of Tyndale's antagonist: Sir Thomas More. Frequently accorded the status of the most eminent literary figure in earlier sixteenth-century England, More continues to attract scholarly and critical attention of a magnitude befitting such a reputation. There is much about him as a person to command the highest admiration: his learning, his literary sensibility, his wit, his loyalty to principle, his martyr's courage. Among his writings, *Utopia* is an undoubted masterpiece of humanist Latinity. Yet his English prose, the aspect of More's work with which I shall be concerned, has been the object of extremely diverse assessments. It is useful to focus consideration of More as a vernacular stylist by inquiring into the gist and grounds of these judgments.

The most familiar and most influential tribute to More's literary importance has come from R. W. Chambers, whose continuity hypothesis, developed in an essay of 1932, pronounced More "the great restorer of English prose" and of a tradition reaching back to King Alfred.[58] Since Chambers's essay was written as an introduction to a sixteenth-century life of More, the circumstances may explain why this tribute, for all its felt warmth toward the man, proceeds in the most sweeping terms and omits any specific notice of texts. But if Chambers's glowing generalities can draw some extenuation from circumstances, it is less easy to account for Krapp's equally adulatory and undocumented assertion made two decades earlier in *The Rise of English Literary Prose:* "More shows a much

---

[58]Raymond Wilson Chambers, Introduction, *Harpsfield's Life of More,* ed. Elsie V. Hitchcock, Early English Text Society, o.s. 186 (London: Humphrey Milford, 1932), p. clxxi.

more certain feeling for English expression than do any of his learned contemporaries."[59] Over time, a greater number of negative and qualified assessments have been ranged against the strongly positive ones offered by Krapp and Chambers. George Saintsbury, writing in 1898, declared as categorically as they in an opposing vein that "To speak of More as the father of English prose is to apply a silly phrase in a fashion monstrously unhistorical." He concluded, again without troubling with evidence, that "More's place in the strict history of English literature is very small, and not extraordinarily high."[60] J. A. Gee, surveying the state of early sixteenth-century English prose composition in 1928, was the first scholar in the present century to broach an analysis of More as a vernacular stylist. He expressly built on the precedent set by Sir James Mackintosh's comments on More as early as 1831; these run as follows:

In the combination and arrangement of words, in ordinary phraseology and common habits of composition, he differs widely from the style prevalent among us for over two centuries. His diction seems a continued experiment to discover the forms into which the language naturally runs. In that attempt he has frequently failed. . . . The structure of his sentences is frequently not that which the English language has finally adopted. The language of his countrymen has decided, without appeal, against the composition of the father of English prose.[61]

Gee's own examination of the defining features of More's vernacular prose style issues in a thoughtfully tempered view which deserves wider recognition than it has hitherto received. He finds that the best sense to be made of claims on More's behalf arises from considerations of priority, not quality. First establishing that a tension between relying on native sentence forms and attempting to domesticate what he can of Latinate sentence forms shows through More's writing of English from beginning to end, Gee argues that More should be credited with introducing a hybrid sentence type to serve as the basis of a specialized style for learned purposes in the vernacular. He traces More's hybridizings of native and Latinate sentence forms back to 1510, the date of More's original though very brief preface to his translation of the *Lyfe of J. Picus Mirandula;* and he cites the following sentence as an illustration:

But for asmuch as the love & amitie of christen folke should be rather ghostly frendship then bodily: sith that all faithfull people are rather spirituall then

---

[59]George P. Krapp, *The Rise of English Literary Prose* (New York: Oxford University Press, 1915), p. 101.

[60]George Saintsbury, *A Short History of English Literature* (New York and London: Macmillan & Co., 1898), p. 212; cf. his *History of English Prose Rhythm* (London: Macmillan & Co., 1912), pp. 122–23: "More . . . did not do much of real importance in English."

[61]J. A. Gee, *The Life and Works of Thomas Lupset* (New Haven: Yale University Press, 1928), p. 195, quoting Sir James Mackintosh, "Eminent British Statesmen," *The Cabinet Cyclopaedia* (London, 1831), I, 23.

carnall (For, as thapostle saith: We be not now in flessh, but in spirit, if Christ abide in us), I therfore myne hertely beloved sister in good lucke of this new yere, have sent you suche a present, as maie beare witnesse of my tender love and zele to the happy continuance & graciouse encreace of vertue in your soule.[62]

It will prove useful for the ensuing discussion of More's English prose style to pause over this example of Gee's and register some points about its syntax. The basic source of tension between native and Latinate sentence forms lies in the differential requirements of the two languages regarding (1) the sequential arrangement of major constituents within clausal units and (2) the overall intactness of those units in surface sentential structure. Modern English, as we have been seeing, enforced comparatively high demands on both fronts from the outset. Thus "open sentence" could be achieved by means of full or only somewhat reduced clausal units that exhibited the fairly invariant internal structure of Subject $NP + V$ ($+$ Object NP) ($+$ Adverb) ($+$ Complement). There could at most be some relatively compact and uncomplicated adjunction of other syntactic material within the clausal units in question, if "open sentence" was to be sustained. These constraints lead in the direction of a more general stylistic principle: as successiveness is the dynamic governing the arrangement of lexical and phrasal elements within the clause, so, too, it is the dynamic operating over the wider compass of English sentence form. Accordingly, it is preferable as a rule to adjoin material at the end rather than in the middle of a clausal unit, for end positioning respects the intactness of the "canonical sentoid" on which syntactic perception and comprehension depend. Pattern-loading figures at best as a calculated risk for the writer of English; the complications introduced by this means can be tolerated only so far as they avoid interfering to any serious degree with sentential processing. By contrast with English, Latin sentence structure quite freely admits adjunction within clausal units, and it is virtually unconstrained as well with respect to the ordering of lexical and phrasal elements in the clause. Latin, moreover, makes heavy use of participial (tenseless VP) constructions, while English tends to employ fuller clause structure together with a conjunctive particle. The net effect of these particular differences is to increase the likelihood that a main clause in a Latin sentence will physically incorporate an appreciable proportion of the total material in the sentence, just because of its receptivity to various kinds of internal adjunction and its consequent expansions in size. This familiar and fundamental property of the clause in Latin is the single most important factor in what is conventionally called "suspended" or "periodic" sentence form. To image the distinction, one might analogize from English clausal units to

---

[62]Thomas More, Preface, *The Lyfe of J. Picus Mirandula*, cited in Gee, *Life and Works of Thomas Lupset*, p. 195.

rows of overlapping shingles, and from a Latin clausal unit to a piece of sheet roofing. The two are equally adequate means of coverage, but they utilize alternative modes of disposing material over the area to be covered.

The sentence from More which Gee quotes signals itself as a fairly transparent effort to Latinize English sentence form by spreading and suspending the main clausal unit. Suspension gets underway immediately in the adjunction of syntactic material at the head end of the main clause. After opening with "But" and before proceeding to the subject *NP* (which turns out to be "I"), More exercises the stylistic option of "fronting" no fewer than three complex subordinate clauses that delay the advent of the structural and semantic nucleus of the sentence: the $NP + V (+NP . . .)$ sequence of its main clause. It would appear from the triad of fronted participles at the opening of Wilson's parodic letter (see the first section of this chapter) that the multiple fronting of complex subordinating constructions such as More performs here carried learned and Latinate associations in sixteenth-century English. But, significantly, More's fronted material shows a predominance of native syntactic types and tendencies: first a loose correlative construction ("for as much") of the kind labeled characteristic of fifteenth-century English prose by Workman; then a similarly loose "since" construction and "for" construction, both adjoined together in the English fashion at the extremities of clausal units, so that they trail rather than interrupt and suspend structure. As for More's main clause unit, there is ample evidence—in the insertion of "therfore," of the vocative "myne hertely beloved sister," and the adverbial phrase "in good lucke of this new yere" between the subject *NP* "I" and the *V* "have sent"—that an attempt is being made to spread its form by spacing out the succession of major constituents. However, there are equally important native tendencies in the handling of syntax in this main clause. For example, apart from the wedge driven between the subject *NP* and the *V* to achieve what I shall be calling "clausal spread," the major *VP* elements follow in unbroken succession ("have sent you suche a present"). Moreover, the bulk of the expansion of the main clausal unit is performed by the *such . . . as* construction that adjoins the object *NP*, "a present." Compounded though it is with internal pattern-loading, this construction nevertheless trails the object *NP* to expand the clause in native fashion by filling up its tail end. We will find, indeed, as discussion continues that manner and degree constructions with *such . . . as* and *so . . . that* bear watching as amenable means for combining Latinate suspensiveness with English successiveness—the divergent syntactic impulsions which More's style undertakes to reconcile effectively (as Pecock's style had not managed to do).

But just how effective is More's hybridizing of Latinate and native principles of sentence form? Gee, as noted, credits More with limited but genuine early success. This also seems to be the gist of Richard S. Sylvester's view of More's style in his *History of King Richard the Third* (1513).[63] Notwithstanding these acknowledgments of early success, Gee reaches far severer judgment on the style of More's subsequent English works and on the overall quality of his prose. Gee alleges two chief, related faults: first, overelaboration of sentence content with a concomitant loss of formal control ("the main thought is lost because of its having too many modifiers") and, second, such excessive recourse to English approximations of absolute constructions and verb-final word order as to place meaning frequently in doubt.[64] On the whole, subsequent critics have not disputed Gee's view of early promise vitiated by later practice in More's vernacular works, but the sense of promise has dimmed with an understandable shift of interest away from his comparatively derivative youthful output (translation, adaptation) to the massive original prose compositions of his maturity. Arthur I. Taft's introduction to his edition of More's *Apology*, a work first published in 1533, dwells on the deleterious effects of Latinisms and, above all, repetitiousness in the handling of syntax in the later English prose. Although Taft perceived a certain functionality in the authorial determination "never to leave meaning in doubt," he was finally forced to conclude as follows: "When the redundance and looseness concur in endless, rambling sentences, More's style is at its worst."[65]

C. S. Lewis's comparative judgment on More and Tyndale as vernacular prose writers has probably been as influential in its way as Chambers's "continuity" essay, but unfortunately it, too, takes the form of generalization all the while that it pioneers in recognizing the More-Tyndale controversy as an effectual gauge of the two men's stylistic achievements. Lewis sides with the negative majority in his "serious reservations" regarding the "great claims made in modern times . . . for More's English prose," finding "nothing at all in him which, if further developed, could possibly lead on to the graces of Elizabethan and Jacobean literature." Style, according to Lewis, is a precinct "where Tyndale is most obviously and continually superior to More."[66] Most recently, in the wake of Lewis, counterefforts have been mounted to rehabilitate

[63]Richard S. Sylvester, Introduction, *The History of King Richard III*, in *Complete Works of St. Thomas More*, vol. 2 (New Haven and London: Yale University Press, 1963), pp. lxxx–civ.

[64]Gee, *Life and Works of Thomas Lupset*, pp. 195–96.

[65]Introduction, *The Apologye of Syr Thomas More, Knyght*, ed. Arthur Irving Taft, Early English Text Society o.s. 180 (London: Humphrey Milford, 1930), pp. lii–liii.

[66]C. S. Lewis, *English Literature in the Sixteenth Century, Excluding Drama* (Oxford: Clarendon Press, 1954), pp. 180–81, 192. Extending Lewis's emphasis on the literary interest of the More-Tyndale exchanges, Norman Davis surveys some points of linguistic (and stylistic) interest in *William Tyndale's English of Controversy*, Chambers Memorial Lecture, University College, London (London: H. K. Lewis & Co., 1971).

More's critical reputation while leaving in force the shift of attention to the later English writings, but it is noteworthy that these counterefforts bypass stylistic considerations in favor of other dimensions of literary form. Leonard Miles's claims about More's greatness as a writer on the basis of the late *Dialogue of Comfort against Tribulation* (1534) are indicative: these address the factors of suspense, climax, dramatic engagement, and pacing in the handling of dialogue form as well as the employment of source materials and the creation of allegory.[67] Miles's markedly more inclusive critical outlook, however, has as its concomitant an obtrusive editorial policy that carries implications for stylistic concerns; there are repeated excisions and bracketed insertions of phrases and clauses throughout the body of the text. In the absence of any explanation for such strenuous reshaping, it is hard not to infer that even such an advocate of More as Miles finds the sentence forms of the *Dialogue of Comfort* too problematical to stand on their own. As for my approach here in discussing More as an English stylist, I shall not so much reargue the pros and cons of evaluation as aim to describe and explain the characteristic features of sentence form in his mature original works. Although I own to agreeing with Lewis that the Tyndale-More controversy comprises a crucial body of stylistic evidence which reveals Tyndale as the better writer, the real issue needing to be addressed is the dearth of analysis of More's later vernacular prose. Why did the hybridizing of native and Latinate sentence forms so perceptively noted by Gee prove to be the unstable and finally unworkable compound seen in More's mature writing? If any light can be thrown upon the answer to this question, it will help us to see our way beyond blanket or impressionistic judgments in the vexed matter of More's net standing in English literary history.

In March 1528 Cuthbert Tunstal, bishop of London, wrote in Latin to More, a layman, praising him as "an ardent defender of Catholic truth" and soliciting the use of his demonstrated abilities "in our vernacular tongue, no less than in Latin," for the composition "in our own language" of "such books as may show to simple and unlearned men [*simplicibus et ideotis hominibus*] the cunning malice of the heretics, and fortify them against these impious subverters of the Church."[68] Up to

[67]Thomas More, *A Dialogue of Comfort against Tribulation*, ed. Leonard Miles (Bloomington and London: Indiana University Press, 1965), pp. xli–liv; cf. the note taken of "obstacles to reading," pp. xcix–ci.

[68]Tunstal's commission to More is reprinted from David Wilkins, *Concilia Magnae Britanniae* (London: R. Gosling, 1737), III, 711–12, in *The Correspondence of Sir Thomas More*, ed. Elizabeth F. Rogers (Princeton: Princeton University Press, 1947), pp. 387–88. The translation is T. E. Bridgett's, from his *Life and Writings of Blessed Thomas More* (London: Burns, Oates & Washbourne, 1935), pp. 281–82. Why More was cast as the sole vernacular defender of Catholicism in England remains a puzzle, although his lay status would have been a special advantage in coping with the high tide of anticlerical sentiments.

this date More had not written at all extensively in English, but on accepting Tunstal's commission he redressed the proportion of his vernacular output many times over. Of the group of works centering on Tyndale which figure in the present discussion, More's *Dialogue concerning Heresies,* or *Dialogue against Luther and Tyndale* (1529), runs to 175,000 words, Tyndale's *An Answer unto Sir Thomas More* (1531) to 80,000 words, and More's *Confutation of Tyndale's Answer* (1532) to 500,000 words.[69] Thus there is a sheer physical reckoning to be made with the linguistic—not to speak of other—energy elicited by the advent of the Reformation in England.

Although More wrote against other Reformers too, he astutely registered the surpassing threat to ecclesiastical authority constituted by Tyndale in his twin role as translator of Scripture and apologist for the "new learning" that so emphatically affirmed its foundation in Scripture. How very well More perceived the subversive import of Tyndale's appeal to individual and personal lay judgment may be gathered from the set of terms he singles out in the *Dialogue concerning Heresies* as the basis for condemning Tyndale's New Testament as heretical. More defends the reading "church" in place of Tyndale's "congregation," "priest" in place of Tyndale's "senior" (later, "elder"), "penance" in place of "repentance," and "charity" in place of "love." The debate over vocabulary that first focused the opposition between the two men is a remarkable joint demonstration of linguistic ingenuity and delicacy of perception regarding the expressiveness of the native tongue. Tyndale recognized that centuries of accrued usage would operate to give clerical authority and the Catholic sacrament of ordination a claim to Scriptural warrant if he translated *ekklesia* as "church" and *presbuteros* as "priest," while similarly accrued meanings of "doing penance" and "giving charity" would undergird the religion of works which he considered un-Scriptural anathema. Philologically there might be a defense for the etymologizing efforts by which Tyndale sought to retrieve apostolic Christianity in its first forms of organization and formulations of doctrine. Yet it would have been wholly disingenuous to represent such lexical choices as mere philological niceties—especially to More, who saw so clearly and said so roundly that the Scripturalism (and Lutheranism) of Tyndale would undermine the established rule and prerogatives of the papacy and the Roman Church.

A glance at the larger context is useful at this point, for issues of religious vocabulary go considerably beyond the More-Tyndale controversy to focus essential differences between the Catholic and Protestant positions in England during the Henrician era. A. F. Pollard's *Records of*

---

[69]The figures for More's works are given by Nugent, *Thought and Culture of the English Renaissance,* pp. 433–34.

the English Bible reproduces a letter written in early 1527 by Robert Ridley, Tunstal's chaplain, to Henry Gold, a chaplain to William Warham, the archbishop of Canterbury. Ridley's letter prefigures in brief many of More's criticisms of Tyndale in the *Dialogue concerning Heresies* which appeared in print the next year. It is also noteworthy and symptomatic in the consistency with which Ridley manages to make a preliminary statement of his objections in English, only to shift into Latin whenever he wants to clinch a point. In part he shifts in order to cite the Vulgate, but he also employs Latin generically as a mode of authoritative discourse. Thus Ridley faults Tyndale for maintaining

that by good warkes we do no thyng merite, *contra illud ad Corinthos ut referat unusquisque prout gessit sive bonum sive malum et illud genes ad Abram quia fecisti hanc rem* etc. *item illud Matthaei quod sitivi et dedistis mihi potum* &c. *et venite benedicti patris mei*. . . . As for the texte of the godspell, first the title is hereticall saying that it is prent as it was writen by the evangelistes: *cum neque consentiat cum antiqua translatione neque cum erasmica*. . . . By this translation shal we loose al thies christian wordes, penance, charite, confession, grace, prest, chirche, which he alway calleth a congregation, *quasi turcharum et brutorum nulla esset congregatio nisi velit illorum etiam esse ecclesiam.*

Ridley's parting words to Gold, however, couch his chief objection to Tyndale's Scripturalism in blunt English: "It becummyth the people of truste to obey & folowe their rewellers which hath geven study & is lerned in such matters as thys. People showd heer & beleve, thai showd not judge the doctrine of paule ne of paules vicares & successors."[70]

This insistence upon maintaining clerical authority (and superiority) through retention of a traditional and specifically Latinate vocabulary becomes the core of the English Catholic position regarding Biblical translation.[71] Stephen Gardiner, its leading spokesman, submitted a list of one hundred words from the Vulgate to Convocation in 1542; he argued that these should be transliterated as exactly as possible from Latin into English, out of reverence for what he characterized to his fellow bishops as "their germane and native meaning and the majesty of their matter" (*pro eorum germano et nativo intellectu et rei majestate*). The words on Gardiner's list include *ecclesia, poenitentia, pontifex, adorare, sacramentum, ceremonia, mysterium, religio, caritas, episcopus, confessio, sa-*

[70]Letter from Robert Ridley to Henry Gold (Brit. Lib. Cotton MS. Cleopatra E.v.362ᵇ), cited in *Records of the English Bible,* ed. Alfred F. Pollard (London: Henry Frowde for Oxford University Press, 1911), pp. 123–25. See, further, Robert E. McNally, "The Council of Trent and Vernacular Bibles," *Theological Studies* 27 (1966): 204–27, for a circumstantial account of conciliar developments between 1546 and 1564 that crystallized in "the unbiblical atmosphere of the post-Tridentine Church."

[71]Gardiner's speech (as preserved in Wilkins's *Concilia*, III, 860–62) is excerpted in Pollard, *Records of the English Bible*, pp. 272–75. The preface to the Rheims New Testament (1582) is cited on pp. 305–6.

tisfactio, Dominus, and *sanctus* among the manifold entries. This articulated Catholic position persists in the preface to the Rheims New Testament (1582): first, in the assertion that lay access to Scripture is no necessity but rather a gesture of "special consideration" made by the clergy; second, in the various explanations given for certain renderings in the English text. "Amen," for example, replaces "verily," "Alleluia" replaces "Praise ye the Lord," "Pasche" replaces "Passover," "the advent of our Lord" replaces "the coming," and "the imposing of handes" "the laying on of hands." It is explained that the last two renderings were thought advisable "because one is a solemne time, the other a solemne action in the Catholike Church," and that terminology generally in translating Scripture should "signifie to the people, that these and such like names come out of the very Latin text of the Scripture. So did *Penance, doing penance, Chalice, Priest, Deacon, Traditions, aultar, host* and the like (which we exactly keepe as Catholike termes) procede even from the very wordes of Scripture." These "very wordes of Scripture," however, have consistent Latin origins, not Hebrew or Greek ones.

Against this backdrop of sixteenth-century evidence that vocabulary remained a crucial issue for the duration of the Reformation, the More-Tyndale controversy stands out in all the sharper relief as evidence that the handling of sentence form and affiliated aspects of discourse are at least as vital an index to the ideological opposition between Protestantism and Catholicism in England as are any other features of language use. Indeed, in this controversy syntax finally emerges as an even more incisive register than vocabulary because Tyndale and More evolved along mutually exclusive lines of thinking on a pair of stylistically essential questions: first, how to utilize the relation between spoken and written language in dealing with substantive religious matters in English; and, second, how far to countenance the exercise of individual reflection and expression on such matters in English. The results are, as we shall see, two starkly contrasted conceptions and styles of authoritative utterance.

More began his labors as a controversialist in English by writing dialogues. The choice of this form was felicitous and natural for several reasons: it had long-standing didactic associations both in classical antiquity and in Christian tradition, whether the writing was being done in Latin or in the vernacular; More also shared Erasmus's fondness for writers of dialogue (Lucian especially), and he had employed the form himself in *Utopia.* Yet, for all of these predisposing literary considerations, there is little in More's antecedent writings—except some of the dialogue in his *History of Richard III*—that prepares us for the recurrently speechlike turns of the prose in the *Dialogue concerning Heresies.* Evidently More set out to address the readership of "simple and unlearned men" which Tunstal had assigned him by the promising expedient of putting a persona of this very type into his work. The *Dialogue* represents itself as a discussion between More and a young Londoner, the trusted friend of a friend sent to More's house with some confidential information about heretical goings-on in the city. A letter of recommendation written by More's friend for the young man praises him "not onely for hys trouth & secretnesse, but also for his memory," also for being "more then meanlye lerned, with one thing added where with ye wont weel to be content, a very mery wit." Above all, the young man is said to be "of nature nothing tongetayed." The characters of the two personae— the Lord Chancellor More and the forthright young man—can therefore be expected to clash tellingly on the issue of religious authority, as the alleged letter from More's friend anticipates: "I have . . . boden him more to mynde his matter, then his curtesye, & frely to lai forth, . . . gyvyng no fote in disputing unto your authority, but yf he bee borne back with reason." Nevertheless, it is noteworthy that More's friend (as represented by More the author) has no doubts of the outcome:

Thus may ye se I am bolde on your goodnes/ to put you to labour and busynes/ and sende one to face you in your owne house. But so moche am I bolder/ for that in such chalenges I know you for a redy and sure defender. And of suche laboure your wysdome well seeth/ that God is the rewarder/ who longe preserve you & all yours.[72]

More's care in contriving the fictive circumstantiality of the *Dialogue concerning Heresies* suggests strongly that his strategy was to address the thinking of typical Londoners in 1527 on recent challenges to the authority of the Church and to do so in language that would have its effect through colloquial informality. Accordingly, the selection of the first topics for discussion was crucial both for launching a familiar, conversational mode and for preparing the eventual triumph of the More authority figure within this mode. These topics turn out to tap directly into current sources of lay discontent: imputation of vice and hypocrisy to the clergy, suspicion of miracles and of the efficacy of pilgrimages and prayers to saints. They conduce superbly to the launching of the desired conversational mode as More and the young man recount to each other various personal experiences with the folk mentality and exchange civil pleasantries in between. Accordingly, the prose of the opening section of the *Dialogue* is firmly based in oral expression: expletives, pleonasm, anacoluthon (or "special syntax"), and loosely additive clausal sequences as staples of the style. Here is a typical progression which begins with the I-figure's—that is, More's—good-natured twitting

[72]*A Dialogue concerning Heresies*, ed. Thomas M. C. Lawler et al., in *Complete Works of St. Thomas More*, vol. 6 (New Haven and London: Yale University Press, 1981), p. 26. Subsequent references are abbreviated *DCH* and incorporated in the text. In quoting, I have expanded printer's contractions and modernized *i, j, u,* and *v*.

of the young man for his skepticism and continues with the young man's attempt to justify his skepticism toward ecclesiastical authority by telling an eyewitness tale of humble candor:

Well sayd I/ what yf I sholde tell you now/ that I had sene the same?

By my fayth quod he merely I wold byleve it at lesour whan I had sene the same/ and in the meane whyle I coulde not let you to say your pleasure in your owne house/ but I wolde thynke that ye were disposed merely to make me a fole.

In good fayth quod I/ I mene good ernest nowe/ and yet as well as ye dare trust me I shall as I sayd yf ye wyll go with me provyde a couple of wytnes of whome ye wyll byleve any one better than twayne of me/ for they be your nere frendes/ and ye have bene better acquaynted with them/ and suche as I dare say for theym be not often wont to lye.

Who be they quod he I pray you?

Mary quod I your owne two eyen/ for I shall yf you wyll brynge you where ye shall se it/ no ferther hens than evyn here in London.

Mary syr quod he these wytnes in dede wyll not lye. As the pore man sayed by the preste/ yf I may be so homely to tell you a mery tale by the way.

A mery tale quod I/ commyth never amysse to me.

The pore man quod he had founde the preste over famylyer with his wyfe/ and bycause he spake it a brode and coulde not prove it/ the preste sued hym before the bysshoppys offycyall for dyffamacyon/ where the pore man upon payne of cursynge/ was commaunded that in his parysshe chyrche/ he sholde uppon the sondaye/ at hygh masse tyme/ stande up and say mouth thou lyest. Wherupon for fulfyllynge of hys penaunce/ up was the pore soule set in a pew/ that the peple myght wonder on hym/ and here what he sayd. And there all a lowde (whan he had rehersyd what he had reportyd by the preste) than he set his handys on his mouth/ and sayd mouth mouth thou lyest. And by and by thereupon he set his hande uppon bothe his eyen and sayd/ but eyen eyen quod he/ by the masse ye lye not a whytte. And so syr in dede/ and ye brynge me those wytnes they wyll not ly a whyt . . . / yet am I never the more bounden by reason to byleve them/ that wolde tell me a myracle. [DCH, pp. 67, 69]

As long as the topics are objections to abuses of ecclesiastical customs and prerogatives, the More persona remains relaxed and informal in conversing with the young man. Their styles of expression are, in fact, nearly indistinguishable in the earlier sections of the *Dialogue*, for when More admonishes the young man on some matter, the colloquial syntax and homely exempla suggest a latter-day Mirk. Here is a piece of the More persona's admonition in this vein, aimed at the perennial youthful tendency to indiscriminate reactions:

Well quod I ye speke merrely/ but I wote well ye wyll do better what so ever ye saye. . . . For though the Jewes were many so noughty/ that they put Cryste to dethe/ yet ye be wyser I wote well/ than the gentylwoman was/ whiche in talkynge ones with my father when she harde say that our lady was a Jewe/

fyrst could not byleve it/ but sayd what ye mocke I wysse I pray you tell trouth. And whan it was so fully affermed that she at laste byleved it/ & was she a Jewe quod she/ so helpe me God and halydom I shall love her the worse whyle I lyve. I am sure ye wyll not do so/ nor mystrust all for some/ neyther men nor myracles. [*DCH*, p. 92]

But the evocation of a realistic contemporary speech context is not the sole function of the early stylistic homogeneity of More's *Dialogue*. In the sections where the I-figure and the young man use undifferentiated colloquial expression, the contextual implication is that they are discoursing essentially as equals. At certain junctures in these earlier sections, the I even takes pains to affirm their shared humanity—for example, in the following passage where the More persona irrelevantly but effectively invokes sexuality to defuse an anticlerical outburst by the young man that has nothing whatever to do with sexuality. The quotation picks up near the end of the young man's inveighings against pilgrimages and offerings to images:

And men reken that the clergye is glad to favour thies wayes/ and to norysshe this superstycyon under the name and colour of devocyon/ to the parell of the peoples soules/ for the lucre and temporall advauntage that them selfe receyve of the offryngys.

Whan I had hard hym say what hym lyked I demaunded yf he mynded ever to be preste/ wherunto he answered nay verely/ for me thynketh quod he that there be prestes to many all redy but yf they were better. And therfore whan god shall sende tyme I purpose he sayd to marry.

Well sayd I than syth I am all redy marryed twyse/ & therfore never can be preste/ and ye be so set in mynde of marryage/ that ye never wyll be preste/ we two be not the most metely to ponder what myght be sayd in this matter for the prestys parte. [*DCH*, p. 53]

Throughout the *Dialogue concerning Heresies* the young man remains the mouthpiece of colloquial expression. So successful and suggestive is the link forged between Protestant sympathies and speech-based prose that we must consider it a conscious authorial creation. Nevertheless, while the young man is in no danger of losing his voice, overall as the *Dialogue* proceeds he is given less and less to say. The I is gradually but inexorably brought into greater and greater prominence as an interlocutor; in the process he begins more and more to suspend his own conversational manner when he has anything substantive to say. This trend toward sharp stylistic differentiation and disproportionate allocation of speaking roles between the two personae sets in unmistakably when the young man raises and presses for an extended stretch his point that Scripture is the ultimate authority over the Church, and not vice versa, as the I contends. It is, then, the issue of Scripturalism and individual lay judgment that precipitates new measures on the part of the More persona to sustain authoritative utterance.[73] What these new measures entail will emerge as we trace them from the observable origins of a developing stylistic differentiation between the young man and the I in chapters 26 and 27 near the end of Book 1. As the differentiation in speaking manners becomes more pronounced, an imputation of inequality in the relation of the two personae grows as well. The following excerpts illustrate by turns the young man's continuing colloquialism in arguing for the authority of Scripture, and the More persona's increasingly magisterial manner in affirming the authority of the Church:

Truely syr quod he/ me thynketh it is well sayd that ye have sayd. And in good faythe to say the truthe I se not what I shold answere it withall. And yet whan I loke backe agayne upon holy scrypture/ and consyder/ that it is Goddes owne wordes/ whiche I wote well ye wyll graunte/ I fynde it harde in myne hart to byleve all the men in the hole worlde/ yf they wold say any thynge/ wherof I sholde se that the holy scrypture sayth the contrary/ syth it is reason that I byleve God alone far better than them all.

But where shall it appere that God commaundyth us in all suche thynges to byleve the chyrche? For fyrst me thynkyth that were a very straunge maner of commaundynge. For of the chyrche be all we that sholde (as ye say) be by God commaunded to byleve the chyrche/ and all we togyther make the hole chyrche. And what reason were it than to commaunde us to byleve the chyrche. Whyche were no more in effecte/ but to byd us all byleve us all/ or eche of us to byleve other? And then yf we fell at dyvers oppynyons/ why sholde the one parte more byleve the other/ than be byleved of the other/ sythe bothe the partys be of the chyrche and make the chyrche amonge them? savynge that alway that parte semeth to be bylevyd whiche best and most clerely can alledge the scrypture for their oppynyon. For the wordes of God must breke the stryfe. [DCH, pp. 154, 162–63]

Ye take that quod I for a grete doubte and a thynge very perplex/ whiche semeth to me very playne. For eyther fyrste the chyrche hathe the truthe and byleve all one way tyll some one or some fewe begynne the chaunge/ and than thoughe all be yet of the chyrche/ tyll some by theyr obstynacy be gone out or put out/ yet is it no doubte but yf I wyll byleve the chyrche I must byleve them that styll byleve that waye/ whiche all the hole byleved before.

Or els yf there were any thyng that was peradventure such/ that in the chyrche somtyme was doubted and reputed for unreveled and unknowen/ yf after that the hole chyrche fall in one consent upon the one syde/ eyther by common determynacyon at a generall counsayle/ or by a perfyte perswasyon and byleve so receyved thrughe crystendome/ that the crysten people thynke it a dampnable erroure to byleve the contrary/ than yf any wolde after that take the contrary waye/ were it one or mo/ were it fewe or many/ were they lerned or unlerned/

---

[73]On the larger ramifications of the issue at stake in this passage, see George H. Tavard, *Holy Writ or Holy Church: The Crisis of the Protestant Reformation* (London: Burns & Oates, 1959).

were they ley people or of the clergye/ yet can I nothynge doubte whiche parte to byleve yf I wyll byleve the chyrche.

That is trouthe quod he/ but ye prove me not yet that God hath boden me byleve the chyrche.

Ye somwhat interrupted me quod I with your other subteltye/ by whiche ye wolde it sholde seme an absurdytye to bydde us byleve the chyrche.

But surely this is moch to be marked. For it is the perpetuall order whiche our lorde hath contynued in the governaunce of good men from the begynnynge/ that lyke as our nature fyrst fell by pryde to the dysobedyence of God with inordynate desyre of knowledge lyke unto God/ so hath God ever kepte man in humylyte/ straynynge hym with the knowledge & confessyon of his ygno-raunce/ & byndynge hym to the obedyence of byleve of certayne thynges/ where-of his owne wyt wolde verely wene the contrary. And therfore are we bounden not onely to byleve agaynste oure owne reason/ the poyntes that God sheweth us in scrypture/ but also that God techeth his chyrche without scrypture & agaynst our owne mynde also/ to gyve dylygent herynge/ ferme credence/ and faythfull obedyence to the chyrche of Cryst/ concernynge the sence and under-standynge of holy scrypture. Not doubtyng but syth he hath commaunded his shepe to be fedde/ he hath provyded for them holesome mete and trewe doc-tryne. And that he hathe therefore so farre inspyred the olde holy doctours of his chyrch with the lyght of his grace for our instruccyon/ that the doctryne wherin they have agreed/ & by many ages consented/ is the very trewe fayth and ryght way to heven/ beynge put in theyr myndes by the holy hande of hym/ *qui facit unanimes in domo*/ that maketh the chyrche of Cryst all of one mynde. [*DCH*, pp. 164, 166]

The stylistic differentiation between the young man and More consists fundamentally in their disparate approaches to the handling of clausal units in sentence structure. The young man relies on asymmetric and trailing sequences of clauses in which conjunction—including sentential and nonrestrictive relative constructions—plays the major role. *For* is nearly as frequent as *and*, signaling as surely as in the prose of Wyclif and Fortescue the adaptation of native syntactic resources to a forensic purpose. The young man also intermittently uses loose temporal and conditional connectives together with his asymmetric conjunctions, for example, in his third sentence: "*And yet whan* I loke backe . . . *and* consyder . . . *whiche* . . . ye wyll graunt, I fynde it harde in myne hart to byleve all the men . . . , *yf* they wold say any thynge/ *wherof* I sholde se . . . the contrary, *syth* it is reason that I byleve God." But what is most essential of all in the syntax of the young man's discourse is that he manages both the internal structure and the adjunction of clausal units so as to respect the "successiveness" of English and preserve "open sentence." To these ends, in the first place, the Subject $NP + V + ($Object $NP) + ($Complement$)$ order of major constituents within the clause is kept highly constant: there is only one inversion (the sentence beginning "For of the chyrche be all we . . ."). In the second place, and even more requisitely for openness, the intactness of the grouping of major constituents in clausal units is rarely broken, and then by brief insertions that neither obscure nor encumber the internal structure of the clause (e.g., "I fynde it harde *in myne hart* to byleve . . ."). Thus, the sustaining dynamic of the young man's sentence forms is readily perceived as a succession of clausal units to which most modifying material is adjoined at clausal boundaries rather than internally. There is some adjunction at the heads of clauses (e.g., "And *in good faythe to say the truthe* I se not . . . ," "For *fyrst* me thynkyth . . . ," "that *alway* that parte semeth . . ."), but the brevity and syntactic simplicity of this material render adjunctions inconspicuous and unproblematic in this position. By far the more common arrangement in the young man's sentence forms is for various additions and expansions to be located at the tail ends of clauses where they elaborate without complicating the line of thought, usually by bolstering or shoring up a plainspoken question or assertion.

In the evolution away from colloquial expression that can be observed in the More persona's style, there is still quite appreciable utilization of the recursive potential of conjunctive syntax. The crucial difference is that recursion is put into effect a great deal more at the phrasal level, where clustered coordinate structures "load the patterns" of major constituents, as, for example, in "a grete doubte and a thynge very perplex," "was doubted and reputed for unreveled and unknowen," "by a perfyte perswasyon and byleve," "to gyve dylygent herynge/ ferme credence/ and faythfull obedyence to the chyrche of Cryst," "the sence and understanding of holy scrypture," "the very trewe fayth and ryght way to heven." Among these pattern-loading coordinate structures, there is a significant and obvious proportion of (near-)tautological word pairs, the staple of earlier English attempts at authoritative style. Despite these divergences, however, no categorical distinction can yet be drawn between the young man's and the More persona's style in the use of loose binary connectives to join sentences and clauses; this remains a shared native resource. Notable in this regard are the second and third sentences in the More persona's rejoinder—the one beginning "For eyther . . . ," the other "Or els . . ."—and the extent to which other binary constructions like *thoughe . . . yet, yf . . . than,* and *eyther . . . or* organize the internal syntactic workings of this sentence pair.

On balance, from this point onward in the *Dialogue,* the young man's discourse preserves "open sentence" but the More persona's increasingly does not. Again the handling of clausal units becomes the crucial factor. While Gee's strictures on excessive modification resulting in the loss of a main idea must be acknowledged, in my view the principal source of complication and perplexity in More's authoritative sentence forms is the distension to which he regularly subjects his main clauses. This is not necessarily or even primarily a matter of modification, in the sense of appended qualifiers. More contrives to suspend and enlarge the boundaries of main clauses so that, instead of retaining a perceptual intactness as syntactic units, they seem headed for coextensiveness with the domain of the sentence as a whole. He achieves this effect, which I term "clausal spread," by a pair of means in combination: one more general, the other more particular. The more general means is to construct a clause containing semantically minimal elements in one or more of its key subject-verb-object or complement positions, which in turn require some suppletory construction (often itself a clause) in order to deliver a full quota of sentential meaning. The commonest minimal structures for clauses make heavy use of pronouns and of the verb *to be*, but there are numerous additional possibilities with a range of verbs that take clauses as subject or predicate complements.[74] The more particular of More's means for achieving clausal spread utilizes *so . . . that* and *such . . . that* complements as the suppletory constructions for minimal main clause elements.

In the speech by the More persona quoted above, it is remarkable how clauses are spread by these combined means. Together they account for the syntactic superstructure of more than half of the sentences, as can be demonstrated in skeletal outline as follows, with the minimal elements and the *so* and *such* connectives italicized:

Or els yf *there were any thyng that was* peradventure *such/that . . .* , than yf *any* wolde after that take the contrary waye *. . .* , yet can I *nothynge* doubte *whiche* parte to byleve. *. . .*

But surely *this is moch to be* marked.

For *it is* the perpetuall order *which* our lorde hath *so* contynued *. . . that . . . so* hath God ever kepte. *. . .*

And *that* he hathe therfore *so* farre inspyred the olde holy doctours *. . . that* the doctryne *. . . is* the very trewe fayth and ryght way to heven, *that* maketh the chyrche of Cryst. *. . .*

These examples show why *so* and *such* clausal complements contribute so prominently to spreading clausal structure. Unlike more ordinary clausal complementation with *that*, which in English sentences overwhelmingly occurs in predicate position at the tail end of a higher clause, *so . . . that* and *such . . . that* complements insert the particle *so* or *such*

[74]My colleague Joseph M. Williams of the University of Chicago has proposed the label "metadiscourse" for the class of such semantically minimal locutions as, e.g., 'It may be the case that . . .' or 'What is now evident is that. . . .' Metadiscourse is an apt term, for it bespeaks the special function performed by expressions of this type in training attention upon a following predication. William A. Vande Kopple, "Experimental Evidence for Functional Sentence Perspective" (Ph.D. diss., University of Chicago, 1980), has found that metadiscourse is more difficult to recall than is ordinary discourse.

into the internal phrase structure of the higher clause unit, thereby precluding any sense of closure in that unit and complicating the successiveness which is so essential to the workings of English syntax. That the cultivation of clausal spread puts real strain on the language (and its users) can be gathered, moreover, from the frequent resumptive constructions that help one to regain one's bearings in sentence forms. There are resumptive constructions in two of the four outlined sentences: the *so*s in "which our lord hath *so* contynued . . . that . . . *so* hath God ever kepte," and the *that*s in "And *that* . . . he hathe therfore so farre inspyred . . . , *that* maketh the chyrche of Cryst." In particular, in the latter example, where the *that*s join the beginning and end of the entire sentence in one great spreading which at last fills in for the semantically empty elements of the main clause, one finds a sentence form that is virtually the converse of a native type. It is, however, a creditable approximation of Latinate periodic or "circular" composition, which in English tends oftener to circuitous realizations than to truly circular ones.

The foregoing observations suggest a first answer to the question that naturally arises regarding the stylistic cleavage that develops in the *Dialogue concerning Heresies:* Why would More, with his proven capabilities in the native, colloquial mode, increasingly adopt in his vernacular controversial writings principles of sentence construction that replaced successiveness with suspensiveness and deliberately departed from English norms for speech and prose? One evident motive for such a departure stems from the profound allegiance to Latinity that was bred in More jointly by his Catholicism and his humanism. With respect to this dual orientation, the more Latinate English could be made, the closer it would come to being a condign medium for articulating and defending his values. Moreover, in the light of his commission from Tunstal to defend the Roman faith to a vernacular readership, More's efforts at domesticating Latinate periodic sentence form as clausal spread in English take on a symbolic appropriateness. The mounting associations between authoritativeness and a turning away from indigenous syntactic patterns in More's English prose can thus be interpreted as a positive and deeply impelled stylistic program. And yet there are equally marked negative aspects of this development in More's vernacular style. A second look at the question why the Latinizing took place at all in the work of a writer who was a master of colloquial expression suggests that the turn was not as unforced an option as might initially appear. For why could English prose not achieve authoritativeness with its native resources? The sense that emerges from a reading of the *Dialogue concerning Heresies*—as well as *The Supplication of Souls* (1529), More's defense of the dogma of purgatory, and the *Confutation of Tyndale's Answer*—is that More by degrees closed off any such possibility for his style by assigning a derogatory function not simply to colloquialism but also to the resources of conjunctive sentence form. This claim, I know, requires substantiation.

As Pineas has noted, a prime objective of the *Dialogue* was to exculpate to a contemporary readership the proceedings of Church authorities in the case of Richard Hunne, a London merchant tailor who had had the temerity to lodge a civil suit against a priest and who subsequently was imprisoned on a heresy charge and then found hanged in his cell.[75] The case was a notorious spur to anticlericalism in the capital; justifiably so, it would appear from twentieth-century research confirming that Hunne's death was murder and not suicide. The tactic employed by More to defend the clergy's role is to rehearse what he represents as the verbatim testimony of several witnesses on the Hunne side at the inquest. In the following supposed testimony of a man who claimed to have an informed opinion about the manner of death because he had worked as an almoner's assistant, the satirical undertones in the colloquialism would have sufficed to disparage the witness, without the More persona's commentary. The quotation below picks up with the question to the witness on the manner of Hunne's death:

The man . . . was moche amased/ and loked as though his eyen wolde have fallen out of his hed into the lordys lappys. But to the questyon he answered and sayd/ that he sawe that very well/ for he sawe hym bothe ere he was taken downe and after.

What than quod the lordys so dyd there many mo/ whyche yet uppon the syght coulde not tell that.

No my lordys quod he but I have another insyght in suche thyngys than other men have.

What insyght quod they?

Forsothe quod he it is not unknowen that I have occupied a great whyle under dyvers of the kyngys almoygners/ and have sene and consydered many that have hanged theym selfe/ and therby yf I se one hange I can tell anone whyther he hanged hym selfe or not.

By what token can you tell quod the lordys.

Forsothe quod he I canne not tell the tokens/ but I perceyve it well ynoughe by myne owne syght.

But whan they herde hym speke of hys owne syght/ and therewith sawe what syght he had/ lokynge as though his eyen wolde have fallen in theyr lappys/ there coulde fewe forbere laughynge/ and sayd we se well surely that ye have a syghte by youre selfe. . . .

Why quod another lorde meryly your offyce hathe no more experyence in hangynge than hath an hange man. And yet he can not tell.

Naye syr quod he and it lyke your lordshyp he medleth not with theym that hange theym selfe as I do.

[75]Pineas, *Thomas More and Tudor Polemics*, pp. 92–95; cf. Dickens, "The Hunne Affair and Its Sequels," *The English Reformation*, pp. 90–96.

Well quod one of the lordys howe many of theym have ye medled with in your dayes?

With many my lorde quod he/ for I have bene offycer under two almoygners and therefore I have sene many.

Howe many quod one of the lordys?

I can not tell quod he howe many/ but I wote well I have sene many.

Have ye sene quod one an hundred?

Nay quod he not an hundred.

Have ye sene foure score and ten? thereat a lytell he studyed as one standynge in a doute and that were lothe to lye and at last he sayd/ that he thought nay not fully foure score and ten. Than was he asked whyther he hathe sene twenty. And thereto without any styckynge he answered nay not twenty. Thereat the lordys laughed well to se that he was so sure that he hadde not sene twenty/ and was in doute whyther he hadde sene foure score and ten. [*DCH*, pp. 322–23]

Similarly derisive connotations attach to predominantly conjunctive syntax after the change in roles and styles late in the first book of More's *Dialogue*. Here, to illustrate, is a run of additive sentential conjunction employed for the purpose of discrediting the line of Scripturalist thinking which More so reprehends in Tyndale:

For this one poynt is the very fond foundacyon and grounde of all his greate heresyes/ that a man is not bounden to byleve any thynge but yf it may be provyd evydently by scrypture. And there uppon goth he so farforth/ that no scrypture can be evydent to prove any thyng that he lyst to deny. For he wyll not agre it for evydent be it never so playn. And he wyll call evydent for hym that texte/ that is evydent agaynst hym. . . . And because the olde holy doctours be full and hole agaynst hym/ he settyth them all at nought. And with these worshypfull wyse ways he proclamyth hym self a conquerour/ where besydes all the remenaunt/ wherin every chylde may se his proud frantyke foly/ he is shamfully put to flyght in the fyrst poynt/ that is to wyt that no thynge is to be byleved for a sure trouth/ but yf it appere proved and evydent in holy wryt. [*DCH*, pp. 148–49]

This is an interesting passage. More's stylistic consciousness shows in his recognition that the native resource of asymmetric conjunction was well suited to the presentation of a series of accusations. His stylistic self-consciousness shows, moreover, in his careful differentiation of sentence forms. Thus, before launching upon the run of coordinate sentences that lampoon Protestant reasoning, More makes a decisive Catholic pronouncement in a pair of sentences that bid for authoritativeness in a tautological doubling ("foundacyon and grounde") and clausal spread (here achieved by empty main clause elements combined with predicate complementation in the first sentence, and by a *so . . . that* construction in the second). Analogously, in drawing his indictment to a close in the last sentence, More again uses a tautological doubling ("proved and evydent") in combination with clausal spread, as if to ratify formally the authority of his authorial pronouncements.

In the *Confutation of Tyndale's Answer* a further prominent feature of Tyndale's Scripturalist style—the Pauline catalogue—comes in for frequent and increasingly savage parody. It is doubly revealing that More recognizes only the negative semantic and rhetorical functions of Tyndale's catalogues and exaggerates these in his own wholly negative applications. The following excerpt from the *Confutation* demonstrates how More undermines the resources of conjunctive syntax by suffusing his sentence forms with recursions to the point of stupefaction and then intimating that he is only addrssing Tyndale in Tyndale's own mode of expression:

Then wyll we say to Tyndale and ask hym why do not you Tyndale and your spyrytuall felowes accordynge to your owne wordes, love out of your hartes the pope, the cardynals, the clergye, the prynces, the people, and so forth, beynge as your younger brothern not yet borne agayne/ and why do you not forbere them wyth all love and pacyence & so forth, and wayte on them and serve them and suffer them and so forth/ and when they wyll not wyth you come forth, why do you not then speke them fayre and flater them and promyse them fayre and so forth, and so drawe them forth and so forth. And yf that for all thys they wyll not come forth: why do you . . . use at your yonger brothern to laughe them to skorne, to mocke, to jeste, to checke, to chyde, to brawle, & rybaldously to rayle/ callynge them apyshe, pevysshe, popysshe, juglers, theves, murderers, bloodsuppers, tormentours, and traytours, Pylatys, Cayphaas, Herodys, Annaas, & Antecrystes, Judaas, hypochrytes, motenmongers, pryapystes, idolatres, horemaysters, and sodomytes, abomynable, shamles, stark madde, and faythlesse beestes, hangemen, martyr quellers, and Cryste kyllers, serpentes, scorpyons, dremers, and very dyvels/[76]

As the conclusion of the quotation indicates, and as the rest of this passage and many others state, More associated Tyndale's affective manner of writing and its attendant stylistic features with a concerted program to overthrow the established authority of the Roman Church. Taken altogether, the attenuation of any real dialogic give-and-take and the denial of positive stylistic functions for native speech-based prose and sentence forms in More's later controversial writings can scarcely be fortuitous developments. It is difficult to avoid the inference that More deliberately resigned to Tyndale—and to English Protestants generally—the exercise of native resources for prose composition, in part because he sought to cultivate a superior style for authoritative expression modeled on Latinity, but also in part because he viewed the native resources as tainted instruments of subversion. It remains to us, finally, to consider

---

[76]*The Confutation of Tyndale's Answer*, ed. Louis A. Schuster et al., in *Complete Works of St. Thomas More*, vol. 8 (New Haven and London: Yale University Press, 1973), pp. 58–59, and cf. p. 79.

what the degree of More's accomplishment was in attempting to evolve an authoritative Latinate sentence form for the writing of English prose.

As the enormous combined size of the *Dialogue concerning Heresies* and the *Confutation of Tyndale's Answer* alone attests, any assessment of More as a prose stylist is perforce an extremely selective—and, hence, subjective—undertaking. My own view is that More on occasion handles clausal spread with a judiciousness that remarkably anticipates Richard Hooker, and this is when More's mind appears genuinely engaged by both sides of an issue. Such occasions are exceedingly rare in the *Dialogue* and the *Confutation*, for More there is primarily as intent, singleminded, and unrelenting in his defense of Catholic authority as Tyndale is in his Scripturalism. A notable exception, however, is found in More's excursus on English translations of the Bible in the third book of the *Dialogue*. Since the anti-Lollard *Constitutions* of 1408, the official Catholic policy in England had been to forbid and to prosecute for heresy anyone who made or owned an English Bible. More frankly abominated Lollardy and Tyndale's Scripturalism. Nevertheless, his mind and feelings were engaged in this particular issue with exploring how allowance might be made for regulated access to vernacular Scripture on the part of a trusted few. Accordingly, his reiterated use of clausal spread to test the tenability of a moderating position between the extremes of Catholic authority and radical Protestantism results in a set of measured, grave, and lucid formulations. I cite several of these sentence forms in which the suspensiveness of clausal spread figures centrally, in order to document what I consider the finest achievements of More's Latinizing mode and style:

And surely howe it hathe happed that in all this whyle God hath eyther not suffered or not provyded that any good vertuous man hath had the mynde in faythfull wyse to translate it/ and therupon eyther the clergy or at the lest wyse/ some one bysshop to approve it/ this can I nothynge tell. [*DCH*, p. 331]

Nor I never yet herde any reason layde/ why it were not convenyent to have the byble translated in to the englysshe tonge/ but all those reasons semed they never so gay & gloryous at the fyrste syght/ yet when they were well examyned they myght in effecte for ought that I can se/ as well be layde agaynst the holy wryters that wrote the scrypture in the ebrue tonge/ & agaynste the blessyd evangelystes that wrote the scrypture in greke/ & agaynst all those in lykewyse that translated it out of every of those tonges in to latyn/ as to theyr charge that wolde well and faythfully translate it out of latyn in to oure englysshe tonge. [*DCH*, p. 337]

For no doubte is there/ but that God and his holy spyryte hath so prudently tempered theyr speche thorowe the hole corps of scrypture/ that every man may take good therby and no man harme/ but he that wyll in the study therof lene prowdely to the foly of his owne wytte. [*DCH*, p. 339]

Nowe yf it so be that it wolde happely be thought not a thynge metely to be adventured/ to set all on a flushe at ones/ and dashe rashly out holy scrypture in every lewde felowes tethe/ yet thynketh me there myght suche a moderacyon be taken therin/ as neyther good vertuous ley folke sholde lacke it/ nor rude & rashe braynes abuse it. . . . so that as nere as may be devysed/ no man have it but of the ordinaryes hande/ & by hym thought and reputed for suche/ as shall be lykely to use it to Goddes honoure & meryte of his owne soule. [*DCH*, p. 341]

As impressive and achieved as the style of the foregoing sentences is, the other, far larger, and more conspicuous aspect of More's efforts to domesticate an authoritative Latinate manner of expression in English prose is ultimately, in my view, a negative one. The stylistic stance cultivated by More in the course of his controversy with Tyndale became, as Pineas has remarked, increasingly "one of great self-confidence. . . . In conformity with his habit of constant repetition, More never tires of reminding his readers how completely he has overcome his opponent. . . . The air of superiority, and almost of infallibility, which he adopts toward his opponents is assumed on behalf of the Church he is defending."[77] The unfortunate ramifications of arrogating "superiority" if not "infallibility" in More's handling of suspensive syntax too often invite judgment either as faulty management of larger sentence form (Pecock's and Caxton's besetting problem) or as studied disregard of comprehension in favor of swamping the opposition. Either alternative does damage as an explanation of More as a stylist, for the one casts him as inept—which I think unlikely—and the other represents him as having confused authoritarian with authoritative expression. Whichever explanation one adopts, the fact remains that suspensive sentence form more and more strains the limits of linguistic capacity and human capabilities as the enormous reaches of the *Confutation* follow upon the momentous stylistic shift made in the *Dialogue*.[78] To document the growing strain on sentence form and sentence processing, here is a sentence from the *Dialogue* in which the I-figure elaborates what appears to be a complete argument on behalf of Catholic authority by loading patterns and spreading clauses in a single sentence:

[77]Pineas, *Thomas More and Tudor Polemics*, pp. 114–15. More's views on Scripture in the vernacular also become more and more negative with time; see his *Apologye*, ed. Taft, pp. 12–13.

[78]My interpretation of More's development as a stylist in his later English works has been anticipated in part by Taft's remarks on the greatly increased redundancy of expression from one tract to the next: "After 1531 this becomes his chief fault, and in the *Apology* it is certainly conspicuous. . . . Writing, as he was, for a popular audience, he tried to write down to that audience. It is to be feared that he sometimes underestimated the intelligence of his readers almost as much as he overestimated their patience. . . . This theory seems to me to account satisfactorily for the unnecessary elaboration and repetition, . . . and may also account in part for the looseness of his sentence-structure" (Introduction, *Apologye*, p. liii, and cf. pp. lx–lxiii).

Nowe then yf his chyrche be and ever shall be contynuall without any tymes bytwene (in which there shall be none) & without fayth it maye never be/ and no parte of the faythe is as ye say els where had/ but in holy scrypture/ and all it must be had/ and also as we were agreed a lytell whyle afore/ there must be none erroure adjoyned therto/ and therfore as far as toucheth the necessyte of fayth/ no parte of scrypture maye be mysse taken/ but all must be understanden ryght/ & may be ryght understanden eyther by hap/ reason/ or helpe of grace/ it necessaryly foloweth that by one or other of these wayes/ the chyrch of Cryst hath alway and never fayleth/ the ryght understandyng of scrypture/ as farre as longeth for our necessyte. [*DCH*, p. 118]

I have said that this sentence appears to encompass an argument for the infallibility of Scriptural interpretation in the Roman Church. Actually the inferences that suspend the sentence turn on an equivocation between two senses of "must" and of "necessyte": the one in which *must* means 'needs to,' 'is obligated to,' as in 'We must obey God,' which is the sense the young man had been pursuing; the other sense one of material (and logical) necessity, in which *must* has the force of 'cannot be or do otherwise than it is or does.' There is also an attendant equivocation on *may*, between 'is allowed to be' and 'is possible for it to be.' The strategy of the syntax is to proceed as if the two senses were equivalent, in order to affirm an agreement between the young man's and the More persona's positions, while rendering the nonequivalence of the two senses less noticeable by interpolating a good deal of pleonasm (e.g., "be and ever shall be contynuall," to which is added "without any tymes bytwene (in which there shall be none)"; also, "there must be none erroure adjoyned therto," to which is added "and . . . no parte of scrypture maye be mysse taken/ but all must be understanden ryght"). It is clear that this sentence form may be characterized as a strategy and even as one which More applies confidently, for when the long-postponed main clause arrives at last near the end of the sentence, it is the I-figure's meaning that shapes its predication ("it necessaryly foloweth that . . . the chyrch hath alway and never fayleth the ryght understanding of scrypture") while the young man's meaning is subsumed to this ("as farre as longeth for our necessyte").

In More's controversial works after the *Dialogue concerning Heresies* the prose tends toward ever greater utilization of multiple embeddings to suspend sentence forms and also toward greater readiness to apply these forms for overtly rhetorical as opposed to discursive ends. The following single sentence from the *Confutation* documents the sheer linguistic lengths to which More would seek to carry his bid for authoritative Catholic utterance in English:

> In thys poynte they stycke styffely/ and when they be answeryd that all though we serve god with good workes wrought with his gracyous helpe, to thentent to please hym the better therby/ as hymselfe

hath in many places of holly scrypture commaundyd us/ & hope also that suche good workes shall the rather helpe us to hevyn, so that we shall in hevyn be rewarded for theym and for the respecte of goddes commaundement/ and for thys entent also we do them

Mar. 9

as Cryste hath also gyven us good occasyon, where he saythe that who so gyve so mych as a draught of colde water shall not lese hys

Lucae. 16

rewarde, and where he byddeth us gyve unto the poore to thentent

Math. 25

that they may receyve us in to the eternal tabernacles, and where he sheweth that at the daye of dome men shall have hevyn for theyr charytable almesse dedes done here in erthe: nowe when we tell them thus, and that we do never the lesse knowlege and confesse therwyth that we neyther do nor can do any good worke wythout the specyall grace & helpe of god, and that our deades be commenly so defectyve that though good deades well done be rewardable, yet every man maye fynde in hymselfe great cause to mystruste hys owne, and that we tell them also that all the best that the best man may do is yet no more than hys deutye for every man is of his deutye bounden to labour for hevyn and to serve and please god aswell and asmych as he maye, and notwythstandynge that we also tell them that the best worke that any man worketh wyth goddys helpe and grace, is not yet rewardable with hevyn of the nature or goodnes of the worke it selfe, all though he suffred every daye in a longe

Rom. 8

lyfe a dowble martyrdome accordynge to the wordes of saynt Paule, the passyons of thys worlde be not worthy the glory that is to come that shall be reveled and shewed uppon us/ and notwythstandynge that we tell them to/ that all the hevynly rewarde of mannes good workes cometh onely of goddys owne lyberall goodnes, in that it hath pleased hys hyghe bountye to gyve so great & ryche pryce for so poore and symple ware as are all mennys workes/ & all be it that we tell them also that god wolde not rewarde our workes in such wyse, were it not for the shedynge of hys sonnes bloud/ and so we fynally referre all the thanke and rewarde of our good workes, bothe the begynnynge, the progresse, and the ende, effectually to god and the merytes of Crystes passyon/ when we tell Tyndale and Luther all this, yet fare they as though they herde us not, and styll they synge us on theyr olde songe that it is ydolatrye to serve god wyth any good workes to thentent the better to please god therewyth, and the rather to come to hevyn therfore/ and that we may not wythout synne for any helpe to hevynwarde serve god wyth any good worke savynge onely fayth.[79]

This is a revealing sentence to observe as it simultaneously executes at the cost of frustrating its declared design upon the reader. Its constructive thrust is carried by the huge proliferation of *when* and *if* constructions at the onset; their force is discernible, en masse at least, as signifying

---

[79]*The Confutation of Tyndale's Answer,* in *Complete Works of St. Thomas More,* vol. 8, pp. 53–54.

'Look at the totality of what the Catholic Church acknowledges about the relation of good works and faith, of sin and grace.' Yet the real gist of this enormous sentence, as contained in its main clause, is polemical rather than predicative: in spite of all this, More says, Tyndale and Luther "fare as though they herde us not." The curiously self-defeating thing about the overall construction of the sentence is that, while it offers a compendium of Catholic teaching, it does so in syntactic terms that preclude the reader's being able to absorb this teaching. The effect is, first, to reduce the functionality of the sentence form to something like a rhetorical outburst, exasperation on the order of 'Look at all we acknowledge, and it is still not good enough for Tyndale and Luther.' Interestingly, however, what the main clause says is not 'This is not good enough for Tyndale and Luther'; it says, rather, "Yet fare they as though they herde us not."

The sentence itself indicates why such might be the case. If linguistic perception is overstrained, comprehension in turn fails, and one may then indeed fare as though one heard not. More's vernacular style is too often found bearing this kind of witness against itself as his efforts as a religious controversialist continued on their voluminous course. His style places beyond question the extremity of his commitment to a program of assimilating English sentence form to Latinity, as it does the symbolic appropriateness of undertaking such a program while writing in defense of the authority of the Roman Church. By the same token, the degree of success attained with a vernacular readership by means of More's stylistic program remains very much in question. While the burden of judgment must rest, as I have argued and tried to demonstrate, on interpretation grounded in specific analysis, we may bring to a close this discussion of More by taking note of his authorial proceeding in the last of his works, undertaken while he was a prisoner in the Tower of London, and left unfinished at his death. Having completed in English his *Dialogue of Comfort against Tribulation,* a production very much of a piece stylistically and structurally with his controversial prose, More applied himself to writing *The History of the Passion.* Since I have aimed at insight that would carry us toward explanation, it seems to me a disclosure of More's ultimate course, momentum, and objectives as a vernacular writer that, midway through this final prose work, he shifted his medium from English to Latin. This decision registers as nothing less than a spiritual and stylistic quietus—a gesture for which, fittingly, there is no native name, only the Latin one.

CRANMER'S PRAYER BOOK COLLECTS

The preceding discussion has implied that attempts to achieve an authoritative mode of composition by incorporating Latinate features into English sentence forms were doomed by their very nature, since the suspensiveness of the one language and the successiveness of the other evince such divergent syntactic principles. To the extent that aureate prose and More's controversial writings alike prove incapable of sustaining discourse with such hybrid sentence forms, a negative conclusion appears warranted. However, such a conclusion is wrong if taken as categorical, as an utter denial that Latinate and English sentence forms can be combined for the purposes of authoritative expression. I shall now examine a circumscribed yet major body of evidence which had come into existence by the mid-sixteenth century, and which, by its consummate stylistic achievement, forces qualification of a number of the critical strictures drawn or suggested in what I have said thus far. This body of evidence indicates, first, that an authoritative ecclesiastical style can be created, in English, by hybrid sentence forms; second, that successful hybrid forms of this kind extend the stylistic range of the vernacular in a genuinely new fashion; and, finally, that success in this special vein—which was seen as so imperative in the age in question— fell somewhat improbably to an outspoken Scripturalist and confirmed Protestant. The evidence to which I refer is the sequence of English collects that Thomas Cranmer, as archbishop of Canterbury, composed for the first Book of Common Prayer (1549).[80]

Some preliminary attention to the features and associations of the collect form which worked to Cranmer's advantage in shaping his authoritative vernacular instances will sharpen rather than detract from our understanding of what he achieved by these means. Although the roots of the form lie so far buried in Christian liturgical tradition that its definition and derivation receive varied accountings, there is enough agreement to permit description of the collect as a written prayer, typically of one sentence, which embodies a single impetus of petition or thanksgiving and which is designed for recitation in divine worship by a priest or minister on behalf of the assembled congregation.[81] Functionally and formally the collect is well named, whether one chooses to

---

[80]For discussion of the large degree of original composition in Cranmer's collects, see James A. Devereux, S.J., "The Primers and the Prayer Book Collects," *Huntington Library Quarterly* 32 (1968–69): 29–44, esp. pp. 32, 37.

[81]For further exposition, see W. Bright, "On the Collects," *Prayer-Book Commentary*, ed. F. E. Warren (London: Society for Promoting Christian Knowledge, 1933), pp. 82–95, and Kenneth D. Mackenzie, "The Collect," in W. K. Lowther Clarke and Charles Harris, eds., *Liturgy and Worship: A Companion to the Prayer Books of the Anglican Communion* (London: Society for Promoting Christian Knowledge, 1964), pp. 374–78.

trace its inception to Latin *collectio* (a summation offered by the priest to draw together the various inward responses of the people to the biddings enjoined on them in the liturgy) or to Latin *collecta*, short for *oratio ad collectam* (a prayer said over the gathered people, and hence one that speaks for them all as a group). Either etymology transmits the vital associations of clerical authority, for the power imputed to the collect is that of a definitive corporate utterance—the difference being a slightly more subjective emphasis in the *collectio*, and a slightly more institutional one in the *collecta*. For my purposes, the most important property of the collect form is that it achieves completeness as a species of discourse within the confines of a single sentence. (The collect sentence must, however, meet further requirements which will be noted shortly.) Here we may reflect that this unusual provision in natural language—the provision for an exact coincidence between the limits of a discourse and the boundaries of a sentence—materially facilitates the task of a writer who seeks to engraft Latinisms within English syntax. The task becomes easier, first and quite simply, because the composition of a collect does not count just as a sentence of prose but as a finished production in a particular prose genre. Second and more specifically, the task is easier because the strain on perception and comprehension which rapidly shows when periodic or suspended sentence form is attempted in English may not reach an intolerable level if the domain to be encompassed is, after all, only that of a single sentence. These stylistic advantages accrue automatically with composition in the collect form.

What, then, are the further requisite features of the collect sentence? In its prototypic form, the collect sentence begins with a direct address to God (that is, in the vocative), and this is followed by one or more ascriptive clauses. This stretch of linguistic material is intuitively recognizable as the "subject" half of the collect sentence. Next comes the petition or thanksgiving. Its verb or verbs standardly take the imperative mood, although they may be downgraded to the supplicatory force of *grant* or *give*. Not surprisingly, in view of their semantic function, these verbs belong mainly to the class of transitive verbs taking clausal complements. Recursion of *that* clauses as object complements for the imperative verbs, together with recursion of attributive (nonrestrictive relative) constructions in the ascription section, accounts for the bulk of syntactic elaboration in the collect sentence. Then, after the object—or other—complementation of the main verb(s) has come to a close, the ending completes both the petition or thanksgiving section and the sentence as a whole with an adverbial or ascriptive adjunct—most often, an acknowledgment of divine agency, power, grace, or greatness that literally rounds out the composition by referring back to the person named in the opening vocative. The verb-complement-adjunct sequence intuitively registers as the "predicate" half of the collect sentence, but it also divides perceptibly within itself into the $V + Comp$ and *Adv* segments. There are thus two pivots articulating three syntactic subdivisions in the prototypic collect sentence: one between the end of the subject *NP* with its trailing adjunctions and the onset of the *VP*, and another between the last of the trailing object complements of the main verb(s) and the sentence-final adjunctions.[82]

Viewed in accordance with the stylistic objectives that govern much earlier sixteenth-century religious prose, the sentence form of the collect offers an ingenious solution to the problem posed by the disparate tendencies in English successiveness and Latinate suspensiveness. This solution consists in the fact that the very syntactic recursions which distend the internal structure of the sentence—namely, the attributive constructions adjoined to the subject *NP* and the object complements of the transitive main verb(s)—are also the most prominent stretches of asymmetric material since they follow the subject and follow the verb, respectively. Hence, spreading and trailing figure as concurrent rather than opposing formal tendencies in the composition of an English collect. Having registered this effect of the dynamics of collect sentence form, we may still ask why the concurrence arises. A chief factor is the articulated double-pivot internal structure—the easily located divisions (often marked with colons) between subject *NP* and *VP*, between verbal complement and adverbial coda—which becomes a signal system for maintaining one's syntactic bearings through the course of a collect sentence.

Yet there is another, more potent factor offsetting the inherent pull toward overcomplication and opaqueness in the formal elaboration of the collect sentence: this is the striking maximal explicitness of surface syntactic structure which the form displays. I have pointed out that the prototypic collect has its main verb(s) in the imperative, a mood which customarily triggers deletion of the subject *NP* because sufficient indication of the grammatical subject is felt to attend on the use of direct address. Thus, for example, "Forgive us our trespasses" is a more ordinary form of petition than "You forgive us our trespasses," although the latter is possible with appropriate intonation. The collect sentence form is extraordinary, among other things, for the amount of linguistic redundancy which it incorporates as a matter of convention. No fewer than three sentential components figure in this regard: (1) the vocative *NP* that accompanies the imperative verb(s) of the central section of the collect, (2) the attributive material adjoined to the vocative *NP* that expands upon the naming of the deity, and (3) the adverbial material of

[82]My account of the formal features of the collect sentence is indebted to John Wallace Suter, Jr.'s introduction to his edition of selections: *The Book of English Collects* (New York and London: Harper & Bros., 1940), pp. xxxiii–xxxiv.

the ending, which also serves these naming and ascriptive functions. In transformational-generative terms, the maximal explicitness that characterizes collect sentence form can be represented as an unusually close relation between superficial and underlying structure.[83] Since deep structure is charged in the theory with exhaustive specification of sentential meaning, the nearer the correspondence of surface structure, the more explicit—and, presumably, comprehensible—the sentence will prove to be.

We may approach Cranmer's artistry in the collect form by way of a pair of examples in which the basic double-pivot structure is clearly articulated in an amplitude of phrasing supplied by conjunctive syntax:

Almightie and everlastyng God, which hatest nothyng that thou hast made, and doest forgeve the sinnes of all theim that be penitente: Create and make in us newe and contrite hartes, that wee worthely lamentyng our synnes, and knowlegyng our wretchednes, maie obteine of thee, the God of all mercie, perfect remission and forgevenesse: thorough Jesus Christ. [Ash Wenesday]

O God, the king of glory, whiche hast exalted thine only sonne Jesus Christe, with great triumphe unto thy kingdom in heaven: we beseche thee, leave us not comforteles, but send to us thyne holy ghost to comfort us, and exalt us unto the same place whither our saviour Christe is gone before: who lyveth and

---

[83]If one describes collect sentence form in transformational-generative terms, it is possible to demonstrate a close and systematic kinship among what have been called its three discrete "types": A, B, and C (see, e.g., Suter's remarks in *The Book of English Collects*, pp. xxxviii–xlviii). Type A is the prototypic form which I have been discussing; its structure may be represented as [vocative *NP* + ascriptive adjuncts + petition or thanksgiving— imperative *V* + clausal *VP* complements + ending—*S* adverbial]. Type B differs from Type A in interchanging the order of the vocative *NP* and the petition or thanksgiving section, which in turn prompts elimination of the ascriptive adjuncts. The verb of the petition or thanksgiving in Type B may itself take the form of a deep structure complement to a higher verb of requesting (e.g., "Grant, we beseech thee . . ." from "We beseech thee that thou grant . . ."). The structure of Type B may be represented as [petition or thanksgiving—imperative *V* + vocative *NP* + (request clause +) clausal *VP* complements + ending—*S* adverbial]. In Type C, a further development on Type B, the collect sentence is assimilated to the litany form; this entails that the verb(s) of the petition section be introduced by a "We beseech thee" clause. The structure of Type C may be represented as [request clause + vocative *NP* + petition *V* + clausal *VP* complements + ending—*S* adverbial]. Types A, B, and C can be given the following general representation using the conventions of braces and parentheses to denote, respectively, mutually exclusive choices and indifferent options:

$$\left\{ \begin{array}{l} \text{voc } NP \text{ + (adjuncts +) imperative } V \\ \text{voc } NP \text{ + request cls + petition } V \end{array} \right\} + VP \text{ complement(s) + } S \text{ adverbial(s)}$$

Condition: If the adjunction option is not exercised, the vocative *NP* may then optionally exchange position with its immediately following element—i.e., imperative *V* or request cls.

reigneth with thee and the Holy Ghost, now and ever. [The Sunday after the Ascension][84]

Word pairs are one of the most immediately obvious means by which Cranmer's collects aim at authoritative utterance, and they accordingly find first place in the discussion of style in Stella Brook's *The Language of the Book of Common Prayer*.[85] These word pairs range over the spectrum of what by the mid-sixteenth century were conventional applications of this native resource: stock, often proverbial phrases ("heven & earth," "now and ever"), an English item and its Romance equivalent ("Create and make," "remission and forgevenes"), and partially tautological or semantically overlapping conjunctions that evoke more complexity or intensity than either conjunct in isolation ("almightie and ever lastyng," "lyveth and reigneth," "thee and the Holy Ghost"). As remarked earlier in the discussion of doublings in the last section of chapter 3, the syntactic effect of word pairs is to thicken or reinforce surface sentential structure at nodes to which they attach as a residue of nonidentical—and hence unreduced—constituents after conjunction reduction has applied. By the same token, as we have also noted in the last section of chapter 3, a sentential node whose structure has been elaborated by a cluster of conjuncts will produce local suspension within its containing clause, unless the cluster is positioned at the head or tail end of the clause. Cranmer's general practice is to place his numerous word pairs where they least encumber the succession of major elements in clausal structure—at clause ends or in otherwise discrete units of collect sentence form (e.g., the vocative "Almightie and everlastyng God" or the ascriptive closing "who lyveth and reigneth with thee and the Holy Ghost").

It is, however, significant that the impetus to reduplication in Cranmer's composition extends beyond word pairs to whole phrases and clauses in the collects. The majority of these larger reduplications are binary, like the word pairs, for he typically makes heavy use of antithetical and correlative conjunctions. Examples in the pair of quoted collects include "which hatest nothyng that thou hast made, and doest forgeve the sinnes of all theim that be penitente," "leave us not comforteles, but send to us thyne holy ghost to comfort us," and "worthely

[84]*The Booke of the Common Prayer* . . . (London: E. Whitchurche, 1549) (STC 16274), sigs. Diii[r], Hiiii[r]. In citing this edition (hereafter abbreviated BCP, with references incorporated in the text), I depart from its readings only in modernizing consonantal *i* and *u*. An accessible edition, in old spelling, is *The First and Second Prayer Books of Edward VI*, intro. E. C. S. Gibson (London: Dent–Everyman's Library, 1910).

[85]Stella Brook, *The Language of the Book of Common Prayer* (New York: Oxford University Press, 1965), chap. 3, esp. pp. 64–65, 84–85. Another linguistically oriented study is Anton Adriaan Prins's *The Booke of the Common Prayer (1549): An Enquiry into Its Language (Phonology and Accidence)* (Amsterdam: M. J. Portielje, 1933).

lamentyng our synnes, and knowlegyng our wretchednes." The apparent antecedents for such redundant or overlapping antitheses and conjunction pairs are the Hebraic sense parallelisms of Scripture, to judge from the respective reminiscences here of Ephesians 5:29 ("no man ever yet hated his owne flesh, but nourisheth and cherisheth it, even as the Lord the chirche"); John 14:16, 18 ("And I wil praye the Father, and he shal geve you another comforter. . . . I wil not leave you comforteles"); and Jeremiah 14:2, 20 ("Juda mourneth; . . . and the cry of Jerusalem is gone up. We acknowledge, o Lord, our wickednes . . . : for we have synned agaynst thee"). It is equally true that Cranmer's phrasing, like Tyndale's, exhibits greater syntactic, as opposed to semantic, parallelism than is found in much of Scripture except for the Pauline Epistles. Nevertheless, while marked syntactic parallelism emerges as a defining feature of the stylistic design of English Protestant prose by the mid-sixteenth century, a further distinction between Tyndale and Cranmer must be drawn. Tyndale deploys his binary constructions within larger sentence forms that are predominantly additive and asymmetric, while Cranmer's structural responsions are realized through the more suspensive dynamics of the collect. It is Cranmer's singular genius to have evolved a means of offsetting the inevitable momentum of English word order toward asymmetric, additive sentence form with syntactic structures that promote greater integration and interconnection in the sentential composition as a whole. To this end, the principal formal operations of Cranmer's style in the Prayer Book collects combine complementation with coordination as the most exercised means of sentential recursion, and in so doing, preserve the intactness of phrasal and clausal units while ensuring their careful linking and sequencing. But the sentence forms of Cranmer's collects also exploit the potential for semantic richness that arises from incorporating a measure of syntactic indeterminacy within an otherwise superbly controlled construct. The frequency and prominence of *so . . . as, such . . . as, so . . . that, such . . . that*, and *that* connectives will bear watching as vehicles of a suggestive openness of form and meaning regarding the conformity of man's will to God's, in and through the act of public, authorized Christian prayer.

In the overall dynamic of collect sentence form, it is clear that the series of elements beginning with the direct address to God and running through the main verb of petition or thanksgiving offer a fairly constrained set of compositional possibilities. These reduce, by and large, to options of ordering and emphasis. Thus a collect may begin in one of four ways: "O Lord, grant . . ." or "Grant, O Lord . . ." or "O Lord, we beseech thee to grant . . ." or "We beseech thee, O Lord, to grant . . . ." While the latitude afforded by these options is surely not trivial— either when the ascriptive material appended to the vocative complicates the transition to the next sentential element, or when the choice lies between stylistic focus on the human speech act (*we beseech thee*) and divine agency (*grant*)[86]—nevertheless it is the clausal complements of the main verb(s) of the collect that excite the greatest interest and expectancy. This is so because they constitute the least predictable, most potentially various aspect of overall sentence form. The semantic range of these *VP* complements is, in fact, as unlimited as the possible actions or responses which man might invocate of God, at one or another point, in the great cycle of the liturgical year. Hence these complements may take the form of clausal (or infinitival or gerundive) direct objects of any of a host of transitive verbs, or they may be further shaped as purpose or result clauses. Whatever their specific character, Cranmer typically employs sentential conjunction to proliferate these complements since they are literally the substance of the prayer being offered. It is this midsection of the collect sentence, therefore, which opens up the widest stylistic opportunity to the composer, in the handling of form and meaning alike.

Finally, the ending of the collect sentence emerges too as a relatively determined structural element, even though the fashion in which it is linked to its preceding material becomes a significant formal concern. The majority of Cranmer's collects end with a prepositional phrase of agency (e.g., "through Jesus Christe our Lord") or with an ascriptive clause (e.g., "who lyveth and reigneth with thee and the Holy Ghost, now and ever") or with a combination of the two. Very occasionally the ending is omitted altogether. A responsory *Amen* supplies the terminal element and orally punctuates the close of this comprehensive, freestanding sentence unit. On the evidence of Cranmer's strong preference for agentive and ascriptive constructions as collect endings, the ideal at which his composition aimed was a "circular" sentence form whose close again named the deity addressed by the opening vocative. Such circularity of syntax, beyond its authoritative Latinate associations, had added symbolic appropriateness because the circle, traditionally the most perfect of the plane figures, was an immemorial emblem of the divine nature.[87] However, the ultimate stylistic challenge faced by Cranmer in

[86]I am assuming John R. Ross's analysis of the declarative sentence, according to which every instance of the type contains in its deep structure a highest clause of the general form "I say to you that. . . ." See his "On Declarative Sentences," *Readings in English Transformational Grammar,* ed. Roderick A. Jacobs and Peter S. Rosenbaum (Waltham, Mass.: Ginn & Co., 1970), pp. 222–72; cf. Jerrold M. Sadock, *Toward a Linguistic Theory of Speech Acts* (New York: Academic Press, 1974), pp. 21–50.

[87]The origins of the associations between divinity and circularity trace back at least to Parmenides (ca. 450 B.C.); for references, see Janel M. Mueller, ed., *Donne's Prebend Sermons* (Cambridge, Mass.: Harvard University Press, 1971), pp. 222–23. For a comprehensive treatment of the history of this image, see Georges Poulet, *The Metamorphoses of the Circle,* trans. Carley Dawson and Elliot Coleman (Baltimore: Johns Hopkins University Press, 1967).

attempting to achieve ideal form and authoritative utterance in his English collects was somehow to adjudicate between acknowledgments of God's omnipotence and all-sufficiency, on the one hand, and, on the other, the urgency of human desires and concerns that make a reverently circular close both proper and problematic. We shall now examine in selective detail how Cranmer met and contrived to surmount this stylistic challenge.

As implied in my remarks on the opening and closing functions of ascriptive and agentive constructions in the collect, the achievement of circular sentence form is inseparable from the specific representation made of the nature of God. Here are two illustrations:

Almightye and everlastyng God, whiche haste geven unto us thy servauntes grace by the confession of a true fayth to acknowlege the glorye of the eternall trinitie, & in the power of the divyne majestie to wurshippe the unitie: we beseche thee, that through the stedfastnes of thys fayth, we may evermore be defended from all adversitie, whiche liveste & reignest, one God, worlde without end. [Trinity Sunday, BCP, sig. Hvʳ]

Almightie God, whiche by thy blessed sonne, diddest cal Mathew from the receipt of Custome, to be an Apostle & Evangelist: Graunt us grace to forsake all covetous desires & inordinate love of riches, and to folowe thy saied sonne Jesus Christ, who lyveth and reigneth with thee and the holy Ghost, now and ever. [St. Matthew's Day, BCP, sig. Nvʳ]

Despite the reliance on coordinate constructions to achieve amplitude of expression in both of these collects, the syntax and semantics of conjunction are exploited in divergent ways with regard to the representation of the Godhead and the realization of circular form. The Trinity Sunday collect unambiguously emphasizes the "unitie" of "the eternall trinitie" at its opening (in the second person singular "whiche *haste* geven" of its ascriptive clause) and equally at its close (in the appositional insertion "one God" to reinforce what again are second person singular verbs, "liveste & reignest"). However, while the semantics of the Trinity Sunday collect evince total command, the syntactic transition from the end of the petition section to the onset of the ending is abrupt and discontinuous: I am referring to the juncture ". . . *from all adversitie, whiche liveste & reignest. . . .*" In my view, Cranmer realizes his most felicitous effects in the circular form of the collect sentence when the *NP* "Jesus Christe" is the last, or a near-to-last, constituent of the petition section. Such ordering makes for a smooth joining with the usual ascriptive close, "who lyveth and reigneth," and allows the claims of successive and suspensive syntax equal force in the composition of the sentence as a whole. It is just this arrangement that we find in the St. Matthew's Day collect cited above, of which the relevant portion reads: "Graunt us grace to forsake all covetous desires & inordinate love of

233

riches, and to folowe *thy saied sonne Jesus Christ, who lyveth and reig-neth. . . ."* An essentially analogous though slightly looser effect can be observed in the turn toward circular form in the collect for the Sunday after the Ascension quoted slightly earlier: its transition evolves as follows: ". . . and exalte us unto the same place whither *our saviour Christe* is gone before: *who lyveth and reigneth. . . ."*

Examples of both the stricter and looser type of circularity in Cranmer's handling of the syntax of his collect endings could easily be multiplied. But the formal point has been sufficiently substantiated to proceed to an accompanying aspect of meaning, namely, the measure of semantic indeterminacy (or unspecificity) incorporated in the conjunctions "who lyveth and reigneth with thee and the holy Ghost" as articulations of the divine nature. The following questions arise. Are the conjoined verbs "lyveth and reigneth" to be understood as separate predications with individual meaning, deriving from two underlying sentences, one with *live* as its verb, the other with *reign?* Or are the conjoined verbs to be understood more complexly, as joint predications of the 'laughed-and-cried' type noted in chapter 1 (p. 23)? Although joint predication is a reasonably rare type of construction, it would appear theologically impossible to preclude such a reading as a characterization of perfect existence with God: that to live with him is simultaneously to reign with him, and vice versa. Cranmer's syntax specifies neither reading while accommodating both. A similar question arises regarding the phrase "with thee and the holy Ghost." Does the conjunction carry individual meaning deriving from separate predications in deep structure ("lyveth with thee" and "lyveth with the holy Ghost") or does it carry unit meaning? Again, theological articulation of the kind exercised by Cranmer in the Trinity Sunday collect seems to necessitate the unit, or joint, interpretation, in order to do justice to the unity of Three Persons as One God. Liturgically, however, it is altogether permissible to address a prayer to one among the Persons of the Trinity. Thus the best reading of "who lyveth and reigneth with thee and the holy Ghost" may be a further possibility sanctioned by the conjunctive syntax, namely, a three-way reciprocal construction involving the Son as grammatical subject, the Father as object addressee ("thee"), and the Holy Ghost as a named but not addressed grammatical object. What I wish to imply in raising such questions that resist definite single answers is that the measure of ambiguity in these coordinate structures is the better for being there. Cranmer at one and the same time elicits the recognition that speaking of God and to God stretches natural language to its limits while keeping the possibilities of multiple meaning under sure syntactic control.

It is, however, the development of clausal complementation in the central portions of Cranmer's collects that displays his richest and sub-tlest management of semantic potentiality in man's relation to God through combined use of the resources of Latinate and English sentence form. A convenient entry in this matter is provided by Cranmer's penchant for casting complement constructions into binary, correlative form, as illustrated by the following collects (my italics):

Graunt O mercyfull God, that *as* thyne holy Apostle James, leavyng his father and al that he had, without delay, was obedient unto the callyng of thy sonne Jesus Christ, and folowed hym: *so* we, forsakyng all worldly and carnal affeccions, may be evermore ready to folowe thy commaundements, through Jesus Christe our Lord. [St. James the Apostle's Day, BCP, sig. Niii^{r-v}]

God whiche makest us glad with the yerely remembraunce of the birth of thy onely sonne Jesus Christ: graunt that *as* we joyfully receive him for our redemer, *so* we may with sure confidence beholde him when he shal come to be our judge: who liveth and reigneth with thee and the Holy Ghost, now and ever. [Christmas Day, First Communion, BCP, sig. Bii^v]

In these two collects, the *as* . . . *so* correlatives are made prominent by their central position and by the extent of the sentential material which they enclose. Thus, by implication, the principal shared concern seems to be with the outcome of meritorious human actions: in the St. James's Day collect, the effectiveness of a good example in prompting others to goodness: in the collect for Christmas morning, the reward that those who put their faith in Christ can expect. In both collects it is possible to lose sight of the complement framework for a considerable stretch, since enough material intervenes between the "grant that" and the "we may" portions of the sentence structure to obscure the fact that an action is being invoked of God all the while. The concluding agentive ("through Jesus Christe our Lord") and ascriptive ("who liveth and reigneth . . .") formulas serve, however, as respective reminders that God's action is the object sought; in so doing they redress somewhat the felt imbalance of power in the petition sections of both collects. For overall both are much more weighted syntactically toward affirmations of human virtue than toward the need for divine aid and grace, which is given merely conventional acknowledgment.

In other uses of correlatives to shape complement structures, Cranmer comes closer to incorporating an essential balance in the collect form between what God is being asked to do and what man can claim to be able to do. The most accomplished instance of this type, in my opinion, follows—a collect worthy of additional note for its exceptional double inclusion in the first Communion for Easter Sunday and in the order of service for Easter Monday:

Almightie GOD, whiche through thy onely begotten sonne Jesus Christe, hast overcome death, and opened unto us the gate of everlastyng lyfe: we humbly beseche thee, that *as* by thy speciall grace, preventyng us, thou doest put in our myndes good desires, *so* by thy continuall helpe we maie bryng the same to good effect: through Jesus Christ our Lorde, who liveth and reigneth with thee and the Holy Ghost, now and ever. [BCP, sigs. Giii^r, Giiii^v. My italics]

While the "we beseche thee that . . . we may" framework of this collect is no less distended than in the two preceding examples, the difference here is that the *as . . . so* correlatives are apportioned to convey the constant cooperation of God's grace with man's free will in the doing of good works. As the age of the Reformation was to discover afresh, the relation of grace to free will poses one of the most difficult problems for formulation in Christian theology, but Cranmer's Easter collect represents this relation as a harmonious and vital interplay through its sequence of clauses and phrases. Man acts in asking ("we humbly beseche thee"), but acts to ask God to act as he has acted before ("that as by thy speciall grace, preventyng us, thou doest put in our myndes good desires"). In turn, God's action and man's are brought into such close cooperation that the two join as instrument and agent in the latter half of the correlative ("so by thy continuall helpe we maie bryng the same to good effect"). The semantic implications of this syntax strengthen associative links between the *so* of likeness (correlative *so*) and the *so* of a manner or means construction. Yet in the Easter collect Cranmer's syntax is not itself ambiguous, even though it readily conduces to manifold associations. The framework of the petition is demonstrably that of a transitive verb ("we beseche thee") and a clausal object complement ("that . . .") containing the correlative in question.

However, there are collects in which Cranmer combines *as . . . so* correlatives with complements of other types to achieve varied semantic implications by means of these connectives. In the following composition, a straightforward plea for grace in the initial clausal complement ("we beseche thee . . . powre thy grace into our hartes") gives way to appreciable elaboration in a later clausal complement containing a correlative (the italicized *that, as . . . so*). The collect reads:

We beseche thee Lord, powre thy grace into our hartes, *that, as* we have knowen Christ thy sonnes incarnacion by the message of an Aungell: *so* by hys Crosse and passion we maie be brought unto the glory of his resurrecion: Through the same Christe our Lorde. [The Annunciation of the Virgin Mary, BCP, sig. Miii^r. My italics]

Here the syntax—in particular, the *so* construction—is genuinely ambiguous. It appears both to complete the correlative and to contribute to the articulation of instrumentality ("powre thy grace . . . that . . . so we maie be brought . . ."). But the ambiguity is highly functional in rendering the soul's constancy in its knowledge of Christ inseparable from God's grace as the means to that knowledge. This is the sort of effect that enables Cranmer's localized and controlled openness of meaning to enrich rather than subvert the prose style of his English collects.

In exploring the richness contributed by semantic indeterminacy in the expansions of collect predicates, we must pay special attention to Cranmer's *so . . . that* and *such . . . that* constructions. The *so . . . that* constructions, which enclose verbs (infinitive or finite) and thus invest actions with circumstantiality, are the more numerous group. They are typically ambiguous. On the one hand, the *so . . . that* may seem to be an adverbial expression of means or manner (one answering the question 'How?'—'By this means,' 'In this way'). On the other hand, the *so . . . that* may seem to be an expression of magnitude or extent (one answering the question 'How much?'—'This much').[88] Here are two characteristic specimens:

Almightye God whiche hast buylded the congregacion upon the foundacion of the Apostles and prophetes, Jesu Christe hym selfe beyng the head corner stone: graunt us *so* to be joyned together in unitie of spirite by their doctrine, *that* we maye be made an holye temple acceptable to thee, through Jesu Christ our Lorde. [Simon and Jude Apostles' Day, BCP, sig. Nvii^v. My italics]

O God, who for our redempcion diddest geve thyne onely begotten sonne to the death of the Crosse: And by his glorious resurreccion hast delyvered us from the power of our enemie: Graunte us *so* to dye daily from synne, *that* wee maie evermore lyve with hym in the joye of his resurreccion, through the same Christ our Lorde. [Easter Sunday, Matins, BCP, sig. Gii^r–v. My italics]

In the first of these two collects, the construction "so to be joyned together in unitie of spirite" is ambiguous between senses of extent (so joined in unity = to become one) and of manner (so joined = made a holy temple). The effect is to intensify the reference to the communion of saints in the Church with both connotations and to suggest that both are necessary to make the Church "acceptable" to God. In the construction "so to dye daily from synne, that wee maie evermore lyve with hym" the second collect expresses the traditional Christian mystical notion of dying to the world and living for Christ which traces ultimately to a Pauline source in Scripture (Romans 6–8). This construction—"so to dye daily from synne, that wee maie evermore lyve with hym"—exhibits a multivalence of no fewer than three possible senses: (1) manner (so to die = to die from sin), (2) extent (so to die = to die daily), and (3) result or purpose (so to die that we may evermore live).

Cranmer's *such . . . that* constructions, though fewer in number, also supply productive ambiguities in the same semantic categories of manner, extent, and result or purpose. However, since the *such . . . that* constructions enclose nouns, not verbs, they have a correspondingly

---

[88]Joan W. Bresnan has argued for the underlying linguistic relatedness of *so* and *such* on the basis of a shared abstract semantic feature, [SO + MUCH]. See her "Syntax of the Comparative Clause Construction in English," *Linguistic Inquiry* 4.3 (1973): 299–305, which, however, does not address the type of *so* and *such* constructions being discussed here.

distinct stylistic function: they focus on adjuncts of substantives (nouns, noun phrases) rather than actions (verbs) that have important spiritual implications. The following collect, for example, devolves into a concise Scripturalist manifesto as what begins as specification of the right reception of God's Word ("in suche wise") modulates into a depiction of the life of faith:

> Blessed Lorde, whiche hast caused al holy scriptures to be written for our learnyng: graunte us that we maie in *suche* wise hear theim, read, marke, learne, and inwardly digest theim, *that* by pacience and comfort of thy holy word wee maie embrace and ever holde fast, the blessed hope of everlastyng life, whiche thou hast geven us in our Saviour Jesus Christe. [Second Sunday in Advent, BCP, sig. Avii^v. My italics]

Cranmer exploits the indeterminacy of his *such . . . that* construction to bring within the compass of right reception of Scripture great specificity—specificity regarding the manner (in the recursively accumulated conjuncts "hear, read, marke, learne, and inwardly digest") as well as specificity regarding the result of reception in this manner, including an expression of magnitude or extent in the adverb "ever" ("wee maie embrace and ever holde fast, the blessed hope of everlastyng life"). In a similar fashion the *such . . . that* construction of the collect for St. Andrew's Day first evokes what is entailed in receiving the grace to become a martyr by combining senses of magnitude, manner, and result, and then analogizes, in the complements of the main clause verb "Graunt," to the implications of the grace given to ordinary Christians for living their lives:

> Almightie God, whiche hast geven *suche* grace to thy Apostle sainct Andrewe, *that* he counted the sharp and painfull death of the crosse to be an hye honour and a great glory: Graunt us to take and esteme all troubles and adversities whiche shal come unto us for thy sake, as thinges profitable for us toward the obtainyng of everlasting life: through Jesus Christ our Lorde. [BCP, sigs. Lvi^v– Lvii^r. My italics]

As a final example of the significant and enhancing ambiguity of Cranmer's *such . . . that* constructions, we may consider his exquisite collect for the sixth Sunday after Trinity:

> God, whiche haste prepared, to theim that love thee, *such* good thinges *as* passe al mannes understanding: Poure into our hartes *suche* love toward thee, *that* we loving thee in al thinges may obtein thy promises, which exceade al that we can desire: Through Jesus Christe our Lorde. [BCP, sig. Jvi^r. My italics]

In this collect Christian love is evoked in the radically subjective and personal character that it assumes in the later fourteenth-century English devotional writers and in the works of the English Reformers. (The "love" here, that is, connotes the affectivity on which Tyndale insisted in translating the New Testament, as opposed to the "charity" rendering which More defended, with its associations of charitable works like almsgiving and poor relief.) What is more, as the sense of the word "love" is shaped by the form of Cranmer's collect sentence, it comes to reflect an increasingly specific Protestant conception. Although initially this love is alluded to in the ascriptive clause adjoined to the vocative as a species of human attainment ("theim that love thee"), it is subsequently invoked as God's gift in the main clause predicate: "Poure into our hartes *suche* love. . . ." The chief properties ascribed to it combine means, manner, extent, and result in a fluid semantic continuum that richly expresses love in its fullness: "suche love toward thee, that we loving thee in al thinges may obtein thy promises, which exceade al that we can desire." The "promises" here, a key Tyndalian term taken over by Cranmer, do not remain mere tokens of futurity, but instead are treated as obtainable certainties through God's and man's mutual exercise of love. The ambiguities of the *such . . . as, such . . . that* constructions figure centrally in the richness of Cranmer's signification regarding the nature and effects of Christian love, even as his phrasing affirms its incomprehensibility and transcendence in other dimensions: "such good thinges as passe al mannes understanding," "thy promises, which exceade al that we can desire."

What continues to stand out under close analysis as the most remarkable aspect of Cranmer's stylistic achievement in his English collects is not merely how he manages to combine the disparate tendencies of spread and trailing sentence form but also, and especially, how he generates semantic indeterminacy as much through the use of subordinating constructions as through coordinating ones. It is not readily apparent how he can turn his hybrid syntax to such effects, for one of the cardinal assumptions that undergirded earlier philologists' grand evolutionary view of sentence form as progressing from parataxis to hypotaxis was, quite simply, that the former left clausal relations imprecise while the latter articulated them clearly (see pp. 13–17). However, a transformational-generative approach to the analysis of asymmetric conjunction uncovers no categorical identification of dependent or contingent meaning with subordinating constructions. For the fact of sequencing itself frequently carries with it the imputation of some temporal, causal, or intentional force, which in turn registers the fact that the conjuncts stand in an asymmetric—that is, noninterchangeable—relation with one another.

There is a class of simple-seeming but imperfectly understood coordinate constructions in English which it is useful to note briefly, since they exhibit functional ambiguity in connecting the order of conjuncts

with implications of result or purpose.[89] Because these typically colloquial, asymmetrically conjoined predicates seem to operate on a bor-
derline between coordinate and complement constructions, they may
shed some glimmerings of light on our final topic for consideration, the
indeterminacy between result and purpose arising from the recursively
elaborated predicates of Cranmer's collect sentences. This class of asymmetric conjunctions is commonly exemplified by English imperatives,
exhortations, invitations, and the like; Scriptural instances of the class
are particularly easy to find: "Taste and see that the Lord is good"; "Be
fruitful and multiply, and replenish the earth"; "Come and join us."
Insofar as these conjunctions submit to an accounting they bespeak the
existence of an intuitive semantic continuum that originates in the natural association of a necessary order of events with a sense of their
mutual interdependence—specifically, the relation of later conjuncts as
outcomes or realizations of earlier ones. The existence of such a semantic
continuum is indicated by the equivalence of certain explicitly binary
sentence types: the asymmetric *VP* conjunctions instanced above, and
correlative and complement constructions involving the same pairs of
terms. The following equivalence will illustrate: *Taste and see that the Lord
is good = When you taste, then you see that the Lord is good = Taste to see
that the Lord is good.* Actually, however, the third sentence is equivalent
only in its result sense to the other two; it is ambiguous in itself between
result and purpose. This ambiguity between result and purpose is endemic as well in certain *that* complements of Cranmer's collects, and it
functions to a lesser degree in his coordinate and correlative constructions. He evidently finds this particular syntactic and semantic ambiguity
essential to his enterprise in the collect mode of composition. We shall
conclude by inquiring how and why this should be so.

In addition to the Ash Wednesday collect cited earlier, here are two
collects which manifest the characteristic ambiguity between result and
purpose in Cranmer's handling of *that* constructions:

Almightie God, whiche haste geven thy holy sonne to be unto us, bothe a
sacrifice for synne, and also an example of godly life: Geve us the grace *that* wee
maie alwaies moste thankfully receive that his inestimable benefite, and also
daily indevor our selfes, to folowe the blessed steppes of his moste holy life:
through Jesus Christ our Lord. [Second Sunday after Easter, BCP, sig. Gviii^r.
My italics]

Mercyfull Lorde, we beseche thee to caste thy bryght beames of light upon thy
Churche, *that* it beyng lyghtened by the doctryne of thy blessed Apostle and

---

[89]See Susan F. Schmerling, "Asymmetric Conjunction and Rules of Conversation," in
Speech Acts, ed. Peter Cole and Jerry Morgan, Syntax and Semantics no. 3 (New York:
Academic Press, 1974), pp. 210–31.

Evangelist John may attayne to thy everlastyng gyftes: Through Jesus Christe our Lorde. [St. John Evangelist's Day, BCP, sig. Bv^v. My italics]

A requisite step in beginning an analysis of these two collects is to observe that neither of the constructions whose *thats* have been italicized is a clausal complement of a main verb. In the collect for the second Sunday after Easter, the main verb, "Geve," already has a direct object, "the grace," and in any case would be ungrammatical with a clausal complement (we do not say *Give that* . . . in English). Although the main verb of the collect for St. John's Day could take a clausal complement (we do say *we beseech that* . . .), nevertheless the possibility is precluded here because "beseche" already has an infinitive complement: "we beseche thee to caste thy bryght beames of light." Once the possibility of object complementation has been set aside, the *that* constructions in the two collects appear equally receptive to interpretations of result or purpose. In the collect for St. John's Day, God may cast his beams on the Church either with the result that the Church will attain his everlasting gifts or for the purpose that it attain them. Similarly, in the collect for the second Sunday after Easter, the *that* construction following the main verb may be articulating either the result or the purpose of God's giving of grace. The semantic indeterminacy is clearly vital to the meaning of the entire collect sentence and to its function as authoritative utterance. Hence it will be worth pursuing our analysis of the syntax and semantics of Cranmer's *that* constructions a last step or so further, if we can.

In an interesting argument in her monograph, *Abstract Syntax and Latin Complementation*, Robin Lakoff remarks that the *that* clauses having purpose interpretations take subjunctive verbs in Latin dialogues. She goes on to propose that the deep structure of purpose clauses be formulated to differ from the deep structure of result clauses in just this respect: purpose clauses would contain an underlying verb expressive of desire or intention, but result clauses would not.[90] Lakoff's proposal turns on the undoubtedly correct perception that, if we do something *on purpose*, we do so because we want to, or because we intend that something else happen. By contrast, the result construction conveys only the sense of making something happen. Thus, if we undertake to represent the result sense of the *that* construction in the St. John's Day collect by procedures used in generative semantics to decompose features of meaning into abstract underlying predicates, we would arrive at something like the following disposition. The highest clause in the sentence would be *We beseech thee*; its *VP* object complement, the next lowest clause, would be *thou cast thy light upon the Church*. Its *VP* object complement, lower still,

[90] See Robin T. Lakoff, *Abstract Syntax and Latin Complementation* (Cambridge, Mass.: MIT Press, 1968), pp. 195–207.

would be this sequence whose abstract verb is given in capitals: [*thou cast thy light upon the Church* + MAKE HAPPEN + *the Church attains gifts*]. The last and lowest sequence encapsulates the meaning of the result construction. However, a different deep structure is needed to represent the purpose sense of the *that* construction; it, according to Lakoff, must have an additional underlying predicate with an abstract verb of inclination or desire. We can represent the purpose sense of the *that* construction in the St. John's Day collect as a conjunction between desire for an event and its happening. Thus, again, the highest clause in the sentence would be *We beseech thee*; its *VP* object complement, the next lowest clause, would again be *thou cast thy light upon the Church*. Its *VP* object complement, however, would be a conjunction of two underlying clauses, each with its abstract verb—the encapsulation of the result sense plus the encapsulation of the purpose sense, schematically represented thus: [*thou cast thy light upon the Church* + MAKE HAPPEN + *the Church attains gifts*] *and* [? + DESIRE + *the Church attains gifts*]. Even allowing for the provisional character of these formulations, we encounter an important uncertainty in the abstract clause representing the purpose sense, namely, the question mark that occupies the subject *NP* position preceding the verb [DESIRE]. The English verb *desire* requires an animate, sentient subject, as does a relevant analogue, *intend*. Presumably the abstract verb [DESIRE] is also analogous in this essential respect. The question, therefore, is, Who is the subject of the abstract verb [DESIRE] in the purpose constructions of Cranmer's collects?

There are two possible answers to be drawn from the immediate sentential context: God (referred to as "thou") may be the subject of the abstract [DESIRE] clause or man (referred to as "we") may be. In the composition of Cranmer's collects both possibilities resonate with promise. To take "thou" as the subject of the underlying [DESIRE] clause in the St. John's Day collect is tantamount to affirming that the God who casts his light upon the Church, with the result that the Church attains his gifts, is the same God whose purpose in casting his light is that the Church attain those gifts. Such an interpretation clearly falls within the range of possibility; the purpose sense is significantly ambiguous to this extent. However, the structure of the highest clause of all in collect sentence form—namely, "we beseech thee"—weights the probabilities in favor of the other possible interpretation: since "we" are invoking the result, "we" may also be taken to have the result as our purpose. The latter interpretation may appear the likelier, moreover, in view of the predominantly petitionary character of the collect, and of prayer in general: we pray to God, ordinarily, for what we want rather than what he wants. Yet because the great objective of Christian spirituality, tracing back to Paul, is the conforming of the "old man," or Adam, of the self to God to bring into being a "new man" in Christ, the semantic ambiguity of Cranmer's result or purpose constructions remains profoundly functional in its controlled multiplicity of possible implications.

Hence, in the first collect under discussion (Second Sunday after Easter), we ask God to give us the grace that results in thankful reception and daily following of Christ—results, however, that depend on his and our desire. In the collect for St. John's Day, we ask God to cast his light on the Church and to bring it about that the Church attains his gifts—again, his result, but again and equally, his and our desire. Thus the class of predicate complements that promote indeterminacy between result and purpose meanings operates, perhaps more powerfully than any other aspect of sentence form in Cranmer's collects, to enforce the sense that what God wills to effectuate are the same things that man can be brought in the public worship of the Church to desire. What we have been tracing in some particularity here is a manifold display of mastery in a mode of single-sentence discourse that specially conduced to combining Latinate suspensiveness with English successiveness for authoritative religious expression. Whatever guidance in creation Cranmer gained from his set form of composition, it also gave ample rein to his genius for encompassing a rich range of implications while expressly formulating means for the worshippers of the Church of England to collect themselves and their thoughts in addressing God. The collect sentence, in Cranmer's handling, synthesized the principal strengths of native English prose style—its speech basis, its demonstrated resources of conjunctive syntax—with more learned and ornate features to produce a hybrid form that at once exploited and enlarged the capabilities of the vernacular. In so doing, Cranmer's collects supplemented the evidence of Tyndale's Bible translations that English, by the mid-sixteenth century, had confirmed its full modern stature as a literary medium, at least in the domain of religious prose.

5. Prose in the Earlier Half of the Sixteenth Century: Sententious Sentence, or Forms of Counsel

PROSE OF COUNSEL: A DEFINITION

In chapters 2–4 I have attempted to substantiate the guiding hypothesis of this study—that English prose in its formative, early modern period can be treated as a self-contained body of materials, a subject for critical examination in its own right—and I have done so by addressing stylistic developments along with pertinent historical and conceptual developments over a century and a half, from 1380 onward. On the linguistic plane, I have identified the joint Englishness and modernity of this prose with a group of interrelated defining features. These include the stabilizing of word order within clausal units into the $NP + V$ ($+ NP$) ($+$ Adverb) ($+$ Complement) pattern which creates the "canonical sentoid" so vital to "open sentences," the evident oral basis or speechlikeness of writing which importantly relies on coordinate structures in all aspects of sentence form and discourse, and the comprehensive resources of conjunction itself as recursively applied, whether asymmetrically or symmetrically, whether reduced or unreduced in the surface configurations set down on the page. I have also pointed out certain historical and conceptual signs of a modernity above and beyond the identification of linguistic features that emanates from the vigorous vernacular prose produced between the late fourteenth and the early sixteenth century. This upsurge of activity and confidence in writing in the native tongue is inseparable from the rise of nationalistic sentiment accompanying the sensed possibility and need for effective centralized government (variously attested in Fortescue and the continuations of *The Brut*), inseparable also from the confirmed siting of a capital for such a government in the London-Westminster area, and the steady growth in power, visibility, and voice of a commercial and mercantile bourgeoisie in a number of cities throughout the realm, most notably London. (These developments are variously attested in the guild records, the early English wills, the how-to-do-it manuals, the Paston, Cely, and Stonor letters, *The Book of Margery Kempe,* and the readerships who spurred the literary activities of Pecock, Malory, and Caxton.)

While in no way discounting the operation of such modern forces as nationalism, early capitalism, secularization, and incipient democratization through the spreading of the economic, political, social, and educational power base to broader levels in the gradual course of this period, I wish to make a specific case for the stylistic impact in early modern English prose of the combined conceptual position and compositional process which I term Scripturalism: a writer's molding of his thought and language forms after a recognizable mode or model from the Old or New Testament. That the literary impact of Scripturalism predates the Wycliffite movement is attested by the superb responsiveness shown by a late fourteenth-century devotional writer like Hilton to the syntactic and semantic modalities of the sacred text. Nonetheless, with Wyclif and his associates vernacular Scripturalism attains much greater impetus as a factor in the development of prose style. The impetus shows in the energizing confidence regarding the adequacy of English and its native speakers to receive and register the Word of God as it echoes first in Wyclif's English sermons and reechoes with equal if not greater intensity in Tyndale's prose. The impetus also shows in the reflectiveness about English as a medium and the stylistic self-consciousness about handling the vernacular in an effective fashion for a broad popular readership that produce such lucid, lively results in Purvey's and Tyndale's Biblical translations and original writings. However, because the history of securing popular access to the Bible in English is as beleaguered in its way as the history of securing the lifeline of English itself as a language, it is evident that the impact of Scripturalism as I have defined it can only begin to be traced in earnest in the writing of English prose after about 1537–38, when Thomas Cromwell and Thomas Cranmer began to implement widely Henry VIII's authorization of an English Bible—Tyndale's work, supplemented by Miles Coverdale and John Rogers—to be set up for reading in every church in the realm.

In continuing to argue for the stylistic impact of Scripturalism upon English prose composition, I have no intention of claiming that its weight was absolute or that it was felt in isolation from other factors like nationalism, secularization, and the demands and desires of a contemporary vernacular readership which remained in force. Indeed, for the very reason that the Bible in English requires authorized circulation—immensely furthered, as it happened, by the confirmed economic viability of the printing press by 1530—before Scripturalism can be assessed for its stylistic impact on the writing of prose, the same authorized status of the English Bible and its prominent place in widely attended divine services and sermons can be expected to promote the assimilation of Scriptural thought and language forms into the mainstream of national consciousness. Oddly, however, the possible impact of Scripturalism upon the writing of English prose in the sixteenth century has been all but ignored by literary historians. Only Richard Foster Jones, in "The Moral Sense of Simplicity," has broached concerns akin to mine in documenting a broad spectrum of sixteenth-century writers of English, secular as well as religious, who claimed for their own prose the qualities of direct, instrumental communication that were standardly praised in Biblical language.[1] Yet Jones's study is not fully Scripturalist in my sense because his interest is exhausted by ideas about style; it does not extend to the analysis of style.

Nor can the lack of attention to the possible stylistic impact of Scripturalism be explained by disagreement over the object of analysis—the overall character and identifying traits of sixteenth-century English prose—for scholars and critics concur widely on what these are. This prose is, first, thoroughly and overtly rhetorical: it seeks to persuade, whatever its subject. Often the author adopts the stance of a speaker, incorporating various hallmarks of earlier oral-based prose (pleonasm, expletives, colloquial idioms and bywords, first- and second-person forms of address) and not infrequently opting for dialogue as the genre of discourse.[2] Second, this prose, in which the resources of recursively applied conjunction continue to generate the preponderance of linguistic energy, displays a greater and greater tendency toward schematic design which culminates, at the end of the century, in the much studied vogue of Euphuism. It is indisputable, moreover, that this greater and greater tendency toward schematic design both provides the major momentum in English prose from about the middle of the century and makes for its quite remarkable stylistic uniformity toward the end of the century. Thus, for example, John Lyly in 1580 can appropriate sizable portions of the *Description of England*, which William Harrison prepared for the first (1577) edition of Holinshed's *Chronicles*, and insert them into *Euphues and His England* without any felt incongruity; and it is not much later that the link between Euphuism and sermon style consolidates in the highly patterned preaching of Thomas Playfere which delighted Nashe and the other University Wits who were Lyly's associates and coevals.[3] To show how—and, if possible, to suggest why—the internal dynamic

[1]Richard Foster Jones, "The Moral Sense of Simplicity," *Studies in Honor of Frederick W. Shipley*, Washington University Studies, n.s., Language and Literature, no. 14 (St. Louis, 1942), pp. 265–87.

[2]See the suggestive discussion by Walter J. Ong, S.J., "Oral Residue in Tudor Prose Style," *PMLA* 80 (1965): 145–54.

[3]For discussion, see George Williamson, *The Senecan Amble: A Study in Prose Form from Bacon to Collier* (Chicago: University of Chicago Press, 1966), pp. 89–95; on Lyly's borrowings from Harrison, see R. Warwick Bond, ed., *The Complete Works of John Lyly* (Oxford: Clarendon Press, 1902), I, 133, II, 191–96.

of English prose style eventuated in Euphuism remains an acknowledged task of literary history for the sixteenth century.

At the present time, a phase of relative inactivity in the study of Euphuism after the massive surge of inquiry and speculation which came to a head in the early twentieth century, there are two schools of thought that persist in exercising explanatory weight even though they stand at least partly in opposition. The first, the creation of Eduard Norden, is broadly inclusive in outlook: it traces the set of formal features which define Euphuism to an ultimate source in the sophistic techniques for discourse developed by Gorgias and refined by Isocrates, through intermediary stages in the degenerate Ciceronianism of the late Roman Empire in which major Latin Church Fathers received their training and spread their influence in Christendom, down to the latter-day and equally extravagant Ciceronianism of Antonio de Guevara, a Spanish bishop and noted neo-Latin stylist of the early sixteenth century.[4] The second school, that of Morris Croll, insists on a categorical distinction between positive, classical influences and detrimental, medieval ones in the creation of Euphuism; it accordingly locates prototypes and sources in the schematic Latin prose of the Middle Ages.[5] Since Norden and Croll, various scholars have attempted to mediate between the vast perspective entailed by the one and the polarization entailed by the other.[6] Increasingly we have come to realize that the origins of Euphuism defy tracking down to some exclusive model or models for formal composition. This is so because the composite of syntactic, semantic, and sound features which produce the elaborate Euphuistic consonances and correspondences is demonstrable common property of the classical languages and the European vernaculars as well—what in transformational-generative theory is called a set of linguistic universals and, hence, potentially a set of stylistic universals. Designation as a "universal" means a feature that can be replicated from language to language. We shall be seeing in chapters 5 and 6 that the chief reason why the composite of syntactic, semantic, and sound features in Euphuism qualifies as a set of stylistic universals is that a number of these features trace to a source in sentential conjunction, which is itself a linguistic universal.

[4]Eduard Norden, *Die antike Kunstprosa vom VI. Jahrhundert vor Christi bis in die Zeit der Renaissance*, 2 vols. (Leipzig: Teubner, 1909).

[5]Morris W. Croll, "The Sources of the Euphuistic Rhetoric," in John Lyly, *"Euphues: The Anatomy of Wit" and "Euphues and His England,"* ed. Morris W. Croll and Harry Clemons (New York: Dutton, 1916); rptd. in *Style, Rhetoric, and Rhythm: Essays by Morris W. Croll,* ed. J. Max Patrick et al. (Princeton: Princeton University Press, 1966), pp. 241–95.

[6]See, for example, William A. Ringler, Jr., "The Immediate Source of Euphuism," *PMLA* 53 (1938): 678–86; James Wortham, "Sir Thomas Elyot and the Translation of Prose," *HLQ* 11 (1948): 219–40; Williamson, *Senecan Amble*, pp. 11–60.

But we have also increasingly come to realize, with regard to standing accounts of Euphuism, that it will not suffice for the purposes of literary interpretation to uncover a more or less plausible range of formal sources and prototypes for a given mode of composition. What demand interpretation, specifically, are the factors making the choice of some source or prototype more rather than less plausible than the choice of some other(s). In this connection, Alvin Vos has offered an admirable specimen of interpretation in "The Formation of Roger Ascham's Prose Style." Remarking that formalistic analysis can build an essentially equivalent case for Isocrates or the schematic early orations of Cicero as models for Ascham's English style, he proceeds to offer on behalf of a Ciceronian model a number of biographical and ideological considerations which establish Ascham's impressionability regarding the tastes and crotchets of his longtime mentor and correspondent Johannes Sturm, a German humanist and evangelical Protestant schoolmaster. Vos makes no exclusive claims about Ascham's prose style, but argues the strong relative probability that Sturm's adulation of Cicero's youthful excesses in patterning language influenced Ascham's own thinking and writing. The multiple yet discriminating approach which Vos espouses in prose study shows clearly in his concluding words:

Our conceptions of the development of prose style in the Renaissance have readily been over-simplified. The forces and influences in Renaissance prose style are both more elusive and more numerous than we have thought. The most vexing problem in Renaissance prose, the question of influences and sources, needs to be examined more fully. Further studies are necessary before we can be sure of the complete history of the rise of English literary prose.[7]

I concur wholeheartedly with Vos that what the study of sixteenth-century English prose style now needs most is the exploration of yet unexamined possibilities for addressing "the question of influences and sources"; and in due course, in chapter 6, I shall try to shed some different, but still plausible light on Ascham. The possibilities I shall pursue are continuations of the concerns that have shaped discussion up to this point: first, and more comprehensively, the dynamic inherent in the syntax and semantics of conjunction which remains in this period the greatest single resource for vernacular prose style; and second, and more particularly, the stimulus supplied by Scripturalism as its forcibly repressed and delayed impact upon modes of composition came into its own with the English Reformation. However, by the standards which I have just been endorsing, it is insufficient for me merely to demonstrate formal grounds for supposing that Scripturalism stimulated awareness of syntactic and semantic likenesses which motivate sentential conjunc-

[7]Alvin Vos, "The Formation of Roger Ascham's Prose Style," *SP* 71 (1974): 344–70; quotation from pp. 369–70.

tion and in turn, if systematically cultivated, conduce to schematic style. It is necessary to show in addition that English prose writers after 1530 conceived Scripturalism in a fashion that would make it an amenable mode for treating the subjects and issues that draw their efforts and elicit increasing schematism. Happily there is widespread evidence to the effect that Scripturalism from the later 1530s onward assumed a clear character and equally definite connotations that recommended it highly as a model for diverse kinds of prose composition. I shall be dealing in specifics for individual writers in subsequent sections of chapters 5 and 6; at this point I shall merely sketch the larger picture in bald outline.

The conceptual heart of Scripturalism in the sixteenth century lies in the Protestant insistence on the supremacy of the Bible both as the source for truths necessary to salvation and as the highest authority on a range of other fundamental matters. Which matters these were eventually occasioned dispute and divisiveness as Nonconformity solidified in the later course of the Reformation in England. But at its inception, in the period with which we are dealing, there was a quite remarkable consensus among thinkers who became writers regarding the scope and character of the authority to be ascribed to Scripture. We can look for delineation of this scope and character to the writings of Tyndale himself. His urgent affectivity and concomitant schematic tendencies deriving from the style of the Pauline Epistles—the means by which he sought to bring home to the soul the amazing grace of the Gospel promises— did not prevail as the single mode by which Scripturalism was to be implemented in prose, not even in his own prose. A number of scholars have called attention to the emergent bent of Tyndale's thought in his last years—that is, after 1530, when he was engaged in translating the Pentateuch—which lays emphasis on the directives of Old Testament Law and moral counsel.[8] Correspondingly, Tyndale's writing exhibits a heightened sententiousness and a proclivity toward Hebraic sense parallelisms, although he was not to live long enough to write much in his later style. Besides the effect of labors on an English version of the five books of the Mosaic Law, the slaughter and upheaval being wreaked in Germany at this time by Thomas Münzer and his Anabaptist adherents may have moved Tyndale toward a conception of the message of Scripture that downplayed personal and subjective elements and stressed strong civil authority, social order, and practical morality. Certainly the latter associations inform the great English consensus of the sixteenth century, for in its middle and later decades there is no writer who does not cling to them as norms, no writer with whom Anabaptism gained

[8]See, for example, William A. Clebsch, *England's Earliest Protestants, 1520–1535* (New Haven and London: Yale University Press, 1964), pp. 169–85; Arthur G. Dickens, *The English Reformation* (New York: Schocken Books, 1964), p. 73.

so much as a toehold. Religious and social persuasions of this sort and degree of strength thus led to a steady focus on the ethical and sententious content of the Bible, preponderantly the prophetic and wisdom books. The sermons of Hugh Latimer, justly the most renowned of English mid-century preachers, bear ample witness to the thematic and stylistic ramifications of a Scripturalism conceived mainly as prophetic outcry against social evils and as moral precepts by which a nation could be governed under a godly king. His showpiece in this line is the series of sermons in recurrently schematic prose, suffused with citations from Jonah, Jeremiah, Amos, and others, which Latimer delivered at court before the young Edward VI in 1549 and 1550.[9]

Notwithstanding the shaping influence of Old Testament Scripturalism on mid-sixteenth-century prose composition as a reaction to felt social and moral ills, probably the most important factor of all in predisposing English writers to associate the authoritativeness of God's Word quite specifically with the Old Testament was political in character, and distinctively English in its circumstances. This was the historic sequence of actions by which Henry VIII broke with the authority of the papacy to assume the title of Supreme Head of Church and State within his dominions. Through this train of events set in motion by royal fiat, the English Reformation was transformed from a protest movement of uncertain status into a cornerstone of national policy and self-definition. Obviously, though, no monarch could effect changes of so drastic and fundamental a character unless he was able to count on widespread popular support—a commodity which Henry both possessed and accrued at a great rate. Thus the sweeping Act of Supremacy (1534), which constituted him the sovereign ecclesiastical as well as temporal power in the realm, not only received ready Parliamentary ratification but, in fact, derived the strength of its formulations from an earlier enactment (1531) in Convocation, by the bishops of the realm. In longer terms, however, the way to authenticate the office of the king as constituted by Henry VIII was to authorize it—in practice, of course, by the effective imposition and exercise of rule, but also in theory, which in that age essentially meant demonstration by authority. It is here, above all, that Old Testament Scripturalism came to play a vital and indispensable role. For while there were important New Testament texts—Jesus' "Render unto Caesar the things that are Caesar's" and Paul's "Submit yourselves unto the higher powers"—a far richer source of authentication for the idea that the king ruled over God's people in God's stead by God's express directive was afforded by the Old Testament. Beyond useful

---

[9]See Allan G. Chester's indispensable edition (which restores outspoken passages suppressed in earlier printings) and its useful introduction: *Selected Sermons of Hugh Latimer,* Folger Documents of Tudor and Stuart Civilization no. 11 (Charlottesville: University of Virginia Press for the Folger Shakespeare Library, 1968).

single texts like Psalm 82:6, "I have said, ye are gods," which was interpreted as a direct divine imparting of earthly sovereignty to kings, by far the most compelling Scriptural authority was felt to derive from the historical narrative in which God institutes monarchy among the Jews at their own urging by commanding the judge and prophet Samuel to anoint Saul king (1 Samuel 8–11) and the later confirmation of hereditary kingship under David, Saul's successor (2 Samuel 2 ff.). There is appreciable evidence to support the inference that a predominantly Old Testament Scripturalism attained the hold it did in sixteenth-century English thought and expression principally because of the reverence and the assiduity with which this age looked to the founding and governance of the kingdom of Israel as a model—and, somehow, a certification—for the rule of the Tudors.

In undertaking to argue the case for the impact of Scripturalism on English prose style between 1530 and 1580 while also keeping in focus the concern with modernity in prose and prose study that has guided my inquiry from the first, I have sought to identify a body of writing that would reflect the major developments then taking place: the impact of the English Reformation compounded with the growth of nationalism, public-spiritedness, and the cultural and political power of the gentry and the middle class in a gradual, sustained, and finally decisive process of secularization. I have constituted this body of writing as a species by affixing it with a label—"the prose of counsel"—one not strictly of my creation, but adapted to my purposes. In *The Articulate Citizen and the English Renaissance*, Arthur B. Ferguson traces a process of transformation that takes place between the late fourteenth and the mid-sixteenth century in a body of writing—almost wholly, vernacular works—which he terms "the literature of counsel."[10] For Ferguson, the interest of the literature of counsel inheres in the ultimately significant changes in the assumptions and thinking of English writers who address political and social problems in the realm with the intent of offering constructive advice. The earlier works see problems for the most part in religious and static terms, as evidence of human perversity in deviating from a God-given order of things. Although this perspective is tenacious and, in many cases, inveterate in the English writers who figure in Ferguson's study, he is nonetheless able to document the gradual emergence of a more empirical, pragmatic approach to the powers and functions of government—one which takes a problem-solving rather than a purely sin-decrying line to propose concrete ways of dealing administratively with various political, social, and economic issues. Since Ferguson's clear concern is with intellectual history—specifically, with the history of the

---

[10]Arthur B. Ferguson, *The Articulate Citizen and the English Renaissance* (Durham, N.C.: Duke University Press, 1965), especially pp. 3–41, 133–61.

emergence of a practical political consciousness—he has no cause to reflect on the possible literary-historical ramifications of a species labeled "prose of counsel." Yet there are suggestive leads in that direction, and I propose to build on them.

By enlarging more than departing from Ferguson's conception, I use "prose of counsel" as a selection principle for tracing at once salient and representative developments in the vastly increasing literary domain of the mid- and later sixteenth century; the term, moreover, designates a gathering of works and authors whose signficant common features will serve to test the broader and more general impact of Scripturalism beyond the confines of explicitly religious writing. The works to be considered as "prose of counsel" are oriented rather toward secular than toward religious subjects, they are predominantly discursive and non-narrative (narrative, where it figures, is kept subordinate to discursive elements), and, of course, they have an overtly advisory and hortatory cast—they offer counsel. The authors of "prose of counsel" also share important characteristics as a group: those who will bear the brunt of attention are all laymen, and humanists in one way or another; furthermore, they address a readership of persons who (like the authors) interest themselves in contemporary problems and issues.[11] These authors and their works constitute a prose of counsel for the most part expressly, because they offer reflections and recommendations for life in their times. Yet, even where the aspect of counsel operates more obliquely, as in the recurrent use of the dialogue form or the fiction from the close of the period, the conceptual and stylistic approach of these writers remains geared to political, social, or moral problematics, as is clear from the sententious and generally schematic texture of their discourse. It is this group, then, who will absorb consideration as we pursue the concerns of this study to their conclusion in chapters 5 and 6—a group comprising Sir Thomas Elyot, various handbook compilers (among them, Nicholas Udall, William Baldwin, and Thomas Becon), Sir Richard Morison, Sir John Cheke, Roger Ascham, Sir Thomas Wilson, George Pettie, and John Lyly.

[11]A. G. Dickens has documented an interesting mid-century shift in the reading interests of provincial Englishmen. Before 1550 the materials are overwhelmingly religious, but beginning in the decade 1550–60 a broadening and diversification occur, reflected in interests in medicine, science, natural history, law, social and economic problems, genealogy, and poetry. See his discussion in *Transactions of the Royal Historical Society*, 5th ser., no. 13 (1963): 49–76.

Toward a Generalized Scripturalism: The Precedent of Elyot

Sir Thomas Elyot has secured a position of honor in English literary history as a prolific humanist who, at a remarkably early date (by 1531), had made a binding choice of the vernacular as the medium by which to transfuse the educative and ennobling values of antiquity into the lifeblood of his nation. As all of his works, original and translated, attest, Elyot was typical among thoughtful Englishmen of his era in responding ardently to Erasmus and, like the master, resisting any propensity to divide classical from Christian strains in the inherited wealth of antiquity. Elyot's four translations—*The Doctrinal of Princes Made by the Noble Orator Isocrates* (1534), *The Rules of Christian Life* of Pico della Mirandola (1534), *A Sweet and Devout Sermon of Holy St. Cyprian of the Mortality of Man* (1534), and *The Education or Bringing Up of Children Translated Out of Plutarch* (1535?)—are surpassed more than twice over in number, length, and eclecticism by his original works: *The Book Named the Governour* (1531), *Pasquil the Plain* (1532), *Of the Knowledge Which Maketh a Wise Man* (1533), *The Banquet of Sapience* (ca. 1534), *The Castle of Health* (ca. 1536), The Latin-English *Dictionary* (1538), *The Defense of Good Women* (1540), *The Image of Governance* (1541), and *A Preservative against Death* (1545). Although two book-length studies—a biography and an account of his place in Renaissance intellectual history—have confirmed Elyot's stature as an early English humanist, he is still comparatively underacknowledged for his contributions to the development of prose style.[12] By and large his linguistic interests have exhausted the notice paid him in this line: Elyot is credited for progressiveness in choosing to write in English, but he is viewed in a mixed light as a coiner and borrower, even something of an aureator and inkhornist. There is much more to the story, however, as I shall try to show. The size and variety of Elyot's canon coupled with his expressed self-consciousness in building and diversifying his stylistic repertory make him a subject of exceptional interest. The interest is not simply intrinsic to Elyot either, for his career as a writer takes on a paradigmatic aspect as it reflects backward and forward by turns on directions in English prose style in the 1530s and 1540s.

At the outset of his enterprised career, in his important first work, *The Book Named the Governour*, Elyot's approach to authorship, whether declared or implicit, has much in common with that of Caxton half a century before. As Caxton had courted royal (and near-royal) patronage in the persons of Margaret of Burgundy and Lord Rivers, Elyot dedicates

---

[12]The book-length studies are Stanford E. Lehmberg's *Sir Thomas Elyot: Tudor Humanist* (Austin: University of Texas Press, 1960), and John M. Major's *Sir Thomas Elyot and Renaissance Humanism* (Lincoln: University of Nebraska Press, 1964). Elyot is, however, treated seriously as a stylist by Wortham ("Sir Thomas Elyot") and Holmes ("The Significance of Elyot's Revision of *The Governour*," *RES*, n.s. 12 [1961]: 352–63).

his *Governour* to Henry VIII as the first of a succession of studious "labours" which he hopes will meet with the king's approbation. Elyot also concurs with Caxton in emphasizing historical materials as the prime source of the teaching power and the celebration of greatness which literature must provide. Thus, although there is proportionately more exposition and commentary than narration in *The Governour* and Elyot's other works, he relies very heavily on historical exempla and anecdotes throughout because, as he explains, they are invaluable for the vicarious experience they offer and for the notable deeds and wise sayings they contain.[13] Accordingly, Elyot represents his authorial role in *The Governour* very much as Caxton had his: he will "describe in our vulgare tunge the fourme of a just publike weale: . . . to the intent that men which wil be studious . . . may fynde the thinges therto expedient compendiously writen, . . . trustynge therby tacquite me of my dueties to god, your hyghnesse, and this my contray" (Proheme, p. xxxi). What is more, Elyot's patriotism as a writer eager to be of use to his king and countrymen in the native tongue impels many of Caxton's stylistic choices; *The Governour*, particularly the first, unrevised edition, abounds in word pairs, neologisms, proverbs, and grandiloquent sentence forms.[14] The premium on elegance, cultivation, and prescriptivism in language which shapes the composition of this work shows clearly in Elyot's recommendations that wellborn children, the future governors of the realm, be brought up by nurses selected (among other things) for their pure English and then entrusted to competent tutors who will teach them to converse in correct Latin as young as possible (I.v, x, xiii; pp. 23, 34, 54).

Like Caxton, Elyot at the beginning of his career aimed to discharge his authorial responsibilities by gracing English with fine writing, by styling his prose at a perceptible remove from speech. Besides his excursuses into definition and vocabulary-building in order to make the vernacular a more adequate and more eloquent means to knowledge, Elyot's every point of emphasis in *The Governour* is set out in the loaded patterns of earlier sixteenth-century authoritative utterance, whether or not accompanied with aureate diction. His pronouncement on the true end of

---

[13]Sir Thomas Elyot, *The Boke Named the Governour,* ed. Ernest Rhys, intro. Foster Watson, Everyman's Library (London: J. M. Dent; New York: E. P. Dutton, 1907), The Proheme, p. xxxii. All subsequent references will be to this edition of *The Governour* and will incorporate Elyot's book and chapter numbers as well as the page numbers in parentheses in the text.

[14]See the informative discussion of Elyot's earlier and later conceptions of style and authorship in Elisabeth Holmes, "The Significance of Elyot's Revision of *The Governour*," pp. 352–63. Norman F. Blake comments on the listed features of style which the early Elyot shares with Caxton in *Caxton and His World* (New York: London House & Maxwell, 1969), pp. 158–61.

rhetorical study illustrates the survival of Caxtonian ideas and practice alike regarding vernacular prose style:

Undoubtedly very eloquence is in every tonge where any mater or acte done or to be done is expressed in wordes clene, propise, ornate, and comely: whereof sentences be so aptly compact that they by a vertue inexplicable do drawe unto them the mindes and consent of the herers, they beinge therwith either per-swaded, meved, or to delectation induced. [I.xiii; p. 55]

The compositional repertory to be observed here is virtually identical with Caxton's, as is Elyot's use of it: the enlargement of nodes of phrase structure with recursively elaborated, near-tautological conjuncts ("any mater or acte done or to be done"; "clene, propise, ornate, and comely"; "mindes and consent"; "either perswaded, meved, or to delectation induced") combined with the loose, asymmetrical expansion of sentence form at the clausal level ("every tonge where"; "whereof sentences be so aptly compact that"; "they beinge therwith"). However, it is much more characteristic of Elyot's sentence forms in *The Governour* to avoid the additive, rambling movement of Caxton's, and instead to combine pattern-loading at the phrasal level with spreading of the main clause unit, as illustrated in the first sentence of the following quotation: the opening portion of Elyot's definition of sapience. Besides its accomplished handling of clausal spread, the quotation is notable for its profuse doublings, its self-conscious reaching after "a more elegant worde," and the complacent implication of its magniloquent design—that, as God is sovereign over nature, so the king must be absolutely supreme in the "publike weale":

All be it that some men which have hiderto radde this boke will suppose that those vertues whereof I have treated be sufficient to make a governour vertuous and excellent, nethelas for as moche as the effecte of myne enterprise in this warke is to expresse, as farre furthe as god shall instructe my poore witte, what thinges do belonge to the makinge of a perfeyte publike weale, whiche well nigh may no more be without an excellent governour than the universall course of nature may stande or be permanent without one chiefe disposer and mever, which is over all supereminent in powar, understanding, and goodnes. Wherfore because in governaunce be included disposition and ordre, whiche can not be without soveraigne knowlege, procedynge of wisedome, in a more elegant worde called Sapience, therfore I will nowe declare as moch as my litle witte doth comprehende of that parte of Sapience that of necessitie must be in every governour of a juste or perfeyte publike weale. [III.xxiii; p. 268]

Despite the extensive affinities between Caxton and Elyot in conceptions of literature and authorship and in such stylistic practices as near-tautological doublings and aureate pattern-loading, *The Governour* is a far more able and variegated composition than anything we have from Caxton's pen. In particular, it is worth considering at closer range Elyot's

systematic capacity to do without the trailing sequences of native conjunctive syntax in handling his largely expository and even narrative
materials. How, we may inquire, does he manage to pursue his commitment to *historia* without these familiar and all but inevitable trailing
sequences? What sentence form does Elyot substitute? The answer to
the first question depends upon particulars, but the second admits of a
general answer. Elyot's substitute sentence form traces to the authoritative Latinate mode of utterance which we have observed in More and
seen prefigured to some extent in Love and Pecock. Its staple is a subclass
of conjunctively originating constructions—appositives, parentheticals,
nonrestrictive, continuative, and sentential relatives—whose syntactic
common denominator is their adjunction within a higher, containing
clause at the position occupied by the primary element to which they
have some identity relation.[15] Thus, as we have seen, this species of
constructions creates a sentence form that concurrently loads the patterns and spreads the larger units of clausal structure. We find this
sentence form from first to last, from *The Governour* to *The Image of
Governance*, wherever Elyot's recourses to historical exempla lead us to
expect what we do not get—the predominantly asymmetric conjunctions
of the native mode. Here is an illustration from late in *The Governour*, a
passage intrinsically interesting for its heroic portrayal of King Edgar's
outfacing of challenges to his rule of England, and a very proper subject
for a writer who was courting Henry VIII's approbation:

Edgare, who in the tyme that the Saxons had this realme in subjection, hadde
subdued all the other Kynges Saxons, and made them his tributaries. On a tyme
he hadde theim all with hym at dyner, and after it was shewed hym that Rynande, kynge of Scottes, hadde sayde that he woundred howe it shulde happen
that he and other kynges, that were tall and great personages, wolde suffre
them selfes to be subdued by so litle a body as Edgare was. Edgare dissembled
and answered nothinge, but faynynge to go on huntynge, he toke with him the
Scottishe kynge in his company, and purposely withdrewe hym from them that
were with hym; and causynge by a secrete servaunt two swerdes to be convayed
in to a place in the forest by hym appointed, as soone as he came thither he
toke the one sworde, and delyvered the other to Rinande, byddinge hym to
prove his strength, and to assay whither his dedes wolde ratifie his wordes.
Wherat the Scottisshe kynge beinge abasshed, beholdynge the noble courage of
Edgare, with an horrible feare confessed his errour, desirynge pardon, whiche
he with moste humble submission at the laste optayned. That noble kynge
Edgare declarynge by his Magnanimitie that by his vertue, and nat by chaunce,
he was elected to reigne over so noble a region. [III.xiv; p. 241]

In the alternative to native, trailing sentence form that Elyot employs
for narrative material, we note a cultivated distance from orality. Every

---

[15]Several branches of this family of constructions are treated in Mats Rydén, *Relative
Constructions in . . . Thomas Elyot* (Uppsala: Almqvist & Wiksells, 1966).

bit of dialogue in the foregoing passage is converted into indirect discourse and tucked into embedded or adjoined phrases ("it was shewed hym that Rynande . . . hadde sayde that he woundred howe it shulde happen that"; "byddynge hym to prove . . . and to assay whither"; "confessed his errour, desirynge pardon, whiche he . . . optayned"). But, all the while that these sentence forms preserve a studied distance from speech-based prose, the adjunctions that spread their clauses are constantly used to interpose commentary. Elyot asserts an imperious presence in his narratives, although not as a speaking voice. Some of these conjunctively arising insertions have a nearly neutral expository function—for example, the nonrestrictive relatives in the first and second sentences ("who in the tyme that"; "that were tall and great personages"). Elyot regularly uses this species of constructions, however, to impute express psychological and moral significance to each development in a narrative, so that as we receive history at his hand, we are also directed how we are to receive it. Some italicizing will illustrate how instrumental these constructions are in giving such direction: "Edgare . . . answered nothinge, *but faynynge to go on huntynge,* he toke with him the Scottishe kynge"; "*Wherat* the Scottishe kynge *beinge abasshed, beholdynge the noble courage of Edgare,* with an horrible feare confessed his errour"; "That noble kynge Edgare *declarynge by his Magnanimitie".*

For my purposes it is significant, moreover, that the Elyot of *The Governour* subjects Biblical narrative to the same strenuous recasting in his directed sentence forms. An example is provided in the following passage, which recounts an episode involving King Saul, David and Abner in order to demonstrate the enduring truth that "all they, in whome is any portion of gentill courage, endevoure them selfes to be all wayes trustye and loyall to their soverayne":

What tyme that Saull for his grevous offences was abandoned of all mighty god, who of a very poore mannes sonne did avaunce him to the kyngedome of Israell, and that David, beinge his servaunt and as poore a mannes son as he, was elected by god to reigne in Israell, and was enointed kynge by the prophet Samuell, Saulle beinge therfore in a rage, havinge indignacion at David, pursued hym with a great hooste to have slayne hym, who (as longe as he mought) fledde and forbare Saule, as his soveraygne lorde. . . . And in a night, whan Saull and his armye were at reste, and that David by an espiall knewe that they were all faste on slepe, he toke with him a certayne of the moste assured and valiaunt personages of his hoste, and in most secrete wise came to the pavilion of king Saul, where he founde hym suerly slepynge, havinge by him his speare and a cuppe of water. Wherfore one of the company of David sayde that he with the speare of Saulle, wolde stryke hym through and slee hym. Nay, sayd David, our lorde forbede that I suffre my soveraigne lord to be slayne, for he is enointed of god. And therwith he toke the speare with the cuppe of water, and when he was a good distaunce from the hoste of Saulle, he cried with a loude voyce to Abner, which was than marshall of the armye of Saul. Who answered and sayde, What arte thou that thus diseasest the kyng, which is nowe at his reste? To whome David said, Abner, thou and thy company are worthy deathe, that have so negligently watched your prince; where is his hede? suerly ye be but dede men whan he shall know it. And there with he shewed the speare and cuppe with water. Whiche Saulle perceyvinge and hearynge the voyce of David, cried unto him saienge, Is nat this the voice of my dere sonne David? I uncurtaisely do pursue him, and he nat withstandinge doth to me good for evill. With other wordes, whiche to abbreviate the mater I do passe over. This noble historie and other semblable . . . of particuler persones, whiche have showed examples of loyaltie, I praye god may so cleve to the myndes of the readers, that they may be all way redy to put the semblable in experience. [III.vi; pp. 214–16][16]

Again, in this passage, Elyot reveals his studied disinterest in reproducing speech by the dismissive remark, "With other wordes, whiche to abbreviate the mater I do passe over," and by the elegant rephrasing which he performs on the dialogue of 1 Samuel 26. Where Abner's words read "What art thou that cryest to the king?" in the Great Bible, Elyot's rendering is: "What arte thou that thus diseasest the kyng, whiche is nowe at his reste?" In the Great Bible Saul says, "Is this thy voyce my sonne David? . . . I have synned, come agayn my sonne David, for I will do thee no moare harme." Elyot reworks the colloquialism into formality: "Is nat this the voice of my dere sonne David? I uncurtaisely do pursue him, and he nat withstandinge doth to me good for evill." These observations constitute our first piece of evidence that the religiously conservative Elyot, from first to last a loyal Catholic in his beliefs, had no sympathy with the newly resurgent Scripturalism of Tyndale. But there also seems to be more at stake than Erasmian elegance in the distance Elyot puts between prose composition and speech as he applies his style to historical materials, sacred no less than secular. His indirection and periphrasis in handling Abner's and Saul's speeches infuse them with an inescapable judgmental coloration: Abner's question is made a reproach to those who disturb the king, and Saul's speech (with the inserted sentential adverbs "uncurtaisely," "nat withstandinge") is turned to self-reproach, although there is no Biblical warrant for either.

More generally, the subclass of conjunctively arising constructions that function to spread clauses also attests to the encompassing directive aim of Elyot's alternative sentence form for narrative. His self-styled authorial role is a strongly managerial one; he operates through his syntax to build the lessons of history into historical passages. Thus, in the Saul and

[16]David and Saul, along with Alexander the Great, are the most frequent subjects of historical exempla in *The Governour*; for other examples, see pp. 87, 117, 269–70 (I.xx, II.i, III.xxiii).

David episode, the appositives, parentheticals, and nonrestrictive relatives bulk large as interpretive obtrusions in sentence form—for example, "What tyme that Saull for his grevous offences was abandoned of all mighty god, *who of a very poore mannes sonne did avaunce him to the kyngedome of Israell,* and that David, *beinge his servaunt and as poore a mannes son as he,* was elected by god to reigne in Israell," "Saule *beinge therfore in a rage, havinge indignacion at David,* pursued hym with a great hooste to have slayne hym, *who (as longe as he mought) fledde and forbare Saule, as his soveraygne lorde,*" "Whiche Saulle *perceyvinge and hearynge the voyce of David,* cried unto him" (my italics). The systematic use of pattern-loading and clausal spread to steer the reader along Elyot's course by adjoining reflections on the motives and inner feelings of agents within ostensibly repertorial sentences reveals this style as a quite deliberate contrivance. Even though schematism plays no noticeable role, its sentence units qualify as a kind of directed syntax because they undertake to rule the reader's perceptions while they are in the making; nothing of significance is left unsignaled or unspecified. These sentence units announce themselves as early ancestors of what Francis Bacon in time would characterize as "magistral" as opposed to "initiative" method.[17]

Thus far I have been inferring Elyot's authorial purpose from the consistent nature of the syntactic evidence, but his own pronouncement on the desired effect of a knowledge of history at the end of the Saul and David episode puts the matter beyond doubt. God is invoked to do what Elyot's directed syntax is also designed to do: to "so cleve" the lesson of respect and obedience "to the myndes of the readers, that they may be all way redy to put the semblable in experience" and transfer the learning on the page into life. For this author and others who produced prose of counsel in the sixteenth century, styling English away from the loosely additive sentences of speech was undertaken as an act of guidance and stabilization. Hence the apparent impersonality of the spread and loaded sentence form which Elyot made a staple of the narration and exposition in his works, since there is no identified speaker for the interpretive and evaluative language of his insertions. Here, to illustrate its expository application, is a brief passage in which Elyot not only conveys the information that governors are customarily selected from among the wellborn and wealthy but also insists on the reason and propriety in the custom by means of adjuncts that serve a directive function. For clarity, I have italicized these adjuncts:

[17]See *Of the Proficience and Advancement of Learning* and *De dignitate et augmentis scientiarum* in *The Works of Francis Bacon,* ed. James Spedding, Robert Leslie Ellis, and Douglas Denon Heath (London: Longman & Co., 1857–59), III, 403, IV, 449, 452. For discussion, see Karl R. Wallace, *Francis Bacon on Communication and Rhetoric* (Chapel Hill: University of North Carolina Press, 1948), pp. 18–24, 134–35.

Fyrste it is of good congruence that they, *whiche be superiour in condition or haviour*, shulde have also preeminence in administration, if they be nat inferiour to other in vertue. For *they havinge of their owne revenues certeine wherby they have competent substance to lyve without takyng rewardes*: it is lykely that they wyll nat be so desirous of lucre, (*wherof may be engendred corruption*), as they whiche have very litle or nothynge so certeine. Also suche men, *havyng substance in goodes by certeyne and stable possessions, whiche they may aporcionate to their owne livynge, and bryngynge up of theyr children in lernyng and vertues*, may, (*if nature repugne nat,*) cause them to be so instructed and furnisshed towarde the administration of a publike weale, that a poure mannes sonne, onely by his naturall witte, *without other adminiculation or aide*, never or seldome may atteyne to the semblable. [I.iii; p. 17]

It is important to register that top priority is given to the directive function, if analysis of Elyot's prose style is not to dissolve into unrelated observations or, even, the sense of working at cross-purposes. We have been considering one aspect of his instrumental approach to composition, the spread and loaded sentence form that figures conspicuously in narration and exposition, and we have remarked on its generally unspeechlike, impersonal, and unschematic effects. But Elyot's style as a whole makes no pretense at having eliminated direct address; there are many passages in *The Governour* and the subsequent works that utilize first or second person pronouns, represent something as a quotation or saying, or assume the hortatory mood. In these contexts, necessarily, Elyot's expression takes on a more personal character and his prose comes into closer relation with the spoken language. What is striking, however, is that such contexts also tend to show sentences in schematic form, as if direct address required this kind of stylization in the prose of counsel.

Under the sway of the directive function, schematics becomes the other major aspect of Elyot's instrumental approach to composition. It can be broken down into two categories, more as a matter of convenience than of strict syntactic principle—since the members of both are mainly comprised of conjunctively originating constructions that emphasize, by means of binary responsion, the identity of sense and form that motivates sentential conjunction. Nevertheless, if one thinks in terms of the size of discourse units, it is possible to differentiate a schematics of the sentence (aphorism, byword, riposte) from a schematics of the passage (runs of correlatives, conjunction pairs, and so on).

With regard to the former, Elyot, like so many rhetorically sophisticated sixteenth-century prose writers, is an inveterate quoter. The adducing of sayings not only fostered *copia*, endowing writing with something like the fluency of speech, but also gave testimony an evidentiary weight, leading to *auctoritas* by a time-honored route. I have already pointed out that the authorities for Elyot's Christian humanism were manifold, classical as well as Biblical; we shall now see that, as components of his discourse, they display a remarkable stylistic homogeneity. He is one of the earliest sixteenth-century writers in whom the point registers forcibly that there was not merely quotable matter. There was, additionally, a more or less canonical quotable form, to which the bulk of quotable matter adhered. In general, the quotable form of a sentence in the sixteenth century had a pair of clauses in parallel structure joined by some type of binary connectives (antithetical, correlative, or coordinate). This is also, in general, the form of Hebraic wise sayings—the mode of the Old Testament prophecies and wisdom books, of the Psalms, and of Jesus' own Sermon on the Mount—but it is by no means exclusively so. Gnomic utterance in Greek and Latin exhibits much the same form, a fact which confounds the respective attempts by Croll and Whallon to distinguish classical from nonclassical, and classical from Biblical sententiousness.[18] Even the addition of a semantic distinction based on Hebraic sense parallelism—synonymy rendered in different words with correspondent phrase structure—will not strengthen formal criteria sufficiently to yield reliable results. It seems that we must accept sententious sentence form as a stylistic universal; at least this is the implication encouraged by the frequent and eclectic quotations in Elyot's prose and that of many other Renaissance writers. Here, to illustrate their easily recognized canonical form, is a trio from *The Governour*:

Aristotle saieth that frendship is a vertue, or it joyneth with vertue; whiche is affirmed by Tulli, sayenge, that frendship can nat be without vertue, ne but in good men onely. [II.xi; pp. 161–62]

Saynt Ambrose saieth in his boke of offices, Better is he that contemneth injurie, than he that sorroweth. For he that contemneth it as he nothynge felte, he passeth nat on it: but he that is sorrowfull, he is therewith tourmented as though he felt it. [III.xi; p. 233]

The wise kinge Salomon sayeth, Amonge proude men be all way contentions, and they that do all thinges with counsayle, be governed by wisedome. [III.xv; p. 242]

[18]Croll ("The Sources of the Euphuistic Rhetoric," pp. xv–xvii) attempted to distinguish between antithesis in classical writers as a trope (figure of thought) and antithesis in medieval writers, and preeminently in Lyly, as a schema (figure of syntactic arrangement). William Whallon tried to argue that Biblical sententious form combined parallelism and synonymy while classical sententious form was characterized either by parallelism and antithesis or by synonymy without parallelism; see his "Hebraic Symmetry in Sir Thomas Browne," *ELH* 28 (1961): 335–52. But the Crollian distinction proves arbitrary and unfounded; and Whallon's proposed distinction on the basis of antithesis will not hold either, since antithetical parallelism was in fact the second major Biblical type identified by Lowth (see the second section of chap. 1, above). More generally, parallelism and nonparallelism of synonymous conjunctions will be found to crisscross any putative Biblical-classical division.

We can be quite certain that attempts to differentiate types of senten-tious form as well as content would have seemed futile and misguided to Elyot at the time he wrote *The Governour*, for a resounding theme in his long, climactic discussion of sapience is the consonance of all words of wisdom, whatever their provenance. Thus he notes of a character-ization given by "the noble philosopher and moste excellent oratour, Tullius Cicero, in the iv. boke of his Tusculane questions": "This defi-nition agreeth wel with the gifte of sapience that god gave to Salomon, king of Israell" (III.xxiii; pp. 268–69). He proceeds to expatiate at some length on the "auctoritie" of Solomonic utterance:

The auctoritie of sapience is well declared by Salomon in his proverbes. By me (sayth sapience) kynges do raigne, and makers of lawes discerne thinges that be juste. By me prynces do governe, and men havynge powar and auctorytie do determyne Justyce. I love all them that love me, and who that watcheth to have me shall fynde me. . . . Better is the frute that commeth of me than golde and stones that be precyouse. The same kynge sayth in his boke called Eccle-siastice: A kynge without sapyence shall lose his people, and cities shall be inhabited by the wytte of them that be prudent. Whiche sentence was verefied by the sonne and successour of the same kynge Salomon, called Roboaz, to whome the sayd boke was written. Who neglectinge the wise and vertuous doctrine of his father, contempned the sage counsayle of auncient men and imbraced the lyte persuasions of yonge men and flaterers; wherby he loste his honour and brought his realme in perpetuall devision. [P. 270]

For all of the lingering appreciation (and quotation) that Elyot accords to Solomon's sentences, his ultimate objective is to document "to every Catholyke man that hath the liberall use of reason" the unitary, divine source of "all maner of understandyng and knowlege" in "that hyghe sapience whiche is the operatrice of all thynges." Accordingly, he presses an ever more encompassing series of claims: first, that "Orpheus (one of the eldeste poetes of Grece)" conceived of wisdom as enthroned in heaven exactly as "Salomon, or Philo, or who so made the boke called *Sapientia*" did; second, that "Eustathius (the expositour of Homere)" and "Pythagoras, or some of his scholers writynge his sentence" defined the divinity in man as "the knowlege of the soule, and . . . a thyng divine as the soule is," thus encapsulating a universally acknowledged truth: "Whiche sentence of Pythagoras is nat rejecte eyther of Plato, whyche approched nexte unto the Catholike writars, or of divines whiche in-terprete holy scripture, takynge the soule for the ymage and similytude of god" (pp. 272–73). As a final and revealing step, Elyot focuses on what sages have said about the transmission of divine wisdom from one soul to another, once again finding a broad concurrence of sense and "sentence":

Semblably the foresayde Socrates in Platons boke of Sapience sayeth to one Theages: Never man lerned of me any thinge, all thoughe by my company he became the wiser. I onely exhortynge and the good spirite inspyringe. Whiche wonderfull sentence, as me semeth, may well accorde with our catholyke fayeth, and be receyved in to the commentaries of the mooste perfect divines. For as well that sentence, as all other before rehersed, do comprobate with holy scripture that god is the fountayne of Sapience, lyke as he is the soveraygne begynnynge of all generation. [III.xxiii; p. 274]

The foregoing sampling can only begin to suggest the texture of the most sustained tissue of sententia in *The Governour,* a passage that attests Elyot's cognizance of the psychological and semantic instrumentality of gnomic or aphoristic sentence form and, hence, of the contexts in which it is most effectively employed. There is nothing fortuitous in the fact that the subject of this long chapter is sapience: Elyot's term—following the nomenclature of medieval philosophy and theology—for the highest kind of human knowledge, the truest wisdom. It is also particularly characteristic of Elyot that he understood the specific nature of what language renders in an aphorism as moral truth. Thus he attributes peculiar efficacy to "quicke and wise sentences, comprehending good doctrine or counsailes" because they are fit vehicles of ethical insights (II.iii; p. 126). In holding that such sentences show the unity, integrity, and harmony that goodness itself does, Elyot has a principled basis for praising the pithy formulations of Solomon, Pythagoras, and Socrates; the basis derives from Christian Platonism.[19] However, it is less through his insistence on the special congruity between sententious form and moral truth than through his instinct for the psychological saliency of aphorism that we come to regard this sentence type, too, as a species of directed syntax, quite as much as the spread and loaded forms used to shape historical and discursive understanding. Citing Aristotle, Elyot remarkably anticipates another tenet of Baconian stylistics, namely, that aphorism consolidates the content of a sentence to make it amenable to the mind's grasp—first as cognition, later as memory.[20] In Elyot's own words, the mind, "the principall sense of manne," is enabled to take hold of "a thynge" by virtue of a set of unitary properties inhering in the thing, "whiche by the same sense is perceyved as longe as it is retayned intiere or hole, and, (as I mought saye), consolidate, pure,

---

[19]Major (*Elyot and Renaissance Humanism,* pp. 171–269) discusses the manifold aspects of Elyot's Platonism (excluding style). An admirable account of the larger intellectual-historical background for Elyot's concern with sapience is provided by Eugene F. Rice, Jr., *The Renaissance Idea of Wisdom* (Cambridge, Mass.: Harvard University Press, 1958).

[20]Bacon would pronounce famously in Book I of the *Advancement* that "Aphorisms . . . cannot be made but of the pith and heart of sciences; for discourse of illustration is cut off; recitals of examples are cut off; descriptions of practice are cut off; so there remaineth nothing to fill the Aphorisms but some good quantity of observations" (*Works of Francis Bacon,* ed. Spedding, Ellis, and Heath, III, 405).

manifeste, or playne and without blemmishe, in suche wise that in every part of it the mynde is stered or occupyed, and by the same mynde it may be throughly perceyved and knowen" and "retayned in the mynde" (III.xxiii; p. 275). To Elyot's own mind, aphorism offered the linguistic equivalents of the properties he names; its form was "intiere or hole," "consolidate, pure, manifeste, or playne and without blemmishe." Hence, he incorporates as the centerpiece of his definition of eloquence (quoted earlier in this section) "sentences" that "be so aptly compact that they by a vertue inexplicable do drawe unto them the mindes and consent of the herers" (I.xiii; p. 55).

It is also fairly clear that Elyot recognized the oral provenance and character of sententious form, for shortly before he offers his definition of eloquence in *The Governour* he pronounces as follows: "And to be playne and trewe therein, I dare affirme that if elegant speking . . . be nat added to other doctrine, litle frute may come of the tonge; . . . and the frute of speche is wyse sentence, whiche is gathered and made of sondry lernynges" (I.xiii; p. 54). The difficulty in construing this pronouncement lies in being sure that "wyse sentence" is specifically aphorism. However, an inference to that effect is strengthened by other evidence that, for Elyot, aphoristic sentence form was intimately bound up with speech: it consists in his habit of shifting to direct address whenever he begins to cite "wyse sentences" from other authors—especially from Solomon, the wisest author of all by his reckoning. Here is a typical pair of examples:

Howe vigilant ought a christen man beinge in autoritie, howe vigilant (I say), industrious, and diligent ought he to be in the administration of a publike weale? Dreding alway the wordes that be spoken by eternall sapience to them that be governours of publik weales; . . . For moste harde and grevous jugement shall be on them that have rule over other. To the poure man mercy is graunted, but the great men shall suffre great tourmentes. He that is lorde of all excepteth no persone, ne he shall feare the gretnes of any man; for he made as wel the great as the smal, and careth for every of them equally. The stronger or of more mighte is the persone, the stronger payne is to him imminent. Therfore to you governours be these my words, that ye may lerne wisedom and fal nat. This notable sentence is nat only to be imprinted in the hartes of governours, but also to be often tymes revolved and called to remembraunce. [II.i; pp. 117–18]

Dothe nat Salomon saye, A man moche sweringe shall be filled with iniquitie, and the plage shall nat departe from his house? O mercifull god, howe many men be in this realme which be horrible swerers and commune jurates perjured? Than howe moche iniquitie is there, and howe many plages are to be feared, where as be so many houses of swerers? Suerly I am in more drede of the terrible vengeaunce of god, than in hope of amendement of the publike weale. [III.vii; p. 222]

I remarked earlier that the categories separating a schematics of the sentence from a schematics of the passage in Elyot's style could not be rigid. Nowhere is the force of such a remark felt more keenly than in the disquisition on sapience surveyed earlier, or in the continuation of the first of the foregoing pair of quotations, where Elyot adds a series of his own maxims for governors in Solomonic sentence forms that swell the whole to more than twice the size of the material he cites. In such passages, what begin as schematic sentences modulate into schematic discourse. There are at least a couple of reasons why this modulation should be so easy, not just in Elyot but in prose composition generally; both have to do with the dynamic inherent in sentential conjunction and the stylistic impetus which this dynamic provides. For a start, schematic discourse often employs the same predominantly binary linkages—whether correlative or antithetical—that figure in schematic sentences; these binary linkages, moreover, are motivated by some linguistic identity relation. Hence, a writer who is dealing in antitheses, correlatives, or conjunction pairs is also drawing on an intuition of an identity relation sufficient to bring one or another of these forms into play. The activated sense of identity—syntactic or semantic sameness of some kind—is therefore fundamental. Yet like would still not come to beget like except for the further fact, also a matter of linguistic intuition, that these binary connectives belong to the larger (and potentially infinite) range of coordinate expressions—one recursively empowered by the operation of sentential conjunction. The dynamic, then, can become a stylistic impetus in prose composition when a writer proceeds from intuitions of relevant linguistic likeness in the genesis of compound sentences to intuitions that such likeness can be multiplied as long as there is a communicative or rhetorical reason for doing so.

Nevertheless, despite a substantial overlap between the two, schematic discourse in Elyot and subsequent sixteenth-century writers does not altogether contain itself within the resources of conjunctive syntax which are the main determinants of aphoristic form. In particular, Elyot and subsequent writers are prone to expand upon their intuitions of identity and correlation so as to engross a semantic field that includes a variety of equative locutions and comparative and degree constructions. I am inclined to view such expansions as developments in directed syntax that were prompted by the character of the age. England under the Tudors remained assertively authoritarian, hence given to pronouncements on what was what (equative locutions), and no less assertively commited to specifications of order and rank (requiring comparative and degree constructions). We shall be seeing how pervasive schematizations of discourse using these sorts of constructions become in sixteenth-century prose of counsel. But the patterns are already

entrenched in *The Governour,* as the following passages (with their semantically affiliated elements italicized) will serve to indicate:

Justice *all though it be* but *one* entier vertue, *yet is it described in two* kyndes. . . .
The one is named justice distributive, which is in distribution of honour, money,
benefite, or *other thinge semblable; the other is called* commutative or by exchaunge,
and of Aristotell *it is named* in Greeke Diorthoticē, which is in englysshe corrective. . . . Justice distributive *hathe regarde* to the persone; justice commutative
hath no regarde to the persone, but onely considerynge *the inequalite wherby the
one thynge excedeth the other,* indevoureth to brynge *them both* to *an equalitie.* Nowe
wyll I retourne agayne to speke firste of Justice distributive, leavinge Justice
commutative to an other volume, whiche I purpose shall succede this warke,
god givynge me tyme and quietnes of mynde to perfourme it. [III.ii; pp. 195–
96]

For *if* vertue . . . *consisteth* in *a meane,* which is determined by reason, *and that
meane is the verye myddes of two thynges* viciouse, *the one* in surplusage, *the other*
in lacke, *than* nedes *must* Beneficence and Liberalitie *be* capitall vertues. . . . But
Beneficence *can by no menes be* vicious and retaine still his name. *Semblably* Liberalitie (as Aristotle saith) *is a measure, as well* in gyving *as* in takyng of money
and goodes. . . . Therfore *it maye be saide* that he usethe every thynge *best* that
exerciseth the vertue whiche is to the thinge *most appropred.* [II.x; pp. 158–59]

Beholde *the ordre* that god hath put generally in al his creatures, begynnyng at
the most inferiour or base, and assendynge *upwarde:* he made not only herbes to
garnisshe the erthe, but also trees of a *more eminent* stature *than* herbes, and yet
in *the one and the other* be *degrees* of qualitees; *some* plesant to beholde, *some*
delicate or good in taste, *other* holsome and medicinable, *some* commodious and
necessary. *Semblably* in byrdes, bestis, and fisshes, . . . where any is found that
hath many of the said propreties, he is *more* set by *than* all *the other,* and by that
estimation *the ordre* of his place and *degree* evidentlye appereth: . . . *so* that in
every thyng is *ordre,* and without *ordre* may be nothing stable or permanent;
and it may nat be called *ordre,* excepte it do contayne it in *degrees, high* and *base,
accordynge to* the merite or estimation of the thyng that is *ordred.*

   Nowe to retourne to the astate of man kynde, . . . hit semeth that in hym
shulde be *no lasse* providence of god declared *than* in the *inferiour* creatures, *but
rather* with a *more perficte ordre* and dissposition. And therfore hit appereth that
god gyveth *nat* to *every* man *like* gyftes of grace, or of nature, but to *some more,
some lesse, as* it liketh his divine majestie. . . . Nat withstandyng *for as moche as*
understandynge is *the most excellent* gyfte that man can receive in his creation
. . . : it is therfore *congruent,* and *accordynge* that *as one excelleth an other* in that
influence, *as* therby beinge *next to the similitude* of his maker, *so* shulde the astate
of his persone be *avanced in degree* or place where understandyng may profite
. . . for the lyving and governance of mankynde.

So the husbande man fedeth hym selfe and the clothe maker: the clothe maker
apparayleth hym selfe and the husbande: they *both* soccour *other* artificers: *other*
artificers *them: they and other* artificers *them* that be governours. But they that
be governours *nothinge* do acquire by the sayde influence of knowlege for

theyr owne necessities, but do imploye *all* the powers of theyr wittes, and theyr diligence, to *the only* preservation of *other* theyr *inferiours:* amonge whiche *inferiours* also behoveth to be a disposition and *ordre accordynge to* reason, . . . whiche impresseth a reverence and due obedience to the vulgare people or communaltie; and *with out* that, it can be *no more* said that there is a publike weale, *than* it may be affirmed that a house, *without* his propre and necessarye ornamentes, is well and sufficiently furnisshed. [I.i; pp. 3, 4–6, 7]

I have cited extensively from specimens of Elyot's schematic discourse because the convictions about the divinely ordained nature of the universe and the correspondingly necessary character of human institutions that structure his sentence forms are not his alone; they are shared with other Tudor writers virtually without exception. As the earliest vernacular stylist to produce an encomium on the relations of order and degree by which God constituted the whole of creation, Elyot attained extraordinary heights of authoritativeness and articulation, as Shakespeare recognized in drawing upon the last long quotation from *The Governour* when he wrote Ulysses' speech on the same subject in *Troilus and Cressida*. The italics in the quotations isolate the linguistic elements that principally conduce to making the sentence forms instruments of Elyot's meaning: the correlative, comparative, and degree constructions are so placed and reiterated as almost to enact the semantics of the discourse. Together with the articulation they provide, the large number of equative constructions with *to be* and various predicate complements infuse the style with authoritativeness. This authoritativeness, moreover, is enhanced by Elyot's recourses to direct address ("Nowe wyll I retourne agayne to speke"; "whiche I purpose shall succede this warke"; "Beholde the ordre that god hath put generally in al his creatures"), for at these junctures the style signals an authorial presence with an express outlook of his own. No reader who becomes familiar with this outlook from reading Elyot is surprised at the failure of the promised "other volume" on commutative justice to appear, since Elyot so emphatically expresses his sense that distributive justice—giving each his due—is the moral and social reflection of the constitutive principle of the universe.

Nor are the designs of his sentence forms merely a subjective register. The schematics of the preceding passages are put forward as representations of how the world really, inherently is. Elyot's recurrent ontological claims stress the certain and self-evident character of the values it embodies; thus he asserts that virtue "consisteth in a meane, which is determined by reason" and its practice in exercise of "the vertue whiche is to the thinge most appropred," while the later grand excursus defines its social and political results as "a disposition and ordre accordynge to reason." If we are to give Elyot's authorial self-consciousness its due in conceiving of his style, we must not merely credit his schematics as rhetorical constructs, adept appeals to the psychologies of his readers, but also see them in the way he intended, as mimetic forms, reflections of the nature of things. Elyot, moreover, never wavered in his assurance that hierarchy is God-ordained and founded wholly on reason, although his later discursive works show him occupied at great length in securing the foundations—demonstrating the inequalities and correspondences that proportion the natural and social orders in *Of the Knowledge Which Maketh a Wise Man*, insisting on strict, impartial, and searching laws and civil administration in *The Image of Governance*, so as to prevent abuse of power by those who have it, and insubordination by those who do not. Elyot is nowhere found probing the foundations of the Tudor world view because he never saw cause to doubt them.

Yet while Elyot's certainty about the essentials of the cosmic and moral order remained unshaken, and his faith in reason undimmed, from time to time he evinces a more troubled, qualified, and urgent outlook in reflecting on his task as a prose writer. The objective is clear: to bring his readers to "wysedome," which for Elyot consists in regulating life according to reason and morality. But how is this to be done? In a remarkable late excursus in *The Governour,* he expounds his interdependent notions of writing, reading, and living which in the process supply an incisive commentary on the diverse stylistic aspects of his own work. Since he identifies "wysedome" with an active, internalized capability to judge rationally and do rightly, he is much concerned with the means of acquisition: instruction and practice. Whatever instruction and practice are gotten through experience in living, one must supplement these, Elyot insists, by the vicarious experience afforded specifically in the reading of "historie." He then proceeds to an interesting etymological argument (his etymology and definitions are accurate); the argument holds that, as "in greke Historeo . . . dothe signifie to knowe, to se, to enserche, to enquire, to here, to lerne, to tell, or expounde unto other," so "must historie whiche commeth therof be wonderfull profitable, whiche leaveth nothinge hydde from mannes knowlege, that unto hym may be eyther pleasaunt or necessarie" (III.xxv; p. 281).

What is striking in Elyot's argument from etymology is, first, the warrant it purports to give for conceiving of history as the summation of everything that anyone could want or need to know and, second, the basis it provides for understanding the reading and writing of history as a transactive, reciprocal relation along a continuum. In this relation, the reader undertakes "to knowe, to se, to enserche, to enquire, to here, to lerne," and the writer undertakes "to tell, or expounde unto other." For Elyot the literary process, as traced in the etymology of "Historeo," is on the one hand a serious inquiry, and on the other a serious exposition "whiche leaveth nothinge hydde from mannes knowlege, that unto hym may be eyther pleasaunt or necessarie." Here the most telling feature of Elyot's characterization of history is the affinity it bears in language and connotation to contemporary representations of Scripture as affording the soul the knowledge leading to salvation, which is all it needs and desires, and of the role of the minister as the declarer and interpreter of the sense of Scripture to the soul. That this affinity was manifest to Elyot and even, it seems, deliberately induced becomes clear in the series of reflections on which he embarks after finishing "the exposition of the verbe Historeo":

Nowe let us se what booke of holy scripture, I meane the olde testament and the newe, may be saide to have no parte of historie. The five bokes of Moises, the boke of Juges, the foure bokes of Kynges, Job, Hester, Judith, Ruth, Thobias, and also the historie of Machabees (whiche from the other is seperate), I suppose no man wil denie but that they be all historicall, or (as I mought say) intier histories. Also Esdras, Nemias, Ezechiel, and Daniel, all though they were prophetes, yet be their warkes compacte in fourme of narrations, whiche by oratours be called enunciative and only pertaineth to histories, wherin is expressed a thyng done, and persones named. All the other prophetes, thoughe they speake of the tyme future or to come, which is out of the description of an historie, yet either in rebukinge the sinnes and enormities passed, or bewayling the destruction of their contray, or captivitie of the people, and suche like calamitie or miserable astate, also in meving or persuading the people, they do recite some circumstaunce of a narration. But nowe be we commen to the newe testament, and principally the bokes of the Evangelistes, vulgarely called the gospelles, which be one contexte of an historie. Do nat they contayne the temporall lyfe of our savyour Christ, Kinge of Kinges and lorde of the worlde, untill his glorious assention? And what thinge lacketh therin that doth pertayne to a perfect historie? There lacketh nat in thinges ordre and disposition, in the context or narration veritie, in the sentences gravitie, utilitie in the counsailes, in the persuasions doctrine, in expositions or declarations facilitie. The boke of actes of Apostels, what thinge is it but a playne historie? The epistles of saint Paule, saint Peter, saynt John, saynt James, and Judas the apostles do contayne counsailes and advertisementes in the fourme of orations, reciting divers places as well out of the olde testament as out of the gospelles, as it were an abbreviate, called of grekes and latines, Epitoma. This is well knowen to be true of them that have hadde any leasure to rede holy scripture, who, remembringe them selfes by this my little induction, wyll leave to neglecte historie, or contemne it with so generall a disprayse as they have been accustomed. [III.xxv; pp. 282–83]

Ostensibly the foregoing passage develops a Scriptural defense for Elyot's comprehensive claims regarding the writing and reading of history as the means of transmitting all wisdom needful to man. He takes the Bible as the paradigm of what an utterly indispensable work must contain, and then subjects its contents to analysis. Finding that the Bible is essentially history, he particularizes at some length on the inclusiveness of the genre. It has its outer framework, what Elyot calls a "context" of narration, a "fourme . . . whiche by oratours be called enunciative and only pertaineth to histories, wherin is expressed a thyng done, and persones named." Besides its enunciative form, history also contains "the fourme of orations," a mode of direct address, in which Elyot distinguishes a more impassioned prophetic strain used "in rebukinge the sinnes and enormities passed, or bewayling . . . calamitie . . . , also in meving or persuading the people," and a more tempered apostolic strain found in the New Testament Epistles which administer "counsailes and advertisementes," that is, admonitions by way of "reciting divers places" in "as it were an abbreviate" or epitome. Elyot singles out the Gospels as "perfect historie," proceeding to specify its defining features: "There lacketh nat in thinges ordre and disposition, in the context or narration veritie, in the sentences gravitie, utilitie in the counsailes, in the persuasions doctrine, in expositions or declarations facilitie."[21] This set of specifications, in turn, bolsters a Scripturalist reading of the fore-going passage, for the features which define Biblical style for Elyot accord with those which we have found in his own prose style: one mode reserved for narration and exposition, another—a dual mode—of direct address, with a brief form for "sentences" and a more expansive one for "counsailes" and "persuasions." "Order and disposition" are also Elyot's governing compositional principles, as we have noted in the directedness and instrumentality of his syntax. Overall, then, the ac-count which he gives of the writing of history—with the Bible as the supreme instance—appears to fit his own prose style.

But there are other passages in *The Governour* and biographical side-lights on his religious stance which prevent us from treating this excursus as a straightforward Scripturalist brief. Elyot had some temporizing sides in the matter of religion, as he almost inevitably would have to have had to secure the successive patronage of Thomas Wolsey and Thomas Cromwell. He was also sufficiently intimate with Thomas More to feel the need of palliating the association after More's execution. In what has become a notorious letter written in 1536 or 1537, Elyot implores his patron Cromwell "now to lay apart the remembraunce of the amity betwene me and sir Thomas More which was but *usque ad aras,* as is the proverb, considering that I was never so moche addict unto hym as I was unto truthe and fidelity toward my soveraigne lord." Elyot also dilates in this letter to Cromwell on the aspects of his public image that make him anxious:

---

[21]Again, in his conception termed "perfecte historie" (although not in his equation of it with the Gospels), Elyot appears to anticipate Bacon, who appropriated the identical term to secular usage in *De augmentis,* II.6, 7. What made a history "perfect" in Bacon's eyes was the supplementing of bald narration of facts with speeches, counsels, and com-mentary on motives, designs, and causes (*Works of Francis Bacon,* ed. Spedding, Ellis, and Heath, IV, 302–8).

I perceyve that ye suspect that I savor not truely holy scripture. I wold Godd that the King and you mowght see the moste secrete thowghts of my hart. Surely ye shold than perceyve that, the ordre of charity savyd, I have in as moche detestacion as any man lyving all vayne supersticions, superfluous ceremonyes, sklanderouse jouglings, countrefaite myrakles, arrogant usurpacions of men callid spirituall and masking religious, and all other abusions of Christes holy doctrine and lawes. And as moche I injoy at the Kinges godly proceeding to the due reformacion of the sayde enormyties as any his Graces poure subject lyving.[22]

The content of the above disclaimer has no bearing on the charge it purports to address: Elyot's attitude toward vernacular Scripture. On the evidence of his printed works up through the date of the letter in question, this attitude was self-consistent, but out of keeping with the growing strength of the demand for an authorized Bible in the native tongue. Elyot shared More's deep aversion for the individualistic reliance on one's own reading and understanding of Scripture compounded with equally individualistic theologizing that Tyndale and other early English Reformers fostered. Accordingly, Elyot adopted a strategy that yields to close inspection in the excursus from *The Governour* which we have been considering. The strategy is bold, but un-Tyndalian in the extreme. Elyot moves to set aside, to rule out of account, the inducements to speculation and introspection which others found in the Bible. In effect he defines these away by defining Scripture, after his fashion, as a sovereign compendium of history: a book of narrative exempla from which morality and sound reason can be learned better than by experience, a book of practical wisdom which reinforces this morality and sound reason through its well-designed sentences, its forms of counsel.

Elyot minced no words in print about his attitude. He did not overtly declare against involvement in the "many thynges harde to be understande" in Paul, "whiche they that be unlerned and not constaunt doo pervert, as they doe the residue of scripture, unto their owne perdicion" until his last work, *A Preservative against Death* (1545).[23] But the exemplum

---

[22]The letter (British Library MS. Cotton Cleopatra E.IV, fol. 260) is quoted in the "Life of Elyot" prefaced to Henry H. S. Croft's edition of *The Governour* (London: Kegan Paul, Trench, & Co., 1880), I, cxxix–cxxxi. *Usque ad aras*—literally, "as far as the altars"—is read as meaning "so far as religious obligations permit." For discussion, see Lehmberg, *Elyot: Tudor Humanist*, pp. 153–54; Richard S. Sylvester's review of Lehmberg in *Renaissance News* 14 (1961): 179–80; and Major, *Elyot and Renaissance Humanism*, pp. 90–92.

[23]Sir Thomas Elyot, *A Preservative agaynste Deth* (London: T. Berthelet, 1545) (STC 7674), sig. Diiii^v. There is also this less revealing because more oblique reflection in Elyot's Proheme to *Of the Knowledge Which Maketh a Wise Man:* "For somme doo chiefly extoll the study of holy scripture (as it is rayson) but while they do wrest it to agree with theyr willes, ambition, or vayne glory: of the mooste noble and devoute lernynge, they doo endevor them to make hit servile and full of contention." I cite Edwin Johnston Howard's old-spelling edition (Oxford, Ohio: Anchor Press, 1946), p. 11.

of Uzza struck dead for having laid his hand on the Ark of the Covenant (2 Samuel 6) cited in *A Preservative* to warn against "presumynge on the power of our propre wittes . . . to enter boldely" God's "Tabernacle, whiche is holy scripture" had already been used in a highly analogous connection early in *The Governour*. The connection exhibits the consistency of Elyot's position on the interpretation of Scripture throughout his career as a writer. The early passage from *The Governour* also dispels any doubt whether Elyot intended, as a practical matter, that Scripture reading be circumscribed. He did so intend, for the following are all of his stipulations regarding the Bible in his chapter on "the moste commodious and necessary studies" for a prospective governor:

The proverbes of Salomon with the bokes of Ecclesiastes and Ecclesiasticus be very good lessons. All the historiall partes of the bible be righte necessarye for to be radde of a noble man, after that he is mature in yeres. And the residue (with the newe testament) is to be reverently touched, as a celestiall jewell or relike, havynge the chiefe interpretour of those bokes trewe and constant faithe, and dredefully to sette handes theron, remembrynge that Oza, for puttyng his hande to the holy shryne that was called Archa federis, whan it was broughte by kyng David from the citie of Gaba, though it were waverynge and in daunger to fall, yet was he stryken of god, and fell deed immediately. [I.xi; p. 48]

As these pronouncements intimate, what Elyot did as a prolific writer of vernacular prose in yet another foreshadowing of Baconian tactics was to dichotomize sharply between the sacred and the secular—in this case, within the canon of Scripture itself—and then stake out the secular as his domain of literary operation. It is meaningful, as we shall close this discussion of Elyot by seeing, to speak of his Scripturalism in the terms defined for this study, but we can only come to do so by the paradoxical route of secularization which rendered the vernacular Bible a viable stylistic and compositional model for Elyot. As long as he could conceive of his authorial enterprise as taking a parallel and hence non-convergent course with the cure of souls which was the priest's vocation, he was capable of writing in a genuinely Scripturalist mode (subject, of course, to his self-set limitations) and of producing works which so appealed to a contemporary English readership that they went through multiple editions. Three works are distinguished in this way by their publication records: *The Governour*, with eight editions between 1531 and 1580; *The Banquet of Sapience*, with six editions between 1534 and 1564; and *The Castle of Health*, with fourteen editions between 1536 and 1595.[24] Of these three works, *The Governour* is the most sporadic in its Scripturalism for the very reasons of stylistic range and variety which we

---

[24]This bibliographical information is given by Lehmberg in his *Elyot: Tudor Humanist,* pp. 197–98.

have examined in some detail. It does, however, set the pattern that persists: Elyot's Scripturalism follows in the line of Solomonic sentence. An especially interesting manifestation which combines secular content with effective replication of Hebraic sense parallelism is to be found in his "VII articles" enumerating essential "thynges" to be pondered before accepting appointment or election as "governour of a publike weale." These excerpts will illustrate:

> They shall nat thynke howe moche honour they receive, but howe moche care and burdene. Ne they shall nat moche esteme their revenues and treasure, considerynge that it is no buten or praie, but a laboriouse office and travaile.
>
> Let them thynke the greatter dominion they have, that therby they sustayne the more care and studie. And that therfore they must have the lasse solace and passetyme, and to sensuall pleasures lasse opportunitie.

> The most sure fundation of noble renome is a man to be of suche vertues and qualities as he desireth to be openly publisshed. For it is a fainte praise that is goten with feare or by flaterars gyven. And the fame is but fume which is supported with silence provoked by menacis. [II.i; pp. 118–19]

The Banquet of Sapience, which its title page and dedicatory epistle to Henry VIII describe as a compilation "of sondry wyse counsels, gathered by me out of the warkes of moste excellent persons, as wel faithfull as gentyles," takes Elyot an appreciable distance further in the Solomonic line of composition begun in *The Governour.*[25] The personification of Sapience as the gracious preparer and server of a feast of many dishes whose varied tastes will both please and nourish the king and other readers after their Lenten fasts is a deliberately eclectic projection of Elyot's Christian humanism: she is at once the transposed Sapience of *The Governour,* the highest form of human wisdom that accordingly befits a ruler, and the allegorical figure of that name who bids citizens to her public feast in the book of Proverbs: her banquet, likewise, partakes both of this Solomonic feast and a Greek symposium as described by Plato or Plutarch. Despite its eclectic sources, *The Banquet of Sapience* is notable overall for its high amount of stylistic homogeneity, which tends to confirm the universality of the aphoristic mode as perceived and practiced in the sixteenth century. Stanford Lehmberg's tabulation of Elyot's marginal references helps in reconstructing the master recipe and the several ingredients in Sapience's dishes: among authors cited more than ten times, the Solomonic canon (Proverbs, Ecclesiastes, Song of Solomon) receives 86 entries, Seneca 64, Cicero 56, Augustine 41, Jerome

[25]I cite the photographic facsimile of *The Bankette of Sapience* included in *Four Political Treatises by Sir Thomas Elyot,* intro. Lillian Gottesman (Gainesville, Fla.: Scholars' Facsimiles and Reprints, 1967), pp. 103–5.

26, Paul 23, Plutarch 14, and Ambrose 11.[26] The aphoristic texture of the work may be sampled in the contents of the section labeled "Sapience":

Tullius tusc. 5	Men called wise menne are not to be honored for every worde that they speake, but for their stabilitie & constancie in vertue.
Euripedes	Princis become wyse, by companye of wyse men.
Ecclesiast.	The rote of wysedome is to fere god, & the braunches therof be of longe lyfe.
	A wyse harte and that hathe understandynge, wyll absteyne from yll dedes, and in warkes of justice, his purpose shall prosper.
	The thoughts of a wise manne at noo tyme, nor for any feare shall be depraved.
Seneca	The greattest token and offyce of sapyence, is that the dedes do agree with the wordes, and that the persone be ever one, and lyke to hym selfe.
	Let thy minde and thoughtes herto extende: onely wishe and busily care, for to be with thy selfe alwaye contente, and satisfied with the desires that of thee do procede: al other desyres referrynge to god.[27]

However, Elyot's most sustained piece of Scripturalist composition in *The Banquet of Sapience* is the framing device for introducing the various dishes of counsel. It takes the form of an open invitation to the feast which Sapience proclaims in a loosely assembled collection of excerpts from the first, eighth, and ninth chapters of the Solomonic book of Proverbs. It is thoroughly typical of Elyot's secularizing approach to Biblical material that no sacramental overtones attach to this meal of bread and wine; it consists solely of wholesome counsel. Significantly, too, Sapience caters to the authoritarian as well as the aphoristic pro-clivities of the age by incorporating her credentials into her summons, which Elyot entitles 'The Introduction to the Banket":

Salomon Proverbi Cap. 9. Cap. 1. Cap. 8.	Sapience hath builded a house for her selfe, she hath prepared her wine & laide forth her table, she calleth out abrode in the stretes, & in the chiefe assembly of people, and at the gates of the cytie she speketh with a loude voice: Ye babies, how long wil ye delyte in your childyshnes? And how longe wyl fooles covete those thynges whiche shall hurt them? And they which lacke wit hate knowlege & lernyng? Come on & eate ye mi brede & drinke my wyne that I have ordeined now for you. To me do belong Counsayll & equitie:

---

[26]Lehmberg, *Elyot: Tudor Humanist*, p. 131. Also see the unfortunately undemonstrated claim by William G. Crane that *The Banquet of Sapience* derives "almost entirely" from Nannus Mirabellius Dominicus's *Polyanthea* (Venice, 1507): *Wit and Rhetoric in the Renaissance: The Formal Basis of Elizabethan Prose Style* (New York: Columbia University Press, 1937), pp. 31–32.

[27]*The Bankette of Sapience*, fol. 41[r-v], in *Four Political Treatises*, pp. 191–92.

mine is prudence, & mine also fortitude. By me kynges do reign, & makers of lawes do determyne those thynges that be ryghtwyse. By me pryncis do governe, & men in autoritie do give sentence accordyng to justice. I love them that love me, & they that wake erely shal finde me, with me do remaine both substance & renoume, stately richesse, & Justyce, my fruyte doth excell gold & stones precious, and my branches are better than fyne tryed silver, my walkes be in the high waies of justice, & in the middel of the pathes of jugement, to the intent that I wil make them ryche that do love me, and fil up their treasures.[28]

Increasingly in the 1530s Elyot's attempts to assure himself of Cromwell's continuing favor, as revealed in his private correspondence, were directed on the public side into a literary program aimed at accommodating his patron's strenuous advocacy of a vernacular Bible and his own religious conservatism.[29] The mode of accommodation remained that of a generalized Scripturalism which Elyot takes to its farthest reaches in *The Castle of Health,* the most popular of his works. In undertaking to provide his English readers with basic knowledge that would enable them to avoid certain dysfunctions and cope with common ailments, Elyot was certainly acting in consonance with the humanist emphasis on proper care for both body and mind as well as literalizing the Platonic image of wisdom as a cure, a restorative medicine for the sick soul.[30] However, Elyot's self-defense for venturing to compose the first English health manual does not build on Platonic or humanist considerations. Instead, the preface which he added to the third (1541) edition of *The Castle of Health* devolves as a systematic and transparent analogue of the arguments that had been adduced in support of vernacular Scripture for over a century and a half, and had at last carried in the authorization of the Great Bible four years earlier. After protesting his wholly benevolent intentions and rehearsing his qualifications to compile a book of "commoditie" for physicians as well as their patients, he continues with an irony that is strikingly Tyndalian (even Wycliffite) in its reflections on the Christianity of the medical profession:

But yf phisitions be angry, that I have wryten phisike in englishe, let theym remembre, that the grekes wrate in greke, the Romayns in latyne, Avicena, and

[28]Ibid., p. 108 in Gottesman's numbering. Elyot's cento from Proverbs uses verses in the following order: 9:1–2, 1:20–22, 9:5, 8:14–21.

[29]On relevant correspondence of Elyot's from these years, see Lehmberg, *Elyot: Tudor Humanist,* pp. 148–62.

[30]Plato's *Gorgias* was a chief source for this metaphor, which was Christianized by Augustine and other Church Fathers. On its influence in English prose in the succeeding century, see Stanley E. Fish, *Self-Consuming Artifacts: The Experience of Seventeenth-Century Literature* (Berkeley and Los Angeles: University of California Press, 1972), especially chap. 1.

the other in Arabike, whiche were their owne propre and maternal tonges. And yf they had bene as moche attached with envy and covatyse as some nowe seeme to be, they wolde have devysed somme particuler language, with a strange syphre or fourme of lettres, wherin they wold have writen their science, which language or lettres no man shoulde have knowen that hadde not professyd and practised phisycke: but those, although they were painimes and Jewes, in this parte of charitye they farre surmountid us Christianes, that they wolde not have soo necessary a knowledge as phisicke is, to be hyd frome them, whych wolde be studiouse aboute it.[31]

Elyot also expressly links his *Castle of Health* with the progress of the English Reformation, drawing a parallel between his labors to make known "thynges apte for medicine" and "our soveraygne lord the kinges majesty, who dayly preparith to stablyshe among us true and uncorrupted doctrines" (*CH*, sig. Aiii'). In keeping with his popularizing objectives and his conception of this work as a gathering of useful counsel, Elyot's style in *The Castle of Health* is adjusted to the plainspokenness which he had begun to commend as a political tactic in his dialogues, *Pasquil the Plain* (1532) and *Of the Knowledge Which Maketh a Wise Man* (1533), written immediately after the more florid *Governour*. Here plainspokenness is applied to shear away any technicality or obscurity in medical lore, "for asmoche as it dothe requyre a reder havynge some knowlege in philosophye naturall, or els it is to harde and tedyouse to be understande" (*CH*, fol. 13').

The stylistic ramifications of the secularizing and popularizing objectives that find expression in *The Castle of Health* entail a departure from the spread and loaded sentence forms that had been Elyot's chief narrative and expository vehicles in *The Governour*. The concomitant readjustment in his inventory of syntactic resources brings his two schematic modes into greater prominence through greater use. Accordingly, the text of *The Castle of Health* is largely compounded, on the one side, of aphoristic entries with the general cast of Hebraic sense parallelisms, as illustrated by the following series from the section on poultry in the long second book on diet:

Partryche,

Of all fowles is most sonest digested, and hath in hym moche nutriment: comforteth the brayne, and maketh sede of generation, and receiveth lust whiche is abated.

[31]Sir Thomas Elyot, *The Castel of Helthe (1541),* intro. Samuel A. Tannenbaum (New York: Scholars' Facsimiles and Reprints, 1937), sig. Aiiii'. Subsequent references, abbreviated *CH*, are incorporated in the text.

Quayles,

Although they be of some men commended, yet experience proveth them to increace melancolye: and are of a small nourisshinge.

Larkes,

Be as well the fleshe as the broth very holsom: eaten rosted, they do moche helpe ageinst the colyke, as Dioscorides sayth.

A plover,

Is slowe of digestion, nourysheth lytell, and increaseth melancolye.

Blacke byrdes or ousyls,

Amonge wylde fowle hath the chiefe prayse, for lyghtnesse of digestion: and they make good nouryshment, and lyttell ordure. [*CH,* fol. 20^v]

On the other side, there are a considerable number of longer passages in schematic discourse that set out and apply the governing notions of proportion and opposition in humoral physiology and psychology: that an ill humor is redressed by its contrary, and a healthy body has its humors in balance. In such passages the schematizing functions of antitheses and correlatives sustain this mode of directed syntax for the joint purposes of informing and counseling, as a pair of representative excerpts will show:

Where nature is offended or greved, she is cured by that, whiche is contrary to that, which offendeth or greveth: as colde by heate, heate by colde, drythe by moysture, moysture by drythe. In that wherby Nature shoulde be nourysshed, in a hole and temperate body, thinges must be taken, whiche are lyke to the mannes nature in qualitie and degree. As where one hath his bodye in a good temper, thynges of the same temperaunce doth nouryshe hym. But where he is out of temper, in heate, colde, moysture, or drythe, temperate meates or drynkes nothynge do profyte hym. For beinge out of the meane and perfytte temperature, nature requyreth to be therto reduced by contraries, remembrynge not oonely, that contraryes are remedye unto their contraryes, but also in every contrary, consideration be hadde of the proporcion in quantitie. [*CH,* fol. 40^r]

The moderation of slepe must be measured by helthe and syckenes, by age, by tyme, by emptynesse or fulnesse of the body, & by naturall complexions. Fyrst to a hole man having no debilitie of nature, and digesting perfytly the meate that he eateth, a lytel slepe is sufficient: but to them, which have weake stomakis, & do digest slowly, it requireth that sleape be moch lengar. Semblable temperance is required in youth and age, wynter and sommer. The body beinge full of yll humors, very lyttell slepe is sufficient: except the humors be crude or raw, for than is slepe necessary, whiche digesteth theym better than labour. Semblably, where the body is long empty by long syknesse or abstinence, slepe comforteth nature: as well in the principall members, as in all the other. [*CH,* fol. 45^{r-v}]

The stylistic and tonal equilibrium which the foregoing passages reveal goes far in accounting for the great appeal exercised by *The Castle of Health* in its time as well as the unusual authorial satisfaction which Elyot took in the work. Two passages advert clearly to his sense that, with this addition to his canon, he had fulfilled his literary vocation as a wise counsellor to his nation. In the one, a brief excursus on psychological and spiritual ailments, Elyot represents *The Castle of Health* as an outgrowth of his earlier political and moral concerns, referring any reader oppressed with "ire" or "hevynesse of mynde" to the aid to be had from predictable portions of Scripture—the Old Testament historical books, the Gospels, and the sayings of Solomon—as well as "my warke, callyd the Governour, wher I therof do write more abundantly" (*CH*, fols. 62^r–64^v). In the other passage, an envoi added to the third edition, Elyot appeals to "all honest phisitions" not to impede the reception of "this treatyse" with "enviouse dysdayne," but to recognize that his layman's efforts have been faultlessly patriotic and Christianly. He has written, he urges, "for the love that I beare to my countrey," adding that "the intent of my labour was, that men and women redinge this warke, and observinge the counsayles therin," should be more aware and informed about the state of their health and the readier "to receyve more sure remedy by the medicines prepared by good phisitions in dangerous syckenesses." This ingenious defense, analogizing both to the traditional priestly cure of souls and to Protestant accountability of the individual for his or her own state, culminates in a benediction on his English readers and on his own layman's efforts by way of a characteristically free compounding of two sentences from Ecclesiasticus 38:4, 12: "The hyghest god dyd create the phisition, for mans necessitie, And of the earth created medicine, and the wyse man shall not abhore it. Thus fare ye wel gentyll reders, and forget me not with your good reporte, and praye to God that I be never wars occupyed" (*CH*, fol. 94^{r-v}). With this Solomonic valedictory, Elyot closes the most circulated of his works and his most Scripturalist production in the generalized mode for which he created the precedent in England.

SENTENTIOUS COMPILATIONS IN THE SCRIPTURALIST MODE

Although I have used the testimony of Elyot's letters and writings to document his encounter with the resurgent Scripturalism of the 1530s and 1540s, the context in which he worked was clearly energized by cultural and historical currents that encompassed considerably more than the issues of doctrine, religious practices, and ecclesiastical sovereignty dividing Protestants from Catholics, exacerbated as these issues were. Elyot himself identified the challenges which he faced and met with his literary enterprise as questions about his commitment to the king's and Cromwell's reforming measures or to the "savor" of "holy scripture." Yet the successful popularizing and secularizing measures which Elyot took in jointly pursuing his course as a vernacular writer and bypassing religious issues are, I think, to be construed as evidence running with rather than against the momentum of a larger ideological movement—in the first place because popularizing and secularizing were real options for Elyot, and in the second place because he was able to make them work. Given our present state of knowledge, even as advanced by Elizabeth Eisenstein's study of the printing press as an agent of cultural change,[32] we are constrained to deal symptomatically and speculatively for the most part with the complex of energizing developments—in which printing, humanism, and the Reformation figured prominently with social and economic changes—that ushered in the modern era of the book. The hallmarks of this era—the appeal to an inclusive and not merely specialized readership, the attendant premium on vernacular works, the notion that knowledge is to be shared and disseminated, not left as the jealously guarded preserve of experts—were already emerging in the 1530s and 1540s when Elyot's literary activities reached their height. As a committed, able, and perceptive writer of English prose, he was responding along with numbers of his contemporaries to the forces that were bringing modern book culture into being, and his response, like theirs, was to try to secure the place of a participant in that culture.

It is a speculative venture at this point, though not a wholly uninformed one, to try to specify the broader impact of Scripturalist habits of mind and composition within the complex of developments that led to the modern era of the book. At appropriate earlier junctures in this study we have been on demonstrably firm ground in registering the connections between an outpouring of energies in vernacular works aimed at a wide popular audience and the two concentrated accesses of Scripturalist activity in England: that of Wyclif and his collaborators and, again, that of Tyndale and his supporters. Yet once the Bible passes into the mainstream of English life and language, its influence becomes far more vast and more elusive as it mingles with other energizing forces for vernacular literature aimed at a wide readership in the late 1530s and onward. Certainly Scripturalism alone does not account for the production of such literature, but just as certainly we may take it to have had its effect. The problem remains: How do we trace this effect? My continuing attempt has been to make Scripturalism a manageable critical

[32]Elizabeth L. Eisenstein, *The Printing Press as an Agent of Change: Communications and Cultural Transformations in Early Modern Europe,* 2 vols. (Cambridge: Cambridge University Press, 1979).

referent by defining it not simply on the ideological plane, but also and particularly as a stylistic program for transposing and extending to the works of human authors engaged in serious concerns the features of expression that render the Bible a uniquely inspired and efficacious creation, to the extent that these features can be brought over from text to text, and from language to language. I shall presently be resuming consideration of Scripturalism in terms of replicable features of sentence form. Before doing so, however, I wish to suggest and explore what I think may be a specific, isolable contribution of Scripturalist habits of mind and composition to the emergence of modern book culture: this is the absolute premium placed on both reading and writing as interpretive activities. In examining the rationale for the singularly privileged status of the Bible as a norm and prototype of all significant human purposes in using language, we find it at least as important to the Scripturalist way of thinking that this text could be counted on to yield universal and personal meaning as that it issued from the ultimate authorship of God. Since at this era it was taken for granted that all of life was divinely disposed and ruled, God's acts and power were subject to far less uncertainty than was the reading of his intentions. To the Scripturalist, the most exciting prospect offered by the Bible and the strongest reason for making it available in the native tongue was to let people see for themselves what God said and meant, for he could be trusted to say what he meant and mean what he said. The Scripturalist, moreover, did not construe the determination of Biblical meaning as passive reception of a Word from on high but, rather, as an earnest, participatory engagement—a search for the sense, an inquiry into the truth. What made engagement with this text hopeful and compelling besides the faith to be placed in its divine author was the credit accorded by Scripturalism to the good faith of the individual reader: the soul could and would find God's message for it within the plenum of vital meaning encompassed by the Word.

I am suggesting that Scripturalism invigorated and intensified the genial standing assumption that vernacular works would benefit a popular readership, first, by removing associations of inferiority with such works and readers (for if God's Word could be made fully available in English, what book could not?) and, second, by positing an active, interpretive paradigm for the relation contracted by the writer and the reader of a text. The activity was seen as mutual, the interpretive relation as reciprocal: the writer was bound to efforts and means that would convey what he had to communicate, while the reader was bound to efforts and expectations that would promote communication and make it the property of both parties. If we now pursue the implications of the dual stimulus which I propose to ascribe to the Scripturalist cast of mind in the sixteenth century, we can see immediately that the removal of limiting conceptions of works and readers as well as the cooperative engagement of author and reader with respect to the sense of a work are factors easily extended beyond the case of the Bible to other kinds of composition. But we can also see that certain kinds of works would be more amenable than others to functioning as sites of meaning transactions—specifically, those in which the reader's investment of interest in the interpretation of a subject was such as to make him a viable counterpart of the author who was offering an interpretation.

It seems to me that "prose of counsel" affords good potential instances of serious authorial intentions regarding the Scripturalist interpretive paradigm, for writers of such works, by the very nature of the works, have a message to convey, knowledge to impart, advice to give. It also seems to me that if we look at well-received, highly popular works of this kind, we have reasonable enough presumptive evidence of reader interest. We can then undertake to test the working hypothesis that Scripturalism operated in a generalized fashion to add impetus to the bringing of vital information other than the Bible within popular reach and to foster the production of works which, in their overall form as well as more localized features of style, embodied an active approach to interpretation as their basic principle of composition. From Elyot's prolific career and its ongoing adjustments to the impulsions of Scripturalism, the pronounced popularity of *The Castle of Health* and *The Banquet of Sapience* leads in the direction of two vernacular genres—the medical handbook and the anthology of aphorisms—as likely places to look for the more generalized influence of the Scripturalist mode in the period. In addressing the genres of the medical handbook and the anthology of aphorisms during the decades of Elyot's literary activity, we find his perceptiveness confirmed and illuminated in two very different ways. These are indeed exceptionally popular genres with English readers and, hence, ones which attract numbers of English writers, but the great majority of these writers are Protestants. Can we proceed from these externals of popularity and mainly Protestant authorship to find evidence of the more generalized influence of Scripturalism in the two genres in question?

H. S. Bennett has called attention to the comparatively little interest shown by printers in works of science and related information during a half century and more after Caxton began printing at Westminster in 1476, even though the supply of such works had grown considerably in the fifteenth century.[33] One noteworthy indication is the survival of the vernacular treatise *The Seynge* (or *Judgement*) *of Urynes* in more than

---

[33]H. S. Bennett, *English Books and Readers, 1475–1557* (Cambridge: Cambridge University Press, 1952), p. 97; also see his "Science and Information in English Writings of the Fifteenth Century," *MLR* 39 (1944): 2.

seventy manuscripts. Yet Elyot's *Castle of Heath*, with its date of 1536, was "the earliest important manual of health originally written in English,"[34] and it was preceded in print by only a handful of translations. Elyot himself cites a single precedent, "a compendiouse and profitable treatyse, callyd the Governaunce of helthe, in latyne *Regimen sanitatis*," or *Schola Salernitana*, a collection of advice on diet and hygiene first assembled in the twelfth century, which Thomas Paynell translated into English and published in 1528; this work, according to Elyot, raised the estimation of "physicke in this realme" (*CH*, sig. Aiiiʳ). Elyot may well have been prompted to cite the *Regimen* because its translator was a canon of Merton Abbey, but, if so, his circumspection typically got the upper hand: Paynell is not named. Besides the *Regimen*, Paynell translated and published another short work, *A Moche Profitable Treatise against the Pestilence* (ca. 1534). To round out the early translations in this genre that saw their way into print before *The Castle of Health*, Bennett instances a trio of herbals, essentially compilations of home remedies or first aid measures utilizing leaves or flowers: the so-called *Bankes' Herball* (1525), *The Grete Herball* (1526), and *Macer's Herbal Practysed by Dr. Linacre* (1530), all anonymous preparations issued by various printers. *The Seynge of Urynes*, first printed in 1525, reached a tenth edition by 1555.[35] With these must be grouped two English translations of works by Jerome of Brunswick (1450?–1500?): the anonymously produced *Noble Experyence of the Vertuous Handywerke of Surgeri* (1525) and Lawrence Andrewe's translation of *A Vertuose Boke of Distyllatyon* (1527)—Jerome's voluminous instructions on how to prepare tinctures by steeping herbs and flowers—written, as Andrewe affirms, "not only to the synguler helpe and profyte of the Surgyens, Phisycyens, and Pothecaryes, but also of all maner of people."[36] Only this last popularizing stipulation portends what would ensue in the genre of vernacular medical manuals after the appearance of *The Castle of Health*.

It is a fact too striking to dismiss as coincidence that the peak of Thomas Cromwell's influence with Henry, the years 1537–40, which saw the authorization of the Great Bible, also saw the launching of a spate of English medical manuals which display significant common features. All, with one later exception, in which the author is at pains to explain himself, were prepared under Protestant auspices; and all, again with the one exception, justify their existence with analogues of the Scripturalist argument that knowledge should not be left to those in authority but should be opened to the people, who will judge and use it rightly.

---

[34]Lehmberg, *Elyot: Tudor Humanist*, p. 133.

[35]Bennett, *English Books and Readers, 1475–1557*, pp. 97–99, 103. *Bankes' Herball* saw at least sixteen editions between 1525 and 1560.

[36]Andrewe's preface, *A Vertuose Boke of Distyllatyon* (STC 13435), sig. iʳ, cited by Bennett, *English Books and Readers, 1475–1557*, p. 99.

Perhaps the earliest of all these manuals was Thomas Moulton's *The Myrrour or Glasse of Helth*, which appeared about 1539; it was reprinted thirteen times by 1550. Moulton represents his advice as "necessary and nedefull for every person to . . . kepe theyr body from the sekenes of the Pestylence," and he pays only token respect to "Surgyons" before sturdily asserting of his book that he has "set it in prynt so in Englysshe that every man lerned, and lewde, rich and pore may the better understand it and do therafter."[37]

An especially interesting illustration of the insistence on broadening access to vital medical information during Cromwell's ascendancy is afforded by Richard Jonas's translation of a treatise by Eucharius Rösselin, the city physician of Worms (d. 1526), under the title, *The Byrth of Mankynde, Otherwyse Named The Womans Booke* (1540). All that is known of Jonas is that he died in prison in Mary's reign (1557); this fact and the declaration of his intentions in translating *The Byrth of Mankynde* align him with other exponents of a popularizing movement with many affinities to Scripturalist aims. Jonas says he has made his translation "for the syngular utilite and profete that ensueth unto all such as rede it, and most speciallye unto all women (for whose onely cause it was wrytten) . . . for that there be fewe matrones and women . . . but yf they can rede, wyll have this booke alwayes in readynesse . . . if it be set forth in the Englyshe speche." The prefatory "Admonicyon to the Reder" candidly acknowledges the risk of dispensing obstetrical lore in the native tongue, for it may be abused in loose talk. Nonetheless, Jonas rejoins, he has been emboldened by a spirit of praise for "the mightie God of nature in al hys workes" and by a spirit of sympathy for "our evyn-christens, the wymmen, whych susteyne & indure for the tyme a grete dolour and peyne for the byrth of mankynde and delyveraunce of the same into the worlde." In this spirit, he admonishes his readers "to knowe moche and to saye lytel, but onely where it maye do good," remembering always the proverb (Ecclesiastes 3:1), "Everythyng, as sayth Salomon, hathe hys tyme."[38] *The Byrth of Mankynde* was corrected and enlarged at mid-century by the physician Thomas Raynalde; it reached a twelfth edition by 1634. Long thereafter it continued in use as the standard English text on obstetrics.

---

[37]Thomas Moulton, *The Myrrour or Glasse of Helth* (STC 18219), sig. Avii[r], cited by Bennett, *English Books and Readers, 1475–1557*, p. 98.

[38]*The Byrth of Mankynde*, trans. Richard Jonas (STC 21153), sigs. ABii[v], Aii[v]; reprinted in modern spelling in Gertrude Annan's useful section, "Tradition and Early Tudor Medicine," in Elizabeth M. Nugent's *The Thought and Culture of the English Renaissance: An Anthology of Tudor Prose, 1481–1553* (Cambridge: Cambridge University Press, 1956), pp. 291–92. On the work's later history, see Sir D'Arcy Power, "The Birth of Mankind or the Woman's Book," *The Library*, 4th ser., 8 (1927): 1–37.

Sustaining the popularizing trends of the English medical handbooks and the express insistence on making essential knowledge freely available that so perceptibly tallies with Scripturalism, Andrew Borde brought out *A Dyetary of Helth* (1542); Thomas Phaer translated from the French *The Regiment of Life, Wherunto Is Added a Treatise of the Pestylence, with the Boke of Children* (1544); Robert Recorde compiled *The Urinal of Physick* (1547), Christopher Langton another book on physic (ca. 1550); and William Turner, having begun with his Latin *Libellus de re herbaria novus* (1538), announced his principled decision to write for a broader audience in English, which he did in *The Names of Herbes* (1548) and, chiefly, in his masterwork, *A New Herball* (vol. 1, 1551; vol. 2, 1562; vol. 3, 1568). Besides Turner's *New Herball*, the most scientifically important English medical publication of the sixteenth century was Nicholas Udall's translation of a Latin manual on dissection techniques, *Compendiosa totius anatomie delineatio* (1545), which had been written by Thomas Geminus, surgeon to Edward VI and onetime student of the great Vesalius at Padua; Udall's English text circulated under the title, *A Compendyouse Rehersall of All Anatomie* (1553).[39] The foregoing is an all but exhaustive list of the works that comprised the vogue of vernacular medical handbooks in the middle decades of the sixteenth century. Their propounders, moreover, are uniformly men with Protestant leanings, in some cases men with reputations for outspoken antiauthoritarian views that surface in these very works. Audrey Eccles has suggested in an essay on "The Reading Public, the Medical Profession, and the Use of English for Medical Books in the Sixteenth and Seventeenth Centuries" that the defensiveness in Elyot's *Castle of Health* and the strident vindication of the people's right to know in Phaer's *Regiment of Life* evince "a powerful anti-English lobby" on the issue of "having medical books available to all who could read."[40] Fortunately for our purposes, learned opposition availed least in Edward VI's reign, and it is prose from that era that resounds with the most defiant challenges to the monopolistic control of knowledge by professionals.

William Turner, a physician himself and an early Nonconformist divine, acknowledges in the preface to the first volume of *A New Herball* that he has suffered much reproof from his colleagues, who call his decision to write his treatises in the vernacular "unwysely done, and

---

[39]Bennett, *English Books and Readers, 1475–1557*, pp. 98–108; Annan in Nugent, ed., *Thought and Culture of the English Renaissance*, pp. 276–77, 288–90. Annan also considers the *Compendiosa* a "pirated edition of Vesalius's *Epitome*" (pp. 298–99).

[40]Audrey Eccles, "The Reading Public, the Medical Profession, and the Use of English for Medical Books in the Sixteenth and Seventeenth Centuries," *Neuphilologische Mitteilungen* 75 (1975): 145–56. Also see Bennett on the mounting opposition to vernacular medical books in the latter half of the sixteenth century: *English Books and Readers, 1558–1603* (Cambridge: Cambridge University Press, 1965), pp. 179–81.

agaynst the honor of my art that I professe, and agaynst the common profit, to set out so muche knowledge of Physick in Englysh." But Turner slyly discloses the prejudice in the alarmism of his fellow doctors by quoting them—"Now (say they) every man . . . nay every olde wyfe will presume, not without the mordre of many, to practise Physick"— and he then proceeds to his own defense by making exactly the analogues of Scripturalist arguments made by Elyot fifteen years before. Like the Gospels, the works of Galen and Dioscorides were vernacular writings for their original readers, and "if they gave no occasyon unto every olde wyfe to practyse Physike, then gyve I none. If they gave no occasyon of murther, then gyve I none." Indeed, Turner, like Elyot, adds patriotic to Scripturalist echoes in claiming to further "the study of lyberall sciences" by "wrytyng unto the English my countremen an Englysh herball."[41] Yet while Turner tempers his apologia with an effusion of nationalism, Christopher Langton, writing within a year of Turner, is much angrier against the doctors who accuse him of corrupting Galen by making him popularly known in English. Langton lashes out, likening these men to papists. Then, stepping up the force of this particular comparison, he contends that King Edward should undertake a reformation of the medical profession as a fitting extension of the reformation of religion in the realm. Of the doctors Langton hints darkly to his readers:

Yf I were dysposed I coulde prove that there is a moch jugglyng and deceyvyng of the people now a dayes amongest our phisitions (I wyll name none, but everye man knoweth his owne weakenesse and infirmitie) as ever was amongest the Popysh preestes, and a redresse myght be had, yf it pleased the kynges hyghnesse, that none myght be suffered to practyse but suche as be lerned.[42]

The conspicuous exception to the Protestant tenor of vernacular medical handbooks at mid-century is John Caius's *A Boke or Counseill against the Disease Commonly Called the Sweate, or Sweatyng Sicknesse* (1552). Trained at Padua during Vesalius's student days, he became an associate of the great anatomist and, ultimately, one of the most distinguished members of the medical establishment. After returning to England in 1544, Caius lectured on anatomy at Henry VIII's command in the Hall of the Company of Barbers and Surgeons, becoming reader of the Company in 1546. In 1547 Caius was appointed a fellow of the College of Physicians of London, a foundation of Henry VIII's; in due course he held a number of its governing offices, including its presidency. Caius also served as court physician under Edward, Mary, and Elizabeth, although Elizabeth

---

[41]William Turner, *A New Herball* (STC 24365), sig. Aiii^v, cited in Bennett, *English Books and Readers, 1475–1557*, pp. 101–2.

[42]Christopher Langton, *An Introduction into Phisycke, Wyth an Universal Dyet* (London, 1550?) (STC 15204), sig. Bii^v, cited in Bennett, *English Books and Readers, 1475–1557*, p. 109.

is reported to have dismissed him in 1568 because of his unconcealed Catholic leanings.[43] We have Caius's own word for what an untypical production *A Book or Counsel against the Sweat* is for him; at its beginning he announces that it is his only work in English among the seventy-odd he has written. He explains his several reasons for preferring to write "either in greke or latine": to enable the "commoditie" of his works to reach beyond England, to secure more than a "halfe" learned readership, "to avoide the judgement of the multitude, from whome in maters of learnyng a man shalbe forced to dissente, in disprovyng that whiche they most approve, & approvyng that whiche they most disalowe," and to escape the imputation of publishing "phisicke unperfectly" and "undiscretly" which arises from "the common settyng furthe and printing of every foolishe thyng in englishe." Indeed, as Caius continues to reflect on the vernacular, he finds less and less reason "to stonde onely in the Englishe tongue," and he proceeds to exhort his "countrie men" who wish to be "comparable in learnyng to men of other countries"

to leave the simplicite of thesame, and to procede further in many and diverse knowleges bothe in tongues and sciences at home and in universities, to the adournyng of the common welthe, better service of their kyng, & great pleasure and commodite of their own selves, to what kinde of life so ever they shold applie them. [*BCS*, fols. 4ᵛ–5ʳ]

Caius's candor makes his opening declaration a valuable piece of testimony, for it reveals how a scholar with other modern sentiments—nationalism, scientific commitment, utilitarian goals—nevertheless divides, as a Catholic presumably, from Protestant contemporaries on the language issue in which the medical treatises so nearly recall the great English conflict over a vernacular Bible. The relation of *A Book or Counsel against the Sweat* to the rest of Caius's writings is, he explains, that of an exception to a rule—a rule requiring suspension on account of two recent epidemics of the sweating sickness which had brought England alone to dire extremity. Since he wants to help his country thus uniquely afflicted, Caius can for once rejoice in the option of writing in his native tongue, "thinkynge it also better to write this in Englishe after mine own meanyng, then to have it translated out of my Latin by other after their misunderstandyng." Accordingly, he justifies his decision by envisaging his readership:

Therfore compelled I am to use this our Englishe tongue as best to be understande, and moste nedeful to whome it most behoveth to have spedy remedie, and often tymes leaste nyghe to places of succourre and comforte at lerned

---

[43]This information derives from Archibald Malloch's introduction to John Caius, *A Boke or Counseill against the Disease called the SWEATE (1552)* (New York: Scholars' Facsimiles and Reprints, 1937), pp. ii–vii. Subsequent references to this edition, abbreviated *BCS*, are incorporated in the text.

mennes handes: and leaste nedefull to be set furthe in other tongues to be understand generally of all persons. [*BCS*, fol. 7ᵛ][44]

Having seen his way to writing a medical handbook in the vernacular, the learned Caius sets to work with a will as great as that of any of his Protestant contemporaries in utilizing the transactive literary paradigm that characterizes this genre. Considerable stretches of his text exhibit the open sentences, the asymmetrically conjoined clauses, which had been the staple resource of native prose composition for well over a century and a half before Caius; here, to illustrate, is an excerpt from his section on alternatives for treatment:

But if the sicke on this wise beforesaid cannot sweate kyndly, then nature must be holpen, as I sayd before. And for so moch as sweat is letted in this disease fower waies, by disorder, wekenes of nature, closenes of the pores in the skinne, & grosnes of the humoures: my counseil is to avoide disorder by suche meanes as hetherto I have taught, and next to open the pores if they be close, and make thinne the matter, if it be grosse, and provoke sweat, if nature be weke. Those you shal doe by gentle rubbynges, this by warme drinckes as hereafter streight I will declare. And for that every man hath not the knowlege to discerne which of these is the cause of let in sweatyng, I wil shewe you plainly howe to do with moste suretie and lesse offense. I wyll beginne with wekenes of nature. [*BCS*, fol. 33ʳ⁻ᵛ]

Yet, as Elyot's precedent in *The Castle of Health* prepares us to discover, Caius's sentence forms recurrently distinguish themselves from those of fifteenth-century prose by pronounced outcroppings of schematics: parallelistic phrasing, binary or serial. Its function in context is clearly to keep up the author's end of his reciprocal relation with the reader by marking material which he considers indispensable to understanding and interpretation—in the first place, to lessen the chance that it will be overlooked and, in the second place, to shape it for retention in the memory. Thus Caius particularizes on "the souddeine sharpenes" by which his readers might learn to identify the onset of this peculiarly English disease

that immediately killed some in opening theire windowes, some in plaieng with children in their strete dores, some in one hour, many in two it destroyed, & at the longest, to them that merilye dined, it gave a sorowful Supper. As it founde them so it toke them, some in sleape some in wake, some in mirthe some in care, some fasting & some ful, some busy and some idle, and in one house sometyme three sometyme five, sometyme seven sometyme eight, some-

---

[44]Bennett, *English Books and Readers, 1475–1557*, p. 102, cites what appears, for this period, to be a unique middle position taken by Humphrey Lloyd in the preface to his English translation of John XXI's *The Treasuri of Helth* (1550?) (STC 14652). Lloyd defends vernacular medical handbooks for "the use and profyte of . . . honest persones," but wants their use limited to occasions when a physician's advice cannot be had.

tyme more sometyme all. . . . With what grieffe, and accidentes it helde theym, herafter then I wil declare. . . . In the mene space, know that this disease (because it most did stand in sweating from the beginning until the ending) was called, the Sweating sickenesse: and (because it first beganne in England), it was named in other countries the englishe sweat. [*BCS*, fol. 9^{r-v}]

What is noteworthy about passages of this type in the vernacular medical manuals after Elyot is the recognizable connection between the interpretive paradigm for composition which I have been proposing as a possible extension and generalization of Scripturalist concerns and the tendency for schematics to take over sentence form and cast it into the correspondent units of aphorism when something vital is being said. This recognizable aphoristic tendency in such contexts, moreover, is not confined to learned authors like Elyot and Caius; it is common property among vernacular writers who address an inclusively conceived readership on matters of their welfare. Thus, for example, the popular writer Andrew Borde uses aphorisms of his own devising in his *Dyetary of Helth* to counsel "all maner of men and women, beynge sycke or hole" to compose their spirits and settle their manner of life before considering what foods might or might not agree with them:

There is no man nor woman the which have any respect to them selfe, that can be a better Phesycion for theyr owne savegarde, than theyr owne self can be: To consyder what thynge the whiche doth them good, And to refrayne from suche thynges that doth them hurte or harme. And let every man beware of care & sorowe, pencyfulnes, and of inwarde anger. Beware of surfettes, and use not to moche veneryouse actes. Breke not the usuall custome of slepe in the nyght. A mery herte and mynde the whiche is in reste and quyetnes, without adversyte and to moche worldly busynes, causeth a man to lyve long: and to loke yongly, althoughe he be agyd. Care and sorowe bryngeth in age and deth: wherefore let every man be mery.[45]

Borde's homely aphorisms bring us by a short step from the vernacular medical handbooks to one border, at least, of the extensive field of sententious compilations where, following the precedent of Elyot's *Banquet of Sapience*, we are led to seek the more generalized impact of Scripturalist habits of mind and composition in another genre—the vernacular anthology of "sentences." As Tilley has observed in the introduction to his *Elizabethan Proverb Lore*,[46] sententious forms of utterance in the Tudor period are a rich, if difficult subject for scholarship because they constitute a nexus in which the distillations of folk speech and the elegant

[45]Andrew Borde, *A Compendious Regyment, or A Dyetary of Helth*, ed. Frederick J. Furnivall, Early English Text Society e.s. 10 (London: N. Trübner & Co., 1870), p. 300.

[46]Morris P. Tilley, *Elizabethan Proverb Lore in Lyly's "Euphues" and in Pettie's "Petite Pallace,"* *with Parallels from Shakespeare*, University of Michigan Publications in Language and Literature no. 2 (New York: Macmillan Co., 1926), pp. 1–52.

turns of literary aperçus can prove indistinguishable from one another. Although Tilley appears puzzled by such a situation, we need not be, having recognized in aphoristic sentence form a durable and widely replicable set of defining features—chiefly binary and correspondent units of constituent structure—that, by virtue of their origins in sentential conjunction, become a stylistic universal. Our concern in examining the vernacular anthology of "sentences" or aphorisms is twofold: on the one hand, certainly, to be alert for formal consonances between their entries and identifiable Scriptural models for expression, but equally, on the other, to inquire whether the generalized Scripturalist literary program, with its steady premium on vernacular composition and interpretive activity, recognized any particular value or instrumentality in aphorism. The latter concern raises the further interesting possibility of some overt accommodation, on the circumscribed ground of the aphorism, between Scripturalism and formal rhetoric—an art which tended to be conceived in opposition to the plainspokenness with which Scripturalism was commonly identified. For in sixteenth-century England the notion of an anthology of aphorisms was indelibly associated with the name of Erasmus and with his methods and materials for cultivating a versatile Latin style.

It is one of the more familiar facts of literary history that Erasmus published his initial collection of eight hundred sayings, or adages, gathered from Greek and Latin authors in *Collectanea Adagiorum veterum* (1500), and in successive new editions so augmented and reorganized his materials that the *Adagiorum chiliades* of 1517 offered more than five thousand entries.[47] The English vogue of Erasmus's *Adagia* was enormous even beyond the scope to be expected from its enforced use by most teachers of Latin composition; more than ninety editions, including selections and abridgments, had been printed in England by 1550, and by 1599 the total had reached more than one hundred and thirty editions. In his Prolegomena to *Adagia* Erasmus includes a disquisition on the nature of sententious formulation, in which he finds four benefits: enhanced understanding of philosophy (conceived primarily as morality for living); support for reasoning and argument; appealing ornament for speech and writing; and aid in reading classical texts, where, he says, many of the best authors obtain from aphorisms the very benefits he has identified. Although the value of aphorism as ornament would assume disproportionate importance in the cult of Euphuism later in the

[47]See DeWitt T. Starnes's introduction to *Proverbs or Adages by Desiderius Erasmus, Gathered Out of the "Chiliades" and Englished by Richard Taverner (1569)* (Gainesville, Fla.: Scholars' Facsimiles and Reprints, 1956), pp. v–xii, on which I have drawn for material in this and the following paragraph. Also see Crane's survey discussion of the vogue of Erasmus's sententious compilations in sixteenth-century England (*Wit and Rhetoric in the Renaissance*, pp. 26–31).

century, it is significant, I think, that the three other benefits ascribed to aphorism by Erasmus are intellectual and, specifically, interpretive in character. Their prospective instrumentality for writers under Scripturalist impulsions appears obvious.

In turning to the genre of the vernacular anthology of aphorisms, we find even more conclusively than with the English health manuals that Elyot's intuitions hold true: a writer seriously committed to winning a readership among native speakers with prose of counsel would have to accommodate somehow to the motive forces of the Scripturalist program from the 1530s onward. After Elyot, there is a monopoly of activity by declared Protestants in the production of anthologies of aphorisms. (Even his Latin-English *Dictionary*, which had relied on Erasmus's *Adagia* for illustration of appreciable numbers of terms, was shepherded through its later, larger editions by the staunchly Protestant Thomas Cooper.) In the wake of *The Banquet of Sapience*, Elyot's principal successor was another of Cromwell's protégés, Richard Taverner, who from 1536 until the accession of Mary held the office of Clerk of the Privy Seal. Taverner's weariless efforts as a vernacular compiler have multiple significance for us. First, they are concentrated in the years 1538–40, when Cromwell, at the height of his power, assured the public dissemination of the newly authorized Great Bible. Second, half of Taverner's compilations—three in number—are explicitly scriptural: his *Commonplaces of Scrypture* (1538), his *Epitome of the Psalmes* (1539), and his independent English version of the Bible (1539). Finally, the more humanistic half of Taverner's compilations—his *Proverbes or Adagies Gathered out of the Chiliades of Erasmus* (1539), *The Garden of Wysdom* (1539), and *The Second Book of the Garden of Wysedome* (1540)—evinces the ready embrace accorded by Protestant Scripturalists to Erasmus's promotion of the aphoristic mode.[48] In the three last named collections Taverner emerges as all too eager to extend upon Erasmus's procedure of citing a saying in elliptical form, then in full aphoristic form, and then adding interpretive commentary, for Taverner's additions recurrently show an at once patriotic and Protestant virulence. To illustrate, his *Proverbes or Adagies* reproduces Erasmus's entry *Frons occipicio prior* faithfully in its elliptical form, "The foreheade is afore the hinder parte of the face," and in its full aphoristic form, "The thing a man seeth done afore his face, and in his own presence, is for moost parte better done, then that done behinde his backe." But Taverner proceeds to a fierce admonition to kings, cardinals, bishops, prelates, "and sondry other officers and Magistrates in Christendome, which do al by vicares and deputies, but themselves live in most idlenes, and in all kindes of pleasure like Popes": "Would God," he exclaims, "these

---

[48]See, further, Olive B. White, "Richard Taverner's Interpretation of Erasmus in *Proverbes or Adagies*," *PMLA* 59 (1944): 928–43.

woulde take example of our most vigilant Prince & soveraigne Lorde Kinge Henry the eyght, who . . . loketh him selfe right busely uppon his charge committed unto him of God."[49] The case of Taverner is a telling one for the joint future course of Erasmian humanism and Protestant prose of counsel in this genre.

Taverner's aphoristic compilations, Scriptural and Erasmian, for English readers were followed by Nicholas Udall's translation of Erasmus's free Latin rendering of the *Apophthegmata* ascribed to Plutarch—a compendious work, again, due to Erasmus's practice of formally recasting and commenting on each entry. Udall issued his translation as *Apophthegmes, that is to saie, prompte, quicke, wittie and sentencious saiynges, of certaine Emperours, Kynges, Capitaines, Philosophiers and Oratours, as well Grekes, as Romaines, bothe veraye pleasaunt & profitable to reade, partely for all maner of persones, & especially Gentlemen* (1542); the characteristically verbose title of the period reveals even more about the qualities esteemed in sententious form, and the readership to whom the form appealed, than it does about the contents of the work. In Udall as in Taverner we find a staunch Protestant and an obtrusive interpreter in his own right, one who alerts the reader in his prefatory epistle to look out for additions "of mine owne noting, over and besides the woordes and matter of the Latine werke, . . . somtimes in the middes of the text with this marke of mine * if the place semed to require some more light."[50] While many of Udall's interpolations are explanatory—identifications of persons, places, or allusions—he quite consistently moves to comment where he can maximize the moral force of a "sentence." His handling of the saying of the philosopher Aristippus to a young scholar chagrined at being found in a brothel will exemplify Udall's Protestant uprightness in matters of conduct and style alike, as he translates the apophthegm and Erasmus's commentary and then asterisks his own addition:

> *Young man, to entre into soche a place as this, is no shame at al: but not to be able to go out again in deede is a foule shame.*
>
> He meaned that it is but a veniall and a pardonable matter, if a man dooe moderately use the companie of women, not offendyng the lawe. But to be a thing worthie no pardon or forgivenesse, if one be as a bond servaunt, under the continual yoke of filthie pleasures of the body. This saiyng might in that worlde be well taken, when no temporall lawe, nor civile ordinaunce did forbid men to companie with harlottes: but now beside the wittines of makyng a readie excuse of his sinne, there is in it nothyng worthie laude or praise.

[49]*Proverbs or Adages . . . Gathered . . . by Richard Taverner*, fols. 7ᵛ–8ʳ.

[50]*The Apophthegmes of Erasmus, Translated into English by Nicolas Udall, Literally Reprinted from the Scarce Edition of 1564*, ed. Robert Roberts (Boston, Lincolnshire: Robert Roberts, 1877), p. vi. Subsequent citations, abbreviated *Apoph.*, are incorporated in the text.

* And this was the saiyng of a corrupt Gentile, to whom the lawe of God was no parte of his profession, and not of a christian man. That excuse of sinne, that may seeme to serve a Gentile, maie not serve a Christian man. [*Apoph.*, p. 51]

However, the peculiar character of the larger Scripturalist habit of mind as it takes shape in what I have been calling an interpretive or transactive paradigm for prose of counsel emerges especially clearly in a passage where Udall struggles his way far beyond Erasmus in dealing with a highly condensed and schematic saying by Diogenes the Cynic. The entry begins by rendering Erasmus's elliptical and fuller citations of Diogenes straightforwardly: "He used customably to saie, that in our life we should oftener provide λόγου ἢ βρόχου, that is, *be rather a talker, then an halter.*" Udall's English aptly enough transposes the *parison* and *homoioteleuton* of the Greek while also preserving its sense, as the neat fit with Erasmus's commentary shows. This is how Udall renders Erasmus:

The Greke woorde λόγος signifieth in Latine *sermonem*, in Englishe communicacion or talkyng. And the Greke vocable βρόχος, is in Latine, *lagoeus*, in Englishe an halter or a strynge, soche as a bodie maie by the necke be hanged withall. Whiche he spake, for that soche persones as ar werie of their lives, and are in soche despaire, that thei would fain be out of the worlde, do many of them by and by hange and strangle theim selves, whereas thei ought rather to have recourse to good communicacion, that might recomforte their spirites, and bryng them again from despaire. For, to the hart beyng in heavines and utter discomfort: the beste Phisician is good and wholsome communicacion.

These Erasmian reflections on language stir Udall strongly, as evidenced by two separate asterisked additions on "taking λόγου, for talking":

* I thinke *Diogenes* mened that menne ought so to provide, that their wordes and communicacion at all times be vertuous and fruitfull, aswell to the hearer, as to the speaker, and not of soche sorte as the speaker maie afterwarde have cause to repent, and wishe within his bealie again. So that *Diogenes* would no mennes communicacion to be soche as might afterward bee found hanging matters, and redounde to their owne confusion, but rather to be fruitfull and vertuous. For, onelie soche woordes and none other, been worthie the appellacion, or name of communicacion and talkyng, of whiche redoundeth aswell to the hearer, as to the speaker some fruite, profite, and edifying: and for whiche bothe parties maie be the better, and not have cause afterward to beshrewe them selves. And soche as usen naughtie and pernicious babeling doen often times procure their owen harmes, and been autours and workers of their owne confusion.

* No man ought to leate escape wordes, which muste afterwarde come home again by the throte. No woordes ben worthie the name of talkyng, but such as been fruitefull. Suche as use pernicius wordes are commenlie autoures of their owne confusion. [*Apoph.*, pp. 80–81]

Udall's own commentary supplies an extraordinarily vivid and revealing instance of the more generalized literary impulsions for which I have been proposing a source in Scripturalism—specifically, the commitment to vernacular expression and to a view of "wordes" as profoundly and mutually efficacious for author and reader on the model of God's Word. In his earnestness to divest Diogenes' saying of all cynicism, Udall leaves Erasmus behind to strain toward what might well be hoped from so elegant an "apophthegm"—an entire code of ethics for all linguistic transactions. "Onelie soche woordes and none other," affirms Udall, "been worthie the . . . name of communicacion and talkyng, of whiche redoundeth aswell to the hearer, as to the speaker some fruite, profite, and edifying: and for whiche bothe parties maie be the better." No less vivid and revealing here is the motive force attached to sententious form, as Udall's next original addition gives a culminating admonition on how "wordes" are to be used in a trio of aphorisms of his own making: the two antitheses and the equative construction that follow the second asterisk.

In the 1540s the vernacular anthology of aphorisms can be discerned to enter a second phase, one in which it more nearly comes to resemble Elyot's pioneering venture in *The Banquet of Sapience*. This phase is marked by far less adherence to Erasmus's tripartite format of tag, full formulation, and paraphrase with commentary for each entry; the later anthologies tend to be comprised, like the *Banquet*, of serial runs of aphorisms under specified headings. Yet the attenuation of the paraphrase and commentary in no way diminishes the values imputed to sententious formulation as summed up in Udall's title. By all odds the most popular of this later type of vernacular anthology was William Baldwin's so-called *Treatise of Morall Philosophie* (1547), which saw twenty-three editions in the sixteenth century, some of them in the revised and augmented form given the compilation by Thomas Palfreyman.[51] More precisely characterized, Baldwin's *Treatise* exhibits a transitional form: its first book incorporates vestiges of the older, Erasmian organization (four expository chapters on the origins of philosophy, its branches, the origins of moral philosophy, and the means by which it teaches, plus fifty-nine capsule biographies of notable framers of "sentence" in antiq-

[51]See Robert Hood Bowers's introduction to *A Treatise of Morall Philosophie Wherein Is Contained the Worthy Sayings of Philosophers, Emperours, Kings, and Orators: Their Lives and Answers (1547) by William Baldwin, Enlarged by Thomas Palfreyman* (Gainesville, Fla.: Scholars' Facsimiles and Reprints, 1967), pp. v–xiii. Crane (*Wit and Rhetoric in the Renaissance*, pp. 24, 34–36) finds Baldwin's original compilation indebted to an early Caxton publication, Lord Rivers's *The Dictes and Sayengis of the Philosophres* (1477), which itself drew heavily on Diogenes Laertius's *Lives and Sayings of the Philosophers*; he also claims Guevara, Lagnerius's collection of Cicero's *sententiae*, and Elyot as main sources for Palfreyman's enlargement. In its turn, *A Treatise of Morall Philosophie* would furnish materials and an overall arrangement for *Politeuphuia: Wits Commonwealth* (1597).

uity) which give way to unbroken runs of aphorisms, topically sorted, in the ensuing three—and, in later editions, eleven—books. The primary explanation for the huge popularity of Baldwin's *Treatise* would seem to be the ever increasing number of aphorisms it made available under a wide range of headings including, for example, "Of God, of his Workes, of his Mercy and Justice," "Of the Soule, and the government therof," "Of Policie, and government of Common-weales" (with subheadings "Of the necessity of Order," "Of Kings, Rulers, and Governours, and how they should rule their Subjects," and "Of Counsell or Councellors"), "Of Obedience," "Of Wit, and Discretion," "Of Friends, Friendship, and Amitie," "Of Death, not to be Feared," "Of Praise and Dispraise," "Of Lust and Lecherie," "Of Faith and Truthe," "Of Women." There is remarkable congruity between the aphoristic contents of such an anthology and the fiction of Pettie and Lyly, while the attention accorded by Baldwin to the forms and functions of aphorism also anticipates the intensely rhetorical consciousness of the two later vernacular stylists.

Given the enormous circulation achieved by Baldwin's *Treatise* from 1547 onward, it is worth noting its account of the uses and chief types of sententious expression. In an early chapter Baldwin affirms the didactic and ethical origins of aphorism, and then proceeds to trace its joint classical and Scriptural provenance, which he divides into "three kindes" as developed by "all that have written" or "for the most part taught" moral philosophy:

The first is, by Counsels, Lawes and Precepts, of which *Licurgus, Solon, Isocrates, Cato,* and other more have written much, counselling and admonishing men to vertue by precepts, and by their lawes fraying them from vice.

The second kind of teaching is by Proverbs and Adages: which kinde of Philosophie most commonly is used: in which they shew the contraries of things, preferring alwaies the best: declaring thereby both the profits of vertue, and the inconveniences of vices, that we considering both, may imbrace the good, and eschew the evill.

The third kinde is by Parables, Examples, and Semblances. Wherin by ease and familiar truth, hard things, and more out of use, are declared, that by the one the other may be better perceyved and borne in minde: Our Saviour Christ himselfe, when hee taught the grosse Jewes any divine thing, most commonly he used parables, Semblables, and Examples, which (though differing in somwhat) draw all to one end, and therefore are of one kinde.[52]

For our purposes, Baldwin's observations are immensely illuminating. Recognizing, in effect, that sententious formulation is a stylistic universal (used by "all that have written of Moral Philosophy" or "have for the most part taught it"), he distinguishes three several "kindes" in accor-

---

[52]Baldwin, *A Treatise of Morall Philosophie* (1547), sig. Biii^{r-v}. Subsequent citations, abbreviated *TMP,* are incorporated in the text.

dance with joint semantic and syntactic criteria which are often made remarkably precise. The first kind, "Counsels, Lawes and Precepts," we infer to be discrete sentences of the *thou shalt* or *thou shalt not* form, since they work by "counselling and admonishing men to vertue . . . , and . . . fraying them from vice." Baldwin's second kind, "Proverbs and Adages," is defined syntactically by its antithetical form ("in which they shew the contraries of things") and also psychosemantically characterized in a fashion anticipatory of the dynamics of assent attributed to antithesis by Kenneth Burke (see chap. 1, second section). Baldwin ascribes to the antithetical cast of proverbs and adages the funtion of weighting or swaying judgment on the side of virtue: "preferring alwaies the best: declaring thereby both the profits of vertue, and the inconveniences of vices, that we considering both, may imbrace the good, and eschew the evill." His third kind, "Parables, Examples, and Semblances," is defined syntactically by its comparative or correlative form and semantically by its function of making "hard things," things "more out of use," and "grave and waighty matters" better able to be "perceyved and borne in minde" by articulating their likeness to "easie and familiar truth." Again, considerable cognitive and linguistic insight is suggested by Baldwin's reference to the instrumentality of the underlying relation of likeness in "Parables" and "Semblables."

More generally, these observations of Baldwin's are noteworthy for the constant reliance made on an interpretive paradigm and the concomitant cooperation of writer and reader in order to render an account of the moral efficacy of sententious formulation—especially in its antithetical and correlative (or comparative) "kindes." Nor are Baldwin's insights left merely as preliminary observations in *A Treatise of Morall Philosophie*, for the concluding three sections of the anthology suspend the topical headings that have hitherto ordered its contents and replace these with the three identified types of sententious formulations, under the headings "Of Precepts and Counsailes," "Of Proverbs and Sayings of the Wise," and "Of Parables and Semblables." Baldwin's *Treatise* thus significantly culminates with a renewed emphasis on the formal and functional aspects of the three "kindes" of aphorism rather than on their variety of contents. To illustrate this highlighting of the three "kindes" as discrete semantic and syntactic types, here, first, are specimens of the opening entries in the section "Of Precepts and Counsailes":

Solon. Worship God.
Reverence thy father and mother.
Helpe thy friend.
Hate no man. Maintaine truth.
Sweare not. Obay the lawes.
Thales. Honour thy King. Try thy friends.
Abstaine from vice. Love peace.

Desire honour and glory for vertue.
Take heed to thy selfe, and be circumspect.
Cast whisperers and tale bearers out of thy company.

[*TMP*, fols. 164ᵛ–165ʳ]

Next, here are typical specimens of the entries under the heading "Of Proverbs and Sayings of the Wise":

Mar. Aur.	The great cities full of good inhabitants ought to be praysed, and not the great buildings.
	He is not to be accounted strong, that cannot away with labour.
Seneca.	He is very valiant, who never rejoyceth much, nor soroweth out of measure.
	That which a man hath accustomed long time, seemeth pleasant, although indeed it be painefull.
Plato.	Manners are more requisite in a Childe, then playing upon instruments, or any other kinde of vaine pleasures.
Aristotle.	Exercise eyther hurteth or profiteth nothing.
	When a man doubteth of doubtfull things, and is assured of them that be evident, it is a signe of good understanding.

[*TMP*, fols. 174ᵛ–175ʳ]

And here, finally, are some of the "Parables and Semblables" collected under three subheadings, attributions to "*Hermes, Socrates,* and *Plato*," to "*Anaxagoras, Aristippus, Alexander, Solon,* and *Marcus Aurelius*," and to "*Aristotle, Plutarch,* and *Seneca*," respectively. The continuing stylistic homogeneity, despite the diversity of authorship, witnesses to the universal character of sententious formulation, which the physical presentation of Baldwin's volume likewise helps to enforce. The three triads of "Semblables" that follow are drawn, in order, from Baldwin's three subheadings as listed above:

As Plants measurably watred, grow the better, but watred too much, are drowned and dye: so the minde with moderate labour is refreshed, but with overmuche is utterly dulled.
Like as a ship that hath a sure anker, may lye safe in any place: so the minde that is ruled by perfect reason, is quiet every where.
As fire smoaketh not much that flameth at the first blowing, so the glory that shineth at the first is not greatly envied.

As arrogancy, pride, and presumption, are notably hated of God, and had in derision every where among men: So contrariwise, lowlinesse, meekenesse, and an humble spirit, purchaseth both the favor of God, and knitteth unto man the benevolence of man.
As the knowledge of God ought not to be unperfect or doubtfull, so prayer should not be faint or slacke, without courage and quicknesse.
As the body is neere to health which (though it be' wasted) is yet free and out of the danger of noysome humours: even so is the minde more receivable of

296

the blessing of God, which is not defiled with grievous offences, though shee yet lacke true and perfect vertues.

Like as the Hare both delivereth, nourisheth, and is with young all at once: so an Usurer before hee hath beguiled one, deviseth how to deceive another by making a false bargaine.

Like as an Horse after he hath once taken the bridle, must ever after beare one or the other: so hee that is once falne in debt, can lightly never after be throughly quit there from.

Like as Physitians with their bitter drugs doe mingle sweet spices, that they may be the better receyved: so ought checkes to be mingled with gentle admonitions. [*TMP*, fols. 186ʳ, 188ᵛ, 189ᵛ]

The foregoing survey of the sixteenth-century vogue of vernacular anthologies of aphorisms documents the steady growth of awareness in such compilers as Udall and Baldwin of the integral stylistic functions that converge in sententious form. Nevertheless, for all the sensitivity of insight offered into the workings of antithesis and correlation in the joint domains of syntax and semantics, the handling of "sentences" in these anthologies remains sentential, geared to the discrete unit. This was also Elyot's procedure in serving up the various "dishes" of topically organized counsel in the main body of *The Banquet of Sapience*. If we seek, however, for ramifications of the precedent afforded by the framing device of *The Banquet of Sapience*—the inclusive summons to dine issued by Sapience in a sustained tissue of verses from the book of Proverbs— there is, so far as I know, only Thomas Becon's series of Scripturalist compilations to cite. But this series ran to several volumes, most of them huge, and one of them, at least, a phenomenal bestseller. In tracing for the anthology of aphorisms a modulation analogous to that between a schematics of the sentence and a schematics of discourse in Elyot's style, there is some precedent to cite in Taverner's *Commonplaces of Scrypture* (1538), mentioned earlier, or in Becon's own *Newes out of Heaven* (1541), which Derrick Bailey calls "simply a cento of biblical passages relating to man's redemption through Christ" that "shows to advantage Becon's favorite method of allowing scripture to speak for itself, piling text upon text . . . , and relying for effect upon the selection and arrangement of his material."[53] Becon also used this method of composition in three other anthologies of Scripture texts: *The Governaunce of Vertue, teachinge all faithfull Christians, howe they ought daily to leade their life, and frutefully to spend theyr time, unto the glory of God, and the healthe of theyr owne soules* (1543), *The Principles of Christen Religion necessary to be knowen of the fayhtfull* (1550?),and *The Commonplaces of the Holy Scripture: containing certayne articles of Christen religion, moste necessarye to be knowen of all true Christians*

---

[53]Derrick S. Bailey, *Thomas Becon and the Reformation* (Edinburgh and London: Oliver & Boyd, 1952), p. 19.

in thys wicked and troublous time, both for the purenesse of the doctrine, and for the quietnesse of their conscience (Preface dated 1562). What is lacking in all these works, however, is the dramatic and circumstantial context provided by a speaker figure like Elyot's Sapience, who energizes the inert mass of sententia into direct address to an identified audience.

Precisely such a speech context is provided in a series of works which Becon composed as question-and-answer dialogues between an authorial mouthpiece, the householder Philemon, who is unfailingly adept in the Scriptures and in Protestant doctrine, and a group of Philemon's neighbors, to whom he plays host for some godly social events that provide the settings for discourse. When one recalls that Elyot offered his *Banquet of Sapience* to his king and countrymen as a worthy means of breaking their Lenten fast in 1536, it is hard not to see in this genial conceit the literary inspiration for the colloquies which Becon elaborated in the successive occasional settings of *A Christmas Bankette, garnyshed with many pleasaunt and deynty dishes* (December–January 1541), *A Potation or Drynkynge for this holi time of Lent* (February–March 1542), *A pleasaunt newe Nosegaye, full of many godly and swete floures* (May 1542), and *A New Yeares Gyfte more precious than golde* (1543). These works additionally attest the marked affinities with the vernacular anthology of aphorisms that persist throughout Becon's vast corpus; his prose hovers constantly on the verge of direct Scriptural quotation, with only the barest syntactic adjustments utilized as needed to shape discrete verses into continuous dialogue.

In keying this series of works to the intersection of the church year with the seasonal round of social events in the life of his day, Becon's evident purpose was to domesticate the Scripturalist habit of mind and expression for his English readers in their ordinary dealings with one another and thus, presumably, to mitigate the radically subjective character of Scripturalism in its earliest Tyndalian phase. These works are accordingly colloquial and didactic in their overall design, as well as interpretive in the specific sense that we have been associating with Scripturalism as a literary program and with the cultivation of sententious forms of utterance in this period. At the outset of each work, Becon's characteristic title signals to the reader what direction the reciprocal effort after meaning on the level of plot will take. In each, Philemon convenes his neighbors to present them with a banquet or potation or nosegay or gift appropriate to the occasion, but, since the presentation itself always takes the form of a composite of Biblical texts, the group activity—a kind of parlor game played in high earnest—is to discover through dialogue just how Philemon can be claiming to present his neighbors with this or that object in particular. Thus the controlling form of these works is that of a "Parable" or "Semblable," in Baldwin's terminology, and they further sustain their resemblance to the vernacular anthology of aphorisms in their subdivisions into topics of conversation analogous to thematic groupings.

Becon's Philemon sets forth his Christmas banquet in four courses whose natural and even necessary order, as determined through discussion, yields food for thought and sustenance for the neighbors' souls. The "fyrste dishe" comprises excerpts from the Mosaic Law, which convict man of sinfulness; the second, texts from the Gospels and Paul on Christ's redemption; the third, pronouncements on the necessity of repentance gathered from all over Scripture; and the fourth, similarly compiled pronouncements on the necessity of Christian good works. In the Psalmist's terms, the neighbors under Philemon's guidance "taste and see that the Lord is good," Philemon making sure that their diet is healthful by Protestant standards through prohibiting any admixture of good works with Christ's redemption. Again, at Lent, the penitential season of self-denial, Philemon offers his neighbors only a drink, but its salubrious blend emerges in the give-and-take of their conversation. The ingredients include a base—Philemon's exposition of penance according to its three stages of contrition, confession, and satisfaction—and a set of indispensable additives: consideration of the true manner of fasting, of Lenten ceremonies in the Church and what they mean, and of how to prepare for worthy reception of Easter Communion, all the latter in the form of Biblical citations. Becon's interpretive paradigm for the composition of *A Potation for Lent* is especially conspicuous and interesting, for his Philemon can only stomach giving his neighbors such a draught of tradition upon satisfying himself of their concomitant intake of Scriptural truth, so that they will trust to their own relation to Christ and not depend on priestly absolution in readying themselves for Easter.

Continuing in this vein, the "pleasaunt newe Nosegaye" which Philemon presents to his neighbors "for the Maye seson" draws its shaping "Semblable" from the Song of Solomon as standardly allegorized as a love song between Christ and his Church. The five goodly flowers of the nosegay are five Biblical texts which emit a sweet spiritual savor: they introduce the topics of "Unfayned Humilitie," "Pure Innocencie," "Faythfull Obedience," "Readie Assistaunce," and "Christian Charitie," which also turn out to be the names of the flowers themselves. As for the *New Year's Gift*, a plethora of proof texts that salvation comes by Christ alone, Philemon surprises his neighbors (and the reader) by confessing that he has studied his Bible scarcely at all for half a year, "so turmoyled and vexed" has he been "with the cares & troubles of thys worlde."[54] This admission on the part of the authorial persona that the

---

[54]Thomas Becon, *A New Yeres Gift*, in *Worckes: The first Part* (London, 1560) (STC 1710), fol. clxii^r; modern-spelling version in *Early Works of Thomas Becon*, ed. John Ayre, Parker Society vol. 2 (Cambridge: Cambridge University Press, 1843), p. 309.

need to practice Scripturalism increases with the sense of its difficulty in effect marks the onset of a new, appreciably more ambitious phase in Becon's prose composition. Hereafter the works in this series will address crises of one or another kind, not simply the spiritual interpretation of customary aspects of life. Accordingly, these later works will exhibit far less of the complacent amassing of Biblical texts that sustains their earlier counterparts—as, for example, the house tour episode in *A Christmas Banquet*, where Philemon rehearses his tidy rationales for his Bunyanesque interior:

> *Theophile.* I pray you, what is there written upon your parclose dore?
>
> Joh. 10   *Philemon.* The saying of Christ. I am the dore. By me if any man entreth in, he shalbe safe, and shal goe in and oute and shall find pasture. This is done to put me and my housholde in remembrance that Christ is the dore, by whom we must enter into the favoure of God, and obtaine the glory of heaven, as he himself witnesseth,
>
> Joh. 14   saying: I am the way, the trueth and the life. No man cometh to the father, but by me. *Eusebius.* This is Christenly done. What is this, that is written upon your chimney? *Philemon.* The saying of the
>
> Isa. 66   Prophet Esay. The fier of them shall not be quenched. *Christopher.* This is a terrible and hard saying. *Philemon.* I have paynted this sentence in that place, that as the other fixed upon the dore maketh me to rejoyce and to put my whole affiaunce in Christe, so this in like manner should abstere and feare me and mine from doynge evil, when by loking on this text we consider with our selves the
>
> Psal. 111   unquencheable flames of hell fier, and most grevous paynes, which are there prepared for the wicked transgressoures and breakers of
>
> Prov. 1, 9   Gods lawe. This doeth incute and bere into our harts the feare of
>
> Ecclus. 1   God, which expelleth syn, and is the beginning of wisedome. For
>
> Psal. 112   he that feareth God shall do good things, saith the Scripture, and shal have all his pleasure in the Lordes commaundements.[55]

It is not without interest that Becon's Philemon of the early works so manages his household effects as to impress them with the major kinds of sententious form detailed in Baldwin's *Treatise:* "Precepts" in the individual inscriptions, "Adages" in the antithetical pairings of inscriptions (door and chimney) which teach relationally, as Philemon explains, and "Semblables" in the correspondences between the object on which text is inscribed and the meaning of the text which is its inscription. However, the works from the later phase of Becon's Scripturalist composition exhibit a Philemon no less certain of the encompassing relevance of God's Word to every aspect and eventuality of human experience, but an expositor better able to assemble great constructs of texts on one or another topic (like poverty or patience or sorrow, analogous to Bald-

---

[55]Becon, *A Christmas Banket,* in *Worckes: The first Part,* fol. xvii[r]; Parker Society vol. 2, p. 63.

win's subdivisions) which then become his instruments for dealing with crisis. This later series includes *The Jewel of Joy* (1547–48), which asks with Job why the righteous must suffer; *The Fortresse of the Faythfull agaynst the cruel assautes of povertie and honger* (1550), which considers the dearth resulting from enclosure, rack-renting, rising prices, and a succession of bad harvests; *The Christen Knighte* (1552?), which debates how to vindicate true Protestant faith against the heretical persuasions of others and the doubts that Satan levels at one's soul; and, finally, the celebrated *Sycke Mans Salve* (1561), a book on how to make a godly end that became not only a middle-class mainstay but also a byword in Elizabethan drama as it went through fifteen editions by the century's end.[56]

Becon's return from more far-flung fronts to the domestic sphere in *The Sick Man's Salve*, there to confront the most ultimate of personal issues—how one faces one's death—is by all odds the most successful projection of a problem and a Scripturalist solution to emerge from this later phase of works. For all of their sensitivity to contemporary ills and grievances, *The Jewel of Joy, The Fortress of the Faithful,* and *The Christian Knight* are finally driven back on the interpretive plane to sheer reflex—mechanical reiteration of God's goodness, man's sinfulness, and the necessity of bearing patiently what surely must be constructive trials and corrections administered by a loving heavenly Father to his children. As Arthur B. Ferguson has argued, the resort by Tudor writers of counsel to such an interpretive strategy displays a reversion to an inherited traditional outlook, an inability to sustain the developing modern consciousness that human agency—in particular that of the national government—should formulate and implement measures to ameliorate social and cultural ills.[57] Nevertheless, what Becon was not able to achieve in the way of modern political consciousness by means of his Scripturalism he was able to adumbrate in the familial and psychological sphere through his study of Philemon's dying neighbor, Epaphroditus. The bestselling appeal of *The Sick Man's Salve* to three generations and more of English readers is not difficult to appreciate if one traces through the uneven, plausibly fitful process by which Epaphroditus comes not just to a pious acceptance of his death but, specifically, to a movement beyond self-pity and self-absorption to dispose constructively of his goods and benefits and provide for the household which will survive him. The considerable realism of the characterization achieved by Becon in portraying

---

[56]Bailey (*Becon and the Reformation*, p. 68) cites Lady Haughty's remark in Jonson's *Silent Woman*, IV.ii, "And one of them, I know not which, was cured with The Sick Man's Salve," and Wolf's claim in Marston, Jonson, and Chapman's *Eastward Ho*, V.ii: "He can tell you almost all the stories of the Book of Martyrs, and speak you all the Sick Man's Salve without book."

[57]See Ferguson, *The Articulate Citizen and the English Renaissance*, pp. xv–xvi, 19–22, 31–33, 42, 47, 57–58, 63, 68–69.

Epaphroditus is the more striking in that its means are not those of freely composed dialogue but, as always, a thickly woven texture of Biblical citations and allusions.

To illustrate Becon's accomplishments in the writing of sententious Scripturalist prose for application to a wider context of contemporary concerns than those constituted only by theological and doctrinal issues, some selective exposure to Epaphroditus will serve well. The following quotation is from his initial outpouring upon realizing that he is mortally ill; his flood of grief, bitterness, and *contemptus mundi* is borne along by a number of ejaculatory sense parallelisms from the prophet Jeremiah:

Jere. 20   O cursed be the day, wherin I was born: unhappy be the day wherin my mother brought me forth. . . . O that my mother had bene my grave her selfe, that the birth might not have come out but remayned still in her. Wherefore came I forth out of my mothers wombe to have experience of labour & sorow? Ah how sycke am I; my strength is gone. My syght fayleth me: my toung flottereth in my mouth. My hands tremble & shake for payne, I can not hold up my head for weaknes.[58]

Epaphroditus's despair at learning he must die finds its stylistic counterpart in the complete derivativeness of his sentence forms and his sentences alike from Jeremiah. But, as he comes at length to cope as well as he can with the prospect of dying, he begins to speak quite systematically in correlatives, which mirror the orderly disposition he is making for his family and servants. "First as touching my wife," he says,

Isa. 54   *albeit* I doubt not, but that God, after my departure according unto
Jer. 31   his promis, wil be unto her an husband, yea a father, a patrone and defender, and wil not suffer her to lack, if she go forth to live in his
Psal. 116   feare, to serve him, and diligently to cal on his holy name, *yet forasmuch as* God hath blessed me with worldly substance, and she is
1 Tim. 5   mine own flesh, and whosoever provideth not for his, hath denied the faith, and is worse than an infidel, I bequeth and geve unto her for tearme of her life, this house wherin I now dwel, with the appurtenances, and al the houshold stufe contained therin. Moreover
Jer. 31   as concerning my children, *albeit* I am fully perswaded that God
Psal. 115   according to his promise wil be a father unto them, and *if* they live in his fear, *then* he wil not se them lack, *yet both* the law of God, *and* of nature requireth that I shuld also have some care for them. Therfor unto my sone I bequeath the house and the land, which I have geven my wife for tearm of her life, . . . and to my ii. daughters . . . I geve

[58]Becon, *The Sycke Mans Salve*, in *Worckes: The seconde Part* (London, 1560), fol. ccxxʳ; modern-spelling version in *Works of Thomas Becon: The Catechism and Other Pieces*, ed. John Ayre, Parker Society vol. 4 (Cambridge: Cambridge University Press, 1844), pp. 93–94.

unto eche of them ii.C. pounds, of good and lawful money to be paid in the day of their mariage.

To conclude this process of disposition, Epaphroditus eventually bestows on every one of his servants "*such* portion of mony *as* shal declare some part of my thankful and wel willing hart," before taking his leave of them as a group in an exceptional concentration of correlatives: "*As* ye have hitherto faithfully, truly and ernestly served me in my life time, *even so* after my departure *so* long *as* ye tary here, shew *the like* faithfulnes, truth and honesty toward your mistres."[59] In the immediate context, Epaphroditus's correlatives become the functional expression of the well-balanced providing that he is doing for his wife, his children, and his servants, but they also hint at his resignation of himself to his Savior in deriving their ultimate Scriptural warrant and prototype from the "Semblables" in which, as Baldwin records, Christ habitually spoke. Since Epaphroditus himself, however, is portrayed as the source of these constructions which encase his Biblical allusions and echoes, his syntax most distinctly symbolizes his attainment of inner equilibrium, integrating the Word into the forms of his stipulations exactly as his creator Becon wished by his example to integrate Scripturalism into the fabric of everyday English speech and life.

Schematism and Scripturalism in Morison and Cheke

Becon's efforts to generalize Scripturalist habits of mind and modes of composition in vernacular prose concerned with the social—most specifically, the domestic—sphere were by no means a solitary undertaking in the later 1530s and 1540s, as is perhaps to be inferred from the large popular appeal of his works. In the final decade of Henry VIII's reign and even more conspicuously in the reign of Edward VI there was a swelling vein of prose of counsel, often produced under pressure from the Crown or its chief ministers, which carried Scripturalism into issues of national concern and policy. This prose has its place in the present study, first, because it shows what a permeable membrane divided religious and secular preoccupations in sixteenth-century England as well as the live interactions that resulted and, second, because it documents an increasingly firm bond of association between Hebraic sense parallelisms—conceived as the major Biblical mode of expression due to the gravitation of the age toward the Old Testament canon—and schematic sentence form of whatever provenance. This bond apparently solidified through the growth in consciousness which we have traced from Elyot through such representative writers as Udall and Baldwin: the con-

[59]Ibid., fols. ccxxxv^v–ccxxxvi^r, ccxlvi^r; Parker Society vol. 4, pp. 117–18, 134. My italics.

sciousness that certain fundamental types of syntactic design—espe-cially, antithesis, correlation, and parallelism—were potent instruments for an author who entered a transactive relation with definitely for-mulated ends in mind. Certainly such a state of consciousness was ready for extension from single sentences to the composition of connected discourse, and writers dealing with national issues are in the vanguard which leads in that direction. The earliest as well as the most prominent exponent of this type of prose of counsel was Richard—later, Sir Rich-ard—Morison.

W. Gordon Zeeveld has provided an invaluable account of Morison's career as Cromwell's secretary and as the most highly esteemed pro-pagandist for Henrician policies between 1536 and 1540, preceded by a steeping in Italian humanism at Padua as a member of Reginald Pole's circle and followed, after Cromwell's fall, by a term of service as the English ambassador to the imperial court of Charles V in the 1540s and 1550s.[60] An unusual fascination attaches to Morison, for no one of the obscurely born "new men" of the Tudor era achieved such preferment and distinction as he did on the strength of his pen; the very few who rose higher—Wolsey, Cranmer, Cromwell himself—did so by other means. Since we are concerned precisely with Morison as a writer, it is the years 1536 to 1540 that claim our attention. They open with *A Remedy for Sedition, wherein are conteyned many thynges, concernynge the true and loyall obeysance, that commens owe unto their prince and soveraygne lorde the kynge* (1536), a tract commissioned as an answer to the popular elements who had united with disaffected nobility and ecclesiastical leaders in Yorkshire to form the curious, threatening coalition which styled itself the Pilgrimage of Grace. Henry and Cromwell at the time, like historians since, were able to discern which parties to the Pilgrimage were moti-vated by which alleged grievances: the nobility, by the affront and the reduction of their power attendant on the rise of the king's "new men"; the higher clergy, by the dissolution of the monasteries and other Church "reforms"; the people, preeminently by poverty and loss of livelihood which they attributed to the enclosure for sheep grazing of formerly tilled land. Briefly, in the early autumn of 1536, it looked to the Crown like the whole north might rise in support of the Pilgrimage of Grace. Morison wrote his *Remedy for Sedition* under the urgent imperative of defusing popular motives for joining the insurrection.

In the conventional ideas and authoritarian emphases which furnish its point of departure, Morison's most celebrated tract at first seems to

---

[60]W. Gordon Zeeveld, *Foundations of Tudor Policy* (London: Methuen & Co., 1948), chaps. 1, 4, 5, 7 and 8. Also see Zeeveld's "Richard Morison, Public Apologist for Henry VIII," *PMLA* 55 (1940): 406–25. Other light is cast on other aspects of this important and com-paratively underacknowledged figure in James K. McConica, *English Humanists and Ref-ormation Politics under Henry VIII and Edward VI* (Oxford: Clarendon Press, 1965), chap. 6.

belie its claim to be a "remedy" for popular grievances. It invokes the venerable commonplace, the image of the "body politic" with its implications of fixed functions for the various members, to insist on distinguishing ranks and degrees among men and enforcing the rule of law. "A comune welthe is lyke a body, and soo lyke, that it can be resembled to nothyng so convenient, as unto that," Morison asserts:

The handes are content, the fete go: the tethe pleased, that the tongue tell the hole tale: the eare doth not desire to see, nor the eie to here. . . . A comune welth is, as I thynke, no thynge elles but a certayne nombre of cities, townes, shires, that all agre, upon one lawe, and one hed, unyted and knytte together, by thobservation of the lawes: these kept, they must nedes florishe, these broken, they must nedes perisshe. The heed muste rule, if the body woll do well: and not every man make hym selfe ruler, where only one ought to be. Thynges be not doone in this worlde by chaunce, neyther ought to be governed by rasshenesse. God maketh kynges, specyally where they reigne by successyon. God toke awaye prynce Arthure, & wold king Henry the eyght, to be our heed, and governour. Woll we be wyser than god? wol we take upon us, to know who ought to governe us, better than god? God made hym kynge, and made also this lawe, Obey your kynge. How can ye obey hym, that refuse his lawes? that seke his dishonour?[61]

What is chiefly notable in Morison's elaboration of the "Semblable" of the body politic is the pervasive extension of its motivating semantic likeness into the sentence forms of the ensuing discourse, which takes on a markedly schematic cast. Short, parallel clauses become the vehicles for the sure, darting movement of Morison's mind, either in conjunction pairs used to affirm correspondences ("The handes are content, the fete go: the tethe pleased, that the tongue tell the hole tale: the eare doth not desire to see, nor the eie to here") or in antithetical pairings which champion one alternative and disparage another ("The heed muste rule, if the body woll do well: and not every man make hym selfe ruler, where only one ought to be"). This author, moreover, lacks all diffidence as an interpreter of God's will in his Word ("God made hym kynge, and made also this lawe, Obey your kynge") and as a commentator on recent or contemporary events in the light of divine purposes, as the asymmetrically conjoined pair of declaratives on Prince Arthur and King Henry reveals. Yet, as the tract proceeds, the stylistic interest of its schematism increases. The sharply incised forms of Morison's sentences are not the exclusive instruments of his own persuasions; he is willing to use them also, in the larger implicit framework of the interpretive paradigm, to

[61][Sir Richard Morison,] *A Remedy for Sedition* (London: Thomas Berthelet, 1536), sigs. Biii^v–Biiii^r. Subsequent citations, abbreviated *RS,* are incorporated in the text. Morison's authorship of *A Remedy* was demonstrated by Charles R. Baskervill, "Sir Richard Morison as the Author of Two Anonymous Tracts on Sedition," *The Library,* 4th ser., 17 (1936): 83–87.

bring the rebels' ideas into clear focus. For the sanguine Morison, such clarity cannot possibly foster error; instead, it will cause error to be seen for what it is and rejected.

Accordingly, he applies his schematic mode of presentation to the two major mistakes he finds in the thinking of the popular party supporting the Pilgrimage. The first is the supposition that an equalizing of means will end the dissension arising from poverty and restore stability to the English commonwealth. Here Morison creates ironic *sententiae*, laced with sarcasm, to function as a *reductio ad absurdum* under the onslaught of his serial questioning:

> We love to be disceyved, we ymagyne a certayne common welthe in worde and in outward appearance, whiche if we baptyse right, and not nyck name it, we must nedes cal a comon wo. We think it is very evyll, that soo many of us be poore: we thynke it were a good worlde, if we were all riche. I pray you for a seson let it be as we desyre: let us imagine, we be al ryche. Doth it not streight folow, I am as good as he, why goeth he before, I behynde? I as ryche as he, what nedeth me to labour? They mayde as prowde as her dame, who mylketh the cowe? The fermour having no more cause to toyle then he that loketh for the rentes, who shal tyll the grounde? . . . What were more to be wayled, then suche welth, that shuld brynge eyther every man, or the mooste parte of men, to extreme confusion? [*RS*, sig. Aiii^{r-v}]

The use of parallelisms to parody the equalizing impulsions of the populace in their misguided thinking is taken by Morison far beyond Elyot's similarly formulated dismissal of commutative justice in *The Governour*. Indeed, directed syntax in *A Remedy* can reach extremes never envisaged in Elyot's precedent, as in the following denunciation of popular proposals for settlement which Morison literally casts as reversals: "No, no, take welth by the hande, and say farewell welthe, where luste is lyked, and lawe refused, where up is sette downe, and downe sette uppe" (*RS*, sig. Aii^{v}).

So far the positions of the rebels and of the defender of the Crown seem predictable enough, but as Morison addresses himself to the second mistake which he finds in the thinking of the popular party supporting the Pilgrimage, the positions begin to shift and realign: the rebels are identified with tradition and conservatism, the Crown with what are now billed as salutary new policies. It is no small tribute to Morison as a thinker and stylist that he steers his discourse through so drastic a turnabout. Its pivot is the characterization of the "order" which Henry VIII has brought to the civil administration of the realm by promoting persons who display the "vertue" that consists in "lernynge, wysedome & other pryncely qualities," for "our mooste gratiouse soveraygne lorde the kynge . . . hath evermore welle declared, that trewe nobilitie is never, but where vertue is." Thus, "in gyvyng offices, dignities & honour," the king has "well testified, that he woll all his subjectes to contende, who may obteyne mooste qualities, mooste wytte, moste vertue: and this onely to be the way to promotion, and here nobilitie to consyste" (*RS*, sig. Bi^v). The foregoing is an arrestingly modern view of a competitive civil service in which appointments go to the best qualified candidates, but the careful retention of standing terminology (the wholly redefined "nobilitie" and "vertue") and the sententious casting of vital assertions in the form that Baldwin would call "Precepts" ("trewe nobilitie is never, but where vertue is") identify the perspective of the Henrician era. By contrast, says Morison, the rebels fail to understand "nobilitie" and "vertue" as the king does, clinging instead to their class-bound preju-dices. On these, in turn, Morison undertakes to perform a reductio ad absurdum:

They be angry, that vertue shulde be rewarded, whan she cometh to men, that had no lordes to their fathers. They wyl that none rule, but noble men borne. Let them have that they require: whome towcheth this soo soore, as them selfe, and al their posteritie? What doo they leave unto theirs, whan they also take away the possibilitie of better fortune?

Agayn, what desyre shall good wyttes have, to employe them self to the knowl-ege of thynges, and to passe thother, whome slouthe woll not lette growe any higher, when good & evyl be equally estemed? What shall we nede to endevour our selfes unto, whenne what so ever we do, we must be tryed by our byrth, and not by our qualities? [*RS*, sigs. Bi^v, Bii^r]

Nonetheless, the pragmatic Morison concedes, the logic of uncon-strained opportunity does not govern popular sentiment, and the north is in revolt. The king has called all men "here to occupie theyr wyttes" to think how "the cause of rebellion may utterly be taken awaye," since it is obviously preferable "to fynde a waye, that none might have wylle to rebell, then to trusse up rebellious people." It is in this context and to this intent that Morison broaches some bold counsel that only makes sense and only even becomes conceivable within the framework of a generalized Scripturalism, as we shall see. To stop rebellion at its source, poverty must be eliminated; but the sole way to do this is to replace "evyll education" with equal access for all Englishmen to good educa-tion, which will fit them with a means of livelihood and keep them law-abiding:

For where so many lacke honest occupations, wherby al men, that can not otherwise lyve by their landes, ought to maynteyne them selves, howe canne we lacke any kynd of mischief? . . . The lacke of honest craftes, and the ha-bundauncie of ydlenes, all be it they be not the hole cause of sedicyon, yet as they brede theves, morderers, and beggers, so not a lytle they provoke men, or thynges lyke men to rebellion. There is a parte in man, whiche is named the mynde, that is of this nature, yf it be galyarde and lusty, either to do moche good, or contrary to do moche hurt. If this lacke good institution, if this be not handeled and ordered as it shulde be, men maye lacke sedition, but they can not lacke a thynge within them to styre them to sedition. This must be so taught, that there be no rebellion within our selfes, we must conquere our lustes, and compell the appetites, to obeye all such statutes, as reson and honestie shall thynke worthye to be enacted. [*RS*, sig. Dii^{r-v}]

In this passage we are taken to the core of Morison's at once religious and secular understanding of man as a striving, restless being bent on acquisition and self-advancement—a being who, on account of these drives, is most constructively socialized through education which will "handel," "order," and provide "good institution" for the "parte in man, whiche is named the mynde, that is of this nature, . . . either to do moche good, or contrary to do moche hurt." The secular dimension of Morison's outlook on human nature shows in his factual acceptance of the desire for wealth and advancement as something to be channeled for society's benefit—specifically, into public office attained by superior qualifications—and not reprehended simply as depravity or sin. Zeeveld refers Morison's frank acceptance of man as he is to the influence of Italian civic humanism, above all, Machiavelli's.[62] Yet the religious dimension of Morison's outlook on human nature comes to the fore as he proceeds to specify that a crucial component of the universal education he proposes is a grounding of the kingdom in the faith of the prince. For the nobility will not be loyal to a king from whom they dissent "in opinions of religion," and tenants and servants will adopt whatever creed their overlord does. This, then, is a paramount educational objective: "The nobles muste be of one beleve, of one fayth, of one religion, they must all agre upon one heed. The gentylmen wyll folowe, the comunes can not tary longe behynde" (*RS*, sig. Div^r). But how is such uniformity of belief to be attained? Morison's stress falls squarely and explicitly upon Scripture:

It is only Christis religion, that can make Christen men one of us love an other, as we shulde do. The preceptes of philosophie, and good education, coude make many of the Grecians, mo of the Romans, not only to forsake riches, to banyshe pleasures, & to put them selfes in a thousande perilles: but also to dye for their countrey. And can not the knowlege of the worde of god, the swete adhortations, the hyghe and assured promyses that god maketh unto us, kepe christen men from contempning the judgemente and lawes of god, from undoinge theyr countrey, from fyghtyng against theyr prince?

I can not thinke, but if Christis promyses were surely prynted in our hartes, that we shulde, and that a great sorte, testife the worde of god, to be of moche more puissaunce, then vaine fame. Goddis worde is potent, and to saye as I

---

[62]Zeeveld, *Foundations of Tudor Policy*, pp. 184–89; cf. McConica, *English Humanists and Reformation Politics*, pp. 172, 213.

thynke, almost omnipotent, if it be well handeled, and of suche as it shulde be. It is moch that good men maye do.

Men saye wel that do wel. Goddis lawes shal never be so set by, as they ought, before they be well knowen. We must fyrst lerne to kepe goddis lawes, or ever we ernestly passe of the kynges statutes. All be it he that kepeth thone, wylle also kepe thother, . . . the mynd well pourged, that is restored into the good and pure nature, that fyrst god made it in. . . . He that can fynde a better way, to avoyde sedition, than fyrste to brynge in the worde of god, which our most lerned kyng, and true lieutenant of god in this realme of England, hath holly intended this many yeres, . . . shall do ryght wel to shew it: I fynde none. [*RS*, sigs. Ei^v, Eii^{r-v}, Eiii^r]

In belaboring his insistence on a thorough grounding in Scripture as the basis of universal education in England, Morison seems at certain junctures merely to be restating contemporary commonplaces—for example, in drawing a proof text for the royal supremacy out of 1 Samuel: "The kyng is our heed, though popyshe say nay, yet lette us beleve the prophete Samuel, Lo saythe he unto kynge Saule, God hathe anoynted thee, and made thee prince of all his inheritance" (*RS*, sig. Diii^v). However, in the longest passage by far in *A Remedy for Sedition* devoted to what Scripture can do to make "the mynd well pourged, that is restored into the good and pure nature, that fyrst god made it in," this audacious propagandist for the king builds on the consonance of the Old and New Testaments in an effort to establish unconditional loyalty to the Crown as requisite to faith in Christ. First observing that "God sayth, Honour thy father and mother, Love thy neyghbour as thy selfe," Morison embarks upon the textual enchaining by which he seeks to enforce the association of England's earthly and heavenly kings:

[Gen. 4:4, 5]	Thus he sayth, but he is nothynge herde, where as sedition is. For what sacryfice can the father offre to god and his countrey, more acceptable, than to kylle with his owne handes his sonne, now no lenger his sonne, being a traytour? What act can be more worthy
[Lk. 15:19]	prayse, than the son to slee his owne father in such case? He is none of myne, saythe Christe, nor worthy to be my servaunt, that can
[Mat. 10:36, 37]	not, if juste cawse require hym so to do, forsake his father & mother to do me servyce. He is none of myne, sayth Englande, that canne not hate his father and mother, that canne not kyll them bothe, sooner than ones consente to my destruction. [*RS*, sig. Cii^r]

Such projection of Scriptural pronouncements as directives for conduct in contemporary England is not confined to *A Remedy for Sedition*, but extended and elaborated in Morison's subsequent vernacular writings. The whole of *An Invective ayenste the great and detestable Vice, Treason* (1539), written to vindicate the trials and executions in June 1538 of three near relatives of Reginald Pole, Henry VIII's self-exiled cousin, for their overt support of Pole's efforts to induce the pope to invade England,[63] is organized as a demonstration that God has shown more protective mercy toward England and Henry than he is recorded as having shown toward the children of Israel and any of their judges, prophets, or kings. Morison recapitulates incidents involving Moses, Joshua, Isaiah, Jeremiah, Ezekiel, Daniel, Job, Gideon, Judith, and, supremely, David, through sustained Biblical quotation or close paraphrase; as a result, the tract unfolds from end to end as a reading of current events through the text of Scripture. Here, to illustrate, is part of Morison's lengthy recrimination against Pole for siding with the pope instead of Henry; it makes an effective modulation into self-recrimination for treason by way of the same passages from Job that Becon would use for his dying Epaphroditus:

O Pole . . . , god be thanked, thou arte nowe a Pole of lytel water, and that at a wonderfull lowe ebbe. . . . Hast not thou moch greater cause to say, as Job dyd, than ever had Job? who ever myght better say, than thou? who ought sooner to crie than thou? Cursed be that day that I was borne in, let that daye perish, & the night also, in the which it was said, there is a knave child conceived. Let that day be turned in to darknes, . . . let never light shine upon it: . . . let not the daye that I was borne in, be rekened amonge the dayes of the yere, nor counted in the monethes. Let them that dispise that night, and curse the day, curse also the mornynge that folowed my birthe, let it loke for lyght and see none, bycause it shut not uppe the wombe that bare me. Alas whye died I not even in my birth? Why dydde not I perisshe as sone as I came out of my mothers wombe?[64]

However, Morison's *Exhortation to styrre all Englyshemen to the Defence of theyr Countrye,* which appeared late in 1539, affords a yet more flamboyant and lengthy extrapolation from the text of Scripture in order to obtain a topical reading of current events and a directive for action. In a climactic passage of too grand proportions to be conveniently cited or even excerpted, Morison rehearses in lavish detail a prophecy from the fourth book of Esdras, which involves the vanquishing of a proud eagle by a greathearted lion. He interprets this prophecy as a guarantee that King Henry will overcome the power of the pope and the eagle-bearing legions of the Holy Roman Empire, and hence as a complete sanction for the war policy that Cromwell was then pressing with a temerity that

[63]For contextual particulars, see McConica, *English Humanists and Reformation Politics,* pp. 181–82; Zeeveld, *Foundations of Tudor Policy,* pp. 228–30.

[64][Sir Richard Morison,] *An Invective ayenste the great and detestable Vice, Treason* (London: T. Berthelet, 1539) (STC 18111), sigs. Biv^v–Ci^v. Subsequent citations, abbreviated *Inv.,* are incorporated in the text.

precipitated his fall from power.[65] Beyond such bold use of the interpretive paradigm as the motive force in his prose composition, Morison's Scripturalism carries through in recurrent passages in both the *Invective* and the *Exhortation* where sentences assume the cast of Hebraic sense parallelisms to render their contents maximally telling. Here is a series of illustrations, the last being the final call to England in the *Exhortation* to take up arms against the papal armies:

Englande, haste thou no cause to folow David, to make himnes and dities of thankes unto god? When wolt thou perceyve goddis love towarde thee, as yet thou perceyvest it not? . . . Thou must confesse dette: thou canste nat denie it without thy greatte shame. All nations wonder at thy felicitie: All men knowe what jeoperdies thou hast escaped, how nighe sorowes brink thou hast ben brought: and straight howe sone thou haste ben made gladde. [*Inv.*, sigs. Aiv^v–Av^r]

Man maye seke to destroy, that god wolle have saved: but he shall doo as they that seke to make stronge rockes fall, with a knocke of theyr hedes. For as these labour folyshely, and doo but breake theyr owne braynes, so do they that thynke to pull downe a prynce, whom god hath chosen to reigne over his people. [*Inv.*, sig. Av^v]

Some truste in charyottes, some in horses, but we, in callynge uppon the lorde. God can and oft tymes doth pyne man and beast, yea, even in the myddes of all plentie. God whan his wyll is, fedeth, where no foode is to be founde. And as folyshenes, whan hym lusteth, confoundeth the wyttes of the wyse: so weakenes, where god setteth to his hande, worketh wonders, and sturdy strength standeth in no stede. [*Exh.*, sig. Bv^v]

Our countreye is refreshed, our hope fyxed in the judgement of the lorde, and our affiaunce sette faste in goddis mercy. . . . Let this yelling Egle approche towarde us, let her come with all her byrdes about her, & let a traytour cary her standard: doth not god say, her wynges shall be cut, her kyngedome waxe feble, the Lyon waxe stronge, and save the residue of goddes people, filling them full of joye and comfort, even while the worlde endureth. Let us therfore worke lustely nowe: we shall play for ever hereafter. Let us fight this one fielde with englysshe handes, and englysshe hartes: perpetuall quietnes, rest, peace, victorie, honour, welthe, all is owers. [*Inv.*, sig. Dviii^r]

We may sum up on the major characteristics of Morison's able and vigorous prose style by noting two systematic tendencies in expression within a general continuum of speechlikeness signaled by first and second person forms of address, expletives, and colloquialisms. The first is the

---

[65]For the prophetic extrapolation in its entirety, see Sir Richard Morison, *An Exhortation to styrre all Englyshemen to the Defence of theyr Countreye* (London: T. Berthelet, 1539) (STC 18110), sigs. Div^v–Dviii^r. Subsequent citations, abbreviated *Exh.*, are incorporated in the text.

more tightly schematic and insistently patterned syntax that Morison employs for analysis and argument in dealing with the rebels' demands and imputed illogicalities. This syntax serves negative or corrective functions: either it formulates errors and absurdities clearly so that they can be recognized as such, or it obtrudes with its designs to affirm and impose some notion of order. The second is the considerably looser schematism that gains the ascendancy in Morison's prose when he is projecting Scripture into a contemporary issue as a means both of understanding it and of ascertaining the course of action to be taken; it is looser schematism precisely because Morison hews closely to his Scriptural texts in his own phrasing, reproducing its Hebraic sense parallelisms in the passages he cites and conforming his own sentences to the same mode. It follows, of course, that the looser schematism of the Scripturalist passages carries active and, for Morison, constructive connotations, for it is the regular vehicle of directives from God on how to remedy sedition, proceed against traitors to the Crown, and resist the pope.

More broadly, it may be possible to infer from the stylistic connections between Scripturalism and positive proposals in Morison's writing an underlying link between his religious reformism and his social reformism; for, as Ferguson and other scholars have shown, the energetic advancement of moves against the Roman Church as an institution in England that gets underway during the period of Cromwell's influence with Henry was also accompanied by an upsurge in preaching against economic and social ills. Where Protestant persuasions were especially ardent and the Scripturalist cast of mind deeply engrained, as in the most outspoken and most eminent preacher in this reforming line, Hugh Latimer, one might find even in a Court sermon a pronouncement like the following: "The poorest ploughman is in Christ equall wyth the gretest prynce that is."[66] It was no more part of Latimer's intention than of Morison's to countenance any politically or socially radical implications of the equality of all men and women as Christian souls before the throne of God. Nevertheless in the era extending from the later years of Henry's reign through Edward's one can find the compartmentalizing of the spiritual and social realms recurrently dissolving in prose written under an impulsion to relieve or reform the ills of England as expeditiously as human agency could, by attending to God's will in Scripture. Both Morison's and Latimer's writings are infused with this Scripturalist

[66]Hugh Latimer, *The Fyrste Sermon . . . whiche he preached before the Kinges Majestie* (London: J. Daye & W. Seres, 1549) (STC 15271), sig. Dvᵛ, cited in Helen C. White, *Social Criticism in Popular Religious Literature of the Sixteenth Century* (New York: Macmillan Co., 1944), p. 123. For a perceptive discussion of Latimer's self-styling in the native, vernacular tradition of religious social criticism, see Robert L. Kelly, "Hugh Latimer as Piers Plowman," *SEL* 17 (1977): 13–26.

impulsion. Since this is so, and since Latimer's writings also reveal a division of stylistic labor between a more schematic, indicting or satiric mode of expression and a less schematic, reconstitutive one based on the Old Testament prophets (and selective use of the Pauline Epistles), the considerable affinities between his prose and Morison's may trace to a shared outlook on the Word, the world, and the most compelling linguistic linkages to be made between them.

Whether or not one opts to posit or explore connections between religious and social reformism in the era in question, it remains a fact that such connections—for whomever they may have existed—were of exceedingly brief duration in the writing of sixteenth-century English prose. The next specimen of prose of counsel to claim our attention is the tract entitled *The Hurt of Sedition, howe grevous it is to a Commune welth* (1549), which Sir John Cheke published at the time of the uprising of the Devonshire farmers and of Ket's Rebellion in Norfolk.[67] Only thirteen years had intervened since Morison had offered *A Remedy for Sedition* to ameliorate much the same grievances—agrarian unemployment and poverty, class antagonism, religious conservatism—that had actuated the Pilgrimage of Grace. Indeed, the likenesses between the two crises were recognized at the time, and Cheke's tract unmistakably echoes Morison's at one critical juncture. What had altered in the interim, however, was the disposition of the newer generation of writers, who saw "sedition"—agitation against the Crown's authority—no longer as a problem calling for solution but as criminal madness to be halted. The difference in the wording of Morison's and Cheke's titles encapsulates the change of outlook that had occurred.

Since Cheke's *Hurt of Sedition* offers a wholly conventional and uncompromising brief for submission to higher powers, its inclusion in the present discussion may need some explaining. This treatise struck its early readers as a remarkable composition, and it won its author renown as a stylist (and propagandist) for nearly a century. Cheke, a declared Protestant and younger associate of Morison's in the circle of intellectuals patronized by Cromwell, rose to distinction for his scholarship and godliness through two appointments: he was named first Regius Professor of Greek at Cambridge in 1540 before Cromwell's fall from power, and continued to hold his professorship after becoming Edward VI's tutor upon the boy king's accession in 1547. Thematic similarities between *The Hurt of Sedition* and an oration composed as a Latin exercise by Edward in the summer of 1549—both works addressing the proposition that war and rebellion attract only those ignorant or heedless of the

---

[67]The standard account is Frederic W. Russell's *Kett's Rebellion in Norfolk* (London: Longmans, Brown, Green, Longmans, & Roberts, 1859). Stanley T. Bindoff has considered why Northumberland's government reacted with such consternation to these events in *Ket's Rebellion, 1549* (London: G. Philip for the Historical Association, 1949).

consequences—make it likely that Cheke wrote to supply a vernacular model for his tutee to work from. In any event, *The Hurt of Sedition* was promptly published, and reprinted in 1569, 1576, 1577, and 1641. Gabriel Harvey's *Letter Book* terms it "a prettie elegant treatise," also the vein in which it is praised by Richard Carew in his "Epistle on the Excellencie of the English Tongue," while Thomas Wilson's *Arte of Rhetorique* and Ben Jonson's *New English Grammar* reflect admiration in their use of *The Hurt of Sedition* for several illustrations. Finally to be noted is Milton's tribute to Cheke as the crowning glory of the advent of the English Reformation—"at that time the learnedest of Englishmen, and for piety not inferior"—in *Tetrachordon*.[68]

The sustained, highly wrought schematism of the sentence forms is the most notable feature of Cheke's composition throughout, and it must have figured prominently in attracting contemporary approbation of his style. We have, accordingly, to inquire not only into the linguistic resources used to execute the design of *The Hurt of Sedition* but also into the possible reasons why it was judged so admirable. Cheke begins much as Morison had, in a posture of confrontation: you rebels stand there, he says in effect; and true subjects stand with me here. The initial representation of the two positions is handled in a remarkable display of mimetic syntax. Here is the rebels' position conveyed in a clausally spread and suspended sentence which involves itself in a thicket of embeddings scarcely to be distinguished from anacoluthon at the italicized juncture:

Ye whiche be bound by Gods worde, not to obey for feare, like men pleasers, but for conscience sake like Christians, have contrari to gods holy wil, whose offence is everlasting death, & contrari to the godly order of quietnes, set out to us, in the Kinges Majesties Lawes, the breach wherof, *is not unknowen to you taken in hande* uncalled of god, unsent by men, unfit by reason, to cast away your bounden duties of obedience, & to put on you, agaynst the magestrates, goddes office committed to the magestrates for the reformacion of your pretended injuries.[69]

In fact, the sentence form proves consistent from end to end; the spread main clause with its predicate complements is "ye . . . have . . . taken in hande . . . to cast away your bounden duties . . . & to put on you . . . goddes office. . . ." But its parts work at cross-purposes, creating confusion and loss of sense. The faltering construction mirrors Cheke's

[68]Norman Roundy Atwood, "The Influence of Ancient, Medieval, and Early Renaissance Stylistic Theory and Practice Concerning Prose upon the Style of the *Hurt of Sedition* by Sir John Cheke" (Ph.D. thesis; Columbia University, 1965; Ann Arbor: University Microfilms no. 68-8538), pp. 2–4, 58.

[69]Sir John Cheke, *The Hurt of Sedition, howe grevous it is to a Commune welth* (London: J. Daye & W. Seres, 1549) (STC 5109), sig. Aiii^{r-v}. Subsequent citations, abbreviated *HS*, are incorporated in the text.

view of rebellion. In stark contrast, Cheke states both the loyalists' position and the principal heads on which they are proceeding against the rebels in parallel constructions that develop point-for-point correspondences between constituents in respective clauses (*parison*), so that the morphology of the constituents filling parallel positions tends to coincide (*paromoion*) and the clauses tend to have the same number of elements (*isocolon*), except where the principle of making the last item in a series the largest is applied for some slight variety and formal elegance. I suspect that, in performing these concurrent manipulations, Cheke may be punning synctactically on the Greek root of the term for sentential word order (*suntaxis*)—literally, the drawing-up of soldiers in battle formation—for he makes phrasal and clausal parallelism the dominant formal feature of the sentences in which he affirms and defends the necessity of fixed order and degree. Here, successively, are Cheke's initial representation of the loyalist position, its almost literal advance against the rebel position in a sentence comprised of degree constructions, and the serial enumeration of the four kinds of offense that compound the crime of rebellion, rounded off in a final antithesis that renews the posture of opposition:

And so for oure selves, we have greate cause to thanke God, by whose religion and holy word dayly taughte us, we learne, not onely to feare him truely, but also to obey our kinge fayethfully, and to serve in our owne vocacion lyke subjectes honestlye. And as for you, we have suerlye just cause, to lament you as brethren, and yet juster cause, to rise agaynste you as ennemies, and most just cause to overthrowe you as rebelles. For . . . ye have fyrst fauted grevously agaynst God, next offended unnaturally our Sovereigne Lorde, Thirdly troubled miserably the hole commune welth, undone cruelly many an honest man, and broughte in an utter misery both to us the kynges Subjectes & to youre selves, beynge false rebelles: but yet ye pretende, that partelye for goddes cause, and partelye for the commune welthes sake, ye do aryse. [HS, sigs. Aii^v, Aiii^v]

Cheke also proceeds like Morison in schematizing his representation of the rebels' grievances as a means of exposing the errors they contain. The difference in argumentative strategy, however, reflects a basic difference in authorial outlook. Morison employed reductio ad absurdum because he perceived some human desires, not reprehensible in themselves, carried to excess, but Cheke can find nothing but fatal contradictions in the grievances alleged by the rebels of 1549. He hammers this judgment home in serial antitheses, their semantics reinforced by parallel (often mainly identical) phrasing. The following sequence is excerpted from Cheke's rehearsal and reprehension of the rebels' religious demands:

Ye rise for religion, what religion taught you that? . . . For religion ye kepe no religion, and nother wol followe the councell of Christe, nor the constancye of martyrs. Why rise ye for religion: have ye anythyng contrary to goddes boke: yea, have ye not all thynges agreeable to goddes worde? But the newe is differente from the olde, and therefore ye wyl have the olde.

Ye seke no religion: ye be deceyved, ye seke traditions. They that teach you, blynde you, that so instruct you. . . . What other religion would ye have nowe then this religion? Ye would have the bybles in againe.

Christe saythe to everyone, Serche ye the scriptures, for thei beare witnes of Christ. You saye, Pul in the scriptures, for we wyll have no knowledge of Christe. The appostles of Christe, wyl us to be so readye, that we maye be hable to geve every man an accompt of our fayeth. Ye wyll us not ones, to rede the scriptures, for feare of knowynge of our fayeth. Sayncte Paule prayeth that everye man maye encreace in knoweledge, ye desier that our knowledge might decay agayne. [*HS*, sigs. Aiv^v, Av^r, Av^v–Avi^r]

The Norfolk rebels' demand that a commonwealth be established by making the wealth of England literally common is handled in analogous fashion; antithesis, rendered more conspicuous by parallelism, serves to expose an alleged contradiction between intention and result. This is an especially revealing passage in *The Hurt of Sedition*, as Zeeveld and Ferguson have remarked,[70] because in paraphrasing part of Morison's argument against equality Cheke ends by showing how disparate in tenor and direction his own thought is from that of his predecessor. Morison, it will be recalled, envisaged equality as a leveling upward: if everyone had the same means, everyone would think himself or herself too good to work, and nothing would get done. Cheke, however, discloses his elitist class bias in only being able to imagine social and economic equality as a leveling downward. This is the nub of the contradiction he alleges: under equality, which the rebels think a desirable thing, people would in fact be worse off. Obviously not all people would be worse off, just those with more wealth to lose than to gain in an equalizing process. Significantly, to Cheke this is everyone—everyone, at least, who can find place among the "Gentylmen" in his discourse. "The other rable of Norfolke rebelles" at most "pretende a common welth," "a mervelous tanned common welth" which Cheke represents conjointly as vicious illogic and illogical vice:

If riches offend you, bycause ye would have the lyke, then thyncke that to be no commen welth, but envie to the commen welth. Envye it is, to appaire an other mannes estate, wythout the amendement of youre owne: & to have no Gentylmen, bycause ye be none youre selves, is to brynge downe an estate, and to mende none. Would ye have all a lyke riche? that is the overthrowe of laboure, and utter decaye of worke in thys realm. For who wil laboure more, if when he hath gotten more, the idell shall by lust wythout ryghte, take what

---

[70]Zeeveld, *Foundations of Tudor Policy*, pp. 222–24; Ferguson, *The Articulate Citizen and the English Renaissance*, pp. 275–76.

hym lust from hym, under pretence of equalitie wyth hym. Thys is the bringinge in of Idlenes which destroieth the commen welth, and not the amendement of laboure that maynteyneth the commenwelthe. . . . And bycause ye seke equalitie, whereby all cannot be riche, ye would that by like, whereby everye man should be poore. [*HS*, sigs. Avi^v, Aviii^r–v]

Beginning with this revealing divergence on the equality issue, Morison's *Remedy for Sedition* and Cheke's *Hurt of Sedition* pursue quite separate conceptual and stylistic courses. There is, for example, nothing in *The Hurt of Sedition* corresponding to the modulation from tighter to looser schematism in Morison's sentence forms when he undertakes to extrapolate his remedy, his constructive course of action, from the text of Scripture and consequently begins to adapt his own expression to its characteristic sense parallelisms, with the looser design as a result. Cheke's style remains tightly schematic from end to end. At first it seems strange that Scripturalism should exert so little shaping influence upon his sentence forms, for Cheke supported the free circulation of vernacular Scripture. This is not merely affirmed in *The Hurt of Sedition* but verified in his opposition to the move to Latinize and to inhibit access to the English Bible that Stephen Gardiner and other conservative clergy had mounted in Convocation in 1543. Even stronger evidence of Cheke's persuasions regarding the Scripturalist program is the fact that he began to translate the New Testament from Greek himself. This incomplete effort (it survives as an English version of the Gospel of Matthew, from which a few leaves have been lost, plus half of the first chapter of Mark) is thought to date from about the time of *The Hurt of Sedition*—that is, around 1550.[71] Hence it is worth considering how Cheke proceeds in incorporating his frequent Biblical references into his prose and why there is little formal resemblance between the sentences of the original and his own.

Not unlike Love and Fisher in earlier eras, Cheke deals with Scripture by citing or paraphrasing brief, discontinuous segments, which he places within syntactic envelopes of his own fashioning. Thus, despite the great frequency with which he adverts to the Bible, it is not permitted, as it were, to speak in its own terms; Cheke's own sentence forms become a gridwork through which the Scripture is filtered. Two brief illustrations follow; for each, after italicizing the elements of direct quotation, I have added the readings of the relevant texts from the Great Bible:

If ye seke what the old doctours saye, yet loke what Christe the oldeste of all sayeth, for he sayeth *before Abraham was* made, *I am*. If ye seke the truest waye,

---

[71]In the introduction to his edition, *The Gospel According to Saint Matthew and Part of the First Chapter of the Gospel According to Saint Mark, Translated into English from the Greek, With Original Notes*, by Sir John Cheke (Cambridge, Eng.: J. & J. J. Deighton, 1843), James Goodwin states: "With respect to the date of the translation, it was probably made by Cheke about the year 1550" (p. 9).

he is *the* very *truth,* if ye seke the rediest waye, he is *the* verye *waye,* if ye seke everlastynge lyfe, he is *the* very *life.* [*HS,* sig. Av^{r-v}]

Compare John 8:58: "Jesus sayd: Verely verely I saye unto you: ere Abraham was borne, I am"; John 14:6: "Jesus sayeth unto him: I am the waye and the trueth and the lyfe."

Remembre ye not, that if ye come nyghe to God, he wyll come *nyghe unto* you? If then ye go from God, he wyll go from you. Doth not the Psalme saye, he is *holy wyth the holy,* and *with the* wycked man he is *froward.* Even as he is ordred of men he wil order them agayne. If ye would folow hys wyll, and *obaye* hys *commaundementes,* ye shold eate the fruites of the earth sayth the Prophet, if not, *the sword* shal devoure you. [*HS,* sig. Bii^v]

Compare Psalm 145:18: "The Lorde is nye unto all them that call upon him, yee all soch as call upon hym faythfully"; Psalm 18:25, 26: "With the holy thou shalt be holy, and with a perfecte man thou shalt be perfecte. With the cleane thou shalt be cleane, and with the frowarde thou shalt lerne frowardenes"; Jeremiah 11:4, 8; 12:12: "Obay my voyce, and do accordinge to my commaundements. . . . Yet they obayde not, nor enclynde theyr eare . . . : therfore . . . The destroyers come over the heeth every waye, for the sweard of the Lorde doth consume from the one ende of the land to the other, and no flessh hath reste."

Comparison of the wording of the Great Bible with Cheke's makes clear what has happened in the process of transposing the Hebraic sense parallelisms which exert their period fascination upon him: the Scripture is assimilated to Cheke's schematics rather than the reverse, unless—as in the case of the conflation of Psalm 18:25, 26—the cast of the quoted sentence and the larger design of Cheke's passage coincide. The deformation undergone by Scriptural texts provides a vital index to the imperiousness of the compositional strategy applied in *The Hurt of Sedition,* for it is, I think, neither ineptitude nor hypocrisy that interferes with the attainment of a genuinely Scripturalist prose style by so committed an advocate of the vernacular Bible as Cheke. Rather, I think it is precisely because he takes an aspect of the more generalized Scripturalist literary program—the authorial side of its interpretive paradigm—with such extreme seriousness that he is propelled beyond replication of sense parallelisms into the avid cultivation of linguistic identity that characterizes the schematic type of directed syntax. *The Hurt of Sedition* is an extraordinarily overmastering composition. It is devoted throughout to the objective not simply of inducing some one interpretation of the crisis at hand but, more strenuously, of reinterpreting everything in the outlook that rebellious eyes train upon the world and doing so in a way that at once convicts and persuades the rebel of being wrong. To gauge the stylistic stridency that Cheke attains principally by schematic means, we may consider the following passage on the providence of God:

Ryches and inheritaunce be goddes providence, and gyven to whom of hys wysdome, he thyncketh good. To the honest, for the encreace of their godlines, to the wycked for the heapyng up of their damnacion, to the simple, for a recompence of other lackes, to the wise, for the greater settyng out of Gods goodnes: why wyl youre wysdome nowe stoppe goddes wisdome, and provide by your lawes that God shal not enrich them, whom he hath by prudence, appoynted as him liketh? God hath made the pore, and hath made them to be poore, that he myght shew his might, and set them aloft when he listeth, for such cause as to hym semeth: and plucke downe the riche, to hys state of povertie, to shew his power, as he disposeth. Why do not ye then being pore bere it wisely, rather then by lust seke ryches unjustly? [*HS*, sigs. Aviii^v–Bi^r]

The syntactic dynamic in this passage works through its early parallelisms, and their constituent identity, to suggest that God treats everybody fairly by treating everybody in equivalent fashion; similarly the parallelisms reinforcing the binary antitheses toward the end of the quotation evoke a sense of evenhanded justice. Yet the powerful pull of the syntax in the direction of these associations is remarkable, for the semantics of the passage taken alone bespeaks an arbitrary, voluntaristic God whose demonstrations of "might" and "power" are entirely and only his own business.

In reflecting upon the admiration which *The Hurt of Sedition* commanded in its time, we can find an immediate reason in its highly wrought style, its conversion of the resources of language to display, for the response proper to such effects is a kind of wonder. But Cheke's style will bear further probing into what we are being made to wonder at. Certainly we are offered the spectacle of the lashed-up energy of natural language—in particular, exploitation of options in sentential conjunction that recursively proliferate units of structure and suffuse them with reinforcements of its identity condition through various consonances of form and sound. But we are also offered a schematic prose that can be made an endlessly convertible instrument of meaning: serial parallelisms that can function, for example, as a list of accusations against the rebels or as a vindication of the distributive justice of God's providence. To be sure, such a promiscuous application of schematic design will and did cloy with time, but it seems to me a necessary exercise of critical imagination to try to reintuit the principal factors that led to the Euphuistic vogue. A sense of exuberant potential and creativity in the formal fashioning of English sentences was one such factor, and a sense of the semantic interconvertibility of these formal means was another. Cheke, writing in 1549, must have contributed toward strengthening the latter sense at a time when recursive schematism still seems to have been weighted more toward negative (denunciatory or satiric) associations than toward positive ones. Yet another factor, I believe, was the growth through the middle decades of the sixteenth century of a distinctly rhetorical sense of the utility of identity or likeness relations in aiding the understanding and the memory. Among works which we have examined, this sense has been most explicitly registered and related to the generalized Scripturalist literary program by William Baldwin in his remarks on the "Semblables" by which Christ in his parables so effectively taught. The force of such a recognition helps us to make sense of Euphuism as an integrated set of linguistic functions centering on the relations of likeness and identity, and ranging from the phonological level (assonance, alliteration, rhyme) through the syntactic level (various correspondent schemes) to the semantic level (similes—especially ones involving implications from the realm of nature to human conduct).

As one might expect from a translator of the Gospels, Cheke in *The Hurt of Sedition* contributes in this third sense to the heightening of appreciation for the appeal of "Semblables" to the mind and memory. Besides frequent incidental occurrences of similes and analogies, there is a sustained and conspicuous passage in which Cheke develops a number of analogies between animal behavior and human behavior to enforce the ironic (and presumably instructive) recognition that, even if the brutes are set as a norm of behavior for men, men will fall below this norm as rebels. The pertinent section of this passage reads as follows:

For we se that the shepe wyll obaye the sheperd, and the nete be ruled by the nete herde, and the horse wyll knowe his keper, and the dogge wilbe in awe of hys master: and every one of them wil fede ther, and of that, as his keper and ruler doth appoynt him, and goe from thens, and ther, as he is tobydden by hys ruler. And yet we have not hearde of, that any herd or company of these, hath risen agaynst their herdeman, or governoure, but be alwayes contented not onely to obeye them, but also to suffer them to take profit of theym. And we se furdermore, that all herdes, and all sorts, be more eger in fersnes against all kyndes of strangers, then they be against their owne rulers: and wil easlier offend hym, who hath not hurte theym, then touche theyr ruler who seketh profet on theym. But ye that ought to be governed by your magestrates, as the herdes by the herdman, and ought to be lyke a shepe to your kynge, who oughte to be lyke a shepard unto you, even in that time when your proffit was soughte, and better redresse was intended than your upstirres and unquietnes coulde optaine, have beyond the crueltie of all beastes fouly risen agaynste your ruler, and shewe your selves worthy to be ordered lyke beastes, who in kynd of obedience wyll falle from the state of menne. A dogge stoppeth when he is beatten of hys master, not for lake of stomake, but for natural obedience: you beynge not striken of your head, but favoured, not kepte downe, but soccoured, and remedyed by lawe, have vyolentlye agaynste lawe not onely barcked lyke beastes, but also bitten like hel houndes. What? Is the myschiefe of sedition, other not knowen unto you, or not feared? [*HS*, sigs. Bvi^r–Bvii^r]

It seems to me not unlikely that we have in the foregoing passage a Chekian counterpart to an extended "Semblable" or parable, although, once again, the resemblance to a Gospel (or, for that matter, a secular) prototype cannot be pursued beyond the homely materials and the express analogizings because of the characteristically intrusive authorial presence and its directed syntax, both working to enforce the moral all the while that the exemplum is in the telling. Nevertheless, Cheke clearly demonstrates his sense of the serviceability of simile and analogy as well as schematism in writing that pursues the interpretive objectives of vernacular prose of counsel to their fullest. Subsequent major steps, which we will trace in chapter 6, involve the integration of simile and schematism with Scripturalism in a comprehensive design for prose style.

6. Prose in the Later Half of the Sixteenth Century: The Belletristic Circuit—From Scripturalism to Euphuism, and Back

CICERO AND SCRIPTURE: ASCHAM'S ACCOMMODATION

The four sections of chapter 6—discussions of Roger Ascham, Sir Thomas Wilson, George Pettie, and John Lyly—will bring this study to a close by tracing the implications of the increasingly belletristic motives that become discernible in the generalized Scripturalist program for English prose of counsel as the sixteenth century continues on its course. As I have declared previously and now propose to show, the vogue of Euphuism constitutes the first clear terminus of the belletristic motives of this program. Yet before any connection between Scripturalism in a generalized form and Euphuism can seem intelligible, let alone plausible, two pivotal figures require some close attention. They are Roger Ascham and Sir Thomas Wilson.

From the perspectives of current criticism, it may seem odd to the point of perversity to postulate a relation between Ascham and even the generalized Scripturalist program for prose which I have been discussing, for important essays by Thomas M. Greene and Alvin Vos have reaffirmed the correctness of Lawrence V. Ryan's characterization of Ascham's style and outlook in his prior critical biography: with them Ascham registers as the first full-fledged exponent of what Vos terms "English Ciceronianism."[1] Some of the possible oddity in proposing Ascham for consideration as a Scripturalist recedes, however, when we reckon in turn with the extensive overlap between what I have been calling the interpretive or transactive relation between writer and reader

---

[1]See Lawrence V. Ryan, *Roger Ascham* (Stanford: Stanford University Press, 1965), pp. 25, 34, 147–49, 243, 260–67, 277–86; Thomas M. Greene, "Roger Ascham: The Perfect End of Shooting," *ELH* 36 (1969): 609–25; and Alvin Vos's three essays, "The Formation of Roger Ascham's Prose Style," *SP* 71 (1974): 344–70; "Form and Function in Roger Ascham's Prose," *Philological Quarterly* 55 (1976): 305–22; and " 'Good Matter and Good Utterance': The Character of English Ciceronianism," *SEL* 19 (1979): 5–18.

and Greene's and Vos's representations of Ascham's brand of Cicero-nianism. For his part, Greene insists on the importance of "a continuum properly aligning style, thought, judgment, and action" that "underlies page after page" of Ascham. Accordingly, he contests the categorization (one as old as Bacon) that lumps Ascham with Continental apes of Cicero who cultivated manner at the expense of matter in prose composition. In Greene's words, "the real risk Ascham runs is not the empty love of pure style but rather the apparent naiveté of entangling style too much with all that it is not," for he anticipated "a calamity which is real and modern—the gap between language and feeling, the 'devorse betwixt the tong and the hart' " which we have also seen Udall concerned in his way to prevent:

Ascham thought, as Bacon did not, that the activity of choosing words sharpened the judgment to enable it better to choose actions. The series of manifold tiny decisions required to write a paragraph resembles, he thought, the larger decisions required to act judiciously in society. . . . The line between the morality of proper conduct and the esthetics of verbal composition was not, for him, very well-defined. Barbarous writing involved something like moral failure.[2]

Vos's work on Ascham's English Ciceronianism has similarly probed its impassioned insistence on the indisseverability of speech and style from religious, political, and social values. Yet, curiously enough, in reviewing Cicero's key conception of oratory as effectuating the merger of wisdom (*sapientia*) with eloquence through a freely inquiring mentality and a frank receptivity to diverse forms of excellence in the Greek philosophers and rhetoricians who were his joint models, Vos finds just these traits of mind lacking in Ascham. His English Ciceronianism substitutes "right judgment in doctrine" and "a reforming zeal in literature and religion" for Cicero's intellectual and speculative orientation, while also enjoining a set design for prose style in place of Cicero's eclectic utilization of models and effects.[3] This set design, which Vos views as the stamp of the influence of Sturm, Ascham's German humanist colleague, "is given to a striking degree of parallelism":

More exactly, it is a style leaning heavily on isocolon (corresponding members having similar length) and parison (corresponding members having similar structure), frequently reaching for antithesis (as a *schema verborum*), and on occasion rather liberal with paromoion (corresponding members having similar sound).[4]

As one reads Greene's and Vos's sympathetic and respectful discussions of Ascham as a thinker and writer, it becomes evident, nonetheless, that

[2]Greene, "Ascham: The Perfect End of Shooting," pp. 614–17.
[3]Vos, " 'Good Matter and Good Utterance,' " pp. 6–16.
[4]Identical in Vos, "The Formation of Roger Ascham's Prose Style," p. 346; "Form and Function in Roger Ascham's Prose," pp. 307–8.

the term "English Ciceronianism" as defined by Ascham's stylistic views and practice occasions genuine dissatisfaction and perplexity of a kind. The classification leaves us confronting a pair of serious questions, which may be phrased thus: (1) Can we somehow account for the aspects of Ascham's Ciceronianism that so markedly modify its original as to constitute, finally, a departure from Cicero? (2) Why, among the features of Ciceronian sentence form that Ascham prescribes for imitation, does he fix upon the ones he does as hallmarks of eloquence? What I propose to argue is that the continuing focus of the present study on the creative potentiality of sentential conjunction, together with reference to the native English context of prose writing that sought to develop secular counterparts to Scripturalism, will materially aid our understanding of the stylist of *Toxophilus* and *The Schoolmaster*.

Upon its publication in 1545, *Toxophilus, The Schole of Shootinge conteyned in Two Bookes*, announced itself as an unequivocal specimen of English prose of counsel and as a brilliantly self-aware period piece—one as brilliant, moreover, in its anticipations as in its recapitulations of stylistic attainments in vernacular composition. Among the diverse strains in its literary inheritance, the most readily apparent resemblances are to several of Elyot's works—above all, *The Governour*. In probing these resemblances and remarking that Ascham's first work appeared in the same year as Elyot's last (followed by Elyot's death in 1546), we sense in *Toxophilus* an implicit claim by an aspiring Elisha to a secular English equivalent of Elijah's mantle. *The Governour* seems clearly to prefigure Ascham's dual dedication of *Toxophilus* to King Henry and "To all Gentle men and yomen of England," as a work "pleasaunt for theyr pastyme to rede, and profitable for theyr use to folow, both in war and peace." For *Toxophilus* answers extensively to the defining features of Elyot's prose of counsel in *The Governour*: there is the same adulatory patriotism in recounting Henry's greatness, the same declared commitment to educating the classes of youth who will supply the Crown's civil service, the same burden of complaint that learning and the learned are disregarded in England, the same Christian Platonic assumptions that increased knowledge will breed increased virtue, and the same pride in advancing the literary status of the vernacular by writing "this Englishe matter in the Englishe tongue, for Englishe men."[5]

In matters of substance and presentation that impinge upon style, moreover, Elyot's precedent is evident in *Toxophilus*. The suggestion by several scholars that Ascham's work may be a deliberate outgrowth of

[5]Roger Ascham, *Toxophilus*, in *English Works*, ed. William Aldis Wright (Cambridge: Cambridge University Press, 1904), pp. ix, xii, xviii; modern-spelling text in *The Whole Works of Roger Ascham*, ed. J. A. Giles (London: John Russell Smith, 1864), Vol. II, Part 2, pp. 1, 4. Subsequent citations, abbreviated *Tox.*, will supply page references to Wright's and Giles's editions, in that order, and will be incorporated in the text.

the last chapter of book 1 of *The Governour*—"That shotynge in a long-bowe ys the pryncipall of all other exercyses"—accrues plausibility from Ascham's story of having asked Elyot whether he knew anything "concernynge the bryngynge in of shootynge in to Englande: he aunswered me gentlye agayne, that he had a worcke in hand which he nameth, *De rebus memorabilibus Angliae*," and that it would document the Saxon king Vortiger's conquest of the native Britons by means of the then "straunge and terrible" new weapon, the "bowe and shaftes" (*Tox.*, p. 53; II:2, 77–78).[6] But beyond Elyot's presumed involvement in Ascham's choice of his main subject, the composition of *The Governour* appears to have showed Ascham how to assemble classical and Biblical histories as teaching examples of the use that princes and commonwealths have made of shooting. Not only does he select and organize his material like Elyot, he also styles it like Elyot, injecting authorial commentary into the sequences of exempla in *Toxophilus* by the same syntactic means used in *The Governour:* appositives, parentheticals, and nonrestrictive relative clauses. I have italicized the onset of conjunctively arising commentary elements in the following characteristic presentation of exempla from *Toxophilus:*

> God, when he promyseth helpe to the Jewes, he useth no kynde of
> Deut. 32 speakyng so moch as this, *that he wyll* bende his bowe, *and* dye his shaftes in the Gentiles blood: *whereby it is manifest,* that *eyther* God wyll make the Jewes shoote stronge shotes to overthrowe their enemies: *or at leeste* that shotinge is a wonderful mightie thing in warre, *wherunto* the hygh power of God is lykened. David in the Psalmes
> Psal. 7, calleth bowes the vessels of death, *a bytter thinge, and* in an other
> 63, 75 place a myghty power *and other wayes mo, which I wyll* let passe, bycause everye man readeth them daylye: *But yet* one place of scripture I must nedes remembre, *which is* more notable for the prayse
> 1 Regum. 31 of shoting, then any that ever I red in any other storie, *and that is,* when Saul was slayne of the Philistians, *being* mightie bowmen, *and* Jonathas *his sonne* with him, *that was* so good a shoter, *as the scripture sayth,* that he never shot shafte in vayne, *and yat* the kyngdome after
> 2 Regum. 1 Saules deathe came unto David: the first statute and lawe that ever David made after he was king, was this, *that* al the children of Israel shulde learne to shote, according to a lawe made many a daye before that tyme for the setting out of shoting, *as it is written (sayeth Scripture)* in libro Justorum, *whiche booke* we have not nowe: *And thus* we se plainelye what great use of shoting, and what provision even from the begynnynge of the worlde for shotyng, was amonge the Jewes. [*Tox.*, pp. 40–41; II:2, 61–62]

---

[6]On Ascham's putative indebtedness to Elyot, see Major, *Sir Thomas Elyot and Renaissance Humanism*, p. 25; and Ryan, *Roger Ascham*, pp. 62–66.

While the foregoing passage shows Ascham's assimilation of Elyot's syntactic techniques for simultaneously narrating and interpreting "historie" joined with a Scripturalist concern in grounding his subject, it also reflects one thoroughgoing difference between the youthful styles of the two writers: Ascham was never the aureator or neologizer that Elyot briefly was. Yet it is arguable that Elyot's steady implementation of a more idiomatic, even colloquial mode as well as a more binary and schematic form of expression as he sought to fashion a literary enterprise based on generalized Scripturalism secured for English prose precisely the position from which Ascham himself began to write. For *Toxophilus* evidently harks back to *The Governour* in the particulars of subject, compositional method, and directed syntax for narrative which we have just noted. It also appears to have drawn the prototype for its Platonic dialogue form from *Of the Knowledge Which Maketh a Wise Man*[7] and its strongest directives for style and authorial self-consciousness from *The Castle of Health*, the most overtly Scripturalist of Elyot's works.

Both the dedicatory letter to the king and the one to the gentlemen and yeomen of England link the choice of English for the writing of *Toxophilus* with Ascham's professed motive of offering healthful counsel and wholesome ministration in the same way that these concerns are linked in the analogue of the apologia for vernacular Scripture which Elyot developed in the preface to the third edition of *The Castle of Health*. But the reduplicated linkage of linguistic and moral concerns in the prefatory material of the two works is reinforced by Ascham's adoption of the later Elyot's binary schematics to impress on his readers what he intends to promote and what to discourage in treating the neglected subject of shooting with the longbow. Henry is given a sententious distillation of Ascham's proposed subject as "a pastime, honest for the minde, holsome for the body, fit for everi man, vile for no man, using the day and open place for Honestie to rule it, not lurking in corners for misorder to abuse it." Elegantly offsetting the predominance of antithesis in shaping his statement of purpose to the king, Ascham employs another binary sentence form, a conjunction pair, to convey reassurance about his comprehensive purposes in *Toxophilus*: "Therefore I trust it shal apere, to be bothe a sure token of my zeele to set forwarde shootinge, and some signe of my minde, towardes honestie and learninge" (*Tox.*, p. x; II:2, 2–3). However, the schematic strategy in Ascham's declaration of his intentions to the gentlemen and yeomen of England re-

---

[7]That the dialogue form of *Toxophilus* (like that in *Of the Knowledge Which Maketh a Wise Man*) is conceived after a Platonic model becomes clearest at the close of book 1 and the beginning of book 2 where, respectively, Philologus employs the method of elenchus to expose a contradiction in Toxophilus's assertions, and Philologus formally assumes the role of questioner—by agreement, a fixed one in Socratic dialectic. See *English Works*, ed. Wright, pp. 63–72; *Whole Works*, ed. Giles, II:2, pp. 89–101.

mains relentlessly—and recursively—antithetical. The antitheses enact his concern not simply to articulate a running distinction between good and bad uses of one's time and energies but to impart a stabilizing, therapeutic balance to his readers' whole outlook:

My minde is, in profitynge and pleasynge every man, to hurte or displease no man, intendyng none other purpose, but that youthe myght be styrred to labour, honest pastyme, and vertue, and as much as laye in me, plucked from ydlenes, unthriftie games, and vice: whyche thing I have laboured onlye in this booke, shewynge howe fit shootyng is for all kyndes of men, how honest a pastyme for the mynde, howe holsome an exercise for the bodye, not vile for great men to use, not costlye for poore men to susteyne, not lurking in holes and corners for ill men at theyr pleasure, to misuse it, but abiding in the open sight and face of the worlde, for goodmen if it fault, by theyr wisdome to correct it. [*Tox.*, p. xiii; II:2, 5–6]

From the outset, the pronounced schematic styling of all essential content and emphases in *Toxophilus* bears witness to Ascham's peculiarly intense conception of the transactive paradigm, the mutual collaboration to get at a constructive sense, that binds the author and reader of a text in the Scripturalist literary enterprise. Ascham's first vernacular work is already fully informed with the conviction that style should both be and do specific things: it should be morally consonant and transparent, and it should transmit these qualities. But is such transmission really possible? And, if so, how is it achieved? In determining to answer both questions with a positive demonstration, he began where Elyot had left off in *The Castle of Health*, by representing the vernacular writer's role as a secular counterpart to the cure of souls and making literal stylistic application of the principle that the physician works by contraries to restore the equilibrium identified with the state of health:

Ar. Pol. 7   A pastyme, saith Aristotle, must be lyke a medicine. Medicines stande by contraries, therfore the nature of studying considered, the fittest pastyme shal soone appeare. . . . If . . . a man woulde have a pastyme holesome and equall for everye parte of the bodye, pleasaunt and full of courage for the mynde, not vile and unhoneste to gyve ill example to laye men, not kepte in gardynes and corners, not lurkynge on the nyght and in holes, but evermore in the face of men, either to rebuke it when it doeth ill, or els to testifye on it when it doth well: let him seke chefely of all other for shotynge. [*Tox.*, p. 18; II:2, 33–34]

Accordingly, Ascham's summation in praise of shooting as a pastime is couched in binary schematics that affirm the principle of working "by the contrarye, lykewyse as all physicions do alowe in physike," to draw the youth of England from "suche unlawfull games" as the nocturnal pastimes of dicing and card playing to the exercise of archery "upon the daye light, in open syght of men, havynge such an ende as is come to by conning, rather then by crafte: and so shulde vertue encrease, and vice decaye. For contrarye pastimes, must nedes worke contrary mindes in men, as all other contrary thinges doo" (*Tox.*, p. 30; II:2, 48–49).

But in other comments on aspects of his directed syntax in *Toxophilus*, Ascham far outstrips the stylistic self-consciousness of Elyot. What he has to say in particular about what Kenneth Burke termed the "dynamic of assent" created by certain binary schemes predates by a couple of years what Baldwin had to say about the antithetical cast of "Proverbs and Adages" and the correlative cast of "Parables, Examples, and Semblances" in his *Treatise of Morall Philosophie* (see the third section of chapter 5). According to the eponymous spokesman of Ascham's work, "comparisons, sayth learned men, make playne matters" because they formulate the "difference" by which we discern "honest thynges . . . from unhonest thinges." Toxophilus is personally "loth" to compare "the natures of shooting and gamming, whiche is good, and which is evyl," for to his mind the likeness which should motivate comparison has its vanishing point in their utter difference: "I thinke ther is scarse so muche contrariousnes, betwixte hotte and colde, vertue and vice, as is betwixte these ii. thinges: for what so ever is in the one, the clean contrarye is in the other." Yet he consents to pursue a presumptive minimal likeness "not bicause there is any comparison at al betwixte them, but therby a man shal se how good the one is, how evil the other" (*Tox.*, pp. 22–23; II:2, 39–40).

The syntax and semantics of conjunction provide appreciable confirmation for the cognitive force which Ascham attributes to antithesis, correlatives, and conjunction pairs and seeks to harness for his purposes. It is a fundamental fact of the way we process connected speech and, even more, the way we read a text that we attune ourselves to occurrences of closure—most obviously, at the ends of sentences. Our attunement is a good deal finer than a simple on-off switch, for we distinguish reliably between broken-off sentences (even at ends of utterances or texts) and completed sentences. Binary connectives become instrumental by managing our attunement to closure as a two-step process: the first member focusing the opening of the construction, the second focusing its completion, all the while keeping our expectations under sure direction and control. To illustrate, here are some first members of binary schemes from earlier quotations; the italics clarify their function in context as openers of form, eliciters of expectation:

it shal apere, to be *bothe* a sure token of my zeele to set forwarde shootinge
evermore in the face of men, *either* to rebuke it when it doeth ill
not lurking in holes and corners
For what so ever is in *the one*

And here are the schemes' second members, whose italicized connectives supply the closure the reader has been primed to expect:

and some signe of my minde, towardes honestie and learninge
or els to testifye on it when it doth well
but abiding in the open sight and face of the worlde
the clean contrarye is in *the other*

In addition, serial conjunction of words, phrases, and clauses offers a different but related means of arousing and satisfying expectations of sentential closure. This Ascham recognized clearly, as the frequency of triads and larger multiples shows—for example, "labour, honest pastyme, *and* vertue," "ydlenes, unthriftie games, *and* vice," "*not* vile and unhoneste to gyve ill example to laye men, *not* kepte in gardynes and corners, *not* lurkynge on the nyght and in holes, *but* evermore in the face of men." Closure in serial constructions is forestalled by suspended intonation (or the comma which by this era functions as a typographical equivalent), so that the reader's expectation is propelled forward to the terminal element signalled expressly by *and* or *but*.

Although the degree of linguistic intuition raised to stylistic self-consciousness that is attested in the density of Ascham's binary and serial conjunctions is remarkable in itself, these by no means exhaust the evidence of his awareness of the workings of conjunctive sentence form or his determination to manipulate this major resource of style for his particular purposes. Ascham's prose is energized by an extraordinarily keen sense of the identity relation which is required to motivate any conjoining of elements in natural language (see the second section of chapter 1). We have registered something of this sense in Toxophilus's declaration that comparisons, even ones that dissolve in difference, "make playne matters" by localizing points of sameness and difference in what is being compared, and, hence, triggering recognition of the nature and extent of the identity involved. But a still more revealing and self-conscious passage on syntax and style occurs in the second prefatory letter to *Toxophilus*, where Ascham develops his notion that writing is like archery as a species of activity: both are oriented toward hitting a target. An introductory syntactic example distinguishes the point of comparing two things, "whether shuld be better then the other," from the point of conjoining two things, so that "the one shoulde be alwayes an ayde and helpe for the other": a writer should know how to apply these discrete uses of the identity relation (*Tox.*, p. xiii; II:2, 5). Ascham then proceeds to a virtuoso application of his own, sustaining his comparison of writing and archery (announced in the italicized correlative construction of the first sentence following) through a parallel series of conjunctions (the sentences beginning "Some," "Other," and "Other"). These are the vehicle for the identity relation which is the overall point of the passage:

In our tyme nowe, whan every manne is gyven to knowe much rather than to lyve wel, *very many do write,* but after suche a fashion, *as very many do shoote. Some* shooters take in hande stronger bowes, than they be able to mayntayne. This thyng maketh them *summtyme,* to outshoote the marke, *summtyme* to shote far and perchaunce hurte summe that looke on. *Other* that *never* learned to shote, *nor yet* knoweth good shafte *nor* bowe, wyll be *as* busie *as* the best, *but* suche one commonly plucketh doune a syde, *and* crafty archers which be agaynst him, will be *bothe* glad of hym, *and also* ever ready to laye *and* bet with him: it were *better* for suche one to sit doune *than* shote. *Other* there be, whiche have verye good bowe and shaftes, and good knowledge in shootinge, *but* they have bene brought up in suche evyl favored shootynge, that they can *neyther* shoote fayre, *nor* yet nere. Yf any man wyll applye these thynges togyther, he shal *not* se *the one farr differ from the other.* [*Tox.,* pp. xiii, xv; II:2, 5, 8. My italics]

What is chiefly remarkable about this passage is the steady pressure brought to bear by Ascham's conjunction pairs, serial conjunctions, and correlatives (indicated by italics) in order to enforce and elaborate the likeness between the dynamic of a sentence and the trajectory of an arrow: each requires the most carefully calculated and precisely executed movements on the part of its launcher if it is to hit its mark. Clearly, for Ascham, the writer's careful calculation and precise execution attach to the heightening of formal linguistic likeness, in the creation of parallelism and concomitant sound similarities, to keep on target in the reader's perceptions and memory the syntactic and semantic workings of coordinate structure which are the mainstay of the moral design of his prose. Indeed, at major transitions in his discourse—in summations of prior discussion or introductions of new topics—the forms of Ascham's sentences regularly evince a schematism raised to the level of total design, as in the declaration of intent cited earlier, whose higher- and lower-order binary responses unfold as follows in surface structure:

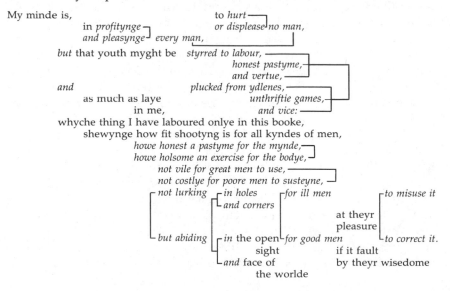

This sentence and numerous others resembling it have been referred by Vos to the ideal for prose composition which Ascham esteemed and emulated in Cicero: a style notable for parallelisms wrought to the exactitude of *parison* and *isocolon*, a style prolific in antithesis at one end of the sound-meaning continuum and in *paromoion* at the other. Vos has also defined Ascham's English Ciceronianism in terms that carry causal implications for the schematism of Ascham's own prose, arguing that he understood Cicero's insistence on fusing eloquence with wisdom to mean that a writer's sentence forms should so manipulate a reader's linguistic consciousness as to compel the continual making of relative judgments regarding the subjects of discourse. According to Vos, once Ascham arrived at this identification of style with what I have been calling directed syntax, he was never able to conceive Cicero's eloquence in any other terms than the flamboyant Gorgiastic patterns which the older orator himself criticized in reflecting upon his youthful productions.[8]

It will be obvious that Vos's account of the peculiar features and specific implications of Ascham's English Ciceronianism and my account of essentially the same phenomena—stylistic self-consciousness impelling the systematic use of schematics to enforce a jointly moral and rhetorical point—stand simply as alternative critical approaches unless some basis emerges for preferring one to the other. For all of the real merits of Vos's approach to Ascham as an English Ciceronian, it seems to me to involve a major blind spot in the failure to find any rationale, only grounds for reprehension, in binary recursions that produce what Vos says "first appears to be mere redundancy, but which in fact is a more complex fault of style." Commenting on the sentence just parsed above in terms of its formal responsions, he complains that "Ascham's tendency toward schematization can be a bane":

In this period . . . the second member of each pair adds little to the import of the first. If Ascham pleases everyone, he need not add that he displeases no one; if he stirs youth to virtue, obviously he restrains them from vice. . . . Although antithesis may be useful even when it merely provides an added emphasis (as it does here), it loses some of its functional value. Without appreciably sharpening meaning, the second member merely rephrases the first in the negative, parallelism becoming virtually an end in itself.[9]

Just as surely as Sturm and Ascham limited what they could register of the range and variety in Cicero's style by the set of preconceptions which they brought to their reading, so, too, Vos's evaluation here is conditioned by a priori associations of "functional value" with avoidance of semantic redundancy, and of "mere redundancy," where it appears to

---

[8]Vos, "Form and Function in Roger Ascham's Prose," pp. 307–12; "The Formation of Roger Ascham's Prose Style," pp. 349–54, 366–68.

[9]"Form and Function in Roger Ascham's Prose," pp. 312–13.

be a systematic tendency rather than an isolated accident, with a "fault of style." It is my view that Scripturalism enters as a useful critical referent at exactly this point. It serves to elucidate and even to justify this aspect of Ascham's prose by providing a normative precedent in Hebraic sense parallelism for redundant material in binary (and, sometimes, serial) responsions of clausal form. In the remainder of this section I shall be concerned with showing that Scriptural modes of sententious expression—and in *Toxophilus* particularly, Hebraic sense parallelism—came more and more to figure as model features of the prose style which Ascham cultivated in his vernacular writings.

Admittedly, the most obtrusive manifestation of Scripturalism in *Toxophilus* occurs at the level of content. Ascham makes repeated recourse to Biblical antecedents—Davidic ones above all—in order to state what he represents as his strongest argument from authority and antiquity for the practice of shooting with the longbow. We have noted one such characteristic passage in which textual allusions are loosely concatenated as exempla in the manner of Elyot in *The Governour;* other passages of this kind are readily found (e.g., *Tox.*, pp. 39–40, 61–62; II:2, 60–61, 88). But the impress of Scripturalism on the style of these passages is only intermittent, as in the following sentence where Ascham's correlative envelope replicates the binary structure of the embedded quotation from 1 Maccabees 1:3: "And *although* I knowe, that God is the onely gyver of victorie, and *not* the weapons, *for* all strength and victorie (sayth Judas Machabeus) cometh from heaven: *yet* surely strong weapons be the instrumentes wherwith god doth overcome that parte, which he wil have overthrown" (*Tox.*, p. 39; II:2, 60; my italics for connectives). Nonetheless, it is vital to see that the motive force for the proliferation of antitheses to establish moral distinctions between archery and other, pernicious pastimes in *Toxophilus* is specifically Scriptural and Psalmic in origin. We have already had occasion to examine two of the several schematic excursuses which Ascham develops in support of the claim that archery is a genuine preventative against evildoing because it is an activity which takes place in the daylight, in the open air, in the full sight of other persons. Eventually, near the midpoint of book 1, Toxophilus elucidates for Philologus the source of the antithetical associations distinguishing shooting from such pastimes as carding and dicing and "all these unthriftie ydle pastymes"; these he identifies as the "very bugges, that the Psalm meaneth on, walking on the nyght and in corners" (*Tox.*, p. 31; II:2, 50). The marginal reference is to Psalm 90 (in the Vulgate numbering) or 91 (in the numbering of the English versions). Significantly, it is possible to pinpoint Ascham's allusion to Miles Coverdale's Psalter of 1535, for it is the only version to read "bugges" in the fifth verse where the other sixteenth-century vernacular versions read either "terrour" or "feare." The sequence of relevant verses from Psalm 91 runs as follows in Coverdale:

He shal saye unto the Lorde: o my hope, & my stronge holde, my God, in whom I wil trust. For he shal deliver thee from the snare of the hunter, & from the noysome pestilence. He shal cover thee under his wynges, that thou mayest be safe under his fethers: his faithfulnesse and trueth shal be thy shylde and buckler. So that thou shalt not nede to be afrayed for eny bugges by night, ner for arowe that flyeth by daye: for the pestilence that crepeth in the darcknesse, ner for the sicknesse that destroyeth in the noone daye. A thousande shal fall besyde thee, and ten thousande at thy right honde, but it shal not come nye thee. Yea with thyne eyes shalt thou beholde, and se the rewarde of the ungodly.[10]

These are the accumulated Psalmic associations—the intermingled correlative and antithetical sense parallelisms on the "arowe that flyeth by daye" and "the pestilence that crepeth in the darcknesse"—that provide the dynamic for the recurrent passages in *Toxophilus* where archery is compared, always to its advantage, with other recreations or arts. Here, to demonstrate the stylistic repercussions of Ascham's source, is a final instance of his handling of this emphatic theme:

Yet even as I do not shewe all the goodnes, which is in shotynge, whan I prove it standeth by the same thinges that vertue it selfe standeth by, as brought in by God, or Godlyelyke men, fostered by labour, committed to the savegarde of lyght and opennes, accompanied with provision and diligens, loved and allowed by every good mannes sentence: Even likewise do I not open halfe the noughtines whiche is in cardyng and dising, whan I shewe howe they are borne of a desperate mother, norished in ydlenes, encresed by licence of nyght and corners, accompanied wyth Fortune, chaunce, deceyte, and craftines: condemned and banished, by all lawes and judgementes. [*Tox.*, pp. 24–25; II:2, 42]

Reference to Psalm 91, Ascham's acknowledged source for his controlling images and associations, makes it possible to account semantically for much of a sentence like the preceding, even the redundancy of content to which Vos objects. Syntactically, however, while there is the same intermingling of antitheses and correlatives, Ascham's sentence more closely resembles those of Cheke in its composition and progression than it does those of the Psalms. Where Hebraic sense parallelisms typically take their course of development in full or only slightly reduced clausal units that are the containing (or "highest") constituents of sentence structure, Ascham's parallelisms in book 1 of *Toxophilus* are most characteristically local (and "lower") syntactic units—noun phrases from clauses which have undergone extensive conjunction reduction, or verb phrases whose main verbs have been gapped to leave a residue

[10]Psalm 91:2–8 in Miles Coverdale's 1535 Psalter, reproduced in *The Hexaplar Psalter, Being the Book of Psalms in Six English Versions*, ed. William Aldis Wright (Cambridge: Cambridge University Press, 1911), pp. 226, 228.

of objects and complements. Because their conjunctively elaborated elements are, as a rule, words and phrases in clusters positioned deep in subsentential structure, Ascham's schematic sentences in book 1 comprise a species of directed syntax whose impetus is felt in a stroke-upon-stroke rhythm quite unlike the processional, almost strophic pace of Hebraic sense parallelisms, and quite like Cheke's own. Thus, if there were only the evidence of book 1 and of its Old Testament (and Apocryphal) source materials for Ascham's putative Scripturalism in *Toxophilus*, the accounting would have to be markedly qualified. Book 2, however, alters the givens of analysis and the appropriate referents alike.

Any attempt to reckon with the whole of *Toxophilus* in characterizing its style must confront the decided modulation from schematic design to loosened sentence units that takes place in the movement through its two books. While highly wrought forms are frequent at the outset, sentences in the familiar native, trailing style produced by asymmetric conjunction combine in growing numbers with more highly wrought ones in the course of book 1; by book 2—essentially a how-to-do-it manual on archery in an active vernacular tradition going back well over a century—the trailing sentences predominate. What is of special interest in the light of our concern with Ascham's Scripturalism is how certain narrative passages function in a gradual transfer of directive force from schematic to trailing sentence forms. These passages show sustained correspondences with another dimension of Biblical sententiousness, that of the Gospel parables or "Semblables"; and Ascham's narratives serve as these do, to recast moral truths and imperatives in a more humanly immediate mode of expression while simultaneously placing them in a figurative light. The following is an example of Ascham's parabolic style and manner from the earlier and highly schematic portion of book 1; Toxophilus offers it to buttress his claim that "surelie the best wittes to lerning must nedes have moch recreation and ceasing from their boke, or els they marre them selves, when base and dompysshe wittes can never be hurte with continuall studie":

The same I finde true in two bowes that I have, wherof the one is quick of cast, tricke, and trimme both for pleasure and profyte: the other is a lugge, slowe of cast, folowing the string, more sure for to last, then pleasunt for to use. Now sir it chaunced this other night, one in my chambre wolde nedes bende them to prove their strength, but I can not tel how, they were both left bente tyll the nexte daye at after dyner: and when I came to them, purposing to have gone on shoting, I found my good bowe clene cast on the one side, and as weake as water . . . ; and as for my lugge, it was not one whyt the worse, but shotte by and by as wel and as farre as ever it dyd. And even so I am sure that good wittes, except they be let downe . . . and unbent like a good casting bowe, they wil never last and be able to continue in studie. [*Tox.*, pp. 3–4; II:2, 14–15]

Manifestly, despite the colloquialisms ("as weake as water," "not one whyt the worse") and the direct address with an expletive ("Now sir") that impart an oral flavor to this homely "Semblable," its composition attests the ascendancy of schematics. This is no longer the case, however, in the most protracted and stylistically self-conscious of the anecdotally developed similitudes in *Toxophilus*. Near the end of book 1, Ascham places nothing less than a full-blown secular analogue of Christ's parable of the sower (Matthew 13, Mark 4, Luke 8) in the mouth of his fictive alter ego. The secularized Scripturalism of content and style alike in this remarkable passage become Ascham's deliberate, only slightly oblique contrivance for claiming a seriousness and efficacy in his joint vocation as prose writer and pedagogue that can bear comparison with one who preaches the Word (the gist of the original Gospel similitude):

All Englishe men generally, be apte for shotyng: and howe? Lyke as that grounde is plentifull and frutefull, whiche withoute any tyllynge bryngeth out corne, as for example, yf a man shoulde go to the myll or market with corne, and happen to spyl some in the waye, yet it wolde take roote and growe, bycause the soyle is so good: so England may be thought very frutefull and apte to brynge oute shooters, where children even from the cradell, love it: and yong men without any teachyng so diligentlye use it. Agayne, lykewyse as a good grounde, well tylled, and well husbanded, bringeth out great plentie of byg eared corne, and good to the falle: so if the youthe of Englande being apte of it selfe to shote, were taught and learned how to shote, the Archers of England shuld not be only a great deal ranker, and mo then they be: but also a good deal bygger and stronger Archers then they be. This commoditie shoulde folowe also yf the youth of Englande were taught to shote, that even as plowing of a good grounde for wheate, doth not onely make it mete for the seede, but also riveth and plucketh up by the rootes, all thistles, brambles and weedes, whiche growe of theyre owne accorde, to the destruction of bothe corne and grounde: Even so shulde the teaching of youth to shote, not only make them shote well, but also plucke awaye by the rootes all other desyre to noughtye pastymes, as disynge, cardyng, and boouling, which without any teaching are used every where, to the great harme of all youth of this realm. [*Tox.*, pp. 58–59; II·2, 84–85]

This passage is an achieved Scripturalist composition which replicates both the serial progression through different kinds of ground and tilling that structures the Gospel parable of the sower and the clausal basis of Hebraic sense parallelism—for example, "Lyke as that grounde is plentifull and frutefull, whiche without any tyllynge bryngeth out corne," "where children even from the cradell love it: and yong men without any teachyng so diligentlye use it." In its larger implications, the passage bespeaks the generalized Scripturalism of Baldwin and Cheke in responding to the parabolic modes of thought and expression in the Gospels. Its pivotal persona, moreover, the sower who becomes a diligent tiller of the English soil, interestingly anticipates the central figure of

Hugh Latimer's famous Sermon of the Plough (1548), which was preached three years after the appearance of *Toxophilus*. But the immediate contributions of this strategically placed secular parable and its loosening of phrasal schematics into "open sentence" are to affirm Ascham's settled sense of his literary vocation by the end of book 1 and to launch the far more genial, relaxed, and discursive manner of book 2, whose staple sentence form is one predominantly composed of clausal units asymmetrically or correlatively combined in order to instruct English youth in the practice of archery. As Ascham moves in sequence through the various aspects of the necessary lore—the kinds of shafts and bows and their respective uses; how to stand, take aim, draw and release the shaft cleanly; how to avoid common mistakes and injuries; how to reckon with the vagaries of wind and weather—book 2 of *Toxophilus* enlarges on its self-declared objective of writing "this Englishe matter in the Englishe tongue, for Englishe men" by sustaining exposition or process description in updated counterparts of the recursively elaborated, asymmetrically conjoined clauses building to a crux or climax which we examined as the staples of vernacular resources for prose composition in chapter 3 of this study.[11] Accordingly, its net stylistic result is to place in abeyance for the duration any identifiable impetus either from English Ciceronianism or from Scripturalism.

During the more than two decades intervening between *Toxophilus* and the publication of *The Schoolmaster* one year after its author's death in 1569, a major shift can be discerned in Ascham's declared sense of literary vocation and in the prose style which was its instrument. What vanishes is the genial, expatiating manner of book 2 of *Toxophilus*. As a consequence, the parabolic and additive mode of composing in asymmetrically conjoined sentences assumes far less importance in Ascham's writing. Indeed, apart from his 1566 letter dedicating *The Schoolmaster* to Queen Elizabeth—a text structured as an exhortation to mark the correspondences between the events which brought her to the throne and God's replacement of Saul with David as king of Israel—there is little sign of influence from either the Old Testament historical books or the Gospel parables to be found in the latter work. Nonetheless, Ascham's sense of vocation and its attendant impetus toward a secular

---

[11]Book 2 of *Toxophilus* provides, in effect, a brilliant retrospective on the stylistic potential of conjunctive sentence forms. Both the sentence on the use of a shooting glove, which Vos faults as "too unstructured, too rambling" ("Form and Function in Roger Ascham's Prose," p. 316), and the protracted description of blowing snow, which Greene calls "the most beautiful page Ascham ever wrote" ("Ascham: The Perfect End of Shooting," p. 622), yield straightforwardly to analysis as specimens of asymmetric composition leading to or away from a semantic crux or pivot. The passage on the shooting glove is found in Wright's edition on p. 71, and in Giles's at II:2, p. 101; the passage on the blowing snow on pp. 112–13, and at II:2, pp. 154–55, respectively.

adaptation of Scripturalism become demonstrably stronger in *The School-master*, where his new heights of moral concern for England raise to new power his attraction to varieties of sententious formulation. In brief, what happens to Ascham as a prose stylist under his conviction that Protestant England is convulsed by a cultural crisis is that he finds himself more and more driven back from the binary responsions of sense parallelisms to the urgent, affective schematics whose model is the Pauline Epistles. Thus, in secularized form and inverse order, the mainstays of Tyndale's Scripturalism make their reappearance in vernacular prose.

The observations on Scripture in the dedicatory letter to Queen Elizabeth mirror the guiding conceptions of *The Schoolmaster* at its outset: an allusion to Romans 15:4 registers approval for the Apostle Paul's claim that all Scripture is written for all men's learning, but the approval is directly tempered by Ascham's own claim that the fittest reading "for all men, both learned and lewed," is the Book of Wisdom and the Proverbs of Solomon and Jesus Sirach.[12] Next Ascham's Preface elaborates his own aims in the work as a witty parallel to his characterization of Scripture as, supremely, wisdom literature; he will offer as his "Will and Testament" (and as a memorial to his beloved friends, Cheke and Sir Richard Sackville) his wisest thoughts on how to conduct a child's earliest education (*Sch.*, pp. 175–81; III, 78–87). In the text proper, this declared purpose of laying down basic educational precepts for a broad English audience compounds with Ascham's always lively stylistic self-consciousness. The results are frequent formulations in the binary clausal responsions of Biblical wisdom literature. The heart of the famous disquisition on "quick wittes" in book 1 yields a pair of early instances:

Soche wittes delite them selves in easie and pleasant studies, and never passe farre forward in hie and hard sciences.

They be like trees, that shewe forth, faire blossoms & broad leaves in spring time, but bring out small and not long lasting fruite in harvest time: and that only soch as fall, and rotte, before they be ripe, and so never or seldome cum to any good at all. [*Sch.*, pp. 188–90; III, 96, 97]

As discourse proceeds, however, the declarative and the antithetical or correlative types of sententious sentences—respectively, Baldwin's "Counsels and Precepts" and his "Proverbs and Adages"—are reserved for the elaboration of key themes. Thus, the following series of sense parallelisms in precept form introduces Ascham's excursus on the superiority of study to experience (one of several points in which his ideas about education concur with Elyot's):

[12]Ascham's Dedication, *The Schoolmaster*, in *Whole Works*, ed. Giles, III, 70. Subsequent citations, abbreviated *Sch.*, will supply page references to Wright's and Giles's editions, in that order, and will be incorporated in the text.

Learning teacheth more in one yeare than experience in twentie: And learning teacheth safelie, when experience maketh mo miserable then wise. He hasardeth sore, that waxeth wise by experience. An unhappie Master he is, that is made cunning by manie shippewrakes: A miserable Merchant, that is neither riche or wise, but after some bankroutes. It is costlie wisdom, that is bought by experience. [*Sch.*, p. 214; III, 136]

However, to concentrate the pith of his famous assertion that "all languages, both learned and mother tongues, be gotten, and gotten onelie by *Imitation*," he has recourse to the form of "Proverbs and Adages," which, in Baldwin's words cited earlier, "shew the contraries of things, preferring alwaies the best." Ascham's own proverbs on imitation run as follows:

For as ye use to heare, so ye learne to speake: if ye heare no other, ye speake not your selfe: and whome ye onelie heare, of them ye onelie learne. And therefore, if ye would speake as the best and wisest do, ye must be conversant, where the best and wisest are: but if yow be borne or brought up in a rude contrie, ye shall not chuse but speake rudelie. The rudest man of all knoweth this to be true. [*Sch.*, pp. 264–65; III, 210]

In a further specialization of rhetorical function, Ascham tends to reserve the sententious analogizing of "Semblables" for his summary last word on a given topic. Thus he concludes the section advising the admixture of play with teaching to bolster the retentiveness of very young children: "For, the pure cleane witte of a sweete yong babe, is like the newest wax, most hable to receive the best and fayrest printing: and like a new bright silver dishe never occupied, may receive and kepe cleane, anie good thyng that is put into it" (*Sch.*, p. 200; III, 115). And thus, similarly, he concludes his account of the natural symptoms of "a good witte in a child for learning," namely, the wellspokenness joined with aptness of mind and will which he terms Εὐφυής (*Euphues*): "And even as a faire stone requireth to be sette in the finest gold, with the best workmanshyp, or else it leseth moch of the Grace and price, even so, excellencye in learning, and namely Divinitie, joyned with a cumlie personage, is a mervelous Jewell in the world" (*Sch.*, p. 194; III, 107). So instrumental, overall, are the types of sententious formulation characteristic of generalized Scripturalism in the sustaining of pedagogic and, especially, moral seriousness in *The Schoolmaster* that Ascham at one point is even found declaring as follows with respect to the classical myth of those charmed into beasts by Circe:

Hieremias.
4. cap.

The trewe meenyng of both *Homer* and *Plato*, is plainlie declared in one short sentence of the holy Prophet of God *Hieremie*, crying out of the vaine & vicious life of the *Israelites*. This people (sayeth he) be fooles and dulhedes to all goodnes, but sotle, cunning and bolde, in any mischiefe. [*Sch.*, p. 227; III, 154]

Notwithstanding their recurrence at vital junctures of the discourse, the outcroppings of Hebraic sense parallelisms and related types of sententious formulation in *The Schoolmaster* are ultimately less conspicuous than the recursively elaborated moral exhortations and admonitions that become Ascham's secular counterpart to the pastoral counsel in the Epistles of Paul. In this last work, Ascham's sentence forms and turns of phrase take on a decidedly Pauline cast at impassioned moments, exhibiting a characteristic instinct for decorum in representing the conflict of true Christianity with the ways of the world. Yet, as noted earlier, to cite Paul as a stylistic model for the writing of English prose is inevitably also to recall Tyndale, which a number of the most urgent and strident passages in *The Schoolmaster* do: for example, Ascham's repeated injunctions to revere God's Word as the sole foundation of all learning, to be mindful of the special providence with which England is favored above all other nations, and to shun the blandishments of the papistical brood of Antichrist.[13] Since such tonalities—which rise to a head in the long fulminations against the corrupting effects of travel in Italy upon young English gentlemen—are an exceedingly familiar aspect of the standing conception of Ascham, it is well to recall that they are viturally confined to *The Schoolmaster*. By contrast, I find only two Tyndalian reminiscences in *Toxophilus:* the pair of widely separated passages that extol vernacular chronicle history as a faithful record of God's dealings with his Englishmen and dismiss romance as the base feigning of monks and poets (*Tox.*, pp. xiv–xv, 55; II:2, 7–8, 79). The quarter century that intervened between *Toxophilus* and *The Schoolmaster* made the latter a very different piece of English prose of counsel. The Ascham who circumspectly weathered successive upheavals in Church and State as writing instructor to Edward, tutor to Elizabeth and Lady Jane Grey, and Latin secretary under Mary and Elizabeth declares himself at last as an outspoken Reformer whose religious convictions suffuse and ground his classicizing pedagogy from end to end. It is for the purposes of limning and authenticating the self-portrait of the schoolmaster which he left as his legacy to England that the prototype of Pauline style becomes indispensable to Ascham.

By far the most common resemblance between Ascham's prose and the Apostle's involves recursion of conjunctively reduced sentential elements in the heaping catalogues compounded with antitheses that bear so much of the burden of moral intensity in the pastoral portions of the Epistles. Ascham displays his sensitivity to specifics of sentence form in a number of passages which build catalogues out of the same (or similar) constituents as their Pauline prototypes. To illustrate, I offer a

---

[13]For passages on these subjects, see *The Schoolmaster* in *Whole Works*, ed. Giles, III, 86, 122–24, 128–30, 138, 144, 159–66, 201, 211–13, 227–28.

series of three comparisons in which a passage from Ascham, with relevant constituents italicized, is paired with analogues from the Geneva Bible, the closest version in date and phrasing to *The Schoolmaster:*[14]

(1) Hard wittes be hard to receive, but *sure to keepe: painefull without werinesse, hedefull without wavering, constant without newfanglenes: bearing heavie thinges,* thoughe not lightlie yet willinglie: *entring hard thinges,* though not easilie, yet depelie. . . . They be grave and stedfast, *silent of tong, secret of hart: Not hastie in making, but constant in keping any promise: Not rashe in uttering, but ware in considering every matter:* and therby, *not quicke in speaking, but deepe of judgement,* whether they write or give counsell in all waightie affaires. [*Sch.,* p. 191; III, 101]

Compare 2 Corinthians 4:8–9: "We are *troubled on every syde, yet* are we *not in distresse:* we are *in povertie, but not overcome of povertie;* we are *persecuted,* but *not forsaken* therin . . ."; Romans 12:10–13: "In geving honour, go one before another, *not slothful to do service, fervent in sprite, serving the Lorde: rejoycing in hope, patient in tribulation,* continuing in prayer . . ."; and Colossians 1:10: "That ye myght walke worthy of the Lord in all thinges that please, *being fruteful in all good workes, and increasing in the knowledge of God."*

(2) An other propertie of this our English Italians is, to be mervelous *singular in all their matters: Singular in knowledge, ignorant of nothyng:* . . . *Common discoursers of all matters: busie searchers of most secret affaires: open flatterers of great men: privie mislikers of good men: Faire speakers, with smiling countenances* and much curtessie openlie *to all men: Ready bakbiters, sore nippers, and spitefull reporters* privilie *of good men.* [*Sch.,* p. 236; III, 165–66]

Compare Romans 1:28–32: "And as they regarded not to knowe God, even so God delivered them up, . . . that they should do those thinges which are not comly, being *ful of all unrighteousnes,* . . . *takyng all things in the evyl parte, backbyters, haters of God, doers of wronge, proude bosters, inventers of evyl thynges, disobedient to father and mother: without understanding, covenant breakers, without natural affection* . . ."; 2 Timothy 3:1, 2, 4: "This understande, that in the laste dayes . . . men shal be *lovers of their owne selves,* . . . *without charitie, trucebreakers, false accusers, riatours, despicers of them which are good: traytours,* . . . gredy upon volupteousnes *more than the lovers of God:* having a similitude of godly lyvyng, but having denyed the power therof: and turne away from suche."

(3) Εὐφυής [*Euphues*] Is he, that is *apte* by goodnes of witte, *and appliable* by readines of will, to learning, *having all other qualities of the minde and partes of the bodie,* . . . *not trobled, mangled, & halfed, but sounde, whole, full, & hable to*

[14]Excerpts from the Geneva Bible are cited from *The English Hexapla, Exhibiting the Six Important English Translations of the New Testament Scriptures* (London: Samuel Bagster & Sons, 1841).

do their office: as a tong, *not stamering,* . . . *but plaine, and redie* to deliver the meaning of the minde: . . . a countenance, *not werishe* and crabbed, *but faire* and cumlie: a personage, *not wretched* and deformed, *but taule* and goodlie: for surelie, a cumlie countenance, with a goodlie stature, geveth credit to learning, and authoritie to the person. [*Sch.*, p. 194; III, 106–7]

Compare Titus 1:7–9; 2:1, 7–8: "For a bishop must be *fautlesse,* as it becommeth Gods steward: *not frowarde,* not angry, . . . *not geven to fylthy lucre: but harberous,* . . . *wise, righteous, holy, temperate:* and suche as holdeth fast the true word of doctrine, that he may exhorte with wholsome learning. . . . But speake thou that which becommeth wholsome learnyng, . . . *shewing thy selfe an ensample of good workes* with uncorrupt doctrine, with gravitie, and with the wholsome worde, which can not be rebuked . . .."; 1 Timothy 3:2, 3: "A byshop therfore must be faultlesse, . . . watching, sober, modest, harberous, *apt to teache: not geven to wyne,* . . . *not geven to fylthy lucre: but gentle, abhorring fyghtyng, abhorring covetousnes.*"

Beyond the remarkable structural correspondences between Ascham's catalogues and the Apostle's extend semantic correspondences that are no less resonant and exact. The second example, Ascham's denunciation of "our English Italians" in the mode of Paul's characterization of the reprobate in Romans and of the equally damnable hypocrites "having a similitude of godly lyvyng, but having denyed the power therof" in 2 Timothy, is the most conventional of the three, for it utilizes the predominantly negative associations of the catalogue. The other two examples, Ascham's commendation of "hard wittes" in the mode in which Paul praises steadfast Christians and, especially, Ascham's portrayal of his model scholar, Euphues, in the mode of Paul's portrayal of a model bishop, are proportionately the more interesting and suggestive creations, for they extend upon the earlier advances noted in Tyndale and Cheke toward establishing a positive valency for the catalogue in Scripturalist style. Other examples could be adduced without difficulty,[15] but the foregoing will suffice to illustrate how peaks of moral intensity in *The Schoolmaster* tend to coincide with schematic composition in an identifiably Pauline mode—so much so, in fact, that passages of this kind can be used as an index to expressions of Ascham's deepest concerns and convictions. Since the correspondences exhibit such a consistent pattern, we may properly conclude this discussion of Ascham's prose of counsel by considering what evidence there is for viewing his secular appropriations of Pauline schematics as a conscious stylistic strategy, and how such a strategy might sort with his commitment to English Ciceronianism.

[15]For other passages in a Pauline mode, see *The Schoolmaster,* ed. Giles, III, 98–99, 102, 129 (benediction), 138, 139–40, 151, 160.

In assessing Ascham's self-consciousness as a stylist with respect to a Pauline model, there are two important passages in *The Schoolmaster*. The earlier one is a frank apologia for his plainspoken audacity, which he justifies by the precedent of the Apostle's preaching—and in reprises of Pauline schematics:

> But, perchance, som will say, I have stepte to farre, out of my schole, into the common welthe, from teaching a yong scholer, to monishe greate and noble men: . . . Who, if they do, as I wishe them to do, how great so ever they be now, by blood and other mens meanes, they shall becum a greate deale greater hereafter, by learninge, vertue, and their owne desertes: which is trewe praise, right worthines, and verie Nobilitie in deede. Yet, if som will needes presse me, that I am to bold with great men, & stray to farre from my matter, I will
>
> Ad Philip. aunswere them with *S. Paul, sive per contentionem, sive quocunque modo, modo Christus praedicetur, &c.*: even so, whether in place, or out of place, with my matter, or beside my matter, if I can hereby either provoke the good, or staye the ill, I shall think my writing herein well imployed. [*Sch.*, p. 222; III, 146–47]

The explicitly instrumental and active conception of writing which Ascham here associates with Paul ("if I can hereby either provoke the good, or staye the ill") receives further important development—again, on the Apostle's authority—in the midst of the impassioned excursus on Italianate Englishmen:

> Ad Gal. 5 *S. Paul* saith, that sects and ill opinions, be the workes of the flesh, and frutes of sinne: this is spoken, no more trewlie for the doctrine, then sensiblie for the reason. And why? For, ill doinges, breed ill thinkinges: and of corrupted maners, spryng perverted judgementes. And how? There be in man two speciall thinges: mans will, mans mynde. . . . Where will inclineth to goodnes, the mynde is bent to troth; where will is caried from goodnes to vanitie, the mynde is sone drawne from troth to false opinion. And so, the readiest way to entangle the mynde with false doctrine, is first to intice the will to wanton livyng. Therfore, when the busie and open Papistes abroad, could not, by their contentious bookes, turn men in England fast enough, from troth and right judgement in doctrine, then the sutle and secrete Papistes at home, procured bawdie bookes to be translated out of the *Italian* tonge, whereby over many yong willes and wittes allured to wantonnes, do now boldly contemne all severe bookes that sounde to honestie and godlines. [*Sch.*, p. 230; III, 158–59]

As a theoretical statement that draws the practical implications for vernacular composition from faculty psychology construed in Paul's mordant terms, what Ascham says could not be less equivocal—or more Scripturalist. He derives his authority specifically from Galatians 5:16–

17: "I say, walke in the Spirite, and ye shal not fulfil the lustes of the fleshe. For the fleshe lusteth against the Spirite, and the Spirite against the fleshe: and these are contrary one to the other, so that ye can not do the same things that ye would" (Geneva rendering). When the circumstances for discourse are envisaged as a two-front war—the contention of God's Spirit with the lures of the flesh in the world, and the inward strife of the human spirit against bodily incitements—what a speaker or writer requires is a literally inspiriting style, one that can animate the will to good actions. For Ascham, as we have been seeing, this requirement was met by employing antitheses, correlatives, and serial conjunctions for overt cognitive direction. But an inspiriting style has a further dimension, one of encouraging and enlivening, and this for Ascham was evidently realized in the insistent, even agitated rhythms and linguistic nervous energy of Pauline catalogues with their conjunctively reduced constituents in sporadic parallel formations. This sense of energy transmuted to urgency arises from the crescendo of aggregated elements that strain at the limits of sentence form by postponing its final intonational downturn and thus holding off the expected closure. It is not, finally, Cicero but rather the Apostle, through Ascham's close attention to the informing conceptions of the Spirit, the world, and the duality of human nature that shape the style of the Epistles, who can enlighten us most regarding the premium on schematics and the particularly favored patterns in the style of *The Schoolmaster*. The Pauline prototype represents the process of schematizing—channeling content to make its way into the heart no less than the mind—as the essential component in the formulation of good counsel.

A last piece of evidence to be considered in weighing the influence of Pauline notions, objectives, and modes of expression upon Ascham's English style is provided in a letter he wrote to Sir William Cecil from Brussels in March, 1553, close to the midpoint of the long interval between *Toxophilus* and *The Schoolmaster*. Ascham begins to reflect to Cecil on the futility of a wise saying "used for the most part in the mouth of such as either know not what they say, of ignorance, or care not what they speak, of spite." Instead, he continues, if one wishes one's wisdom to be availing, one must use every resource at one's command to impress it upon one's audience, as the Apostle Paul unfailingly did. Ascham then proceeds in macaronic terms to describe the rhetorical challenge he confronts as a reduplication of Paul's in addressing worldly hearers and readers:

And after these men's opinions, if a man be not πολυπράγμων [officious, a busybody] in doing, or will not πλεονεκτεῖν [claim more than his due] in all matters for profit, or list not καιροφυλακεῖν [watch for the right moment with] all persons for favour, or cannot πραπελιζεῖν [perform turnabouts] at all times

343

for pleasure, or, to speak most fitly in Saint Paul, if he do not wholly σχηματίζειν τοιούτω [assume a form, figure, or posture in this same way], he shall be counted of them ἰδιώτης ἀπειρόκαλος [odd and tasteless, ignorant of the beautiful] and *ineptus,* how learned, well mannered, and fit to many good qualities soever he be.[16]

The verb σχηματίζειν *(schematizein)*—literally, to schematize—is identified by Ascham in this passage as the means by which the Apostle gained credit and established favor with his worldly audiences. *Schematizein* occurs four times in the Pauline Epistles, always in a compounded form. There are three occurrences, in close contiguity, of *metaschematizein* ('transform') in 2 Corinthians 11:13–15—a passage where Paul affirms that the true preacher of the Gospel transforms himself into a minister of righteousness to counter the deceitful self-transformations of those who pretend to be Christ's apostles, and of the devil himself who pretends to be an angel of light. While this passage points to the metaphysical struggle that comprises one context for the verb *schematizein* in Paul, the remaining occurrence seems still more pertinent to Ascham's conception of Pauline style. The compound *suschematizein* ('fashion like') is used in Romans 12:2, "And fashion not your selves lyke unto this world, but be ye changed in your shape, by the renuying of your myndes, that ye may prove what is the wyl of God, which is good, acceptable, and perfect" (Geneva rendering). In this verse we are taken to the core of the Pauline associations that schematic style in a Scripturalist mode came to acquire for English writers like Ascham. Schematism offered a means for at once resisting conformity to worldliness while effecting the transformation of a renewed mind and an energized will that would "prove"—that is, ascertain—"the wyl of God, which is good, acceptable, and perfect."

How do such imputations of an ethically transforming and inspiriting effect to the schematic language of Scripture fit with the broader program of Ascham's English Ciceronianism and the pedagogy of *The Schoolmaster?* On the formal level of antithesis, correlation, and recursion of parallelisms where we are dealing with stylistic universals, there can be no question of discordance or, even, of categorical distinction—a major reason, it would seem, why the two strains have gone undistinguished in Ascham's prose. On the conceptual level, too, Ascham's Scripturalism and his Ciceronianism accord in his pedagogical methods, especially in his stress on training in composition through the Chekian technique of double translation: turning a passage from the original into English, and then back again, with careful scrutiny of the results to ensure that the

---

[16]Letter CXLV in Ascham's Letters, *Whole Works,* ed. Giles, I:2, p. 352. The bracketed translations of Greek words are mine.

versions remain equivalent to one another. Thus Ascham can exclaim of the divinely willed consonance which his methods sustain:

But behold the goodnesse of Gods providence for learning: . . . those that were wisest in judgement of matters, and purest in uttering their myndes, the first and chiefest, that wrote most and best, in either tong, as *Plato* and *Aristotle* in Greeke, *Tullie* in Latin, be so either wholie, or sufficiently left unto us, as I never knew yet scholer, that gave himselfe to like, and love, and folow chieflie those three Authors but he proved, both learned, wise, and also an honest man, if he joyned withall the trewe doctrine of Gods holie Bible, without the which, the other three, be but fine edge tooles in a fole or mad mans hand. [*Sch.*, p. 266; III, 213]

Although such an integration of Cicero and Scripture might seem delusive to a later mind, there are no grounds for accusing Ascham, or any other Renaissance aspirant to the same objective, of not knowing what he was about. In an excellent essay which includes discussion of Ascham's double translation as a technique aimed equally at imitation and creation, Marion Trousdale reaches some generalized reflections which can help to conclude this consideration of Ascham's vernacular style by placing our findings about the mixed provenance of its schematics in a wider historical perspective:

When Ascham talks of Cicero's use of the same thought in two different passages and wishes that he had the original pattern in Demosthenes which Cicero used, he is seeing ideas as forms. . . . On the one hand, they exist independent of the matter which they express, and, on the other hand, independent of the words by which they are expressed. . . . By definition they represent that which can be copied, reproduced, shared. I have suggested earlier that they are perceived by acts of mind, and we might see them as concepts which can be abstracted from phenomenal things. But such hidden images seem to have had more substance for the Elizabethans than for us. . . . They suggest perfection, original pattern, cause, and, as such, if they exist in an ontological sense, these ideas, in Aquinas for instance, exist in the mind of God. But such ideas exist, as well, in their diverse and manifold variations in the world around us, and they constitute what it is possible for us to know in the world which we see. . . . Thus the intellectual abstractions by which we define were assumed to be part of our own minds as well as the defining part of the reality which we perceive.[17]

If we augment Trousdale's remarks on concept formation with the affective force that shapes character, we can find our way to an understanding of the vital workings attributed by Ascham to his schematic style—a style whose profoundest impulsions are seen truly for the Prot-

[17]Marion Trousdale, "Recurrence and Renaissance: Rhetorical Imitation in Ascham and Sturm," *ELR* 6 (1979): 156–79; quotation from 176–77.

estant humanism they bespeak, when their Scripturalist component is recognized along with their English Ciceronianism.

THE PREMIUM ON WIT: WILSON'S PROTESTANT AMBIVALENCE

Sir Thomas Wilson, the author of *The Rule of Reason conteinying The Arte of Logique* (1551) and *The Arte of Rhetorique, for the use of all such as are studious of Eloquence, set forth in English* (1553), has several claims for inclusion in the account of the English prose of counsel which is the subject of chapters 5 and 6. Some of these arise from Wilson's perceptible ties to the line of succession reaching back to Elyot and the impetus to evolve a generalized Scripturalism that especially marks his later work. Wilson's determination in *The Rule of Reason* not to leave logic "hidden in the Greke, or Latine tongue" but to make it "an arte, as apt for the Englishe wittes, and as profitable for their knowlege, as any thother sciences" by setting it forth "in the Englishe" with "simple and plain wordes" which yet have "grace"[18] recalls the 1541 Preface to *The Castle of Health*, while early statements in *The Arte of Rhetorique* also cast Wilson's rhetorician in a role analogous to a minister of the Word. In the Preface of the *Arte*, eloquent speakers are represented as having been sent by God after the Fall to alleviate the warring, precarious state of their fellow humans by persuading them "to live together in fellowship of life, to maintain Cities, to deale truely, and willingly obeye one an other," and the "learned and wise men" who subsequently formulated the "purpose" and "use" of rhetoric in order to teach it to others are represented as at once the repairers and enhancers of imperfect human nature.[19] But the nearest resemblances of all in the *Arte* to Elyot's conception of his vocation as a secular ministrant of beneficial counsel are found in the early offerings of the specimen compositions that make Wilson's work so pragmatic and revealing: these range from praises of youthful virtue and "commendation of Justice, or true dealing" through advice (adapted from various sources) to embrace the study of law or the state of matrimony to, finally, a consolatory address to the duchess of Suffolk on the sudden death of her two young sons from the sweating sickness (*Arte*, pp. 14–17, 23–29, 31–35, 39–63, 66–85). Wilson concludes his address to the duchess with a declaration that doubly recalls Elyot—in

[18]Sir Thomas Wilson, *The Rule of Reason conteinying The Arte of Logique,* ed. Richard S. Sprague, Renaissance Editions no. 6 (Northridge, Calif.: San Fernando Valley State College, 1972), pp. 1–2. Subsequent citations, abbreviated *Rule*, will be incorporated in the text.

[19]Sir Thomas Wilson, *The Arte of Rhetorique,* ed. G. H. Mair (Oxford: Clarendon Press, 1909), sig. Avii^r, pp. 5, 8–9. Subsequent citations, abbreviated *Arte*, will be incorporated in the text.

what it says about the value of exempla, in what it says about ministering to the cure of souls as a layman: "Thus the rather to make precepts plaine, I have added examples at large, both for counsaile giving and for comforting. And most needful it were in such kinde . . . to bee most occupied, considering the use hereof appeareth full oft in all parts of our life" (*Arte*, p. 85; cf. *Rule*, pp. 81–82).

Overall, however, Wilson's most binding ties are with the outspokenly Protestant strain in sixteenth-century English prose of counsel. Though he makes no identifiable reference to Elyot, one admiring allusion seems to attach to Morison's *Invective against . . . Treason*, while other passages redouble praise for Cheke's *Hurt of Sedition* and Hugh Latimer's preaching as outstanding contemporary illustrations of ordered discourse in the native tongue that conduces to civil and religious order.[20] Wilson also makes two allusions in the *Arte* (pp. 66, 184) to his collaboration with the distinguished Latinist, Walter Haddon, on the *Vita et Obitus duorum fratrum* (1551), a memorial tribute to the forementioned sons of Katherine Willoughby, duchess of Suffolk, herself a staunch Protestant and the patroness of Latimer's last years. (Wilson's specimen composition in English obviously adapts its Latin precursor.) In reflecting on the origins of these various ties, it is well to recall that the circle of Wilson's intimates at St. John's College, Cambridge, between 1545 and 1549 included Cheke and Ascham among others, for it is to Ascham supremely among English writers that Wilson bears affinity—a fact, as we shall see, that makes their differences the more crucial in the end.

Like *Toxophilus* and *The Schoolmaster*, *The Rule of Reason* and *The Arte of Rhetorique* are imbued with an educational concern that figures centrally in both authors' sense of their literary vocation. The strength of the concern in Wilson's case is all the more borne out by his inability to abide by the resolve voiced in the Prologue to the second (1560) edition of the *Arte*: to write no more because of the torture and imprisonment which he had suffered under the Inquisition in Italy, where he had gone in self-exile during Mary's reign.[21] That Wilson should have incurred heresy proceedings is not surprising, given the insistent anti-Catholicism

[20]See, respectively, *Rule*, p. 120; *Arte*, pp. 181, 202, 123, 147. The topicality of these passages is compounded with Wilson's scornful asides on the Ket of Ket's Rebellion as a Jack Straw *redivivus*, and on the Pilgrimage of Grace and the concurrent Norfolk uprisings (*Arte*, pp. 123–24, 210, 216).

[21]Wilson's *Discourse uppon Usury by way of Dialogue and Oracions* was completed by 1569 and published in 1572; in 1570 he published vernacular versions of seven of Demosthenes' orations—a project in which he may have been assisted by Cheke. Russell H. Wagner, "Thomas Wilson's *Arte of Rhetorique*," *Speech Monographs* 27 (1960); 11, cites the opinion of the late seventeenth-century antiquary John Strype that Cheke translated the first three orations.

of both the *Rule* and the *Arte*.[22] Indeed, because he was considerably more forthright about his Protestantism at an earlier date than Ascham, *The Arte of Rhetorique* anticipates *The Schoolmaster* in repeatedly analogizing between secular and sacred eloquence, between the would-be improver of his fellow Englishmen and the worthy minister of the Word (e.g., *Arte*, pp. 36, 87, 88, 105, 108). Wilson, moreover, shares with Ascham in the endeavor of English Ciceronianism to join wisdom with eloquence. Accordingly, in the opening section of the *Arte*—a compilation from Cicero's various writings on oratory, Quintilian, the *Ad Herennium*, and Erasmus's manual for sermon style, *Ecclesiastae*, freely interlarded with Wilson's own commentary[23]—Cicero's authority is used to define rhetoric as "a learned, or rather an artificiall declaration of the mynd," "an Arte to set foorth by utteraunce of words, matter at large." The "matter at large" in which the orator must be knowledgeable and "able to speake fully" comprises "al those questions, which by lawe & mans ordinance are enacted, and appointed for the use and profit of man, such as are thought apt·for the tongue to set forwarde" as well as "all such matters, as may largely be expounded for mans behove, and may with much grace be set out, for all men to heare them" (*Arte*, p. 1). It could be argued that Wilson comes a good deal closer than Ascham to Cicero's intellectualist identification of wisdom with the study of philosophy, although the branch of philosophy which Wilson stresses is logic, not Cicero's moral and natural philosophy. In any case, wisdom nowhere contracts for Wilson merely to Ascham's "sound doctrine." The *Rule* and the *Arte* attest the range of interest in methodology and materials which characterizes earlier Renaissance treatments of logic and rhetoric; they are innocent of any connections with the Ramistic campaign to compartmentalize the two which had begun shortly before their composition.

The affinity between Wilson and Ascham centers in their basic assumptions about the relationship of art and human nature that governs the rhetorician's (and the logician's) enterprise. As surely as Ascham structures *Toxophilus* along a progression from aptness—or proper preparation—to learning to use of the art of shooting with the longbow, Wilson sees the arts he teaches as working by "the very ordre of nature" to activate and train the capabilities of a would-be reasoner or persuader

---

[22]For the autobiographical narration, see *Arte*, sigs. Aiiii^v–Av^v. For evidence of Wilson's anti-Catholicism, see *Rule*, pp. 120, 123, 132, 139, 147–52, 171, 178, 199, 216; *Arte*, pp. 87, 140–43, 146, 151, 154, 163–64, 197, 203, 217.

[23]Mair describes Wilson's work as a "judicious compilation" whose main source for two books (pp. 1–160) is Quintilian, adding, however, that the third book (pp. 160–222) "owes almost as much to Cicero" (Introduction, *Arte*, pp. xix–xx). A more varied enumeration of Wilson's sources for the *Arte* is given in William Crane, *Wit and Rhetoric in the Renaissance*, pp. 101–3. A fully annotated critical edition of *The Arte of Rhetorique* is much to be desired.

(*Rule,* pp. 38, 44–45; cf. pp. 153–56). In two passages on disposition of material in the *Arte,* he expounds the order of nature as the governing principle of all human life, political and individual, and hence of anything we "devise, learne and frame . . . to good purpose" (pp. 156–57), and he specifies how this order of nature is to be implemented in discourse as follows:

By no meanes better shall the standers by knowe what we say, and carie awaie that which they heare, then if at the first we couch together, the whole course of our tale in as small roome as we can, either by defining the nature and substaunce of our matter, or els by dividing it in an apt order, so that neither the hearers be troubled, with confounding of matter, and heaping one thing in an others necke, nor yet their memorie dulled with overthwart rehearsall, and disorderly telling of our tale. [*Arte,* pp. 100–101]

To bring what one knows and would transmit to others into proper order, eloquence is required. Thus Wilson anticipates the famous outcry in *The Schoolmaster*—"Ye know not what hurt ye do to learning that care not for wordes, but for matter, and so make a devorse betwixt the tong and the hart" (*Sch.,* p. 265; III, 211)—as he himself exclaims on the indispensability of eloquence to learning: "I much mervaile that so many seke the onely knowledge of things, without any mind to commend or set forth their intendement: seing none can know either what thei are, or what they have without the gift of utterance" (*Arte,* p. 161). Thus, too, Wilson concurs with Ascham in prescribing imitation as the means for acquiring eloquence, citing in his support the Biblical authority of "the Proverbe, By companying with the wise, a man shall learne wisedome" (*Arte,* p. 5; the allusion is to Proverbs 13:20).

As we shall be seeing, the affinity between Ascham's and Wilson's basic assumptions as expositors and practitioners of rhetorical composition issues in joint espousal of a markedly schematic style for which a generalized Scripturalism supplies a large share of the warrant. Yet while their positions on style ultimately converge, they are reached for the most part by independent routes. In the preceding section we examined the awareness of the workings of language that ensues on Ascham's highly self-conscious deployment of certain resources—chiefly, antithetical, correlative, and serial conjunctions—to achieve the directed syntax of his schematic style. But Wilson comes into his own much more notably as a commentator than as a stylist. Indeed, as a commentator, he has few if any equals among English Renaissance writers in the incisiveness and scope of the linguistic and literary insights which he distills from his manifold sources in the *Rule* and the *Arte.* Wilson's attainments in this regard deserve some specific notice, since they amount to what by any standard is a quite fully articulated modern view of the nature of English prose.

Wilson is the first English writer to insist on the dual sustaining connections between prose and speech, on the one hand, and between prose and the faculty of thought, on the other. The "composition" section of the *Arte* (pp. 162–69) adapts to the native tongue Cicero's norms for "plainnesse" and "aptnesse" in individual word choice and for idiomatic phrasing judged by current spoken usage; it is in this connection that Wilson adduces his letter parodying aureation which we considered in the first section of chapter 4. As for the function of prose as an instrument of thought, Wilson treats the overlap between logic and rhetoric in his day as an advantage. Noting that the "places of invention" make proper to both arts a concern with "externals" (cause, effect, purpose and realization, location, time, circumstances) and with "accidents" (the name of a thing, its parts, wise sentences about it, things similar and dissimilar, or concordant and opposing), he welcomes this commonality, affirming that the handling of "externals" and "accidents" is the likelier to be effective because it joins the art of reasoning with the art of eloquence (*Rule*, pp. 91, 120–38; *Arte*, p. 23, 112–13, 124–25). This stress on the cognitive as well as persuasive character of prose composition, in turn, has important ramifications in the value ascribed by Wilson to schematic style in later discussion.

Beyond his general manifestation of a modern sense of the nature of prose, the acuteness of Wilson's comments on aspects of the syntax and semantics of conjunction at various points in the *Rule* and *Arte* assumes special interest in the context of this study—in particular, the linguistic findings discussed in the second section of chapter 1. To begin with, his proposed distinction between sentences that are merely "like" and sentences that are "like among themselves" bespeaks recognition of the fundamental identity relation that motivates sentential conjunction. Wilson's "like" sentences correspond to Chomsky's sentences with "constituents of the same type" in their "final shape" and "history of derivation"; the example in the *Arte* of "like" sentences is: "Lust hath overcome shamefastnesse, impudence hath overcome feare, and madnesse hath overcome reason." The matching phrase structure of these sentences empowers the creation of their containing coordinate sentence. Sentences "like among themselves," however, exhibit both a stronger and a more pervasive identity relation in their respective constituents; hence their containing coordinate sentence can be expected to show the effects of conjunction reduction. "As thus," says Wilson: "Is it knowne, tried, proved, evident, open and assured that I did such a deede? An other. Such riot, Dicing, Carding, picking, stealing, fighting, Ruffians, Queanes and Harlottes must needes bring him to naught" (*Arte*, p. 204).[24]

[24]Wilson also adverts to the tendency of like sentences to exhibit parallel form in discussing the rhetorical figure, *paria paribus* ("when the one half of the sentence answereth

On the semantic level, similarly, Wilson's directives for composing a "narration," the early section of an oration in which "the matter must be opened, and every thing lively tolde, that the hearers may fully perceive what we goe about, nowe in reporting an act done, or uttering the state of a controversie," turn on a sensitivity to the principles governing asymmetric sentential conjunction. In judging what material to include and how to arrange it, the principles to be applied are, as Wilson explains, (1) a controlling notion of the main subject—what he calls "the whole in a grosse somme" and Robin Lakoff the "common topic"; and (2) a sense of the dynamics relating the conjuncts to one another—what Wilson terms "the verie purpose of all the devise" and Lakoff a recognizable "crux" to which a train of coordinated clauses leads. He explains the first as speaking "no more then needes we must, not raving it from the bottome, . . . nor yet touching every pointe, but telling the whole in a grosse somme. . . . that all may understand it, . . . every thing in order so much as is needful." Of the second, he declares that "the reporting of our tale, may sone appere plain . . . if we orderly observe circumstances, and tell one thing after an other . . . , if we speake directly as the cause requireth, if we shewe the very purpose of all the devise, and frame our invention, according as we shall thinke them most willing to allowe it, that have the hearing of it" (*Arte*, pp. 106–7). Later remarks on composition warn, in effect, against two dangers—against disorienting one's listeners if a common topic is not sustained and against the tedium of recursive sentential conjunction that is not clearly motivated:

Composition therfore is an apt joyning together of wordes in such order, that neither . . . any man shalbe dulled with over long drawing out of a sentence, nor yet much confounded with mingling of causes such as are needelesse, being heaped together without reason, and used without number. For by such meanes the hearers will be forced to forget full ofte, what was sayd first, before the sentence bee halfe ended: or else be blinded with confounding of many things together. [*Arte*, p. 166]

Wilson proceeds to discussion of factors governing conjunct ordering. An anecdote illustrates that temporal or causal priority is to be respected: a man came home "in haste, after a long journey" and said to his servant, "Come hether sir knave, help me of with my bootes and my spurres." At this Wilson interposes roundly: "I praie you sir, give him leave first to plucke of your spurres, er he meddle with your bootes, or els your man is like to have a madde plucking" (*Arte*, pp. 167–68). In the same context he offers instructions on how conjunct ordering should proceed when temporal or causal factors are lacking: here the principle is an extension of "First things first," where 'first' is understood as meaning

---

to the other, with just proportion of number"), and the following one, *gradatio* ("when a sentence is dissevered by degrees"): *Arte*, pp. 204–5.

'of greater eminence, importance, or power.' Thus Wilson asks with typical Tudor complacency about the existing social hierarchy: "Who is so foolish as to say, the Counsaile and the King, but rather the King and his Counsaile"? Similarly, who would say, "My mother and my father are both at home, as though the good man of the house did weare no breches" (pp. 168, 167)? Still other remarks bearing on conjunct ordering anticipate experimental evidence of a much later date regarding the natural prominence of the first and last positions in a series:

And in proving of our matters we had neede evermore, rather to weye our reasons, then to number them. . . . And first of all the strongest should be used, and the other placed in the middest, the which being heaped together will make a good mustar. And yet this also would be learned, whereas we used the best reasons at the first, wee should also reserve some that were like good for the latter end: that the hearers might have them fresh in their remembrance. [*Arte*, pp. 158–59]

To my mind, however, the single most remarkable insight offered by Wilson into the syntax and semantics of conjunction is reached not in the rhetorical domain of the *Arte*, but in the logical domain of the *Rule*; this is the distinction he registers between individual meaning and unit meaning—that is, the separateness or jointness of elements—in coordinate structure. The distinction arises in the course of his discussion of the fallacy of *Disjunctio conjunctorum*: "a dividing of thinges, whiche should be joigned together, and making of woordes severall, or elles a dissevering of twoo partes, whiche should be all one." He gives as an example the following invalid syllogistic inference: "The Lawe and the Gospel, are twoo diverse thinges; the woorde of God, is the lawe and the Gospel; Ergo the woorde of God, is twoo diverse thinges." Wilson then spells out the error involved in conceiving of the "woorde of God" as "partes severallie understanded, . . . not both together as thei should be": "For the woorde of God is not the lawe onelie, or the Gospel onelie, although it stand of these two, but is the lawe and the Gospel bothe joigned together: . . . whiche are nothing elles but the whole." And he proceeds to warn against failing to preserve unit meaning but instead reducing all to individual meaning, as "both divines and lawiers oftentimes ful ungodlie have dooen, not regarding the whole . . . , but takyng out patches and pieces, to serve their ungodlie purposes: neither thei themselves dooe understand what thei bring, when thei doe not marke the whole," the unitary character, of God's Word (*Rule*, pp. 169–71).

Having paid due respect to the often incisive comments on features and functions of coordinate structure in Wilson's treatments of logic and rhetoric, we are now in a position to examine his recommendations regarding prose style in what unquestionably became the most influential sections of his *Arte* for English readers. But in order to discern the rationale for these recommendations as a body, we shall find it essential to attend at all points to the circumstances for discourse which Wilson is presupposing. We may begin with the ordinary or standard ones that are in force through much of the *Arte:* namely, a speaker (or writer) whose purposes lie "first, in apt teaching the hearers what the matter is, next in getting them to give good eare, and thirdly in winning their favor" and an audience which is open to the possibility of being taught, delighted, and persuaded, by turns or all at once (*Arte*, p. 100; cf. pp. 2–4). Under these ordinary circumstances, in keeping with the well-disposed receptivity of the audience, Wilson soon collapses any distinctions between teaching, delighting, and persuading by recommending an all-purpose approach to prose composition through "amplification"—the presentation of "plentifull matter" in "apt words and picked Sentences" by a method he regularly calls "heaping" (*Arte*, pp. 6, 35, 112, 116; cf. pp. 23, 151). Such is Wilson's regard for well-managed copia that, as Crane has remarked, the treatment of the figures of amplification comprises the largest section on style in the *Arte*.[25] But while Cicero and Erasmus in particular among Wilson's sources provide important precedents for favoring amplification as a stylistic resource, Wilson himself outdoes them in representing the "heaping" of "matter" as, in effect, a mode of argumentation or persuasion:[26]

When we have declared the chiefe points, whereunto we purpose to referre all our reasons, wee must heape matter, and finde out arguments to confirme the same to the uttermost of our power. [*Arte*, p. 112]

And now because non shal better be able to amplifie any matter, then those which best can praise or most dispraise any thing here upon earth, I thinke it needfull first of all, to gather such thinges together which helpe best this way. Therefore in praising or dispraising, wee must be well stored ever with such good sentences, as are often used in this our life, the which thorowe art beeing increased, helpe much to perswasion. [*Arte*, p. 116]

Againe, sentences gathered or heaped together, commende much the matter. As if one should say, Revengement belongeth to GOD alone, and thereby exhort men to pacience. He might bring in these sentences with him, and give great cause of much matter. No man is hurt but of himselfe, that is to say: adversitie or wrong suffering is no harme to him that hath a constant heart, and lives upright in all his doings. [*Arte*, pp. 117–18; cf. pp. 65, 130, 194–95]

[25]William Crane, *Wit and Rhetoric in the Renaissance*, p. 101.
[26]On the precedent offered by Erasmus, see Ong, "Oral Residue in Tudor Prose Style," *PMLA* 80 (1965): 147–48. Also useful is Ong's "Tudor Writings on Rhetoric," *Studies in the Renaissance* 15 (1968): 39–69. Further insight into Wilson's regard for amplification in argument may be gained from his discussion in the *Rule* (pp. 82–83) of "Sorites, An heaping Argumente," as an alternative to syllogistic formulation.

For Wilson, surveying the native resources of English from a Christian humanist's outlook, the essential provision for prose writing was sententious sentences in ample supply. The last of the foregoing passages is noteworthy, moreover, in what it reveals of Wilson's implementation of Scripturalism in sententious form. First invoking Romans 12:19, "Vengeaunce is myne, and I will rewarde, sayth the Lorde," itself an echo of Deuteronomy 32:35, "To mee belongeth vengeaunce, and recompense," he proceeds to amplification with a sense parallelism of his own devising: a first clause, "No man is hurt but of himself," on which he expatiates in two succeeding clauses that form a pair of the third, so-called incomplete type. The functionality of Hebraic sense parallelism as a resource of style which we see in small in this passage proves important to Wilson throughout the *Arte*. In this connection he at one point lists apt sentences in the manner of Elyot's *Banquet of Sapience* and Baldwin's *Treatise of Moral Philosophie* (*Arte*, pp. 118–19), but the commoner manifestation of Wilson's regard for Scripturalist modes of expression occurs in the intermittent specimen passages of composition that amplify sense parallelisms and accentuate their predominantly binary form, for example:

Jhon 14	If you love me (sayth Christ) followe my Commaundementes. Christes
Math. 19	will is such, that wee should love God above all things, and our
Mark 10	neighbour as our self. Then if we doe not justice (wherein love doth
Prov. 16	consist) we do neither love man, nor yet love God. The Wiseman
Prov. 4	saith: The beginning of a good life is to do Justice: yea, the blessing
Psal. 96	of the Lord, is upon the head of the just. Heaven is theirs (saith David) that doe justly from time to time. What else then shall we doe but the will of God, and live justly all the daies of our life? . . . Where right beareth rule, there craft is compted vice. The liar is much hated, where trueth is well esteemed. The wicked theeves are hanged, where good men are regarded. [*Arte*, pp. 26–27; cf. pp. 74–75, 191]

With his characteristic articulateness regarding the workings of language, Wilson makes clear what, besides the inherent authority of Scripture, accounts for the effectiveness of sense parallelism: in stating the desiderata for sententious utterance, he stresses the avoidance of "vaine repetitions" of the same things in the same words, which "declare both want of witte and lacke of learning," and the reinforcement of one's points through artfully varied restatement that "handsomely gathers up" matters (*Arte*, pp. 169, 114).

Yet, while sense parallelism is a basic component of effective prose style for Wilson, it is by no means the only one. His interest in means of amplification that combine cognitive and affective impact takes him beyond the fundamental similarity-and-difference relations that inform synonymic and antithetic parallelism to a wider sphere of devices which he, like Ascham, perceives as being of a kindred function: "Also similitudes, examples, comparisons, from one thing to an other, apt translations, and heaping of Allegories, and all such figures as serve for amplifying, doe much commend the lively setting forth of any matter" (*Arte*, p. 178). Of the listed devices, Wilson particularly promotes the use of similitudes "not onely . . . to amplifie a matter, but also to beautifie the same, to delite the hearers, to make the matter plaine, and to shewe a certaine majestie with the report of such resembled things"—indeed, "to prove thinges" by drawing correspondences between "the nature of divers beastes, of mettalles, of stones, and al such as have any vertue in them," and "mans life" (*Arte*, pp. 188–89). For fuller discussion of the effectiveness of similitudes, Wilson refers the reader to his "booke of *Logique*" (*Arte*, p. 190); its emphasis falls on the keenness of observation required for framing arguments from the properties of natural objects and on the consequent mental sharpening that a writer can induce in his readers by compelling them to judge how apt a likeness he has proposed. The appended illustrations of proof by similitude in *The Rule of Reason* are strikingly proto-Euphuistic:

For like as water by continuance weareth a stone, so there is nothing so hard but by time it maie be compassed or brought to passe. As spiders make their awne copwebbes without any other helpe: so some good felowes can bring up newes, and tel straunge tales, without any hearing, when there is not one word true. As the Palme tree beyng overlaied with weightes, riseth higher, and buddeth upwarde more freshely: So a noble stomache vexed with moche adversitie is evermore the stouter. [*Rule*, p. 124]

Other pronouncements in the *Arte* on the use of examples, imagery, and "translations" (tropes or turnings of language from literal to figurative significations) enlarge upon the perceptual and cognitive saliency that Wilson finds in similitudes. He sounds much like Elyot and Ascham, and comparatively conventional, in urging that a writer who "mindeth to perswade, must needes be well stored with examples" from the "Historie of Gods booke to the Christian" and from "Chronicles of all ages" (*Arte*, p. 190). But his more distinctively analytical bent emerges as he pursues his reflections to note that "Unegall examples commend much the matter . . . when the weaker is brought in against the stronger, as if children be faithfull, much more ought men to be faithfull" or that "Contraries being set the one against the other, appeare more evident," so that "if one should set . . . a faire woman against a foule, she shall seeme much the fairer, and the other much the fouler" (*Arte*, pp. 191, 195). The high point of Wilson's treatment of analogies and illustrations, however, is reached in his speculations on the origin of tropes in natural language in the *Arte*. He proceeds by extending a point made previously in the *Rule*, that "the whole matter seemeth by a similitude to be opened," and raising it to a generalization about figurative speech, in which

the hearer is ledde by cogitation uppon rehearsall of a Metaphore, and thinketh more by remembraunce of a worde translated, . . . because every translation is commonly, and for the most part referred to the senses of the bodie, and especially to the sense of seeing, which is the sharpest and quickest above all other. For when I shall say that an angrie man fometh at the mouth, I am brought in remembrance by this translation to remember a Bore, that in fighting useth much foming, the which is a foule and lothly sight. And I cause other to think that he brake pacience wonderfully, when I set out his rage comparable to a bores foming. [*Arte*, p. 171]

In this picturelike visual concomitant of what we recall most vividly, Wilson locates the germ of figurative language. He envisages a primordial "want of words" which compelled "learned and wise men" who "sought with great utterance of speech to commende causes" to "borowe wordes translated" in order "to inlarge their tongue." Their tropes "time and practize made . . . to seeme most pleeasaunt, and therefore they are much the rather used"—so much so at present, he adds with a shrewd glance at stylistic fashions, that "Men coumpt it a point of witte, to passe over such words as are at hand, and . . . of a purpose . . . use such as are farre fetcht and translated" (*Arte*, p. 171; cf. pp. 207, 213, 217). The disparagement of extremism does not cancel Wilson's larger insistence that figurative language is both witty and effective.

Throughout *The Arte of Rhetorique*, the specimen passages in which Wilson demonstrates the use of his recommended set of resources for prose composition reveal that the style being held up as a model is emphatically and in every way a product of wit—to be understood, for the moment, as the cognitive faculty. The staple of this model style is the sententious sentence of sixteenth-century English prose of counsel: predominantly a binary clausal conjunction of an antithetical or correlative type, and usually characterized by the semantic redundancy that identifies Hebraic sense parallelism. As we have been seeing with Wilson's guidance, the creation of this kind of sentence requires an observant, discriminating mind, and the judgment of the "aptnesse" of its form to its content calls upon the same powers of mind in the hearer or reader. Additionally, the similes and examples with which the sense parallelisms are interlarded exercise the wits of both parties in the same fashion. But maneuvers on the boundary of linguistic likeness and difference are not restricted in this style to semantics. Extensive syntactic parallelism characterizes the phrases and clauses of the binary conjunction pairs, both as pairs and as members of recursively elaborated series. Some sound similarities arise as a matter of course from the extensive syntactic parallelism—for example, those stemming from like grammatical affixes on nouns and verbs or the matching in number of constituents that is the likelier to result from matching phrase and clause structure. (These two side effects are the *paromoion* and *isocolon* of rhetoricians like Wilson.) Sound similarities become a further matter of stylistic choice, exercised in superadditions of alliteration, assonance, and rhyme—varieties of the well-named though miscellaneous rhetorical category of *paronomasia*, or sound play. This play is with linguistic likeness and difference on the phonological level, but, again, is not restricted to it. For the hearer or reader whose wit has been roused by the cognitive goadings of such a style will be on the alert for sound-sense correspondences—puns and equivocations, but also figurative language as analyzed by Wilson—which work to return the mind suddenly full circle, to the level of semantics once more. Such a return understandably ranks as "a point of witte" and is obviously at a high premium in a style like this one, whose whole dynamic is to exploit and enforce the identity relation that underlies the operation of conjoining in natural language. A couple of excerpts from representative passages in Wilson's model style will document the combination of featural constants which I have just enumerated:

> If lowlinesse and charitie maintaine life, what a beast is he that [John 15:12] through hatered will purchase death? If God warneth us to love one [Matt. 11:29] an other, and learne of him to bee gentle as he was gentle and humble in heart: How cruell are they that dare withstande his Commaundement? . . . Beastes and birdes without reason love one an other, they shroude and flocke together: and shall man endued with such giftes, hate his even Christian, and eschue companie? When Sheepe doe stray, or Cattle do strive, one against an other, there are Dogges readie to call them in: yea, they will bite them (as it hath beene full often seene) if two fight together: and shall man want reason, to barke against his lewd affections, or at the least shall he have none to checke him for his faultes, and force him to forgive? [*Arte*, pp. 116–17; I have added the bracketed Biblical references here and below.]

> You must measure your children by their vertues, & not by their Sap. iv yeares. For (as the Wiseman saith) a mans wisedome is the greye heares, and an undefiled life is the old age. Happie is that mother that hath had godlie children, and not she that hath had long living children. For, if felicitie should stand by length of time, some Tree were more happie then any man, for it liveth longer: and so like wise brute beastes, as the Stagge, who liveth (as *Plinie* doth say) two [Psal. 8:3] hundred yeres and more. If we would but consider what man is, we should have small hope to live, and little cause to put any great assurance in this life. Let us see him what he is: Is his bodie any [Gen. 2:7] thing els, but a lumpe of earth, made together in such forme as we [Psal. 39:4] doe see? A frail vessel, a weake carion subject to miserie, cast down [Psal. 31:12] with every light disease: a man to day, & to morowe none. A flowre

[Psal. 103: 15]   that this day is fresh, & to morrowe withereth. Good Lord doe wee not see, that even those thinges which nourish us, doe rotte and dye, as hearbes, birds, beastes, water, and al other, without the which we cannot live. And how can we live ever, that are sustained with dead thinges? Therefore, when any one doth dye, why doe wee not thinke, that this may chaunce to every one, which now hath chaunced to any one. [*Arte*, p. 83]

Manifestly, the prose style which Wilson advocates draws its force from the directed syntax of schematic sentences as much as Ascham's does. Since the two writers share Scripturalist proclivities tracing to stout Protestant convictions and an appreciable number of the same resources for prose composition, we may well inquire whether there are any significant differences either in their notions of style or in their outlooks on the capacities of language and language users. The first differences to emerge seem ones merely of degree. Comparatively speaking, Wilson's model style exhibits greater vehemence over longer stretches of discourse than even the impassioned Pauline mode found at intervals in *The Schoolmaster*. Ascham's vehemence is associated with essentially one device—catalogues of lexical primaries plus whatever formal likenesses they may entail—and essentially one kind of context—issues of what, to him, are fundamental values. Vehemence for Wilson, however, is not just an effect of style that always commands favorable notice in the *Arte*.[27] It is, more exactly, the one great objective at which all the features of his model style aim. Wilson's "heaping together" of coordinate constructions tends to be more conspicuous than Ascham's because the units are larger (generally full or only slightly reduced clauses)[28] or semantically more insistent (question form is endemic in the clausal recursions of the *Rule* and the *Arte*). But the difference in the degree of vehemence is perhaps most to be accounted for by Wilson's assaults on his readers' sensibilities through visual and aural stimuli—the use of imagery in examples and similitudes, and the incessant undertone of sound similarities. Yet, for all of the systematic excitation of eye and ear in *The Arte of Rhetorique*, Wilson is no unreflective advocate of some "the more the merrier" principle in setting out his amplified, vehement style.

[27]See, for example, the section "Of moving pittie, and stirring men to shewe mercie" (*Arte*, p. 65); the remarks on "augmenting and vehemently enlarging" (p. 114); the recommendation of "notable and strange" examples "to make our talk appear vehement" (p. 120) and, in general, of "Vehemencie" in words (p. 128); the definition of the orator's objective as "a stirring or forsing of the minde, either to desire, or els to detest and loth any thing, more vehemently then by nature we are commonly wont to do" (p. 130); and, finally, the specific remarks on "vehement" and "stirring" figures (pp. 186, 201, 205, 208).

[28]Wilson does, however, take explicit notice of the rhetorical figure constituted by a recursively elaborated *NP* catalogue in the section on "Reckening" or *dinumeratio* (*Arte*, p. 206). There are also some rare uses of this device in his specimen passages; see *Arte*, p. 33, and cf. pp. 128, 179.

His exposition redounds with warnings to be moderate in handling the potential for elaboration that language offers its user in so many forms. "Therfore not onely is it wisedome, to speake so much as is needefull, but also it is good reason to leave unspoken so much as is needelesse," he advises in an early section (*Arte*, p. 9). Other passages to this effect cluster in the sections devoted to "Composition," "Exornation," and the sound figures "Like ending, and like falling":

Some use overmuch repetition of some one letter, as pitifull povertie praieth for a penie, but puffed presumption passeth not a point, pampering his panch with pestilent pleasure, procuring his passeport to poste it to hell pit, there to be punished with paines perpetual. [*Arte*, p. 167]

Some end their sentences all alike, making their talke rather to appeare rimed Meeter, then to seeme plaine speeche, the which as it much deliteth being measurably used, so it much offendeth when no meane is regarded. [*Arte*, p. 168]

These two kindes of Exornation are then most delitefull, . . . when that once againe is uttered which before was spoken: when sentences are turned and letters are altered. . . . This may be an example: where learning is loved, there labour is esteemed: but when slothe is thought solace, there rudenesse taketh place. . . . Divers in this our time delite much in this kinde of writing, which beeing measurably used, deliteth much the hearers, otherwise it offendeth, and wearieth mens eares with sacietie. . . . I speake thus much of these ii. figures, not that I thinke folie to use them (for they are pleasant and praise worthy) but my talke is to this ende, that they should neither onely nor chiefly be used, as I know some in this our time, do overmuch use them. [*Arte*, pp. 202–3]

The odd thing about Wilson's warnings to observe moderation in cultivating similarity features that schematize one's prose is that they raise the very problem which they purport to be laying to rest. Even as he admonishes, his own prose remains heavily schematic—a systematic endeavor, as we have been seeing, to manipulate the identity-difference relation at all levels of linguistic structure in the service of various rhetorical ends. It is possible to bring the problem to a head in an impatient demand: Why does the sharp-witted Wilson fail to see that his practice and his preaching are at variance with regard to stylistic excess? Yet a question so formulated closes off any possibly informative answer because it makes an irony of Wilson's considerable powers as an observer and analyst of language. I would prefer to ask: Why is Wilson's toleration for schematics in prose style pitched at so high a level? This strikes me as a better question. It allows, I think, for an interesting answer—one which casts further light on specifically Protestant aspects of thinking which, through the influence and agency of Wilson, propelled the generalized Scripturalist program for prose along its course to the ne plus ultra of Euphuism in Lyly. A start on an answer to the question just posed may be found by returning to the last passage quoted from the *Arte*. There Wilson acknowledges of "like ending, and like falling" that "*S. Augustine* had a goodly gift in this behalfe, and yet some thinkes he forgot measure, and used overmuch this kind of figure." The excuse for Augustine which Wilson instantaneously offers reflects in a trenchant continuing fashion upon human nature, not only in Augustine's time but in the earlier era of Tacitus and (in the shift to present tense "speake" in the final sentence of the quotation below) Wilson's time as well:

Notwithstanding, the people were such where he lived, that they tooke much delite in rimed sentences. . . . Yea, thei were so nice and so waiward to please, that except the Preacher from time to time could rime out his sermon, they would not long abide the hearing. Tacitus also sheweth that in his time, the Judges and Serjantes at the lawe, were driven to use this kinde of phrase, both in their writing, and also in their speaking. Yea, great Lordes would thinke themselves contemned, if learned men (when they speake before them) sought not to speake in this sort. [*Arte*, p. 203]

The final contemporary turn taken in this excursus on the waywardness and intractability of human nature in distant ages of the Roman Empire indicates the immediacy of Wilson's concerns in the apparently involuntary manner in which he reveals them. The larger fact is, however, that both *The Rule of Reason* and *The Arte of Rhetorique* project a recurrently negative view of audience psychology and, in a number of instances, connect this view with the need for a vehement style that makes potent appeals to the ear and eye.

Only on slight acquaintance can Wilson's view seem indistinguishable from Ascham's own high seriousness in implementing the generalized Scripturalist program for prose in *The Schoolmaster*, where accesses of cultural and moral intensity take the form of heaping catalogues—the mode of Paul in delivering his most urgent pastoral counsel. Overall, Wilson's Protestantism entails a decidedly more negative outlook on human nature than does Ascham's. The quotient of patriotism in *Toxophilus* and *The Schoolmaster* is so ample that these works remain sanguine about the humanity embodied in Englishmen, at least. Thus the earlier work represents the progression from native aptitude to learning to use in handling the longbow—and in its concomitant, living morally—as accessible to every male in the realm, with allowances only for differences in proficiency. The later work, while admittedly virulent against Italianate ways and any form of papistry, holds firm in its optimism that English readers can be brought to their senses through doses of right-mindedness administered in directed syntax, just as it is optimistic about the prospects of shaping English schoolboys into good Latinists and virtuous souls even without beating them. Such is not the outlook of Wilson, who wrote *The Rule of Reason* to expose what he brands as the pernicious errors and brazen fallacies of the Papists and Anabaptists in the land and who takes the offensive directly in pronouncing on the aim of persuasion at the opening of *The Arte of Rhetorique:*

Such quicknesse of witte must bee shewed, and such pleasaunt sawes so well applied, that the eares may finde much delite, whereof I will speake largely, when I shall intreate of moving laughter. And assuredly nothing is more need-full, then to quicken these heavie loden wittes of ours, and much to cherish these our lompish and unweldie Natures, for except men finde delite, they will not long abide: delite them, and winne them, wearie them, and you lose them for ever. And that is the reason, that men commonly tarie the ende of a merie Play, and cannot abide the halfe hearing of a sower checking Sermon. Therefore even these auncient Preachers, must now and then play the fooles in the pulpit, to serve the tickle eares of their fleting audience, or els they are like sometimes to preach to the bare walles: for though their spirite bee apt, and our wil prone, yet our flesh is so heavie, and humours so overwhelme us, that we cannot without refreshing, long abide to heare any one thing. Thus we see that to delite is needfull, without the which weightie matters will not be heard at all. [*Arte,* pp. 3–4]

This passage discloses allusively but surely the grounding for all of Wilson's proceedings as a rhetorician: the truth of Christ's own char-acterization of the human self as divided against itself (Matthew 26:41, Mark 14:38) compounded with the deeper overtones of the willing spirit but weak flesh and the futility of unaided moral effort with which this Gospel characterization was invested by Paul (Romans 7:23, Galatians 5:17). For Wilson, two principles were entailed by the complex truth of this characterization of human nature. First, as we have seen, the aims of teaching, delighting, and persuading stood their best chance of being realized if they were pursued conjointly; and, second, a practitioner of eloquence had to be ready at all times to take a combative approach to the negative facets of his audience's psychology—ready, that is, to "winne them" or "lose them for ever." It is, of course, demonstrable that the phraseology of striving for victory, of "getting the overhand," that recurs in the *Arte* harks back to Cicero and Quintilian, two of Wilson's main sources, as a reflection of the adversary system by which cases were argued in the law courts of the Roman Empire (and, likewise, in Wilson's and our society). What is significant, however, about Wilson's use of the phraseology is that he regularly applies it not just to the opposing parties in an argument or to tactics for dealing with judges—the ordinary classical contexts—but generalizes it to represent the relation of a speaker to any hearers, or a writer to any readers. The net consequence of this broader use of adversative phraseology is to evoke as a possibility, which might arise at any time, another set of circumstances than the ordinary ones posited for discourse by Ascham and by Wilson, too, at other junctures in the *Arte*. In the latter circumstances, as opposed to the

ordinary ones, what I have termed the transactive or interpretive paradigm for the relation between a speaker and hearer or a writer and
reader is suspended, for the speaker or writer is denied the cooperation
and receptivity of his audience. These may therefore be thought of as
special circumstances, but hardly infrequent or unusual, given Wilson's
view of the intractability of human nature. What they require is that the
speaker or writer use every effective means at his disposal to combat
the audience's indisposition to attend for any length of time to what is
being said.

Thus, advises Wilson, "if moving affections can doe more good, then
bringing in of good reasons, it is meete alwaies to use that way, whereby
wee may by good helpe get the overhand" (*Arte*, p. 8; cf. pp. 9–10, 100,
115–16). In particular, "because the beautie of amplifying, standeth most
in apt moving of affections," he pauses to develop the larger negative
dimensions of audience psychology in order to show what a powerful
resource amplification is for the rhetorician and how much he stands in
need of it:

Affections therefore (called Passions) are none other thing, but a stirring or
forsing of the minde, either to desire, or els to detest and loth any thing, more
vehemently then by nature we are commonly wont to do.

If an evill man finde much favour, we envie his good hap, yea, it greeveth us,
that any one such, should have such favor shewed: and not onely do we hate
the evill that are come to any wealth, but also we envie commonly all such as
come to any preferment, especially, if either they have bene as poore men as
we are, or else came of a meaner house then we have done. Noe one man would
have any to be better then himself.

And thus we can never be content to give our neighbour a good worde. Yea,
though they have served right well, and deserved a greater reward, wee must
needes finde some fault with them to lessen their praises, and say that though
their desertes be greate, yet their natures are nought: none so proude, though
fewe bee so hardie: none so envious, though fewe so faithful: none so covetous
though fewe so liberall: none so gluttonous, though fewe keepe such an house.
And thus, though we graunt them one thing, yet we will take an other thing
as fast againe from them. [*Arte*, pp. 130–31]

For the most part—indeed, overwhelmingly—Wilson uses his pessimistic view of human psychology to sanction the more obtrusive devices
in his recommended style, namely, the aural appeal of sound figures
and the imaginative appeal of exempla and similitudes, as necessary
means for stirring the affections of one's audience to desire and practice
virtue (*Arte*, pp. 166, 169, 198, 218). Here the implicit assumption
throughout is that the rhetorician exerts his wit to activate the wits of
his audience and motivate them constructively. Yet from time to time in
Wilson's *Arte* the negative outlook on human nature translates as a great

divide between a select few who are learned and witty and the many who are ignorant or dullwitted—as in this observation: "Considering the dulnesse of mans Nature, that neither it can be attentive to heare, nor yet stirred to like or alow any tale long told, except it be refreashed, or finde some sweete delite: the learned have by witte and labour, devised much varietie" (*Arte*, p. 134; cf. pp. 10, 108).

As the foregoing quotation indicates, the emphasis at those junctures which convey the sense of a great divide falls on the "witte and labour" by which the audience is brought, in spite of itself, to attend to "the learned." The divide notwithstanding, Wilson implies that all is well in such proceedings, for it is "the learned" who are outwitting human frailty—a class which he, like Ascham, consistently identifies with the morally upright. No doubt we are meant to find reassurance as well in the easily inferred analogy with an able, conscientious minister and his congregation of ordinary, erring souls. However, just as Wilson goes beyond Ascham in recognizing circumstances caused by the perversities in human nature that pit a rhetorician against his audience, so, too, Wilson sometimes reflects the candor that flickers in classical writers when he confronts the possibility that the way of wit may diverge from learning or morality in deploying the resources of eloquent expression. "Now an eloquent man being smally learned can much more good in perswading by shift of wordes, and meete placing of matter: then a great learned clarke shalbe able with great store of learning, wanting words to set forth his meaning," he remarks at one point (*Arte*, p. 161). And at another: "Such art may bee used in this behalfe, that though the cause bee very evill, yet a wittie man may get the overhand, if he be cunning in his facultie" (*Arte*, p. 115). Hence the most intriguing passages in the *Arte* are ones which set out Wilson's reflections on how wit can triumph over the innate resistance of humankind by manipulating the powerful instrument of natural language.

The longest sequence of such reflections occurs in the section on means "Of deliting the hearers, and stirring them to laughter," which Crane has identified as deriving in considerable measure from chapters 62–71 of the second book of Castiglione's *Courtier*, a treatment in turn based on the treatment of wit in Cicero's *De oratore*.[29] At the outset of this section Wilson moves quickly to quash objections to his claim that every speaker, even a preacher, needs versing in the techniques which he is about to describe. His self-defense assumes remarkably combative undertones as it depicts the redoubtable figure of a wit:

Pet. 5   But some perhaps wil saie unto me, *Facite quantum in vobis est*, to
Mat. 10   whom I aunswere, *estote prudentes*. And now because our senses be

[29]William Crane, *Wit and Rhetoric in the Renaissance*, pp. 19, 101–2, 128. This section of the *Arte* occupies pp. 134–56 in Mair's edition.

such, that in hearing a right wholsome matter, we either fall a sleepe
when we shoulde most harken, or els are wearied with still hearing
one thing, without any change, and think that the best part of his
tale, resteth in making an ende: the wittie and learned have used
delitefull sayings, and quicke sentences, ever among their waightie
causes, considering that not only good will is got therby (for what
is he that loveth not mirth?) but also men wonder at such a head,
as hath mens hartes at his commaundement, being able to make
them merie when he list, and that by one word speaking, either in
aunswering some thing spoken before, or els oftentimes in giving
the onset, being not provoked thereunto. Againe, we see that men
are full oft abashed, and put out of countenance by such taunting
meanes, and those that have so done are coumpted to be fine men,
and pleasaunt fellowes, such as fewe dare set foote with them. [*Arte*,
p. 137; cf. p. 135]

Wilson's ensuing anecdotal rehearsal of linguistic triumphs of wit focuses on effects of surprise or of irony, or of both combined, that are
attainable by playing on the identity-difference relation in the sound
and sense of isolated words or of larger constituent structures. I shall
use "punning" to designate such play at the word level, and "equivocation" to designate play involving phrases, clauses, or sentences. Later
passages in this section extend the notion of playing with language to
encompass role-playing; in them Wilson's most interesting observations
concern exaggeration, dissimulation, figuration (with which he closely
associates fabulation), and conjecture.

In the treatment of punning and equivocation, the illustrations from
Wilson's own experience frequently distinguish themselves by the gravity of the subject or issue which they involve and which he manifestly
considers a factor in their effectiveness. One anecdote illustrating equivocation pays grudging but genuine tribute to the quip of a witty "Span-
yard" who watched "an earnest Gospeller" suffer "death in Smithfielde"
for "words spoken against an Ecclesiasticall lawe." "*Ah miser, non potui
tacere et vivere?*" Wilson records the onlooker as saying. "Ah wretch that
he was, could he not live and hold his peace?" (*Arte*, p. 138). Another
anecdote illustrating punning conflicts Wilson. He acknowledges that
"it is wel liked, when by the chaunging of a letter, or taking away some
part of a word, or adding sometimes a sillable, we make an other meaning," but he finds "full unhappely" meant the quibble of one who in-
veighed against "those that held of Christes spiritual being in the
sacrament": "Some (quoth he) wil have a Trope to be in these words:
This is my body: but surely I would wish the T. were taken away, &
that they had for their labour which is left behind" (*Arte*, pp. 141–42).
But when the punning is Protestant, Wilson's compunctions disappear.
Here is his possible tribute to Morison:

Many wittie men take occasion, to reason pleasauntly upon the interpretacion of a woorde. As I remembre a wittie man, and a woorthie man also did, who enveighyng at a time against Cardinall Poule, and beyng vehement in the cause of his countrie, saied thus in the middest of his heate, o Poule, o whurle Poule, as though his name declared his evill nature. [*Rule*, p. 120]

More interesting still, however, are Wilson's observations on sustained role-playing in language as manifestations of wit, for by degrees the distinction that comes to figure is not just one of linguistic identity or difference but one of truth or falsehood. Regarding exaggeration, he can remark amiably enough on its humorous potential: "In augmenting or diminishing without all reason, wee give good cause of much pastime" (*Arte*, p. 146). Yet in discussing the Scriptural warrant that attaches to exaggeration, as a figure of speech, he is plainly uneasy that "God promised to Abraham, that he would make his posteritie equal with the sandes of the earth." Wilson does his best to explain: "Now it was not so saied, that there should be so many in deede, but that the number should be . . . very great." "Mounting above the trueth, is when wee doe set foorth things exceedingly and above all mens expectation. . . . Therefore in this speech we must understand there is a mounting, called of the Grecians *Hyperbole*: wee use this figure much in English," he adds in a tone that is hard to catch. But the uneasiness creeps back into his last words: "In all which speeches we mount evermore a great deale, and not meane so as the wordes are spoken" (*Arte*, p. 183). The possibility that hyperbole may produce misunderstanding become a matter of overt anxiety in a third passage on the subject, where Wilson adverts to Cicero's supremacy in rhetorical exaggeration: he "did herein so excell, that lightly he got the victorie in all matters, that ever he tooke in hand," whether he was called upon for praise or dispraise. This momentary tribute breaks off with the following troubled comment: "I doubt not but the wittiest wil take most paines in this behalfe, and the honest for ever will use it for the defence of most honest matters. Weapons may be abused for murther, and yet weapons are onely ordeined for safegard" (*Arte*, pp. 115–16).

Wilson's comments on "dissembling" exhibit a like gradation into dubiety. His principal treatment, in the section "Of deliting the hearers," invokes two eminent older contemporaries by name: Sir Thomas More, who "had an excellent gift, not onely in this kinde, but also in all other pleasant delites, whose witte even at this hower, is a wonder to all the worlde," and "our worthie *Latimer*," who once "set out the Devill for his diligence wonderfully, and preferred him for that purpose, before all the Bishops in England." Wilson declares of these precedents: "It is a pleasaunt dissembling, when we speake one thing merily and thinke an other earnestly: or els when we praise that which otherwise deserveth dispraise, to the shaming of those that are taken not to be most honest" (*Arte*, pp. 146–47). Subsequent remarks on dissembling are marked by an increasing meanness rather than pleasantness of effect and an attendant obscuring of moral point, even as the premium on wit is maintained. In defining and illustrating the figure *Dissimulatio*, Wilson continues to insist, although somewhat hollowly, on its utility as a social corrective by retailing a story about a vainglorious monetary expert who was given "a frumpe even to his face" by a courtier in one of the recurring crises exacerbated by Tudor devaluations of the currency. The courtier's leading on of the other man is acknowledged by Wilson as jesting "closely, & with dissembling meanes" to "grig our fellowe, when . . . we see one boasting himselfe, . . . to holde him up with ye and nay, and ever to add more to that which he saieth" (*Arte*, pp. 184–85). But he never explains what is "pleasaunt" about his vignette entitled "Pleasaunt dissembling in outward behaviour":

There is a pleasaunt kinde of dissembling, when two meete together, and the one cannot well abide the other: and yet they both outwardly strive to use pleasaunt behaviour, and to shewe much courtesie, yea, to contend on both partes, which should passe other in using of faire wordes, and making of lively countenaunces: seeking by dissembling, the one to deceive the other. [*Arte*, pp. 155–56]

Other, related passages on "a close understanding, . . . when more may bee gathered, then is openly expressed" and on "bitter Jestes . . . which have a hid understanding in them" encourage the inference that the pleasure in these species of linguistic dissimulation is mainly self-satisfaction in the triumph of one's own wit at the expense of another's feelings. For all three of Wilson's illustrative anecdotes display this pattern: Demosthenes' insinuation that a man who faulted him for burning so much lamp oil in preparing his speeches was himself a thief in the night; an anonymous retort to one who disputed another's choice of dinner meat, to the effect that experience with fish did not make for expertise in meat (a humiliating allusion to a fishmonger father); and, lastly, Diogenes the Cynic's well-known importuning of a man for some slips of a fig tree on which the man's wife had hanged herself, so as to grow a whole orchard (*Arte*, pp. 180, 151).

Figurative expression, moreover, ranks consistently with Wilson as a sign of special wit. We have already noted his view that the origination of tropes is a lasting credit to the wit of "learned and wise men" who enriched the common resources of language by "borrowing" words into "translated" meanings. He pays like tribute to those who can delight others with "pleasaunt tales" and "Fables" of their own devising: "For undoubtedly no man can doe any such thing, except they have a great mother wit, & by experience confirm such . . . whereto by nature they

were most apt" (*Arte*, pp. 144–45). In a late section of the *Arte* he spec-
ulates anew on the motives of the ancient poets who began to devise
fables—which he conceives, like a true Renaissance thinker, as sustained
figurations of meaning, or allegories. Significantly, Wilson considers
fabulation to have begun in dissimulation:

> The Poetes were wisemen, and wished in hart the redresse of things, the which
> when for feare, they durst not openly rebuke, they did in colours painte them
> out, and tolde men by shadowes what they should doe in good sooth, or els
> because the wicked were unworthie to heare the trueth, they spake so that none
> might understande but those unto whom they pleased to utter their meaning.
> [*Arte*, p. 196]

The anachronistic allusion to reprobate ears in this passage shows Wilson
projecting the perceived conditions of his day back into antiquity, where
he accordingly finds much of value in "the saying of Poetes and all their
fables": "By them we may talke at large, and win men by perswasion,
if we declare before hand that these tales were not fained of such wise-
men without cause, . . . either to the amendment of maners, to the
knowledge of the trueth, to the setting forth of Natures work, or els the
understanding of some notable thing done" (*Arte*, p. 195). Such feigning
in order to pursue constructive purposes lends further support to the
adversative model for the relation between the speaker or writer and
his audience which the formulations of the *Arte* recurrently imply.[30]
Hence Wilson can close his discussion of fables with a recommendation
that merges the adversative model for discourse with the Pauline characterization of the Gospel as foolishness to the worldly-wise (1 Corinthians 1:17–27, 2:14, 3:18–19):

> I would thinke it not amisse to speake much, according to the nature and phansie
> of the ignorant, that the rather they might be won through Fables, to learn more
> weightie and grave matters. . . . The multitude must needes be made merie: &
> the more foolish your talke is, the more wise will they compt it to be. And yet
> it is no foolishnesse, but rather wisedome to win men, by telling of Fables to
> heare of Gods goodnesse. [*Arte*, p. 198]

[30]Wilson has similar observations to make on *periphrasis* or "circumlocution," which he
calls "a large description, either to set forth a thing more gorgiously or els to hide it, if
the eares can not beare the open speaking: or when with fewe words, we can not open
our meaning to speake it more largely" (*Arte*, p. 175). With what Wilson says about
figuration and fable it is interesting to compare Puttenham's strikingly similar (but more
trenchantly articulated) characterization of allegory as "the figure of false semblant or
dissimulation," "which is when we speake one thing and thinke another, and that our
wordes and our meanings meet not." Puttenham also views allegory as "the chief ring-
leader and captaine of all other figures, either in the Poeticall or oratorie sciences"; see
The Arte of English Poesie, ed. Gladys D. Willcock and Alice Walker (Cambridge: Cambridge
University Press, 1936), p. 186.

It is preeminently in Wilson's treatment of "things gathered by conjecture," however, that his acknowledgment of how rhetorical discourse may play by means of wit at the boundary of truth and falsehood assumes the most ominous overtones of all. Although he asserts that "Things gathered by conjecture, to seeme otherwise then they are, delite much the eares being wel applied together" (*Arte*, p. 152), his two display pieces on the rhetorical use of conjecture—one a full-blown "Oration conjecturall," another a specimen of "Amplification by conjectures"— make extremely disquieting reading, for all their indebtedness to Latin, especially Ciceronian, antecedents. Both pieces are accusations of murder against a man who entirely denies the act, and they are composed by such strategies as "heaping of words and sentences together," "as when by many conjectures and great presumptions, we gather that one is an offendour, heaping them all into one plumpe," "to the intent that our talke might appere more vehement" (*Arte*, p. 128) or recourse to the *"Places of confirmation, to prove things by conjecture,"* which are, baldly enough, "i. Will to doe evill" and "ii. Power to do evill." Since by Wilson's own admission, these places are amplified "by suspitions gathered, and some likelihood of thing appearing," it is insufficiently reassuring to be told at the end of the presentation that "The person accused beeing innocent of the crime that is laied to his charge, may use the selfe same places for his owne defence, the which his accuser used to prove him giltie" (*Arte*, pp. 90–91, 94).

To conclude discussion of Wilson, it is illuminating to consider that the greater part of the linguistic resources with which he credits the power of wit to elicit delight in *The Arte of Rhetorique* had been catalogued and reprehended as "deceiptfull" only two years earlier in his *Rule of Reason*. The final section of the *Rule* is a lengthy survey of "the places of false conclusions, or deceiptfull reasons" developed by Wilson from a lead in Aristotle's *Rhetoric*.[31] It opens with a striking evocation of current tactics for confuting an opponent by other than logical means which recalls distinctly the witty mover to laughter of the *Arte*:

We make thargument appere slendre, when we receive it laughyngly, and declare by woordes, even at the first, that it is nothing to the purpose, and so abashe the opponent. Again, wee tourne another argument in our adversaries necke, when wee bryng another example against him. Or els when . . . we shift awaie, . . . by makyng some digression, or gevyng occasion of some other talke, whereby the adversarie, either is driven to forget his argument, or els beeyng blinded with to moche matier, is forced either to goe no foorther, or els to thinke himself content. In all whiche maner of confutacion, when we purpose to put a man to

[31]Wilson signals his indebtedness to Aristotle at the outset of this long section of the *Rule* (pp. 156–219); his editor, Sprague, supplies the exact reference (p. 233) to *Rhetoric* 1401a–2a—a passage of only five pages in the compact Loeb edition. Obviously, Wilson has enlarged upon Aristotle many times over.

silence, I would wish great moderacion to be used, and as little advauntage taken by soche meanes, as maie be possible. . . . It is a worlde to see the subtle brain, of many braggyng bodies whiche with held countenaunce, beare an outward shadowe of wisedome havyng onely the maskyng visage, and lackyng the naturall face. Thei will stand stoutely in mainteinaunce of an untruthe, and with countenaunce seme to shewe it: yea, and by their bolde bearyng it out, almoste perswade the hearers, that thei onely have the true part, and that others are altogether deceived. Thei will saie, that no wiseman, would ones thinke that for shame, which their adversarie uttreth with out al shame: yea, . . . last of all, thei will trifle and toie merely, and so with impudent laughyng make thother past speaking. [*Rule,* pp. 157–58]

As the survey proceeds to castigate particular linguistic maneuvers as illegitimate substitutes for logical argument, it is surprising to find repeated counterparts of devices that are praised for wit and delightfulness in the *Arte*. For example, the first two means of "deceiptfull arguments" identified in the *Rule* are "these folowyng: i. The doubtfulnesse of wordes. ii. The double meanyng of a sentence"—that is, punning and equivocation, respectively, as I have used these terms to capture Wilson's distinction between lexical and syntactic play in the *Arte*. In the *Rule,* Wilson traces the possibility of punning to "*Homonymia,* whiche maie be called in Englishe, the doubtfulnesse of one woorde, when it signifieth diversly." He proceeds to reflect adversely on it as "a manner of subtletie, when the deceipt is in a woorde that hath mo significations then one. . . . Of no one thing riseth so moche controversie, as of the doubtfulnesse, and double taking of a woorde" (*Rule,* pp. 161–63). For its part, equivocation—"when sentences be spoken doubtfullie, that thei maie be construed twoo maner of waies, and the partes diverslie poincted"—derives from ambiguity, another property of natural language which incurs only negative comment in Wilson's *Rule:* "The Ambiguitie is, when the construction bringeth errour, having diverse understandinges in it" (*Rule,* pp. 164–65). Yet a third, specifically verbal means of "deceiptfull argumente" is "*Figura dictionis,* called otherwise in good Latin, *forma orationis,* the maner of speache"—a category in which Wilson includes all nonliteral modes of expression "when the phraise bredeth errour, and the propertie of the tongue not well knowen engendreth ambiguitie" (*Rule,* p. 171). Interestingly enough, his examples of figurative speeches that have occasioned misunderstanding derive entirely from Scripture—most from the enigmatic utterances of Jesus in the Gospels, but some from the Old Testament and the Pauline Epistles. Although in each case Wilson deflects responsibility for these misunderstandings upon the obtuse or perverse minds of the hearers in question, the net effect of his treatment of figurative language in the *Rule* is to emphasize its deceptive—and, hence, problematic—character.

The problematic note continues in the section devoted to "Thinges spoken above measure." Here Wilson has nothing to say about delight or wit in a sequence of cautionary remarks regarding exaggeration in language, for example, those on hyperbole—"that is to saie, when a thing is spoken beyonde measure uncrediblie, and yet is not so largelie mente"—which evoke an Icarian flight: "We must diligently take hede, when soche speches are used, that we take them not as thei bee spoken, but as thei are mente. . . . And alwaies be wise in our mounting, that ascending over highe, we be not commaunded to come doune as fooles" (*Rule*, p. 184).

Dissimulation, another major species of linguistic role-playing which figures as a source of pleasure produced by wit in the *Arte*, becomes Wilson's most constant object of opprobrium in the section on "false conclusions, or deceiptfull reasons" in the *Rule*. Besides the three sources of deception which he traces to properties of natural language—homonymy, ambiguity, and figurative expression—Wilson lengthily discusses no fewer than seven means by which a fallacious argument can be made to look like a valid one. He emphasizes, however, that three fundamental faults characterize "all soche false conclusions as are in the matier": "either in the wrong definyng, and not well settyng foorthe the nature of any thing, or els in not aptly dividyng, or lastly, not advisedly weighyng the causes of thinges, but heapyng them up without ordre or reason" (*Rule*, pp. 175–76; cf. p. 204). Significantly, two of the three material sources of fallacious argument enumerated by Wilson trace to the procedures of definition and division which the arts of logic and rhetoric share. The disconcerting possibility that rhetorical concerns may be at fault in the framing of specious reasoning begins to seem the likelier when one notes the utterly disparate representation of "heaping matter" in Wilson's two works—as a source of false conclusions in the *Rule*, as the essential technique of eloquent expression in the *Arte*.

The severest if not the most constant opprobrium in the treatment of "false conclusions" in the *Rule* is reserved for the deceitfulness of representing doubtful or conjectural matters as if they were certainties. Of special note in Wilson's discussion of conjectural reasoning is his stress on how common it is in everyday life and how great an incentive to its use is provided by the human penchant for self-deception. Thus, for example, he comments on the fallacy of "*secundum non causam, ut causam*, that is, whan a cause that is not able to prove the matier, is brought in, as though it were of force, and strength" under the rubric "Badde excuses": "This deceiptfull argument is moche used in this our life, and made a buckelar for diverse matiers. As when I am lothe to be of a quest, or that any . . . should trouble mee, beeyng sent for, I fain my self sicke. . . . This is as thei saie in Englishe, better a bad excuse, then none at all" (*Rule*, pp. 188, 190–91). In a related vein, Wilson notes a fallacy that flouts the rule "*A posse ad esse, non est bona consequentia:* because a thing maie be, it shall not therefore followe that it is," and he finds it operative in such inferences as "He is pale in countenaunce. Ergo he is in love." Wilson rejoins: "Of signes that be not propre, neither tary long, no strong argument is made. . . . Paleness maie come of studie, or care, and thought, of abstinence, of watchyng, of some distemperature in the bodie, and many other waies besides" (*Rule*, p. 194). The immediately following section casts disapproval on the conjectural strategy of "*plures interrogationes*, many questions," that is, "when of one thing many are asked, one maie easely be enveigled and brought to an inconvenience, before he be ware" (*Rule*, pp. 195, 197); what strikes the reader of these warnings is their lack of fit with the recurring "many questions" in the amplified and vehement style promoted in the later *Arte*. Finally, to round out the literarily pertinent observations made on varieties of deceitful conjectural reasoning, note must be taken of Wilson's expanded definition of the fallacy of "*Repetitio principii*, the cuckoes song, that is, repetyng of that wholy in the conclusion, which before was onely spoken in the first Proposicion: or els by thinges doubtful to prove thinges that are as doubtfull." Wilson elaborates sardonically on this fallacy which he has so picturesquely named:

Self willed folke that folowe lust, and forsake reason, use oft the cuckowes song. As beyng asked why thei will dooe this and that, thei aunswere streight, Marie because I will dooe it, or because it pleaseth me best, so to dooe. . . . For though it be a plaine deceipt, and by reason should be overthrowen, yet . . . reason is out of ceason, and dooeth but litle helpe. Some women are subjecte to this aunswere, whiche in witte dooe excell, though in the eighte partes of reason, fewe scholars can hardely finde them. Well, God graunt all our willes, to stande ever with his will, and then I doubte not, but this harme shall with ease be avoided, and al deceipt for ever sette aparte. [*Rule*, p. 198]

Notwithstanding this pious expression of hope for a conforming of refractory human wills to the divine will which would put an end in this life to deceitful language and argument, the remarkable ambivalence attested in *The Rule of Reason* and *The Arte of Rhetorique* toward the exercise of human wit makes it clear that Wilson cannot devoutly enough wish such a consummation to make its attainment seem a real possibility in the here and now. Even the *Rule*'s lengthy treatment of "the places of false conclusions, or deceiptfull reasons" pays scattered tribute to the brilliance of the very faculty whose waywardness is being anatomized. Thus Wilson can tell the story of "a wonderfull good shifte" practiced by a boy who lied to his mother to keep from having to divulge a state secret, he can exclaim over the "singulare" wit displayed in the creation of a notable metaphor, and he can digress upon the traps to be set in "certaine wittie questions and argumentes, whiche can hardely be avoided, beyng very pleasaunt, and therefore not unworthie to be knowen" (*Rule,* pp. 191, 208, 210). The sum total of such tributes is not large, but on balance it is sufficient to foreshadow the appreciation for wit in argument and language that figures so conspicuously in the *Arte.*

Wilson's two handbooks, published within a pair of years, may be regarded jointly as projections of a peculiarly Protestant sense of human ways with language—one compounded of acknowledgment of what Sidney's *Defence of Poetrie* would subsequently term an "infected will" and an "erected wit."[32] It is even possible to find the balanced perspective implied by Sidney's phrasing in the work of Wilson, whose admiration for the exercise of wit in the *Arte* succeeds—and largely seems to supersede—the more wary outlook embodied in the *Rule.* To put the matter another way, it is clear that the Wilson of *The Rule of Reason* would have endorsed the celebrated distinction in Ascham's *Schoolmaster* between quick wits, which are too fickle and shallow to become learned, and hard wits, which are less impressionable but have the steadiness to attain wisdom. But it is unclear whether the Wilson of *The Arte of Rhetorique* would have agreed to any such distinction, and more unclear still, if he were to agree, whether he would have sided with Ascham against quick wits in favor of hard ones. In his portentous disclosure of an ambivalence that is finally more receptive than guarded toward wit and its array of shifts, Wilson leaves the way open for the generalized Scripturalist program for prose composition to devolve from its hitherto upright course into the errancy with which Lyly so dazzlingly and deliberately experimented in writing his *Euphues.*

MANNER AND MODALITY: EUPHUIZING IN PETTIE AND LYLY

Comparatively early in the great philological hunt for the sources of Euphuism that began over a century ago, Friedrich Landmann claimed George Pettie's *A Petite Pallace of Pettie His Pleasure* (1576) as the English work with the strongest title to being the stylistic prototype for John Lyly's *Euphues: The Anatomy of Wyt* (1578), if not to having originated Euphuism itself. Landmann's claim for Pettie focused on conspicuous and frequent instances of *isocolon, parison, paromoion,* and *paronomasia* as well as runs of rhetorical questions, proverbs, exempla, and similitudes derived from mythical properties of natural objects—in short, the ample presence of those features that, by scholarly agreement, defined Eu-

---

[32]*A Defence of Poetry* in *Miscellaneous Prose of Sir Philip Sidney,* ed. Katherine Duncan-Jones and Jan van Dorsten (Oxford: Clarendon Press, 1973), p. 79. For relevant discussion, see Andrew D. Weiner, *Sir Philip Sidney and the Poetics of Protestantism: A Study of Contexts* (Minneapolis: University of Minnesota Press, 1978).

phuism.[33] With the publication of Tilley's findings that "more than half of Pettie's two hundred and sixty-one proverbs . . . are repeated in *Euphues*," the imputed connection between the two writers became a verified debt.[34] As shown in the following parallel excerpts—the first from Pettie, the second from Lyly—the latter could make close use of the former:

He ought to injoy you which joyeth most in you, which loveth you best, & indureth most paine for your sake: & for proufe of natures lawes, it may please you to consider the quality of the shee woulfe who always choseth that woulfe for her make who is made most leane and foule by following her. . . . Your Wolves example . . . doth inforce no sutch proofe to your purpose, . . . but therin truly you observe *decorum* very duly, in usyng the example of a Beast in so beastly a cause: for like purpose, like proofe: like man, like matter.

I esteeme him more worth then any, he is to be reputed as chiefe. The Wolfe chooseth him for her make, that hath or doth endure most travaile for hir sake. . . . Brute beastes give us ensamples that those are most to be lyked, of whom we are best beloved. . . . And in that you bringe in the example of a beast to confirme your folly, you shewe therein your beastly disposition, which is readie to followe suche beastlinesse.[35]

Although Tilley demonstrated Lyly's pillaging of Pettie for similitudes, exempla, and sententious sayings with which to amplify his composition in the approved sixteenth-century manner, Jacobus Swart argued that there were formal grounds for retaining Lyly's title as the originator of Euphuism, specifically, that Lyly makes an integrated stylistic system out of Pettie's mere appliqué work: "In Pettie's prose we are struck by the alliteration rather than the balance of phrases. By restricting the alliteration, shortening the isocolon—thereby making it more obvious—and combining parison and patterned alliteration to a higher degree than had been done by Pettie, Lyly created a systematic style."[36] Swart's insights and conclusion are surely correct, despite his failure to discriminate clearly between considerations of frequency and system or to explain how the features of Lyly's style are "systematic" in a way that

[33]Friedrich Landmann, "Shakspere and Euphuism," *New Shakspere Society Transactions*, Part II (1880–85), p. 255, where Pettie's *Petite Pallace* is said to have "exhibited already to the minutest detail, all the specific elements of euphuism."

[34]Morris P. Tilley, *Elizabethan Proverb Lore in Lyly's "Euphues" and in Pettie's "Petite Pallace,"* *with Parallels from Shakespeare*, University of Michigan Publications in Language and Literature no. 2 (New York: Macmillan Co., 1926), p. 2.

[35]George Pettie, *A Petite Pallace of Pettie His Pleasure*, ed. Herbert Hartman (London and New York: Oxford University Press, 1938), pp. 17–18; *The Complete Works of John Lyly*, ed. R. Warwick Bond (Oxford: Clarendon Press, 1902), I, 239–40. Subsequent citations from these editions of these works—abbreviated *PP* and *Euph.*, respectively—will be incorporated in the text.

[36]Jacobus Swart, "Lyly and Pettie," *English Studies* 23 (1941): 18.

Pettie's are not. There is indeed a difference in kind and not just in degree to be drawn between a style in which such features as *isocolon*, *parison*, and *paromoion* occur discretely (even if frequently) and a style in which the same features are made functions of one another. The syntax and semantics of conjunction as investigated under transformational-generative analysis can help to illuminate the nature and workings of the linguistic system that identifies the style of full-blown Euphuism.

While the compilations of figures in handbooks like Wilson's *Arte* suggest no way of viewing combinations of *isocolon*, *parison*, and *paromoion*, for example, as anything but discrete effects, the very etymologies of the terms (the morphemes *iso-* and *homoio-*) bespeak the shared existence—or creation—of linguistic likeness as vital to the effects being wrought. If we look for possibly relevant aspects of likeness or identity in natural language, we are drawn immediately to the motivating conditions for clausal conjunction, which require likeness both at the semantic level (a "common topic") and at the syntactic level (constituent structure of "the same type"). The dynamism of likeness in clausal conjunction, moreover, regularly manifests itself in conjunction reduction: an operation governed by an identity principle so powerful that it imposes a necessary connection between form and meaning. Iteration in surface structure implies nonidentity, while noniteration in surface structure implies identity; thus, 'A woman was waiting and a woman was singing softly' is interpreted as referring to two individuals, but 'A woman was waiting and singing softly' to one. In turn, as we have noted from time to time, the surface phrases produced by obligatory reduction of strongly identical elements in the underlying structures of conjoined clauses tend to exhibit a certain amount of point-for-point correspondence, while necessarily falling short of the full identity of tautology. Hence, the familiar phenomenon of syntactic parallelism, which ranges through degrees of completeness and incompleteness. ('A woman was waiting and singing softly' illustrates a typical intermediate degree.) Whatever the degree of realization, however, the phenomenon of syntactic parallelism at once evinces and elicits recognition of the likeness and identity relations which inform all the separate operations, as well as the general process, of conjunction in natural language. Not the least salient factor in such recognition is a sense of the limits on identity. For if conjoined elements are totally identical—in effect, the situation of tautology—then the conditions for conjunction reduction are also met, putting an end to the discrete existence of the totally identical conjuncts as elements of surface sentential structure.

Returning, now, to the question of the nature of the "system" in Euphuism raised by Swart's argument regarding Pettie and Lyly, it is obvious that *parison*, *paromoion*, and *isocolon* all depend to a greater or lesser extent on syntactic parallelism. As Jonas Barish pointed out in his now classic essay on Lyly's prose style, the dependence is so great in the case of *parison* that without reference to syntactic parallelism any definition of "like form" is simply inconceivable.[37] With *paromoion*, parallel structure becomes a principal resource both for creating and for signaling sound similarities, since the grammatical functions of words (their roles in syntax) are closely bound up with the morphological features they display. Put most simply, the rhetorical effects of various like-beginnings and like-endings are standardly realized by way of prefixes and suffixes or through lexical items that are performing correspondent functions in their respective phrases and clauses. Without syntactic parallelism these effects could not be achieved with anything like the same regularity. In the case of *isocolon*, or equality of clausal units reckoned by number of syllables, the absence of any necessary dependence on syntactic parallelism does not detract from the quite strongly indicated role for parallelism in ensuring the perceptibility of *isocolon*—and, hence, its very utility as a resource of prose style. What I am suggesting is that Swart's important insights regarding the systematic interrelation of the major formal features of Euphuism as practiced by Lyly attain most cogency and force if the conception of "system" invoked is the identity-equivalence-likeness relation that empowers the creation of coordinate structures in natural language. Once this identity-equivalence-likeness relation is recognized for its central role in creating Euphuistic effects, it also becomes possible to see other defining features of this style—the similitudes, the sense parallelisms of the sententiae, the serial runs of these, and of antitheses and questions—as ancillary if more heterogeneous means for exploring the reciprocal limits of similarity and difference at every level of organization in the linguistic continuum from sound to sense that is spanned by the operations of sentential conjunction. Viewed from this vantage, an appreciable share of the stylistic interest of Euphuism attaches to the lavish exercise of optional recursion in its characteristic formal features—features which bring full circle, though certainly not to an end, the creative potentialities of the native conjunctive sentence forms that supply the substratum as well as the finished shape of much earlier modern English prose.

Having taken the position, with Swart, that there is a crucial literary distinction to be drawn between mere superaddition and system in the use of the defining formal features of Euphuism, we are ready to examine some specifics in which Pettie distinguishes himself on this very basis from Lyly. Not only the existence of the distinction but also the nature of the superaddition which Pettie practices is clarified by turning to specimen passages: these show recursions of exactly identical surface elements which are not blocked by the conditions triggering conjunction

---

[37]Jonas A. Barish, "The Prose Style of John Lyly," *ELH* 23 (1956): 14–27, esp. 15, 16.

reduction. The most prevalent kind of identical elements is simple alliteration or assonance in a string of adjacent lexical items—the very effect which Wilson had parodied for its exaggeration in the *Arte*. Pettie's prose is redolent with such runs as "Loe yonder stands the *p*eereles *p*aragon *pr*incely *Pr*ogne"; "yea, all her *p*artes so *p*erfectly *p*roportioned, that nature sought to winne great commendation in *c*arving *so c*unningly *so c*urious a *c*arkas"; "I *meane is it meet if I purpose* to *p*ossesse so *p*roper a *p*eece"; and "for a *mother to murther, to mangle, to make man*s meate of her own childe" (*PP*, pp. 44, 211, 14, 54; my italics). What is noteworthy in these excerpts, besides Pettie's heavy hand in disposing his sound similarities, is the adventitious way they play across constituent structure. Thus, while in the first the paired *p*s and *pr*s reflect the boundary between the two noun phrases in apposition, the runs on *p*, *c*, and *m* in the second and third entirely override the phrase and clause boundaries of their containing sentence. In the fourth excerpt there is a curious but typical Pettiean standoff produced by the repeated *-ther*s which enforce the cohesion of the initial *for . . . to* infinitive phrase but do so at the price of downplaying the parallel *VP* series of which "to murther" is the first conjunct. The literary implications of such handling of sound similarities tend noticeably toward the sporadic rather than the systematic. A closely analogous kind of mere superaddition practiced by Pettie is nonanaphoric, verbatim repetition of lexical items, their randomness of effect deriving mainly from the lack of parallelism in their containing structures, as the following examples will indicate. (The first is additionally interesting because the lack of parallelism in the two thirteen-syllable segments whose final constituent is "studdy" renders their *isocolon* all but imperceptible.)

This youth stood staryng in her face in a great *studdy*, which shee perceivynge to bryng him out of his *studdy*, prayed him to reach her a boale of Wyne. [*PP*, pp. 56–57]

I can not (sayth he) but count your commaundement a commodytie, only in that *you* shall thinke me *worthy to doe you service*: neither will I wish any longer to live, then I may be able, or at least willing, *to doe you* due and dutifull *service*. If sir (saith she softly unto hym) it were in my power to put *you* to sutch *service* as I thought *you worthy* of, you should not continue in the condition of a servant longe. [*PP*, p. 189; my italics]

The ultimate application of the distinction between Pettie's sporadic and Lyly's systematic deployment of the defining formal features of Euphuism involves nothing less than the composition of their respective works as wholes. What we have been seeing in small samples as the on-again, off-again character of Pettie's stylizing holds true at large in the sequence of twelve "Hystories" recounted in *A Petite Pallace*, where Euphuizing always and only appears in three types of contexts: (1) exchanges of speeches by characters affected in some way by love; (2) soliloquies and letters about love; and (3) authorial commentary on individual tales, appended by way of introduction or conclusion. Admittedly, Pettie's overall strategy, as outlined, can not only be explained but cleared from disparagement as patchwork by remarking the perfect conformity of his contexts for Euphuizing with the guidelines given in handbooks like Wilson's *Arte* for the use of amplification and its attendant figures. But the more germane point with regard to the stylistic distinction between Lyly and Pettie is that there is only the one, continuously sustained style in the narrative portion of *Euphues*—an encompassing mode of expression used at every juncture by the narrator and the characters. While each of the even dozen of tales in *A Petite Pallace* is an independent and self-contained discourse with a worked-out plot and its own cast of characters, *Euphues* is a single narrative of a love triangle and its aftermath so laconically and incompletely told that various appended tracts and letters, which altogether equal the size of the narrative, are required to furnish an ending. Without the addition of the ostensibly nonfictional materials, there would be no conclusion at all for the fiction of *Euphues*. This contrast between their relative commitments to narrative is the final index to the stylistic distinction we are pursuing: with Pettie, the demands of the story count for more than do the systematic effects of the style; with Lyly, the choice is the reverse. That the choice did lead in genuinely divergent directions in prose composition—essentially the two modalities constituted by asymmetric and symmetric conjunction—can be ascertained from any stretch of narrative in Pettie's *Pallace*. For in these stretches we observe the inevitable appearance of the native, trailing sentence forms to replace the temporary Euphuistic equipoise achieved through various kinds of binary construction and responsion.

Beyond the evidence which can be gleaned to substantiate a difference in kind between the prose styles of Pettie and Lyly in their respective handling of the defining formal features of Euphuism, I find it significant that a corresponding difference can be demonstrated in the rhetorical and semantic dimensions of discourse developed by these two writers with the same formal means. I shall be arguing in the next section that the taut symmetries of Lylyan style in the narrative portion of *Euphues* make for a prose that is enigmatic, studiedly opaque. To prepare the way for that argument, what I aim to establish here is the transparency of meaning, the obviousness of design and its attendant rhetorical objectives in the sentence forms of Pettie's *Petite Pallace*. The larger point to be registered about Pettie's use of his resources for schematic display is that we discover nothing whatever that is new in kind: he is just another practitioner of the directed syntax that we have been establishing as a principal factor in the continuity of the generalized Scripturalist program for English prose of counsel that finds its precedent in Elyot.

If the authorial voice at the opening of *A Petite Pallace* is taken at face value, it was no part of Pettie's conscious intention either to write prose of counsel or to dabble in directed syntax when he began the work. His prefatory letter to R. B. invites his friend to consider the twelve "discourses" in the light of two Italianate genres of secular prose then fashionable in England—the *novella* and the *tratatto d'amore*, the former a tale of love (and, usually, intrigue) involving highborn personages, the latter the exploration of some amatory topic or issue (a *questione d'amore*) in cultivated conversation in mixed society, as a species of entertainment. Pettie is equally insistent that his stories have their origins in gatherings of witty sophisticates which he attended and that their intent is to give pleasure: these "Tragicall trifles" (the oxymoron striking the desired mondaine note) are offered "as a token of good will," "whether they seeme unto you good or ill" (*PP,* p. 5). For its part, R. B.'s letter recommends Pettie's stories as "wittie and pithie pleasantnes" to a readership addressed as "gentle Gentlewomen Readers," thus projecting the social convention of the *questione d'amore* as the apparent shaping principle of the work (*PP,* p. 3). At its outset, then, *A Petite Pallace* promises diversion and mind play freed from any predisposing influences; when they have read a tale, the ladies will declare their will and pleasure. In actuality, however, it is only in the conclusion to the first tale that Pettie manages to leave judgment genuinely open in a functional use of balanced, parallelistic constructions:

Therefore Gentlewomen I leave it to your judgements to give sentence, whether be more worthy reprehension, hee or she. He had the law of love on his side, shee had the lawe of men and of marriage on her part: love led him, which the goddes themselves cannot resist, chastitie guided her, whiche the goddes themselves have lost: he killed him whom he counted his enemy, she killed him whom she knew her fleshly friende: shee with reason might have prevented great mischiefe, his wings were to mutch limed with lust to fly forth of his folly. [*PP,* pp. 38–39]

The remaining eleven discourses of *A Petite Pallace* reveal the narrator's mounting tendency, first, to preempt the passing of judgment on the relative responsibility of participants in some complicated and fatal chain of action, and, second, to advance an interpretation of a story by importing significance into it (usually by allegorizing physical details) or by representing the story simply as corroborating some maxim or generalization stated at the start. In order to assert his increasingly imperious control over the possible responses to each story, the narrator alters his style and his tone: his schematics direct rather than suspend or elicit judgment, and his initial deference toward "gentlewomen" gives way to a complex of patronizing attitudes—officious advice, sly teasing laden with sexual innuendo, pat declarations on woman's nature and place. Since the shifts in the narrator's stance in *A Petite Pallace* are inseparable from the rhetorical and semantic functions served by the style, to illustrate the one is to illustrate the other.

As early as the conclusion of the second tale, "Tereus and Progne," the narrator's gesture of submission to the audience's judgment—"It were hard here gentlewomen for you to give sentence, who more offended of the husband or the wife"—is rendered hollow by his already having pronounced judgment two pages earlier: "so that I thinke your selves wil say her fury exceeded his folly, and her severity in punishyng his cruelty in offending" (*PP*, pp. 55, 53). This arrogating of judgment by the narrator goes hand in hand with his announcement at the beginning of "Tereus and Progne" that this horror story of incestuous rape, mutilation, and infanticide has a moral which he can specify without undue difficulty: "The history I meane to tell shall not bee altogether estraunged from the argument of my former discourse, for though it manifest not our manyfolde misery, yet shall it at least set foorth the frailty of felicity" (*PP*, p. 42).

Subsequent tales do not even go through the motions of bidding "Gentlewomen" to judge the action; concomitantly, the narrator obtrudes not merely his interpretations but what he represents as practical lessons for his readers' conduct as well. Yet it is hard to find the practicality in the lesson drawn at the end of "Icilius and Virginia," a tale in which a virgin chooses death at her father's hand rather than submit to the lustful and vicious judge Appius: "Therefore, if I were either in wit able or otherwise worthy to give you counsayle, I would advise you to avoyde the traines of sutch tyrauntes" (*PP*, p. 42). By its nature tyranny denies its victims choices about what "to avoyde." But the narrator's ensuing jest intimates that his "counsayle" is not intended for use in the political arena, rather, in the boudoir; the real reason for avoiding *Senes fornicatores* like Appius, he suggests, is that they prove unable to satisfy young wives. Such slyness, however, remains incidental. The predominant means employed by the narrator of *A Petite Pallace* to enforce his readings and directives for conduct upon his female readership is that of allegorizing; and the success of the allegory, in turn, depends crucially on the rhetorical and semantic functioning of the schematic devices in Pettie's style. What emerges overall is a rigid, recursively labored use of parallelism and sound similarities within an explicit correlative framework to evoke a fixed universe of correspondent meanings. The rigidity and the recursion in the style of Pettie's schematic passages function, in effect, as a guarantee on the stable relationship of form and meaning. For just as the correlation pairs amass a concordant set of considerations without jarring or reduplicating one another, so, too,

these sentence forms imply, the world will patently yield up the significance of outward things—especially the traits of subhuman creatures—
for the inner life of humankind. Thus the Pettiean narrator employs his
jointly allegorical and schematic mode to instruct his readers how they
are to understand Apollo's restoration of Alcest to life at the end of
"Admetus and Alcest":

This seemeth straunge unto you (Gentlewomen) that a woman should die and
then live againe, but the meaninge of it is this, that you should die to your
selves and live to your husbandes, that you should counte their life your life,
their death your destruction: that you should not care to disease your selves to
please them: that you should in all thinges frame your selves to their fancies:
that if you see them disposed to mirth, you should indevour to bee pleasaunt:
if they bee solemne, you should be sad: if they hard, you havinge: if they delight
in haukes, then you should love Spanniels: if they hunting, you houndes: if
they good company, you good housekeeping: if they be hastie, then you should
be pacient: if they bee jelous, then you should lay aside all light lookes: if they
frowne, then you feare: if they smile, then you laugh: if they kisse, then you
cleepe, or at least give them two for one: and so in all thinges you should
conforme your selves to their contentacion: so shall there bee one will in two
minds, one hart in two bodies, and two bodies in one flesh. [*PP*, pp. 145–46]

Neither the overt echoes here of the Gospel and Pauline characteriza-
tions of marriage as a husband's and wife's becoming one flesh (Matthew
19:5–6, Mark 10:8, I Corinthians 6:16, Ephesians 5:31) nor the quoting
of Solomon (Proverbs 30:17) at the end of "Scilla and Minos" to the effect
that ravens will pick out the eyes of a daughter who flouts her parents'
choice of a mate for her (*PP*, p. 165) provides any needed clue to the
stance adopted with greater and greater intransigence by the narrator
of *A Petite Pallace* in the course of telling his tales. The stance, as surely
as that in the cultural commentary passages of Ascham's *Schoolmaster*,
is one of a secular counterpart to a preacher of the Word. Moreover,
Pettie's style, like Ascham's, exhibits unmistakable connections with the
generalized Scripturalist program. If one major reason for the stable and
correspondent character of meaning in both writers is the point-to-point
responsion which their schematics sustain and proliferate, a no less
important factor is the contribution of sense parallelisms as vehicles,
now, of a wholly secular sententiousness. Sense parallelisms—in particular, synonymic ones—are a more obtrusive staple of Pettie's style
than that of any other writer we have considered, except Becon, who
cleaves so closely to Biblical citation. Indeed, in Pettie, they emerge as
the most reliable resource for amplifying sentence form:

his patrimony was not great, neither his living more than might suffice to maintain
the porte of the place and the countenance he carried in the citie.

The Astronomers are of this opinion, that *the Planets have preheminence over us, and* that *the Starres stir us up to all our enterprises:* but I am rather setled unto this sentence, that *not the Planets but our passions have the cheife place in us, and* that *our owne desires not the destines dryve us to all our doynges.* [*PP,* pp. 104, 56; my italics]

However, as the preceding quotation begins to indicate, the most vital function served by secular sense parallelisms in Pettie's style is to provide semantic grist for the schematic mill. The following pair are representative of the large number of such passages in *A Petite Pallace:*

I am of this minde, that *nothynge doth more argue a mad minde, then to desire goods which never did good, but which have been always the cause of all our calamities. What a world of men hath desire of wealth wasted in war? what huge heapes hath it drowned in the Sea?* . . . But you will say *though the desire of goods be detestable, yet the possession is profitable.* Wherto I pray you? . . . But *though the immoderate desire of ritches bee to bee reprehended, yet* must I needes say that *moderately to account of them is not to be misliked,* for they are given us by God to passe the pilgrimage of our life withall, and *we may use them and yet not abuse them, wee may make of them and yet not make our Goddes of them.*

And *as* a sience grafted in a strange stalke, *their natures being united by grothe, they become one,* and together beare one fruite: *so* the love of the wife planted in the breast of her husband, *their harts by continuance of love become one,* one sence and one soule serveth them both. And *as the sience severed from the stocke withereth away,* if it bee not grafted in some other: *so a loving wife seperated from the societie of her husband, withereth away in woe, and leadeth a life no lesse pleasant then death,* as the sequele of this history shall shew, wherin you shall see a mervaylous Mirrour of blessed Matrimony, and a terrible tipe of beastly tyrannie. [*PP,* pp. 85–86, 11–12; my italics]

The interplay of the schematism with the various italicized sense parallelisms is obvious enough to require no comment. Instead I wish to call attention to the fact that the numerous sense parallelisms in *A Petite Pallace* comprise a major redundancy feature on the semantic level of discourse and, as such, a feature closely analogous to the identical reiterated elements discussed earlier as a formal redundancy feature and a distinguishing trait of Pettie's prose. Just as the conditions governing conjunction reduction do not filter out the heavy alliteration and assonance in Pettie's sentences, so, too, they do not eliminate such redundancies of meaning as "the Planets have preheminence over us, and . . . the Starres stir us up to all our enterprises," "goods . . . never did good, but . . . have been alwayes the cause of all our calamities," "their natures being united by grothe, they become one," and she "withereth away in woe, and leadeth a life no lesse pleasant then death."

Having documented redundancy at all levels of linguistic organization as a stylistic option that individuates Pettie's Euphuizing, we may inquire finally about its larger rhetorical function. While amplification construed as sheer verbal mass is a motive never entirely to be discounted among writers of this period, it is evident to me, at least, that Pettie's redundancies—like those of Reginald Pecock over a century earlier—are contracted in an effort to endow his style with maximal explicitness and clarity. In this regard Pettie, unlike Pecock, achieves appreciable success precisely because of the extent to which he utilizes sense parallelisms and respects the intactness of clausal units which this kind of composition demands. The more compelling comparison, however, is that between Pettie and Lyly as stylists on the grounds of clarity and explicitness. I have already stated my view that Lyly is by design an opaque and enigmatic writer and Pettie a transparent and accessible one—even to and past the point of superfluity. A not inconsiderable share of Pettie's easy comprehensibility derives from the redundancies of the identical linguistic elements and the sense parallelisms in his prose, for these operate, as redundancies do at large in natural language, to ensure the transmission of the message. To substantiate the difference between the two writers and also to introduce the discussion of *Euphues* in its own right, here is, first, a typical display of Pettiean redundancy in specifying a correlation which, then, Lyly's abbreviated adaptation can be seen equally typically to complicate:

And so mutch the lesse I lyke this lot, by how mutch the lesse I looked for it, and so mutch the more sower it is, by howe mutch the more soddaine it is. [*PP*, p. 187]

Well, *Lucilla* (aunswered *Euphues*) this case breedeth my sorrowe the more, in that it is so sodeine, and by so much the more I lament it, by howe muche the lesse I looked for it. [*Euph.*, I, 239]

In the excerpt from Pettie, extensive verbal identity buttresses the paired members in each of the two correlations, which are themselves developed in a straightforward use of the likeness relation: "so mutch the lesse" is paired with "by how mutch the lesse," and "so mutch the more" with "by how mutch the more." Alliteration, too, as sound identity reinforces the pairing of "lyke" with "looked" and "sower" with "soddaine." The resources of style specify while they clarify the semantics of the sentence. By contrast, Lyly pares away all identical verbal elements in the syntax of his first two clauses, at once dispensing with parallelism and leaving the force of the comparative unspecified, so that the reader must infer (or supply) the relation between "so sodeine" and "more sorrowe." As for the second pair of clauses, while they articulate a correlation, they do so with seeming perversity, on the basis of a difference: "so muche the more . . . by how muche the lesse." The effort of making sense, if full sense can be made, of this correlation pulls the mind in opposite directions simultaneously; under such strain the alliterating verbs "lament" and "looked" may register with more mockery than clarification. Prompted by the extent of parallel structure to accept the relatedness of the two clauses, but unable to perform the verbal manipulation equivalent to an inverse relation in mathematics, the reader can settle for an approximate reading with the gist of "I lament it much, since I looked for it little." But the sense of the Lylyan double correlative remains elusive, and the style—in spite or because of its surface symmetries—enigmatic.

THE CRISIS OF WIT: LYLY'S *EUPHUES*

The sense of the problematic which I have indicated will guide my discussion of Lyly's Euphuism is far from being unique to me; it merely marks my response as something other than an immediately contemporary one. The story of this style's irresistibility to writers and readers of English prose for a full decade after the publication of *Euphues: The Anatomy of Wyt* in 1578 has become one of the best known in Renaissance literary history through several learned and expert retellings.[38] But these retellings sound prophetic as well as historical notes in recording the first accesses of disenchantment, for the enduring pattern of reception that Lyly's style has met is a hostile—or, at least, an openly critical—one. We seem still to be in the throes of the initial counterreaction: agreed only in withholding adulation, but unresolved how (and how far) to construe Lyly positively as a stylist. I think, however, that the moment is propitious for considering the Euphuism of *Euphues* as a creation in its own right rather than a period craze or a proving ground for source study.

The debate over the origins of Euphuism which absorbed great scholarly energy in the later nineteenth and earlier twentieth century began to spend its force as the scope of inquiry at once widened and came ever more surely home to England. Landmann's early certainty that Guevara was Lyly's model incurred qualification along with support from Bond, Child, Feuillerat, and, especially, Norden, whose work showed both how eclectic a borrower and refashioner Lyly was with regard to other ascertainable sources like Plutarch, Pliny, and Erasmus and what extensive currency could be documented for the word and sound schemes of Euphuism—as near at hand as Pettie and as distantly

---

[38]See, especially, Albert Feuillerat, *John Lyly: Contribution à l'histoire de la Renaissance en Angleterre* (Cambridge: Cambridge University Press, 1910); George Williamson, *The Senecan Amble: A Study of Prose Form from Bacon to Collier* (Chicago: University of Chicago Press, 1951), pp. 11–120; and G. K. Hunter, *John Lyly: The Humanist as Courtier* (Cambridge, Mass.: Harvard University Press, 1962), pp. 257, 280–89.

as the oratory of Gorgias and Isocrates.[39] But the overt opposition to Landmann's claim did most to redirect source hunters toward a prospective English quarry. Hence, Croll's argument for the prototypic schematics of patristic and medieval Latin writers acknowledged the presence of the same schemes in the English prose of Hugh Latimer, Thomas Lever, and John Jewel; and William A. Ringler's case, adhering to a Latin source, nonetheless focused on a series of lectures by John Rainolds which Lyly, as an Oxford undergraduate, was in a likely position to have heard.[40] Today the origins of Euphuism are a dormant issue, but questions about the interpretation of Lyly's style and work are very much alive. While Croll's categorical view that Euphuism consists in figures of sound rather than figures of thought has been discredited, there is no agreement on what cognitive or rhetorical functions the style primarily (or ultimately) serves. Although Walter King, Jonas Barish, and G. K. Hunter have severally argued that Lyly's Euphuism must be treated as a product of Renaissance humanism, the three critics end by viewing the style quite disparately. King maintains that the sophistical conduct of speeches by the youthful Euphues functions as a means of characterization; Barish, that Lylyan antitheses operate as reflectors of the changeful, contrarious experience of lovers and courtiers; Hunter, that Lyly's Euphuism is true to humanism in the high value it sets on order and on the capacities of the human mind for conceiving and creating order, for bringing unity out of multiplicity.[41]

At present there is also widespread disagreement regarding the interpretation of *Euphues* as a fictional construct. Taking a biographical approach, Feuillerat saw the work as evidence of Lyly's efforts to ingratiate himself with the Puritanically inclined William Cecil, Lord Burghley; Hunter, however, has argued no less biographically to the contrary effect that *Euphues* objectivizes Lyly's chagrin at finding himself the possessor of B.A. and M.A. degrees but without career prospects in the university

[39]Friedrich Landmann, "Shakspere and Euphuism"; *Der Euphuismus: sein Wesen, seine Quelle, seine Geschichte: Beitrag zur Geschichte der englischen Literatur des sechszehnten Jahrhunderts* (Giessen: W. Keller, 1881); Clarence G. Child, *John Lyly and Euphuism* (Erlangen and Leipzig: G. Böhme, 1894); R. Warwick Bond, *Works of John Lyly*, I, 119–20, 135–43, 154–59; Feuillerat, *John Lyly*, pp. 444–75; Eduard Norden, *Die antike Kunstprosa vom VI. Jahrhundert vor Christi bis in die Zeit der Renaissance*, 2 vols. (Leipzig: Teubner, 1909).

[40]Morris W. Croll, "The Sources of the Euphuistic Rhetoric," in John Lyly, *"Euphues: The Anatomy of Wit" and "Euphues and His England,"* ed. Morris W. Croll and Harry Clemons (New York: Dutton, 1916); rptd. in *Style, Rhetoric, and Rhythm: Essays by Morris W. Croll,* ed. J. Max Patrick, et al. (Princeton: Princeton University Press, 1966), pp. 241–95; William A. Ringler, Jr., "The Immediate Source of Euphuism," *PMLA* 53 (1938): 678–86.

[41]Walter N. King, "John Lyly and Elizabethan Rhetoric," *SP* 52 (1955): 149–61; Barish, "The Prose Style of John Lyly"; Hunter, *Lyly: The Humanist as Courtier*, pp. 6–7, 10, 34, 268, 272, 275–77.

or at court.[42] In a more directly literary line, Dover Wilson has advanced an influential twofold argument that *Euphues* owes to the popular neo-Latin school drama *Acolastus* (1st ed., 1529) both its own playlike condensation into discrete episodes where speechmaking is primary and its concern with the prodigal son theme. Wilson's argument is rendered the more plausible by the fact that the names, if not the precise identities, of the characters Eubulus and Philautus derive from *Acolastus*.[43] In subsequent literary discussion, Hunter has stressed the felicitous disposition of the thematic material of *Euphues* in a barely fictionalized analogue of Terentian five-act comic structure; but Joseph Houppert inverts these emphases, finding more thematic than formal interest in *Euphues'* parlaying of the prodigal son motif into a prodigal daughter one, and claiming superiority as a formal construct for Lyly's sequel, *Euphues and His England* (1580). Recently, Madelon Gohlke has proposed a radical new reading of at least the subtext of *Euphues* as a homosexual brief, based on the discontinuities of form and the difficulties recurrently posed by Lyly's style.[44] In such ongoing ferment, the lack of any settled critical opinion regarding Euphuism as a style or *Euphues* as a work is obvious, and I shall proceed on the assumption that I need to explain somewhat the line of approach that my own discussion of Lyly will take. My point of departure is an assumption that does not seem liable to cause dispute: that the multifarious contents of *Euphues*, as much as the more homogeneous "Hystorics" of *A Petite Pallace*, subsist easily within my classification of "English prose of counsel" and hence within the continuing framework of chapters 5 and 6 of this study. Next, my approach undertakes to reckon in two ways with the multifariousness that the assemblage of minimal narrative, abundant speechmaking, letters, and tractates on love remedies, education, and Protestant theology compels us to acknowledge in Lyly's work. I shall argue, first, that the style of *Euphues* is not so uniform in its operation and effects as its tight and showy set of defining features might lead one to suppose, and, second, that an appreciable amount of the diverse critical response to *Euphues* ought to be accommodated in any interpretation that seeks, as mine does, to cope with its genuine complexity.

To set the context for the specifics of my argument, some note must be taken of the affinities which Lylyan source study has shown to exist between *Euphues* and antecedent works on education that were either

[42]Feuillerat, *John Lyly*, pp. 43–68; Hunter, *Lyly: The Humanist as Courtier*, pp. 36–62.

[43]John Dover Wilson, "Euphues and the Prodigal Son," *The Library*, n.s. 10 (1909): 337–61. Willem de Volder (1493–1563), known internationally as Fullonius or Gnapheus, was the author of *Acolastus*; John Palsgrave made the English translation (1st ed., 1540).

[44]Hunter, *Lyly: The Humanist as Courtier*, pp. 54–57; Joseph W. Houppert, *John Lyly*, Twayne's English Authors (Boston: G. K. Hall & Co., 1975), pp. 22–41; Madelon Gohlke, "Reading *Euphues*," *Criticism* 19 (1977): 103–17.

produced in the heat of Renaissance enamorment with rhetoric or accorded special currency then. It has long been realized that the hero's name and his outstanding natural endowments—ready and brilliant wit, displayed in comely speech and enhanced by good looks and a graceful bearing—hark back to the vignette in Ascham's *Schoolmaster*, as do the keynotes in Lyly's exposure of wit corrupted through immersion in Italianate culture.[45] *Acolastus*, one of the period compositions aimed expressly at providing schoolboys with pure Latin phrasing and equally pure Christian doctrine, seems unquestionably to have influenced Lyly to cast his hero's errancy in the Scripturalist mold of a prodigal rather than simply as a portrayal of wasted youthful promise. Crane has pointed out, in addition, that Cicero's remarks on wit in *De oratore* allude self-consciously to two Platonic contexts in which the term *euphues* ("well-natured," hence, "naturally witty") is employed: one in the *Phaedrus*, where this trait contributes to defining the true orator, and another in the *Laws*, where it is alleged that one who is *euphues* may, if ill-intentioned, do the state more harm than an ignorant person.[46] Since it is altogether likely that Lyly and Ascham, in their turn, were self-consciously alluding to the Ciceronian source in utilizing the term, it is the more significant that both contrive a Christian context for its introduction in English. Ascham does so through the Pauline sentence forms previously noted, Lyly through early exposition which stresses that his Euphues is not a Ciceronian-Platonic danger to the state, but a private individual who squanders his store of good advice and fit companionship more disastrously, even, than he does his inheritance. The most we are told at any one point about the patrimony which prospectively qualifies Lyly's hero as a prodigal is that "the son being left rich by his fathers Will" became "retchles by his owne will." The rest are widely scattered allusions: to Euphues' Neapolitan companions who try to "soake hys purse to reape commoditie," to the hero's later being able to offer only "good manners" as over against a rival's "great mannors," and to his still later regret at having wasted his "lands in maintenance of braverie," of which we otherwise know nothing (*Euph.*, I, 186, 225, 241). In the generalized Scripturalist tradition of English prose of counsel, Lyly is far less concerned with Euphues' external circumstances than he is with probing the state of mind and soul in a highly gifted youth who

havinge the bridle in hys owne handes, either to use the raine or the spurre, disdayning counsayle, leavinge his countrey, loathinge his olde acquaintance, thought either by wytte to obteyne some conquest, or by shame to abyde some

---

[45]Bond, *Works of John Lyly*, I, 327; Feuillerat, *John Lyly*, pp. 48, 54, 62; and Hunter, *Lyly: The Humanist as Courtier*, pp. 49–50, 58, who cite prior scholarship.

[46]Crane, *Wit and Rhetoric in the Renaissance*, pp. 3, 10–11, 82, 127.

conflicte, and leaving the rule of reason, rashly ranne unto destruction. [*Euph.*, I, 185]

Other important connections between *Euphues* and the literature of education include the fact that "Euphues and His Ephebus," the longest of the nonfictional appendages to the narrative, is substantially a translation and paraphrase of Plutarch's *De educatione puerorum* interspersed with borrowings from Erasmus's *Colloquium puerpera*.[47] Notably, Plutarch's tract is the very one which Elyot had chosen to translate and publish about 1535 under the title *The Education or Bringing Up of Children*. Further putative links between Lyly and Elyot include their shared fervor in celebrating the ideality of youthful male friendship (not excluding the possibility that Lyly may have modeled the relationship of Euphues and Philautus on the long story of Titus and Gisippus in *The Governour*) and, less conjecturally, Lyly's inversion in his narrative of the three-stage pattern projected in *The Governour*, by which a child's development progresses from natural needs and appetites to the acquisition of reason and self-control through training and, thence, to the constructive exercise of his educated capabilities as an adult.[48]

Besides the influence of a heavily subjectivized conception of a prodigal youth which Lyly found in antecedent Christian humanist works on education and extended greatly in his characterization of Euphues, there are links between his work and Wilson's *Arte of Rhetorique* which are germane to my argument. Feuillerat has insisted most fully on these to build his case—now a commonplace of critical commentary—that the *Arte* is the one handbook above all others in which the defining features of Euphuism come in for praise amounting, virtually, to promotion as a stylistic program. I have reviewed much of the evidence on which Feuillerat's case rests, though without explicit reference to Lyly, in my account of Wilson's preferred resources of style, for it is the sections on "egall members," "contrarietie" in words and sentences, "like ending" and "like falling," similitudes, exempla, and the "sayinges" and "fables of Poetes" that Feuillerat cites. He also remarks perceptively on the special appositeness to Lyly's style of Wilson's assertion: "To delite is needful, without the which, weightier matters will not be heard at all" (*Arte*, p. 4).[49] The angle from which I propose to approach the interpre-

---

[47]Bond, *Works of John Lyly*, I, 352; and Croll and Clemons, *Euphues*, p. 111. Both editions cite prior scholarship.

[48]Elyot himself derived this three-stage pattern from Plutarch; see Major, *Elyot and Renaissance Humanism*, pp. 157–59. Its appeal to Ascham shows in the shaping use he made of it—overtly, in *Toxophilus*, more subtly, in *The Schoolmaster*. Lyly, however, was no mere traipser in Elyot's and Ascham's footsteps. As Hunter points out (*Lyly: The Humanist as Courtier*, pp. 52–53), at the beginning of "Euphues and His Ephebus" he appears to have lodged a cavil against valuing study over experience (*Euph.*, I, 260).

[49]Feuillerat, *John Lyly*, pp. 464–67, 257–58.

tation of style and content in the "prodigal" or narrative portion of
Euphues—almost exactly the first half of the work—extends Feuillerat's
insights regarding the links between Lyly and Wilson, especially as pin-
pointed in the foregoing assertion. I shall argue that Lyly posits as the
circumstances of discourse at the outset of *Euphues* the adversative situation which Wilson treats as nonstandard, but scarcely infrequent because of the refractoriness of human nature: the situation in which the
audience is not open and predisposed, but has to be inveigled, won
over to attending to what the speaker or writer has to say. I shall argue,
further, that Lyly follows Wilson's lead in two other crucial determinants
of style and rhetorical strategy: first, that he assimilates the Gospel-
derived, negative view of the self-divided psychology of humankind
which, in Wilson, accompanies and explains the notion of a recalcitrant
audience; and second, that he acts on Wilson's sense of the best tactics
to be applied in such circumstances with such an audience—namely, to
disarm them by delighting them, using wit to move them to mirth.

Since Wilson specifies a group of linguistic and rhetorical resources
as particularly effective for wittily moving an audience, I will need to
show that these—the posture of dissimulation, the modes of equivocation, exaggeration, figuration, and conjecture—operate to shape the
style of the first, narrative half of *Euphues*. This will, indeed, occupy
much of my concern. In addition, I shall attempt to establish a larger
correlation between the work's two-part structure and the rhetorical and
stylistic assumptions that inform its respective halves through exploring
the radically disparate character and psychology of Lyly's hero. This
hero, as a prodigal, shares as fully in the negative manifestations of
human nature as any other character, but, in his repentant and reformed
state, he becomes an image—and, ultimately, a spokesman—for the
redemption which the Gospel promises the faithful. As prima facie support for the larger dimensions of my argument, there is Lyly's own full
title to cite—an announcement and brief characterization of the binary
division of the work in the apt syntactic form of two successive binary
conjunctions: "Euphues. The Anatomy of Wyt. Very pleasant for all
Gentlemen to reade, *and* most necessary to remember: Wherein are contained the delights that Wyt foloweth in his youth by the pleasauntnesse
of Love, *and* the happynesse he reapeth in Age, by the perfectnesse of
Wisedome" (*Euph.*, I, 177; my italics).

Remarkably enough, Lyly does not await the establishment of his
narrative framework to put into effect either the assumption of a dis-
inclined audience or the projection of a witty persona who is working
obliquely and at cross-purposes with himself; both are in evidence in
the prefatory letters. The one to "the Gentlemen Readers" opens jauntily
by "heaping matter"—exempla compounded with similitudes—to make
a purely defensive point: every article of manufacture, above all, a book,

soon ceases to be in fashion or command any notice at all. What expectations, then, can the author of *Euphues* have of his readership, with respect to himself and his work? The other letter, his dedication to Lord Delaware (a figure whose relation to Lyly remains mysterious),[50] multiplies paradoxes as it plays with this question. The first rhetorical gesture is a self-ingratiating one:

I hope I shal not incur the displeasure of the wise, in that in the discourse of Euphues I have aswel touched the vanities of his love, as the vertues of his lyfe. . . . If then the first sight of Euphues, shal seeme to light to be read of the wise, or to foolish to be regarded of the learned, they ought not to impute it to the iniquitie of the author, but to the necessitie of the history. . . . And certes I thinke ther be mo speaches which for gravitie wil mislyke the foolish, then unsemely termes which for vanitie may offend the wise. Which discourse (right Honorable) I hope you wil the rather pardon for the rudenes in that it is the first, & protect it the more willingly if it offend in that it shalbe the laste. . . . Howsoever the case standeth I looke for no prayse for my labour, but pardon for my good will: it is the greatest rewarde that I dare aske, and the least that they can offer. I desire no more, I deserve no lesse. [*Euph.*, I, 179–80]

As the quotation shows, the vehicle for the important rhetorical posture of self-ingratiation in Lyly is a recognizable type of sentence. It has a concessive or optative or tentative first member which provides a designedly weak opening ("I hope I shal not . . . ," "If then the first sight shal seeme . . . ," "And certes I think ther be . . . ," "Which discourse I hope . . . ," "Howsoever the case standeth . . ."). This opening is followed at varying distance—usually some, sometimes none—by members that suddenly and intensively display semantic symmetry and accompanying formal responsions to make a designedly stong close ("as wel . . . the vanities of his love, as the vertues of his lyfe," "not . . . the iniquitie of the author, but . . . the necessitie of the history," "mo . . . which for gravitie wil mislyke the foolish, then . . . which for vanitie may offend the wise," "the rather pardon, in that it is the first, & protect in that it shalbe the laste," "the greatest rewarde that I dare aske, and the least that they can offer"). As the dynamics of the self-ingratiating sentence type make clear, the mode is dissimulating and ironic: it gestures toward playing down the claims of the self while continuously playing up their linguistic formulations. Indeed, the latter are allowed to stand alone, without a weak opening, in the last sentence of the passage quoted: "I desire no more, I deserve no lesse."

But this sentence type—binary clausal parallelism—has another, more specific function in Lyly's style as early as the prefatory letters to *Euphues:* it may follow one or more self-ingratiating sentences in order to urge a point of argument or a purported truth which the speaker now appar-

---

[50]See Feuillerat, *John Lyly,* pp. 44, 235; Hunter, *Lyly: The Humanist as Courtier,* pp. 67–68.

ently considers himself in a position to register with his audience. Thus, the dedication to Delaware proceeds:

Euphues beginneth with love as allured by wyt, but endeth not with lust as bereft of wisedome. He wooeth women provoked by youth, but weddeth not himselfe to wantonesse as pricked by pleasure. I have set down the follies of his wit without breach of modestie, & the sparks of his wisedome without suspicion of dishonestie. . . . Though the stile nothing delight the dayntie eare of the curious sifter, yet wil the matter recreate the minde of the courteous Reader. The varietie of the one wil abate the harshnes of the other. . . . For . . . thinges make most against me, in that a foole hath intruded himselfe to discourse of wit. But as I was willing to commit the fault, so am I content to make amendes. . . . It is a world to see how English men desire to heare finer speach then the language will allow, to eate finer bread, then is made of wheat, to weare finer cloth then is wroght of Woll. But I let passe their finenesse, which can no way excuse my folly. [*Euph.*, I, 180–81]

These binary clausal parallelisms are instantly recognizable as the principal type of sententious sentence in sixteenth-century English prose and, therefore, appropriate vehicles for any vital declarations that Lyly has to make. But the curious thing about the foregoing conjoined declaratives is how little straightforward declaring they manage to do. The first two sentences, likely vehicles for antithesis as *but* conjunctions, thwart closure of that sort by a surplusage of contrastive elements. We saw in the second section of chapter 1 that the identity conditions governing conjunction with *but* involve a combination of sameness with difference—specifically, two elements in which the conjoining clauses differ. This condition would have been routinely met, and antithetic closure attained, if Lyly had written 'Euphues beginneth with love, but endeth with lust' (differing elements: *begin/end, love/lust*) or 'He wooeth women, but weddeth wantonness' (differing elements: *woo/wed, women/ wantonness*). Lyly's actual sentences, however, contain a third element of difference apiece, a negation in their second conjuncts: "but endeth *not* with lust," "but weddeth *not* himselfe to wantonesse." These negatives open up the meaning of their respective sentences to let in an indeterminacy which allows Lyly to evade the reader's expectation of being given some longer-term information about what happens to Euphues. While such sentences may be well-placed baits to curiosity in a prefatory letter, what I am concerned to stress is their opaqueness—a recurrent peculiarity of Lyly's style at junctures in the first half of *Euphues* which seem to have been set up as moments of truth or disclosure.

To continue with the elusiveness of these apparently sententious sentences, the indeterminacy which perplexes the third is easily identified, though not so easily resolved: in the conjoined phrases "without breach of modestie, & . . . without suspicion of dishonestie," whose "modestie," whose "suspicion," and, hence, whose "dishonestie" are being referred to—Lyly's or his readers'? Is the referent the same throughout, or is it varied? The style gives us no help with these questions. But the syntactic and semantic indeterminacy of subsequent sentences is more perplexing still. How are the nouns "stile" and "matter" to be paired off with the nouns "varietie" and "harshnes"? Why, moreover, does Lyly advert to his writing of *Euphues* as a "fault" committed, as an inexcusable "folly"? If, as he says, what he has done "can no way" be excused, why does he raise the possibility of making "amendes"? And if he has been at fault in presuming, as "a foole," "to discourse of wit," why does he blame the "desire" of Englishmen "to heare finer speach then the language will allow"? Lyly's self-presentation in the dedicatory letter to Delaware leads into a paradoxical blind: we are given a writer wise and witty enough to tell the true, full history of Euphues for the judgment and approbation of wise readers, yet also a writer who will be condemned for a fool and who, knowing and accepting this, asks pardon for his folly while simultaneously declaring it inexcusable. How are we to construe the dizzying displays of Lylyan volte-face regarding himself, his readership, and his work?

I think the way to construal lies through Wilson's body of comments in *The Arte of Rhetorique* on the resistance of human nature to sound teaching unless a speaker or writer can appeal to the auditory and visual senses of his audience and charm them into attention. Thus Lyly's castigation of his English contemporaries for their superfineness and dainty curiosity of taste is neither an impertinence nor a mere shifting of blame; it becomes an indispensable factor in his account of why he has written in the style that he has. Wilson had conceded the possibility of "overmuch" aural appeal in Cyprian's and Augustine's sermons, but he sanctioned their styles as necessary means of winning credit with their auditories. Lyly suggests a like rationale for his "fault" and "folly," which "can no way" be excused since they are called into being jointly by the facts of human nature and the character of the objectives at which rhetoric perforce aims. If this line of interpretation can be found to hold, it also helps us to discover a plausible motivation for the obliqueness and opaqueness of Lyly's Euphuism: he needs to conceal his negative working assumptions about human psychology and the adversative rhetorical stance entailed by them in order for his style to have its effect. Before we proceed to consider the pertinence of the pessimistic and manipulative strain in Wilson's *Arte* to the stylistic effects in the first, narrative portion of *Euphues*, it is proper to ask a last question about the larger plausibility of the approach I am taking: Is there any reason, beyond the envisaged interpretive benefits, to suppose that Lyly was operating on such negative and adversative grounds in his cultivation of Euphuism? The answer seems to be yes, given the information regarding the period context and Lyly's personal history for which we have Feuillerat and Hunter, variously, to thank.[51] To be sure, Hunter has gone on record as rejecting Feuillerat's view that Lyly wrote *Euphues* as a fervent moral and cultural campaigner against profligacy masquerading as the latest Italian fashion. It is Hunter's view that Lyly wrote *Euphues* out of a profound desperation and alienation brought on by the experienced contradictions between his humanist ideals of enlightened public service and the realities of the Elizabethan court, where power politics left no place or need for scholars. What Hunter has to say about Lyly's situation and frame of mind makes it easy to see the attraction of a negative view of human nature and an adversative stance toward an audience that was to be won over to esteem for the author (and, doubtless, to patronage in due course). But, by the same token, we are not obliged to dismiss Feuillerat as wrong about the high—even, ultimately, religious—seriousness of *Euphues*, for the negative conception of human nature projected in Wilson's *Arte* was altogether compatible with the increasingly Calvinistic character of later sixteenth-century English Protestantism, if not, indeed, traceable to it. The Wilsonian framework accommodates a range of possible impulsions—from the most secular to the most sacred—in interpreting the style and composition of *Euphues*. This, I maintain, is just the latitude we require.

In the speeches and the few letter exchanges that comprise the bulk of the first, narrative half of *Euphues*, all the evidence indicates that one cannot trust to a direct approach to others in language, but instead must strategize carefully to get anywhere. Without exception, every speech that goes straight to its point proves a disaster. This may be because the speaker is acting on an inadequate or mistaken sense of his addressee, as in the instantaneous contracting of friendship by Euphues and Philautus, Ferardo's notification to Lucilla that she should prepare forthwith to marry Philautus, Euphues' "How you must have missed me!" speech to Lucilla, and Ferardo's heartbroken plea that Lucilla return to Euphues or Philautus, but in any case desist from her passion for Curio (*Euph.*, I, 198–99, 227, 237, 243–44). Or the disaster may be due to the unexpected bad news that the frankness brings, as in three speeches of Lucilla's, two to Ferardo and one to Euphues, informing them of her arbitrary shifts of erotic "fancie" (*Euph.*, I, 228–29, 237–39, 244–45); this group takes to grotesque extremes Lyly's employment of speech as a form of (anti-)social behavior and compulsive self-will in his characters. No less remarkable, as a fact in its own right and as further evidence of the consistently negative and adversative conceptions that shape the narrative of *Euphues*, is the distinctive organization exhibited by the soliloquies. The four examples—two by Euphues (*Euph.*, I, 208–11, 240–

---

[51]Feuillerat, *John Lyly*, pp. 50–68; Hunter, *Lyly: The Humanist as Courtier*, pp. 30–35, 58–62.

42) and one each by Lucilla (205–7) and Philautus (232–33)—proceed uniformly in an order which is the inverse of that observable in the dialogues. The beginning of a soliloquy is candid, going straight to the point of the emotion or intention—presumably as a sign of the constraint that lifts when one is alone. But, after intervening ruminations, the ending of a soliloquy resolves on a scheme for action that reflects badly on the speaker as well as on his or her associates—presumably as a sign of an imminent return to society. In summary terms, the indications to be gathered from language behavior in the narrative portion of *Euphues* enforce negative assumptions and adversative relations throughout.

Accordingly, the largest component of the narrative, the dialogue exchanges in speeches and letters, evince the manipulations of language by which Wilson's *Arte* instructs a speaker to overcome the common human proclivity not to pay attention. The especially relevant means are those specified in the section "Of deliting the hearers," and the most relevant of all to Lyly is dissembling. Virtually from the outset, the narrator insists and shows that dissimulation is the covering law for speech and action alike. Thus, we read of Euphues upon his arrival in Naples that "hee behaved hymselfe so warilye, that he singled his game wiselye. Hee . . . welcommed all, but trusted none, hee was mery but yet so wary, that neither the flatterer coulde take advauntage to entrap him in his talke, nor the wisest any assurance from his friendship" (*Euph.*, I, 186). Ensuing speeches by the hero consistently transmute this description into verbal dissembling.

Euphues' treatment of Eubulus, the old man who tries to advise him, closely answers to Wilson's description of how to "grig" or "abashe" a victim and "put him out of countenance" by leading him on in his speech and then suddenly rounding on him with a taunt or insult. The initial blandishments ("Father and friende . . . I am neither so suspitious to mistrust your good will, nor so sottishe to mislike your good counsaile," "I meane not to cavill wyth you as one loving sophistrye, neyther to controwle you as one having superioritie") give place to a volley of taunts and insults ("The similytude you rehearse of the waxe, argueth your waxinge and meltinge brayne," "you shal assone catch a Hare with a Taber, as you shal perswade youth, with your aged & overworn eloquence," "So these olde huddles having overcharged their gorges with fancie, accompte all honest recreation meere folly") (*Euph.*, I, 190–94). Later there is a major sequence of episodes structured by verbal dissimulation which turns suddenly to flouting; it begins with Euphues' letter in response to Philautus's charge of bad faith in wooing Lucilla, and it continues through Lucilla's cat-and-mouse game with Euphues that ends in her shocking disclosure of love for Curio (see *Euph.*, I, 235–39). The savage irony unifying this sequence arises from Euphues' initial certainty that he is the archdissembler; he boasts in writing to Philautus: "No, no, he that cannot dissemble in love, is not worthy to live. I am of this minde, that both might and mallice, deceite and treacherie, all perjurie, anye impietie may lawfully be committed in love, which is lawlesse" (I, 236). But Lucilla proves him wrong by triumphing in the very dissembling tactics of which Euphues boasts.

Verbal dissembling to "grig" or "abashe" another person exposes quite nakedly the negative assumptions regarding human nature and the adversary stance of the witty speaker both in Wilson's instructions for delighting hearers and in Lyly's fictional world. But, remarkably, Lyly also riddles ostensibly positive contexts with verbal dissembling, as characters gesture toward each other in courtesy or reach out in love or friendship. Thus Euphues secures Philautus's friendship with two claims openly belied by the narrative: that he had been seeking a single true friend, and that long acquaintance has convinced him of Philautus's surpassing worth (*Euph.*, I, 198); Euphues also makes his first trial of his friend's trustworthiness with the lie that he loves Livia (I, 211–14). The narrative's father-daughter relationship, too, is riddled with this kind of verbal role-playing: we are told that Ferardo "dissembled his fury, to the end he might by craft discover hir fancie" and that "*Lucilla* perceiving the drifte of the olde Foxe hir Father, wayed with hir selfe what was best to be done, & at the laste . . . shaped hym an aunswere" (*Euph.*, I, 229–30). The climax of dissimulation in the narrative, however, is reached in Euphues' declaration of love to Lucilla and her response, an interchange which Lyly orchestrates elaborately to bring out the sustaining impetus of verbal deception. In the *tratatto d'amore* scenes played out in Don Ferardo's household, Euphues and Lucilla take turns espousing positions which (we are shown) they do not in fact hold at the time that they speak—he, that gifts and graces of the mind are to be esteemed above those of the body; she, that women are the frailer, more fallible sex; he, that women are capable of sublimating desire and repulsing their lovers' importunity (*Euph.*, I, 201–4, 216–17). Counterposing the two scenes in company, Lucilla's and Euphues' respective soliloquies set the pair on their convergent course by revealing their equally firm intent to manipulate words and appearances to gain their ends. She concludes with herself:

Albeit I can no way quench the coales of desire with forgetfulnesse, yet will I rake them up in the ashes of modestie, seeing I dare not discover my love for maidenly shamefastnes, I wil dissemble it til time I have opportunitie. And I hope so to behave my selfe as *Euphues* shall thinke me his owne, and *Philautus* perswade himselfe I am none but his. [*Euph.*, I, 207]

For his part, Euphues reasons and resolves thus in his soliloquy:

Shall I not then . . . deceive *Philautus* to receive *Lucilla?* Yes, *Euphues,* where love beareth sway, friendshippe can have no shew. . . . Let *Philautus* behave himselfe never so craftely, hee shal know that . . . because I resemble him in wit, I meane a little to dissemble with him in wyles. [*Euph.,* I, 210]

Finally, in the lovers' private meeting, Lyly brilliantly compounds thematic and psychological ironies by couching Lucilla's acceptance speech in the form of a diatribe against dissimulation in love. Its projection of the battle of the sexes discloses negative views of human nature and the speaker's adversative stance as unmistakably as any flout could. The following excerpts will show Lucilla's disingenuous drift:

But yet I am not angry *Euphues* but in an agony, . . . if this love to delude mee bee not dissembled. It is that which causeth me most to feare, not that my beautie is unknown to my selfe but that commonly we poore wenches are deluded through lyght beliefe, and ye men are naturally enclined craftely. . . . I did at the first entraunce discerne thy love but yet dissembled it. . . . Eyther therefore dissemble thy fancie, or desist from thy folly. But why shouldest thou desist from the one, seeinge thou canst cunningly dissemble the other. . . . Alas we silly soules which have neyther witte to decypher the wyles of men, nor wisedome to dissemble our affection, . . . wee I say are soone enticed, beeing by nature simple and easily entangled, beeinge apte to receive the impression of love. . . . Although as yet I am disposed to lyke of none, yet whensoever I shall love any I will not forget thee, in the meane season accompt me thy friend, for thy foe I will never be. [*Euph.,* I, 220–21, 223–24]

Demonstrably, then, dissimulation is the constantly shifting ground which wit creates for its own exercise in the narrative portion of *Euphues.* Because it is the mode of virtually all speech and behavior, it is impossible to associate with any particular verbal resources or stylistic devices; yet, for all that, its inverse operation with regard to the generalized Scripturalist program for prose is clear: the joint search for meaning which bound writer and reader cooperatively has been put in abeyance. As for the other means of eliciting pleasure through wit which Wilson promotes and Lyly prominently utilizes—word play, with its two forms of realization, lexical (punning) and syntactic (equivocation), as well as the other role-creating modes of discourse, conjecture, exaggeration, and figuration—these, as we shall see, find their respective expressions in precisely specifiable major features of Euphuistic style.

It is appropriate to begin discussion with word play, for Wilson assigns pride of place in his section "Of deliting the hearers" to punning and equivocation as tactics for taking others off their guard, tickling their fancies, and certifying one's own wit. While Lylyan word play recurs so frequently throughout *Euphues* that it is difficult to tell who finds it more indispensable, the narrator or the characters, one of its most prominent systematic functions is to heighten the impact of a speaker's first words at some critical juncture of the narrative. Thus Euphues makes his entrée in Neapolitan mixed society with a tripled *polyptoton* on the stem *strange*, compounded with an equivocation on *will come/welcome*: "If it be the guise of Italy to *welcome straungers* with *strangenes*, I must needes say the custome is *strange* . . . , if the manner of Ladies to salute Gentlemen with coynesse, then I am enforced to think the women without courtesie to use such *welcome*, and the men past shame that *will come*" (*Euph.*, I, 206; my italics). Thus, too, the old counselor figure Eubulus, having made the decision to speak out, undertakes to lodge his words in Euphues' resistant bosom. Such is the Lylyan premium on linguistic manifestations of wit that the hero is represented as attending in spite of himself to Eubulus's repellent advice, which gets underway with the following manifold equivocations and puns:

Young gentleman, although my acquaintance be *small* to intreate you, and my authoritie *lesse* to commaund you, yet my *good will* in giving you *good counsaile* should induce you to beleeve me. . . . Having therefore *opportunitie* to utter my *minde*, I *meane* to bee *importunate* with you to folowe my *meaninge*. As thy *birth* doth shewe the expresse and lively Image of *gentle bloude*, so thy *bringing up* seemeth to mee to be *greate blotte* . . . , so that I am enforced to thincke that either thou dyddest *want one* to give thee *good instructions*, or that thy parentes made thee a *wanton* wyth to much cockeringe. [*Euph.*, I, 187; my italics]

As I remarked, the narrator in *Euphues* employs punning and equivocation of a sort indistinguishable from that of the characters' and does so, too, at analogous junctures of the discourse: that is, when he enters to introduce a new piece of information or to announce a new turn in the story. It seems to me arguable, in addition, that Lyly reserves for his narrative voice most of the best exhibitions of wit in word play, in the sense of the subtlest strikings of nuanced meaning from like sounds. These include such remarks as "Heere ye may beholde gentlemen, how lewdly wit standeth in his owne lyght, . . . seeing for the moste parte it is *proper* to all those of sharpe capacitie to esteeme of themselves, as most *proper*," made after Euphues has flouted Eubulus (*Euph.*, I, 195); and the narrator's interposition to describe Euphues' reaction to Lucilla's riddling answer to his suit: "*Euphues* was brought into a great quandarie and as it were a colde shivering, to heare this newe *kinde* of *kindenesse*" (I, 224; my italics).[52] Yet the finally important point about the punning and equivocation in *Euphues* consists less in whatever fine distinctions can be drawn between the narrator and the characters on this basis than in the fact that the word play—like every other major feature of Euphuistic style—is an equally accessible resource to both. Feuillerat, citing

---

[52]Undoubtedly the best play on words, however, is the Freudian slip from "lyst" to "lust" made by Lucilla in the privacy of her chamber (*Euph.*, I, 207).

L. H. Vincent, was one of the earliest critics to stress the stylistic homogeneity of *Euphues*, but King's useful qualification holds that this homogeneous style leaves room for local "differentiation" in, say, the density or paucity of shared features, and that the differences can be expressive.[53] For my purposes, the high degree of stylistic homogeneity becomes instrumental in confirming that the same assumptions about human nature and effective discourse hold in the characters' fictional world and in the narrator's more omniscient outlook. As readers we are brought by the style to realize that, at least for the duration of the narrative, the designs that Lyly has upon us are effectually those that the characters have in dealing with each other.

In proceeding from word play to note other witty linguistic means of giving pleasure, Wilson had urged that "Things gathered by conjecture, to seeme otherwise then they are, delite much the eares being wel applied together," and he had also declared that "many conjectures and greate presumptions" serve to "encrease our cause" and make "our talke . . . appere more vehement . . . by heaping of words and sentences together, touching many reasons into one corner" (*Arte*, pp. 152, 128). Besides its inherent wit, conjecture, according to the *Arte*, is an especially potent resource when the hearers' disposition or the state of the case does not favor the speaker. Thus Wilson's specimen "Oration conjecturall" develops its charge against a presumed murderer through a lengthy recursion of *if . . . then* sentences which fill the blank left by the absence of material evidence or eyewitness testimony. By the same syntactic means—clausal correlations with *if . . . then*—Lyly's characters offer the reader frequent access to this dubious species of witty delight by arguing conjecturally with themselves or one another. Euphues' speech at Lucilla's soirée, for instance, depends crucially on the manipulation of conjecture to make its transition from flattery and alleged idealization to a final carpe diem appeal. In the former vein the hero employs conjecture to voice high-sounding sentiment without committing himself to what he is saying: "*If* it be so, that the contemplation of the inwarde qualitie ought to be respected more, than the view of the outward beautie, *then* doubtlesse women eyther doe or should love those best whose vertue is best" (*Euph.*, I, 201); in the latter vein, however, he is swept

---

[53]Feuillerat (*John Lyly*, p. 290) invokes the langue-parole distinction to insist that there is no individual characterization in terms of parole: "Ces personnages s'expriment tous en une langue uniforme, celle de l'auteur." Walter King ("Lyly and Elizabethan Rhetoric," p. 153) concedes that Lyly's characters all "speak and act in the same way and possess few if any individualizing traits. Nevertheless," he continues, "what they say and how they say it always indicate their state of mind and allow for differentiation between them. The characters also represent in a pseudo-allegorical fashion certain common types of humanity. Thus Euphues stands for facile intellectuality synonymous with sophistry, which it is Lyly's purpose to expose and condemn."

up in the recursive dynamic of his own sentence forms and uses conjectural argument to "heape" his exhortations with Wilsonian vehemence:

If you will be cherished when you be olde, be curteous while you be young, *if* you looke for comfort in your hoary haires, be not coye when you have your golden lockes, *if* you would be embraced in the wayning of your bravery, be not squeymish in the waning of your beautie, *if* you desyre to be kept lyke the Roses when they have loste theyr coulour, smell sweete as the Rose doth in the bud, *if* you would be tasted for olde wyne, be in the mouth a pleasant Grape. [*Euph.*, I, 203; my italics]

If Lyly's syntax of conjecture consisted only in his profuse *if . . . then* correlations, his Euphuism would remain neatly within Wilson's confines and within the grand antithetical design that Barish finds in his prose, with the *if . . . then*s as illustrations of "the second type of antithesis, which proposes alternatives but does not resolve them."[54] It is interesting to observe, however, that Lyly systematically expands the syntax of conjecture in *Euphues*, allocating *if . . . then* correlations to what might be called weak (hypothetical or conditional) uses and introducing *either . . . or* conjunction for strong, "vehement" purposes, the compelling of choice between posited alternatives. The strong, *either . . . or* forms of Euphuistic conjecture are indispensable, moreover, to the characters' adversarial dealings with one another: the use of these conjunction pairs betokens attempted or actual dominance, the weak *if . . . then* correlations submission. To illustrate, the old Eubulus nerves up himself and his language to give Euphues a needed reproof:

I am enforced to thincke that *either* thou dyddest want one to give thee good instructions, *or* that thy parentes made thee a wanton. . . . For *either* they were too foolishe in using no discipline, *or* thou too froward in rejecting their doctrine, *eyther* they willinge to have thee idle, *or* thou wylfull to bee ill employed. [*Euph.*, I, 186; my italics]

But, true to his origins as a Lylyan hero, Euphues can spot amplification by conjecture instantly. He scorns the mode as invalid argument and the old man into the bargain; rhetorically, his ad hominem aspersions make his return volley of *either . . . or* sentences the more devastating while also ironically confirming Eubulus's suppositions that the young man's wit is out of control:

Whereas you argue I knowe not uppon what probabilyties, but sure I am uppon no proofe, that my bringing up shoulde bee a blemish to my birthe, I aunswere, and sweare too that you were not therein a lyttle overshot, *eyther* you gave too muche credite to the report of others, *or* to much lybertie to your owne judgement. . . . *Eyther* you would have all men olde as you are, *or* els you have quite forgotten that you your selfe were young, or ever knew young dayes: *eyther* in

[54]Barish, "Prose Style of John Lyly," p. 19.

your youth you were a very vicious and ungodly man, *or* now being aged very supersticious & devoute above measure. . . . You measure my affections by your owne fancies, and knowing your selfe *either* too simple to rayse the siege of pollycie, *or* too weake to resist the assault by prowesse, you deeme me of as lyttle wit as your selfe, *or* of lesse force, *eyther* of small capacitie, *or* of no courage. [*Euph.*, I, 190, 192, 193; my italics]

This syntactically conducted showdown ends with Euphues turning heel on Eubulus upon finishing his speech, even though the old man is a guest in Euphues' house. The rude dismissal turns out to be absolute, both for Eubulus as a character in the narrative and for his well-intentioned adoption of strong forms of conjecture with respect to the hero. The old man signals his defeat by murmuring farewell to Euphues in weak *if . . . then* sentence forms and by finding place for strong forms only in soliloquy, as he leaves the scene for good:

Ah *Euphues* litle dost thou know that *if* thy wealth wast, thy wit will give but small warmth, & *if* thy wit encline to wilfulnes, that thy wealth will doe thee no great good. *If* the one had bene employed to thrift, the other to learning, it had bene hard to conjecture, *whether* thou shouldest have ben more fortunate by riches, *or* happie by wisdome, *whether* more esteemed in the common weale for welth to maintaine warre, *or* for counsell to conclude peace. But alas why doe I pitie that in thee which thou seemest to praise in thyself. [*Euph.*, I, 195; my italics]

What is left to conjecture and its associated weak and strong syntactic realizations until the penultimate events in the narrative emerges as an ever more sophistical and cynical range of applications. In the paired soliloquies where Lucilla and Euphues respectively rationalize their passion for one another, Lyly makes masterly use of heaping conjecture to portray self-doubt overcome by willed self-deception. Lucilla's grand recursion of conjectures directed against herself ("If thou haste belyed women, he will judge thee unkynde, if thou have revealed the troth, he must needes thincke thee unconstant, if he perceive thee to be wonne with a Nut, he will imagine that thou wilt be lost with an Apple . . .") terminates abruptly in a shift to hopeful use of the same mode, even though none of the recriminations have been answered: "But suppose that *Euphues* love thee, that *Philautus* leave thee . . ." (*Euph.*, I, 206). As the reader moves on to Euphues' juxtaposed soliloquy, an individually characterizing, local function of the syntax of conjecture comes into play. While Lucilla frames her conjectures in the weaker *if . . . then* form in keeping, presumably, with her female role, Euphues conjectures in the stronger *either . . . or* form about himself and their mutual relation, intermixing *if . . . then*s only to reflect on Lucilla independently: "Ah my *Lucilla*, wold thou wert either lesse faire or I more fortunate, eyther I wiser or thou milder, either would I were out of this madde moode, eyther I would we were both of one minde. But how should she be perswaded . . . ? will she not rather imagine me to be intangled with hir beautie, then with hir vertue? . . . Yes, yes, she must needs conjecture so" (*Euph.*, I, 209). These local differentiations in the lovers' wilfully witty use of conjecture are integrated with larger thematic developments in the charged scene where Lucilla riddlingly communicates her passion to Euphues. In framing her speech, Lucilla ironically echoes the distinction between positive and only probable argument on which Euphues had insisted so strongly in rebuffing Eubulus. The echo is doubly ironic because it is unwitting on Lucilla's part—though duly marked by the attentive reader—and because it occurs in a calculating defense of conjecture: "Pardon mee *Euphues* if in love I cast beyond the Moone, which bringeth us women to endlesse moane. . . . Though I as yet never tryed any faithles, wherby I should be fearefull, yet have I read of many that have bene perjured, which causeth me to be carefull: though I am able to convince none by proofe, yet am I enforced to suspect one uppon probabilyties." Again, the weaker *if . . . then* form of conjecture becomes indispensable to Lucilla as the vehicle for her gesture of surrender. By representing herself as helpless to repel his importunity, she schemes to bind Euphues the more firmly to her:

And then no mervaile it is that if the fierce Bull be tamed with the Figge tree, that women beeing as weake as sheepe, be overcome with a Figge, if the wilde Deare be caughte with an apple, that the tame Damzell is wonne with a blossome, if the fleete *Dolphin* be allured with harmony, that women be entangled with the melodie of mens speach, fayre promises and solemne protestations. [*Euph.*, I, 222–23]

It is, however, neither Lucilla nor Euphues but the victim of their joint betrayal, Philautus, who is assigned the last major use of conjecture in the narrative, thus bringing the larger thematic developments associated with this witty rhetorical resource to a close. The style of Philautus's letter to Euphues effects a vital Lylyan play on semantic identity and difference; for, like Eubulus at the beginning, Philautus near the end of the action cannot make any sense of the prodigal Euphues' expenditures of wit: "If thou diddest determine with thy selfe at the first to be false, why diddest thou sweare to bee true? If to be true, why arte thou false?. . . If the sacred bands of amitie did delyght thee, why diddest thou break them? if dislyke thee, why diddest thou prayse them?" (*Euph.*, I, 234). But the differences between Eubulus's proffered counsel and Philautus's letter end by grossly outweighing the likenesses, thus trenchantly exposing the isolation which the hero has brought upon himself by his bad faith. While Eubulus had spoken out of solicitude, Philautus writes as if from the far side of a divide to one whose actions have set him apart as a moral monstrosity.

Notwithstanding the essential contribution of conjecture to the negative, adversative grain of the narrative and to developments in plot, theme, and character, it remains the case, as one would expect, that the bulk of argumentation in the narrative portion of *Euphues* is carried out in the positive mode. Once again, the best gloss on Lylyan positive argumentation is the treatment of witty exaggeration and figuration in *The Arte of Rhetorique*. Of exaggeration Wilson had said: "In augmenting or diminishing without all reason, wee give good cause of much pastime." Certainly the narrator and characters of *Euphues* are extremists if not always irrationalists in this respect; and to implement their rhetoric of exaggeration two (related) syntactic resources are vital: superlatives and correlative expressions of quantity.

As I suggested in differentiating Pettie and Lyly in the preceding section of this chapter, correlative expressions of quantity are a reliable individuating feature of the style of *Euphues*. In their simple, semantically transparent form the correlating connectives are joined with respective occurrences of the same adverbial (e.g., *by how much the more . . . by so much the more*) to give a witty turn of phrase to an assertion bearing intensive force. In this manner Eubulus appeals to Euphues for a hearing: "for by howe much the more I am a straunger to you, by so much the more you are beholding to me" (*Euph.*, I, 187). Yet, as noted, in this form this type of correlative is rare almost to the point of nonoccurrence in Lyly, although it is common in Pettie. We are now in a better position to see why. The simple, transparent form of the correlative expression of quantity makes a fairly straightforward report on the speaker's thinking. But, as we know from our consideration of dissimulation and conjecture, such moments are programmatically excluded from the narrative of *Euphues*. I have been able to find only one other pure instance—a brief lapse into candor on Lucilla's part, which the narrator represents as a glimpse of her brazenness: "Gentlemen . . . by so much the more you are welcome by how much the more you were wished for" (*Euph.*, I, 215). Two other possible examples involving the direct expression of feeling are significantly complicated—and compromised—at the moment of utterance. Lucilla, soliloquizing about her passion for Euphues, cannot do so without being driven to rationalize it (in a correlative expression of quantity in the opaque form created by antithetical adverbials): "*By so muche the more* therefore my change is to be excused, *by how much the more* my choyce is excellent: and *by so much the lesse* I am to be condemned, *by how much the more* Euphues is to be commended" (*Euph.*, I, 206; my italics). By the same means Philautus puts half a brave face on his heartbreak in addressing Lucilla's father: "Certeinely *Ferardo* I take *the lesse* griefe *in that* I see her *so* greedy after *Euphues*, and *by so much the more* I am content to leave my sute, *by how much the more* she seemeth to disdayne my service" (*Euph.*, I, 231–32; my italics). This anomalous example attests all the more to the systematic integration of features in Lyly's Euphuism because Philautus uses a simple, transparent form of the correlative expression to signal his break with the intrigue of the narrative. We are left, then, as the complications in even the infrequent simple forms show, with the opaque, antithetical form of the correlative expression of quantity as the standard type in the narrative portion of *Euphues*. Its occurrences operate uniformly, whether the narrator or one of the characters is speaking, to set human psychology and behavior in a contrarious light. Thus the narrator informs us that the cross-workings of Euphues' mind are reflected in Philautus's also: "*Philautus* by how much the lesse he looked for thys discourse, by so much the more he liked it" (*Euph.*, I, 198). Thus, too, Don Ferardo utters sentiments to Lucilla of the same riddled and riddling sort: "Neyther doe I like thee the lesse, in that thou lykest *Philautus* so little, neyther can *Philautus* love thee the worse, in that thou lovest thy selfe so well" (*Euph.*, I, 229).

However, as Barish has finely noted, it is the superlatives—the other syntactic category that contributes in a major way to the rhetoric of exaggeration in *Euphues*—which carry a heavier share still of the semantic burden in the work. Despite the social ambiance of the narrative, superlatives scarcely function as colloquial intensifiers like 'We had the best time at your house,' or 'You were the prettiest girl at the party.'[55] Instead they are pressed into service of a quasi-metaphysical kind, to express a ruling perception which Barish describes as follows: "The notion that things contain within them their own contraries, or the power to work contrary effects, occurs so often in *Euphues* . . . that by virtue of sheer frequency of repetition it comes to be felt as a major insight." As vehicles for this insight, he continues, "two comparatives are better than two positive adjectives, because they double the distance between the antithetic terms, and superlatives are best of all, since they drive the terms as far apart as they will go."[56] What Barish identifies is indeed a ubiquitous (and uniform) feature of Lylyan composition: recursive clausal conjunctions of superlative expressions that assert over and over, from everybody's point of view, "the precarious closeness of extremes" in the constitution of the natural and human realms. The narrator sets the syntactic and semantic pattern in the opening expository section: "The freshest colours soonest fade, the teenest Rasor soonest tourneth his

---

[55]The only instances I have found of this rare use of superlatives in *Euphues* occur at I, 198, 217–18. The latter, Lucilla's sardonic interruption of Euphues' flattery, wittily but incompletely anticipates the controlling conceit of Donne's "Lecture upon the Shadow": "In faith *Euphues*, I woulde have you staye there, for as the Sunne when he is at the highest beginneth to goe downe, so when the prayses of women are at the best, if you leave not, they wyll beginne to fayle."

[56]Barish, "Prose Style of John Lyly," pp. 20–21.

edge, the finest cloathe is soonest eaten with Moathes, and the Cam-
bricke sooner stained then the course Canvas: whiche appeared well in
this Euphues" (*Euph.*, I, 184–85), a declaration soon borne out by the
hero's choice of licentious Naples for his residence—"whereby it is evidently seene that the fleetest fishe swalloweth the delicatest bayte, that
the highest soaring Hawke trayneth to the lure, and that the wittiest
skonce is invegled wyth the soddeyne viewe of alluringe vanities" (*Euph.*,
I, 186). It is altogether unsurprising to find Eubulus the first character
to ratify the narrator's world view by the same syntactic means: "The
fine christall is sooner crazed then the harde marble, the greenest Beeche
burneth faster then the dryest Oke, the fairest silke is soonest soyled,
and the sweetest wine tourneth to the sharpest vineger, the pestilence
doth most ryfest infect the cleerest complection" (*Euph.*, I, 189). But it
is at least initially surprising that Euphues and Lucilla both bear identical
testimony in the identical style to this perception of the constitution of
things. "Doe we not commonly see that in paynted pottes is hidden the
deadlyest poyson? that in the greenest grasse is the greatest Serpent?
in the cleerest water the uglyest Toade?" inquires Euphues grandly of
the mixed company assembled at Don Ferardo's (*Euph.*, I, 202). And
Lucilla, soliloquizing, reminds herself that this world view will work
against her with Euphues, for as surely as he knows "that the glass once
crased will with the leaste clappe be cracked, that the cloath which
staineth with Mylke, will soone loose his coulour with vineger," so surely
does he know "that she that hath been faythlesse to one, will never be
faythfull to any" (*Euph.*, I, 205).

This class of recursively elaborated superlative expressions, like every
principal individuating feature of Euphuism, poses a variety of challenges to interpretation. There is, first, the rhetorical challenge: Are the
archdissimulators Lucilla and Euphues dissembling when they claim to
share with the narrator and Eubulus a knowledge of the fatal proneness
of best things to become worst? If so, then it is hard to know what to
make, in turn, of the central generalization in the repentant Euphues'
soliloquy as he prepares to return from Naples to a life of study at home
in Athens: "The proofe of late hath bene verefied in me, whome nature
hath endued with a lyttle witte, which I have abused with an obstinate
will, most true it is that the thing the better it is, the greater the abuse,
and that ther is nothing but through the mallice of man may be abused"
(*Euph.*, I, 241–42). Both in isolation and in context this appears to be
anything but dissembled speech, but it cannot be distinguished rhetorically or stylistically from the same claim in the prodigal Euphues' mouth.
Yet if we construe Lucilla's and Euphues' claims to such knowledge
straightforwardly through the narrative, then their self-conscious and
self-chosen commitment to evil becomes not less but more baffling. Are

Lyly's characters hopelessly inconsistent psychologies that defy understanding?

Beyond the rhetorical challenge lie ones posed by the syntax and semantics of Lyly's superlatives, and these are no easier to confront. The narrator asserts, in the passages quoted above, that the meaning of such conjunctions "appeared well," "is evidently seene." Actually, what we discover when we look closely is something quite different. To begin with, there is no apparent logic to the selection and arrangement of these serial conjunctions, either as evocations of a cosmic interconnectedness or as representations of some process of induction in the mind. Typically the grammatical subjects are drawn miscellaneously from the spheres of the natural and the manufactured—for example, the fine crystal, the greenest beech tree, the fairest silk, the sweetest wine, the pestilence—and they are introduced in no necessary order that we can discover. (Shuffling the order of the conjuncts does not seem to affect the whole series for better or worse.) Lacking evidence to the contrary, then, we tentatively take these serial conjuncts as symmetric—that is, interchangeable—and we look for the semantic identity principle, the "general proposition" that constitutes them as a set, in Wierzbicka's and McCawley's terms (see the second section of chapter 1). If we had only the subject noun phrases as conjuncts—the freshest colors, the teenest razor, and so on—they would quite unproblematically constitute a set: things that are the finest of their kind. While there might be some minor residual sense of incongruity in an assortment of crystal, beech tree, silk, and wine, it would presumably be offset by whatever was being conjointly predicated of them in their shared verb phrase. Hence, if these superlatives were conjoined subject *NP*s only, we could probably relate them without difficulty to Barish's and Hunter's outlook on Lyly's syntax and style as analytic, reflective of the pattern and order that the mind either finds or can superimpose upon things.

But such is not the form of Lyly's serial superlatives; instead he gives us full, unreduced clauses as the domains of our search for the "general proposition" that motivates the composition of the whole. Since the units are clauses, it is entirely possible—in the context of the period and of this study—to try to read them as sense parallelisms, the "same thing" said in "different words." But what semantic identity principle unifies a string of assertions to the effect that the freshest colors fade soonest, that the fleetest fish swallows the most delicate bait, that the greenest beech burns faster than the dryest oak, that the pestilence most rifely infects the clearest complexion? In the frustration of our hunt for semantic identity we are brought to see that, to the extent that these assertions can be treated propositionally at all, it is not at all in the same sense. Perhaps it is in the nature of all beechwood to be more combustible than all oakwood. But we cannot confirm that those with the best complexions incur the worst cases of smallpox or that the freshest colors are the soonest to fade. The best sense to be made of such assertions is that a case of smallpox may seem the worst if it ruins an especially fine complexion, or that the fading of a very fresh color may seem quickest because of our psychological resistance to such occurrences, together with our propensity in grief to magnify the expression of loss. As for the fleetest fish, if the assertion were merely that it could be baited (like the luring of the hawk that soars highest), this might be treated as a fact analogous to the presumed one about the properties of different woods or a truism to the effect that nothing is invulnerable. But what is the significance of "the delicatest bayte"? Is it merely the different truism that what is most irresistible proves most irresistible? Apparently not, for we also have the assertions that the greenest grass hides the greatest serpent, and the clearest water the ugliest toad. In these superlatives the truth content appears most elusive of all. Thus the syntax and semantics of these clauses with redoubled superlatives bespeak not simply "the precarious closeness of extremes," as Barish says and as the subjective readings of the faded color and the pockmarked complexion would bear out, but something more awesomely mysterious: the co-existence of extremes in an identity or interdependency relation whose nature is never clarified yet constantly reaffirmed.

These clausal conjunctions of superlative expressions, then, disqualify themselves as sense parallelisms, for their different words do not say at all the same thing although they might seem to in passing. Physical (or mythical) attributes, emotional reactions to undesired happenings, and metaphysical hints at the mystery of evil do not amount to anything like a well-formed set of conjuncts; but Lyly does nothing to alleviate our perplexity at the absence of a discernible identity relation. Instead he persists with his recursions as if the coordinations were, indeed, perfectly motivated (as the parallel phrasing and the sound similarities additionally suggest). In consequence, what he generates is, in Madelon Gohlke's words, a "peculiarly obstructive . . . style," "a language of self-concealment,"[57] or, in my terms, a powerful extension of the dissimulating modality that envelops the narrative of *Euphues*. What, we may persist in asking, is the net rhetorical effect of affirming over and over through sharply rendered and varied images that the best contains the worst, that the best conceals the worst, that the best becomes the worst—and does so instantaneously, not in the tried-and-true, *ubi sunt* fashion of temporal things? Gohlke says that the joint effects of Lylyan serial superlatives are to articulate the assumption which everyone in *Euphues* shares—"that the object of desire, once achieved, loses its value"—and to stave off its degrading implications through "an elaborate system of

[57]Gohlke, "Reading *Euphues*," pp. 103, 106, 109.

delay": "a barrage of rhetoric" that "serves both to camouflage this process and to postpone the collapse of romantic illusion." Gohlke's reading thus focuses on escapism and sentimentalism as the principal rhetorical effects. I am inclined, however, to discover a more complexly sinister drift in these clausal recursions of superlative expressions— namely, a repeated invitation to identify good and evil, to make no distinction where difference is represented so minimally, in terms of a split second or a tiny contingency or the coexisting properties of a single object. The syntax of these expressions dissimulates because it stops short of affirming such an identity all the while that it points and points again in that very direction. Consequently, these serial superlatives only read as if they were registering perceptions and judgments about the best and the worst. Under scrutiny they can be seen to flirt with a nihilism that (paradoxically) would preclude all possibility of perceiving or judging anything with reference to good or bad.

An analogous train of difficulties attends the interpretation of Lyly's so-called similes from unnatural natural history—perhaps the most notable single feature of Euphuistic style from his day to ours and also the final major aspect in which his composition tallies with Wilson's discussion of the pleasure-giving linguistic resources of wit in the *Arte*. As we observed previously, Wilson commends figuration—the heaping of images and examples—as a compelling means of amplifying one's discourse because it exploits sensory appeal. We have also seen him ascribing to figures and to fables, which he treats as extended figures, a lively ethical force and transparency: winning ways of presenting truths and values so that they will be embraced. For its part, the narrative portion of *Euphues* abounds with images multiplied in recursive clausal conjunctions like the superlatives, with which they not infrequently mingle. Like the superlatives, too, the images—more often images than explicit similes—from unnatural natural history ostensibly function as another device shared by the narrator and characters to illustrate some "general proposition" that is being advanced. Thus Euphues retorts to Eubulus in the opening scene: "The Sun shineth uppon the dungehill, and is not corrupted, the Diamond lyeth in the fire, and is not consumed, the Christall toucheth the Toade, and is not poysoned, the birde *Trochilus* lyveth by the mouth of the Crocodile and is not spoyled, a perfect wit is never bewitched with leaudeness, neyther entised with lasciviousnesse" (*Euph.*, I, 193). Soon, however, Lucilla's beauty infatuates him, and he soliloquizes thus against his initial compunctions:

But why goe I about to hinder the course of love, with the discourse of law? hast thou not redde *Euphues,* that he that loppeth the Vine causeth it to spreade higher? that hee that stoppeth the streame forceth it to swell higher? that he that casteth water on the fire in the Smithes forge, maketh it to flame fiercer?

Even so he that seeketh by counsayle to moderate his overlashinge affections, encreaseth his owne misfortune. [*Euph.*, I, 208–9]

As a carefully executed companion piece, Lucilla's soliloquy likewise moves from self-blame to self-exoneration through runs of natural and nonnatural images:

But can *Euphues* convince me of fleetinge, seeing for his sake I breake my fidelitie? Can he condemne me of disloyaltie, when he is the onely cause of my dislyking? . . . Doth he not remember that the broken boane once sette together, is stronger then ever it was? That the greatest blotte is taken off with the Pommice? That though the Spyder poyson the Flye, she cannot infect the Bee? That although I have been light to *Philautus*, yet I may be lovely to *Euphues?* [*Euph.*, I, 205–6]

At length, Philautus's angry letter to Euphues makes one of the final contributions to this profuse aspect of the style of the narrative through a return to alleged moral directives in nature:

Dost thou not know that a perfect friende should be lyke the Glazeworme, which shineth most bright in the darke? or lyke the pure Franckencense which smelleth most sweete when it is in the fire? or at the leaste not unlyke to the Damaske Rose which is sweeter in the still then on the stalke? But thou *Euphues*, dost rather resemble the Swallow which in the Summer creepeth under the eves of every house, and in the Winter leaveth nothing but durte behinde hir, or the humble Bee which having sucked honny out of the faire flower doth leave it & loath it, or the Spider which in the finest webbe doth hang the fairest Fly. [*Euph.*, I, 234]

What can be said about Lyly's recursive images in terms of the syntax and semantics of conjunction? Obviously these coordinations are as independent of fixed ordering overall as the superlatives appeared to be. However, a sizable number of them attest to a "general proposition" by virtue of which they comprise a set. Euphues' two speeches are of this kind: the first a series of illustrations that exposure to evil need not entail loss of purity, the second a gathering of evidence that restraint augments the force inherent in natural things. Indeed, the combined syntactic and semantic identity of the clausal conjuncts in the hero's speeches is enough to qualify them as sense parallelisms. But the latter two—Lucilla's and Philautus's—just as surely do not attest to some general proposition or submit to analysis as sense parallelisms. Lucilla purports to conjoin two individual predications, themselves ill-sorted, with a generic one: a broken bone that has healed, a blot removed by the pumice stone, and the spider that infects the fly but not the bee. Comparable incoherence characterizes the conjoined images in Philautus's letter. What can be made of such mixed findings? Is any unifying perspective possible?

Shimon Sandbank offers an interesting critique of Lyly's image conjunctions together with a proposal for their general interpretation. Distinguishing essentially the two types just remarked on—the "strictly synonymous" and the "not strictly synonymous" image conjunctions— he complains (with justice, in my view) that the latter type, Lucilla's and Philautus's, "seem to confuse the issue rather than 'analyze' it." But Sandbank also faults the former type, multiply reiterated expressions of the same idea, for the constantly attenuating effect he finds the whole coordination to have upon its individual components. In his words, Lyly's "multiplication of images . . . means that no single image is given the opportunity to realize itself. The 'presence' of the images is neutralized and all possible conflict with the meaning is prevented." Furthermore, we find that "the more multiple and thus disparate" the image conjuncts are, "the less do their physical qualities count, and the more formalized and empty becomes their common denominator . . . until they become totally abstracted—the faceless carriers of a logical relationship, mere exempla."[58] Since they fail by the criteria of sensory concreteness standardly applied to figurative language, Sandbank proposes to view Lyly's image conjunctions as the products of a rhythmic impulsion: an urge to constitute a prose style in balanced structures and even strokes.

Although I find the rhythmic explanation too limiting to be persuasive, I think Sandbank is right about the generally reductive semantic effect of Lyly's image conjunctions. But the ultimate difficulty I see is not that these discrete images become "faceless carriers" of some one "logical relationship"; rather, that they can be marshaled in support of any view or any course of action whatever, at any juncture. As the narrative of *Euphues* unfolds through almost uninterrupted exhibitions of characters using image conjunctions to argue opposing sides of a question with one another or within themselves, Lyly also discloses why this rhetorical resource is so infinitely adaptable, and that the hero, at the very least, recognizes it as being so. The adaptability, of course, derives from that of nature itself, both in the variety of its contents and in the variousness of aspect that the human mind can discern in a single object. (Thus, in the preceding quotations, the bee images purity to Lucilla but faithless ingratitude to Philautus.) As for express recognition that one can prove anything whatever by manipulating images and exempla, Lyly makes Euphues his self-conscious spokesman in the scene where he repudiates Eubulus's counsel:

As you have ensamples to confirme your pretence, so I have most evident and infallyble argumentes to serve for my purpose. . . . Infinite and innumerable were the examples I coulde alleadge and declare to confirme the force of Nature, . . . were not the repetition of them needelesse having shewed sufficient, or

[58]Shimon Sandbank, "Euphuistic Symmetry and the Image," *SEL* 11 (1971): 1–13; quotations from pp. 7, 12–13.

bootelesse seeinge those alleadged will not perswade you. . . . It is the disposition of the thought that altereth the nature of the thing. (*Euph.*, I, 191, 193; cf.
I, 239)

What Euphues roundly declares is what the usage of the characters and
the narrator alike confirms. The serial image conjunctions of Lyly's narrative do not create clarity and moral transparency even though Wilson's
directives are in force; instead they produce a dense atmosphere of
relativistic reasoning. "It is the disposition of the thought that altereth
the nature of the thing." To ends such as these, obviously, both the
integrated and the incoherent types of serial images which we have
remarked conduce with equal effectiveness; hence it may be in ethical
relativism that we find the unifying interpretive perspective for which
we have been looking. The relativism which is indeed the overriding
rhetorical effect brings us close to our desired perspective, but it remains
imprecise as a characterization in its focus on the "relative"—the diverse,
the shifting. For under scrutiny the connotations with which these images surround their paired references to human traits or behavior do
finally build to a single implication: namely, that man is just another
animal, and woman, too, for that matter. This is the ultimate reduction
worked by Lyly's serial image conjunctions: they not only crowd and
neutralize one another as vehicles, but they also downgrade their tenor
to a literally brutish level, one which owes its existence less to Pliny
than to Ovidian erotic naturalism.

Yet here, as always, the syntax dissimulates, never straightforwardly
asserting that humans are merely animals and only intermittently re-
sorting to the overt comparative form "as the deer . . . so a woman."
This evasiveness is the reason for stickling over nomenclature, over
references to Lyly's "similes," for these heaps of material are most often
not shaped into simile form in the narrative portion of *Euphues*. Instead
they tend to be cast as conjoined declaratives proceeding matter-of-factly,
or as binary correlations (e.g., *though . . . yet*) shedding an aura of equa-
ble reflection, or as questions—most insidiously, rhetorical questions
implying that bestial behavior is no news to anyone: "Did not *Jupiter*
transforme himselfe into the shape of *Amphitrio* to imbrace *Alcmaena*?
Into the forme of a Swan to enjoye *Laeda*? Into a Bull to beguyle *Io*? Into
a showre of golde to winne *Danae*? Did not *Neptune* chaunge himselfe
into a Heyfer, a Ramme, a Floud, a *Dolphin*, onely for the love of those
he lusted after?" (*Euph.*, I, 236). Yet the sense that leads readers to think
of these image conjunctions as similes is not, after all, fundamentally in
error, for there is such persistent argument by analogy being conducted
on the basis of this material that at last the freight of alleged affinities
collapses a kinship between humans and animals into a functional identity. Lyly achieves this result obliquely, through recursions of conjunctive

409

syntax that turn on the presence of an identity relation. Human animality evoked in coordinate structures, however, is an implication hinging on nothing more explicit than the contiguity and the parallelism afforded by paratactic linkage. The syntax operates, one might say, as a kind of innuendo. In this connection Gohlke's observations on the serial image conjunctions (in her terms, "analogies" or "simile") are suggestively developed within her framework of patent and latent functions of style:

Euphuism is designed in part to provide a medium in which desire is acceptable. The elaborately constructed rhetoric masks a reality which is perceived as shameful. If everyone is in false face it is because they can neither renounce their desires nor admit them fully into their awareness. . . . What is repressed in surface communication and awareness finds expression elsewhere, primarily in the proliferation of analogies which attends every major decision of the book. It is in simile that the characters express their deepest impulses and their deepest fears. Here what one finds is an erotic energy which is perceived as violent and destructive.[59]

But violence and destruction are not all that the serial image conjunctions connote with regard to the erotic energy of the human animal. They also work with and through the elaborate formal responsions to be found at every linguistic level in Euphuistic style to aestheticize sexual appetite in particular and the exercise of self-will generally—to render it exotic, curious, rich, and strange that there should be such force felt, but always at the same time "natural" that it should. Lucilla's major speech to Euphues illustrates: "I have read that the Bull being tyed to the Figge tree loseth his strength, that the whole herd of Deare stande at the gaze, if they smell a sweete apple, that the *Dolphin* by the sounde of Musicke is brought to the shore. And then no mervaile it is . . . that women be entangled with the melodie of mens speach, fayre promises and solemne protestations" (*Euph.*, I, 223).

Taken all in all for the brilliantly integrated system of play with the potentialities of conjunctive sentence form that it is, the style of the narrative portion of *Euphues* registers a triumph for wit's winning ways— not merely in the fictional world of the characters as shaped by the negative and adversative conditions for discourse that Wilson projected in *The Arte of Rhetorique*, but also in the historical record of its adulatory reception by Lyly's contemporaries. Although the savor of the triumph has long since faded, the showiness of the style has continued to obscure an interesting and remarkable fact, namely, that Lyly himself was the first to react negatively (though not altogether dismissively) toward the Euphuism that he had created. The stylistic reaction takes place in the latter half of *Euphues*, beginning at the point of the betrayal, reversal, disillusion, and repentance which the prodigally witty hero undergoes

[59]Gohlke, "Reading *Euphues*," pp. 107–8.

and which in turn precipitate his homeward flight to Athens. My final subject here will be the nature and manifestations of Lyly's stylistic counterreaction and its relation to the larger concerns of chapters 5 and 6 of this study.

Of all Lyly's critics, Feuillerat has offered the most useful view of the interworkings of structure and style in the whole of *Euphues*. Building on Dover Wilson's recognition that Euphues' experience is modeled after that of the prodigal son of the Gospel parable, Feuillerat remarks that the fictional and ostensibly nonfictional halves of *Euphues*—the latter an assemblage of letters including "A Cooling Carde for Philautus and All Fond Lovers," and the two tracts entitled "Euphues and His Ephebus" and "Euphues and Atheos"—fit together like a traditional story-sermon (in the manner of the *Legenda aurea* or Mirk's *Festial*): first the tale, then its edifying gloss. Feuillerat also praises Lyly for not succumbing to what he calls the "narrow pessimism" of "Protestant humanists" like Ascham in the catastrophic ending of the *novella* section, but instead proceeding to supplement the narrative with the almost entirely nonnarrative letters and tracts in which Euphues retains his psychological and moral self-possession.[60] What needs to be added to this outline sketch of the relation between the two halves of *Euphues* and of the relation of the style to them is this: Lyly's mode of composition closely mirrors the inner state of his hero, to the extent that Euphuism as a stylistic program submits to a stiff reckoning and a process of reformation along with the life and character of Euphues himself. The larger attendant implication of the correspondent changes in the style and in the eponymous hero in the latter half of Lyly's work seems to be that Euphuism is, in its own author's eyes, a prodigal misuse of wit and a willful squandering of the resources of his linguistic patrimony, which could otherwise be employed constructively, with the "wisdom" at which sixteenth-century English prose of counsel consistently aimed after the precedent set by Elyot.

What, then, are the nature and manifestations of the change in Lyly's style? Their thoroughgoing—hence, presumably deliberate—aspects are most clearly traceable in terms of Wilson's inventory of the chief pleasure-eliciting resources of wit which we have observed to figure so conspicuously in the Euphuism of the narrative portion of the work. First, there is an abrupt end put to dissimulation as a mode of conduct and utterance even before the fictional appurtenances of dialogue, soliloquy, and declamation have been dispensed with; and it comes at the moment when Lucilla bluntly informs Euphues that Curio has replaced him in her affections. The style accordingly sheds its oblique mannerisms and takes on an overall directness. This registers forthwith in sentence form

---

[60]Feuillerat, *John Lyly*, pp. 257–59, 62, note 4, 64, note 1.

as a great outcropping of binary clausal conjunction, oftenest in anti-thetical or correlative pairings. Thus Lucilla speaks in this newly straight-forward, semantically transparent style: "Certes *Euphues* you spend your wind in wast: for your welcome is but small, & your chere is like to be lesse. Fancie giveth no reason of his chaunge, neither wil be controlled for any choice. This is therfore to warne you, that from hencefoorth you neither sollicite this suite, neither offer any way your service" (*Euph.*, I, 238). And thus Euphues employs this style to soliloquize slightly later, in unmitigated self-reproach:

I have lost *Philautus,* I have lost *Lucilla,* I have lost that which I shall hardlye finde againe, a faythfull friende. Ah foolishe *Euphues,* why diddest thou leave *Athens* the nourse of wisdome, to inhabite *Naples* the nourisher of wantonnesse? Had it not bene better for thee to have eaten salt with the Philosophers in *Greece,* then sugar with the courtiers of *Italy?* But behold the course of youth which always inclineth to pleasure: I forsooke mine olde companions to search for new friends, I rejected the grave and fatherly counsayle of *Eubulus,* to follow the brainesicke humor of mine owne will. [*Euph.* I, 240–41]

This new plainspokenness with its associated binary clausal conjunctions in predominantly antithetical or correlative pairings—the staple, as we have seen, of sixteenth-century sententious sentences—continues to hold throughout the latter half of *Euphues*. Notably, also, the end of linguistic dissembling coincides with Lyly's all but complete abandonment of fic-tional presentation, a shift that may reflect rather more "narrow pessi-mism" regarding the feigning in fables than Feuillerat was prepared to acknowledge. But there is an accompanying positive development that leaves the way open for the sort of fabulation that Wilson envisaged and for Lyly's return to fiction-writing in *Euphues and His England;* this development is the setting up of an interpretive paradigm linking speaker and hearer, writer and reader, in a posited relation of mutual seekers after the sense of things—the hallmark of generalized Scripturalism in English prose. Euphues appears to advert specifically to the role of sententious sentences in implementing this paradigm when, in a late letter to Philautus, he weaves a thick texture of directed syntax in binary forms to convey to his friend the truth about himself as Euphues sees it:

Thou wilt muse *Philautus,* to heere *Euphues* to preach, who of late had more minde to serve his Ladye then to worshippe his Lorde. Ah *Philautus* thou art now a Courtier in *Italy,* I a scholler in *Athens,* and as hard it is for thee to follow good counsayle as for me to enforce thee, seeing in thee there is little will to amend, and in mee lesse authoritie to commaunde: yet will I exhort thee as a friende, I woulde I myght compell thee as a Father. But I have heard that it is peculiar to an *Italian* to stande in his owne conceite, and to a courtier never to be controlde: which causeth me to feare that in thee which I lament in others.

That is, that either thou seeme to wise in thine owne opinion thinking it scorne to be taught, or to wilde in thine attempts in rejecting admonishment. The one proceedeth of self love, and so thy name importeth, the other of meere folly, and that thy nature sheweth: thou lookest I should crave pardon for speaking so boldly, no *Philautus*. [*Euph.*, I, 306–7]

The foregoing passage is a certain specimen of later sixteenth-century prose of counsel, but it is not certifiably a production by the Euphuizing Lyly of the narrative first half of the work because the style lacks any of his distinguishing opaqueness. Indeed, the passage takes various countermeasures against such effects—in its explanatory nonrestrictive and sentential relative constructions ("who of late had more mind," "which causeth me to feare"), in its equally explanatory appositives ("I a scholler in Athens," "That is, that either thou seeme to wise . . . or to wilde," "and so thy name importeth," "and that thy nature sheweth"), and in its regular recourse to sense parallelisms as well as binary conjunctions as units of composition ("I have heard that it is peculiar to an *Italian* to stande in his owne conceite, and to a courtier never to be controlde," "either thou seeme to wise in thine owne opinion . . . or to wilde in thine attempts in rejecting admonishment"). In addition, the schematics of the passage is tempered to a level well below the heights systematically scaled in the earlier half of *Euphues*. The shift from relentless parisonic structures to sense parallelisms is significant in this regard, as are the local irregularities produced by gapping verbs ("thou art now a Courtier . . . , I a scholler," "The one proceedeth of self love, . . . the other of meere folly") and the diminished premium on sound similarities. Significantly, the very features that lessen the distinctiveness of the passage are the ones that figure most in Lyly's stylistic reformation. Further confirmation of the event and of the prodigal's return to normative modes of expression for the age comes from the narrator's introduction of Euphues to his readership—in an asymmetrically elaborated sentence containing only local symmetries—as the author, now, of the tract entitled "Euphues and His Ephebus" (the combined translation and paraphrase of Plutarch on the education of youth):

And calling to minde his former losenes, & how in his youth, he had mispent his time, he thought to give a Caveat to all parents, how they might bring their children up in vertue, and a commaundement to al youth, how they should frame themselves to their fathers instructions: in the which is plainly to be seene, what wit can, & will do, if it be well employed, which discourse following, although it bringe lesse pleasure to your youthfull mindes then his first course, yet will it bring more profite: in the one being conteined the race of a lover, in the other, the reasons of a Philosopher. [*Euph.*, I, 259]

Among the other major Wilsonian devices for eliciting pleasure in witty language, word play survives the Lylyan stylistic reformation essentially intact. It is evident that there are considerably fewer instances of punning and equivocation in the latter half of *Euphues*,[61] but what instances there are still function as tokens of the hero's born wit and as sources of his appeal as a sententious speaker quite as much as a profligate one. Thus Euphues can initiate discourse punningly even in such serious cirumstances as his colloquy with Atheos, the spokesman for a species of natural religion who comes off effectually as an atheist: "If my hope (*Atheos*) were not better to converte thee, then my happe was here to conferre with thee, my hearte would breake for griefe" (*Euph.*, I, 292). While it is equally symptomatic of the chastened style of the latter half of *Euphues* that the remaining sixteen pages of the tract contain no further word play, the presence of any instances at all calls for comment. Wilson's remarks on the sermon styles of Cyprian and Augustine as well as his reiterated admiration for Latimer's preaching may go some way toward accounting for Lyly's retention of word play in what amounts to homiletic contexts. Yet it seems to me that what Wilson says about word play in his *Rule of Reason* is more apposite to Lyly's stylistic practice than are any remarks in the *Arte;* I have in mind the comment on the play by a "wittie" and "woorthie" man on Reginald Pole's name: "o Poule, o whurle Poule, as though his name declared his evill nature." Like the larger Renaissance interest in a variety of sources dealing with the mystical properties of names and numbers, this comment bespeaks an intuition that the potential for word play inheres in the givens of language—that it is there for the taking by a mind with ready responses to, say, the incidence of homonyms. Not only does the view of language that undergirds such an intuition seem quite plausible, it also allows word play itself to be classed as an "invention" in the Renaissance sense of a discovery rather than in our sense of a contrivance. Hence we see that there is more than one possible account to give of Lyly's retention of word play as an occasional feature of a reformed and chastened mode of composition. Clearly, what the latter half of *Euphues* repudiates are perversions and subversions of language by wit, not witty language itself. In support of this point we can invoke literary history: it was fortunate for a sensibility like Lyly's that there would be no inclination among English writers for half a century and more after *Euphues* to regard punning and equivocation categorically as vices.

Unlike word play with its inherent potential for relating sound and sense, the resources of conjecture, exaggeration, and figuration are problematic to a greater or lesser degree in a style that has put linguistic

[61]I have noted only the following instances in the latter half of *Euphues:* women/woe unto men (I, 241); cockney/cockescombe (I, 244); pleased/deceased, annoy/joy, choice/chance (I, 245); slip (*N*) /slipped (I, 265); cast/cast away (I, 284); sweate/sweete, sweete/sower (I, 288–89); hope/happe, convert/conferre (I, 292); contemne/condemned, excuse/accused (I, 321).

dissimulation at an end. The handling of these respective resources in the latter half of *Euphues* exhibits considerable intrinsic interest as well as further confirmation that a stylistic reform is in effect. Predictably enough, conjecture is no longer a unilateral option for a writer or speaker. As a result the passages of character analysis or reflections on possible courses of action in the late letters read very differently from those in the early speeches, with their recursions of *ifs*, *whethers*, and *either . . . ors* introducing clauses in the hypothetical mood. Declaratives replace hypotheticals, and conjecture as such virtually disappears. The unique provision for it occurs in "A Cooling Carde for Philautus and All Fond Lovers," a prose redaction, as Feuillerat showed, of parts of Ovid's *Remedia amoris* interspersed with stretches of original writing.[62] Here, to accommodate both the form and the substance of the Ovidian serial recursions of *if . . . then* and *either . . . or* sentences which develop a minute contingency plan for ending a love affair, Lyly admits conjecture as a tactic for placing the beloved in her worst imaginable light and then combating desire with what, admittedly, are fabrications. "*If* she be well sette, *then* call hir a Bosse, *if* slender a Hasill twigge, *if* Nutbrowne, as blacke as a coale, *if* well couloured, a paynted wall, *if* she be pleasaunt, *then* is she a wanton, *if* sullemne, a clowne, *if* honeste, *then* is she coye, *if* impudent, a harlotte." But the essential difference is that this conjecture is not to be employed in speaking to others, only to be self-administered in private, as need dictates: "This is therefore to admonish all young Impes and novises in love, not to blowe the coales of fancie wyth desire, but to quench them with disdayne. . . . *If* thou perceive they selfe to be entised with their wanton glaunces, *or* allured with their wicked guyles, *eyther* enchaunted with their beautie *or* enamoured with their braverie, enter with they selfe into this meditation. What shall I gayne *if* I obtayne my purpose? nay rather what shall I loose *if* I win my pleasure?" (*Euph.*, I, 254, 248; cf. I, 255; my italics).

Thus, with the exception of certain stretches of translated material in "A Cooling Carde" which nonetheless propose only a private, antidotal use for conjecture, Lyly eliminates this witty resource and its attendant syntactic realizations from the latter half of *Euphues*. It does not prove nearly so easy, however, to dispense with exaggeration and its associated superlative expressions in particular—the evident reason being that these are vehicles for the central Lylyan world view that contraries coexist in inseparable closeness. Although I have found only two occurrences of such superlatives in the latter half of *Euphues*, again the count is less important than either the prominence accorded them (positions at the very beginning and the very ending of this portion of the work) or the explicit qualifications added to the expression of the Lylyan world view

[62]Feuillerat, *John Lyly*, Appendix C, pp. 583–94.

in both contexts. The soliloquy of the newly repentant hero supplies the first of these contexts. The sentence reads as follows: "The proofe of late hath bene verefied in me, whome nature hath endued with a lyttle witte, which I have abused with an obstinate will, most true it is that the thing the better it is, the greater is the abuse, and that ther is nothing but through the mallice of man may be abused" (*Euph.*, I, 241–42). The significance of this pronouncement is, first, that Euphues now confirms the very outlook which he had fiercely denied to Eubulus in the opening scene of the narrative and, second, that he encases this outlook in a wrapper of commentary and explanation which insulates it from nihilistic and deterministic overtones. It is such touches as these that suggest and then, in their systematic character, confirm the implementation of a stylistic reformation in *Euphues.* A similar explicitness operates similarly at the end of the work, in Euphues' letter to Eubulus on the death of Eubulus's daughter: a document that brings full circle the expression of the Lylyan world view in the exchanged roles of counselor and counselee. Here, once again, the effect of Euphues' commentary and explanation is to ensure semantic transparency, to drain the outlook of its inscrutability and to reformulate it as a commonplace compounded of Christian consolation and Christian morality (closely reminiscent in theme and style of Wilson's specimen oration on the deaths of the duchess of Suffolk's two young sons):

But thou grauntest that she shold have dyed, & yet thou art grieved that she is dead. Is the death the better if the lyfe be longer? no truly. . . . The chiefe beautie of lyfe consisteth not in the numbering of many dayes, but in the using of vertuous doings. Amongst plants those be best esteemed that in shortest time bringe forth much frute. Be not the fairest flowers gathered when they be freshest? the youngest beasts killed for sacrifice because they be finest? The measure of lyfe is not length but honestie, neyther do we enter into lyfe to the ende we should set downe the day of our death, but therefore do we lyve, that we may obey him that made us, and be willyng to die when he shal call us. [*Euph.*, I, 310–11]

Yet, as the foregoing quotation makes manifest, the effect of the appended commentary and explanation is not merely to rehabilitate the rhetoric of exaggeration for retention in the latter half of *Euphues* but also to bring the style into overt conformity with the Scripturalist mode in prose composition. Lyly's loosening of his sentence forms from the point-for-point responsions of the high Euphuistic style of the narrative in order to replace opaqueness with explicitness repeatedly issues in the creation of sense parallelisms as bearers of the essential sententious content of the passage—for example: "The chiefe beautie of lyfe consisteth not in the numbering of many dayes, but in the using of vertuous doings," "neyther do we enter into lyfe to the ende we should set downe the day of our death, but therefore do we lyve, that we may obey him that made us, and be willyng to die when he shal call us."

The momentum leading toward sense parallelism as the single most vital element in the reformed prose style of *Euphues* becomes still more pronounced in Lyly's altered handling of the resource of figuration. In the earlier narrative, it will be recalled, the profuse images of natural and mythical objects functioned ambiguously in syntax, with the implied but usually unspecified force of analogies, while on a semantic plane they worked no less obliquely to enforce an amoral, libertine perspective on human nature and behavior. Since it is the Book of the Creatures, not that of God's Word, that becomes the proverbial nose of wax to be wrung to any angle in the narrative first half, Lyly accordingly exerts great effort to the latter half of *Euphues* to reclaim and reconstitute imagery within his chastened mode of composition. Notice of a reformulated approach to figuration which will result in a new species of imagery is summarily served by the hero at the crux of the narrative, as Euphues articulates his rude awakening to Lucilla's depraved nature and its ramifications in her language:

And in that you bringe in the example of a beast to confirme your folly, you shewe therein your beastly disposition, which is readie to followe suche beastlinesse. . . . Shall the lewdenesse of others animate thee in thy lightnesse? why then dost thou not haunt the stewes because *Lais* frequented them? why doest thou not love a Bull seeing *Pasiphae* loved one? why art thou not enamoured of thy father knowing that *Mirha* was so incensed? These are set down that we viewing their incontinencie, should flye the like impudencie, not follow the like excesse: neither can they excuse thee of any inconstancie. [*Euph.*, I, 240]

Yet, for all of Euphues' assurance in moralizing here, it is important that the recognition of variability in individual subjective responses to objects and experiences holds as firmly in the latter half of the work as in the former; Euphues himself says as much outright in his letter to the exiled Botonio (adapted from Plutarch's *De exilio*): "It is not the nature of the place but the disposition of the person that maketh the lyfe pleasaunt" (*Euph.*, I, 316). Accordingly, it is imperative for Lyly and his reformed prodigal to control the allusiveness and indeterminacy of an image if the newfound confidence in their ethical transparency which Euphues expresses in the foregoing quotation is to be sustained beyond this moment of reckoning. For Euphues himself, such control is to be gained principally through the redirected course of study on which he now solemnly resolves: "Philosophie, Phisicke, Divinitie, shal be my studie. O the hidden secrets of Nature, the expresse image of morall vertues, the equall ballaunce of Justice, the medicines to heale all diseases, how these beginne to delyght me" (*Euph.*, I, 241; cf. I, 286). With Lyly, however, the control emerges much more immediately and strikingly in the

417

handling of imagery in the latter half of *Euphues* by two chief means: (1) the regular, explicit use of correlative syntax (*like . . . as, as . . . so*) as a frame, and (2) the addition of explanatory comment, which at points takes on an allegorizing character. It is by the latter means particularly that the images are driven again and again toward incorporation in sense parallelisms, where the image, on the one hand, and its gloss, on the other, become the "different ways" of saying the "same thing." From an abundance of possible examples, these selections will illustrate the altered handling of imagery in the latter half of *Euphues* in order to harness its vivid sensory appeal to some edifying point:

For as the fire stone in *Liguria* though it bee quenched with milke, yet againe it is kindled with water, or as the rootes of *Anchusa*, though it bee hardned with water, yet it is againe made softe with Oyle, so the heart of *Euphues* enflamed earst with love, although it be cooled with the deceites of *Lucilla*, yet will it againe flame with the loyaltie of some honest Ladye, and though it bee hardned with the water of wilynesse, yet will it bee mollified with the Oyle of wisedome. [*Euph.*, I, 258]

But as in manuary craftes though they bee all good, yet that is accompted most noble, that is most necessary, so in the actions and studies of the minde although they be all worthy, yet that deserveth greatest praise which bringeth greatest profit. And so we commonly do make best accompt of that which doth us most good: we esteeme better of the Phisition that ministreth the potion, then of the Apoticarie that selleth the drugges. [*Euph.*, I, 289]

It is sayde that Thunder bruseth the tree, but breaketh not the barke, and pearceth the blade, and never hurteth the scabberd: Even so doth sinne wounde the hearte, but never hurte the eyes, and infect the soule, though outwardely it nothing affect the body. [*Euph.*, I, 309; cf. I, 242, 261, 266, 267, 268, 272, 277]

In sum, the evidence from every crucial aspect of stylistic practice for a consciously reformed mode of composition in the nonfictional latter half of *Euphues* attests the undoing of the negative and adversative set of working assumptions by which wit is allowed the use of any rhetorical or linguistic means to gain what Wilson called "the overhand" with others—and even, in an ironic Lylyan twist, to delude its own possessor. Instead, as the repudiation of dissembling and conjecture together with the rehabilitation of hyperbole and simile show in a systematic fashion, Lyly turns Euphuism back from the stylistic excesses with which he explored the pessimistic extremes of available views of human nature and the uses of eloquence, rededicating the cognitive and affective power of its schematics to the constructive ends that had hitherto characterized English prose of counsel in the sixteenth century. Notwithstanding the interest and importance of the evidence from various aspects of style that we have been considering in some detail, the most critical single development of all in the reformation effected in the latter portion of

Euphues is the witness borne by the tract entitled "Euphues and Atheos" that Lyly has conformity to Scripturalist modes of composition in view as an express major objective. He undertakes to dramatize his thorough revaluation of norms for prose style by assimilating the speech of his characters to the very words of Scripture as the ultimate source and model for the profoundest reaches of human expression.

Our sole preparation for this momentous development is provided in the hero's soliloquy at the end of "Euphues and His Ephebus," a projection of his state of mind long after his return home, at the end of ten years spent as "publyque Reader" in natural philosophy at the University of Athens. Euphues begins to reason with himself in an orthodoxly inverse anticipation of Dr. Faustus's self-reckoning. "Why *Euphues* art thou so addicted to the studye of the Heathen that thou hast forgotten thy God in Heaven? shal thy witte be rather employed to the attaining of humayne wisedome then devine knowledge?" Reaching the realization that only the "gladde tidings of the Gospell" can minister "comforte" and "hope of the resurrection" to his "guiltie conscience," the hero makes his second—and, this time, exclusively literary—self-reversal in the work:

I my selfe have thought that in divinitie there coulde bee no eloquence, which I myght imitate, no pleasaunt invention whiche I might followe, no delicate phrase, that myght delyght mee, but nowe I see that in the sacred knowledge of Gods wyll, the onely eloquence, the true and perfect phrase, the testimony of salvation doth abide: and seeing without this, all learninge is ignoraunce, all wysdome meere folly, and wytte playne bluntnesse, all Justice iniquytie, all eloquence barbarisme, all beautie deformytye: I wyll spend all the remainder of my lyfe, in studying the olde testament, wherein is prefigured the comming of my saviour, and the newe testament, wherein my Christ doth suffer for my sinnes, and is crucified for my redemption. . . . Farewell therefore the fine and filed phrases of *Cicero*, the pleasaunt *Eligies* of *Ovid*, the depth and profound knowledge of *Aristotle*. Farewell Rhetoricke, farewell Philosophie, farewell all learning which is not sponge from the bowels of the holy Bible. [*Euph.*, I, 287–88]

The dramatic disclosure of the Scripturalist Euphues ensues in "Euphues and Atheos," a tract which, as an apparently original composition (no source being known beyond scanty introductory borrowings from Cicero's *De natura deorum*), represents an anomaly among the long nonfictional pieces of the latter portion of *Euphues*. Although this tract has met disparagement bordering on open hostility from earlier critics and at best cursory notice from more recent ones,[63] it has a claim to acknowl-

---

[63]Bond annotates with exactitude only the two Ciceronian borrowings in "Euphues and Atheos" (*Works of John Lyly*, I, 365–67), sketchily indicating or passing over the multitudinous Biblical citations that come later in the tract. He offers the opinion that Lyly's "critical faculty" was "perhaps swamped by the real strength of his religious convictions"

edgment as a product of specifically English Scripturalist impulsions and, hence, to final notice in this study on at least two counts. The first is its early and striking representation of the identifiably Protestant conversion experience of Atheos, a godless natural man on the exterior who yet can feel the saving motions of the Spirit in his heart. The second is Lyly's remarkable fidelity and adeptness in composing after the precedent of Thomas Becon, in whose voluminous works characters speak in centos of Bible verses while also going about their everyday rounds of activity (see the third section of chapter 5). Both the Greek names of the characters and the pastiche of citations worked into colloquial dialogue are strongly and specifically reminiscent of Becon's manner. It is not in the least inconceivable that if Lyly has a sizable indebtedness to anyone in "Euphues and Atheos," it could be to Becon's vast corpus. But source hunting and extensive discussion alike lie beyond my present purposes, which are well enough served by illustrating concurrently the two substantive bases of Lyly's claim to our notice as a Scripturalist.

Having reasoned his way to an impasse with Atheos by a late point in the dialogue, Euphues decides to take his leave. At this point it appears that no means in the shared medium of language can be mustered by the man of faith to gain the "overhand" in persuading an adherent of natural religion (a credo which itself recalls the insistent naturalism of the stylistic overtones in the first half of the work). However, as he is on the verge of departing, Euphues suddenly breaks into an urgent, personal affectivity of address which at the same time strikes down to Tyndalian theological bedrock by invoking the inward motions of "feelyng faith":

I meane not to wast winde in proving that which thine infidellitie wyll not permit thee to beleeve, for if thou hast as yet felt no tast of the spirit working in thee, then sure I am that to prove the immortalitie of the soule were bootlesse: if thou have a secrete feelinge, then it were needlesse. And God graunt thee that glowinge and sting in conscience that thy soule may witnesse to thy selfe that there is a living God, and thy heart shed drops of bloud as a token of repentance, in that thou hast denied that God, and so I commit thee to God. [*Euph.*, I, 300]

---

in its composition, also noting: "His euphuism is little felt, because the pamphlet is so largely composed of the actual words of Scripture" (I, 364). A greater short-temperedness emerges in Croll and Clemons's *Euphues:* "Lyly combines quotations from Exodus, Deuteronomy, and Isaiah, without proper indications of where one begins and another ends" (p. 150); "Lyly has an unjustifiable way of quoting the substance of a passage as if he were quoting literally" (p. 156); "The quotations in this passage are so familiar that it is not necessary to give the references" (p. 159). Feuillerat, for his part, finds in the tract "a menacing and imperious will" to convert the atheist, "the spirit" of a "rigorous Protestantism with a certain Puritan intransigence" which accords "Biblical citations the place of proofs" (*John Lyly*, pp. 66–67; translations mine).

Atheos reacts in fear and desperation to the prospect of being left alone by Euphues in his present state of mind, but, since he is actually the first Lylyan character to begin to speak Scripture, his ultimate spiritual welfare is put beyond doubt by the style:

> Nay stay a while good *Euphues* & leave not him perplexed with feare, whom thou maist make perfect by faith. For now I am brought into such a double & doubtfull distress that I knowe not howe to tourne mee: if I beleeve not the Scriptures, then shall I be damned for unbeliefe, if I believe them then I shall be confounded for my wycked lyfe. I knowe the whole course of the Bible. . . . Where threates are poured out agaynst sinners, my heart bleedeth in my bellye to re-
> [Psal. 50: member them. I wyll come unto you in judgement sayth the Lorde,
> 3–4, 7] and I wyll be a swifte and a severe witnesse. . . . Great is the day of the Lord and terrible, and who is he that may abide him? What-
> [Joel 2:11] shall I then doe when the Lord shall arise to judge, and when hee
> [Job 31:14] shall demaund what shal I answere? . . . These things *Euphues* testifie unto my conscience that if there be a God, he is the God of the
> [Psal. 139: righteous, & one that wil confound the wicked. Whither therefore
> 7, 8, 9] shal I go, or how may I avoide the day of vengeance to come? if I goe to heaven that is his seate, if into the earth that is his footstoole,
> [Isa. 66:1] if into the depth he is there also: Who can shrowde himself from
> [Job 34:22] the face of the Lord, or where can one hide him that the Lord cannot
> [Psal: 83:14] finde him? his wordes are like fire, and the people lyke drye woode and shalbe consumed. [*Euph.*, I, 300, 301; my bracketed references]

Like Becon's Philemon, but also like an ordained Church of England minister pronouncing the "comfortable wordes" of absolution from the Order for Holy Communion in the Prayer Book, Lyly's Euphues responds in Scriptural kind to the distressed Atheos as the doctor in divinity which the hero now is:

> Although I cannot but rejoyce to heare thee acknowledge a God,
> [1 Pet. 5:8] yet must I needes lament to see thee so much distrust him. The Divell that roaring Lyon seing his pray to be taken out of his jawes, alledgeth al Scripture that may condemne the sinner, leaving al out that should comfort the sorrowful. . . . Let not thy conscience be
> [Gen. 2:4] agrieved, but with a patient heart renounce all thy former iniquities
> [Rom. 8:15– and thou shalt receive eternall life. Assure thy selfe that as God is
> 16] a Lord so he is a father: as Christ is a Judge, so he is a Saviour: as
> [Acts 10:42] there is a lawe, so there is a Gospel. . . . Heare therfore the great
> [Mat. 1:21] comfort flowing in every leafe & line of the Scripture if thou be
> [John 3: patient. . . . So God loved the worlde that he gave his onely begotten
> 16–17] sonne that whosoever beleeved in him myght not perish but have everlasting life. God hath not sent his sonne to judge the world, but
> [Isa. 49:15] that the worlde might be saved by him. Can the Mother (sayth the Prophet) forget the chylde of hir wombe, & though she be so un-
> [Lk. 15:7] naturall, yet will I not be unmindefull of thee. There shalbe more

[Mat. 9:13] joye in heaven for the repentaunce of one sinner then for nintie &
Mk. 2:17, nine just persons. I came not saith Christ to cal the righteous but
[Lk. 5:32] sinners to repentance. If any man sin, we have an advocate with
[1 John 2: the father, Jesus Christe the righteous, hee is the propitiation for
1–2] our sinnes, and not for our sinnes onely but for the sinnes of the
whole worlde. [*Euph.*, I, 301–2; my bracketed references]

After this barrage of Biblical quotations, the condign sententious sentences for Atheos's spiritual state, Euphues gears his reformed rhetoric to a still higher pitch of working in an access of identifiably Pauline devices: first an *NP* catalogue ("Turne therefore unto Christ with a willyng hearte & a waylyng minde for thy offences, . . . who is the dore to them that knocke, the waye to them that seeke, the truthe, the rocke, the corner stone, the fulnesse of time . . ."), and then a rash of *erotema*, serial question-and-answer: "Who forgave the theefe his robbery and manslaughter but Christ? Who made *Mathew* the Publycane and tollgatherer, an Apostle and Preacher, but Christ? Who is that good shepehearde that fetcheth home the straye sheepe so lovingly uppon his shoulders, but Christ? Who received home the lost sonne, was it not Christ?" (*Euph.*, I, 303–4).

Thus in ranging the gamut of English Scripturalist modes of expression in the sixteenth century and interpreting his own experience allusively as an extension of Scripture (the "lost sonne" "received home" by Christ), the erstwhile prodigal Euphues becomes the ministrant by whom the Holy Spirit makes a new man of faith out of Atheos. To ratify his conversion and his new identity, Atheos, like Saul of Tarsus become Paul, takes a new name at Euphues' lips—Theophilus, meaning God's friend (and also the name of one of Becon's characters). For all we know, the reformation of this atheist is lasting; we do not encounter Atheos-Theophilus again. As for the hero and his creator, however, it occasions little lasting surprise to the reader of earlier modern English prose (including conversion narratives) that the perfect Scripturalist conformity to the very words of Scripture attained in "Euphues and Atheos" should have relaxed, and that Lyly should write in accordance with the more generalized Scripturalist program for prose composition in secular contexts when he took in hand his sequel, *Euphues and His England,* as well as his later prose, dramatic and nondramatic. For significantly neither the creator of Euphues nor any of his imitators or successors would hereafter mount to the heights of schematic preciosity that made the style of the earlier, narrative portion of *Euphues* a self-reflexive, opaque, and ultimately unproductive game played with the limits of linguistic identity in accordance with a view of human nature so negative and adversative that it made the gaining of attention an end in itself. Whatever the measure of delight afforded by the display of wit in language that issued in the Euphuistic vogue, the future course of earlier modern English prose style was to lie with the sententious sentence forms and the varieties of directed syntax afforded by the resources of conjunction that the Scripturalist program for composition had selected, cultivated, naturalized, and secularized in the vernacular during the sixteenth century.

The momentum of the generalized Scripturalist program and the impact of its characteristic modes and forms of expression would persist powerfully in the seventeenth century, as can be gathered from noting its most obvious connections with studies that have mapped out the later field. Brian Vickers's study of Bacon's prose style, and Joan Webber's of Donne's, have a good deal to say about the importance of clausal and phrasal parallelism (with or without sense parallelism) as a compositional unit. To confirm the continuing reliance on binary forms of clausal conjunction, whether antithetical or correlative, there are Barish's analyses of Lyly and of Shakespeare in his study of Jonson's prose style as well as Williamson's comprehensive survey of the "Senecan amble"— a diffused penchant for antithetical, balanced sentence form that seems rather to have been a survival from the generalized Scripturalism of the preceding century than the defining period feature which Williamson took it to be. John Knott's study of various writers' responses to Scripture has contributed vitally to our awareness of the fresh infusion of energy sustained by the Scripturalist program as a consequence of the flourishing of English Puritanism in the seventeenth century. Moreover, the writer's sense of vocation and readership in generalized Scripturalism— on analogy with the physician's office and the minister's cure of souls— continued to be operative in vernacular prose composition; this, Fish's study of diverse major figures has shown.[64] Thus, as even these sketchy references indicate, the present study has done no more than address a part—the formative phase—of the interrelations between the Word and the native tongue in the domain of English prose style. But, since later developments too comprise large subjects in their own right, they are, quite properly, tales for other tellings.

[64]Brian Vickers, *Francis Bacon and Renaissance Prose* (Cambridge: Cambridge University Press, 1968); Joan Webber, *Contrary Music: The Prose Style of John Donne* (Madison: University of Wisconsin Press, 1963); Jonas A. Barish, *Ben Jonson and the Language of Prose Comedy* (Cambridge, Mass.: Harvard University Press, 1960); George Williamson, *The Senecan Amble: A Study of Prose Form from Bacon to Collier* (Chicago: University of Chicago Press, 1966); John R. Knott, *The Sword of the Spirit: Puritan Responses to the Bible* (Chicago: University of Chicago Press, 1980); and Stanley E. Fish, *Self-Consuming Artifacts: The Experience of Seventeenth-Century Literature* (Berkeley and Los Angeles: University of California Press, 1972).

INDEX